Janet Zhiqun Xing (Ed.)
**A Typological Approach to Grammaticalization and Lexicalization**

# Trends in Linguistics
# Studies and Monographs

### Editors
Chiara Gianollo
Daniël Van Olmen

### Editorial Board
Walter Bisang,
Tine Breban,
Volker Gast,
Hans Henrich Hock,
Karen Lahousse,
Natalia Levshina,
Caterina Mauri,
Heiko Narrog,
Salvador Pons,
Niina Ning Zhang,
Amir Zeldes

### Editor responsible for this volume
Daniël Van Olmen

# Volume 327

# A Typological Approach to Grammaticalization and Lexicalization

East Meets West

Edited by
Janet Zhiqun Xing

ISBN 978-3-11-077744-4
e-ISBN (PDF) 978-3-11-064128-8
e-ISBN (EPUB) 978-3-11-063742-7
ISSN 1861-4078

Library of Congress Control Number: 2019945640

Bibliographic information published by the Deutsche Nationalbibliothek
The Deutsche Nationalbibliothek lists this publication in the Deutsche Nationalbibliografie;
detailed bibliographic data are available on the Internet at http://dnb.dnb.de.

© 2021 Walter de Gruyter GmbH, Berlin/Boston
This volume is text- and page-identical with the hardback published in 2020.
Typesetting: Integra Software Services Pvt. Ltd.
Printing and binding: CPI books GmbH, Leck

www.degruyter.com

# Foreword

The articles in this volume were selected from presentations at *the International Symposium on Typological Regularity of Semantic Change in Grammaticalization and Lexicalization* organized by Janet Zhiqun Xing and held at Western Washington University, Bellingham, Washington, in April 2017. The purpose of this symposium was to provide new perspectives on the typological characteristics of grammaticalization and lexicalization in Asian and Indo-European languages.

I wish to acknowledge all the authors for their contributions and for commenting on one another's chapters. My special gratitude goes to Randi Hacker who proofread and copyedited the entire volume. I would also like to thank two anonymous reviewers and Daniel Van Olmen, the editor of *Trends in Linguistics*, for reviewing the complete collection and for providing constructive comments and suggestions for revision. Western Washington University and the Confucius Institute of the State of Washington funded the symposium and this resultant publication. Without it, this project could not have been completed.

# Contents

Foreword —— V

Contributors —— IX

Abbreviations —— XI

Janet Zhiqun Xing
Introduction —— 1

## Part I: Grammaticalization

Walter Bisang
**Grammaticalization in Chinese – A cross-linguistic perspective** —— 17

Ekkehard Koenig
**Establishing transphrastic relations: On the grammaticalization of demonstratives** —— 55

Xiufang Dong
**From denotation to description: Noun-adjective and verb-adjective polysemy in Chinese** —— 75

Alain Peyraube and Thekla Wiebusch
**New insights on the historical evolution of differential object marking (DOM) in Chinese** —— 101

Christine Lamarre
**An associated motion approach to northern Mandarin motion-cum-purpose patterns** —— 131

Janet Zhiqun Xing and Axel Schuessler
**Semantic extension in Old Chinese: Direction, transitivity, and voice** —— 165

Barbara Meisterernst
**A new approach to the development of deontic markers: In Pre-Modern Chinese** —— 191

Shannon Dubenion-Smith
A typology of non-clausal postpositioning in German dialects —— 231

## Part II: **Lexicalization**

Edward Vajda
**Ket polysynthesis, grammaticalization, and lexicalization** —— 257

Ken-ichi Takashima
**A lexical category in Shāng Chinese: $V_{controllable}$ vs. $V_{uncontrollable}$** —— 283

Chaofen Sun
**Non-specific degree: Chinese gradable adjectives** —— 319

Yancheng He and Fuxiang Wu
**Compounding word-formation in Ahou Gelao** —— 351

**Subject Index** —— 385

**Language Index** —— 391

# Contributors

**Walter Bisang**, Department of English and Linguistics, University of Mainz and Department of Humanities, Zhejiang University, wbisang@uni-mainz.de

**Xiufang Dong** (董秀芳), Department of Chinese Language and Literature, Peking University, xdong@pku.edu.cn

**Shannon Dubenion-Smith**, Department of Linguistics and Modern & Classical Languages, Western Washington University, dubenis@wwu.edu

**Yancheng He** (何彦城), College of Foreign Studies, Guangxi Normal University, yanchenghe@126.com

**Ekkehard Koenig**, Institut für Englische Philologie, Berlin Free University, koenig@zedat.fu-berlin.de

**Christine Lamarre**, Inalco-CRLAO (National Institute for Oriental Languages and Cultures/Center for linguistic research on East-Asian languages), christine.lamarre@inalco.fr

**Barbara Meisterernst**, Institute of Linguistics, National Tsing Hua University, bmeisterernst@gmail.com

**Alain Peyraube**, Centre de Recherches Linguistiques sur l'Asie Orientale (EHESS), alain.peyraube@gmail.com

**Axel Schuessler**, Independent Researcher, xschuesa@gmail.com

**Chaofen Sun** (孙朝奋), Department of East Asian Languages and Cultures, Stanford University, cfsun@stanford.edu

**Ken-ichi Takashima** (高嶋謙一), Department of Asian Studies, University of British Columbia, kenichi@mail.ubc.ca

**Edward Vajda**, Department of Linguistics and Modern & Classical Languages, Western Washington University, Edward.Vajda@wwu.edu

**Thekla Wiebusch**, Centre de Recherches Linguistiques sur l'Asie Orientale (EHESS), thekla.wiebusch@hotmail.fr

**Fuxiang Wu** (吴福祥), College of Linguistic Sciences, Beijing Language and Culture University, wufuxiang100@126.com

**Janet Zhiqun Xing** (邢志群), Department of Linguistics and Modern & Classical Languages, Western Washington University, Janet.Xing@wwu.edu

# Abbreviations

| | |
|---|---|
| 1, 2, 3 | 1st, 2nd, 3rd person |
| A | Agent |
| ACC | Accusative |
| ACH | Achievement phase marker |
| ADJ | Adjective |
| ADV | Adverbial marker |
| ANIM | Animate class |
| ANOM | Action nominal |
| APPL | Applicative |
| ASP | Aspect maker |
| AUG | Augmentation |
| BA | for *qǔ, jiāng, chí, zhuō* and *bǎ* in their function as object markers |
| CAUS | Causative |
| CL | Classifier |
| CLD | Cylindrical or stick-like objects |
| CNS | Consultation (Mood) |
| CNV | Convex objects |
| COMP | Complement |
| COMPAR | Comparative marker |
| COND | Conditional |
| CONJ | Conjunction |
| CONT | Continuous aspect |
| COP | Copula |
| COS | Change of State |
| CRS | Current-relevant-state |
| DAT | Dative |
| DEF | Definite (article) |
| DEM | Demonstrative |
| DIM | Diminutive |
| DIR | Directional |
| DIST | Distal |
| DIST | Distributive |
| DO | Direct object |
| DOM | Differential object marking |
| EXPL | Explanation of a situation |
| FEM | Feminine |
| FLT | Flat thin objects |
| FOC | Focus |
| FUT | Future tense |
| GD | Giving disposal |
| GEN | Genitive |
| GNR | Generic |
| HU | Human class |
| IMPF | Imperfective |

| | |
|---|---|
| INAN | Inanimate class |
| INCEPT | Inceptive (start of action or activity) |
| INDF | Indefinite |
| INF | Infinitive |
| INS | Instrument |
| INSTR | Instrumental |
| INTJ | Interjection |
| INTN | Intention (Modality) |
| INTRANS | Intransitive |
| IO | Indirect object |
| IPV | Imperfective aspect |
| ITER | Iterative (= repeated action or ongoing change of state) |
| KNW | Known human |
| LCL | Locative classifier |
| LOC | Locative |
| MASC | Masculine |
| MD | Making disposal |
| MEB | Mother's elder brother |
| MED | Medium size |
| ML.GRN | Grown male |
| MOD | Modal verb |
| MOD | Modification marker (nominal) |
| MOM | Momentaneous (= single action) |
| MQD | Manner-quality-degree (demonstratives) |
| NCL | Numeral classifier |
| NEG | Negation |
| NOM | Nominative marker |
| NP | Noun phrase |
| OBJ | Object |
| OM | Object marker |
| PART | Particle |
| PASS | Passive |
| PD | Placing disposal |
| PF | Perfect |
| PFV | Perfective aspect |
| PHS | Phase complement |
| PL | Plural |
| POS | Positive |
| POSS | Possessive |
| PP | Purposive |
| PRED | Predicate |
| PREP | Preposition |
| PRON | Pronoun |
| PROSEC | Prosecutive (motion across or through) |
| PROX | Proximal |
| PRS | Present tense |
| PST | Past tense |

| | |
|---|---|
| Q | Question marker |
| R | Realis |
| RDP | Reduplication |
| RED | Reduplicated form |
| REFL | Reflexive |
| REL | Relative clause marker |
| RES | Resultative |
| RND | Round or oval objects |
| SBJ | Subject |
| SFP | Sentence-final particle |
| SG | Singular |
| SRN | Surname |
| ST | Site or place |
| SUBORD | Subordinative |
| SUG | Suggestion |
| SVC | Serial verb construction |
| TAM | Tense-aspect-mood |
| TH | Thematic (prefix with no identifiable meaning) |
| TOP | Topic marker |
| TRANS | Transitive |
| TRANSL | Translative |
| VENT | Ventive |
| VLU | Valued or appreciated |
| VP | Verb phrase |
| YNG | Young |

Janet Zhiqun Xing
# Introduction

The collection of articles in this volume is intended to address typological characteristics in the processes of grammaticalization and lexicalization. More specifically, they focus on whether Asian and European languages share similar grammaticalization and lexicalization processes, whether the general processes of semantic change depend on certain typological properties of an Eastern or a Western language, and whether the processes of grammaticalization and lexicalization correlate with other features of genetically unrelated and typologically different languages. This introductory chapter is organized as follows: Section 1 provides an overview of typological clines of grammaticality in both Eastern and Western languages; Sections 2–4 lay out the framework of comparative studies used by all contributions (synchronic vs. diachronic, Eastern languages vs. Western languages, and grammaticalization vs. lexicalization); Section 5 briefly discusses some of the outcomes of this volume; and Section 6 outlines and summarizes the content of each contribution.

## 1 Typological clines of grammaticality

Over the years, typologically oriented research on grammaticalization and lexicalization has been prolific and many universal tendencies have been identified, such as unidirectionality, or "the cline of grammaticality" diagrammed as "content item > grammatical word > clitic > inflectional affix" (Hopper & Traugott 2003: 7). In comparison, research on cross-linguistic variation in grammaticalization and lexicalization has been sporadic. Based on a diachronic study of Chinese texts, Xing (2012, 2015) suggests a cline of semantic accretion, A > AB > ABC, in grammaticalization for languages with isolating properties, competing with the cline of semantic recession, A > AB > B, suggested by Heine et al. (1991) built on Hopper's layering principle (1991). Xing (2013, 2015) argues that the primary explanation leading to the two different clines of semantic change in grammaticalization as well as lexicalization is related to the typological properties of Chinese and Indo-European languages; that is, Chinese being an analytical and isolating language lacks explicit grammatical marking. Consequently, syntagmatic factors become key in the accurate interpretation of the speaker's intended meaning. Most Indo-European languages, on the other hand, are generally characterized as inflectional languages, although they vary in terms of the degree of inflectional marking.

For instance, even though English still marks tense and number, it has lost much of its case system since the 11th century AD (for detailed discussion on the difference between English and German, see Hawkins 1986). This makes English less inflectional than other Indo-European languages, such as German, French, and Spanish, all of which have explicit markings on both nouns and verbs (e.g. case, number, gender, tense, aspect, voice). When comparing word-external properties in English and German, Hawkins (2018: 1) suggests "individual words [in English] carry less syntactic and semantic information in their grammatical and lexical representations and have become more reliant on neighboring words for the assignment of linguistic properties [than in German]." Regardless, the interpretation of the speaker's intended meaning in all Indo-European languages is generally less dependent on discourse and pragmatics than it is in isolating analytical languages, such as Chinese. This analysis aligns with Bisang's characterization of grammaticalization as two different types of maturation: economy-based maturation that dominates in processes of grammaticalization in the East and mainland Southeast Asia and explicitness-based maturation that operates more prominently in English and German (Bisang 2009, 2015, and this volume).

To address the questions raised above, contributions to this volume focus on the properties, grammaticality, and grammaticalization and/or lexicalization of one or more of the following grammatical categories: demonstrative, modal auxiliary, complement, adjective, preposition or object marking, postposition, compounding, conjunction, negation, and aspect in either Asian (e.g. Chinese, Gelao, and Japanese), European languages (e.g. English, German), or Eurasian language (i.e. Ket). Through analysis of both diachronic and synchronic data, contributors discuss the evolution processes and/or typological properties of those grammatical categories. In addition to studies of two major language types (isolating languages as represented by Chinese and inflectional languages as represented by German), the study of a third type, agglutinative languages as represented by Ket, is also included in this collection. Our goal is to provide empirical evidence for the processes and regularities of grammaticalization and lexicalization in these languages.

## 2 Diachronic data

Unlike other collections, this volume includes studies of grammaticalization and/or lexicalization in written texts from the earliest Chinese to modern Chinese: Takashima's study investigates the semantic and pragmatic functions of differentiating two verb types in Shang Oracle Bone Inscriptions (13th–11th centuries BCE); Xing and Schuessler's study discusses the semantic extension of various types of verbs in Old Chinese (11th–3rd centuries BCE); Peyraube and Wiebusch focus their study on the origin and development of object marking in Medieval Chinese (3rd–13th CE); Meisterernst examines the development of modal verbs in pre-modern Chinese, and several other contributors report on different grammatical elements in modern Chinese. These studies of Chinese texts recorded over the past 3000 years (11th century BCE – 21st century CE) present a consistent and coherent analysis of the development of the major categories of the Chinese grammatical system. One overwhelming conclusion reached by the contributors is that Chinese has all along had no obligatory markings of word class (e.g. nouns, verbs, adjective), from the earliest inscriptions to modern texts. The primary factors for accurate interpretation of a Chinese lexeme have been discourse and pragmatics.

## 3 Comparative analysis and typological properties

To demonstrate typological characteristics in grammaticalization and lexicalization, most of the contributions included in this volume are comparative in nature. Some studies compare the processes of grammaticalization or lexicalization in Eastern and Western languages (e.g. Bisang, Koenig, Dong, Meisterernst, Sun, and Xing & Schuessler), and some compare Chinese with or relate it to other Asian languages (e.g. Bisang, Vajda, Peyraube & Wiebusch, Lamarre, and He & Wu). Other contributions are less comparative in nature, focusing more on the typological and grammatical characteristics of pre-Classical Chinese and English (e.g. Takashima). In comparison, Dubenion-Smith's quantitative study takes a different angle from all other chapters by looking into the typological characteristics of postpositioning in German dialects and compares his findings with other related studies of word order variations. His findings, once compared with those of Peyraube and Wiebusch (this volume) and Hawkins (1986, 2018), help us better understand how a new word order has developed in different language types. Based on the results of these studies, we may conclude that inflectional languages (e.g. German) have a more flexible word order than isolating analytical languages (e.g. Chinese).

## 4 Grammaticalization vs. lexicalization

Another unique feature of this volume is the inclusion of studies that address the processes of both grammaticalization and lexicalization. Of the twelve contributions, seven chapters deal primarily with the issues of grammaticalization, four focus on the processes and characteristics of lexicalization, one on typological properties of propositioning. Though there are more chapters on grammaticalization than lexicalization, several chapters discuss the interaction and/or similarities between grammaticalization and lexicalization. For instance, Vajda's study explores the grammaticalization of finite verbs in Ket. When he discusses the pathways involved in the development of the polysemies of those verbs, he necessarily touches upon the morphological issues of those lexemes where grammaticalization and lexicalization are clearly intertwined. In the literature, grammaticalization is traditionally defined as a change or process "from a lexical to a grammatical [form] or from a less grammatical to a more grammatical [form]" (Kurylowicz 1975: 52), while lexicalization, although less consistently, is defined as a process of conventionalization (Brinton & Traugott 2005) or as a diachronic process in which a non-word form becomes a word (Dong 2012). Evidently, these characteristics of the two types of processes entail overlapping cases of change. In other words, the question involves, for instance, whether the change from an intransitive meaning to a transitive meaning is a case of grammaticalization or lexicalization or both. Vajda considers the change in the verbs in Ket as both. A similar situation can be observed in the contributions by Dong, Sun, and Xing & Schuessler. In comparison, other studies included in this collection are relatively clear cases of either grammaticalization (e.g. Bisang, Koenig, Peyraube & Wiebusch, Lamarre, and Meisterernst) or lexicalization (e.g. Takashima, He & Wu).

## 5 Some outcomes

Several conclusions or tentative conclusions can be drawn from the chapters in this volume. Koenig's study of demonstratives in both Eastern and Western languages and Bisang's comparative study of explicitness-based vs. economy-based maturation in grammaticalization support, to a varied degree, the analysis of semantic recession noted earlier. The results of other studies focusing on polysemies in Chinese (e.g. Bisang, Dong, Lamarre, and Sun) appear to be in agreement with the analysis of semantic accretion, which is identified to be associated with isolating languages. However, the case of manner-quality-degree demonstratives in Chinese does not observe the accretion of meanings, due, according to Koenig, to one or several complete renewals of the system in the course of its historical development. It seems to me that the lack of polysemous demonstratives in Chinese is not surprising but rather in alignment with the general tendency of Chinese grammatical forms. We know that Chinese generally does not mark definiteness (cf. Bisang 1999), and the two basic demonstratives, *zhè* 這 'this' and *nà* 那 'that', as noted in Koenig, have been used as demonstratives since the 8th century AD. However, Fang's recent study (2012) shows that *zhè* has emerged as a definite article in Beijing Mandarin. This newly developed polysemy of *zhè*, along with its demonstrative function, could be considered evidence of the accretion of meaning (i.e. A >AB). Additionally, all other subtypes of Chinese demonstratives (e.g. *zhèyàng* 這樣 vs. *nàyàng* 那樣, *zhème* 這麼 vs. *nàme* 那麼) have developed by compounding or lexicalizing the basic demonstratives with another character expressing manner, quality or degree, a typical process of lexicalization in Chinese (cf. Dong 2012).

It should be noted that Peyraube and Wiebusch's study about the grammaticalization of the object markers *bǎ/jiāng* 把/將 appears to be a case against the analysis of semantic accretion. Their study, based on a number of investigations done by Chinese grammarians and their own analysis, have concluded that *bǎ/jiāng*'s object marking function in the disposal construction (*chǔzhìshì* 處置式) emerged and replaced other earlier disposal markers (e.g. *yǐ* 以, *qǔ* 取, *chí* 持, *zhuō* 捉) in Early to Late Medieval Chinese (3rd–10th CE). In a general sense, this replacement may be viewed as an instance of linguistic recession. However, it is not a change of semantic recession (A > AB > B); rather, it is more a form of (syntactic) recession. As to the semantic change in the process of *bǎ/jiāng*'s grammaticalization, Xing (1994, 2003, and 2013) provides historical evidence to show that *bǎ/jiāng* developed a number of polysemies in the process of their grammaticalization and lexicalization. She sorts *bǎ*'s polysemies into two different clines: 1) 'to hold' > 'to take' > causative marker > obj. marker, and 2) 'to hold' > 'handful' > classifier. All of *bǎ*'s polysemies can be found in modern Chinese, serving as either part of a lexicalized compound or a grammatical function, such as a classifier or an object marker. Clearly, this provides evidence for semantic accretion.

But, arguably, the most revolutionary discovery of this collection is Vajda's study of polysynthetic verbs in the Siberian language Ket. Based on years of fieldwork and study of the morphological structures of Ket, a language heavily influenced by the neighboring suffixal agglutinating languages, he provides many examples to show that though the non-polysemous Ket verb stems can be multiplied, the general trend is for Ket polysynthetic verbs to lose their literal, etymological meaning upon being lexicalized or grammaticalized. That is to say that semantic change in Ket exhibits the cline, A > B > C, typologically different from the two explained earlier in that there is no intermediate stage where both meaning A and meaning B coexist. Such a change may be characterized as a change of semantic substitution. This finding leads us to the tentative conclusion that the tendency of semantic change in grammaticalization and lexicalization correlates with the morphological structure of a language.

Although Vajda's finding still needs to be attested in other agglutinative languages, all studies in this collection seem to point to the same conclusion, namely, that language type, specifically pertinent to morphological structures, affects the type of processes in grammaticalization and lexicalization. In other words, we see a three-way correlation: in analytical and isolating languages, such as Chinese, the trend of semantic change in grammaticalization and lexicalization is accretive; in inflectional languages, such as German, the trend is recessive, and in agglutinative languages, such as Ket, the trend is substitutive. These three-way correlations may be further summarized as follows: the more parsimonious the morphological structure of a language, the more polysemous the lexeme may become. Chinese has the most parsimonious morphological structure, therefore it is the most polysemous; Ket has the least parsimonious morphological structure, hence it is the least polysemous.

# 6 Organization of this volume

This volume is divided into two parts: Part I focuses on grammaticalization and Part II on lexicalization. However, it should be noted that the issues discussed in each part are not mutually exclusive as indicated earlier in Section 4.

In Part I, Bisang's chapter explores whether there is cross-linguistic variation in grammaticalization and whether that variation shows certain regularities. Based on the observation that discourse and pragmatic inference are particularly prominent in the processes of grammaticalization in Chinese (and most mainland Southeast Asian languages) (Xing 2015; Bisang 2015), this study shows that the co-evolution of meaning and form is limited in these languages and, more specifically, their grammaticalization products are characterized by non-obligatoriness and multifunctionality. From a more general perspective, the results of this study are modeled after Bisang (2009, 2015) in the context of two different types of maturation in grammaticalization: economy-based maturation as it dominates in processes of grammaticalization in East and mainland Southeast Asia and explicitness-based maturation as it operates more prominently in English and German. It is argued that hidden complexity scores very high in Chinese and that it does so not only in processes of grammaticalization but also in the lexicon. In fact, it is the comparatively high pragmatic flexibility of lexical items that favors and enhances processes of grammaticalization in Chinese. This study concludes that the similarity of grammaticalization and lexicalization as described by Xing (2015) is a reflection of hidden complexity in Chinese.

Koenig's contribution discusses grammaticalization processes among demonstratives in major European languages and two Asian languages – Chinese and Japanese – with special attention paid to a neglected subclass of demonstratives, viz. those expressing the ontological domains of 'manner', 'quality' and 'degree' (MQD-demonstratives). After presenting a general overview of the processes of grammaticalization typically observable in the notional domain under analysis, a variety of such processes are discussed and compared in the relevant languages. It is shown that there are striking parallels within European languages, on the one hand, and with Japanese, on the other, as far as the extension from the exophoric to the endophoric uses is concerned. The relevant processes, and thus the relevant similarities, are not as clearly observable in Mandarin, arguably due to radical renewals of MQD-demonstratives in the history of that language. In addition, two specific points related to the typical developments of function words (interrogatives, demonstratives), the role of losses and renewals, as well the importance of studying grammaticalization from a comparative perspective, are made in support of the view advocated by Diessel (2006, 2013) contra Heine & Kuteva (2005, 2007). One point is that the subclass of demonstratives under discussion provides further evidence for the assumption that not all grammatical categories and markers derive from members of major lexical classes, such as nouns and verbs. The second point is that the relevant processes also differ from other processes as far as their targets are concerned; they typically establish transphrastic relations, relationships across clauses, rather than strengthening intra-clausal relations between the constituents of a clause.

Dong's chapter focuses on semantic extension from denotative meaning to descriptive meaning in Chinese. Through analysis of historical data, this study has identified two major classes of words – nouns and verbs – that have undergone processes of semantic change. It is shown that some nouns originally denoting a concrete object tend to develop a meaning describing the property of that object and thereby also functioning as an adjective. These two meanings often coexist, with the nominal meaning being denotative and the adjectival meaning being descriptive. Similarly, some verbs originally denoting a concrete activity may gain an adjectival meaning describing the quality related to that activity. She argues that from a cognitive point of view, the semantic shift occurring in verbs is the same or similar to that occurring in nouns, namely from denotative to descriptive. After studying the pathways (metonymy and lexical subjectification) of different cases of semantic change from denotation to description, and comparing Chinese cases with English counterparts, Dong concludes that noun-adjective polysemy and verb-adjective polysemy in Chinese are a result of the lack of morphological markings in word classes in Chinese. Consequently, they are more frequently seen in Chinese than in English.

Peyraube and Wiebusch's contribution focuses on the origin and development of the object markers or prepositions *bǎ/jiāng* in disposal constructions. First, they challenge the following three hypotheses about the origins of the disposal construction: 1) all disposal markers including *bǎ* and *jiāng* are derived from and have replaced *yǐ* 以 through an analogical process; 2) the disposal construction developed from the subject-patient construction (*shòushì zhǔyǔ jù* 受事主語句), to which an object marker has been added, and 3) *qǔ* 取 meaning 'to take' in translated Buddhist texts of Pre-Medieval and Early Medieval Chinese (2nd–5th CE) might be the first attested disposal construction in Chinese, with the argument that disposal constructions were borrowed from the original language (a variety of Indo-Aryan or Indic languages known as Prakrits 普拉克利特语) of these Buddhist documents. Then through analysis of various disposal markers in texts of Medieval Chinese (3rd–13th CE), they conclude that the first hypothesis of an analogical phenomenon with *yǐ*, which might have served as a model for *qǔ* 取, *chí* 持, *zhuō* 捉, *jiāng* 將, and *bǎ* 把 in their grammaticalization, is worth maintaining. The second hypothesis, whereby the disposal construction could have developed from the patient-subject construction to which a differential object marker has been added, is not motivated. Finally, they propose that the joint processes of analogy (with the *yǐ* form) and grammaticalization (Verb > Preposition) play a role in the appearance and development of the 'disposal' construction. Their study also touches upon the issue of whether the 'disposal' form in Chinese can be considered a case of differential object marker (DOM) as modeled in Indo-European languages.

Lamarre's study discusses the encoding in Sinitic of motion-cum-purpose, i.e. 'go and buy food', by identifying two distinct patterns: A: *qù mǎi cài* 去買菜 [go + purpose VP] vs. B: *mǎi cài qu* 買菜去 [purpose VP + go]. Previous studies have shown that dialect specificities are key factors in accounting for the distribution of these patterns. Both A and B are attested nowadays in Standard Mandarin to express motion-cum-purpose 'go (and/to) VP', together with a seemingly redundant "blended" Pattern C: *qù mǎi cài qu* 去買菜去 [go + purpose VP + go]. Patterns A, B and C are attested in the case of venitive motion too, with *lái* (lai) 來. Despite the obvious fact that deictic motion verbs in Pattern B have undergone grammaticalization (as attested, for instance, by their phonetic erosion), only Chao (1968: 479) has analyzed the itive or venitive morphemes in Pattern B as "particles of purpose". The various alternative analyses put forward since then fail to convince. Lamarre argues that Chao's "particles of purpose" need to be assigned to a grammatical category and that associated motion is a plausible candidate. This hypothesis complements Yang (2012)'s claim, supported by historical documents, that the intense contact of Chinese with OV Altaic languages was an important factor in the spread of Northern Pattern B. It raises the issue of a possible link between associated motion and deictic directionals, an issue under discussion in other linguistic areas.

Xing and Schuessler's collaboration, built on Schuessler (2007), explores the semantic extension involved in the dichotomy of direction, transitivity, and voice in Old Chinese (11th century BCE–3rd century BCE). Through analysis of semantic extension from introvert to extrovert, from nominal to verbal, and from active to passive, this study provides evidence to show that those semantic and grammatical extensions were triggered either by phonological/morphological factors, such as voicing, or by syntagmatic factors, such as word order. They argue that, although semantic extension in these cases underwent some of the same processes of semantic abstraction (e.g. metaphoricalization and metonymization) as those commonly discussed in the literature of grammaticalization, the primary mechanism found in OC semantic extension is semantic reanalysis (cf. Xing 2013).

Meisterernst's contribution discusses the development of deontic modal markers from typological and morpho-syntactic perspectives. The modal system of Archaic Chinese (11th century BCE – 3rd century BCE) consists mainly of the so-called 'first modals', i.e. modals of possibility, which potentially appear as the first modals in many languages expressing deontic modal values. Modern Chinese by contrast has quite a complex system of modal marking: it starts to develop in the Early Middle Chinese period around the 1st century BCE, when new and more specialized markers of deontic modality emerge. This investigation proposes a connection between the loss of the derivational morphology reconstructed for Archaic Chinese and the development of a more explicit system of modal marking similar to what has been proposed for the Germanic languages.

Dubenion-Smith's contribution presents results of a corpus study of non-clausal postpositioning in modern German dialects, a phenomenon of a constituent not in its expected position in the inner field but in the postfield of the clause to which it is syntactically linked. Taking into consideration that most investigations of postpositioning in modern German examine the spoken and written standard, Dubenion-Smith builds his study on two works (Patocka 1997 and Westphal Fitch 2011) and extends the investigation to more linguistic areas and to the typological characteristics of the phenomenon in those regional dialects, including spoken dialect texts of the Zwirner Corpus (Institut für Deutsche Sprache) from the North Low German, West Central German, and Bavarian linguistic areas. In particular, the empirical focus of this study is base dialects, the most geographically restricted varieties with the greatest linguistic divergence from the standard language. The result of this study shows that prepositional phrases (form) and adjuncts (function) have comprised the vast majority of postpositionings from earlier stages of German, whereas postpositioned NPs have been drastically reduced over time. Evidence from quantitative analysis suggests that the high rate of postpositioned prepositional phrases (PPs) are possibly attributable to the constituent length of PPs, contact placement, and the attraction principle. The goal of this chapter is to provide an exhaustive typology of postpositionings based on their form and function and to compare the results of this study to earlier studies on this topic.

Part II of the volume starts with Vajda's study of Ket's finite verb structure in its process of lexicalization and grammaticalization. Unrelated to any of the other language families of Northern Asia, the polysynthetic Ket language of Central Siberia displays morphological traits absent from most other Eurasian languages. This study finds that the typical cline of semantic change affecting morpheme classes in the Ket verb template is A > B > C, with no evidence that old and new meanings coexisted in the language for any length of time. This pattern contrasts with that typically found in Western Eurasian languages, where the cline is generally known to be A > AB > B (Heine, Claudi, Hünnemeyer 1991; Hopper & Traugott 2003), and also differs from that observed in East Asia's isolating languages, where it has been argued to be A > AB > ABC (Xing 2015). An examination of Ket polysynthesis, lexicalization, and grammaticalization, therefore, strengthens the hypothesis that the varieties of semantic change prevalent in a language depend, at least in part, on its typological profile and formal morphological complexity.

Takashima's contribution investigates the grammatical, semantic, and pragmatic functions of verbs in the Shang Oracle Bone Inscriptions (OBI) (13th–11th Century BCE). He first classifies the earliest class of action verbs into two types: those of actions executable or controlled by humans (e.g., "We make a sacrificial offering of pigs to such and such an ancestor.") and those of actions not executable or controlled by humans (e.g., literal translation "The moon had an eclipse."). He then shows that this lexical feature not only complements the traditional theory of verb class, but also correlates with the use of negative markers, such as *bù* 不, *fú* 弗, *wú* 毋, and *wù* 勿, as well as the negative copula *fēi* 非 and the so-called modal particle *qí* 其. According to him, the categorical distinction of controllable vs. uncontrollable verbs may well be a linguistic manifestation of the Shang worldview which held that actions and events were divided into two realms of reality: those believed to be amenable to control and those – usually of states or events – believed to be not amenable to control. He argues that failure to distinguish between the two can seriously affect how we interpret the inscriptions to which such a categorical distinction and the concurrent behavior of the negatives and the *qí* 其 would certainly have applied during the late Shang dynasty.

Sun's study proposes that Chinese gradable adjectives that lexicalize a non-specific degree meaning are typologically different from English adjectives.

He provides synchronic evidence to show that, for gradable adjectives (e.g. *gāo* 高 'tall/high', *gānjìng* 乾净 'clean') to convey a non-specific degree meaning (e.g. *gāoxìng* 高興 'tall/high happy' > 'very happy', *gāngān jìngjìng* 乾乾净净 'clean clean' > 'very clean'), the co-occurrence of an appropriate context with a fitting degree word in the construction of an adjectival phrase signaling a specific degree is required. He argues that while gradable adjectives are lexically non-specific in terms of degree, closed-scale meanings entailing maximal or minimal degrees are expressed through de-adjectival verbs (e.g. *mǎnle* 滿了 'full ASP' > 'become full'; *kōngle* 空了 'empty ASP' > 'become empty') or denoted in adjectival negation (e.g. *bù mǎn* 不滿 'not full'; *bù kōng* 不空 'not empty'). Sun concludes that there is no absolute adjective in Chinese, as non-specific degree is part of the conventional meaning of all Chinese positive gradable adjectives. The Chinese adjectival system is, therefore, typologically different from English.

He and Wu's collaboration discusses compounding word formation in Ahou Gelao. As one member of the Kra branch of the Tai-Kadai family, Ahou Gelao is an analytic and tonal language. Typologically, it manifests SVO constituent order and a head-initial pattern in nominal phrases. Within the nominal phrase, all modifiers except numerals follow the modified head, with demonstratives coming last. This is just the opposite of Chinese. Even though Ahou Gelao is genetically unrelated to Chinese, it displays similarities with Chinese in quite a few ways due to areal diffusion, with compounding being one of the similar properties. Specifically, compounding serves as a major morphological process in the two languages. From a typological point of view, this chapter provides a brief survey of the compounding processes in Ahou Gelao, touching upon (1) the behaviors and properties that help distinguish compounds from phrases; (2) the syntactic and semantic relations of their constituents, and (3) compounding in different word classes. In addition, a brief introduction is provided to the lexicalization in the compounding process, especially the motivation, mechanism, degree, possibility of and the constraints on the lexicalization of phrases or syntactic constructions into compounds. Meanwhile, special references are made to the lexicalization and other properties of the compounding process in Mandarin Chinese throughout the chapter where applicable, intending to help readers have a better understanding of the compounding process in the Gelao language and Mandarin Chinese as well as other languages in the area.

To conclude, this volume gathers contributions from researchers who have pioneered and/or shaped various theoretical frameworks related to grammaticalization and lexicalization in both the East and the West. By doing so, it aims to provide some new perspectives on the typological characteristics of grammaticalization and lexicalization in Asian and Indo-European languages.

# References

Bisang, Walter. 1999. Classifiers in East and Southeast Asian languages: Counting and beyond. In *Numeral Types and Changes Worldwide*, Jadranka Gvozdanovic (ed.), 113–185. Berlin: Mouton de Gruyter.

Bisang, Walter. 2009. On the evolution of complexity – sometimes less is more in East and mainland Southeast Asia. In *Language Complexity as an Evolving Variable*, Geoffrey Sampson, David Gil, and Peter Trudgill (eds.), 34–49. Oxford: Oxford University Press.

Bisang, Walter. 2015. Hidden complexity – the neglected side of complexity and its consequences. *Linguistics Vanguard* ISSN (Online), 2199–174X, DOI: 10.1515/linvan-2014–1014.

Brinton, Laurel J. and Elizabeth C. Traugott. 2005. *Lexicalization and Language Change*. (Research Surveys in Linguistics). Cambridge: Cambridge University Press.

Chao, Yuen Ren. 1968. *A Grammar of Spoken Chinese*. Berkeley: University of California Press.

Diessel, Holger. 2006. Demonstratives, joint attention, and the emergence of grammar. *Cognitive Linguistics* 17 (4): 463–489.

Diessel, Holger. 2013. Where does language come from? Some reflections on the role of deictic gesture and demonstratives in the evolution of language. *Cognitive Linguistics* 5.2–3: 239–249.

Dong, Xiufang. 2012. Lexicalization in the history of the Chinese language. In Xing (ed.) *Newest Trends in Studies of Grammaticalization and Lexicalization*, 235–274. Berlin: Mouton de Gruyter.

Fang, Mei. 2012. The emergence of a definite article in Beijing Mandarin. The evolution of the proximal demonstrative *zhè*. In *Newest Trends in the Study of Grammaticalization and Lexicalization in Chinese*, Janet Xing (ed.), 55–85. Berlin: Mouton de Gruyter.

Hawkins, John A. 1986. *A comparative typology of English and German: Unifying the contrast*. London: Croom Helm.

Hawkins, John A. 2018. Word-external properties in a typology of Modern English: A comparison with German. *English Language and Linguistics*, 1–27.

Heine, Bernd and Tania Kuteva. 2005. *Language Contact and Grammatical Change*. Cambridge: Cambridge University Press.

Heine, Bernd and Tania Kuteva. 2007. *The Genesis of Grammar: A Reconstruction*. Oxford: Oxford University Press.

Heine, Bernd, Ulrike Claudi, and Friederike Hünnemeyer. 1991. *Grammaticalization: A Conceptual Framework*. Chicago/London: The University of Chicago Press.

Hopper, Paul J. and Elizabeth C. Traugott. 2003. *Grammaticalization*. Cambridge: Cambridge University Press.

Kurylowics, Jerzy. 1975. The evolution of grammatical categories. In *Esquisses Linguistiques II*, 38–54. Munich: Fink

Patocka, Franz. 1997. *Satzgliedstellung in den bairischen Dialekten Österreichs*. Frankfurt am Main and New York: Peter Lang Verlag.

Schuessler, Axel. 2007. *ABC Etymological Dictionary of Old Chinese*. Honolulu: Hawai'i University Press.

Westphal Fitch, Gesche. 2011. Changes in frequency as a measure of language change: Extraposition in Pennsylvania German. In *Studies on German-language islands*, Michael Putnam (ed.), 371–384. Amsterdam: John Benjamins.

Xing, Janet Z. 1994. Diachronic change of object markers in Chinese. *Language Variation and Change*, Vol. 6: 201–222.

Xing, Janet Z. 2003. Grammaticalization of verbs in Mandarin Chinese. *Journal of Chinese Linguistics*, Vol. 31: 1, 101–144.

Xing, Janet Z. 2012. Introduction. In Xing (ed.) *Newest Trends in Studies of Grammaticalization and Lexicalization*, 1–20. Berlin: Mouton de Gruyter.

Xing, Janet Z. 2013. Semantic reanalysis in grammaticalization in Chinese. In Zhuo Jing-Schmidt (ed.) *Increased Empiricism: New Advances in Chinese Linguistics*, 223–246. Philadelphia/Amsterdam: John Benjamins.

Xing, Janet Z. 2015. A comparative study of semantic change in grammaticalization and lexicalization in Chinese and Germanic languages. *Studies in Language* 39(3), 594–634.

Yáng, Yǒnglóng. 楊永龍 2012. Mùdì gòushì "VP qu" yǔ SOV yǔxù de guānlián [The purpose construction "VP qu" in Chinese and SOV order]. *Zhōngguó Yǔwén* [Chinese Language] 6: 525–536.

# Part I: **Grammaticalization**

Walter Bisang
# Grammaticalization in Chinese –
A cross-linguistic perspective

## 1 Setting the stage: Is grammaticalization a cross-linguistically homogeneous phenomenon?

Typologically-oriented research on grammaticalization is usually focused on cross-linguistic generalizations and universal tendencies in the diachronic development of grammatical markers. This type of research has brought to light an impressive number of grammaticalization pathways or clines (Heine & Kuteva 2002) such as the following:

(1) Givón (1979: 209):
 Discourse > Syntax > Morphology > Morphophonemics > Zero

This cline is prominent in research on grammaticalization. It describes the different levels through which grammatical markers develop across time. What used to be a topic at the level of discourse may become a subject at the level of syntax at a later stage. From there, it may further develop into a morphological pattern, a morphophonemic element and ultimately a zero marker. Clines of this type are characterized by a number of properties that are claimed to be universal (Bisang 2016, 2017). They are realized in stages (cyclicity) with the individual stages following a fixed order and they are not reversible (the reversed order of "Morphology > Syntax" in (1) is not possible (cf. Newmeyer 1998, Norde 2009 on unidirectionality). Moreover, there are claims that the source concept determines the outcome of further processes of grammaticalization (Heine & Kuteva 2002) and that processes of grammaticalization are gradual (Traugott & Trousdale 2010). The gradualness of grammaticalization processes manifests itself in the fact that a linguistic sign can have both meanings at a certain historical stage, its source meaning A and its target meaning B (Heine et al. 1991, also cf. Hopper 1991 on "layering"). Thus, the extension from meaning A to meaning B is characterized by an intermediate stage in which both interpretations are possible – a fact that can be formalized as follows: A > A,B > B.[1] Finally, there

---

[1] I follow Xing's (2015: 595) notation.

is the claim that the semantic change of a linguistic sign from a more concrete meaning to a more abstract grammatical function is also reflected in its form. If this assumption of the coevolution of meaning and form is correct, a linguistic sign loses its syntactic flexibility and its morphophonological substance along a cline like the one in (1).

In contrast to the extensive literature on universals and generalizations, the question of cross-linguistic variation in grammaticalization is rarely asked. The present study takes up this topic. It focuses on the observation from Chinese that the coevolution of meaning and form is reduced and that pragmatic inference remains important even if a linguistic sign has undergone grammaticalization (Bisang 2004, 2015b on Sinitic and other East and mainland Southeast Asian languages). The properties that characterize a large number of grammaticalized forms in Sinitic are the lack of obligatoriness and the presence of multifunctionality. This is illustrated in Section 2 with examples from the perfective marker -*le*, the multifunctionality of 'give'-verbs and the use of classifiers to express the two functions of definiteness and indefiniteness with a single marker. Similar phenomena are described by Xing (2013, 2015) under the term of "semantic reanalysis". Xing also emphasizes the relevance of pragmatics in its interaction with the syntagmatic properties of a language.

In Section 3, the lack of obligatoriness and multifunctionality is ascribed to a type of diachronic maturation that is based on economy and the concomitant pragmatic inference of the relevant value of a grammatical category in a given context. This notion of maturation differs from Dahl's (2004) type of maturation, which is argued to be based on explicitness, i.e., the overt expression of values of grammatical categories even in situations in which their semantic content can be clearly inferred from context. It is assumed that products of grammaticalization are the results of a competition between economy-based and explicitness-based maturation in each language (Bisang 2015a, b; also cf. Haiman 1983 on competing motivations).

If economy-based maturation wins over explicitness-based maturation in a lot of individual cases, this may entail a number of further consequences for the structural properties of these languages. Two of them are discussed in this paper. The first one is concerned with the division of labor between grammar and the lexicon and its effects on grammaticalization and lexicalization, respectively. As is shown in Section 4 with examples using the Chinese perfective marker -*le* and the marking of (in)definiteness by numeral classifiers, some of the functions expressed by grammatical markers in languages with more extensive explicitness-based maturation is taken over by the lexicon in Sinitic (and other East and mainland Southeast Asian languages).

The second consequence of more extensive economy-based maturation has to do with the properties of morphological paradigms that arise in such environments. Section 5 starts with the argument of economy and discusses the factors that blocked the development of explicitness-based maturation in Sinitic to the extent that economy-based maturation and the reduced coevolution of meaning and form remained dominant for some 2,000 years. Based on that, it will be claimed that inflectional morphological paradigms that develop out of environments of economy-based maturation preserve certain pragmatics-related properties and therefore constitute a special type of "East and mainland Southeast Asian inflectional morphological paradigm." The argument of explicitness will focus on semantic reanalysis as defined by Xing (2015). It will show that semantic reanalysis is not limited to the absence of morphology in a linguistic sign and that morphology that is the result of extensive explicitness-based maturation creates new options for it.

## 2 Properties of grammaticalization in Chinese: Reduced coevolution of meaning and form and the high relevance of pragmatic inference

The assumption that there is coevolution of meaning and form in processes of grammaticalization is not only reflected in Givón's (1979) cline in (1); it goes right back to Meillet (1912), who introduced the term "grammaticalization". In his description of the development of auxiliaries out of lexical verbs, he states that "the weakening of the meaning and the weakening of the form of the auxiliary word go hand-in-hand"[2] (Meillet 1912: 139). Later on, this assumption seemed to be more or less taken for granted. In some publications, as for instance in Bybee et al. (1994), this issue is addressed explicitly:

> It therefore seems natural to look for a direct, and even causal, link between semantic and phonetic reduction in the evolution of grammatical material, beginning with the earliest stages of development from lexical sources and continuing throughout the subsequent developments grams undergo. Our hypothesis is that the development of grammatical material is characterized by the dynamic coevolution of meaning and form.
> 
> (Bybee et al. 1994: 20)

---

[2] The translation from French is mine (W. B). The original version runs as follows: "L'affaiblissement du sens et l'affaiblissement de la forme des mots accessoires vont de pair" (Meillet 1912: 139).

The coevolution of meaning and form is also part of Lehmann's (1995) conceptualization of grammaticalization in terms of the autonomy of the linguistic sign. In his view, grammaticalization goes with the loss of autonomy:

> [T]he more freedom with which a sign is used, the more autonomous it is. Therefore, the autonomy of a sign is converse to its grammaticality, and grammaticalization detracts from its autonomy. Consequently, if we want to measure the degree to which a sign is grammaticalized, we will determine its degree of autonomy. (Lehmann 1995: 121–122)

The autonomy of the linguistic sign can be determined by Lehmann's (1995) six parameters of grammaticalization, i.e. the criteria of weight, cohesion and variability with their paradigmatic and their syntagmatic sides. Since these parameters are well-known, they will not be extensively discussed in this chapter. What is important, however, is that only one of them, syntagmatic variability (order of linguistic signs, rigidity of word order), shows strong covariation between meaning and form in grammaticalization processes in Chinese. The other parameters are of reduced importance in most cases. The parameter of integrity (paradigmatic weight) is briefly discussed for the purpose of illustration (for more information, cf. Bisang 2008, 2015b). Further below, paradigmatic variability will be discussed in the context of obligatoriness and pragmatic inference.

A linguistic sign needs a certain amount of substance, a certain, integrity, in order to maintain its autonomy (Lehmann 1995). At the level of semantics, reduction of integrity is associated with the loss of concrete meaning, or desemanticization, while the form-related side of reduction manifests itself in the loss of phonetic substance, or attrition. As can be seen from the cline in (1), the combination of desemanticization and attrition ultimately ends in a zero-marking, i.e., the total absence of phonetic substance combined with a highly abstract grammatical meaning. In Chinese, phonetic reduction mostly stops at a much earlier level of phonetic reduction. In the vast majority of cases, grammaticalized markers do not lose their syllabicity. They often lose their tone, as for instance in the case of the experiential marker 過 -guo (derived from the verb guò 'go through, pass, cross') or the general classifier 個 ge (derived from 箇 gè 'bamboo tree'). Even in the case of aspect suffixes like the durative marker -zhe (derived from the verb 著 zháo 'touch, contact') or the perfective marker -le (derived from the verb 了 liǎo 'complete, finish'), the loss of phonetic substance rarely affects the syllabicity of a linguistic sign in Mandarin Chinese. One of the rare examples is the plural marker -men in combination with personal pronouns. Thus, the pronoun of the third person plural 他們 tā-men [3-PL] can be pronounced as [ta:m] in rapid speech. Another good example is the frozen tone on the numeral yī 'one' in contexts in which the classifier in yī ge [one CL] gets lost in spoken Mandarin (Tao 2006).

A corollary of the coevolution of meaning and form is the development from pragmatic inference to semantic meaning or conventionalization (cf. e.g. Hopper & Traugott 2003). Thus, pragmatic inference is generally assumed to be the driving force that initiates and motivates processes of grammaticalization and loses its relevance once a new meaning has been established.[3] Even though this scenario works with many languages, it does not reflect grammaticalization processes equally well cross-linguistically. A look at Chinese (and many other East and mainland Southeast Asian languages) reveals that pragmatic inference remains high even with grammaticalized linguistic signs (Bisang 2008, 2009, 2015b). This is clearly shown by Xing's (2013, 2015) analysis of Chinese in terms of semantic reanalysis, defined as a "syntagmatic process involving semantic interpretation based on contextual, pragmatic, and encyclopedic knowledge" (Xing 2015: 624). As a consequence, grammaticalization does not necessarily follow the cline of A > A,B > B (cf. Section 1) but rather a cline of the type A > A,B > A,B,C, in which a new function is added to the already existing functions A and B. As Xing (2015: 595) points out, such processes favor the "accretion of more meaning over time" (Xing 2015: 595).

The relevance of pragmatic inference in Chinese products of grammaticalization shows up in two properties of markers that express grammatical categories, i.e. the lack of obligatoriness and the presence of multifunctionality. Each of them will be illustrated in the remainder of this Section.

The definition of obligatoriness adopted here follows Lehmann's (1995: 139) paradigm-based view. A grammatical marker is obligatory if a language has a set of markers for expressing values of a given grammatical category and the speaker has to select one of these values in a given syntactic environment. Thus, tense marking is obligatory if the grammar forces the speaker to use a past or non-past marker in an independent declarative clause of a language with a binary tense system of that type.

The absence of grammatical information that can be retrieved from context by pragmatic inference is found in multiple domains of Chinese grammar. A famous instance is radical pro-drop (Huang 1984, Neeleman & Szendrői 2007, Bisang 2014, and many others). In this case, arguments can be omitted without concomitant agreement on the verb. Another example is aspect marking. As is well-known, Chinese has aspect markers like -*le* (perfective), -*zhe* (durative), and -*guo* (experiential) but these markers are not obligatory. While the grammar of languages with obligatory aspect marking forces its speakers to use the perfective

---

**3** Cf. the scenarios presented by the Invited Inference Theory (Traugott 2002) or Heine (2002) and Diewald & Smirnova (2012).

aspect in sequences of events, the use of the Chinese aspect marker -*le* (Li & Thompson 1981: 185–217, Smith 1997: 1997, Xiao & McEnery 2004, and many others) is not compulsory, as is illustrated by the following example:

(2) Chinese (Li 2014: 142, adopted from Chu 1998)
華老栓忽然坐起身，擦著火柴，點上遍身油膩的燈盞，茶館的兩間屋子裏，便彌漫了清白的光。

| *Huá Lǎoshuān* | *hūrán* | *zuò-qǐ* ø | *shēn,* | *cā-zháo* | *huǒchái,* |
|---|---|---|---|---|---|
| Hua Laoshan | suddenly | sit-move.up | body | strike-burn | match |

| *diǎn-shàng* ø | *biànshēn* | *yóunì* | *de* | *dēngzhǎn,* | *cháguǎn* | *de* |
|---|---|---|---|---|---|---|
| light-move.up | allover | grease | MOD | lamp | teahouse | MOD |

| *liǎng* | *jiān* | *wūzi lǐ,* | *biàn* | *mí-mǎn-**le** | *qīngbái* | *de* | *guāng.* |
|---|---|---|---|---|---|---|---|
| two | CL | room-LOC | then | fill-full-PFV | blue.white | MOD | light |

'Hua Laoshan suddenly sat up [in bed], struck a match, lit the grease-covered oil lamp, and then a ghostly light filled the two rooms of the teahouse.'

The above example presents four events ('sit up', 'strike a match', 'light an oil lamp', and 'fill a room with light'), each of which reaches its terminal boundary. Even though this is a clear instance of event sequentialisation, only the last event is marked by -*le*, while the previous three events remain unmarked.[4] As will be explained in Section 4, the use of the classifier -*le* depends on discourse (Li 2014).

Multifunctionality is the other property that reflects the high importance of pragmatic inference in Chinese. A grammatical marker is multifunctional if it combines functions from more than one grammatical domain or if it covers grammatical functions from a single domain that represent different values (Bisang 2015a, b). If such a marker occurs in an utterance, its relevant function must be derived either from the construction in which it occurs or from general context. Xing (2015) discusses many examples of multifunctional markers in Chinese. The present study will additionally present the multifunctionality of 'give'-verbs and of classifiers expressing definiteness as well as indefiniteness. The former example stands for multifunctionality across more than one grammatical domain, the latter illustrates how one and the same marker can express two values within a single domain (referential status).

The multifunctionality of 'give'-verbs is well-known in East and mainland Southeast Asian languages (Bisang 1996, Song 1997, Lord et al. 2002, Rangkupan 2007, Thepkanjana & Uehara 2008 and many others). In Sinitic, 'give'-verbs and

---

4 The ø sign in (2) only indicates the absence of information. It does not indicate a zero marking.

their functional range are discussed by Chappell & Peyraube (2006) and Peyraube (2015). The main functions of these verbs in Chinese are:
- Preposition: Marker of dative/benefactive
- Causative marker
- Passive marker

Each of these functions is associated with a specific construction. While many linguists use the term "coverbs" to describe verbs of an adpositional function (Li & Thompson 1981: 356–369), this study follows Paul (2015: 55–92), who convincingly argues that there is a category of prepositions in Chinese that is clearly different from verbs. The default position of PPs is preverbal (3a), some PPs, among them the ones headed by *gěi* 'give', can also occur postverbally (3b).

(3) Chinese (Wiedenhof 2015: 136)
   a. 我給他寫信。
      wǒ    gěi     tā     xiě    xìn.
      1.SG  P:give  3.SG   write  letter
      (i) 'I'm writing him a letter.'
      (ii) 'I am writing a letter for him.'

   b. 我寫信給他。
      wǒ    xiě    xìn    gěi     tā.
      1.SG  write  letter P:give  3.SG
      'I am writing a letter to him.'

The following examples illustrate the causative construction with its structure [SBJ CAUS NP$_{Causee}$ V] in (4) and the passive construction with its structure [SBJ$_{Patient}$ PASS$_{gei}$ NP$_{Agent}$ V] in (5):

(4) Chinese causative with *gěi* 'give'
    請你給他休息幾天。
    qǐng    nǐ    **gěi**   tā    xiūxí   jǐ       tiān.
    please  2.SG  CAUS     3.SG  rest    a.few    Day
    'Please, let him rest for a few days.'

(5) Chinese passive with *gěi* give' (Chao 1968: 331)
    你眼睛怎麼了？給人打了一拳頭。
    nǐ    yǎnjīng  zěnme   le?   **gěi**  rén   dǎ-le     yī    juàn tóu.
    2.SG  eye      how     PF    PASS    man   hit-PFV   one   fist
    'What's the matter with your eye? It was given a blow by someone's fist.'

Even though each function is part of a specific construction, the possibility of not marking arguments or grammatical categories may create surface structures in which the 'give'-verb can be associated with more than one construction (also cf. Bisang 2015b: 137–139 for a similar situation in Khmer). In example (6), the 'give'-verb can be analysed either as a causative marker or as a preposition (even though the prepositional interpretation is less likely). Similarly, *gěi* 'give' in example (7) can be interpreted either as a preposition or a passive marker.

(6) Chinese (Wiedenhof 2015: 148)
請你給我喫點安眠藥。
*qǐng    nǐ    **gěi**    wǒ    chī    diǎn    ānmiányào.*
please  2.SG  GIVE  1.SG  eat   some   sleeping.pill
(i) Causative: 'Please let me take some sleeping pills.'
(ii) Preposition: 'Please, take some sleeping pills for me.'

(7) Chinese (Wiedenhof 2015: 148)
安眠藥給他喫了。
*ānmiányào     **gěi**    tā    chī-le.*
sleeping.pill  GIVE  3.SG  eat-PFV
(i) Preposition: 'The sleeping pills, [he] took them for him.'
(ii) Passive: 'The sleeping pills were taken by him.'

The type of multiple analyses illustrated in the above two examples can not only be seen as a synchronic fact, it can also be seen as a driving force in processes of grammaticalization (Bisang 2015b). A given linguistic sign may occur in a situation in which the grammatical structure of a language allows analysis of it in light of another construction, which provides it with a new meaning that may then be diffused within a speech community if this situation comes up frequently enough.

The function of numeral classifiers is not limited to individuation (Greenberg 1972) or atomization (Chierchia 1998) in the context of quantification; it also extends to definiteness and indefiniteness in various Sinitic languages (Cheng & Sybesma 1999, Simpson 2005, 2017, Li & Bisang 2012, Jiang 2015, Wu 2017) and other languages of East and mainland Southeast Asia (Bisang 1999, Gerner & Bisang 2008, Simpson et al. 2011). An important construction for expressing (in)definiteness is the bare-noun construction or [CL-N] construction.[5] While this

---

[5] The other important construction is [DEM CL N]. Wu (2017) points out that this construction is ultimately more important in Sinitic.

construction is limited to indefiniteness in the postverbal construction in Standard Chinese (8a), its functional range is broader in other Sinitic languages. In the Fuyang variety of Wu Chinese, it marks definiteness preverbally and indefiniteness postverbally (8b). In Cantonese, it marks definiteness preverbally, while it can expresses indefiniteness or definiteness postverbally (8c):

(8)  The classifier in [CL N] (Li & Bisang 2012: 336)
   a. Mandarin Chinese
      *(\*ge)* lǎobǎn mǎi- le **liàng** chē.
      CL       boss   buy  PFV  CL      car
      'The boss bought a car.'

   b. Wu dialect of Fuyang
      **kɤ** lɔpan ma lə **bu** tsʰotsʰɨ.
      CL    boss  buy PFV CL   car
      'The boss bought a car.'

   c. Cantonese
      **go** louban maai-zo **ga** ce.
      CL    boss   buy-PFV  CL    car
      'The boss bought a/the car.'

In the above examples, the referential status expressed by the classifier in [CL-N] depends on word order. As Wang's (2013) typology of [CL N] constructions in 115 Sinitic languages, shows (cf. Table 1), this is not always necessarily the case. In his Type I, the classifier can express definiteness as well as indefiniteness irrespective of word order. Similarly, in Type V, in which the [CL N] construction is

Table 1: Types of (in)definiteness marking in Sinitic (based on Wang 2013).

| Type | Functions in preverbal position | | Functions in postverbal position | | Number of Languages |
|---|---|---|---|---|---|
| I   | Def | Indef | Def | Indef | 10 |
| II  | Def | Indef |     | Indef | 2  |
| III | Def |       | Def | Indef | 9  |
| IV  | Def |       |     | Indef | 2  |
| V   | –   |       | Def | Indef | 1  |
| VI  | –   |       | –   |       | 6  |
| VII | –   |       |     | Indef | 85 |

limited to the postverbal position, it can mark both functions. Thus, in eleven (ten from Type I and one from Type V) out 115 Sinitic languages, word order has no effect on the (in)definiteness interpretation of the classifier.

The multifunctionality of the classifier as a marker of definiteness and indefiniteness shows up in 24 languages that range from Types I to V. Given the total of 115 languages, the classifier is multifunctional in 21% of the Sinitic languages analyzed by Wang (2013). Type I is found across various subfamilies of Sinitic (Jiangwu Mandarin, Hui, Wu, Xiang, Hakka, Pinghua, Min, Gan), while Type V is found only in the Shangyao (上尧) variety of the Pinghua subfamily in Nanning (Wang 2013: 387). The six languages in which the classifier is not involved in marking referential status (Type VI) are all from the Min family. Type VII, the most frequent type, reflects the situation in Standard Chinese (cf. example (8a)).

In addition to multifunctionality, numeral classifiers are not obligatory as markers of (in)definiteness. Even though more research is needed on this topic, the case of Weining Ahmao (the Hmong-Mien language spoken in Guizhou Province) will be discussed here briefly. This language has even developed a fully-fledged morphological paradigm for classifiers (Wang Fushi's 1957 excellent study; Gerner & Bisang 2008), which combines the categories of number (singular vs. plural), referential status (definite vs. indefinite) and size (augmentative, medial, small). As will be discussed in Section 5, this paradigm shows consistent reduction of the autonomy of the linguistic sign in terms of several of Lehmann's (1995) parameters and may thus be seen as a good example of the coevolution of meaning and form in a language of East and mainland Southeast Asia. In spite of this, (in)definite marking is not obligatory and thus deviates in an important way from the general expectation associated with high degrees of grammaticalization.

The following text in (9) from Wang Fushi (1957: 107–109) illustrates how (in)definiteness is marked in a narrative.[6] The story is about a man who walks through the jungle with a basket of hats. When he falls asleep, the monkeys come and steal them. As soon he becomes aware of this, he gets angry and tries to get his hats back from the monkeys who mock him from the trees. At the end of the story, he gets so furious that he throws his own hat onto the ground. The monkeys imitate him and this is how he ultimately gets his hats back. In this story, the animate protagonists, i.e. the man and the monkeys, are always marked for (in)definiteness, while backgrounded nominal concepts often remain unmarked. The hats, which may be seen as inanimate "protagonists" that remain important

---

6 There are not that many published texts available. For some other texts, cf. Wang Deguang (1986).

throughout the story, are generally marked for (in)definiteness with one exception (cf. (9c) below).

The story begins with the passage in (9a). As one can see in line 1, the protagonist $tu^{55}$ $nu^{55}$ 'human being, man, woman' is introduced by the numeral $i^{55}$ 'one' followed by the classifier in its medium-size indefinite form.[7] Later, the protagonist always occurs with the classifier in its definite form (cf. lines 5 and 7 in (9b) below). Moreover, the protagonist is marked by the medium-size indefinite form ($lae^{35}$) at his/her first mention for expressing that s/he is of average size (on the gender of this noun, cf. below). The second noun of interest in (9a) is 'hats', which is marked as indefinite by the numeral $i^{55}$ 'one' in line 2. This time, however, indefiniteness is marked only by the numeral, because the container noun $g\text{'}œy^{31}$ 'basket' cannot be inflected for (in)definiteness. Finally, the backgrounded noun $tau^{55}$ 'hill' is unmarked (9b).

(9) a.  Weining Ahmao (Wang Fushi 1957: 107)
    $m\text{'}a^{35}$    $i^{55}$    $g\text{'}au^{35}$    $i^{55}$    $lae^{35}$      $tu^{55}$ $nu^{55}$    $ti^{11}$
    there.is one time one CL:MED:INDEF:SG Man carry.on.back
    $i^{55}$    $\textipa{n}\text{'}ie$    $g\text{'}œy^{31}$    $kau^{11}$    $tɕ\text{'}au^{33}$    $v\text{'}ae^{31}$    $i^{55}$    $lu^{55}$    $tau^{55}$.
    one big basket hat pass place one CL[8] hill
    'Once upon a time, **a man** who carried **a big basket of hats** on his back was passing a hill.'

The passage in (9b) illustrates how other backgrounded concepts remain unmarked. Thus, $tɕa^{33}$ 'wind' and $nau^{33}$ $nau^{53/31}$ 'birds' occur as bare nouns. The only exception is $hnu^{55}$ 'sun' (lines 6 and 9), whose occurrence with the classifier may be due to its uniqueness.[9] This passage also illustrates the pervasive definiteness marking of the noun $tu^{55}$ $nu^{55}$ 'man' (lines 3 and 6). As one can see additionally, the man is now marked by a different classifier, i.e., $tsi^{55}$ in its medium-size definite form of $tsae^{55}$. This classifier, which is called an auxiliary classifier by Wang Fushi (1957), specifically serves for marking male gender. Thus, $lae^{35}$ $tu^{55}$ $nu^{55}$ [CL:MED:INDEF:SG human] in line 1 of (9a) is gender-neutral and so it can mean either 'a man' or 'a woman'. With the use of the auxiliary classifier in $tsae^{55}$ $tu^{55}$ $nu^{55}$ [CL$_{aux}$:MED:DEF:SG human], the gender of the noun is specified as male.

---

**7** The selection of the medium-size form indicates that the man was supposed to be of about average size, maybe also that he had no particular social status.
**8** Here, Wang Fushi (1957) uses the augmentative form of the classifier. In his description from 1957, there is no definite/indefinite distinction in the augmentative form (but cf. Section 5).
**9** I do not have enough data to comment on whether or to what extent the definite classifier is obligatory with unique nouns like $hnu^{55}$ 'sun'.

Finally, the previously introduced basket is now marked by the definite form of the classifier ($lae^{55}$) in line 7.

(9) b. Weining Ahmao (Wang Fushi 1957: 108)

| $\text{no}^{55}$ | $v'ae^{31}$ | $lae^{55}$ | $ndlo^{55}$ | $ko^{33}$ | $a^{33}zau^{33}$ | $\text{ni}^{55}$ | | |
|---|---|---|---|---|---|---|---|---|
| be.at | place | CL | inside | root | forest | DEM | | |
| $t\varepsilon a^{33}$ | $ts'a^{55}$ | $gi^{11}$ | $ntsie^{55}ntsie^{55}$, | $tae^{11}$ | $m'a^{35}$ | | $nau^{33}$ | $nau^{53/31}$ |
| wind | blow | ADV | intensive | | also | there.is | bird | RED |
| $G'a^{35}$ | $gi^{11}$ | $nto^{55}$ | $nd'uu$. | $Tsae^{55}$ | | | $tuu^{55}nuu^{55}$ | $\text{ni}^{55}$, |
| call | ADV | make.noise | intensive | CL:MED:DEF:SG | | | man | DEM |
| $z'au^{31}$ | $v'ae^{31}$ | $fae^{35}$ | | $qau^{55}$ | $ntau^{33/11}$ | $tau^{33}$ | | |
| sit | place | CL:DIM:INDEF:SG | | bottom | tree | get | | |
| $py^{33}$ | $l'oey^{31}$. | $Lu^{55}$ | | $hnu^{55}$ | $t'au^{33}$ | $v'ae^{31}$ | $ta^{55}$ | $a^{33}ndl'au^{33/11}$ |
| sleep | go | CL:AUG:DEF:SG | | sun | from | place | some | leaf |
| $pi^{55}$ | $tau^{55}$ | $d'a^{31}$ | $toey^{33}$ | $t\varepsilon i^{33}$ | $tau^{33}$ | $\text{n'i}^{13}$. $Tsae^{55}$ | | $tuu^{55}nuu^{55}$ |
| inside | kick | foot | shine | at | 3.SG | CL:MED: DEF:SG | | man |
| $\text{ni}^{55}$, | $tau^{33}$ | $v'ae^{31}$ | $lae^{55}$ | | | $g'oey^{31}$ | $k'oey^{11}$ | $d'oey^{31}$ |
| DEM | from | place | CL:MED:DEF:SG | | | basket | Take | move.ou |
| $i^{55}$ | $lu^{55}$ | $kau^{11}$ | $l'o^{13}$ | $ntau^{33}$ | | $t\varepsilon ie^{33}$, | $a^{33}li^{33}\text{ni}^{55}$, | |
| one | CL:AUG | hat | come | wear.on.head | | Erect | do.like.this | |
| $lu^{55}$ | $hnu^{55}$ | $tae^{11}$ | $t\varepsilon i^{33}$ | $hi^{33/55}$ | $dau^{31/53}$ | $\text{n'i}^{13}$ | $dau^{11}$. | |
| CL:AUG | sun | so | shine | NEG | RES | 3.SG | SFP | |

'There in the forest, the wind was blowing intensively and all sorts of birds were singing. The man sat down at the bottom of a tree to get [some] sleep. The sun shone [lit. 'kicked and shone'] on him through some leaves. The man took a hat from the basket and put it onto his head. Having done so, the sun was not able to shine [on him].'

In the last passage to be quoted here (9c), the monkeys ($lie^{55}$) enter into the scene. They are first marked as indefinite by the numeral $i^{55}$ 'one' followed by the group classifier in its indefinite form of $mb'a^{35}$ 'group' (cf. line 2; the corresponding basic form is $mb'o^{35}$). The passage also mentions backgrounded nouns like $li^{33} fau^{33}$ 'head', $ntau^{33}$ 'tree' and $a^{55} dz'i^{31}$ 'branch'. All of them occur as bare nouns. The hats ($kau^{11}$, cf. line 4) also occur in their bare form. This is due to the fact that the identification of the individual hats is irrelevant in this context. What matters is only that each monkey is wearing one.

(9) c. Weining Ahmao (Wang Fushi 1957: 108–109)

| $\text{n'i}^{13}$ | $tau^{33}$ | $tşau^{33}$ | $li^{33} fau^{33}$ | $n'a^{31}$ | $tau^{33}$ | $ntau^{33}$ | $a^{55} şa^{55}$, |
|---|---|---|---|---|---|---|---|
| 3.SG | get | raise | head | look | at | tree | above |

| | | | | | | | |
|---|---|---|---|---|---|---|---|
| *m'a³⁵* | *i⁵⁵* | *mb'a³⁵* | | *lie⁵⁵* | *ɲo⁵⁵* | *v'ae³¹* | *a⁵⁵ dzʼi³¹* |
| there.is | one | CL<sub>group</sub>:DIM:INDEF:SG | | monkey | be.at | Place | branch |

*ntau³³ a⁵⁵ ṣa⁵⁵,   tsʻa³³   tu³³              lie⁵⁵           tu³³   ntau³³*
tree   above      each   CL:AUG:DEF   monkey   All   wear.on.head
*kau¹¹   tlʼie³³   mʼau³³   tlʼie³³   lʼo³³   vʻae³¹   a⁵⁵ dzʼi³¹   ntau³³   a⁵⁵ ṣa⁵⁵.*
hat    jump    go     jump    come   place    branch     tree     above

'He raised his head and looked up into the trees above. There was a group of monkeys in the tree branches above. Each of the monkeys was wearing a hat and jumping around in the branches of the trees.'

Example (9a-c) illustrates how (in)definiteness marking in Weining Ahmao depends on prominence in discourse: protagonists are always marked; backgrounded nouns tend to be unmarked. Another factor related to prominence is animacy. In the above texts, the animate protagonists (the man, the monkeys) are always marked, while the hats, as the inanimate "protagonists," are unmarked in one instance.

## 3 Economy-based vs. explicitness-based maturation

Processes of grammaticalization have consequences for the synchronic grammatical properties of a language. As was pointed out by Dahl (2004: 105), it makes sense from an evolutionary perspective "to assume that a system like that of English and other Indo-European languages can only come about after a historical development of significant length, involving a number of intermediate stages". In the process of such developments, a language accumulates grammatical material in its grammar G that was not there at an earlier stage of G' of that language. Such a process is called maturation[10] by Dahl (2004: 103–155). Typical results of maturation are complex word structure (inflectional morphology, derivational morphology, incorporating constructions), lexical idiosyncrasies (grammatical gender, inflectional classes, idiosyncratic case marking), syntactic phenomena that are dependent on inflectional morphology (agreement, and partly case

---

[10] Dahl's (2004: 105) definition of maturation runs as follows: '*x* is a mature phenomenon if there is some identifiable and non-universal phenomenon or a restricted set of such phenomena *y*, such that for any language L, if *x* exists in L there is some ancestor L' of L such that L' has *y* but not *x*.' The above description in terms of accumulation of grammatical material follows Ansaldo & Nordhoff (2009: 358).

marking) and a few other phenomena (cf. Dahl 2004: 114–115 for the whole list). What ultimately characterizes these phenomena is their relatively strong deviation from unrestricted concatenation, i.e. from restrictions which are concerned with the order of linguistic signs and the simple juxtaposition of lexical items by the addition of some fixed elements (compare the juxtaposition in English *much snow* with the insertion of *de* 'of' in French *beaucoup de neige* 'much of snow') (Dahl 2004: 52–53). While phenomena of unrestricted or mildly restricted concatenation are seen as linear phenomena, the non-linear phenomena that go beyond word order and juxtaposition are typically associated with maturation and the structures mentioned above (Dahl 2004: 114).

Maturation as it is described by Dahl (2004) is an important diachronic process of universal relevance but it cannot account for the absence of a lot of the above maturation-related phenomena in an isolating language like Chinese and most mainland Southeast Asian languages with their long histories of grammaticalization. At a closer look, the problem with Dahl's (2004) concept of maturation is that it cannot model characteristic properties of grammaticalization in these languages, i.e. the lack of coevolution of meaning and form and the importance of pragmatic inference.

The coevolution of meaning and form in terms of increasing fusion can be seen as a consequence of increasing maturity in the sense that "[f]usional morphology presupposes that there was affixal morphology at an earlier stage, and affixal morphology presupposes periphrastic constructions" (Dahl 2004: 107). If this process is extended to syntax, we ultimately arrive at a grammaticalization cline that shares quite a few similarities with the one from Givón (1979) presented in (1):

(10) Development of grammatical patterns (Dahl 2004: 106):
 FREE > PERIPHRASTIC > AFFIXAL > FUSIONAL

Since maturation in terms of Dahl (2004) clearly reaches its limits in Sinitic if one gets to the stage of FUSIONAL (but cf. Section 5), there must be other factors of maturation that are not covered by Dahl's (2004) approach.

In the context of discourse, advanced maturation reaches a stage at which the use of a grammatical marker is no longer subject to pragmatic inference and becomes obligatory. As Dahl (2004: 106) points out, "if we find an obligatory grammatical marker in a language, there must have been a stage of that language where the same marker was used in the construction(s) in question, although in a less systematic fashion." Again, maturation in terms of Dahl (2004) does not cover the case in which grammatical markers remain facultative. Similarly, multifunctionality is problematic in this approach. In processes of increasing morphologization that lead to inflectional paradigms, the extent to which a marker stands for different functions that must be pragmatically inferred is significantly reduced. Of course, inflectional systems are characterized by what Haspelmath (2002) calls "cumulation", i.e. the combination of two or more functions in a single portmanteau morpheme (cf. the combination of singular [number], feminine [gender] and accusative [case] in the Latin suffix -*um* in a word like *amic-um* 'a/the friend [ACC]') but this is another type of multifunctionality in which each of the relevant functions represents just one value of its corresponding category and the individual categories cannot be separated as they can in agglutinating languages.

If the above observations from a significant number of processes of grammaticalization in Sinitic and other East and Southeast Asian languages are correct, there must be other factors that matter in the course of diachronic change. As was pointed out in Bisang (2009, 2015a), maturation as it is defined by Dahl (2004) is based on explicitness. In this scenario, grammatical markers aim for obligatoriness and for the expression of a clear-cut grammatical function. In an alternative scenario, what drives the expression of grammatical function is economy. The idea that grammatical structures are the result of competing motivations between a force that aims at explicitness and another one that tries to maximize economy is not new. It goes back at least to von der Gabelentz (1891: 251) and it is discussed in terms of iconicity vs. economy by Haiman (1983). Moreover, it is of central importance in Optimality Theory (cf. the distinction between faithfulness and markedness constraints e.g. in Kager 1999: 4–8).

As was argued in Bisang (2009, 2015a), the motivation of that competition lies in what is called the "articulatory bottleneck" by Levinson (2000: 29). In this model, human speech encoding is by far the slowest part of speech production and comprehension. Other processes like parsing or pragmatic inference can produce much more information in a given time interval than articulation. Thus, grammatical structures can be seen as solutions to the problem of keeping the balance between the needs of being explicit and articulation, and the needs of economy and pragmatic inference. An examination of the grammar G' of a language at any given stage of its development reveals that there is actually a bifurcation. If explicitness wins, the resulting Grammar G at a later stage will be the product of maturation in terms of Dahl (2004). If economy wins, our Grammar G will be of a type that favors pragmatic inference and reduces the coevolution of meaning and form (Bisang 2015a). These two types of maturation will be called "explicitness-based maturation" and "economy-based maturation" in the remainder of this study.

The scenario described in Figure 1 applies to individual processes of diachronic change. What can be observed in Sinitic and other East and mainland Southeast Asian languages is that economy-based maturation wins in many

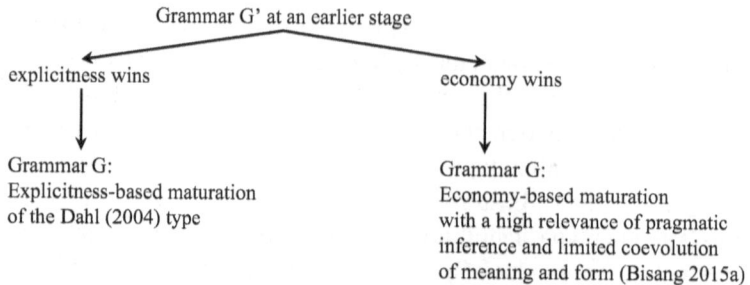

**Figure 1:** Bifurcation: Explicitness-based vs. economy-based maturation.

individual processes. In fact, it looks as if economy-based maturation has reached a level which is rarely seen in other languages. It shows up in the interaction of syntax and pragmatics in general (Huang Y. 1994) and in processes of grammaticalization in particular (Bisang 2009, 2011, 2015a, b). At the level of the lack of obligatoriness, radical pro-drop (cf. Section 2) is a well-known example of the general relevance of pragmatics in the interaction of syntax and pragmatics, while the omission of grammatical markers of tense-aspect (cf. -*le* in (2)) and other categories specifically illustrates the relevance of pragmatic inference in grammaticalization. At the level of multifunctionality, the general relevance of pragmatics in the interaction of syntax and pragmatics shows up in the versatility and coindexation properties of the Chinese anaphora 自己 *zìjǐ* 'self' (Huang Y. 1994). The multifunctionality in the specific context of grammaticalization manifests itself in the examples of 'give'-verbs and the (in)definite functions of classifiers (cf. Section 2) as well as in the examples discussed by Xing (2015).

# 4 The division of labor between grammaticalization and lexicalization in economy-based maturation

The aim of this Section is to show that explicitness-based and economy-based maturation produce different effects in the grammar and in the lexicon. It will be argued that in Sinitic (and in many other East and mainland Southeast Asian languages), grammar and processes of grammaticalization are dominated by economy-based maturation, while the lexicon tends more toward explicitness-based maturation. For that purpose, the grammatical properties of the examples of (i) the perfective marker -*le* and (ii) numeral classifiers as (in)definiteness markers will be analyzed with regard to their interaction with the lexicon.

The fact that the perfective marker -*le* is not obligatory was pointed out in Section 2 in the context of example (2), which is by no means extraordinary. Despite the absence of overt grammatical perfectivity marking, the inference of the sequential relation among the four events in (2) is quite straightforward. To model the way sequences like this are understood, I follow Li's (2014) very insightful analysis, which is based on the two-component view of aspect as developed by Smith (1997). According to her approach, the perfective aspect has two sides: a grammatical side called "view-point aspect" and a lexical side called "situation aspect". In the case of perfectivity in Chinese, grammatical aspect is marked by the perfective marker -*le*, while lexical aspect is expressed by a variety of lexical means that indicate terminal event bounding (Li 2014: 137–139). One lexical expression format is the resultative construction (e.g. 看清楚 *kàn qīngchǔ* [see clear] 'see clearly'), other formats are expressions of event quantification (e.g. 我看了他一眼 *wǒ kàn-le tā yīyǎn* [1.SG look.at-PFV 3.SG one glance] 'I (will) take a look at him') and coverb phrases with a bounding effect (e.g. the coverb [COV] 給 *gěi* 'give' in: 他給我寄了一本書 *tā gěi wǒ jì-le yī běn shū* [3.SG COV 1.SG send-PFV one CL book] 'He sent me a book'). A similar point is also made in Yang (2011: 392), who shows that "-*le* itself does not provide an endpoint to terminate a situation." This information is rather contributed by lexical expressions, the verb reduplicating mechanism and contextual information (Yang 2011: 387).

A look at the verbs in the four events of example (2) shows that all of them are resultative constructions: 坐起 *zuò qǐ* [sit move.up] 'sit up', 擦著 *cā zháo* [strike be.ignited] 'to strike [a match]', 點上 *diǎn shàng* [light move.up] 'to light [the lamp]', and 彌滿 *mí mǎn* [fill full] 'to fill'. Resultative constructions consist of a series of two verbs $V_1$-$V_2$, in which the second verb ($V_2$) expresses a result of the first verb ($V_1$). At the same time, $V_2$ makes a dynamic event expressed by $V_1$ telic and aspectually bounded. The productivity of resultative verbs ($V_2$) varies. A few of them are very productive (e.g. 完 *wán* 'finish'), while a large number are lexically quite restricted, i.e., they can only be combined with a small number of $V_1$ (e.g. 飽 *bǎo* 'be full' in combination with the verb 喫 *chī* 'eat': 喫飽 *chī bǎo* [eat full] 'be full [have eaten enough]'). Given the sheer number of resultative verbs (about 200 – 300; cf. Li and Thompson 1981: 54; also cf. Cartier 1972, Xu *et al.* 2008), it is clear that the resultative construction is a very powerful instrument for expressing situation aspect.

Resultative verbs and other lexical expressions of terminal event boundaries give the speaker enough information to infer the sequential relation between the juxtaposed events. In fact, the information provided by resultatives or other boundary-setting markers is often necessary. In example (2), the first event of *hūrán zuò-qǐ* [suddenly sit-move.up] would be ungrammatical without *qǐ* 'move up' in the V₂ position. Since using a lexical strategy to encode the terminal boundary of an event is sufficient in Chinese grammar, the perfective marker *-le* is free to express additional functions associated with discourse. In Li's (2014) analysis, it is used for grounding. Depending on whether the verb expresses a dynamic activity or a resultant state, perfective *-le* marks either foregrounding or backgrounding. The individual grounding roles depend on the transitivity features of the entire clause and the discourse context rather than on the verb alone (Li 2014: 128). In the case of example (2), the use of *-le* in the final event highlights the peak event (Chu 1998). After three preparatory events, the climax of a ghostly atmosphere as a result of the previous events is reached.

In languages with obligatory grammatical aspect distinctions, grammatical aspect interacts with lexical aspect but cannot be used independently. Thus, what is combined in obligatory aspect systems is split into two parts in Chinese, i.e., lexical expression (situation aspect) and grammatical aspect (view-point aspect). From the perspective of maturation, there is a high degree of economy-based maturation at the level of grammatical aspect (non-obligatoriness of *-le*), while explicitness-based maturation is focused on the lexicon for expressing temporal bounding. In other words, the Chinese aspect system is very explicit at the level of the lexicon but it can be more economic at the level of grammatical aspect because its marking depends on discourse.

The case of numeral classifiers as markers of definiteness and indefiniteness, and the importance of pragmatic inference as it is associated with economy-based maturation was discussed in Section 2. In addition to these indicators of economy-based maturation, classifier systems of East and mainland Southeast Asian languages are additionally characterized by a strong lexical component, which arises from the fact that these languages generally have a rather large inventory of numeral classifiers. The criteria for selecting individual classifiers with individual nouns vary cross-linguistically (Bisang 1999). It is well-known that, in Thai, the assignment of a classifier is rigidly determined by the lexicon (cf. the classical paper by Haas 1942 and many others later). Thus, each noun is either associated with a specific classifier (e.g. *rótyon* 'car' must take the classifier *khan*) or repeated fully or partially in the classifier position as a repeater classifier (cf. *kɔ̀ sǎam kɔ̀* [island three CL] 'three islands' and *ráan-ʔahǎan sǎam ráan* [shop-food three CL] 'three restaurants').

In Chinese, some nouns can occur with more than one classifier. In such cases, the classifier highlights some specific meanings associated with the noun 將軍 *jiāngjūn* 'general', as illustrated in (11). While the general classifier 個 *ge* is used as the default classifier for humans in (11a), other classifiers refer to specific properties of the noun, often linked to the context in which these properties are relevant. In (11b), the honorific classifier 位 *wèi* is used for reasons of politeness. The classifier 名 *míng* in (11c) points out that the general is mentioned on a list of generals, while the classifier 員 *yuán* in (11d) specifically refers to the general in light of his military rank:

(11) Chinese (Zhang 2007)
    a. 一個將軍
        *yī*      **ge**     *jiāngjūn*
        one     CL      general
        'a general'

    b. 一位將軍
        *yī*      **wèi**    *jiāngjūn*
        CL     boss    general
        'an [honorable] general'

    c. 一名將軍
        *yī*      **míng**   *jiāngjūn*
        one     CL      general
        'a general [in a list]'

    d. 一員將軍
        *yī*      **yuán**   *jiāngjūn*
        one     CL      general
        'a general [highlighting his military rank]'

Even from the above rather short discussion, it becomes evident that numeral classifiers as markers of referential status are not only characterized by their lack of obligatoriness but also by a rather complex system of lexical constraints that determine the use of the adequate classifier with individual nouns. In languages in which classifier selection can be employed for semantic specification, the interpretation of the concre te meaning of a noun in a given context depends on a rather complex interaction of lexical-semantic meaning and pragmatic inference.

From the perspective of maturation, one can see again that grammar is characterized by a high degree of economy-based maturation that supports the absence of obligatoriness and multifunctionality in contexts of definiteness and indefiniteness, while the lexicon is characterized by fine-grained semantic distinctions which, depending on the language, modify the semantics of the noun they classify to a smaller or larger extent (cf. Thai with Chinese in (11)). Such a lexically-based system is the result of a long-term diachronic development that accumulates rules of classifier assignment which are highly language specific.

In each of the above examples, the lexicon plays a comparatively prominent role, which is partly expressed by the grammar in other languages outside of East and mainland Southeast Asia. In the case of perfectivity, lexical aspect is sufficient in contexts in which systems with obligatory marking have to use grammatical aspect. In the case of (in)definiteness, the selection of the right classifier follows the same principles as with numeral classifiers. Thus, it is to a considerable extent a matter of the lexicon (with some cross-linguistic variation), while the question of whether the classifier is used is determined by discourse. The higher relevance of the lexicon in systems whose grammar is more strongly dominated by economy-based maturation may also shed some interesting light on Xing's (2015) observation that there is a greater similarity between lexicalization and grammaticalizaton in Sinitic than in German or English. If some of the inferential burden triggered by the lack of obligatoriness and multifunctionality in the grammar is mitigated at the level of the lexicon, the lexicon may partly take over grammatical functions. This different division of labor may then be the reason why the processes of grammaticalization and lexicalization share more similarities in Sinitic (and other East and mainland Southeast Asian languages).

## 5 Grammaticalization in economy-based vs. explicitness-based maturation

Since explicitness-based maturation and economy-based maturation are in permanent competition, explicitness-based maturation is by no means excluded even in East and mainland Southeast Asian languages. After a short explanation of the factors that support the dominance of economy-based maturation over a long period of time in these languages, some rather recently described phenomena of incipient inflectional morphology will be presented. A comparison of the properties of this morphology with the properties of explicitness-based, rich systems of morphology will show that explicitness-based systems of morphology generate options for grammaticalization which are not available in languages with dominant economy-based maturation.

As is well-known, Chinese used to have morphology in the period of Old Chinese (11th – 3rd centuries BC; Downer 1959, Baxter 1992, Sagart 1999, Baxter & Sagart 2014). Even though there are alternative approaches to the reconstruction of Old Chinese morphology, it is quite clear that it is rather of a derivational nature and did not express inflectional categories integrated into morphological paradigms. Moreover, many of its bound morphemes expressed more than one function. The loss of that morphology occurred around the 2nd century AD and was an important factor in the activation of new processes of grammaticalization that gave rise to various new products of grammaticalization, among them the resultative construction, various tense-aspect markers, coverbs and directional verbs (Xu 2006, Bisang 2010, Xing 2013, 2015). Since that time, morphology beyond word formation has developed rather rarely in Standard Chinese and, if it developed, it seldom produced subsyllabic markers (cf. Section 2), nor, with the exception of personal pronouns, did it produce inflectional morphological paradigms, if one disregards personal pronouns (cf. Section 2). What can be seen happening in many cases over the last 1800 years is the effect of economy-based maturation characterized by the lack of obligatoriness and by multifunctionality as outlined in Section 2.

This situation of high economy-based maturation remained stable since for at least two millennia in many varieties of Sinitic. A similar stability can also be observed in many other East and mainland Southeast Asian languages as far as their history can be reconstructed or followed through written documents (cf. Bisang 2014 for some details). Since processes of grammaticalization that follow the full cline of grammaticalization with its coevolution of meaning and form as desribed in (1) and (10) are cross-linguistically frequent, the remarkable degree of stability and economy-based maturation in East and mainland Southeast Asian languages needs explanation. As was pointed out by Bisang (2004, 2008, 2011), there are several factors that contribute to that situation. For that reason, only a brief summary will be provided here.

The first part of the explanation is strongly connected to the lack of obligatoriness and multifunctionality and their blocking effects on the development of inflectional morphological paradigms once they were firmly established. The effects of these two factors are further enhanced by certain phonological properties of the languages involved and sociolinguistic factors of linguistic contact. To understand the blocking effects of the lack of obligatoriness and multifunctionality, it is necessary to briefly look at what makes a morphological paradigm. According to Baerman & Corbett's (2010) definition, a morphological paradigm is defined in terms of the three components of a form paradigm, a content paradigm and the mapping of these two paradigms onto each other. The interaction of these components creates patterns consisting of categories and subcategories (values) with individual cells that are filled by individual markers (e.g. the two categories of number and person with their respective values of singular and plural vs. 1st, 2nd and 3rd person in a prototypical paradigm of verbal agreement).

The conditions that support the development of morphological paradigms are the frequency of their markers and the existence of clearly determined semantic domains such as tense, person or number. Frequency is an important component in the increase of fusion between a lexical item and a grammatical marker (Bybee 1985). If economy-based maturation operates against the marking of a grammatical category even if its marker stands for a highly general concept that can be combined with any number of lexical items (cf. Bybee 1985 on generality), the likelihood of its integration into a paradigm remains low. As for the condition of semantically clear-cut categories: the multifunctionality of markers clearly undermines their integration into such patterns. As a consequence, grammatical markers in a scenario of economy-based maturation strongly tend to lack the momentum that is necessary for paradigm formation.

In addition, processes of morphologization and paradigm formation are generally affected by phonological and sociolinguistic factors. Phonologically, East and mainland Southeast Asian languages are characterized by two rather strong constraints (Ansaldo & Lim 2004, Bisang 2008):
– the discreteness of syllable boundaries and the strong tendency to avoid subsyllabic morphemes,
– phonotactic restraints.

These two constraints together affect the formal side of grammaticalization, which is characterized by phonetic erosion in terms of duration and vowel quality rather than by morphological reduction (Ansaldo & Lim 2004). Of additional importance is tonality. In languages with more than one tonal register, like Cantonese and Hokkien, pitch tends not to be reduced in processes of grammaticalization because tonal contrast must be maintained for reasons of keeping up semantic contrasts. In Sinitic languages like Mandarin with only one tonal register, the distinctiveness of pitch is less important and this facilitates loss of tone in some cases, as one can see from toneless grammatical markers like –*le* (perfective).

The sociolinguistic factor that works against the development of morphology is linguistic contact. Even if there is morphology in an East and mainland Southeast Asian language, the fact that the function expressed by it is marked by an independent word in the surrounding languages may favor the grammaticalization of new markers from the existing lexicon of that language. A good example is the formation of agent nouns in Khmer (Bisang 2011: 115), which can be formed using the infix -*m*- as in *s<m>ò:m* 'beggar (from *sò:m* 'ask, ask a favour') or *ch<m>am* 'guard [n.]' from *cam* 'wait for, guard, keep'. The more productive strategy of agent noun formation in Khmer is identical to the strategies used in Thai, Vietnamese and Sinitic, i.e., the use of a head with the meaning of 'person, man' like Khmer *nèək* 'person'. Thus, compounds of the type *nèək-daə* [person-walk] 'pedestrian' or *nèək-taeɲ* [person-compose/write] 'author, writer, composer,' are much more common in contemporary Khmer. If there is such a tendency in contact situations to avoid morphological strategies at the level of word formation, the probability of using affixation for expressing inflectional categories in Khmer and a vast majority of East and mainland Southeast Asian languages in general is even less likely, since there are no inflectional affixes to start from.

In spite of the above factors that minimize the coevolution of meaning and form in East and mainland Southeast Asian languages, there are examples based on explicitness-based maturation. A particularly remarkable case in point are the paradigms of obligatory case suffixes in the Sinitic languages of the Qinghai-Gansu *Sprachbund*. Such paradigms are found in the Northwestern Mandarin dialects of Linxia (臨夏, spoken in Hezhou), Wutun (五屯, spoken in the Qinghai Tongren district) and Tangwang (唐汪, spoken in the Dongxiang zone of Gansu) (Ma 1982, Li 1993, Dede 2007 and several papers in the edited volume of Cao, Djamouri & Peyraube 2015). In the following example from Tangwang, we find the case markers for dative (*-a*), accusative (*-xa*) and instrumental (*-la*):

(12) Tangwang Chinese (Djamouri 2015: 257)
我那阿羊肉哈碳啦烤給寨。
wɔ　　nə-a　　jãʐʉ-xa　　thẽ-la　　khɔ-ki-tʂɛ.
1.SG　3.SG-DAT　mutton-ACC　coal-INSTR　roast-APPL-IPV
'I roast mutton for him with coal.'

This phenomenon is part of the Qinghai-Gansu *Sprachbund* (Dwyer 1992, Slater 2003), a contact area with languages from four different families (Sinitic, Tibeto-Burman [Amdo Tibetan], Mongolic and Turkic). Since case marking is obligatory and each case marker is monofunctional, this system has all the properties associated with explicitness-based maturation. As it is very likely that this is the result of linguistic contact mainly with speakers of Turkic or Mongolic languages,[11] case marking in the Qinghai-Gansu *Sprachbund* is a good example of how contact can affect the selection of explicitness-based maturation in languages which tend to prefer economy-based maturation.

Other patterns of morphological paradigms are the result of language-internal processes. This is illustrated by incipient systems of inflectional verbal morphology that go beyond concatenative morphology, i.e., (i) fusional tense-aspect marking in various Sinitic languages (mostly Mandarin and Jin languages), (ii) inflected classifiers in Weining Ahmao, and (iii) the agreement clitics of Semelai (Mon-Khmer: Aslian). As will be shown below for each of these examples of explicitness-based maturation, the morphology that arises in situations

---

[11] The identity of the contact languages is not quite clear, since there are no speakers of these languages who currently live in the area of the Sinitic languages that have case suffixes. In spite of this, the presence of speakers of Turkic or Mongolic is historically very plausible.

in which economy-based maturation dominates has still preserved some basic properties of economy-based maturation.

Even though the existence of inflectional verbal morphology that goes beyond concatenative morphology has been described in Chinese linguistics for quite some time, it was Arcodia (2013, 2015) who recently made this fact accessible to Western linguists. As he points out, inflectional tense-aspect morphology is present in Sinitic varieties spoken in the provinces of Henan, Shandong, Shanxi and to some extent also in Shaanxi and Hebei. Most of these varieties belong to Mandarin and Jin varieties. Arcodia (2013 and 2015: 10) proposes three major areal clusters showing fusional morphology in Northern China:

(i) The Northern part of Henan province, possibly including the area around Zhengzhou and Kaifeng plus Southern Hebei,
(ii) Shaanxi,
(iii) Shandong, specifically the central-eastern part.

The morphological patterns found in these areas are derived from grammatical markers which lose their syllabic individuality and get fused more tightly with the rhyme of the preceding syllable. As a result, these languages show *ablaut*, tonal morphology and rhotacisation (the integration of a rhotic consonant into the coda position of the stem syllable). As a consequence of these processes of fusion, verbs often occur in two forms: a basic form and a derived form. This is illustrated by an example from the dialect of Xunxian (浚县, Central Plains Mandarin, Henan), in which the verb with the meaning of 'change' (改, Mandarin pronounciation *gǎi*) has the basic form $kai^{55}$ and the derived form $k\varepsilon^{55}$. In (13), the derived form of the verb is interpreted as perfective:

(13) Xunxian (Jin: Sinitic; Arcodia 2013; Xin 2016a: 47)
會改明個了。
$xuei^{213}$　　$k\varepsilon^{55}$　　　　　　　$m\varepsilon^{42}$ kə　　kə.
meeting　change.GOAL　tomorrow　COS
'the meeting was moved to tomorrow.'

In the Xunxian dialect, 29 rhymes out of 42 rhymes of the verb occur in two forms with regular changes from the basic to the derived form. Thus, verbs with their rhymes in *au*, *ou* and *əŋ* change into *o*, while the rhymes in *i*, *iɛ* and *in* change into *iɛ* (with no difference for *iɛ*) (Arcodia 2015: 16–17). The patterns that arise look like binary *ablaut* paradigms (Arcodia 2015: 17) for expressing two different values of a grammatical category. However, a closer look at these patterns reveals that such an analysis is problematic for at least the following two reasons: (i) the derived form is often multifunctional and (ii) the degree of obligatoriness often remains unclear from the descriptions provided by the individual grammars.

The multifunctionality of the derived verb forms is due to their history of grammaticalization. In its initial phase, the main verb could be followed by a variety of second verbs which expressed different grammatical functions and underwent parallel processes of reduction and fusion. In the case of the Xunxian dialect, the markers involved are cognates of the Mandarin -*le* (perfective marker), -*zhe* (durative marker), 到 *dao* 'arrive' or 上 *shang* 'move up' for marking the subsequent noun phrase as a goal (cf. Arcodia 2013, from Xin 2006b: 89). This multifunctional origin is reflected in the fact that the derived form can express the perfective, the durative and the attainment of a goal in the Xunxian dialect. Many grammatical descriptions do not explicitly address the question of obligatoriness. In spite of this, it is quite clear that the more analytic form with the relevant second verb is still used in addition to the reduced form in many of the dialects having this type of inflectional morphology. Arcodia (2013) describes the use of this alternative construction in terms of social register. Given the multifunctionality of the derived verb forms, one may as well argue that the selection of the analytic form is based on questions of explicitness. If the speaker cannot be sure that the right grammatical function can be inferred by the hearer, s/he adds the relevant grammatical marker. From such a perspective, the selection of either the basic or the derived form is obligatory in the sense that it must be used if one of the grammatical functions associated with it has to be expressed (e.g. derived form for perfective, durative, attainment of goal in the Xunxian dialect) but that form alone may need further specification through more overt information in a given context.

Summarising the two problematic questions concerning the status of binary morphological forms in Sinitic, it can be said that they still show the characteristics of economy-based maturation. They are multifunctional and their multifunctionality can be explicitly specified if necessary for clarity of discourse.

The case of classifier inflection in Weining Ahmao was discussed above in the context of the function and the use of numeral classifiers in discourse (cf. Section 2). What needs to be shown here, then, is the structure of the morphological paradigm as summarized in Table 2[12]):

---

[12] The tones are represented by number combinations. The numbers represent relative pitch on a scale from 1 (lowest) to 5 (highest). The first number represents the beginning of the tonal contour, the second number stands for its end.

**Table 2:** The inflectional paradigm of classifiers in Weining Ahmao (Gerner & Bisang 2008: 721, Gerner & Bisang 2010: 79).[a]

| Gender/ Age Register | Size | Singular | | Plural | |
|---|---|---|---|---|---|
| | | Definite | Indefinite | Definite | Indefinite |
| Male | Augmentative | CVT | C*VT | $ti^{55}a^{11}$ CVT' | $di^{31}a^{11}$ C*VT' |
| Female | Medial | $Cai^{55}$ | $C^*ai^{213}$ | $tiai^{55}a^{11}$ CVT' | $diai^{213}a^{11}$ C*VT' |
| Children | Diminutive | $Ca^{53}$ | $C^*a^{35}$ | $tia^{55}a^{11}$ CVT' | $dia^{55}a^{11}$ C*VT' |

[a] The morphology of numeral classifiers in Weining Ahmao is very well described since Wang Fushi (1957 [1972]) and Wang Deguang (1986, 1987).

The definite singular augmentative form with its structure of CVT (Consonant-Vowel-Tone) is the basic form of the classifier. Each of these elements can be subject to morphophonological change in the other slots. The symbol C* stands for changes in the properties of the consonant in some classifiers. Voicing and aspiration can be used with certain individual classifiers to distinguish between their indefinite and definite forms. The vowel quality [ai][13] is characteristic of the medial size, while [a] marks the diminutive size. The medial-definite form is typically expressed with a [$^{55}$] tone; the medial-indefinite form exhibits a [$^{213}$] tone. The diminutive form displays the tone [$^{53}$] for definite and [$^{35}$] for indefinite. The plural is characterized by a plural marker, whose form is $ti^{55}$ in the case of definite/augmentative. Like the classifiers in their singular form, this marker also inflects for [±definite] and size. The distinction between definite and indefinite is further expressed by different voicing of C, i.e., [t] for definite and [d] for indefinite. The plural marker is followed by $a^{11}$ plus the classifier in its form of C*VT', in which T' indicates that the tone may take a special form with some classifiers. In many cases the tone corresponds to that of the definite augmentative form in the singular.

There are some 100 numeral classifiers in Weining Ahmao (cf. appendix in Gerner & Bisang 2010). To illustrate how the pattern described above works with a concrete classifier, Table 3 shows the inflectional forms of $lu^{55}$, one of the most common classifiers, which is used with nouns denoting inanimate objects.

In Weining Ahmao, the marking of definiteness vs. indefiniteness by means of classifiers is characterized by a comparatively high degree of grammaticalization, as several of Lehmann's (1995) parameters show. The expression formats for definiteness and indefiniteness have lost their phonological substance beyond syllabicity and have become more abstract (paradigmatic weight or integrity).

---

13 Wang Fushi (1957) has [ae] instead of [ai].

**Table 3:** The inflectional paradigm of the classifier $lu^{55}$ in Weining Ahmao (Gerner & Bisang 2008: 722).

| Gender/ Age Register | Size | Singular | | Plural | |
|---|---|---|---|---|---|
| | | Definite | Indefinite | Definite | Indefinite |
| Male | Augmentative | $lu^{55}$ | $lu^{33}$ | $ti^{55}a^{11}\,lu^{55}$ | $di^{31}a^{11}\,lu^{55}$ |
| Female | Medial | $lai^{55}$ | $lai^{213}$ | $tiai^{55}a^{11}\,lu^{55}$ | $diai^{213}a^{11}\,lu^{55}$ |
| Children | Diminutive | $la^{53}$ | $la^{35}$ | $tia^{55}a^{11}\,lu^{55}$ | $dia^{55}a^{11}\,lu^{55}$ |

Moreover, they have been integrated into a morphological paradigm (paradigmatic cohesion or paradigmaticity) and the markers of definiteness and indefiniteness have become tightly connected to the classifier (syntagmatic cohesion or bondedness). If the classifier exhibits that many high grammaticalization values in terms of Lehmann's (1995) parameters, one would expect that classifier use would be obligatory in Weining Ahmao. In contrast, it was shown in Section 2 that classifier use depends on discourse and pragmatics and therefore still shows properties of economy-based maturation. Since the classifier system of Weining Ahmao is by far the most morphologically developed system, this is rather remarkable.

Languages with agreement marking on the verb are relatively rare in East and mainland Southeast Asia. There are some examples in Mon-Khmer languages, whose markers must have developed in more recent times. Of particular interest are languages like Temiar (Benjamin 1976) and Semelai (Kruspe 2004) from the Aslian branch of Mon-Khmer which put person markers on the verb. In Semelai, the person markers are analysed as proclitics (Kruspe 2004). Semelai also has agent marking (A; proclitic *la*=) on the noun plus differential object marking on the patient (O; proclitic *hn*=). A comparison of the proclitic verb forms with the independent forms indicates that verbal cross-reference is a rather recent phenomenon. This follows from the great phonological similarity of the independent pronouns and the verbal proclitics (cf. Table 4). The pronominal forms and the proclitics of the 1st and 2nd person singular for actors (A) are identical for minimal familiar and minimal.[14] In the third person, the forms are clearly related

---

[14] In the first and second person, Semelai has three different forms, "min familiar", "min" and "aug". The minimal (min) or unextended forms are the basis from which additional forms can be derived. There are two minimal forms which stand for politeness distinctions. The forms under "min familiar" are basically used with people of the same age group, while the forms under "min" are more deferential (cf. Kruspe 2004: 171–172). The augmentative forms (aug) are also limited to the 1st and 2nd person. They are formed by the enclitic =ʔən which marks plural. In the 3rd person, there is no politeness distinction and the singular/plural distinction is expressed by

**Table 4:** Pronouns and person proclitics in Semelai (Kruspe 2004: 171).

|  |  | minimal familiar | minimal | Aug | sg | Pl |
|---|---|---|---|---|---|---|
| PRONOUNS | 1 | ʔaɲ | yɛ | yɛ=ʔən | | |
| | 2 | kɒ | ji | je=ʔən | | |
| | 1 & 2 | | hɛ | hɛ=ʔən | | |
| | 3 | | | | kəh | deh |
| | 3S | | | | kəhn | dehn |
| VERBAL PROCLITICS FOR A | 1 | ʔaɲ= | yɛ= | | | |
| | 2 | kɒ= | ji= | hɛ= | | |
| | 3 | | | | ki= | de= |
| | 3UA | | | | ko= | |

(cf. e.g. the identical consonants in the pronominal and the proclitic form in 3rd singular vs. 3rd plural).

In addition, there are several restrictions on the use of cross-reference markers which can be taken as more evidence of their rather recent development because they are atypical of cross-reference systems. Two of these restrictions will be briefly mentioned here. The first one is determined by transitivity. The proclitics mainly occur with transitive verbs (14) and with two classes of intransitive verbs. If used with intransitive verbs (15), cross-reference means "induced by an indirect external cause" (Kruspe 2004: 159). In (15), the event of sleeping is induced by the preceding event of singing.

(14) Semelai (Kruspe 2004: 159)
 jkɔs ki=jəl la=cɔ.
 porcupine 3A=bark.at A=dog
 'The dog barked at the porcupine.'

(15) Semelai (Kruspe 2004: 160)
 yɛ bɲaɲiʔ, ʔarɛh ki=jtɛk.
 1.SG sing new 3A=sleep
 'I sang, (and) just then the child (went) to sleep.'

---

two independent forms rather than by a regular plural clitic. The pronominal system of the 3rd person distinguishes between intransitive subjects (glossed as 3S) and transitive subjects (glossed as 3). The verbal proclitics system of the 3rd person makes an additional distinction between identified and unidentified agents (glossed as UA).

The second restriction has to do with the extent to which events can be individuated. Proclitics only occur with individuated transitive events. They are not used with generic transitive events. Thus, we find cross-reference on the verb in (14) because it reports an individuated event. If the same event is understood generically, there is no cross-reference marking.

(16) Semelai (Kruspe 2004: 159)
cɔ   jəl         jkɔs.
dog  bark.at    porcupine
'Dogs bark at porcupines.'

The example in Semelai clearly shows that its inflectional morphology (person and number marking) is a rather recent phenomenon and does not allow any conclusions concerning the presence of inflectional marking in Proto-Mon-Khmer.

While inflectional morphology can generally be associated with explicitness-based maturation (cf. Section 3), the above three examples of inflectional morphology share properties of economy-based maturation. Since their use still depends on discourse, they are not fully obligatory and there is still multifunctionality in the case of fusional tense-aspect marking. For that reason, one might look at these patterns as instances of a specific type of "East and mainland Southeast Asian inflectional morphological paradigms".

The examples of inflectional morphology discussed so far developed in languages characterized by the dominance of economy-based maturation. The remainder of this Section is concerned with explicitness-based maturation. It will focus on semantic reanalysis (Xing 2015, cf. Section 2) and the observation (i) that the presence of morphology in a linguistic sign does not block it and (ii) that highly developed morphology provides new patterns to which it can be applied.

The first point can be illustrated by examples from Yabem, an Austronesian language spoken in Papua New Guinea (Morobe Province). Yabem verbs are characterized by an obligatory prefix that combines the functions of person and modality (realis [R] vs. irrealis[15] [IRR]) (Dempwolff 1939: 12–18). In the singular, the prefixes for the verb *-moa* 'be at'[16] are *ga-* (1st), *gô-* (2nd) and *gê-* (3rd) in the realis, while the irrealis forms are *jà-* (1st), *ồ-* (2nd) and *ề-* (3rd). In the plural, the forms for realis and irrealis are the same: *da-* (1st PL incl), *à-* (1st PL excl, 2nd PL),

---

**15** Dempwolff (1939: 12) uses the term "modus imaginativus" or "Imaginativ" for irrealis.
**16** There are five inflection classes. I only present the forms which are important for *-moa* 'be at', the verb that undergoes grammaticalization.

*sê-* (3rd PL) (cf. Dempwolff 1939: 14). The verb *-moa* 'be at' in its function as a main verb is shown in (17). Like Chinese *zài* 'be at', it was grammaticalized into a coverb (18) and into an aspect marker that expresses long duration as non-obligatory information on the internal temporal constituency of an event (19).

(17) Yabem (Dempwolff 1939: 77)
    *lao-c*                           **gê-moa**                 *nê*    *kôm.*
    father-in-law-1.SG    3.SG:R-be.at    his    field
    'My father-in-law is in his field.'

(18) Yabem (Dempwolff 1939: 33)
    *sê-janda*       *moc*    **sê-moa**       *gwêc.*
    3.PL-chase    bird    3.PL-be.at    sea
    'They chased birds in the sea.'

(19) Yabem (Zahn 1940: 68)
    *lau*      *sê-kwê*     *àndu*     *kapôêng*    **sê-moa.**
    people    3.PL-build    house    big         3.PL-be.at
    'The people were busy for a long time building a big house.'

These examples show that morphologically complex linguistic signs can still be subject to semantic reanalysis, an option that is excluded in Xing's (2015) analysis. In the case of Yabem, the grammaticalized verb differs from the Chinese verb *zài* 'be at' inasmuch as it still has its own person-modality prefix, which is identical to that of the matrix verb in the above examples. Moreover, the Yabem verb *-moa* 'be at' also shows accretion of meaning of the type A > A,B > A,B,C (for other verbs with similar properties, cf. Bisang 1986). The important lesson to take from Yabem is that the presence of explicitness-based morphology does not necessarily block processes of economy-based maturation that lead to multifunctionality (coverb, aspect marker) and lack of obligatoriness as illustrated by the case of *-moa* 'be at'. Thus, the distinction between the two types of maturation cannot be defined simply in terms of the presence or absence of morphology in the resulting linguistic forms. Needless to say, more research is necessary to further identify and determine the details.

New options of grammaticalization emerge if a language has developed specific slots within a template that can be clearly associated with a specific grammatical category. This can be illustrated with a relatively simple example of a verb in Swahili that has the following preradical templatic structure:

(20) Subject-TAM-Object-Verb- ...

The future marker in Swahili is -ta-. This form corresponds to the verb -taka 'want', which underwent phonological reduction (cf. loss of integrity in terms of Lehmann 1995) in the corresponding slot for expressing tense-aspect-mood (TAM). For such a process of attracting lexical items into certain slots and grammaticalizing them into a value of the grammatical category associated with that slot, a language needs to have reached a certain level of explicitness-based maturation. In that sense, extensive explicitness-based maturation offers mechanisms of grammaticalization which are not available in languages with lower levels of explicitness-based maturation.

A good example is Ket, the last member of the Yeniseian family still spoken by some 200 speakers today in the Yenisei River region of Central Siberia (Vajda 2003, 2004, 2007, 2010). While Yeniseian languages are generally characterized by extensive verbal templates formed by prefixes, Ket verbs have templates which are largely suffixing. The reason for this change has to do with extensive contact with pastoral nomads who speak Ugric, Samoyedic, Turkic, Tungusic and Mongolic languages, all of which have well-developed templates based on suffixation (Vajda 2015). The general pattern of the Yeniseian template is represented by the following schema in (21). Since the only positions needed for the discussion in this paper are the preradical position P07 and the position of the root (P0), the functions of the other slots are not indicated:

(21)  P08 – **P07** – P06 – P05 – P04 – P03 – P02 – P01 – P0 – P-1

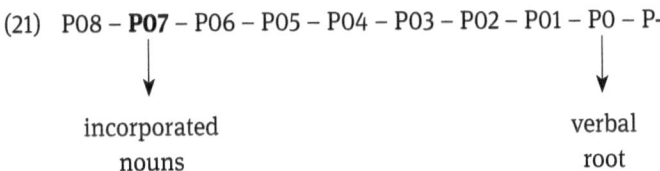

    incorporated          verbal
      nouns            root

Due to intensive contact with suffixing languages, speakers of Ket integrated the verbal roots into P07, a position previously reserved for incorporating nominal roots (Vajda 2015). Thus, a position that was productively filled by nominal lexical items was now used for lexical items from the verbal domain. Only a limited number of verbs remained in P0. Since P0 was no longer associated with the lexical head, the remaining verbs were reanalyzed as tense aspect markers. As a result, Ket has acquired a suffix-based verbal template of the following structure:

(22)  P08 – **P07** – P06 – P05 – P04 – P03 – P02 – P01 – P0 – P-1

      verbal          tense-aspect
       root           markers

The precondition for so remarkable a typological change from a prefix-based template to a suffix-based template is the existence of an extensive morphological paradigm with its functionally defined slots. As soon as speakers start reanalyzing the functions of certain positions in such a template in a different way (induced by linguistic contact in the case of Ket), new processes of grammaticalization arise. In the case of Ket, the position of verbal roots (P0) became the position associated with tense-aspect. From the perspective of maturation, one can argue that for a language to get into the position of triggering such processes of grammaticalization, extensive explicitness-based maturation is needed.

Xing (2015: 604) argues that "isolating analytical languages without grammatical marking develop semantic functions based on syntactic position and pragmatic factors – a process of semantic reanalysis." The data from Yabem (examples (17) – (19)) show that the presence of morphology does not necessarily operate against semantic reanalysis. In spite of this, the question of whether we are in a system of incipient morphology moving away from economy-based maturation or in a system of highly developed morphology as a result of long-term explicitness-based maturation has its impact on the properties of the products of grammaticalization associated with these systems.

# 6 Conclusion

Sinitic and other East and mainland Southeast Asian languages are characterized by the high relevance of discourse and pragmatic inference even with markers that stand for grammatical categories such as aspect, referential status, etc. This has been shown in the context of the non-obligatoriness of the Chinese perfective marker *-le*, for the multifunctionality of the verb 給 *gěi* 'give' in Chinese, and for the non-obligatoriness (Weining Ahmao) and multifunctionality of numeral classifiers that mark definiteness as well as indefiniteness (various Sinitic languages, among them Cantonese and the Wu variety spoken in Fuyang). The relevance of discourse and pragmatic inference is what supports the accretion of grammatical functions due to semantic reanalysis in terms of Xing (2013, 2015).

On a more abstract level, the situation in Chinese on the one hand and the situation in European languages like English and German on the other can be seen in light of two different types of maturation: economy-based maturation as it dominates in processes of grammaticalization in East and mainland Southeast Asia and explicitness-based maturation as it operates more prominently in English and German.

Since economy-based maturation is pervasive across many different domains of grammar, this has its impact on the division of labor between grammar and the lexicon. High economy-based maturation leaves some work that is done by grammar in explicitness-based systems to the semantics of the lexicon. This may create an even greater similarity of lexicalization and grammaticalization as described by Xing (2015) for Sinitic.

The high importance of economy-based maturation is the result of a long-term development in Sinitic and other East and mainland Southeast Asian languages. It starts out from the erosion of derivational morphology in Old Chinese (11th – 3rd centuries BC) and is further supported by at least the following four factors which exert a strong blocking effect on the development of inflectional morphological paradigms: lack of obligatoriness, multifunctionality, phonological properties (discreteness of the syllable, phonotactic restraints) and linguistic contact. If explicitness-based maturation wins in such an environment, this tends to leave its traces in the properties of the newly arising morphological systems. The cases discussed in this context are (i) fusional aspectual morphology in Northern China (Arcodia 2013, 2015), (ii) classifier inflection in Weining Ahmao (Gerner & Bisang 2008), and (iii) agreement proclitics in Semelai (Kruspe 2004). In each case, the morphological marking still has preserved some features of discourse or pragmatics. Of particular interest is the system of obligatory case suffixes found in the Sinitic languages of the Qinghai-Gansu *Sprachbund*. This system with its properties of fully-fledged explicitness-based maturation is most likely the result of linguistic contact.

In contrast, morphological paradigms in explicitness-dominated environments have options of reanalysis within individual slots of templatic paradigms which are nonexistent in languages with dominant economy-based maturation. Also of interest is the change from prefixal templates in Yeniseian to suffixal templates in Ket, the last surviving language of that family (Vajda 2015). The examples of Yabem and Ket show that semantic reanalysis is not limited to languages with no morphology. In Yabem, the existing morphology does not block the grammaticalization of its lexical roots together with their obligatory person/modality prefixes. In Ket, the morphological templates provide another system of reference with slots for semantic reanalysis.

On the whole semantic reanalysis is a very important mechanism for driving processes of grammaticalization. It can be embedded in the broader framework of two competing types of maturation, namely, economy-based and explicitness-based. Both types produce contexts that, with their specific properties, block or enhance certain processes of grammaticalization in terms of the relevance of discourse and pragmatic inference and in terms of the division of labor between grammar and the lexicon.

# References

Ansaldo, Umberto and Lim, Lisa. 2004. Phonetic absence as syntactic prominence. Grammaticalization in isolating tonal languages. In *Up and Down the Cline – the Nature of Grammaticalization*, Olga Fischer, Muriel Norde, and Harry Perridon (eds.), 345–362. Amsterdam and Philadelphia: John Benjamins.

Ansaldo, Umberto and Nordhoff, Sebastian. 2009. Complexity and the age of languages. In *Complex Processes in New Languages*, Enoch O. Aboh and Norval Smith (eds.), 345–363. Amsterdam and Philadelphia: John Benjamins.

Arcodia, Giorgio Francesco. 2013. Grammaticalization *with* coevolution of form and meaning in East Asia? Evidence from Sinitic. *Language Sciences* 40, 148–167.

Arcodia, Giorgio Francesco. 2015. More on the morphological typology of Sinitic. *Bulletin of Chinese Linguistics* 8, 5–26.

Baerman, Matthew and Corbett, Greville G. 2010. Introduction: Defectiveness: Typology and diachrony. In *Defective Paradigms. Missing Forms and What They Tell Us*, Matthew Baerman, Greville G. Corbett, and Dunstan P. Brown (eds), 1–18. Oxford: Oxford University Press.

Baxter, William H.. 1992. *A Handbook of Old Chinese Phonology*. Berlin: Mouton de Gruyter.

Baxter, William H. and Sagart, Laurent. 2014. *Old Chinese. A New Reconstruction*. Oxford: Oxford University Press.

Benjamin, Geoffrey. 1976. An outline of Temiar grammar. In *Austroasiatic Studies I and II*, Philip N. Jenner, Laurence C. Thompson, and Stanley Starosta (eds.), 129–188. Honolulu: University of Hawaii Press. Oceanic Linguistics Special Publications, No 13.

Bisang, Walter. 1986. Die Verbserialisierung im Jabêm. *Lingua* 70, 131–162.

Bisang, Walter. 1996. Areal typology and grammaticalization: Processes of grammaticalization based on nouns and verbs in East and mainland South East Asian languages. *Studies in Language*, 20.3, 519–597.

Bisang, Walter. 1999. Classifiers in East and Southeast Asian languages: Counting and beyond. In *Numeral Types and Changes Worldwide*, Jadranka Gvozdanovic (ed.), 113–185. Berlin: Mouton de Gruyter.

Bisang, Walter. 2004. Grammaticalization without coevolution of form and meaning: The case of tense-aspect-modality in East and mainland Southeast Asia. In *What Makes Grammaticalization? – A Look from its Fringes and its Components*, Bisang, Walter; Himmelmann, Nikolaus P., and Wiemer, Björn (eds.), 109–138. Berlin: Mouton de Gruyter.

Bisang, Walter. 2008. Grammaticalization as an areal phenomenon – the case of East and mainland Southeast Asian languages and its consequences for concepts of complexity and maturation. 语言学论丛 *Yuyanxue Luncong* 38, 64–98.

Bisang, Walter. 2009. On the evolution of complexity – sometimes less is more in East and mainland Southeast Asia. In *Language Complexity as an Evolving Variable*, Geoffrey Sampson, David Gil, and Peter Trudgill (eds.), 34–49. Oxford: Oxford University Press.

Bisang, Walter. 2010. Grammaticalization in Chinese – a construction based account. In *Gradience, Gradualness, and Grammaticalization*, Elisabeth C. Traugott and Graeme Trousdale (eds), 245–277. Amsterdam and Philadelphia: John Benjamins.

Bisang, Walter. 2011. Grammaticalization and typology. In *Handbook of Grammaticalization*, Heiko Narrog and Bernd Heine (eds.), 105–117. Oxford: Oxford University Press. Elisabeth C.

Bisang, Walter. 2014. On the strength of morphological paradigms – a historical account of radical pro-drop. In *Paradigm Change in Historical Reconstruction: The Transeurasian*

*Languages and Beyond*, Martine Robbeets and Walter Bisang (eds.), 23–60. Amsterdam and Philadelphia: John Benjamins.

Bisang, Walter. 2015a. Hidden complexity – the neglected side of complexity and its consequences. *Linguistics Vanguard* ISSN (Online), 2199–174X, DOI: 10.1515/linvan-2014-1014.

Bisang, Walter. 2015b. Problems with primary vs. secondary grammaticalization: the case of East and mainland Southeast Asian languages. *Language Sciences* 47, 132–147. http://doi.org/10.1016/j.langsci.2014.05.007.

Bisang, Walter. 2016. Linguistic change in grammar. In *The Routledge Handbook of Linguistics*, Allan, Keith (ed.), 366–384. Oxford: Routledge.

Bisang, Walter. 2017. Grammaticalization. *Oxford Research Encyclopedia, Linguistics*. Online publication. DOI: 10.1093/acrefore/9780199384655.013.103.

Bybee, Joan L. 1985. *Morphology: A Study of the Relation between Meaning and Form*. Amsterdam and Phildalelphia: John Benjamins.

Bybee, Joan L., Perkins, Revere, and Pagliuca, William. 1994. *The Evolution of Grammar. Tense, Aspect and Modality in the Languages of the World*. Chicago and London: The University of Chicago Press.

Cao, Guangshun, Djamouri, Redouane, and Peyraube, Alain (eds.). 2015. *Languages in Contact in North China. Historical and Synchronic Studies*. Paris: École des Hautes Études en Sciences Sociales: Centre de Recherches Linguistiques sur l'Asie Orientale (CRLAO).

Cartier, Alice. 1972. *Les verbes résultatifs en chinois moderne*. Paris: Klincksieck.

Chao, Yüan Ren. 1968. *A Grammar of Spoken Chinese*. Berkeley and Los Angeles: University of California Press.

Chappell, Hilary and Peyraube, Alain. 2006. The analytic causatives of Early Modern Southern Min in diachronic perspective. In *Festschrift for Ting Pang-Hsin*, Dah-an Ho (ed.), 973–1011. Taipei : Academia Sinica.

Cheng, Lai-Shen Lisa and Sybesma, Rint. 1999. Bare and not-so-bare nouns and the structure of NP. *Linguistic Inquiry* 30: 509–542.

Chierchia, Gennaro. 1998. Reference to kinds across languages. *Natural Language Semantics* 6: 339–405.

Chu, Chauncy. 1998. *A Discourse Grammar of Mandarin*. New York: Peter Lang.

Dahl, Östen. 2004. *The Growth and Maintenance of Linguistic Complexity*. Amsterdam and Philadelphia: JohnBenjamins.

Dede, Keith. 2007. The origin of the anti-ergative [xa] in Huangshui Chinese. *Language and Lingusitics* 8(4): 863–881.

Dempwolff, Otto. 1939. *Grammatik der Jabêm-Sprache auf Neuguinea*. Hamburg: Friedrichsen, de Gruyter & Co.

Diewald, Gabriele and Smirnova, Elena. 2012. Paradigmatic integration: the fourth stage in an expanded grammaticalization scenario. In *Grammaticalization and Language Change. New Reflections*, Kristin Davidse, Tine Breban, Liselotte Brems, and Tanja Mortelmans (eds.), 111–133. Amsterdam and Philadelphia: John Benjamins.

Djamouri, Redouane. 2015. Object positioning in Tangwang. In *Languages in Contact in North China. Historical and Synchronic Studies*, Guangshun Cao, Redouane Djamouri, and Alain Peyraube (eds.), 251–275. Paris: École des Hautes Études en Sciences Sociales: Centre de Recherches Linguistiques sur l'Asie Orientale (CRLAO).

Dwyer, Arienne M. 1992. Altaic elements in the Linxia dialect: Contact-induced change on the Yellow River plateau. *Journal of Chinese Linguistics* 20, 160–178.

Gabelentz, Georg von der. 1891. *Die Sprachwissenschaft, ihre Aufgaben, Methoden und bisherigen Ergebnisse*. Leipzig: T.O. Weigel Nachfolger. Republished 1972 by Tübingen: Narr.

Gerner, Matthias and Bisang, Walter. 2008. Inflectional speaker-role classifiers in Weining Ahmao. *Journal of Pragmatics* 40, 719–731.

Gerner, Matthias and Bisang, Walter. 2010. Classifier declinations in an isolating language: On a rarity in Weining Ahmao. *Language and Linguistics* 11, 579–623.

Givón, Talmy. 1979. *Understanding Grammar*. New York: Academic Press.

Greenberg, Joseph H. 1972. Numerical classifiers and substantival number: problems in the genesis of a linguistic type. *Working Papers on Language Universals* 9. 1–39. Stanford, CA: Department of Linguistics, Stanford University.

Haas, Mary. 1942. The use of numeral classifiers in Thai. *Language* 18, 201–205.

Haiman, John. 1983. Iconic and economic motivation. *Language* 59: 781–819.

Haspelmath, Martin. 2002. *Understanding Morphology*. London: Arnold.

Heine, Bernd. 2002. On the role of context in grammaticalization. In *New Reflections on Grammaticalization*, Ilse Wischer and Gabriele Diewald (eds.), 83–101. Amsterdam and Philadelphia: John Benjamins.

Heine, Bernd, Claudi, Ulrike, and Hünnemeyer, Friederike. 1991. *Grammaticalization. A Conceptual Framework*. Chicago and London: The University of Chicago Press.

Heine, Bernd and Kuteva, Tania. 2002. *World Lexicon of Grammaticalization*. Cambridge: Cambridge University Press.

Hopper, Paul J. and Traugott, Elizabeth C. 2003. *Grammaticalization* (2nd edition). Cambridge: Cambridge University Press.

Hopper, Paul J. 1991. On some principles of grammaticization. In *Approaches to Grammaticalization, Vol I*, Elizabeth Closs Traugott and Bernd Heine (eds.), 17–36. Amsterdam and Philadelphia: John Benjamins.

Huang, C.-T. James. 1984. On the distribution and reference of empty pronouns. *Linguistic Inquiry* 15, 531–574.

Huang, Yan. 1994. *The Syntax and Pragmatics of Anaphora. A Study with Special Reference to Anaphora*. Cambridge: Cambridge University Press.

Jiang, Julie L. 2015. Marking (in)definiteness in classifier languages. *Bulletin of Chinese Linguistics* 8. 319–343.

Kager, René. 1999. *Optimality Theory*. Cambridge: Cambridge University Press.

Kruspe, Nicole. 2004. *A Grammar of Semelai*. Cambridge: Cambridge University Press.

Lehmann, Christian. 1995. *Thoughts on Grammaticalization. A Programmatic Sketch*. Munich: LINCOM.

Levinson, Stephen C. 2000. *Presumptive Meanings. The Theory of Generalized Conversational Implicatures*, Cambridge, Mass.: The MIT Press.

Li, Charles N. and Thompson, Sandra A.. 1981. *Mandarin Chinese. A Functional Reference Grammar*. Berkeley, LA and London: University of California Press.

Li, Wei. 李炜 1993. 甘肃临夏一带方言的后置词"哈""啦" *Gansu Linxia yidai fangyan de houzhici "ha" "la"* [The postpositions *ha* and *la* in the dialects of Linxia and (the vicinity of) Gansu]. *Zhongguo Yuwen* 6, 435–438.

Li, Wendan. 2014. Perfectivity and grounding in Chinese. *Studies in Language* 38.1, 127–168.

Li, Xuping and Bisang, Walter. 2012. Classifiers in Sinitic languages: From individuation to definiteness-marking. *Lingua* 122, 335–355.

Lord, Carol, Yap, Foong Ha, and Iwasaki, Shoichi. 2002. Grammaticalization of 'give': African and Asian perspectives. In *New Reflections on Grammaticalization*, Ilse Wischer and Gabriele Diewald (eds.), 217–235. Amsterdam and Philadelphia: John Benjamins.

Ma, Shujun. 马树钧 1982. 临夏话中的"名哈"结构 Linxiahua zhong de "ming+ha" jiegou [The structure "noun+ha" in the Linxia language]. *Zhongguo Yuwen* 1, 72–73.

Meillet, Antoine. 1912. L'évolution des formes grammaticales. Scientia (Rivista di Scienza) 12/26, 384–400.

Neeleman, Ad and Szendro_i, Kriszta. 2007. Radical pro drop and the morphology of pronouns. *Linguistic Iquiry* 38, 671–714.

Newmeyer, Frederick J. 1998. *Language Form and Language Function*. Cambridge, Mass.: The MIT Press.

Norde, Muriel. 2009. *Degrammaticalization*. Oxford: Oxford University Press.

Paul, Waltraud. 2015. *New Perspectives on Chinese Syntax*. Berlin: de Gruyter.

Peyraube, Alain. 2015. Grammatical change in Sinitic languages and its relation to typology. In *Diversity in Sinitic Languages*, Hilary Chappell (ed.), 53–78. Oxford: Oxford University Press.

Rangkupan, Suda. 2007. The syntax and semantics of GIVE-complex constructions in Thai. *Language and Linguistics* 8.1, 193–234.

Sagart, Laurent, 1999. *The Roots of Old Chinese*. Amsterdam and Philadelphia: John Benjamins.

Simpson, Andrew. 2005. Classifiers and DP structure in Southeast Asian languages. In *Handbook of Comparative Syntax*, Richard S. Kayne and Guglielmo Cinque (eds.), 806–838. Oxford: Oxford University Press.

Simpson, Andrew, 2017. Bare classifier/noun alternations in the Jinyun (Wu) variety of Chinese and the encoding of definiteness. *Linguistics* 55(2),305–331.

Simpson, Andrew, Soh, Hooi Ling, and Nomoto, Hiroki. 2011. Bare classifiers and definiteness: a cross-linguistic investigation. *Studies in Language* 35, 168–193.

Slater, Keith W., 2003. *A Grammar of Mangghuer. A Mongolic Language of China's Qinghai-Gansu Sprachbund*. London and New York: RoutledgeCurzon.

Smith, Carlotta. 1997. *The Parameter of Aspect*. Dordrecht, Boston, and London: Kluwer, Academic Press.

Song, Jae Jung. 1997. On the development of MANNER from GIVE. In *The Linguistics of Giving*, John Newman (ed.), 327–348. Amsterdam and Philadelphia: John Benjamins.

Tao, Liang. 2006. Classifier loss and frozen tone in spoken Beijing Mandarin: The YI+GE phono-syntactic conspiracy. *Linguistics* 44.1, 91–133.

Thepkanjana, Kingkarn and Satoshi Uehara. 2008. The verb of giving in Thai and Mandarin Chinese as a case of polysemy: A comparative study. *Language Science* 30, 621–651.

Traugott, Elizabeth C. and Trousdale, Graeme (eds.) 2010. *Gradience, Gradualness and Grammaticalization*. Amsterdam and Philadelphia: John Benjamins.

Traugott, Elizabeth C. 2002. From etymology to historical pragmatics. In *Studying the History of the English Language: Millennial Perspectives*, Donka Minkova and Robert Stockwell (eds.), 19–49. Berlin: Mouton de Gruyter.

Vajda, Edward. 2003. Ket verb structure in typological perspective. *Sprachtypologie und Universalienforschung* 56.1/2: 55–92. Berlin: Akademie Verlag.

Vajda, Edward. 2004. *Ket*. Munich: Lincom Europa. (Languages of the World/Materials).

Vajda, Edward. 2007 Ket morphology. In *Morphologies of Asia and Africa*, Vol. 2, Alan Kaye (ed.), 1277–1325. Winona Lake, IN: Eisenbrauns.

Vajda, Edward. 2010. A Siberian link with the Na-Dene. *Anthropological Papers of the University of Alaska*, Volume 5, New Series, 31–99.

Vajda, Edward. 2015. Areal features in Yeniseian grammaticalization. Paper presented at Symposium on Areal Patterns of Grammaticalization and Cross-Linguistic Variation in Grammaticalization Scenarios, Mainz (Germany), March 12–14, 2015.

Wang, Jian. 王健 2013. 类型学视野下的汉语方言"量名"结构研究 [Bare classifier phrases in Sinitic languages: a typological perspective]. *Language Sciences* 12.4, 383–393.

Wang, Deguang. 王德光 1986. 威宁苗语话语材料 Weining Miaoyu huayu cailiao [Language material in the Weining dialect of the Miao language]. *Minzu Yuwen* 民族语文 3, 69–80.

Wang, Fushi. 王辅世 1957. 贵州威宁苗语量词 *Guizhou Weining Miaoyu liangci* [The classifier in the Weining dialect of the Miao language in Guizhou]. *Yuyan Yanjiu* 1957: 75–121.

Wiedenhof, Jeroen. 2015. *A Grammar of Mandarin*. Amsterdam and Philadelphia: John Benjamins.

Wu, Yicheng. 2017. Numeral classifiers in Sinitic languages: Semantic content, contextuality, and semi-lexicality. *Linguistics* 55(2), 333–369.

Xiao, Richard and McEnery, Tony. 2004. *Aspect in Mandarin: A Corpus-based Study*. Amsterdam and Philadelphia: John Benjamins.

Xin, Yongfen. 辛永芬 2006a. 河南浚县方言的动词变韵 *Henan Xunxian fangyan de dongci bianyun* [Rhyme change in the grammar of the Xunxian dialect]. *Zhongguo Yuwen* 1, 45–53.

Xin, Yongfen. 辛永芬 2006b. 浚县方言语言研究 *Xunxian fangyan yuyan yanjiu* [Studies on the grammar of the Xunxian dialect]. Beijing: Zhonghua Shuju.

Xing, Janet Z. 2013. Semantic reanalysis in grammaticalization in Chinese. In *Increased Empiricism: New Advances in Chinese Linguistics*, Zhuo Jing-Schmidt (ed.), 223–246. Amsterdam and Philadelphia: John Benjamins.

Xing, Janet Z. 2015. A comparative study of semantic change in grammaticalization and lexicalization in Chinese and Germanic languages. *Studies in Language* 39.3, 594–634.

Xu, Dan. 2006. *Typological Change in Chinese Syntax*. Oxford: Oxford University Press.

Xu, Dan, Qi Chong, Xu Shuang and Fabienne Marc. 2008. *Les résultatifs du chinois contemporain. Dictionnaire pratique*. Paris: L'Asiathèque – maison des langues du monde.

Yang, Suying. 2011. The parameter of temporal endpoint and the basic function of -*le*. *Journal of East Asian Linguistics* 20.4, 383–415.

Zahn, Heinrich. 1940. *Lehrbuch der Jabêmsprache*. Berlin: Verlag Dietrich Reimer.

Zhang, Hong. 2007. Numeral classifiers in Mandarin Chinese. *Journal of East Asian Linguistics* 16:1, 43–59.

Ekkehard Koenig
# Establishing transphrastic relations: On the grammaticalization of demonstratives

## 1 Introduction

How general and how homogeneous is the historical process of grammaticalization, i.e., the development of grammatical markers from lexical elements? Depending on the phenomena investigated, very different answers can be – and have been – given to this question. The development of a specific construction might be observable in only one individual language. The correlative comparative in English, which is marked by the double use of the definite article (*The more you drink of this water, the slimmer you will get.*) and ultimately derives from a correlative use of the Old English degree demonstrative *swa* (Blick.Hom. 15.19–21 *and swa hie him swyþor styrdon swa he hludor cleopode* 'and the more they punished him the louder he cried') seems to be a case in point. At the other extreme of frequency and generality, there are developments attested in a wide variety of languages. The derivation of reflexive from body parts[1] (cf. Schladt 2000; König and Siemund 2005: 195) and the derivation of existential markers from locative demonstratives (Engl. *There is a car over there*) are well-known cases. *The World Lexicon of Grammaticalization* (Heine and Kuteva 2002) provides comprehensive information on typical and recurrent sources of grammaticalization. In such cases, grammaticalization can be related to or even be explained by terms of cognition (fundamental concepts, metaphorical or metonymic extensions, etc.). In between these two extremes we find processes of grammaticalization only attested in genealogically related groups or families of languages or only attested in specific areas. The development of definite articles from adnominal demonstratives (Lat. *ille* > Romance *le*), from intensifiers (Lat. *ipse*) or possessives and the concomitant development of indefinite articles from the numeral 'one' are usually considered as areal features, attested mainly – or even only – in Standard Average European (cf. Haspelmath 2001: 1494). On the other hand, formulating such areal restrictions can simply be

---

[1] Typical examples of such paths can be found, inter alia, in Caucasian languages (e.g. Abkhaz xata- 'head'), Hamito-Semitic languages (e.g. Hebrew etsem 'bone', Arabic nafs- 'soul') and Niger-Congo languages (e.g. Soninke yinmé 'head').

due to our inadequate knowledge of other areas. In a recent paper by Mei Fang, for example, clear evidence is presented that an extension in the use of the proximal demonstrative *zhè* to the use as definite article can be observed in spoken Contemporary Beijing Mandarin (cf. Fang 2012).

In view of such areal and cross-linguistic variation, the inescapable conclusion is that grammaticalization is not a homogeneous process. The contributions to this volume raise several crucial questions: What kind of role does the typological affiliation of a language – in addition to its geographical location ('East meets West.') – play in shaping processes of grammaticalization? To what extent are the patterns of change observable in European and Asian languages similar and how are they different? To what extent do processes of grammaticalization and lexicalization correlate with other features of a language? To what extent are general processes of semantic change dependent on certain 'typological properties' of a language? The languages selected in my paper for this comparative discussion are various European languages, on the one hand, and Mandarin Chinese and Japanese, on the other. The thematic domain selected is one easily identifiable across languages, namely the domain of demonstratives and their role in the development of grammatical categories and markers. In order to avoid well-known facts and for reasons of space I will concentrate specifically on a neglected subdomain of demonstratives, viz. those expressing the ontological domains of manner, quality and degree ('MQD-demonstratives'), exemplified by *sīc, talis, tantus* in Latin, by *so, solch* and *so* in German and by *þus, swelc* and *swa* in Old English. The reason for selecting two typologically different languages as representatives of the East is that only one of them, Japanese, manifests striking similarities with European languages, whereas the other, Mandarin, does not. In connection with the specific comparative analyses of grammatical markers that such MQD-demonstratives lead to, two general points will also be made:
(a) not all grammatical categories derive from content words (V, N) (Diessel 2006, 2013; contra Heine & Kuteva 2005, 2007)
(b) the targets of demonstratives in processes of grammaticalization are special: establishing transphrastic (interclausal) relations rather than strengthening intraclausal relations. (Diessel 2006)

## 2 Demonstratives: Basic properties

Demonstratives are probably the clearest example of a category found in all languages (Dixon 2003). There may be striking differences in the inventory and use of demonstratives across languages, but all grammatical descriptions both of well-known and of lesser described languages seem to have a chapter on demonstratives as basic deictic expressions of the languages in question. Ontogenetically, at least some demonstratives are acquired early and lost late. In German, for example, the distal locative demonstrative *da* is one of the earliest expressions learnt and used by children. Demonstratives are deictic expressions and can therefore be accompanied by gestures, at least in some of their uses. In contrast to the widespread assumption that the relevant gestures are most frequently pointing gestures carried out with the index finger as the instrument, it is, in fact, the direction of gaze that is primarily used for indicating direction. Moreover, there are also mimicking and enacting gestures in addition to the well-known pointing ones, especially within the thematic domain to be discussed in this paper. As a consequence of the pointing gestures typically accompanying the use of demonstratives, the basic function of demonstratives is often described as identifying a referent relative to a center of orientation and, in their extended use, as establishing and coordinating a joint center of interest (cf. Diessel 1999, 2006).

In general, demonstratives are morphologically simple expressions with a very simple semantic structure comprising (i) a deictic dimension relating to the distance of a referent from the center of orientation and (ii) an ontological or content dimension, differentiating such basic ontological categories as person (*him*), entity (*that*), location (*here*), time (*now*), and direction (EME *hither*), as well as manner (*thus*) , quality (*such*), and degree (*so*), which will be the focus of what follows. This simple semantic structure is shared by interrogatives, which are generally differentiated along the same ontological parameters and which also play an important role in the genesis and development of grammatical markers. In their extended, non-gestural use, demonstratives manifest a high degree of distributional and syntactic versatility and may occur as anaphors for a variety of lexical and phrasal categories (cf. Koenig 2012, 2015; Guerin 2015). It is for this reason that the general term 'demonstratives' is more appropriate than more traditional terms like 'demonstrative pronouns'.

Like interrogatives, demonstratives are the origin of a wide variety of grammaticalization processes which characteristically establish relations across clauses rather than strengthening clause-internal relations. In Diessel (1999, 2006), a distillation of such wide-spread processes of change and development is given in the form of Table 1:

**Table 1:** Demonstratives as source of grammaticalization.

|  | | |
|---|---|---|
|  | Definite article → | Noun class marker |
|  | Personal pron. (3rd) → | Agreement affix |
| Demonstratives → | Relative pron. → | Complementizer |
|  | Complementizer → | Purposive marker |
|  | Clause Linker → | Discourse marker |

# 3 A neglected subclass: Demonstratives of MANNER, QUALITY, and DEGREE

It is only in the last few years that the subclass of demonstratives that is the focus of this paper has received some attention in language-specific and cross-linguistic studies (cf. Koenig 2012, 2015; Koenig & Nishina 2015; Guerin 2015; Umbach & Gust 2014; Koenig & Umbach 2018). One reason for this neglect can probably be traced to the fact that English and many other European languages lack both deictic and ontological differentiations in this domain and that the English adverb *so* (< OE *swa*) has lost its basic exophoric (gestural) use and is therefore often analyzed as an isolated adverbial particle. For an introduction to the basic use of the relevant expressions, and thus to the starting point of the grammaticalization processes to be discussed, I therefore have to resort to German examples and their translational counterparts in Japanese and Mandarin:

(1) a. GERMAN *Maria tanzt so* (+ mimicking gesture).
  'Maria dances like this.' (MANNER)
 b. JAPANESE *hanako-wa koo* (+ mimicking gesture of speaker) odor-u.
 c. MANDARIN *Mǎlìyà zhèyàng wǔdǎo* (+ mimicking gesture).
  (瑪利亞這樣跳舞。)

(2) a. GERMAN *Maria ist so* (+ gesture).
  'Mary is/looks like this.' (QUALITY)
 b. JAPANESE *Hanako-wa koo-da* (+gesture of speaker).
 c. MANDARAIN *Mǎlìyà (xiàng) zhèyàng* (+ gesture of speaker).
  (瑪利亞像這樣。)

(3) a. GEMAN *Der Fisch war so groß* (+ gesture).
  'The fish was so big.' (DEGREE)

b. JAPANESE *sakana-wa konna-ni* (+ gesture) *ookii*.
c. MANDARIN *Nà (tiáo) yú zhèyàng dà* (+ gesture).
（那條魚這樣大。）

Lexical differentiations in the deictic domain (proximal vs. distal, etc.), found inter alia in Armenian and Finno-Ugric languages, are a rare phenomenon in the relevant group of demonstratives in European languages. In the content domain, by contrast, lexical oppositions are quite common, as illustrated by the examples in Table 2.

**Table 2:** Simple systems of oppositions (1–3) in content dimension (European).

|  | Manner | Quality | Degree |
|---|---|---|---|
| German | so | so/solch | so |
| English | (thus) arch./like this | (such) arch./like this | so/this |
| French | ainsi/si | tel/pareil | Comme ça, (au)tant), (tellement) |
| Spanish | asi | Asi | tan |
| Latin | sīc | talis | tantus |
| Polish | tak | Taki | tak |

In Japanese, not only are there systematic differentiations found between all content dimensions expressed by demonstratives, but also consistent three-term distinctions in the deictic dimension, roughly describable as 'speaker-proximal', 'addressee/hearer-proximal' and 'distal'. The system is strikingly transparent in its formal make-up, insofar as the deictic component (*ko-*, *so-*, *a-*) is expressed in the first syllable of demonstratives, while the ontological category is signaled in the second and third syllable (cf. Iwasaki 2013: 290ff.; Hofmann 1993; Koenig & Nishina 2015). Interrogatives have an analogous formal make-up, with the interrogative marker replacing the deictic one of demonstratives, signaling that the relevant information is not available. Table 3 provides illustration for the preceding statements:

**Table 3:** More complex systems with oppositions in both the deictic and the content dimensions (Japanese).

| Deictic dimension ↓ | Ontological dimension → | | | | | |
|---|---|---|---|---|---|---|
|  | Entity | Place | Dir. | Man. | Qual. | Degree |
| S-proximal | kore | koko | kotti | koo | konna | konnani |
| H-proximal | sore | soko | sotti | soo | sonna | sonnani |
| Distal | are | asoko | atti | aa | anna | annani |
| interrogative | dono | doko | dotti | doo | donna | donnani |

In contrast to Japanese and also to Cantonese, Mandarin has no lexical distinction in the relevant content domain and draws a 'proximal' vs. 'distal' distinction by combining the basically local demonstratives *zhè* and *nà* with the expression for manner *yàng* (cf. Table 4). Cantonese has a two-term lexical contrast in the content dimension, differentiated by the second vs. the third tone: *gam2* 'quality/manner' – *gam3* 'degree' (cf. Arsenijević, Boban, František and Johanna Ut-Seong Sio 2018).

**Table 4:** Two term distinctions in deictic and content dimension in Mandarin; combinatorial make-up.[2]

| Deictic Dimension | Content Dimension → | | |
|---|---|---|---|
| ↓ | manner | Quality | degree |
| Proximal | zhè-yàng | zhè-yàng (de) | zhè-yàng |
| Distal | nà-yàng | nà-yàng (de) | nà-yàng |

Please note that this diagram is a simplification, since it omits some available synonymy (*zhèmezhe* 'like this – *nàmezhe* 'like that'), as well as some considerable regional and stylistic differentiations, as described in Wiedenhof (2015: 112ff.) and Fang (2012).

If we take a bird's eye view of the development from the OE *swa* (cf. Schleburg 2002) to the ModE *so*, the following picture emerges: more than forty different and distinct meanings and uses for the ModE *so* can be found in most dictionaries and this expression is part of the most basic vocabulary of English and can be used with a variety of different meanings in different notional domains. In what follows, we will reconstruct these different meanings and uses as the results of processes of grammaticalization in English, as well as examine their counterparts in other European languages, as a basis for a comparison with analogous developments in the two Asian languages.

Before I discuss the individual process of grammaticalization, I will first give an overview of the changes typically observed in European languages (cf. Table 5). The structure of this overview is partly determined by very general extensions in the meaning and use of demonstratives, viz. by the extension of exophoric (gestural) use to endophoric ('within the text') use, either retrospective relations to previous discourse (anaphoric) or prospective relations to following discourse (cataphoric). Such extensions can be found for many demonstratives in many languages. It would

---

[2] Alain Peyraube (p.c.) called my attention to the fact that the relevant distinctions were expressed in earlier stages of Chinese by the forms: *níng*寧/*néng*能 vs. *ruó*偌/*yǔmó*與摩.

be misguided to assume, however, that such extensions existed right from the start in the evolution of a language, since languages may differ considerably in their anaphoric and cataphoric use of demonstratives. The discourse-deictic use of demonstratives is often distinguished from the anaphoric and the cataphoric one: only in the latter case do demonstratives relate to specific expressions in the preceding or following context, rather than to content alone. Among the general developments of grammaticalization found for nearly all demonstratives, we also find the 'recognitional use' (cf. Himmelmann 1997), where the memory is the locus of identification. Further developments from these cardinal points are based on the specific ontological dimensions of specific demonstratives and thus do not have parallels in the development of all other demonstratives. In the case of the group under discussion, the crucial semantic property is that of 'similarity' in the manner of carrying out an action, in manifesting a certain quality and in the degree of a property.

Semantic basis: 'SIMILARITY' (of manner, quality, degree)

**Table 5:** Channels of grammaticalization attested for MQD-demonstratives.

| | | | |
|---|---|---|---|
| (Renovation) ↓ Exophoric → | Anaphoric → | Propositional → (obj., pred., comp, VP) | Affirmation |
| | | Adverbs (conditional/ causal/inferential/ manner/contrastive) | |
| | | Relative marker (such ...as) | |
| Exophoric → | Cataphoric → | Comparative → (as...as) ↓ | Booster (sooo good) |
| | | Additive → (also) | Coordination (as well as) |
| | Cataphoric → | Quotative index (so to speak) | |
| Exophoric → | Recognitional → | Approximative (ten students or so; Lat. quasi) | |

# 4 Loss and reinforcement of exophoric use

As already shown in Examples (1) – (3), English has practically lost the exophoric (gestural) use of the relevant group of demonstratives. For OE this use of *þus*, *swylc* and *swa* is clearly attested, but only in the degree sense is it still possible to use *so* in ModE (*My brother is so tall* + gesture indicating height). Even in this use, however, the demonstrative is typically replaced by one of the two spatial adnominal demonstratives (*Is he this/that tall?*). All other exophoric uses of *so* and *thus* have been replaced by complex expressions with spatial deictics and with separate compositional encoding of the deictic component and the content component: *like this, like that, that's the way to do it*; (dial. *like so*)

(4)  John dances like this. John looks like this. John is this tall. Is John as tall as that?

This process of renewal of exophoric deictic expression for manner through presentational deixis can be observed in Latin and Romance languages: Italian: *ecco + si > cosi*; Fr. *accum sic > ensi > ainsi*; Latin *si + ce > sīc*. In Swedish, spatial deixis is used to renew manner deictics (*såhär – sådär*; proximal – distal). In Japanese and in German, by contrast, the exophoric use of the MQD-demonstratives is still found alongside their further grammaticalized uses and no analogous processes of renewal are found.

# 5 From exophoric to anaphoric

Subsets of the following processes of grammaticalization can be observed in a wide variety of European languages, both Indo-European and Finno-Ugric, and in fact in many more language families across the globe (cf. Koenig 2012). Striking similarities among the patterns found in European languages can also be found in Japanese, though not in Mandarin. These largely parallel grammatical patterns among Western languages and Japanese will now be discussed in tandem. Subtle differences are typically due to the differentiations made by Japanese in the deictic dimension. Most of the Japanese examples used in the following sections have been taken from a previous comparative study on Japanese and German (cf. Koenig & Nishina 2015).

## 5.1 Propositional anaphors

The extension of the exophoric use of a demonstrative to an anaphoric one, where the expression does not relate to an external situation but retrospectively to a referential item or stretch of text in the previous discourse, is a very general phenomenon, attested for most demonstratives in most languages. Demonstratives of manner manifest the same extension of use, but given their basic meaning, it is not an entity they relate to, but rather a whole predication or proposition.

In addition to the uses as VP-anaphor (5a) and pro-ADJ (5b), we also find a use of *so* in English where the demonstrative relates to a whole proposition (cf. (6)) and it is exactly this use of a propositional anaphor that is also available for the hearer-proximal ('medial') manner demonstrative *soo* in Japanese (cf. (7)):

(5) a. *John works in his office and Bill does so at home.*
    b. *John is sick and so is Bill. – Is John sick? – Yes. Alarmingly so.*

(6) a. *Our economic situation is pretty difficult.*
    b. *I suppose/think/imagine…so.*

(7) Japanese
    a. *Nihon-no      keizai        zyookyooo-wa   kanari warui.*
       Japan-GEN    economic    situation-TOP    pretty bad
    b. *Watasi-mo    soo        omo-u.*
       1SG-too      so.D2      think-PRS

(8) a. *It may rain tomorrow. If so, we will have to change our plans. – Soo-nara(ba)* 'so-if'.
    b. *Apparently so. – Akirakani soo-da; probably so. – Tabun soo-da.*

Whereas the use of *swa* (> *so*) as VP-anaphor is already attested in OE, the propositional anaphor was a later development. The examples in (8) illustrate further uses of anaphoric *so*: in combination with the conditional connective *if* and in combination with sentence adverbs, which again have a clear parallel in Japanese. Let me note in passing that the cognate demonstrative *so* in German can neither be used as propositional anaphor, i.e. as object after verbs of propositional attitude (the affirmative particle *ja* being used instead), nor in contexts such as (8) which are simply elliptical in German.

## 5.2  SO as sentential connective (conjunct and subordinator)

The Old English *swa* could be used as a sentence-initial adverb, relating to a preceding stretch of text and indicating the manner in which a subsequent event took place. In the course of the historical development of Modern English, these sentence-initial anaphors developed different adverbial meanings, as in the examples in (9) below, even though it is not perfectly clear, whether they represent cases of polysemy or semantic vagueness.

(9) a. *I did not like it. **So** I wrote to him.* (causal)
 b. ***So** you are a linguist, eh? So what? So?* (inferential)
 c. *He is very sick. Even **so**, he goes to work.* (concessive)
 d. *The whole thing was tied up in knots, so that we were not able to undo it.* (resultative)
 e. *He went into lower gear so (that) his car would slow down.* (purposive)

In Japanese, combinations of the medial demonstrative *soo* with various notional components (conditional, causal, concessive, state, etc.) are used analogously as sentential connectives, but it seems that the anaphorically used demonstrative is mainly responsible for the connective, rather than for the adverbial content.

JAPANESE (medial manner demonstrative: *soo*)
(10) a. *soo + s-itara > soositara > sositara* (conditional) 'do so COND'
 b. *soo + iuwake-de > souiuwakede* (causal) 'so say reason-INSTR'
 c. *aa soo > assoo* (inferential/responsive)
 d. *soo-waitte-mo, soredemo* (concessive) 'say so-TOP too', 'so-INSTR too'

## 5.3 Markers of affirmation

The path from anaphoric manner deixis to affirmative expression is a straightforward one: the repetition of a previously uttered opinion in the shape of roughly the content '(it is) like that' amounts to an affirmation of the opinion previously uttered. The path of grammaticalization thus has the following approximate shape:

(11)  manner deictic > anaphoric use > affirmation/confirmation

A development of this kind is observable in a variety of European languages, though not in Japanese, nor in Mandarin, a language which lacks a clear counterpart for the English *yes*.

(12) **affirmation**: Polish *tak*; Russ. *tak*, Ital./Span. *si*; Engl. *yes* (*yeah + swa*); Sh. *even so, just so* (confirmation); Fr. *si* (NEG-Q), Finn. *niin*: 'affirmation + reservation'; Germ. *So ist das* (confirmation); *das ist so > isso* (assertion against doubts of interlocutor);

# 6 From exophoric to cataphoric

## 6.1 cataphoric > quotative index

In the cataphoric (prospective) use of demonstratives it is usually the proximal form that is found, provided a distinction can be expressed in the deictic dimension. In English, we always find *this* rather than *that* in this use:

(13) a. *Let me tell you this*: "*I couldn't care less.*"
 b. *One day this man comes into a pub in Northern Ireland and asks the bartender*:...

Whereas adnominal demonstratives may relate either to some subsequent utterance or to an entity, demonstratives of manner invariably relate to a stretch of speech and typically develop into quotative markers. The following examples from four languages are all translations of the English example 'He put it like this.'

(14) a. *Le ministre s'est exprimé ainsi. "J'ai commis une faute morale."* ; *Pour ainsi dire.* (French)
 'The minister put it like this/ he was like: "I made a moral mistake"';
 'To put it like this'
 b. *Hän sanoi sen näin...* (Finnish)
 'He put it like this: ...' (proximal form)
 c. *Er hat sich so ausgedrückt*: (German)
 d. *kare-wa   koo          it-ta...* (Japanese)
 3SG.M    Manner.PROX  say-PST
 'He said it like this..."

## 6.2 Summarizing a story

In German quotative constructions, *so* may also be inserted into the quotation, rather than prefixed to it, and, what's more, a whole story can be summarized by a coordinated sequence of these quotative markers.

(15) a. *Und ich: so und so und so und so.* (German);
 'And I'm like...' (English)
 b. '*Sie habe', so die Kanzlerin, 'alles versucht.*'
 'The Chancellor said that she tried everything.'

Similar elliptical quotation is possible inter alia in Russian (*i tak, i tak*) and in Japanese:

(16) a. *koo              koo koo koo   iu wake-da*
Manner.PROX    ...................   say reason-COP
b. *aa-de             koo-de              aa-de koo-de*
MANNER.DIST-INSTR   MANNER.PROX-INSTR   ........................

## 7 From exophoric to comparative

In European languages MQD-demonstratives also show up in equative comparative constructions, where they function as degree markers and often also as standard markers, as is shown in the following four examples from Europe:

(17) a. *Karl ist so groß wie Peter.* (German)
[Karl ist so groß [wie Peter groß ist]]
b. *Karl is as tall as Peter.* (English)
*Charles is this tall. Charles is as tall as this.*
c. *Karl est aussi grand que Pierre.* (French)
d. *Kostja takoj umnyj kak ego sestra.* (Russian) (Haspelmath, 2017: 13)
Kostya [so smart]   [as his sister]
'Kostya is as smart as his sister.'
e. COMPAREE – copula – degree marker – parameter – standard marker – STANDARD

In Haspelmath (2017), the type (17e) is described as one of six primary types attested in the world's languages, primarily in European languages. The degree marker is invariably derived from MQD-demonstratives, but, as far as the standard marker is concerned, two subtypes may be distinguished, both of which may also be derived from a demonstrative (cf. English *as...as* < *eall swa*; older forms of German *so... als*) or take the form of an interrogative from the same domain (Modern German, Russian, French). In the latter case, the path of grammaticalization can be reconstructed as follows: an exophorically used degree marker is used cataphorically and combines with a relative clause indicating a standard. German provides very good evidence for such an analysis, which assumes that the predicate of the second clause is deleted under identity with that of the main clause (Thurmair 2001).

(18) a. *Hans ist so groß* + pointing gesture. (indicating standard by gesture)
b. *Hans ist so groß wie Paul ~~groß ist~~.* (providing standard verbally)

The relative-clause-like properties of the second part of such comparatives show up very clearly when the second term of the comparison is embedded.

(19) *Charles is as successful [as I know [he has always wanted [to be __]]]*

There are a few formally related constructions in English with roots in the comparative and correlative use of *swa* in OE, but with slightly different meanings. In (20b-c), for example, the comparee and the standard are the same person.

(20) a. *He did not **so** much as look at me.*
b. *(As) rich as he is, he spends a lot of money on betting.*
c. *(As) poor as he is, he often eats in fashionable restaurants.*

Let us now look at our two Asian languages. The following examples show that there are two ways of expressing equative comparatives, neither of which involves MQD-demonstratives, however. Note, first of all that the property 'high/tall' is not directly predicated on a person in Japanese, but on a dimensional noun 'height' (cf. (21a)). The insertion of a relational noun *gurai* with the meaning 'degree' combined with the proximal adnominal demonstrative *kono* results in a sentence that is used for the exophoric (gestural) identification of a person's height (cf. (21b)). By replacing the demonstrative with a noun, we obtain one type of equative comparative in which the standard is no longer pointed at but rather identified by a noun. In (21c) the standard is expressed by the name *Akio*. This construction is somewhat similar to what we find in German or English, insofar as an exophorically-used demonstrative is replaced by a description. The more frequent equative comparative is, however, a construction in which the comparee and the standard are a single conjoined nominal, so that no distinction is made between a topical comparee and a rhematic standard (Haspelmath's type 3). Moreover, in contrast to what we find in European languages, an equal degree of a property in some dimension is predicated (cf. (21d)).

JAPANESE
(21) a. *Taroo-wa    se-ga          taka-i.*
       Taroo-TOP   height-NOM   tall-PRS
       'Taroo is tall.'
   b. *Taroo-wa    kono-gurai    se-ga         taka-i.*
       Taroo-TOP   this-degree   height-NOM   tall-PRS
       'Taroo is so (+ gesture) tall.'
   c. *Taroo-wa Akio-gurai se-ga taka-i.*
       'Taroo is as tall as Akio.'

d. *Taroo-wa Akio-to onazi-gurai se-ga taka-i.*
   Taroo-TOP Akio-Com equal-degree height-NOM tall-PRS
   'Taroo is as tall as Akio.'

Mandarin has a comparative construction that is largely analogous to (21d) in Japanese: Comparee and standard are expressed in the same phrase and an equal degree of a property is predicated on this conjoined subject (cf. (22a-b)):

MANDARIN
(22) a. *Lǐsì hé/gēn/xiàng Zhāngsān yīyàng gāo/lǎo.*
   (李四和/跟/像張三一樣高/老。)
   Lisi with/with/as Zhangsan same tall/old.
   'Lisi is as tall/old as Zhangsan.'
   b. A + *hé/gēn/xiàng* + B + *yīyàng* + adj.

There is, however, also a comparative construction of the type (23b), exemplified by the token (23a), that manifests grammaticalization of MQD-demonstratives, with a verbal expression of similarity and thus a separate encoding of a standard marker, all quite analogous to the type generally found in Europe. The only difference with the analogous construction in European language is that the standard precedes the degree phrase:

(23) a. *Lǐsì xiàng Zhāngsān zhèyàng/nàyàng gāo/lǎo.*
   (李四像張三這樣/那樣高/老。)
   Lisi resembles/is like Zhangsan this/that degree tall/old.
   b. A+*xiàng*+B+*zhèyàng/nàyàng*+adj.

The negation of (23) is given in (24):

(24) *Tā búxiàng/méi Zhāngsān zhèyàng/nàyàng gāo.*
   (他不像/沒張三這樣/那樣高。)
   He not as/not Zhangsan this degree/that degree tall.
   'He is not as/so tall as Zhangsan.'

# 8 Common patterns in Europe – not found in the two Asian languages

In addition to the targets discussed above, there are many other paths of grammaticalization leading from MQD-demonstratives to (more) grammatical markers in European languages, which have no counterparts in Japanese or Mandarin. The following brief summary of these processes is meant to complete the picture for European languages. Some thoughts on the reasons for their absence in Japanese and Mandarin will be offered in the final section.

A frequent target of semantic change in Germanic languages is the approximate use of manner/quality/degree-demonstratives, which may derived from the recognitional use, but is ultimately based on the notion of 'similarity', expressed by such demonstratives. Here are two examples from English and German:

(25) a. *There are twenty or so students in my class.*
b. *So (etwa) 20 Studenten sind in meinem Kurs.*

A much more frequent phenomenon is focus markers based on MQD-demonstratives. German *ebenso* and *sogar* 'even', English *also*, French *aussi*, Spanish *también* and Swedish *också* are cases in point. A further step in the grammaticalization of additive focus markers can be found in coordinating conjunctions that are used in non-scalar contexts:

(26) a. GERMAN
*ebenso (wie): Karl ist groß und Peter ist ebenso groß.*
'Karl is tall and so is Peter.'
b. FRENCH
*Les garçon sont venus ainsi que les filles.*
'The boys as well as the girls have arrived.'

The following uses of *so* in Modern English are all different, but share a specific feature: they cannot be related to the notion of 'similarity' in any way, nor do they seem to involve comparisons. The most widespread of those uses in European languages is the scalar degree adverb ('booster'). This use is found in combinations of *so* + adjective and its emphatic quality may be represented in writing by repeating the same vowel. Combinations of *such* + noun may be used analogously.

(27) a. *She is SOOO intelligent. Thank you sooo much!*
b. *It was SUCH FUN!*

One could hypothesize that such boosters are the result of reduced comparatives with an ability or situation as second term, but there is no clear evidence for such a historical derivation.

(28) *She is so intelligent* ~~that she can solve any problem~~.

On the other hand, boosters could be seen as deriving directly from an original exophoric use, marginally available in Modern English in the form *like so*, by pointing to a contextually given high point on some scale, provided either by an external situation or by our memory. This latter analysis is the only plausible one for the following cases:

(29)  Her hair is always just so.

(30)  You can only eat so much.

(31)  a.  *Ich hatte keine Eintrittskarte. Ich bin so reingekommen.* (Ger.)
         'I did not have a ticket. I got in without paying.
      b.  *Einfach so?* 'Just like that?'

In (29) *so* identifies a point on a scale that is determined by some 'as it should be' norm. In (30) it is the highest point on some scale achievable by an action or activity. And in (31) the relevant German expressions denote a situation that occurred without relevant or special circumstances. The latter use is also available in English:

(32)  It so happened that my mother called the same day.

GEN-X *so* (Generation X *so*) is the most recent extension in the multifarious uses of *so* in English (cf. Zwicky 2007; Boulonnais 2005). Its characteristic distributional feature is the pre-verbal position and its meaning is glossed by Zwicky as 'definitely, decidedly' or as emphatic negation in negative sentences. All this is similar to the emphatic use of *too* (You did not. – I did too.) as a marker of the verum focus, i.e. of contrastively emphasizing the truth of what follows.

(33)  a.  *I am so going to take a long nap today.*
      b.  *We so don't have time.*

# 9 Summary and conclusion

A variety of conclusions can be drawn from the preceding discussion. The first thing we may note – as has already been noted by Indo-Europeanists such as Karl Brugmann (1904) and philosophers like Karl Bühler (1934) – is that demonstratives are an important source for various processes of grammaticalization. Since demonstratives already straddle the line between lexis and grammar, the processes observed are instances of grammatical elements becoming more grammatical rather than taking members of major lexical classes, such as verbs and nouns, as a point of departure. The focus of our study was on a largely neglected subset of demonstratives, viz. demonstratives of manner, quality and degree, which are atypical insofar as they are frequently associated with enacting and mimicking rather than pointing gestures and insofar as they identify a referent through a relationship of similarity with some salient entity. As far as the targets of grammaticalization processes involving MQD-demonstratives are concerned, however, a generalization can be made for all demonstratives: they typically establish transphrastic relations, relationships across clauses, rather than strengthening intra-clausal relations between the constituents of a clause. This is clearly documented by the list of typical targets listed in Table 1 for the more frequently discussed demonstratives and has been demonstrated by the list of typical targets of MQD-demonstratives in the preceding discussion: anaphora, cataphora, affirmation, adverbial connectives, comparatives, conjunctions, etc. are all cases of relations transcending a single clause. The subclass of demonstratives under discussion thus provides further evidence for the view advocated by Diessel (2006, 2013) contra Heine (2005, 2007) that not all grammatical categories and markers derive from members of major lexical classes.

After previous comparative work on widespread paths of grammaticalization in European languages (Koenig 2012, 2015), the goal pursued in Koenig and Nishina (2015) and in the present paper was to explore also similar and analogous developments in two Asian languages, viz. Japanese and Mandarin. It has been shown that there are striking parallels within European languages and between European languages, on the one hand, and Japanese, on the other, as far as the extension from the exophoric to the endophoric uses is concerned. The relevant processes, and thus the relevant similarities, are not as clearly observable in Mandarin. Why should this be so? Even if no fully convincing explanation can be offered for this difference, there are certainly a few facts worth mentioning which might ultimately contribute to finding such an explanation.

As already briefly mentioned above, MQD-demonstratives have disappeared and have been renewed more than once, so it seems, in the history of Mandarin Chinese. The basic demonstratives *zhè* and *nà* appeared and replaced those of Classical Chinese around the 8th century. At that time, and up to the 14th/15th centuries, the forms *níng/néng* vs. *ruó/yǔmó* were used as MQD-demonstratives, which were replaced around this time by the newly created complex forms *zhèyang* and *nàyang*.[3] A further MQD-demonstrative that more or less disap-

---

[3] I owe these observations to Alain Peyraube, who also called my attention to the relevant Historical Grammar of Chinese: Jiǎng Shàoyǔ 蔣紹愚 & Cáo Guǎngshùn 曹廣順 (2005).

peared in its original function, keeping its concessive use alone or in combination with *suí* is *rán*. *Suí rán* seems to have had a similar semantic development as *even so* in English. Overall, it is quite possible that due to their relative short history rather than as a result of their typological affiliation, the composite MQD-demonstratives *zhèyang* and *nàyang* do not manifest the patterns of grammaticalization found in numerous European languages or in Japanese. On the other hand, the proximal demonstrative of Mandarin is developing a use as definite article, a development not found in Japanese (Fang 2012).

One of the guiding hypotheses of the conference papers assembled in this volume was Janet Xing's claim that Chinese tends to keep older meanings in processes of grammaticalization, i.e. meanings providing the starting points for such developments, thus showing "an accretion of more meanings over time", whereas these meanings and uses are typically lost in the corresponding developments in European languages (Xing 2015: 595). In other words, semantic changes in European languages typically manifest a cline like A > A, B > B, whereas the cline in Mandarin would typically take the shape A > A, B > A, B, C. The loss of the exophoric use of demonstratives in many European languages might be analyzed in this way. At the starting point of a grammaticalization path we often find such a loss of meanings. However the corresponding accretion of meanings cannot be observed in Chinese, due to one or several complete renewals of the system in the course of the historical development of that language.

Overall, the thematic domain selected for the comparative study of this paper does not seem to be the most suitable one for assessing the importance of typological factors in grammaticalization processes. As pointed out above, demonstratives are special in such processes insofar as they tend to establish transphrastic relations, rather than tighter relations within a clause. Moreover, previous comparative work in this domain (Koenig 2012, 2015; Koenig and Nishina 2015) has shown that very similar extensions of meaning and use show up in the inflectional languages of Europe, the agglutinative type as represented by Japanese and in Oceanic languages as representatives of the isolating type (cf. Moyse-Faurie 2016). So, what this paper is primarily about is the notional basis of grammaticalization, the typical developments of function words (interrogatives, demonstratives), the role of losses and renewals as well the importance of studying grammaticalization from a comparative perspective.

**Acknowledgements:** Many thanks to Yoko Nishina, Li Jingying and Alain Peyraube for helping me to find suitable data for Japanese and Mandarin. I am also indebted to two anonymous reviewers and to the editor for critical and helpful comments.

# References

Arsenijević, Boban, Kratochvil, František & Joanna Ut-Seong Sio. 2018. Equative and simulative demonstratives in Sinitic and beyond. www.academia.edu/31817275/Equative_and_simulative_demonstratives_in_Sinitic_and_beyond.

Boulonnais, Dominique. 2005. *So* et les phenomènes d'expansion contextuelle. In *Aux marges du texte: Texte et co-texte*. Etudes réunies par Geneviève Girard. C.I.E.R.E.C. Travaux 128; pp. 49–69. CIEREC: Centre Interdisciplinaire d'Etudes et de Recherches sur l'Expression Contemporaine. Publications de l'Université de Saint-Etienne.

Brugmann, Karl. 1904. *Die Demonstrativpronomina der indogermanischen Sprachen: eine bedeutungsgeschichtliche Untersuchung*. Leipzig: Teubner.

Bühler, Karl. 1934/1982. *Sprachtheorie. Die Darstellungsfunktion der Sprache*. Stuttgart: Josef Fischer.

Diessel, Holger. 1999. *Demonstratives. Form, Functions and Grammaticalization*. Amsterdam: Benjamins.

Diessel, Holger. 2006. Demonstratives, joint attention, and the emergence of grammar. *Cognitive Linguistics* 17 (4): 463–489.

Diessel, Holger. 2013. Where does language come from? Some reflections on the role of deictic gesture and demonstratives in the evolution of language. *Cognitive Linguistics* 5.2–3: 239–249.

Dixon, Robert M.W. 2003. Demonstratives: A cross-linguistic typology, *Studies in Language* 27 (1): 61–112.

Fang, Mei. 2012. The emergence of a definite article in Beijing Mandarin. The evolution of the proximal demonstrative *zhè*. In *Newest Trends in the Study of Grammaticalization and Lexicalization in Chinese*, Janet Xing (ed.), 55–85. Berlin: Mouton de Gruyter.

Güldemann, Tom. 2008. *Quotative Indexes in African languages: A Synchronic and Diachronic Survey*. Berlin: Mouton de Gruyter.

Guérin, Valérie. 2015. Demonstrative verbs: A typology of verbal manner deixis. *Linguistic Typology* 19 (2): 141–199.

Haspelmath, Martin and Buchholz, Oda. 1998. Equative and similative constructions in the languages of Europe. In *Adverbial Constructions in the Languages of Europe*, van der Auwera, Johan (ed.), 277–334. Berlin: Mouton de Gruyter,

Haspelmath, Martin. 2001. The European linguistic area: Standard Average European, In *Language Typology and Language Universals* vol. II. Martin Haspelmath, Matthew Dryer, David Gil and Bernard Comrie (eds.), 1492–1510. Berlin: de Gruyter.

Haspelmath, Martin. 2017. Equative constructions in a world-wide perspective. In *Similative and Equative Constructions: A Cross-linguistic Perspective*, Treis, Yvonne & Martine Vanhoeve (eds.), 9–32 Amsterdam: Benjamins.

Heine, Bernd & Tania Kuteva. 2002. *World Lexicon of Grammaticalization*. Cambridge: CUP.

Heine, Bernd & Tania Kuteva. 2005. *Language Contact and Grammatical Change*. Cambridge: CUP.

Heine, Bernd & Tania Kuteva. 2007. *The Genesis of Grammar: A Reconstruction*. Oxford: OUP.

Himmelmann, N.. 1997. *Deiktikon, Artikel, Nominalphrase: Zur Emergenz syntaktischer Struktur*. Tübingen: Niemeyer.

Hofmann, Thomas R.. 1993. *Realms of Meaning*. London: Longman.

Huddleston, Rodney & Pullum, Geoffrey. 2001. *The Cambridge Grammar of the English Language*. Cambridge: University Press.

Iwasaki, Shoichi. 2013. *Japanese*. rev. ed. Amsterdam: Benjamins.
Koenig, Ekkehard. 2012. Le rôle des déictiques de la manière dans le cadre d'une typologie de la deixis. *Bulletin de la Société de Linguistique de Paris*, CVII. 11–42.
Koenig, Ekkehard. 2015. Manner deixis as a source of grammatical markers in Indo-European Languages. In *Perspectives on Historical Syntax*, Carlotta Viti (ed.), 35–60. Amsterdam: Benjamins.
Koenig, Ekkehard & Siemund, Peter. 2005. Intensifiers and reflexive pronouns. In *The World Atlas of Language Structures*, Martin Haspelmath, Matthew Dryer, David Gil and Bernard Comrie (eds.), 194–197.
Koenig, Ekkehard and Yoko Nishina. 2015. Deixis der Art und Weise, der Qualität und des Grades im Deutschen und Japanischen: Eine kontrastiv vergleichende Analyse. *Linguistische Berichte*, Sonderheft 20, 7–32.
Koenig, Ekkehard & Carla Umbach. 2018. Demonstratives of manner, of quality and of degree: A neglected subclass. In Boef, E., M. Coniglio, E. Schachter & T. Veenstra (eds.) *Atypical Demonstratives: Syntax, Semantics and Typology*. Berlin: Mouton de Gruyter.
Moyse-Faurie, Claire. 2016. Verbal manner demonstratives in Futunan and East Uvean", Unpublished manuscript. Villejuif.
Schladt, Mathias. 2000. The typology and grammaticalization of reflexives. In *Reflexives: Forms and Functions*, Frajzyngier, Zygmunt & Traci S. Curl (eds.), 103–124. Amsterdam: Benjamins.
Schleburg, Florian. 2002. *Altenglisch swa: Syntax und Semantik einer polyfunktionalen Partikel*. Heidelberg: C. Winter.
Shaoyu, Jiang & Cao Guangshun 蔣紹愚、曹廣順 (eds.) 2005. *Hanyu yufa shi* (Historical Grammar of Chinese). Peking: Commercial Press.
Thurmeier, Maria. 2001. *Vergleiche und Vergleichen: Eine Studie zu Form und Funktion der Vergleichsstrukturen im Deutschen*. Tübingen: Niemeyer.
Umbach, Carla & H. Gust. 2014. Similarity Demonstratives. *Lingua* 149: 74–93.
Wiedenhof, Jeroen. 2015. *A Grammar of Mandarin*. Amsterdam: Benjamins.
Xing, Janet. 2015. A comparative study of semantic change in grammaticalization and lexicalization in Chinese and Germanic languages. *Studies in Language* 39 (3): 595–634.
Zwicky, Arnold. 2007. Gen-X so. (https://arnoldzwicky.fileswordpress.com/2011/11/zitsgenx.gif)

Xiufang Dong
# From denotation to description: Noun-adjective and verb-adjective polysemy in Chinese

## 1 Introduction

In the history of the Chinese language, some nouns that originally denoted a concrete object developed an adjectival meaning referring to a property related to the object. In some cases, the previous nominal meaning disappeared, but in some other cases the two kinds of meanings coexisted, and as a result, the words became noun-adjective polysemic. The basic function of nouns is denotation, while the basic function of adjectives is description. Therefore, the path of the above-mentioned semantic change is 'from denotation to description'. Similarly, we find that in the history of the Chinese language, some verbs that originally referred to a concrete activity obtained an adjectival meaning that describes a specific property related to that activity. This kind of semantic change is from predication to description. Since at an abstract level, the function of verbs can be regarded as denoting an activity, the semantic change from verb to adjective can also be seen as from denotation to description. In this kind of semantic change, though the syntactic category changes (either from a noun to an adjective or from a verb to an adjective), the form of the word can remain the same. In this chapter, we analyze some examples of the semantic change from denotation to description, find the regularities in it, explain its mechanisms, explore the diachronic processes it goes through, compare these changes in Chinese with those in English, and finally discuss the relationship of nouns, verbs and adjectives.

## 2 Examples of changing from nominal denotation to adjectival description

In the history of the Chinese language, some nouns underwent a specific semantic change and obtained an adjectival meaning (Song 2008). In this kind of change, the previous nominal meaning denotes a concrete object, while the later obtained

**Note:** The Chinese version of this paper has been published in *Yuwen Yanjiu (Linguistic Research)* 2018, No. 3: 1–7. The content of this English version is slightly different from that of the Chinese version.

https://doi.org/10.1515/9783110641288-004

adjectival meaning describes a property related to that object. For example, *kǔ* 苦 originally referred to a bitter edible plant, i.e. sowthistle, as illustrated in (1), then obtained the adjectival meaning 'bitter' which is obviously related to the nominal meaning, as shown in (2). The two meanings coexisted in Old Chinese.

(1) 采苦采苦，首阳之下。(《诗•唐风•采苓》)
Cǎi     kǔ         cǎi     kǔ,         Shǒuyáng     zhī     xià.
pick sowthistle pick sowthistle mountain-name POSS under
'Gather sowthistle at the foot of Shouyang Mountain.'
(6th century BC, *The Book of Songs*)

(2) 谁谓荼苦，其甘如荠。(《诗•邶风•谷风》)
Shuí weì tú           kǔ,     qí gān     rú     jì.
who say sowthistle bitter it sweet as sheperd-purse
'Who says that sowthistle is bitter? It is as sweet as sheperd's purse.'
(6th century BC, *The Book of Songs*)

Let us look at another example. *Cǎo* 草 originally denoted 'grass', as shown in (3):

(3) 野无青草。(《左传•僖公二十六年》)
Yě     wú     qīng     cǎo.
field NEG green grass
'There was no green grass in the field.'
(4th century BC, *Zuǒzhuàn*)

Overtime, *cǎo* obtained some meanings referring to properties somehow related to 'grass', such as 'lowly, banal, ordinary', as illustrated in (4).

(4) 臣今死罪有馀，乞存草命。(《敦煌变文集•伍子胥变文》)
Chén jīn     sǐzuì             yǒu     yú,     qǐ     cún     cǎo     mìng.
I       now death-penalty have surplus ask keep lowly life
'I deserve more than the death penalty, but please pardon my lowly life.'
(9th-10th century, *Dūnhuáng Biànwén Jí*)

Although the semantic shifts of *cǎo* are not as direct as that of *kǔ*, they are still not too hard to understand: Grass is often stamped on by people or animals and can be seen anywhere, thus it can be associated with the properties of 'lowly, banal, ordinary'. When it has the type of meaning as that in (3), *cǎo* is a noun; when it has the type of meaning as that in (4), it is an adjective.

There are many similar examples. Let us look at some more instances. In the following examples, different meanings are numbered. We first list the nominal meaning, then list the adjectival meaning. Document evidence is given under each type of meaning.

*láo* 牢
①pen, sheepfold
(5) 执豕于牢，酌之用匏。(《诗·大雅·公刘》)
Zhí shǐ yú láo, zhuó zhī yòng páo.
catch pig in pen drink PART use gourd
'Catch the pig in the pen, and drink with the gourd.'
(6th century BC, *The Book of Songs*)

②strong
(6) 東夷之陶者，器苦窳，舜往陶焉，朞年而器牢。
(《韩非子·难一》)
Dōngyí zhī táozhě, qì kǔ yǔ, Shùn
Eastern-barbarian POSS potter utensil suffer low-quality name
wǎng táo yān, jīnián ér qì láo.
go make-pottery there one-year and utensil strong.
'Dongyi (Eastern Barbarian) potters were vexed by the fact that the utensils (they made) were of bad quality. Shun went there to make pottery, and after a year, the utensils became strong.'
(3rd century BC, *Hánfēizǐ*)

*qīn* 亲
①parent
(7) 孩提之童无不知爱其亲者。(《孟子·尽心上》)
Háití zhī tóng wú bù zhī ài qí qīn zhě.
early-childhood POSS child nobody NEG know love their parent PART
'Small children without an exception all know to love their parents.'
(3rd century BC, *Mèngzǐ*)

②intimate
(8) 爱臣太亲，必危其身。(《韩非子·爱臣》)
Ài chén tài qīn, bì wēi qí shēn.
beloved minister too intimate must threat his body
'If beloved ministers have too close a relationship with their monarch, they will surely be a threat to the safety of the monarch.'
(3rd century BC, *Hánfēizǐ*)

*chún* 纯

①silk

(9) 麻冕，礼也；今也纯，俭，吾从众。(《论语·子罕》)
 *Má   miǎn,  lǐ  yě,    jīn   yě   chún, jiǎn,   wú cóng zhòng.*
 linen cap rite PART  now PART silk economical I  follow mass
 'The linen cap is prescribed by the rules of ceremony, but now a silk one is used. It is economical, and I follow the common practice.'
 (5th century BC, *The Analects*)

②pure, elegant

(10) 织作冰纨绮绣纯丽之物。(《汉书·地理志》)
 *Zhī    zuò   bīngwán        qǐxiù           chúnlì   zhī   wù.*
 weave  do   white-thin-silk colorful-silk-fabric elegant POSS thing
 '(They like to) weave white and thin silk, colorful silk fabrics and other elegant things.'
 (1st century, *Hànshū*)

*cūn* 村

①village

(11) 入魏郡界，村落齐整如一，民得财足用饶。(《三国志·魏志·郑浑传》)
 *Rù    Wèijùn     jiè,    cūnluò   qízhěng rúyī,    mín    dé*
 enter place-name territory village  trim    as-one people get
 *cái    zú     yòng    ráo.*
 money enough supply abound
 'Entering the territory of Weijun, you would find that the villages were trim and tidy, and the people there had enough money and supplies.' (3rd century, *Sānguózhì*)

②rustic, vulgar

(12) 我居固已陋，尔鸣良亦村。(宋·唐庚《圆蛤》诗)
 *wǒ    jū      gù    yǐ      lòu,       ěr    míng*
 my   dwelling indeed already simple-crude your cry
 *liáng  yì    cūn.*
 very  too  vulgar
 'My living place is already very simple and crude, and your croak is also very vulgar.'
 (11th century, Táng Gēng's poem)

③bad, poor

(13) 连车载酒来，不饮外酒嫌其村。(宋·苏轼《戏王巩自谓恶客》)
    *Lián        chē      zài      jiǔ      lái,      bù      yǐn      wài jiǔ*
    continuous vehicle carry wine come NEG drink out wine
    *xián     qí     cūn.*
    dislike its bad
    '(He) transported (his) wine in many carts, because he did not want to drink others' wine whose poor quality he dislikes.'
    (11th century, Sū Shì's poem)

When a noun denotes a concrete object, we say it has a 'denotation meaning'; when it is used to describe a quality related to that object, we say it has a 'description meaning'. In the above examples, no matter whether it has a denotation meaning or a description meaning, the form of the word remains the same.

The semantic shift from denotation to description has occurred throughout the history of the Chinese language, and is still active in contemporary Chinese. The following are some recent examples (we list the denotation meaning in ① and the description meaning in ②):

*huǒ* 火 ①fire ②prosperous, popular
*niú* 牛 ①ox ②powerful, formidable, capable
*tiě* 铁 ①iron ②strong, solid
*shíshàng* 时尚 ①fashion ②fashionable

We examined some nouns with a token frequency of more than 13 in Old Chinese, based on the word class labels in the Corpus of Old Chinese made by Academia Sinica of Taiwan, and found that there are at least 32 nouns that obtained description meanings over time. According to the statistics of Meng (2016), there are 298 words with both a nominal meaning and an adjectival meaning in parts of *Xiandai Hanyu Cidian* (Dictionary of Modern Mandarin, 6th edition).[1] Of course, these 298 words include some words that obtained nominal meanings from adjectival meanings but, even if we exclude them, the number of noun-adjective polysemes is still not small. This indicates that the semantic shift from nominal meaning (denotation) to adjectival meaning (description) is a common phenomenon in Chinese.

---

[1] Meng (2016) only surveyed words whose phonological form begins with B, C, D, J, S, Y, Z.

## 3 The types and mechanisms of semantic shift from denotation to description

For some words, the denotation meanings disappeared after they developed a description meaning. For example, *kǔ* 苦, *chún* 纯, etc. This kind of change belongs in the category of 'fundamental change', a term used by Armenakis & Bedeian (1992). For some other words, the denotation meaning does not dissappear but coexists with the description meaning, and the words are noun-adjective polysemic, e.g., *cǎo* 草. This type of change belongs in the category of 'incremental change' (Armenakis & Bedeian 1992). The latter situation is more common in Chinese, which supports the argument of Xing (2015). Earlier studies claim that semantic change follows the cline A>A, B>B. These studies have mostly been done on Indo-European languages (e.g. Heine et al. 1991, Traugott and Dasher 2002). Xing (2015), on the other hand, provides evidence from several case studies suggesting that semantic change in Chinese follows a somewhat different pattern: A>A, B>A,B,C. She argues that such a discrepancy of tendency in semantic change resulted from different grammatical and morphological structures and diachronic evolution between Chinese and Indo-European languages. We believe that the absence of morphological markers makes incremental changes more frequent in Chinese. We will discuss this further in Section 7.

Based on the relationship between the description meaning and the denotation meaning, the semantic shift from denotation to description can be classified into two types.

Type 1: object > inherent property of the object

In this type, the description meaning refers to the inherent property of the object originally denoted by the word. For example, the description meaning 'bitter' of *kǔ* 苦 is a property of that plant which the word denoted originally as shown in (1).

Furthermore, some description meaning is even entailed in the denotation meaning; in other words, the description meaning seems to be a semantic component of the denotation meaning. For example, *jīng* 精 (polished rice → polished, exquisite), *lǐ* 醴 (sweet wine → sweet), *zhòng* 众 (many people, masses → many), *jí* 极 (the highest roof girder → the highest, extreme), *sù* 素 (white silk → white), etc.[2]

---

[2] Though this kind of semantic shift is rather rare in English, it can occasionally be found as in the word 'orange', which can refer to a kind of fruit and can also refer to the color of that fruit.

Type 2: object > property related to the object in people's opinions

In this type, the description meaning is not necessarily a property of the object that was originally denoted by the word, but is, rather, a property related to the object based on the evaluation of language users. That is to say, the description meaning is only associated with the denotation meaning through opinion. For example, the description meaning 'vulgar' of *cūn* 村 is not an inherent property of 'village' which the word denoted originally; instead, it is based on the evaluation of some speakers. The evaluation is made on the property of the people living in villages since some villagers may give people the impression of vulgarity. Apparently, villagers and the village are related closely. The 'rough, sketchy' meaning of *cǎo* (as in *cǎotú* 草图 'preliminary sketch'; *cǎogǎo* 草稿 'manuscript') is not an inherent property of 'grass' either, but a property related to grass according to people's cognition and evaluation, since it is not difficult to associate a field full of grass with an unprocessed, primary state when comparing it with a field full of crops.

In this type, the relationship between description meaning and denotation meaning is not so close as that in the first type.

# 4 Mechanisms of semantic shift from denotation to description

In the first type, the semantic change relies purely on the mechanism of metonymy, since the relationship between description meaning and denotation meaning is largely direct. In the second type, in addition to metonymy, the semantic change relies also on the mechanism of 'lexical subjectification'.

According to Traugott (1989), lexical subjectification concerns shifts from concrete to internal evaluative but still propositional meanings, e.g. when an expression acquires a speaker-related-appreciative or pejorative-component in its lexical semantics. For example, in English, the meaning of the word 'boor' shifted from 'farmer' to 'crude person' and became pejorative according to the evaluation of language users.

The second type of semantic shift from denotation to description involves lexical subjectification. The denotation meaning is comparatively objective, since it can be observed. For example, the denotation meaning of *cǎo* 草 is a kind of plant and it can be seen by the eyes, thus it is comparatively more objective. One description meaning of *cǎo* 草 is 'lowly, banal, ordinary', which is not an inherent property of grass; instead, this meaning is based on a judgment and evaluation made by human beings, so it is more subjective. In this case, the word obtained a pejorative-component during the semantic change. The description meaning can be appreciative or pejorative as can be seen in the examples in the previous section. The result of this type of semantic change is an adjective which can contribute to propositional meaning. Therefore, this type of semantic shift can be regarded as involving a process of lexical subjectification.[3]

An object often has more than one related property. Which property will be chosen by language users to become the new description meaning?

According to our observation, nouns that denote natural objects and nouns that denote artificial objects all can obtain description meanings. For nouns denoting natural objects, the description meaning is always based on the properties that are prominent during interactions between human beings and the object. For example, as for grass, green is one of its properties, however, it is not so prominent in the physical interaction between human beings and grass.[4] Therefore, green is not a decription meaning of *cǎo* 草. People often stamp on grass with their feet and it is from this kind of interaction that grass's property of being lowly is drawn. Therefore, lowly became a description meaning of *cǎo* 草.

For artificial objects, properties related to their functions are most important to people, since artificial objects are made for people to use. Therefore, these kinds of properties are more likely to become description meanings. For example, the function of *láo* 牢 'pen' is to hold livestock thus 'being solide and firm' is its most important property for fulfilling that function. By contrast, properties related to size, shape, materials etc. are not so important. Therefore, *láo* 牢 obtained a description meaning of 'solid, firm, strong'.

It will come as no surprise that the above analysis illustrates that the principle for choosing the descriptive property is anthropocentrism, that is, paying most attention to the perceptions and needs of human beings. The emergence of description meanings is rooted in the interaction between objects and human beings. Those properties that are not much involved in the interaction with people are less likely to become description meanings.

The semantic change from denotation to description generally occurs with concrete nouns, but generally not with abstract nouns. This is because the referent of a concrete noun is more likely to interact with people and therefore receive an evaluation from people.

---

[3] Broadly speaking, we can say that both the two types of semantic shift from denotation to discription involve the mechanism of lexical subjectification, since adjectival meaning is more subjective than nominal meaning in general. But strictly speaking, only in the second type of change (i.e. object > property related to the object in people's opinions), the function of lexcial subjectification is obvious. So here we say that the second type of change involes the mechanism of lexical subjectification to show the difference between the two types. Xing (2013) considers this type of semantic shift as "semantic reanalysis".

[4] For one possible reason, there are a lot of green objects besides grass.

# 5 Paths from denotation to description

The semantic change from denotation to description takes place in language use, just as other semantic changes do. There are three steps involved in this kind of semantic change. Let's examine them one at a time.

Step 1: From denotative meaning to connotative meaning

To understand the semantic change in use more accurately, we need to explore the phenomenon both from the synchronic and diachronic perspectives.

Synchronically, Leech (1983) points out that there are two types of meaning: denotative meaning (or conceptual meaning), and connotative meaning. Denotative meaning is based on truth condition, and is, therefore, objective; connotative meaning is based on the opinions of society or some speakers, and is, therefore, subjective. At a synchronic level, we can see the two types of meanings in the usage of nouns: A noun may exhibit a denotative meaning in some contexts, and a connotative meaning in others.

Dong (2016) analyzes the features of denotative meanings and connotative meanings of nouns. When a noun expresses a connotative meaning, it reflects an evaluation that is usually only associated with some prototypical members but not all members of the category denoted by the noun.

Let's examine the meaning of *nǚrén* 女人 in some contexts:

(14) 问：新来的是个男人还是个女人？
　　 Q: *Xīnlái　　de　　shì　gè　nánrén　háishì　gè　nǚrén?*
　　 Q: new-come PART be CL man or CL woman
　　 'Is the newly arrived [person] a man or a woman?'
　　 答：是个女人。
　　 A: *Shì gè nǚrén.*
　　 A: be CL woman
　　 'It is a woman.'

In (14), *nǚrén* 女人 is used to express a denotative meaning, which refers to all people who are the opposite of men with respect to gender.

In (15)–(17), *nǚrén* 女人 is used to express connotative meanings, which are evaluations focusing on some properties of women. The property chosen is different in different contexts. In (15), the property of being fond of illusion is emphasized; in (16), the property of weakness is emphasized; in (17), the property of insufficiency of strength is emphasized. In these cases, the properties emphasized actually only belong to some women – that is, some prototypical women as seen through the eyes of speakers – but not all women.

(15) 与其说她是一个坚韧不拔的成功者，不如说她是一个女人，因为她善于把自己的幻想和奇妙的梦境，编织成现实，并以此征服世界。
Yǔqí shuō tā shì yīgè   jiānrènbùbá    de   chénggōngzhě,
if    say  she is one-CL firm-indomitable POSS achiever
bùrú          shuō tā shì yīgè   nǚrén, yīnwèi tā shànyú    bǎ  zìjǐ
not-better-than say she is one-CL woman since she be-good-at PART herself
de     huànxiǎng hé    qímiào de     mèngjìng, biānzhī chéng
POSS imagination and fantastic POSS dream      weave    complete
xiànshí, bìng yǐ    cǐ   zhēngfú shìjiè.
reality  and use this  conquer world
'Instead of saying that she is a firm and indomitable achiever, it would be better to say that she is a woman, because she is good at weaving her imaginations and wonderful dreams into reality, and using them to conquer the world.'

(16) 她曾偷偷地哭泣，因为她是女人。
Tā céng   tōutōu    de     kūqì,   yīnwèi   tā shì nǚrén.
she once  furtively  PART   cry    because  she be woman
'She used to cry secretly, because she is a woman.'

(17) 但毕竟她是个女人，渐渐力气不支，歹徒持刀的手终于挣脱出来。
Dàn bìjìng tā    shì gè nǚrén, jiànjiàn      lìqìbùzhī,
but after-all she  be CL woman gradually    lack-physical-strength
dǎitú      chídāo     de     shǒu zhōngyú  zhèngtuō   chūlái.
evil-doer  hold-knife POSS   hand finally    escape    out
'But after all, she is a woman, and gradually she did not have enough strength. Finally, the evildoer's hand that held the knife managed to break free.'

When will a noun be interpreted as having a connotative meaning? This is decided by pragmatics. In short, when the sentence does not make sense if a noun within it is interpreted as having a denotative meaning, a suitable connotative meaning will arise to give the noun a meaning that makes sense in the context.

Speaking specifically, there are two kinds of situations that will stimulate the transition to a connotative meaning. In one, if a noun is interpreted using its denotative meaning, the sentence will not provide any meaningful information. For example, in (15)-(17), it is already known that she is a woman from the context, therefore if *nǚrén* 女人 were to be interpreted using its denotative meaning, the sentence would be superfluous. However, the hearer/reader knows that the speaker/writer must want to express something meaningful, so the appropriate interpretation turns to a connotative meaning. In the other situation, if a noun were to be interpreted as expressing a denotative meaning, the sentence would be contrary to the fact. For example, imagine, if a speaker and a listener all know that 'he' (a man both the speaker and the listener know) is already 40 years old, but the speaker still says that 他是个孩子 'he is a child'. This sentence can be acceptable only if the noun 孩子 *háizi* 'child' is interpreted as expressing a connotative meaning, such as innocent or willful according to different contexts. It seems that language users are able to invoke the connotative meaning of a noun whenever the denotative interpretation is not possible.

No matter whether it expresses a denotative meaning or a connotative meaning, a noun maintains its syntactic category, that is to say, it is still a noun. Connotative meanings usually are not listed separately in dictionaries. However, connotative meanings of nouns indicate that speakers are paying attention to properties related to the object rather than just to the object itself. Thus, the semantic change from denotation to description can find root here. In a sense, getting connotative meaning is the starting point of the subjectification of a noun.

Diachronically, denotative meanings appear earlier than connotative meanings. Take *cǎo* 草 for instance:

(18) 湛湛露斯，在彼丰草。(《诗·小雅·湛露》)
   *Zhànzhàn   lù    sī,    zài bǐ fēng      cǎo*
   heavy      dew   PART   at that luxuriant  grass
   'Heavy lies the dew, on that luxuriant grass.'
   (6th century BC, *The Book of Songs*)

In (18), the meaning of *cǎo* 草 is denotative.

(19) 君子之德，风；小人之德，草。(《论语·颜渊》)
   *Jūnzǐ      zhī    dé,    fēng, xiǎorén        zhī    dé,    cǎo.*
   gentleman  POSS   virtue  wind common-people  POSS   virtue  grass
   'A gentleman's virtue is like the wind, while the common people's virtue is like the grass.'
   (5th century BC, *The Analects*)

In (19), *cǎo* 草 has a connotative meaning, focusing on the property of being soft, weak and easily affected. The connotative meaning is based on the opinion of the speaker, so it is subjective comparing with the denotative meaning in (18).

Step 2: Appearing in the modifier position of a nominal phrase

In Old Chinese, a noun could appear as a subject or an object, or the predicate of a copula-less judgment sentence. At a later stage, a noun might appear in the modifier position, becoming non-referent, and gained the function of description. For example, *cǎo* 草 could appear in the modifier position in the late period of Old Chinese, as seen in (20):

(20) 左右以君贱之也，食以草具。(《战国策·齐策》)
*Zuǒyòu yǐ    jūn    jiàn    zhī yě,    sì    yǐ*
servant because master despise him PART feed with
*cǎo            jù.*
grass (rough) utensil
'Because the master despised him, the servants fed him bad food.'
(1st century BC, *Zhànguócè*)

Let's look at another example. *Jīng* 精 was a noun in old Chinese referring to 'pure and polished rice':

(21) 鼓筴播精，足以食十人。(《庄子·人间世》)
*Gǔ    jiā    bō    jīng,    zúyǐ    sì    shí rén.*
shake fan spread pure-polished-rice enough feed ten people
'(By) shaking the winnowing fan to select good rice (by removing the impurity), he could feed ten people.'
(before 3rd century, *Zhuāngzǐ*)

By the Han Dynasty, *jīng* 精 began to be seen in the modifier position with the meaning 'fine, good':

(22) 怀精白之心，行忠正之道。(汉·桓宽《盐铁论·讼贤》)
*Huái jīng    bái    zhī    xīn,    xíng zhōng    zhèng zhī    dào.*
hold good white POSS heart walk faithful right POSS way
'Have a good and pure heart, and walk in the faithful and right way.'
(1st century BC, *Yántiělùn*)

Song (2008) points out that *sú* 俗 was a noun at the beginning, having the meaning of 'custom, convention'. For example:

(23) 安其居，乐其俗。(《老子》)
*An    qí    jū,    lè    qí    sú.*
satisfied the domicile enjoy the custom
'Be satisfied with the domicile and enjoy the custom.'
(5th century BC, *Lǎozǐ*)

At a later period, *sú* 俗 acquired the meaning of 'banal, vulgar', and initially could only function as a modifier:

(24) 故有俗人者，有俗儒者。(《荀子·儒效》)
 *Gù yǒu sú rén zhě, yǒu sú rú zhě.*
 so exist banal man PART exist banal scholar PART
 'So there are banal men, and there are banal scholars as well.'
 (3rd century BC, *Xúnzǐ*)

The typical function of an adjective is as a modifier in a nominal phrase. Therefore, appearing in the modifier position is a key step in a noun's transformation into an adjective.

Zhang (1994) puts forward the following continuum for word classes (also refer to Ross 1972, which claims that properties of A are "between" those of V and N.):

nouns – non-predicate adjectives - adjectives - intransitive verbs - transitive verbs

From this continuum, we can see that the non-predicate adjectives (that is, words that only appear in the modifier position of a nominal phrase) are located between nouns and adjectives. It is reasonable to regard non-predicate adjectives as the intermediate stage in the diachronic change from nouns to adjectives (Lu & Rao 1981; Li 1996; Tan 1998).

In Chinese, nouns can appear in the modifier position of a nominal phrase. For example:

(25) 妈妈的书
 *māmā de shū*
 mother POSS book
 'mother's book'

If nouns and adjectives can all function as nominal modifiers, then how can we identify the syntactic category of a nominal modifier?

Jespersen (1924) points out that nouns possess a feature of specialization since nouns can involve many characteristics. In contrast, adjectives can only signify one particular property; thus, adjectives can collocate with many nouns and exhibit generalness in semantics. Givón (1984: 55) also argues that the difference between nouns and adjectives is in the complexity of their semantics: Nouns are more semantically complex than adjectives. For nouns, a certain involved property is not crucial; a co-existing property cluster, however, is crucial.

Due to the above-mentioned feature, the meaning of a noun functioning as a modifier is not fixed. Instead, it can vary according to different contexts, similar to the situation of connotative meanings discussed previously. For example, when the noun *háizi* 孩子 'child' appears in the modifier position, its meaning can be varied. For example, in 孩子脾气 *háizi píqì* 'child-temperament', it can be explained as 'innocent' or 'willful, stubborn' depending on the context. Adjectives, on the other hand, express a fixed meaning when they function as nominal modifiers.

When a noun becomes an adjective, its meaning as a modifier becomes specific. The change from multiple interpretations to single interpretation can be regarded as a process of semanticization. During this process, the most common meanings in the usage will be selected and conventionalized as adjectival meanings.

Step 3: Appearing in the predicate position where it can be modified by degree adverbs

Adjectives in Chinese behave like verbs in some ways and can function directly as a predicate. The last step of the semantic change from denotation to description is for the word to appear in the predicate position where it can be modified by degree adverbs.

For instance, *cǎo* 草 has been able to function as a predicate and modified by a degree adverb, as shown in (26), since the Tang Dynasty, later than the time when it was used as a modifier.

(26) 各命仆马，颇甚草草。(唐笔记《纂异记》，出《太平广记》卷 350)
 Gè   mìng pú    mǎ,   pō   shèn cǎocǎo.
 each order servant horse rather very careless
 'They made the servants and horses ready, and (the way they do it) was very careless.'
 (10th century, *Tàipíngguǎngjì*)

*Jīng* 精 was able to appear in the predicate position, as illustrated in (27), in Middle Chinese, later than the time when it was able to function as a modifier.

(27) 临舆执手诀，良诲一何精！(晋•阮侃《答嵇康》诗二首之一)
 Lín    yú    zhí   shǒu jué,      liáng huì      yīhé jīng!
 near chariot hold hand bid-farewell good instruction so fine
 'Holding hands and bidding farewell near the (departing) chariot, what fine instructions you gave me!'
 (3rd century, *Ruǎn Kǎn's* poem)

Let's look at another example. *Sú* 俗 obtained a predicate function and was able to be modified by a degree adverb, as illustrated in (28), after the Six Dynasty, later than the time when it was able to function as a modifier.

(28) 神明太俗，由卿世情未尽。(《世说新语·巧艺》)
 Shénmíng tài sú, yóu qīng shìqíng wèi jìn.
 god too secular due-to you world-emotion NEG end
 'The god (that you drew) is too secular, which is due to the fact that you still have worldly emotion.'
 (5th century, Shìshuōxīnyǔ)

There are some nouns that did not reach Step 3, stopping their transformation at Step 2. That is to say their describing function was limited to that of a nominal modifier. The describing function of these words would be unstable and, therefore, might not be used over a very long period. For example, the adjectival meanings of the following examples are not used nowadays. Note: First we list the nominal meaning, numbered as ①; then we list the adjectival meaning (which could only appear in a modifier position) numbered as ②, followed by illustrations respectively.

*dǐng* 鼎
①an ancient vessel which is the symbol of a dynasty
(29) 楚子问鼎之大小、轻重焉。(《左传·宣公三年》)
 Chǔzǐ wèn dǐng zhī dàxiǎo qīngzhòng yān.
 king-of-Chu ask dǐng POSS size weight PART
 'The king of Chǔ asked (him about) the size and weight of the dǐng (an ancient vessel).'
 (4th century BC, Zuǒzhuàn)

②important
(30) 顷闻上帝震怒，贬黜鼎臣。(《后汉书·李膺传》)
 Qǐng wén shàngdì zhènnù, biǎnchù dǐng chén.
 lately hear emperor furious degrade important minister
 'Lately (I) heard that the emperor was furious and degraded an important minister.'
 (5th century, Hòuhànshū)

*fū* 肤
①skin
(31) 手如柔荑，肤如凝脂。(《诗·卫风·硕人》)
 Shǒu rú róu tí, fū rú
 hand like soft young-white-grass-blade skin like
 níng zhī.
 congealed ointment

'Her fingers were like soft blades of young white grass, and her skin was like congealed ointment.[5]'
(6th century BC, *The Book of Songs*)

②superficial
(32) 澄謏闻肤见，贻挠后昆。(《南齐书・陆澄传》)
Chéng   xiǎowén fū        jiàn,   yí    náo     hòukūn.
name  ignorant superficial  view  leave obstruct posterity
'I (Cheng) am ignorant and only have superficial point of views, and I am standing in the way of the posterity.'
(6th century, *Nánqíshū*)

*hǔ* 虎
①tiger
(33)    履虎尾，不咥人。(《易・履卦》)
         Lǚ     hǔ    wěi,  bù    dié    rén.
        stamp tiger  tail  NEG  bite  people
'[Even if you] stamp on the tail of a tiger, the tiger does not bite.'
(11th century BC, *The Book of Changes*)

②mighty, brave
(34)    矫矫虎臣，在泮献馘。(《诗・鲁颂・泮水》)
         *Jiǎojiǎo*              *hǔ*      *chén,*    *zài Pàn*
        martial-looking  mighty  minister  at river-name
         *xiàn*     *guó*
        present  left-ear (of dead foe)
'(His) martial-looking mighty leaders will present the left ears of (their foes) at the *Pàn* River.'
(6th century BC, *The Book of Songs*)

*guī* 瑰
①precious stone>
(35)    何以赠之？琼瑰玉佩。(《诗・秦风・渭阳》)
         *Hé*    *yǐ*    *zèng zhī?*  *Qiónggūi*        *yù*    *pèi.*
        what  with  give him  precious-stone  jade  pendant
'What did I present to him? Precious stones and jade pendants.'
(6th century BC, *The Book of Songs*)

---

5 The author uses the 'congealed ointment' metaphor here to praise the whiteness and smoothness of the skin of the woman.

②precious

(36) 瑰货方至。(汉·张衡《子虚赋》)
Guī    huò    fāng    zhì.
precious  goods  direction  arrive
'The precious goods arrived from all directions.'
(2nd century, Zhāng Héng's *fu*)

We can summarize the process of change from denotation to description as follows:
　　denotative meaning (noun) → connotative meaning (noun) → describing modification (non-predicate adjective) → describing predicate (predicate adjective)

# 6 From predicate to description

In the history of the Chinese language, some verbs that originally referred to a physical activity changed to express, instead, a property related to the activity (Song 2007, 2008, 2012). As a result, a verb could change into an adjective. This kind of change can be regarded as a move from predicate to description, and can be classified into two types.

　　Type 1: From activity to resultative state
　　Some verbs referring to an activity in Old Chinese changed into adjectives referring to the resultative state of the activity in Middle Chinese. For example, *pò* 破, used only as a verb meaning 'to break' in Old Chinese as illustrated in (37), changed into an adjective having the meaning of 'broken' or 'worn out' in Middle Chinese as illustrated in (38) (Hu 2005, Xu 2005, Xing & Schuessler in this volume). Obviously, the adjectival meaning of *pò* 破 refers to a property related to the resultative state of the activity denoted by its verbal predecessor.

(37) 既破我斧，又缺我斨。(《诗经·豳风·破斧》)
Jì     pò    wǒ fǔ, yòu    quē    wǒ qiāng.
not-only  break  my ax  but-also  splinter  my hatchet
'Not only did I break my axe, but I also splintered my hatchet.'
(6th century BC, *The Book of Songs*)

(38) 是身为譬如破瓶常漏。(东汉·安世高译《道地经》)
Shì shēn wéi pìrú pò    píng    cháng lòu.
this body be like worn-out  bottle  often leak
'The body is like a worn-out bottle that often leaks.'
(2nd century, Buddhist sutra)

The mechanism behind this type of change is metonymy. We will not go into the details behind the process of this change due to limited space.

Type 2: From activity to related property based on speaker's evaluation

In this type of change, the original verbal meaning and the later adjectival meaning are not as closed as they are in Type 1. The mechanisms behind this type of change involve both metonymy (sometimes also metaphor) and lexical subjectification. The semantic change of *dàng* 荡 is a case in point. *Dàng* 荡 originally was a verb, meaning 'swing, shake', as illustrated in (39):

(39) 齐侯与蔡姬乘舟于囿，荡公，公惧。(《左传•僖公三年》)
 *Qíhóu yǔ Càijī chéng   zhōu yú yòu, dàng gōng,*
 name and name ride   boat at park swing man (respectful address)
 *gōng jù.*
 man fear
 'The Marquis of *Qí* and his concubine whose family name is *Cài* rode a boat in the park. She swung the boat and he was scared.'
 (4th century BC, *Zuǒzhuàn*)

At a later stage, *dàng* 荡 obtained the adjectival meaning 'indulgent, libertine', as illustrated in (40).

(40) 其德荡者其行伪。(《淮南子•俶真》)
 *Qí dé     dàng     zhě     qí     xíng     wěi.*
 DEM virtue libertine person his activity hypocritical
 'Those whose virtue is libertine behave hypocritically.'
 (2nd century, *Huáinánzǐ*)

This change involves both metonomy and metaphor. First, through metonomy, the activity of swinging is related to the property 'unstable', and the verb shifts to become an adjective. Then through metaphor, the property in the physical domain extends to the domain of social behavior among human beings. At the same time, this change involves lexical subjectification which, based on language users' evaluation, judges 'being unstable' as 'being bad', thus imparting a derogatory sense to the word after it became an adjective.

Let's look at another example. *Jù* 踞 was a verb meaning 'sit with legs open' in old Chinese, as illustrated in (41).

(41) 庄子则方箕踞鼓盆而歌。(《庄子•至乐》)
 *Zhuāngzǐ   zé     fāng     jī     jù     gǔ     pén*
 name       PART   right-now dustpan sit-with-leg-open beat basin

*ér   gē.*
and   sing
'Zhuangzi was sitting with his legs open like a dustpan and singing while beating on a basin.'
(before 3rd century, *Zhuāngzǐ*)

Sitting with legs open was regarded as impolite in the eyes of the ancient Chinese, and impoliteness can incorporate an element of arrogance. Therefore, because the property of 'arrogant' was imparted to this activity through human evaluation, in Middle Chinese, *jù* 踞 obtained the adjectival meaning 'arrogant', as shown in (42). Obviously, lexical subjectification is involved in this change process.

(42) 捐贫贱之故旧，轻人士而踞傲者，骄人也。(晋·葛洪《抱朴子·外篇·行品》)
*Juān     pínjiàn    zhī    gùjiù,     qīng    rénshì*
abandon  poor-lowly PART  old-friend despise personage
*ér      jù'ào          zhě,   jiāo    rén    yě.*
and     arrogant-proud PART   proud   person PART
'Those who abandon poor and lowly old friends, despise public figures and behave arrogantly are proud person.'
(4th century, *Bàopǔzǐ*)

In some cases, the verbal meaning disappeared after the adjectival meaning came into being. In some other cases, the verbal meaning and adjectival meaning coexisted and resulted in verb-adjective polysemy.

The semantic change from predicative meaning to descriptive meaning involves two steps.

Step 1: Appearing in the predicate position intransitively where it can be modified by a degree adverb

The typical syntactic function of verbs is to be a predicate, therefore the change originated from the predicate position.

Step 2: Appearing in the modifier position of nominal phrases

It is important to note that some verbs only achieved Step 1, but have not reached Step 2. This can be seen in the following contemporary examples of verb-adjective polysemy:

*jǐ* 挤
① verb: jostle
(43) 他挤上了公交车。
    *Tā jǐshàng le gōngjiāochē.*
    he jostle-up ASP bus
    'He jostled his way onto the bus.'

② adjective: crowded
(44) 公交车上很挤。
    *Gōngjiāochē shàng hěn jǐ.*
    bus on very crowded
    'It is very crowded on the bus.'

*shài* 晒
① verb: bask, dry in the sun
(45) 晒被子。
    *shài bèizi*
    dry quilt
    'air the quilt (put the quilt in the sun)'

② adjective: corching
(46) 今天太阳很晒。
    *Jīntiān tàiyáng hěn shài.*
    today sun very scorching
    'Today the sun is scorching.'

In the above two examples, the adjective use only appears in the predicate position and not in the modifier position. Therefore, the adjectival meanings of the two words are not well established. In other words, the changes here are not full-fledged.

# 7 The relationship between noun, verb and adjective

The change from noun to adjective and the change from verb to adjective have something in common: They have similar subtypes and share similar mechanisms. The similarity of the two kinds of changes is rooted in the difference between adjectives on the one hand and nouns and verbs on the other. (Please refer to Shen 2015 for argument from the synchronic perspective. See also Xing & Schuessler in this volume.) Adjectives are more subjective than nouns and verbs. Adjectives refer to properties which are abstract and affiliated with concrete things and activities, thus using adjectives relies on people's judgments to a large degree. In contrast, nouns and verbs refer to objective phenomena which can, for the most part, be observed. The common function of nouns and verbs can be generalized as denotation: Nouns denote things and verbs denote activities. Therefore, the semantic change from predicate (verb) to description (adjective) can also be regarded as a subtype of change from denotation to description at a more abstract level.

Ross (1972) argues that the distinction between verb (V), adjective (A), and noun (N) is one of degree, rather than of kind. From the diachronic perspective, we have shown that both N and V can become A in the history of the Chinese language. Therefore, it is reasonable to believe that N, V and A are not fixed, discrete syntactic categories.

In the history of the Chinese language, adjectives, except for few members, appeared later than nouns and verbs. It can be found that many adjectives are evolved from nouns and verbs. The historical relationship of N, V and A in Chinese can be illustrated as follows:

$$\left.\begin{array}{l} N \\ V \end{array}\right\} > A$$

The original adjectives in Chinese usually express basic, objective properties, which can be observed or measured. In other words, the original adjectives are all prototypical adjectives from the cross-linguistic perspective (Dixon 1982, Dixon & Aikhenvald 2004). The derived adjectives usually express subjective properties that are based on the judgment of human beings and there is no standard way to measure them (Dong & Li 2019).

# 8 Comparison between Chinese and English

The noun-adjective polysemy and verb-adjective polysemy resulting from the semantic changes discussed above are rather common in Chinese as compared to languages with rich morphologies. This is due to the fact that Chinese words generally lack morphological markings which is typical of isolating languages. In languages with rich morphological markings, different word classes have different markings, so there is less likelihood of forming this kind of cross-category polysemy.

Let's compare Chinese with English in this respect. Even in English, whose morphological markings are less rich due to historical changes, the noun-adjective polysemy and verb-adjective polysemy are not so common. Synchronically, at the morphological level, conversion, or zero derivation, which is a change in word class without overt morphological markings, does exist in English. However, according to Qian (2008), most common conversion types in English are the following: (1) Verbs converting to nouns: to have a **look.** (2) Adjectives converting to nouns: the **young**, the **elderly.** (3) Nouns converting to verbs: The doctor **eyed** Bonham with concern. (4) Adjectives converting to verbs: Old newspaper **yellows** with age. (5) Other word classes converting to verbs: Being overweight **ups** the risk of heart disease (adverb → verb). However, noun to adjective and verb to adjective conversion are not among the most common types of conversion in English. The main targets of conversion in English are nouns and verbs, while in Chinese, both nouns and verbs can rather easily convert to adjectives.

In English, there does exist some noun-adjective polysemy, but it is not as common as it is Chinese. For example:

*key*: **key** point (meaning 'critical')

*head*: **head** waiter (meaning 'chief in authority')

Functioning as adjectives, *key* and *head* can only appear in the modifier position; since they can't appear in the predicative position, they are not typical adjectives. Typical adjectives that evolved from nouns in English, such as 'orange', are few.

In English, there are many affixes to mark adjectives derived from nouns or verbs, such as the suffix *-y*. For example, *ice* is a noun, referring to an object, while the related property of this object is expressed by the adjective *icy*, which is different from the noun in form, though morphologically related. There are many other examples: bead-beady, grass-grassy, sleep-sleepy, and anger-angry to name a few. In addition to *-y*, adjectival affixes include *-al, -ic, -ical, -le, -ble, -ly, -like, -ful, -less, -ed, -ite, -ive, -ative, -fold* and others. In Chinese, there are only a few affixes for deverbal nouns and no affixes for denominal adjectives and deverbal adjectives.

# 9 Conclusion

In the history of the Chinese language, there were some nouns referring to concrete objects that changed into words expressing properties related to the objects, and similarly, there were some verbs that changed from referring to physical activities into words expressing properties related to the activities. From this we arrived at the following path of semantic change which frequently occurred throughout the history of the Chinese language and continue to exist in contemporary Chinese:

object/activity > property[6]

This kind of semantic change can be generalized as a change from denotation to description, since both nouns and verbs can denote: Nouns denote objects and verbs denote activities.

As a result, some nouns and verbs obtained adjectival meanings, while maintaining the same form. In some cases, the original nominal or verbal meaning disappeared; while in others, the nominal meaning and the verbal meaning coexisted with the adjectival meaning, resulting in noun-adjective polysemy or verb-adjective polysemy.

The change from noun to adjective involves three stages: (1) from denotative meaning to connotative meaning; (2) appearing in the modifier position of a nominal phrase; (3) appearing in the predicate position where it can be modified by a degree adverb. The change from verb to adjective involves two stages: (1) appearing in the predicate position intransitively where it can be modified by a degree adverb; (2) appearing in the modifier position of a nominal phrase.

The mechanisms behind this kind of change involve metonymy (and sometimes metaphor) and lexical subjectification. Lexical subjectification indicates the important role of speakers in semantic change.

By comparison, we find that noun-adjective polysemy and verb-adjective polysemy are more frequent in Chinese than in English. In English, when a noun or a verb changes into an adjective, usually an affix is involved. The difference between Chinese and English in this respect is due to the typological differences between the two languages: Chinese is an isolating language lacking morphological markings and English is an inflectional language having quite a few morphological markings.

---

[6] This path of semantic change is consistent with the path of metaphorical change put forward by Heine et al. (1991: 48):

Person > Object > Activity > Space > Time > Quality

In this path, both "object" and "activity" are more concrete than "quality" which largely equals to the concept of "property" that we discuss. Therefore, the object and activity all have the possibility of changing into property (quality).

# References

Armenakis, Achilles A. and Bedeian, Arthur G. 1992. The role of metaphors in organizational change: Change agent and change target perspectives. *Group & Organization Management*, 17(3): 242–248.

Dixon, Robert Malcolm Ward. 1982. *Where have All the Adjectives Gone? And Other Essays in Semantics and Syntax*. Berlin, New York, Amsterdam: Mouton Publishers.

Dixon, Robert Malcolm Ward & Aikhenvald, Alexandra Y. (eds.) 2004. *Adjective Classes – A Cross-Linguistic Typology*. Oxford: Oxford University Press.

Dong, Xiufang. 董秀芳 2016. *Zhǔguānxìng biǎodá zài hànyǔ zhōng de tūxiǎnxìng jíqí biǎoxiàn tèzhēng* [On Characteristics of Subjectivity in Chinese], *Yǔyán Kēxué* (*Linguistic Sciences*), No. 4: 561–570.

Dong Xiufang and Li Hongjin. 董秀芳、李虹瑾 2019. *Kèguān xìngzhuàng xíngróngcí yǔ zhǔguān xìngzhuàng xíngróngcí* [Objective adjectives and subjective adjectives]. *Duìwài Hànyǔ Yánjiū* (*Research on Chinese as a Second Language*), No. 19: 96–109. Beijing: Commercial Press.

Givón, Talmy. 1984. *Syntax: A Functional-Typological Introduction*. Vol.1. Amsterdam/Philadelphia: John Benjamins Publishing Co.

Heine, Bernd, Ulrike Claudi and Friederike Hünnemeyer. 1991. *Grammaticalization: A Conceptual Framework*. Chicago and London: The University of Chicago Press.

Hu, Chirui. 胡敕瑞 2005. *Dòngjiéshì de zǎoqī xíngshì jíqí pàndìng biāozhǔn* [Early forms of verb-result constructions and their diagnosis]. *Zhōngguó Yǔwén* (*Studies of the Chinese Language*), No. 3: 214 – 225.

Jespersen, Otto. 1924. *The Philosophy of Grammar*. London: George Allen & Unwin LTD.

Leech, Geoffrey Neil. 1983. *Semantics*. London: Penguin Books.

Li, Yuming. 李宇明 1996. *Fēiwèixíngróngcí de cílèi dìwèi* [Syntactic category status of non-predicate adjectives]. *Zhōngguó Yǔwén* (*Studies of the Chinese Language*), No. 1: 1–9.

Lü Shuxiang and Rao Changrong. 吕叔湘、饶长溶 1981. *Shì lùn fēiwèixíngróngcí* [On non-predicate adjectives]. *Zhōngguó Yǔwén* (*Studies of the Chinese Language*), No. 2: 81–85.

Meng, Kai. 孟凯 2016. *Cóng xíng míng jiānlèicí pèilì de gōngnéng tūxiǎn kàn Xiàndài Hànyǔ Cídiǎn dì liù bǎn de xìtǒng zhàoyìng* [The systematicness of *Dictionary of Modern Mandarin* (6th edition): From the evidence of functional salience in illustrations of words with both nominal and adjective labels], *Císhū Yánjiū* [*Lexicographical Studies*], No. 1: 24–31.

Qian, Jun. 钱军 2008. *Yīngyǔ Cí de Gòuchéng yǔ Dāpèi* [*English Words Structure and Collocation*]. Beijing: Commercial Press.

Ross, John Robert. 1972. The category squish: Endstation Hauptwort. *Chicago Linguistic Society* 8: 316–328.

Shen, Jiaxuan. 沈家煊 2015. *Hànyǔ cílèi de zhǔguānxìng*.[On subjectivity in Chinese word classes]. *Wàiyǔ Jiàoxué yǔ Yánjiū* [*Foreign Language Teaching and Research*], No. 4: 643–658.

Song, Yayun. 宋亚云 2007. *Hànyǔ xíngróngcí de yīgè zhòngyào láiyuán: Dòngcí*. [An important source of Chinese adjectives: Verbs.] *Chángjiāng Xuéshù* [*Yangtze River Academic*], No. 3: 128–144.

Song, Yayun. 宋亚云 2008. *Hànyǔ míngcí hé dòngcí xiàng xíngróngcí zhuǎnbiàn de lìshǐ kǎochá*. [Changes from nouns and verbs to adjectives in the history of the Chinese language]. Postdoc Dissertation of Chinese Academy of Social Sciences.

Song, Yayun. 宋亚云 2012. *Xiàndài hànyǔ shuāngyīnjié míng dòng zhuǎn xíng yánjiū* [On the shift from disyllabic nouns and verbs to adjectives in Modern Mandarin]. *Yǔfǎ Yánjiū hé Tànsuǒ*(*Grammatical Study and Exploration*), Vol. 16: 155–173. Beijing: Commercial Press.

Tan, Jingchun. 谭景春 1998. *Míng xíng cílèi zhuǎnbiàn de yǔyì jīchǔ jí xiāngguān wèntí* [The semantic base and related issues of noun-to-adjective conversion]. *Zhōngguó Yǔwén* (*Studies of the Chinese Language*), No. 5: 368–377.

Traugott, Elizabeth Closs. 1989. On the rise of epistemic meanings in English: An example of subjectification in semantic change. *Language* 65: 31–55.

Traugott, Elizabeth Closs and Richard Dasher. 2002. *Regularity in Semantic Change*. Cambridge: Cambridge University Press.

Visconti, Jacqueline. 2013. Facets of subjectification. *Language Sciences*, Vol. 36: 7–17.

Xing, Janet. 2013. Semantic reanalysis in grammaticalization in Chinese. In Zhuo Jing-Schmidt (ed.) *Increased Empiricism: Recent Advances in Chinese Linguistics*: 223–246. Amsterdam /Philadelphia: John Benjamins.

Xing, Janet Zhiqun. 2015. A comparative study of semantic change in grammaticalization and lexicalization in Chinese and Germanic languages. *Studies in Langue*, 39 (3): 593–633.

Xu, Dan. 徐丹 2005. *Tán 'Pò': Hànyǔ mǒuxiē dòngcí de lèixíng zhuǎnbiàn* [Typological changes of some verbs in Chinese: The case of po (to break>broken)]. *Zhōngguó Yǔwén* (*Studies of the Chinese Language*), No. 4: 333–340.

Zhang, Bojiang. 张伯江 1994. *Cílèi huóyòng de gōngnéng jiěshì* [Explaining conversion from functional perspectives]. *Zhōngguó Yǔwén* (*Studies of the Chinese Language*), No. 5: 339–346.

Zhou, Ren. 周韧 2009. *Cóng lǐxìng yìyì hé nèihán yìyì de fēnjiè kàn tóngyǔshì de biǎoyì tèdiǎn* [The distinction between conceptual meaning and connotative meaning in Mandarin tautological sentences]. *Yǔyán Jiàoxué yǔ Yánjiū* (*Language Teaching and Linguistic Studies*), No. 6: 9–16.

Alain Peyraube and Thekla Wiebusch*
# New insights on the historical evolution of differential object marking (DOM) in Chinese**

## 1 Introduction

Differential object marking (DOM, Chinese: *qūbiéxìng bīnyǔ biāojì* 區別性賓語標記), also called "disposal form" (*chǔzhìshì* 處置式) or "BA sentences" (*bǎzìjù* 把字句), is probably the most studied Chinese construction so far, be it in synchrony or in diachrony. However, the origin of this form is still debated.

What is referred to as DOM in Chinese is the overt marking of direct objects (DO). This overt marking only occurs in the non-canonical preverbal position of the direct object. It is restricted in usage: Whereas both animate and inanimate objects can enter the BA construction, and full nouns, proper names and pronouns can all take the DO-marker, the presence of a marker is usually ascribed to the definiteness – or at least specificity – of the direct object referent. Thus, the more definite an object is, the more likely it is to be used in a BA construction.[1] This reflects the cross-linguistically predominant trend for DOM (see Aissen 2003, Bossong 1982, 1985, Iemmolo & Arcodia 2014).

The term "disposal form", introduced by Wang Li, is used in Chinese linguistics because the marked DO in this construction is supposed to code a semantic patient undergoing an explicit change of state (Wang Li 1947, 1958, Chappell 2013).

(1)  NP$_1$-Agent + BA + NP$_2$-Patient + VP

---

**1** Using a bare noun in a Mandarin BA construction forces the definite reading. *Wǒ bǎ shū gěi nǐ* 我把書給你; I – BA – book(s) – give – you "I give you *the* book(s)" not: "I give you books/a book".

*The order of the co-authors is alphabetical. Authorship is shared equally.
**The first version of this paper was presented by Alain Peyraube at the *International Symposium on Typological Regularity of Semantic Change in Grammaticalization and Lexicalization*, held on April 22-23, 2017, at Western Washington University (Bellingham, WA, USA). We are very grateful to the participants of the symposium for their comments and suggestions, especially Walter Bisang, Dong Xiufang, Ekkehard König, Barbara Meisterernst, Ken Takashima, and Janet Xing. Our profound gratitude goes to the reviewers of this contribution, as well as the editorial assistants.

https://doi.org/10.1515/9783110641288-005

where BA is a disposal marker (usually *bǎ* 把 in Standard Mandarin). *Bǎ* 把, *jiǎng* 將, *qǔ* 取, *zhuō* 捉 or *chí* 持 (see 2.1) can all be observed in this function in Medieval Chinese (3rd–10th c. CE).[2]

The term "differential object marking" that has been frequently used for this construction recently, was first defined by Bossong (1982: 24) as follows:

> "... eine aufgrund einzel- und/oder aussereinzelsprachlicher Gründe als Einheit aufzufassende Kategorie zerfällt morphologisch in zwei Unterklassen, von denen die eine positiv, die andere negativ markiert ist. Eine solche Differenzierung erfolgt ... in Übereinstimmung mit bestimmten semantischen Parametern .... [... a category to be understood as a unit for mono-linguistic or extra-monolinguistic reasons is morphologically divided into two subcategories, one of which is positively, the other one negatively marked. Such a differentiation occurs ... according to certain semantic parameters ...]"

Section 4 will discuss just how far – and since when – the Chinese disposal construction can be considered a genuine example of differential object marking, based on the data and analyses on the development of the BA construction surveyed in Sections 2 and 3.

## 1.1 Restrictions on the use of the BA construction

There exist three main constraints on the BA construction in Contemporary Chinese:

First, the verb "disposes of" the object (hence "disposal construction"). The referent of the object normally must be affected by the action. Thus, BA constructions are typically used with verbs of placing, giving, destroying, finishing etc., but not with certain psychological or perception verbs, such as *xǐhuān* 'like' or *kànjiàn* 'see'.

(2) a. 我 看見 你 了。 *b. 我 把 你 看見 了。
    Wǒ kànjiàn nǐ le     Wǒ bǎ nǐ kànjiàn le
    I see you ASP     I BA you see ASP
    'I saw you'

---

[2] The article uses the periodization of Peyraube (2017b: 46–49), which is based on syntactic criteria. The period of Medieval Chinese (3rd c. CE to 13th c. CE) is divided into Early Medieval Chinese (3rd–6th c. CE) comprising the Wei-Jin-Nanbeichao period (220–581), Late Medieval Chinese I (ca. 7th–10th c. CE) comprising the Tang dynasty (618–907) and the Five-dynasties (Wudai) period (907–960 CE), and Late Medieval Chinese II (ca. 11th c. CE – mid 13th c. CE), comprising the Song (960–1279), and Jin (1115–1234) dynasties. The major developments of the disposal construction take place in EMC and LMC-I. The Sui dynasty (581–618) marks the transition between the two parts.

This restriction could be the only one that was already active in the early phase of the BA construction. See nevertheless Li (2006: section 5.1.3.3 Affectedness) for some apparent counter-examples).

Second, the NP₂ introduced by BA must be definite, or at least typically referential and clearly affected in the event depicted by the verb.[3]

Third, the final VP cannot consist of an isolated monosyllabic verb. If the verb in this VP is monosyllabic, it must be followed by an aspectual marker or by a complement (resultative, directional, locative, etc.) or be preceded by an adverbial phrase.

Even in Contemporary Mandarin, the first two restrictions are not without exception (see Peyraube 1985, Li and Thompson 1981). For Medieval Chinese, the extent to which they are valid is not clear. The third constraint – being the most important one in Contemporary Chinese – has only existed since Pre-Modern Chinese (ca. 14th–15th century). It is also absent in certain Sinitic languages, e.g. in Southern Min (Li & Cao 2013).[4] Thus, the exact constraints of DOM in Medieval Chinese still need to be determined.

## 1.2 Disposal markers in the history of Chinese and their sources

Five or six prepositions – depending on which analyses are consulted – have been ascribed the function of direct object markers or disposal markers at different stages of the (Standard) Chinese language, most of the time overlapping: *yǐ* 以, *yòng* 用, *qǔ* 取, *jiāng* 將, *chí* 持, *zhuō* 捉, and *bǎ* 把. The status of *yǐ* as a disposal marker remains controversial (see below), and *yòng* has only been proposed by Wei Peichuan (1996).

Most of the markers were grammaticalized from full verbs to prepositions, most often in the environment of serial verb constructions, where they acted as V₁ in a 'V₁ ... V₂' sequence (see below). In Archaic Chinese (11thc. BCE – 3rd c. BCE), BA words[5] started out as full verbs, meaning 'to take' (for *qǔ*), and 'to conduct, to lead' (for *jiāng*), 'to grasp, to hold' (for *bǎ*), 'to grasp, to hold' (for *chí*), and 'to clutch, hold, seize' (for *zhuō*). Some of them were used at relatively low frequency.

---

[3] For exceptions see Peyraube (1985: 195).
[4] Li and Chappell (2013: 26) list the characteristics and restrictions of BA sentences in contemporary Sinitic languages.
[5] In this chapter, we will use BA for *qǔ*, *jiāng*, *chí*, *zhuō* and *bǎ* in their function as disposal marker.

*Yǐ* (from 'to lead') and *yòng* 'to use' (from 'to kill and use as sacrifice') differed from BA words as they had already developed into frequently used function words (instrumental 'with' for both *yǐ* and *yòng*) in Archaic Chinese.⁶ While *yòng* retains its verbal meaning 'to use' today, verbal *yǐ* had practically fallen out of use by the Late Archaic Chinese period. For a detailed analysis of the meanings of these verbs, all belonging to the set of TAKE verbs, see Wei Pei-chuan (1996).

The inventory of disposal markers in contemporary Sinitic languages is much richer than that in the historical texts. Apart from TAKE verbs, attested as sources of disposal markers in a large number of contemporary Sinitic languages, especially the Northern Mandarin dialects, GIVE verbs, HELP verbs and COMITATIVE verbs are attested in this function (see Chappell 2007, 2013: 789–791, and Li and Chappell 2013). *Bǎ* 'to take, to grasp' as well as most other markers used in the official language throughout the history of this construction belong to a subtype nowadays found in Chappell's Zone 1 (TAKE verbs I, *nǎ* 'take', *bǎ* 'hold'), found in the Jin languages, Northern dialects, and Northwestern Mandarin, as well as Zone 4 (TAKE verbs II, among them *jiāng*,⁷ *bǎ*, *tí* 提, *zhuō*, and many other synonyms), found in several Cantonese and Hakka dialects.⁸

GIVE markers can be found in many languages of Central and Southwestern China, including Shuang and Gan dialects as well as many Jianghuai Central Plains dialects and Southwestern Mandarin. HELP markers are used in some Southern Wu-dialects, as well as Huizhou (GIVE verbs and HELP verbs form Chappell's Zone 2). COMITATIVE markers can mainly be found in her Zone 3, i.e. many Southern Min dialects, Taiwan Meixian Hakka and Shaoxing and Ningbo-Wu dialects, and Waxiang dialects (Chappell 2013: 802).

As GIVE, HELP and COMITATIVE sources do not play any role in the historical sources available, the question about the origin of these markers in a large group of Sinitic languages is still open. Some of the Medieval disposal markers are still in use in contemporary Sinitic languages (*zhuō*, *jiāng*), while others seem to have completely disappeared.

---

**6** In transmitted Archaic text, the difference in frequency of use between these words is extreme: in all pre-Qin texts of the Scripta Sinica (*Shànggǔ*), *bǎ* occurs only 8 times, *zhuō* 5 times, *chí* 220 times, *qǔ* 1556 times, *jiāng* 2910 times, *yòng* 2994 times, and *yǐ* 22270 times (all meanings). In the earlier (*Shàng shū* and *Máo shī*), texts of this corpus, *yǐ* appears 539 times, *yòng* 190 times, *jiāng* 108 times, *chí* 1 time, *zhuō* 0 time, *bǎ* 0 time, and *qǔ* 26 times.
**7** We provide the Mandarin *pinyin*-pronunciation of the Chinese characters here. The dialect pronunciation is, of course, different.
**8** It is important to note that in some Sinitic languages, *bǎ* has a meaning of 'GIVE' (Chappell 2013: 802).

## 2 The origin of the disposal construction

Since the very first studies of the BA construction, several competing hypotheses about its origin have been suggested, calling upon the three mechanisms of syntactic change: analogy, reanalysis (including grammaticalization) and contact induced change (i.e. external borrowing).

### 2.1 The classical hypothesis

The classical hypothesis on the origin of BA sentences is as follows:

BA verbs have been used as $V_1$ in serial verb constructions (SVC) "$V_1 + O + V_2$" since the Han dynasty (206 BCE – 220 CE). They were grammaticalized and became object markers between the end of the 6th c. CE and the 9th c. CE. (See Zhu 1957, Wang 1958, Li and Thompson 1974, Peyraube 1985, 1989).

Indeed, two subtypes of the serial verb construction were involved in this process, leading to two different forms of the BA construction: the *instrumental form* and the *accusative form* (Peyraube 1985):
(a) $V_1 + O_1 + V_2 + O_2$ (instrumental form)
    with $O_1$ being the object of $V_1$ and $O_2$ being the object of $V_2$.
(b) $V_1 + O + V_2$ (accusative form)
    with O being the object of both $V_1$ and $V_2$.

Consequently, there were two diachronic changes involved in the process:
(a) $V_1$-BA + $O_1$ + $V_2$ + $O_2$ > Instr.Prep: BA + $O_1$+ V (+$O_2$) (instrumental form)
(b) $V_1$-BA + O + $V_2$ > OM: BA + O + V (accusative form)

#### 2.1.1 Instrumental form

The lexical sources of the disposal markers (Section 1.2) show a strong relationship between disposal constructions and instrumental constructions in the history of Chinese.

(3) ...于是　　　　　即　　　　　　將　　　雌劍　　　　　往　　見
    *Yúshì*　　　　　*jí*　　　　　　*jiāng*　*cí_jiàn*　　　*wǎng*　*jiàn*
    then/therefore　immediately　take　female_sword　go　see/visit

楚　　王。
*Chǔ　wáng*
Chu　prince
'... [he] then immediately **took** the female sword and went to see the Prince of Chu.'
(*Sōushén jì, juǎn* 11: 77, ca. 350 CE)

(4) 輕　將　玉　杖　敲　花片。
*Qīng　jiāng　yù　zhàng　qiāo　huā_piàn*
Light　BA[9]　jade　stick　knock　flower_petal
'[She] delicately hits the flower petals **with** a jade stick.'
(*Gōngzǐ xíng*, poem by Zhāng Hù [?-853])

In (3), the serial verb reading appears more plausible (this is how Chinese linguists working on this period interpret the text), but a prepositional reading would not be excluded. In (4), however, the instrumental reading is preferred, and the serial verb reading is awkward: the adverb *qīng* 'delicately' seems only meaningful characterizing the 'knocking' activity, not the grasping activity, i.e. it has scope over the entire verb phrase. For a serial verb reading, the adverb would have to precede *qiāo* 'to knock' immediately.

### 2.1.2 Accusative form

In this classical account, examples of the accusative form appear only from the 8th century on.

(5) 醉　把　茱萸　仔細　看。
*Zuì　bǎ　zhūyú　zǐxì　kàn*
Drunk　**take**　dogwood　fine/careful　look
'Drunk, (he) **took** the dogwood and carefully looked at it.'
(*Jiǔyuè lántiān Cuīshì zhuāng, shi*-poem by Dù Fǔ, mid-8th c. CE)

(6) 啊郎　把　數　都　計算。
*Ā_láng　bǎ　shù　dōu　jì_suàn*
Alang　BA　figure/count　all　calculate
'Alang ("the young guy") did all the calculations.'
(*Dūnhuáng biànwén jí, juǎn* 5/7 [*Dǒng Yǒng biànwén*]: 927, ca. 850–1025)

---

[9] We use BA to gloss BA verbs in cases where we think that they have already grammaticalized to disposal prepositions or markers.

(7) 問　有　將　无　對　　問　無　將　有　對。
　　Wèn yǒu jiāng wú duì　wèn wú jiāng yǒu duì.
　　Ask exist BA not_exist to.answer ask not.exist BA exist to.answer
　　'[If he] asks [if] there is, answer: there is not; [if he] asks [if] there is not, answer: there is.'
　　(*Liù zǔ tán jīng* 10, between 780 and 800)

It is important to note that, at first glance, even the accusative examples (5), (6), and (7) may have two readings in LMC-I: *bǎ* and *jiāng* could be interpreted as verbs in a coordinate or subordinate serial verb construction or as direct object markers. However, a serial-verb interpretation seems more plausible with concrete examples such as (5) and less so with abstract verbs such as *jìsuàn* 'to calculate' and *duì* 'to answer'. Neither is completely excluded.[10] Only sometimes, as in (6), does the use of a quantifier such as *dōu* 'all' or of an adverb favor the reading of BA as a DO marker. It is exactly this ambiguous situation that provides the syntactic environment of the transition phase in the grammaticalization process.

### 2.1.3 Reconstruction of O₂ for the accusative form

According to Peyraube (1989), the second change (b) is not essentially different from the first one (a). Although there is no $O_2$ in (b), a resumptive pronoun (co-referential with $O_1$) can be reconstructed. Several examples involving the resumptive pronoun *zhī* 之 after the $V_2$ can be found during the period preceding that in which single-object examples can be found, as in:

(8) 汝　將　此　人　安　徐　殺　之，
　　Rǔ jiāng cǐ rén ān xú shā zhī,
　　You take DEM man quietly slowly kill PRON
　　勿　損　皮　肉。
　　Wù sǔn pí ròu
　　NEG damage skin flesh
　　'Take this man (and) kill him carefully without damaging his skin and flesh.'
　　([*Fóshuō*] *Cháng Āhán jīng* 7: 69b, 4th–5th c. CE)

---

10 It is quite common cross-linguistically for TAKE-verbs to acquire an abstract meaning extended to cognitive "handling", e.g. English *to take sth. into account*, German *malnehmen* 'to multiply', and *begreifen* 'to comprehend'. Thus, the mere use of BA with abstract objects is not sufficient to prove beyond doubt the interpretation as an object marker.

(9) 船者　　乃　　將　　此　　蟾　　以　　油　　熬　　之。
　　 Chuánzhě nǎi　jiāng　cǐ　chán　yǐ　yóu　áo　zhī
　　 Boatman  then  take   DEM  toad  with  oil   boil  PRON
　　 'The boatman then took that toad and fried it in oil.'
　　 (Zhìguài, 6th–7th c. CE)

The coreferential in BA+Oi+V+PRONi structure has disappeared in contemporary Mandarin, but is still used in a variety of Sinitic languages, e.g. in Meixian Hakka, Shanghai Wu dialect, and Gong'anhua (Southwestern Mandarin), see Chappell (2013: 796).

The grammaticalization of the instrumental and disposal BA are analyzed as equivalent parallel processes in this classical approach, especially for their beginning steps with semantic bleaching and subordination of $V_1$-BA in serial verb constructions. It is important to note that disposal BA and instrumental BA are regarded as distinct functions in different environments ($O_1 \neq O_2$ vs. $O_1 = O_2$).

### 2.1.4 When did the grammaticalization process take place?

Under the aforementioned hypothesis, the process starts with synchronic derivation followed by diachronic change (Peyraube 1989) as shown in Figure 1. However, a question remains: to which period can the grammaticalization process of the diachronic change be dated?

(1) Synchronic derivation:

$$NP_0 + V_1 : BA + NP_1 + V_2 + NP_2 \xrightarrow{NP_2 = NP_1} NP_0 + V_1 : BA + NP_1 + V_2$$

(2) Diachronic change:

$$NP_0 + OM : BA + NP_1 + V$$

**Figure 1:** Process of grammaticalization.

According to the data from translations of Buddhist sutras brought forward by Cao and Yu (2000a, b), Cao and Long (2005) and from other texts, this was a complex process covering several centuries. Part of the complexity is owed to the fact that different BA verbs entered this pathway of grammaticalization at different times: For the verb *jiāng*, which predates *bǎ* in the DOM-function, the process had certainly already begun by the end of the 6th century, as shown by examples found under the Sui dynasty (581–618) in the *Fó běn xíng jí jīng*.

(10) 時　　諸　　比丘　　將　　此　　白　　佛。
　　　Shí　 zhū　 bǐqiū　 jiāng　cǐ　　bái　 Fó
　　　Time　PL　 monks　BA　 DEM　tell/say Buddha
　　　'At this time, the monks narrated this to Buddha.'
　　　(*Fó běn xíng jí jīng* 15, ca. 590 CE)

The TAKE-verb *bǎ* – which is the single disposal marker in Contemporary (spoken) Mandarin – can be found in this function only from the (late) 8th century on (see examples [6] in section 2.1.2 and [13] below).

## 2.2 Another hypothesis: *bǎ* 把 as object marker modeled on *yǐ* 以

In contrast to this classical hypothesis, Bennett (1981), followed by Chen Chusheng (1983), argued that an analogical extension with the *yǐ* 以[11] constructions of Archaic Chinese played a key role in the birth of BA. According to them, *yǐ* was used both in disposal and instrumental constructions in Late Archaic Chinese (5th–2nd c. BCE) and instrumental and disposal *yǐ* phrases could occur in both preverbal and postverbal positions.[12]

(11) 尧　　以　　天下　　　　与　　舜。
　　　Yáo　 yǐ　 tiānxià　　　 yǔ　　Shùn
　　　Yao　 YI　empire/world　give　Shun
　　　'Yao gave the empire to Shun.'
　　　(*Mèngzi* 孟子, Wànzhāng A, 4th c. BCE)

This thesis has also been taken up by Ye Youwen (1988) and, more particularly, by Mei Tsu-lin (1990). Mei drew a distinction between *chǔzhìgěi* 處置給 'giving disposals' (GD), *chǔzhìdào* 處置到 'placing disposals' (PD) and *chǔzhìzuò* 處置作 'making disposals' (MD). He concluded that most of the BA sentences used during the Tang dynasty were inheritors of the *yǐ* 以 forms of Archaic and Han dynasty Chinese.[13]

---

[11] In Late Archaic Chinese, *yǐ* was a high-frequency preposition meaning 'with', 'by means of', 'because of' along with several other functions.
[12] Chen expanded this hypothesis by claiming that *yǐ* disposals already existed in the bronze inscriptions of ca. 1.000 BCE. For him, they represent traces of an old OV order in Chinese, where *yǐ* was only inserted in front of the preverbal direct object.
[13] For a differentiated account of the positions of Bennett (1981), Chen (1983), Mei (1990), Feng (2000), Wu (2003), and Liu (2002) on the broad disposal form and the relationship between *yǐ*, *jiāng* and *bǎ*, see Jiang (2008).

GIVING disposals:
The term "giving disposal" refers to disposal constructions, where the verb denotes a giving action in which the subject denotes the AGENT, the direct object a THEME that is transferred to a RECEIVER/GOAL – ([SUBJECT: AGENT/DONOR] – BA – DO:THEME – GIVE – IO:RECEIVER/GOAL). In Pre-Medieval and Medieval Chinese, verbs of giving (in a broader sense) in GDs include verbs of saying (say = give information). Scholars such as Liu Ziyu (2002) have described in detail giving disposal forms with *yǐ* that were already in use in Late Archaic Chinese, or before.

(12) 陳子 以 時子 之 言 告 孟子。
*Chénzǐ yǐ Shízǐ zhī yán gào Mèngzǐ*
Chénzǐ YI Shízǐ SUBORD.PART word tell Mèngzǐ
'Chenzi told Shizi's words to Mengzi.'
(*Mèngzǐ*, Gōngsūn Niǔ B; 4th c. BCE)

(13) 應 把 清 風 遺 子孫。
*Yīng bǎ qīng fēng yí zǐsūn*
ought.to BA fresh wind bequeath.on child-grandchild
'[One] should bequeath [such a] fresh breeze to one's posterity.'
(From a poem by Fāng Gān 方干 [809–888])

According to the hypothesis of Bennett and Chen, *yǐ* had already begun to develop the function of a disposal marker in Late Archaic Chinese in giving disposals, and *jiāng* replaced *yǐ* in this function during the Sui dynasty (581–618).

PLACING disposals:
The term "placing disposal" refers to disposal constructions in which the action denoted by the main verb consists of displacing the object to a new place. As with giving disposals these verbs require three arguments, in this case a subject (AGENT), a direct object (PATIENT or THEME), and a locative which is a GOAL: (X) BA DO (THEME) V LOC (GOAL).

(14) 復 以 弟子 一人 投 河 中。
*Fú yǐ dìzǐ yī-rén tóu hé zhōng*
again YI disciple one-CL throw river middle
'…and (this time he) threw one disciple into the river again.'
(*Shǐjì, Gǔjī lièzhuàn*, Xīmén Bào yìshì: p. 3212, ca. 100 BCE)

(15) 把    舜子      頭髮    悬      在      中庭        樹      地。
    Bǎ   Shùnzǐ   tóufā   xuán   zài    zhōng-tíng  shù    di
    BA   Shunzi   hair    hang   PREP   courtyard   tree   PART
    '[He] hung Shunzi's hair on the tree in the central courtyard.'
    (*Dūnhuáng biànwén jí* 敦煌變文集: *juǎn* 6/1: 953, 9th–10th c. CE)

The use of *yǐ* in placing disposal constructions can be dated to the Early Han period (1st c. BCE). It was replaced by *jiāng* under the Sui dynasty (581–618). There are many examples in the *Fó běn xíng jí jīng* 佛本行集經 (dated 590 CE), a Sutra translated into Chinese by Jñānagupta (523–600) from Gāndhāra living in Chang'an. *Jiāng* was subsequently replaced by *bǎ* starting during the later Tang (618–907) dynasty.

MAKING disposals:
The term "making disposal" refers to a type of disposal construction in which the V₂ refers to an action transforming the object into something else, using $O_1$ as $O_2$, or assuming $O_1$ to be $O_2$ (Feng 2000: 558). The verb usually does not denote acts of making as a creational or productive process. According to Ōta Tatsuo (1958, in Jiang 2008), making disposals with *yǐ* already existed in Archaic Chinese (14th–3rd c. BCE).

(16) 以    三     公子       為            質。
    Yǐ   sān   gōngzǐ    wéi          zhì
    YI   three prince    make.to.be   pawn
    'Make the third son to be the hostage.'
    (*Zuǒ zhuàn*, Zhāogōng 20, 5th c. BCE)

(17) 將     此     茶芽       為            信。
    Jiāng  cǐ    chá-yá    wéi          xìn
    BA     DEM   tea-bud   make.to.be   evidence/token
    'Make a token of this tea bud.'
    (*Lìdài fǎbǎo jì*, Yǎng tián běn 171, 8th c. CE)

As in the case of GD and PD forms, *jiāng* replaced *yǐ* in MD forms under the Sui dynasty. As mentioned earlier, *jiāng* is found in the *Fó běn xíng jí jīng*.

Thus, according to this account, giving disposals, placing disposals and making disposals (all "broad disposals", see 2.3 below) using BA as object marker during the Tang dynasty were all inheritors of these *yǐ* forms. They had essentially already become *jiāng* forms during the Sui, as examples from *Fó běn xíng jí jīng* cited by Ye Youwen (1988) and Mei Tsu-lin (1990) demonstrate.

## 2.3 Broad versus narrow disposal forms and patient subject sentences

BA sentences have been divided into three broad categories (see Wu Fuxiang 2003: 2–3, for a detailed discussion see Jiang Shaoyu 2008), the narrow disposal form (*xiáyì chǔzhìshì* 狹義處置式), the broad disposal form (*guǎngyì chǔzhìshì* 廣義處置式), and the causative disposal form (*zhìshǐyì chǔzhìshì* 致使義處置式).[14]

The narrow disposal form includes BA sentences with a single final verb (OM + NP + V), as well as sentences where the verb is preceded or followed by a constituent which is neither a receiver, goal, location nor the result of "making": for example, a directional complement or resultative complement.[15] The broad disposal forms include giving disposals, placing disposals, and making disposals. In the causative disposal forms, the subject is the CAUSER, and the direct object is not the PATIENT of the action, as in the narrow disposal form, but a CAUSEE. These forms appear rather late, during the Tang (618–907) and Five dynasties (907–960). They have not been taken into account for the purpose of this chapter.

*Patient subject sentences*
Mei Tsu-lin (1990) emphasizes another point, which seems more important to him. During the 5th and 6th centuries, if one removed *jiāng* from GIVE disposals and PLACE disposals, one would obtain patient subject sentences (*shòushì zhǔyǔ jù* 受事主語句) as Zhu Dexi (1982: 187–189) already noticed for *bǎ* sentences in Contemporary Chinese. In other words, it was enough simply to add *jiāng* to patient-subject sentences to obtain BA sentences. It is this phenomenon, Mei Tsu-lin says, that one should study as one of the main origins of BA disposal forms.

As not all the BA sentences of the 5th and 6th century can be derived from patient-subject sentences by adding BA, particularly those having SVO correlates, it has to be recognized that BA forms may have different origins. Mei (1990: 205) essentially takes the standpoint that there are three of them:
1. Some BA forms (the broad disposal) appeared by analogy with GD, PD, and MD in *yǐ* constructions, which already existed in Archaic and Pre-Medieval Chinese

---

[14] Wu's "broad disposal form" corresponds to Mei's (1990: 193) form A (double object or ditransitive construction), Wu's "narrow disposal form" corresponds to Mei's forms B and C, i.e. single object (transitive) constructions where B contains a verb with modifiers (before and/or after) and C a bare verb.
[15] We consider that it is useful to retain the notion of "narrow disposal forms", but only the verb final cases and not those with constituents following the verb.

2. Others, probably the great majority, came from patient-subject sentences to which BA could be added.
3. Lastly, a new way of forming disposal constructions during the Tang dynasty, arose from the omission of $O_2$ in SVC ($V_1 + O_1 + V_2 + O_2$) with coreferential/identical objects ($O_1=O_2$). This process led to the form "BA + O + V", with a single final verb, a form that flourished during the Song and Yuan dynasties, and disappeared afterwards.

Thus, the classical analysis of the grammaticalization of BA verbs was challenged. These new analyses of Mei Tsu-lin (1990), intriguing as they are, generate several problems, worthy of further discussion. If today there is less doubt that *yǐ* forms played a role in the establishment of BA forms, several questions remain unanswered.

## 2.4 The *qǔ* 取 sentences

Cao and Yu (2000a, b), in an intriguing and very original and detailed analysis, brought new insights to the development of the disposal construction. They found that the earliest BA sentences were not formed with *bǎ* or *jiāng* (or *chí* or *zhuō*), but with *qǔ* 取 (originally a verb meaning first 'to get' and later 'to take'). Their results pushed the origin of narrow disposals back to the 4th c. CE and shed new light on the role of external factors in the development of preposed object constructions.[16]

For their study, Cao and Yu (2000a, b) made a quantitative analysis of a corpus consisting of 15 Buddhist sutras translated into Chinese during the Late Han (25–220 CE) and the Six Dynasties (220–589 CE), as well as four native Chinese texts from the 3rd to 6th century. They found four subtypes of narrow disposal forms using *qǔ*:

A. *Qǔ* + Object + V (26 occurrences)

(18) 還　　取　門　閉，　　前　　　　白　佛　　言 …
　　 Huán　qǔ　mén　bì,　　qián　　　bái　Fó　　yán
　　 Return　BA　door　to.close　go.forward　tell　Buddha　word/say
　　 '[Upon] returning [he] closed the door, went forward and spoke to the Buddha, saying …'
　　 (*Zēngyī Ahán jīng* 44; 561c a 7 [0786b22], late 4th c. CE)

---

[16] For discussions of this phenomenon and new evaluations of the development of the disposal form in Medieval Chinese, see Peyraube (1994), Feng Chuntian (2000), Cao Guangshun & Yu Hsiao-jung (2000a, b), Liu Ziyu (2002), Wu Fuxiang (2003, 2009), Cao Guangshun and Long Guofu (2005), Jiang Shaoyu (2005, 2008), etc.

(19) 當   取   母    殺。
    Dāng qǔ  mǔ   shā
    should BA mother kill (direct speech addressing the mother)
    '[I] must kill you (my mother).'
    (*Chū yào jīng*, j. 4, transl. Former Qin, 351–94)

B. *Qǔ* + Object (+ Adverbial) + V (+ Complement) (3 occurrences)

(20) 諸    人民    取   吾    枉         殺。
    Zhū  rénmín  qǔ   wu   wǎng      shā
    All  people  BA   me   to.wrong.sb. kill
    'All people unjustly sentenced me to death.'
    (*Zēngyī Ahán jīng* 31 [0722c07], late 4th c. CE)

(21) 取   我   身體     碎       如    芥       子, ....。
    Qǔ   wǒ   shēntǐ   suì     rú    jiè      zǐ
    BA   my   body     shatter like  mustard  seeds
    '[Even if you, the king] shatter my body [into small pieces] like mustard seeds, ...'
    (*Chū yào jīng* 23, late 4th c. CE)

C. *Qǔ* + Object + V + *zhi* (25 occurrences)

(22) 是    時    流離    王     即時         拔      劍,
    Shì  shí   Liúlí   wáng   jíshí        bō      jiàn
    DEM  time  Liúlí   king   immediately  draw    sword
    取   守門人          殺    之。
    qǔ   shǒu.mén.rén   shā   zhī.
    BA   guard.door.man kill  PRON
    'At that time, the King Liuli immediately drew his sword and killed the doorman.'
    (*Zēngyī Āhán jīng* 26, late 4th c. CE)

If one considers, as Cao and Yu (2000a, b) did, that *qǔ* 取 has already been grammaticalized into an object marker, then we have the first BA sentences, using *qǔ*, not at the end of the 6th century as previously believed, but rather around the 4th century.

D. *Qǔ* + V + *zhī* (63 occurrences)

(23) 設    當     見     者,    先     截    手     足,    却          取   殺    之。
    Shè  dāng   jiàn   zhě,   xiān   jié   shǒu   zú,    què         qǔ   shā   zhī.
    If   when   see    PART   first  cut   hand   foot   certainly   BA   kill  PRON
    'If [we] see him, [we ought] first to cut his hands and feet, [and then] kill him.'
    (*Chū yào jīng* 16, transl. late 4th c. CE)

All disposal forms with *qǔ*, including the 117 narrow disposal examples, were found only in the five latest translations of Buddhist texts, stemming from the late 4th c. to ca. 600 CE. In the native Chinese texts of the corpus (which are not Buddhist translations), out of ca. 1,000 occurrences of *qǔ* – mainly used as a full verb – there are only 11 instances of its use in a narrow disposal construction.

For Cao and Yu (2000a, b), the constructions A and D both represent the first BA sentences. As they first appeared in Buddhist translations of the Six dynasties, they called upon a phenomenon of contact induced change, i.e. the influence of the source languages that were OV languages and the native languages of the non-Chinese translators: contact induced change.

## 2.5 Possible chains of grammaticalization

In the literature, we find two concurring proposals for chains of grammaticalization for BA rendering different disposal forms. One of them has been suggested by Wu Fuxiang (2003) as diagrammed in Figure 2.

Serial-Verb-Construction
    > Instrumental Forms
        > Broad Disposal Forms
        with 3 forms: GD, PD, and MD
        and the markers *yǐ, qǔ, chí, zhuō, jiāng, bǎ*
            > Narrow disposal forms
            with *qǔ, zhuō, jiāng, bǎ*
                > Causative disposal forms

**Figure 2:** Chains of grammaticalization (Wu 2003).

Cao and Long (2005) provided a quantitative analysis with all occurrences of the different markers in different periods. They concluded that a unique pathway of grammaticalization for all disposal constructions as suggested by Wu (2003) is unlikely. Instead, they argued that the disposal constructions in Early Medieval Chinese can be divided into two groups – the *yǐ* construction and the *qǔ* construction (including *chí, zhuō, jiāng,* and *bǎ*) – and that there were two different pathways of grammaticalization in the second group for the "broad disposal forms" and the "narrow disposal forms" (Cao and Long 2005: 330).

Group I (with *yǐ*)

    Serial verb construction ($V_1 + O_1 + V_2 + O_2$)
        > Instrumental
            > Broad disposal
                > Narrow disposal

Group II (with *qǔ*)
(i) Serial verb construction ($V_1 + O_1 + V_2 + O_2$) > Broad disposal when $O_1$ and $O_2$ are different;
(ii) Serial verb construction ($V_1 + O_1 + V_2 + O_2$) > Narrow disposal when $O_1 = O_2$

# 3 Discussion of the hypotheses on the origin of the disposal form

Section 2 shows that there exist competing approaches to the origin and early development of the disposal form in Chinese. The following discussion aims at showing where they can be reconciled, and which of the contradictory positions accounts better for the data.

## 3.1 The role of patient-subject-sentences

One proposal (Mei 1990) about the origin of the disposal form claims that the great majority of the Medieval disposal sentences come from patient-subject sentences to which *jiāng* and *bǎ* could be added.

Whereas Mei (1990) makes an interesting and important synchronic observation about Early Medieval Chinese syntax and the relationship between passive constructions and disposal constructions, we do not believe that this relationship can serve as a valid diachronic explanation for the origin of the BA construction for two reasons:

First of all, Mei (1990) does not explain where these BA (*bǎ*, *jiāng*, etc.) come from. As we know, *jiāng*, *chí*, *zhuō*, *qǔ*, and *bǎ* were all used as full verbs in Archaic and Pre-Medieval Chinese. As disposal markers, they are no longer full verbs, but function words, markers (or prepositions) that must have grammaticalized from full verbs in a longer process. Only after such a grammaticalization into prepositions could they have been added to patient subjects. The syntactic environment where that would have happened could not have been the patient-subject-sentences, as those did not contain BA. Thus, this hypothesis would need a separate construction, in which BA grammaticalized, in order to subsequently be used in later disposal sentences. We do not think that such a syntactic environment existed in Medieval Chinese.

Moreover, the vast majority of these disposal sentences, which supposedly come from patient-subject sentences, were actually giving disposals and placing disposals, which are also said to have appeared by analogy with the giving disposals and placing disposals using *yǐ* (Mei 1990). These sentences cannot have two different origins. And if it is true that, by removing *jiāng* from the giving disposals and placing disposals of the 5th and 6th centuries, we obtain patient subject sentences, it is equally true that neither can we remove *yǐ* from GIVE disposals nor from PLACE disposal forms to obtain patient-subject sentences.

## 3.2 Lexical replacement of *yǐ*

Could the disappearance of *yǐ* and the increasing use of BA (*jiāng, qǔ, bǎ, chí,* or *zhuō*) during the Suí or even before, in the giving disposals, placing disposals, and making disposals, be the result of a simple lexical replacement as proposed by Chen (1983), Ye (1988), and Mei (1990)?

This does not seem to be the case. It is hard to accept that a preposition (*yǐ*) could be replaced by a verb (*jiāng*). Another and probably better solution would be to say that the disposal markers have been grammaticalized from verbs in serial verb constructions by analogy with some already existing *yǐ* disposals. The two joint processes (analogy and grammaticalization) of *jiāng, bǎ, chí, zhuō*, which first affected serial verb sentences in which the $V_2$ was followed by an indirect object or a resultative/locative complement, would also be possible in serial verb sentences with a final $V_2$. But this explanation still leaves several questions regarding this approach unresolved:

Firstly, there is no way to be sure that *yǐ* can really be considered as a disposal marker, i.e. that *yǐ* BA sentences really exist. Several major differences between *yǐ* constructions and BA constructions cause these doubts:

- *yǐ* + DO can appear both in preverbal (70% of all the cases) and post-verbal (30%) positions whereas post-verbal BA constructions with either *jiāng, bǎ, chí, zhuō* or *qǔ* have not been observed in Medieval or Modern Chinese texts;
- the DO in *yǐ* constructions can be deleted, as can both the DO and IO in double object constructions, as in the following example:

(24) 子路　　　行　　　以　告　。
　　 Zǐlù　　　xíng　　 yǐ　gào
　　 Zilu (NAME) go.away　YI　tell
　　 'Zilu went away [and] told [this] to Confucius.'
　　 (*Lúnyǔ*, Huīzǐ 18, 5th c. BCE)

- the marker *yǐ* can be postponed to DO → DO + *yǐ*, as in:

(25) 是　以　言。
　　 shì　yǐ　yán
　　 this　YI　say
　　 '[He] said this.'
　　 (*Han Fēizǐ*, Bā jīng, 3rd c. BCE)

We thus agree with Liu Ziyu's (2002: 158) conclusion: "*yǐ zì jiégòu bùshì chǔzhìshì* "以"字結構不是處置式 [*yǐ* constructions are not disposal forms]." There is consequently no need to distinguish two groups of disposal construction, i.e. the *yǐ* construction and the *qǔ* construction, as hypothesized by Cao and Long (2005).

Secondly, there is no way to be at all sure that the first BA sentences were broad disposal (*guǎngyì chǔzhìshì*) including the GD, PD, and MD. Indeed, if we accept that the *qǔ* sentences can be considered as BA sentences, it follows that the first BA sentences were the narrow disposals *xiáyì chǔzhìshì* with a single final verb (OM:*qǔ* + NP + V). Then, a few decades later, the grammaticalization of *jiāng, chí, zhuō, bǎ*, which first affected serial verb sentences with a single final verb, was extended to sentences with an indirect object or a resultative/locative complement following the $V_2$.

Thus, we agree with Cao and Long (2005) who hypothesized that there were two distinct origins for the broad disposals and the narrow disposals. We nevertheless suggest that the "narrow disposals" appeared first and that the "broad disposals" came later.

To conclude, the classical hypothesis on the origin of BA sentences can be kept: there was a grammaticalization of a verb with a general meaning 'to take' into an OM (likely a preposition) within a serial verb construction "$V_1 + O_1 + V_2 + O_2$", after the deletion of the $O_2$, identical to or coreferential with $O_1$. This grammaticalization process started no later than the 4th c. CE. The verbs $V_1$ to be grammaticalized were *qǔ, chí, jiāng, zhuō*, and *bǎ*. *Jiāng* and *bǎ* are the only ones remaining today, at least in Mandarin. The resulting structures, after the grammaticalization process, were first narrow disposal forms, and a few centuries later, were extended to create broad disposals:
- Narrow disposal:

    V (*qǔ, chí, zhuō, jiāng, bǎ*, etc.) > OM:BA

through $V_1 + O_1 + V_2 + O_2$ > OM:BA + O + V when $O_1 = O_2$ (pronoun *zhī*)
- Broad disposal:

    V (*qǔ, chí, zhuō, jiāng, bǎ*, etc.) > OM:BA

through $V_1 + O_1 + V_2 + X > $ OM:BA $+ O + V + X$, for both instrumental and accusative forms, X being an indirect object, a resultative or directional complement, or, later aspectual markers, etc.

This grammaticalization process was triggered by the existence in the language of some forms involving the preposition *yǐ*: *yǐ* + Object + Verb + C (where C is a complement or another object in the case of double-object constructions) which resemble disposal forms but cannot be considered as genuine disposal forms.

## 4 Are (all) Chinese disposal constructions genuine cases of DOM?

According to Bossong's (1982) definition, Chinese BA disposal markers qualify as DOM (differential object markers), if we interpret his "morphologisch" in a broad sense, including prepositions or free markers, and not only bound case markers. This interpretation is covered by Bossong's own work and many other studies. Clearly, there are certain direct objects both in Contemporary Chinese and previous stages of the language that are marked, whereas others remain unmarked. Different lexical forms of the BA marker that are partly restricted to certain historical periods or genres can be used in a more or less diverse set of BA structures.

The wealth of studies on the use of *yǐ* in disposal constructions in Archaic Chinese – with scholars coming to very contradictory conclusions – as well as the number of different pathways of grammaticalization suggested for BA constructions – appears to reflect not only the high degree of ambiguity of historical Chinese texts, but also the underspecified use of terms such as "disposal form" or "disposal marker".

Bossong's (1982) definition lacks a strong claim about the lexical status of DOM. For his purposes, it does not seem to play a role, whether marking is achieved by a preposition, a bound morpheme or some other device.

In the diachronic studies on Chinese disposal markers, this question is one of the key issues: because of the analytic nature of the Chinese language, the lack of morphological case marking, and – for historical texts – even the lack of hints for pronunciation or intonation, the question of whether it is necessary or possible to distinguish a disposal/DO *marker* from a *preposition* introducing an accusative argument or a PATIENT, is crucial.

Examples in sections 2.1 to 2.3 show that, over the course of several hundred years, the surface structure of a single sentence often allowed for interpretations of $V_1$ in a SVC ranging from coordinated full verbs through light verbs and prepositions to object markers. In the absence of other clues, scholars rely on the occasional use of adverbs, negations or other clues from context to identify clear examples for either case. In this section, we examine just how far cross-linguistic results for DOM can help assess the nature of disposal constructions in Chinese and evaluate proposed pathways of grammaticalization.

## 4.1 Pathways of grammaticalization

Chinese historical linguists differ in their analysis of the BA markers:
1. Some scholars think that BA words in disposal constructions are prepositions on a par with prepositions in instrumental constructions. (e.g. Cao and Yu 2000b: 154)
2. Other scholars (such as Jiang Shaoyu 2008) distinguish disposal markers from prepositions. They regard disposal markers as semantically more bleached than prepositions. Thus, they posit a step from preposition to disposal marker, which they consider a secondary grammaticalization process.

A grammaticalization process from a lexical preposition to a desemanticized DO marker has also been described for the Romanian *pe* (instrumental preposition *p(r)e* > marker *pe*) (see Lindemann 2018: 5–7). Other studies use the term "prepositional accusative" and talk about "prepositions or morphemes as object markers" (e.g. Schwenter 2014: 238 on Portuguese). The Romanian case bears some resemblance to the Chinese *yǐ*, as the early meaning of the preposition is instrumental as well, and the instrumental and disposal/DOM function continue to coexist.

Lindemann (2018: 7) describes the differences between the contemporary Romanian DO markers *pe* (that she also calls "semantically empty dummy prepositions") and the lexical prepositions *pe*: (1) *pe* as a preposition carries its own semantic meaning (e.g. 'on', 'during', 'through'). It is the syntactic head of the phrases, governs the case of its complements, and assigns theta roles such as GOAL or PLACE to them. Complements are expressed obligatorily. As a semantically empty case marker, *pe* loses its local meaning, theta roles are assigned by the verb.

These criteria to distinguish prepositions from case markers in an inflectional language cannot easily be transferred to the Chinese case: as there are no inflectional case markers in Chinese, we cannot find out, whether case is assigned by BA or the verb.

Starting with *yǐ*, much as scholars differ in their opinion about its status, statistics from Jiang (2008) and Liu (2002) show that in Pre-Qin times, the instrumental preposition function prevails by far over the accusative function. Only giving disposals with three arguments are assumed to belong to the latter type (10%). Even at the later stages, after the Han dynasty, the ratio of instrument arguments of *yǐ* to supposed patient arguments is 3:1, while many PATIENT arguments could be analyzed as WEAK instruments or THEMES. Thus, the initial argument structure of the preposition seems to remain strong. Examples of innovative *yǐ* structures, e.g. an (obligatorily preverbal) *yǐ* + O for placing disposals in the 5th century, could mark the beginning of a development of *yǐ* towards a disposal preposition, maybe by analogy with the emerging BA patterns. However, *yǐ*, even as a preposition, was superseded by others and appears today only in fossilized expressions.

As has been pointed out in Section 2.2, word order constraints and semantic constraints regarding definite reference and animacy do not apply to *yǐ*-constructions in the same way as they do for BA constructions. A post-verbal use of a disposal construction or the use with indefinite referents (in example 25 below) would, of course, not exclude the analysis as a DOM. But a free variance of structural and semantic features is not in accordance with the definition of differential object marking. Example (26) also shows that definite, known (and indefinite) direct objects were used postverbally without *yǐ* in the *Shǐjì*, and indefinite objects were used preverbally with *yǐ*.

(26) 即　　　　使　　吏卒　　共　　　　抱　　大　　巫嫗
　　　*Jí*　　　 *shǐ*　 *lìzú*　 *gòng*　　 *bào*　 *dà*　 *wūyù*
　　　Immediately order servants together hold big witch
　　　'Immediately, [he] ordered the servants to hold the big witch and

　　　投　　　之　　 河　　 中。　 有　　 頃，　　 曰：
　　　*tóu*　　 *zhī*　 *hé*　 *zhōng*　 *yǒu*　 *qǐng*　 *yuē*
　　　to.push PRON river middle exist moment say
　　　to push her into the river. After a while, he said:

　　　「巫嫗　何　　 久　　 也？ 弟子　　 趣　　 之！」
　　　*wūyù*　 *hé*　 *jiǔ*　 *yě*　 *dìzi*　 *cù*　 *zhī*!
　　　witch　 why　 long　 SFP　 disciple　 urge　 PRON
　　　"Why does the witch take so long? A disciple shall hurry her!"

　　　復　　 以　　 弟子　　 一　　 人　　 投　　 河　　 中。
　　　*Fù*　　 *yǐ*　 *dìzǐ*　 *yī-*　 *rén*　 *tóu*　 *hé*　 *zhōng*
　　　again　 YI　 disciple　 one-CL to.push river middle
　　　...and this time (he/they) threw one disciple into the river

　　　有　　 頃，　 曰：「弟子　　 何　　 久　　 也？
　　　*Yǒu*　 *qǐng*　 *yuē*　 *dìzi*　 *hé*　 *jiǔ*　 *yě*
　　　Exist moment say disciple why long SFP
　　　After a while he said: "Why does the disciple take so long?

| 復 | 使 | 一 | 人 | 趣 | 之！」 |
|---|---|---|---|---|---|
| fù | shǐ | yī | rén | cù | zhī |
| again | order | one | person | urge | PRON |

Let another person fetch her!"

| 復 | 投 | 一 | 弟子 | 河 | 中。 | 凡 | 投 | 三 | 弟子。 |
|---|---|---|---|---|---|---|---|---|---|
| fù | tóu | yī | dìzi | hé | zhōng | fán | tóu | sān | dìzi |
| again | push | one | disciple | river | middle | total | push | three | disciples |

And he/they threw a disciple into the river once more. In total, they threw hree disciples [into the river].'
(*Shǐjì*, Gǔjī lièzhuàn, Xīmén Bào yìshì: p. 3212, ca. 100 BCE)

This example allows us to follow the changing use of alternative constructions for basically the same action in the development of a story. In the first sentence, when someone is thrown into the river for the first time – and the person – the witch – is certainly known information, a serial verb construction with two coordinated Vs is chosen, using a resumptive pronoun *zhī* as O$_2$, as O$_1$ and O$_2$ are coreferential.

Moreover, the use of *yǐ* originally seems to be highly preferred for inanimate objects (due to its instrumental origin). Both features are in contrast to cross-linguistic findings about DOM.

As for BA constructions, the forms differ from *yǐ* in nearly every respect: from the very beginning, the V$_1$-position appears to be the syntactic context of grammaticalization, resulting in a preverbal position for the disposal prepositions, as opposed to the freer word order of *yǐ*. From the earliest BA examples on, the referents are usually definite or known, and human and animate reference is frequent, not excluding inanimate and abstract referents. Thus, from the beginning, criteria for marking an object are clearer, and BA words become closer to the status of disposal markers than to prepositions. Still, even BA words retained some of their prepositional meaning, requiring predicates expressing a manipulation of some sort, until Contemporary Mandarin. It is thus questionable whether they fully reached the state of disposal markers.

## 4.2 Criteria for marking/not marking

In the previous paragraph, constraints on the use of disposal markers, forming the required criteria for differential object marking, were discussed. From typological studies, important criteria for DOM include semantic/ pragmatic properties of the argument (a) inherent semantic properties of the object referent, (b) referential properties of the object, (c) topicality or givenness, etc.; semantic features of the predicate (e.g. transitivity parameters); formal features of the noun, and others (see von Heusinger et al. 2008; Aissen 2003). Differential object marking can depend mainly on one of these features, or on a combination of some of them.

For Contemporary Mandarin, as well as for Sinitic languages, referential properties of the object (definiteness or specificity), information structure (given information) and semantic features of the predicate (action affecting the direct object or *disposal*, Li and Thompson 1981), are mentioned most frequently, apart from syntactic constraints. In addition, some authors claim an obligatory marking of animates vs. an optional marking of inanimate objects, and formulate the boundedness of the event as a condition (see Iemmolo and Arcodia 2014: 316).

Li and Thompson (1981) suggest a scale of likelihood for usage of the BA construction as shown in Table 1.

**Table 1:** Continuum of preference for DO marker (Li and Thompson 1981: 487).

| *bǎ* impossible | *bǎ* unlikely | *bǎ* likely | *bǎ* obligatory |
|---|---|---|---|
| indefinite or nonreferential object no disposal | definite objects (low prominence) weak disposal | definite object (DEM) elaborate disposal | definite and highly prominent object strong disposal |

Chappell (2013: 787) proposes similar rules and constraints for disposal constructions in Sinitic languages, with the hint that much variation has been observed. Variation notwithstanding, three constraints familiar from Standard Mandarin, namely (1) a referential direct object – regardless of its inherent properties, (2) a preference for given or old information, and (3) a causativity constraint, phrased as the object denoting "a semantic patient undergoing a change of state", are the most prominent rules for the use of the disposal construction across Sinitic languages. Li and Cao (2013: 26) mention additional constraints, showing that three perspectives are important:
1. The BA verb/disposal marker:
   Several restrictions show that disposal markers have lost their verbal nature (cannot form V + Neg + V, cannot reduplicate)
2. The object, apart from having to be definite, cannot occur with numerals, and BA has to occur before the question pattern the object
3. The predicate is not a bare verb, thus the negation can only occur before BA, and not directly before the main VP

Disposal sentences without result usually do not use the disposal marker.

In Medieval Chinese, animacy does not appear to play a major role in the use of BA. Animate beings can frequently be seen in BA constructions, as can abstract nouns. As in Contemporary Chinese and Sinitic languages, the definiteness scale and information structure seem more important, as diagrammed in Figure 3.

Personal pronouns > Proper names > definite NP > indefinite specific NP > Non-specific NP

**Figure 3:** Definiteness scale (Aissen 2003: 437)

Bare demonstratives, demonstrative phrases, possessive phrases, personal pronouns, proper names, and definite NPs are all found in BA constructions in Medieval Chinese, whereas the use of indefinite referents is rare. It should be remarked that definite vs. specific vs. unspecific reference often remains ambiguous in historical texts. As for personal pronouns: first and second person pronouns are frequently attested, whereas the use of BA with the (3rd person) resumptive pronoun is rare.

The applicability of the disposal construction in general depends on the action denoted by the verb. Such a criterion alone would not qualify as a case of DOM. It would just mean that certain verbs do not take direct objects. But even for actions that do, in principle, allow a disposal construction, this marked construction cannot be used in all cases.

# 5 Conclusion

The grammaticalization process of BA as an object marker started with verbs with the general meaning 'to take, to grasp, to lead' developing into OM (likely preposition) within a serial verb construction "$V_1 + O_1 + V_2 + O_2$", after the deletion of the $O_2$, identical to $O_1$. For several hundred years in Medieval Chinese, several patterns representing different stages of this process coexisted (e.g. BA + O + V + Pron). The verbs $V_1$ to be grammaticalized were *qǔ*, *chí*, *jiāng*, *zhuō*, and *bǎ*. BA forms derived from two or more of these verbs were used during the same period within the same text. Thus, Medieval Chinese shows a pattern of multiple disposal markers also found in numerous contemporary Sinitic languages. Of those five BA markers, *jiāng* and *bǎ* are the only ones remaining today, at least in Mandarin, with *bǎ* being the main colloquial form, and *jiāng* being limited to a more literal style. It was probably not until Late Medieval II or even Premodern Chinese that BA was desemanticized to a degree that it could be considered a pure disposal marker, and not a prepositional object marker.

The grammaticalization process was triggered by the existence, in the language, of forms involving the preposition yǐ: yǐ + Object + Verb + C (where C is a complement or another object in the case of double object constructions). The first verb to have been grammaticalized was most probably the verb qǔ, at the beginning of the Early Medieval period (3rd–4th c. AD). The first "narrow disposal" sentences in Chinese can then be traced back to the 3rd–4th c. and not the end of the 6th c. as thought before.

As these sentences with the marker qǔ appear mainly in the texts translated from a kind of Prâkrit (probably Gāndhārī and not Sanskrit), an influence of the source language – which had SOV word order – on this usage is likely (see Peyraube 2017a). A similar phenomenon can be observed in the use of chí as a preposition in Buddhist texts translated during the Eastern Han: it appeared much more frequently than it did in the native Lùnhéng 論衡 (80 CE). Cao and Long's (2005: 323) statistics also show that the relative frequency of prepositional chí and yǐ varied considerably among translators during the 3rd–6th c. CE.

The exact nature of this influence – i.e. the reasons for the occurrence of such new patterns and usage of lexical items – requires further in-depth research. The language of the source texts, the native language of the translator(s), the exact variety of Chinese they learned or their native dialect in the case of Chinese translators all certainly play a role.

If it is true that the new pattern of narrow disposal construction started in the translated Buddhist texts, this would greatly increase the relevance of this corpus for the diachronic study of Medieval Chinese. This is not so much because they necessarily reflect the vernacular Chinese of their time – in fact, it appears clear, that they often do not, as many translators were not native speakers of Chinese and because they may have tried to remain faithful to a language following rules different from Chinese – but, rather, because it is just this deviation that may have turned them into a place of linguistic innovation, which saw a high degree of dissemination due to the religious prestige of the sutras and the frequency with which they were recited.

To what degree did these texts with their high religious prestige and the frequency of use during several centuries help to promote new structures in the Chinese language? What was the role of intense language contact with different Altaic languages, such as Uighur, Mongolian and Manchurian in the North in subsequent centuries, outside the religious context, further the development of the disposal construction(s)? And where do the local varieties of Sinitic, which display a high diversity of object markers, DOM-structures and semantic constraints, some of them much closer to the situation in Medieval Chinese than to contemporary Mandarin, come in?

We conclude that even though Chinese BA may not conform to all the criteria of differential object markers, BA constructions can certainly be considered as a case of differential object marking. This analysis has shown the potential to deepen our understanding of the functions of BA and its pathway to grammaticalization and to enhance the development of new research questions for the diachrony and typology of the Chinese disposal construction.

## References

Aissen, Judith. 2003. Differential object marking. Iconicity vs. economy. *Natural Language and Linguistic Theory* 21 (3): 435–483.

Bennett, Paul A. 1981. The evolution of passive and disposal sentences. *Journal of Chinese Linguistics* 9 (1): 61–89.

Bossong, Georg. 1982. Historische Sprachwissenshaft und empirische Universalienforschung. *Romanistisches Jahrbuch* 33: 17–51.

Bossong, Georg. 1985. *Empirische Universalienforschung: Differentielle Objektmarkierung in den neuiranischen Sprachen*. Tübingen: Narr.

Cao, Guangshun and Long, Guofu. 曹广顺、龙国富 2005. Zài tán zhōnggǔ Hànyǔ chǔzhìshì 再谈中古汉语处置式 [The disposal construction in Middle Chinese revisited]. *Zhōngguó yǔwén* 中国语文 2005 (4): 320–332.

Cao, Guangshun and Yu, Hsiao-jung. 曹广顺、遇笑容 2000a. Zhōnggǔ yìjīng zhōng de chǔzhìshì 中国译经中的处置式 [The disposal construction translated from Middle Chinese Buddhist sutras]. *Zhōngguó yǔwén* 中国语文 2000 (6): 555–563.

Cao, Guangshun and Yu, Hsiao-jung. 曹广顺、遇笑容 2000b. The influence of translated Later Han Buddhist sutras on the development of the Chinese disposal construction. *Cahiers de linguistique Asie orientale* 29.2: 151–177.

Chappell, Hilary. 曹茜蕾 2007. Hànyǔ fāngyán chǔzhì biāojì de lèixíng 汉语方言处置式标记的类型 [The typology of disposal markers in Chinese dialects]. *Yǔyánxué lùncóng* 语言学论丛 36: 183–209.

Chappell, Hilary. 2013. Pan-Sinitic object markers: morphology and syntax. In *Breaking down the Barriers: Interdisciplinary Studies in Chinese Linguistics and Beyond*, Cáo Guǎngshùn, Hilary Chappell, Redouane Djamouri, and Thekla Wiebusch (eds.), 785–816. Taipei: Academia Sinica.

Chen, Chusheng. 陈初生 1983. Zǎoqī chǔzhìshì lüètán 早期处置式略谈 [On the early disposal form]. *Zhōngguó yǔwén* 中国语文 [Chinese language] 1983 (3): 201–206.

Feng, Chuntian. 冯春田 2000. *Jìndài Hànyǔ yǔfǎ yánjiù*. 近代汉语语法略谈 [Research on the Grammar of Modern Chinese]. Jǐnán: Shāndōng jiàoyù chūbǎnshè.

Heusinger, Klaus von, Udo Klein and Peter de Swart. 2008. Variation in differential object marking. Paper presented at the Workshop on Case Variation. Stuttgart, June 2008.

Iemmolo, Giorgio, and Giorgio Francesco Arcodia. 2014. Differential object marking and identifiability of the referent: A study of Mandarin Chinese. *Linguistics* 52 (2): 315–334.

Jiang, Shaoyu. 蒋绍愚 2005. *Jìndài Hànyǔ yánjiù gàiyào* 近代汉语研究概要 [An outline of Modern Chinese studies]. Běijīng: Běijīng dàxué chūbǎnshè [Peking university press], 205–235.

Jiang, Shaoyu. 蒋绍愚 2008. Hànyǔ guǎngyì chǔzhìshì de láiyuán – jiānlùn cíhuì tìhuàn 汉语广义处置式的来源 – 兼论词汇替换 [The origin of the broad disposal form in Chinese – with a treatment of lexical replacement]. *Lìshǐ yǔyánxué yánjiù* 历史语言学研究 1: 27–39.

Li, Audrey Yen-hui. 2006. Chinese *bǎ*. *The Wiley-Blackwell companion to syntax*. Malden (Mass): Blackwell. 374–468.

Li, Charles and Sandra A. Thompson. 1974. An explanation of word order change: SVO > SOV. *Foundations of Language* 12: 201–214.

Li, Charles and Sandra A. Thompson. 1981. The *bǎ* Construction. In: *Mandarin Chinese. A Functional Reference Grammar*: 463–490. Berkeley, Los Angeles: University of California Press.

Li, Lan and Cao, Xilei (= Hilary Chappell). 李蓝、曹茜蕾 2013. Hànyǔ fāngyán zhōng de chǔzhìshì hé bǎzìjù. 汉语方言中的处置式和把字句 [Disposal form and BA sentences in Chinese dialects]. *Fāngyán* 方言 [Dialects] 35.1: 11–30 (part I); 35.2: 97–110 (part II).

Lindemann, Sofiana Iulia. 2018. *Die diachronische Entwicklung der differentiellen Objektmarkierung im Rumänischen*. Wiesbaden: Springer Fachmedien Wiesbaden, https://doi.org//10.1007/978-3-658-19612-7_2.

Liu, Ziyu. 刘子瑜 2002. Zài tán Táng Sòng chǔzhìshì de láiyuán 再谈唐宋处置式的来源 [The origin of the disposal forms of the Tang-Song period revisited]. In *Hànyǔshǐ* lùnwénjí [Collected essays in the history of Chinese linguistics], Sòng Shàonián 宋绍年 (ed.), 139–168. Wǔhàn: Wǔhàn dàxué chūbǎnshè.

Mei, Tsu-lin. 梅祖麟 1990. Táng Sòng chǔzhìshì de láiyuán 唐宋处置式的来源 [The origin of the disposal constructions during the Tang-Song dynasties]. *Zhōngguó yǔwén* 中国语文 3: 191–216.

Ōta, Tatsuo. 太田辰夫 1958. *Zhōngguóyǔ lìshǐ wénfǎ* 中国语历史文法 [A Historical Chinese Grammar]. Translated from Japanese by Jiǎng Shàoyú and Xú Chānghuá. Běijīng: Běijīng dàxué chūbǎnshè [Peking University Press].

Peyraube, Alain. 贝罗贝 1985. Les structures en BA en chinois médiéval et moderne. *Cahiers de Linguistique Asie Orientale* 14.2: 193–2013.

Peyraube, Alain. 贝罗贝 1989. Zǎoqī bǎzìjù de jǐge wèntí 早期把字句的几个问题 [Some questions regarding the early BA sentences]. *Yǔwén yánjiù* 1: 1–9.

Peyraube, Alain. 贝罗贝 1994. Nouvelles réflexions sur l'histoire des formes accusatives '*ba*' du chinois. *Cahiers de Linguistique – Asie Orientale* 23: 265–277.

Peyraube, Alain. 贝罗贝 2017a. Lùn lìshǐ jùfǎ zhōng Hòuhàn hé Wèi-Jìn-Nánběicháo qiánqī fójīng yìběn de bùkěkàoxìng 论历史句法中后汉和魏晋南北朝前期佛经译本的不可靠性 [On the unreliability of translated Buddhist sutras from the Late Han and early Wei-Jin Nanbeichao period for historical syntax]. *Chángshú lǐgōng xuéyuàn xuébào* (*Zhéxué shèhuì kèxué*) 2017 (1): 63–68.

Peyraube, Alain. 贝罗贝 2017b. Periodization, in *Encyclopedia of Chinese Language and Linguistics*, Rint Sybesma (ed.), 346–349. Leiden: Brill.

Schwenter, Scott A.. 2014. Two kinds of differential object marking in Portuguese and Spanish. In *Portuguese-Spanish Interfaces: Diachrony, Synchrony, and Contact*, Patrícia Amaral and Ana Maria Carvalho (eds.), 237–260. John Benjamins.

Wang, Li. 王力 1947. *Zhōngguó xiàndài yǔfǎ* 中国现代语法 [A Grammar of Modern Chinese], Shànghǎi: Zhōnghuá shūjú.

Wang, Li. 王力 1958. *Hànyǔ shǐgǎo* 汉语史稿. Běijing: Kèxué chūbǎnshè.

Wei, Pei-chuan. 魏培泉 1996. Lùn gǔdài Hànyǔ zhōng jǐzhǒng chǔzhìshì zài fāzhǎn zhōng fēn yǔ hé 论古代汉语中几种处置使在发展中分与和 [On the division and merging of several types of disposal forms in the course of their development in Archaic Chinese]. *Zhōngguó jìngnèi yǔyán jí yǔyánxué* 中国境内语言暨语言学 4: 555–594.

Wú, Fúxiáng. 吴福祥 2003. Zài lùn chǔzhìshì de láiyuán 再论处置式的来源 [Further discussion on the origins of the disposal construction]. *Yǔyán yánjiù* 语言研究 [Studies in Language and Linguistics] 23.3: 1–14.

Wu, Fuxiang. 吴福祥 2009. *Yǔfǎ lùncóng* 语法论丛 [Essays on grammar]. Shànghǎi: Shànghǎi jiàoyù chūbǎnshè 上海教育出版社. 98–114.

Ye, Youwen. 叶友文 1988. On the internal origins of the disposal construction in the Sui-Tang period/ Suí Táng chǔzhìshì nèizài yuányuán fēnxī 隋唐处置式内在渊源分析. *Journal of Chinese Linguistics* 16 (1): 55–71. [In Chinese].

Zhu, Dexi. 朱德熙 1982. *Yǔfǎ jiǎngyì* 语法讲义 [Lectures on Grammar]. Běijīng: Shāngwù yìnshuguǎn [Commercial Press].

Zhu, Minche. 祝敬彻 1957. Lùn chūqí chǔzhìshì 論初期處置式 [On the early disposal form]. *Yǔyánxué lùncóng* 語言學論叢 1: 17–33.

# Appendix 1: Sources

CBETA Hànwén dàzàngjīng 漢文大藏經; Diànzǐ fódiǎn jíchéng 电子佛典集成, "daizokyo" 大正藏 [Electronic collection of Buddhist texts: Tripitaka] http://tripitaka.cbeta.org.

*Chū yào jīng* 出曜经, Taishō 212 T04; transl. from Dharmapâda by Samˊghabhadra and (Zhú) Fónìan 竺佛念 (fl. 365–416 CE) in 399 CE during the Former Qin (351–394). Examples from: *juàn* 4: Yù pǐn 欲品 [Kāmavarga] [0627a21],); *juàn* 16: Fènnù pǐn 忿怒品 [Drohavarga] [0693b21]; *juàn* 23 Ni huán pǐn 泥洹品 Nirvāṇavarga. Electronic edition: CBETA Hànwén dàzàngjīng 漢文大藏經; Diànzi fódiǎn jíchéng 电子佛典集成, Dàzhengzāng.

*Dūnhuáng biànwén jí* 敦煌变文集, ca. 850–1025 CE, Scripta Sinica: Jìndài Hànyǔ zīliàokù 近代漢語資料庫 2: Dūnhuáng biànwén jí xīn shū 敦煌变文集新书.

*Fāng Gān shī* 方干诗 [Fāng Gān's (809–888) *shī* poems] (a poet from modern Zhejiang province). In *Quán Tángshī*: *juàn* 553.

*Fó běn xíng jí jīng* 佛本行集经. Translated between 587 and 591 CE); Taishō T03/T03n0190; Translation of the Abhiniṣkramaṇasūtra by Jñānagupta (Shénàjuéduō 阇那崛多, 527–604) from Gāndhāra, written down (笔受) by Sēng Tán 僧昙, Fēi Chángfang 费长房, Liú Píng 刘平.

*Fóshuō cháng Āhán jīng* 佛说长阿含经 [Long Discourses]. 4th–5th c. CE. Translation of Dīrghâgama (Pāyāsisutta) by Buddhayaśas (chin. Fótuóyéshè 佛陀耶舍, died 413 CE) (Zhú) Fónìan 竺佛念 (fl. 365–416 CE). Example from 7 (*Bìsù jīng* 弊宿经). Taishō Tripitaka 1, vol. 1.

*Gōngzǐ xíng* 公子行, poem by Zhāng Hù 张祜 (785?-849/853?). In *Quán Tángshī* 全唐诗, *juàn* 511.

*Hán Fēizi* 韩非子. 3rd c. BCE. Examples from chapter Bā jīng 八经. Edition: Scripta Sinica.

*Jiǔyuè lántiān Cuīshì zhuāng* 九月蓝田崔氏庄 [Blue field in the ninth month in Cui-clan village]. Mid-8th c. CE. poem by Dù Fǔ 杜甫 (712–770). *Quán Tángshī* 全唐诗, *juàn* 224.

*Lìdài fǎbǎo jì* 历代法宝记 [Record of the Succession of the Dharma-treasure], Yǎng tián běn 仰田本 171, Taishō Tripitaka No 2075, vol. 51; ca. 776, author: Chén Shìqiáng 陈士强 et al.; www.buddhist-canon.com/ history/T51N2075.htm.

*Liù zǔ tán jīng* 六祖坛经 [Platform Sutra of the Sixth Patriarch]. Between 780 and 800. Edition: Scripta Sinica: Jìndài Hànyǔ zīliàokù 近代漢語資料庫 1.

*Lúnyǔ* 论语 [Confucian Analects]. 5th c. BCE. Example from chapter 18 (Huīzi 徽子). Edition: Scripta Sinica, Academia Sinica Taiwan.

*Mèngzǐ* 孟子 [Mencius]. 4th c. BCE. Examples from Wànzhāng A 万章上, Gōngsūn Niǔ B 公孙狃下. In: Scripta Sinica, Academia Sinica Taiwan.

*Quán Tángshī* 全唐诗 [Complete Tang *shi*-poetry], compiled by Cáo Yin 曹寅 from 1705 on during the reign of the Kangxi emperor (1662–1722). Electronic edition: http://ctext.org/quantangshi.

Scripta Sinica (*Hànjí diànzi wénxiàn* 漢籍電子文獻): http://hanji.sinica.edu.tw/ Gǔ Hanyǔ yǔliàokù 古漢語語料庫.

*Shǐjì* 史记 [Records of the Grand Historian], (example from Gǔjī lièzhuàn 估计列传 Xīmén Bào yìshì 西门豹意识), ca. 100 BCE. In Scripta Sinica: Gǔ Hànyǔ yǔliàokù/ Shànggǔ Hànyǔ yǔliàokù 19.

[*Xīnjiào*] *Sōushén jì* [新校]搜神记 [In search of the supranatural, newly annotated] (ca. 350), compiled by Gān Bǎo (干寶, died 336) during the Jin dynasty (317–420). Edition: Scripta Sinica, Gǔ Hànyǔ yǔliàokù: Zhōnggǔ Hànyǔ yǔliàokù 1, 4.

*Zēngyī Āhán jīng* 增壹阿含經 The Ekottara Āgama 'Numbered Discourses' 44; Taishō 125, vol. 2, 561c a 7). Translation of Ekkottaragama sutra. Electronic version: CBETA; translated according to a recitation of Dharmanandin by (Zhú) Fóniàn 竺佛念 (fl. 365–416 CE) and Tan Song in 384–385 CE and revised by Gauthama Saṅghaveda ([瞿曇] 僧伽提婆) in 397–398 CE; Examples from scrolls 26, 31, and 44.

*Zhì guài lù* 志怪錄 6th–7th c. CE (?), compiled by Lù Xūn 陆勋 (fl. 871).

*Zuǒ zhuàn* 左传 [Zuo's Commentaries], 5th c. BCE. Example from Zhāo gōng 昭公. Edition: Scripta Sinica, Gǔ Hànyǔ yǔliàokù, Academia Sinica Taiwan.

Christine Lamarre
# An associated motion approach to northern Mandarin motion-cum-purpose patterns

## 1 Introduction

One of the well-known differences observed between Beijing colloquial Mandarin and southern Sinitic languages such as Cantonese or Taiwanese has to do with the encoding of **motion-cum-purpose**[1] in sentences such as 'go and buy food!'. Sentences (1a) and (2a) illustrate the common Sinitic Pattern A, where the itive verb 'go' is followed by the Verb Phrase which refers to the purpose of the motion (hereafter "purpose VP"). In Pattern B, illustrated in (1b) and (2b), the morpheme expressing motion is located after the purpose VP. Both patterns roughly convey the same meaning 'Go (to) buy food', but the latter has a more northern and a more colloquial flavor.

[Pattern A]                                [Pattern B]
(1a) 去買菜             vs.          (1b) 買菜去
     Qù  mǎi  cài                          mǎi  cài=qu.
     go  buy  food                         buy  food=go[2]
     'Go buy food.'

(2a) 去喝點兒水！       vs.          (2b) 喝點兒水去！
     Qù hē    diǎnr  shuǐ!                Hē   diǎnr  shuǐ=qu!
     go drink some   water                drink some  water=go
     'Let's go and drink some water!'

---

**1** We follow in the present chapter Schmidtke-Bode (2009: 93–99) and use "motion-cum-purpose" for these patterns. This term likely comes from Mesoamerican linguistics. As for the terms "ventive" and "itive", we follow Bourdin (2006).
**2** As one of the aims of the paper is to discuss the status of the morphemes that express deictic motion as handled by the English verbs *go* and *come*, we use the 'go' and 'come' glosses, while marking them as clitics in Pattern B by means of the = symbol. Justification for this treatment is provided in section 3.2. We sometimes add hyphens to the usual Pinyin transcription to separate morphemes, in order to conform to the Leipzig glossing rules. In the pinyin Romanization used here to transcribe Standard Chinese sentences, the lack of a tone mark on a vowel indicates a toneless (unstressed) syllable, as can be seen for *qu* in (1b) and (2b), as opposed to *qù*, which bears a high falling tone (i.e. 51 on the five-level scale widely used in Chinese dialectology).

Previous studies (Chao 1968: 479, Lù 1985) point at dialect background and written vs. spoken style as a key factor to account for the distribution of these patterns: B is typical of the Beijing colloquial. In Standard Mandarin, a variety based on Beijing Mandarin but that integrates features of central and southern varieties and of written Chinese, both patterns are attested nowadays to express motion-cum-purpose 'go (and/to) VP', together with a "blended" Pattern C, where the morpheme expressing itive motion occurs twice in two distinct slots (see Chao 1968: 479, Lù 1985; Zhū 1982: 165), illustrated below in (1c) and (2c).

(1c)  去買菜去！  (2c)  去喝點兒水去！
    *Qù mǎi cài=qu!*      *Qù hē diǎnr shuǐ=qu!*
    go buy food=go        go drink some water=go
    'Go buy food.'        'Go and drink some water!'

Motion-cum-purpose patterns A, B and C may be observed in the case of ventive motion too, with *lái/lai* (see Lu 1989 and example 13 below).

Previous studies also mention that in Pattern B, the itive morpheme that appears after the purpose VP undergoes phonetic weakening and loses its original tone features (Chao 1968: 479, Zhū 1982: 165–166, Lù 1985), which points to some degree of grammaticalization. Despite this, the analysis of *qu* and *lai* in Pattern B as **particles of purpose**, as proposed by Chao (1968: 479), was not taken up by other linguists, probably because there is no available grammatical category in northern Mandarin to which such grammatical morphemes might be assigned. We propose here that "associated motion" is the best candidate as a cross-linguistically valid category likely to be encoded by these "particles of purpose", and discuss several issues related with the grammaticalization of deictic motion verbs into associated motion markers in northern Mandarin.

This chapter is organized as follows. In section 2, after giving an overview of Sinitic motion-cum-purpose patterns and of previous analyses, we argue that the grammatical category encoded by *qu* 'go' in pattern B for motion-cum-purpose markers is **associated motion**, and provide further evidence for a loss of 'verbiness' of deictic motion verbs when they occur after purpose VPs. In section 3, we show that this typological approach is in fact complementary to the analysis developed by Yáng (2012, 2013), who investigated the distribution of these patterns in historical documents, and pointed to the intense contact of Chinese with OV Altaic languages as an important factor in accounting for the spread of Pattern B [purpose VP + *qu*] in northern Chinese. In a concluding section 4, we raise the possible link between the grammaticalization of deictic motion verbs into associated motion markers (particles of purpose) and their grammaticalization into deictic directionals in northern Mandarin.

## 2 Motion-cum-purpose patterns in Sinitic languages

In this section, we first give an overview of the linguistic data under discussion (2.1), further compare motion-cum-purpose patterns A and B (2.2), and examine the treatments proposed for Pattern B in the literature as well as their shortcomings (2.3), then we note the formal similarity of purpose particles and deictic directionals (2.4). In section 2.5 we raise the issue of the grammatical category possibly encoded by the particles of purpose in Pattern B.

### 2.1 Basic facts about motion-cum-purpose patterns

Let us first emphasize that motion-cum-purpose expressions, no matter whether they follow pattern A, B or C, are high-frequency patterns both in dialogues and in narratives. They account for a fair amount of the total number of occurrences of deictic motion morphemes in written as well as in spoken corpora.

In his seminal study, Lù (1985) showed that beyond the northern vs. southern opposition, the issue of written, formal style vs. spoken, informal style is also a key factor in accounting for the distribution of these patterns: B is typical of the Beijing colloquial. Lù noted in his survey that within corpora sharing a northern Mandarin background, pattern B prevails in *xiàngsheng* ('crosstalk') sketches and other corpora reflecting the Beijing colloquial, whereas in literary works by Beijing-based authors such as Lǎo Shě's dramatic work and Chén Jiàngōng's short stories, the proportion of patterns A and B is quite balanced.

**Table 1:** Distribution of Patterns A and B in spoken and written corpora reflecting Beijing Mandarin (from Lù 1985: 27).

| corpus<br>pattern | Lǎo Shě<br>(four plays) | Chén Jiàngōng<br>(short stories) | *xiàngsheng*<br>('crosstalk') | Spoken corpus<br>(interviews) |
|---|---|---|---|---|
| A | 128 | 37 | 4 | 6 |
| B | 132 | 22 | 54 | 66 |

Before we show more data from Standard Mandarin dialogues and narratives, we would do well to provide some information on the way Mandarin expresses deictic motion.

First, motion-cum-purpose patterns also frequently include goal noun phrases (hereafter Goal NPs), located before the purpose VP. Furthermore, in

Standard Mandarin and in many other varieties spoken in northern and central China, the basic deictic motion verbs 'come' *lái* and 'go' *qù* have bimorphemic variants, consisting of a deictically neuter, semantically bleached path verb that may be glossed as 'move.to' and that takes the goal argument when it is overt. A deictic directional is often added after the goal NP. In some of these varieties, deictic motion verbs 'come' *lái* and 'go' *qù* do not bear goal NPs as their argument. This issue is probably closely related to that of the grammaticalization of deictic motion verbs into deictic directionals. Let us first illustrate in (3) the "common Sinitic" pattern, prevalent in southern China, in which deictic motion verbs take goal NPs as their argument, following the regular VO order. We may translate these verbs as 'go to' and 'come to':

(3a) 我去北京。  
    *Wǒ qù Běijīng.*  
    1SG go Beijing  
    'I go to Beijing.'

(3b) 來我這兒！  
    *Lái wǒ zhèr!*  
    come 1SG here  
    'Come to my place!'

In this case, deictic verbs follow the same argument structure as other path verbs such as 'enter' in *jìn zhàn* 'enter the [railway] station' (for a train), 'exit' in *chū-guó* 'leave the country', or 'return (to)' in *huí sùshè* 'return to the dorm'. However, many northern dialects and some central dialects (including colloquial Beijing Mandarin) prefer a bimorphemic pattern where the goal argument is supported by a bleached path verb, and where deictic direction is encoded in deictic directionals located after the goal NP.

The contrast between the "synthetic" (or monomorphemic) encoding in (3) and the "analytic" (bimorphemic) encoding in (4) is illustrative of this.

(4a) 我到北京去。  
    *Wǒ dào Běijīng=qu.*  
    1SG move.to Beijing=DIR$_{ITIVE}$  
    'I go to Beijing.'

(4b) 到我這兒來！  
    *Dào wǒ zhèr=lai!*  
    move.to 1SG here=DIR$_{VEN}$  
    'Come to my place!'

Some northern dialects (for instance the Jilu Mandarin dialects spoken in Hebei and in western Shandong) use *shàng* instead of *dào* as a bleached path verb meaning 'move to' (the former originates in the verb 'to ascend', the latter in the verb 'to arrive'[3]). Many grammarians consider that in this case *dào* must be analyzed as

---

[3] We refer the reader to Lamarre (2008) for a fuller picture of Chinese motion events and deictic motion, including a basic presentation of monomorphemic and bimorphemic patterns.

a preposition 'to' rather than as a path verb: Zhū (1982: 174) and Liú (2000) for instance consider *dào* in (4) as a preposition, whereas Lǚ (1980: 127) analyzes it as a path verb – this is a long-debated issue in the field of Chinese grammar.

As a result, three distinct word order patterns are attested for sentences including both a goal NP and a purpose VP. The pattern [deictic motion verb + goal NP + purpose VP] is the historical pattern; it correlates with Pattern A, and still prevails in Southern varieties. The pattern [bleached motion verb + goal NP + purpose VP + deictic directional] in (5b) is its northern counterpart, and somehow correlates with pattern B. Still, we consider here that *dào* 'move to' is a bleached path verb, and gloss *qu* as an itive directional.

(5a)  去北京讀書  
  *qù Běijīng dúshū*  
  go Beijing study  
  'go to Beijing to study'

(5b)  到北京讀書去  
  *dào Běijīng dúshū=qu*  
  move.to Beijing study=DIR_ITIVE

Another pattern is attested, shown in (5c), where the bleached motion predicate *dào* or *shàng* 'move to' takes the locative goal NP as its argument, whereas *qù* and *lái* are followed by the purpose VP, and seem to recover their "verbiness".

(5c)  到北京去讀書  
  *dào Běijīng qù dúshū*  
  move.to Beijing go study  
  'go to Beijing to study'

These three patterns are illustrated in examples (6a) to (6c), taken from the 1980 novel *By Middle Age*.[4]

(6a)  要不要去醫院看看？  
  *Yào-bu-yào qù yīyuàn kàn-kan?*  
  want-NEG-want go hospital see.a.doctor-RDP  
  'Do you want to go to the hospital to consult a doctor?' [MA 16]

---

That study did not deal with motion-cum-purpose, though, in spite of its high frequency in our data.

**4** *By Middle Age* (*Rén dào zhōngnián*) is a novel by SHEN Rong (also known as CHEN Rong) published in 1980 (the text comprises about 42,370 characters). We chose it to illustrate the frequency of these patterns after an investigation of various corpora, because it proved to be quite representative of late 20th century Modern Written Chinese with respect to the encoding of motion events. The title is abbreviated in [MA] after examples; the number indicates the chapter.

(6b) 剛才孫主任來，勸他到病房外邊的長椅上去歇一會兒……
gāngcái    Sūn       zhǔrèn    lái,    quàn    tā    dào
a.while.ago Sun      Director  come    advise  3SG   move.to
bìngfáng   wàibian   de        chángyǐ=shang    qù    xiē yìhuǐr,...
ward       outside   GEN       reclining.chair=on  go  rest a.while
'… a little while ago Director Sun came and advised him to go and have a short rest on the reclining chair outside the ward,…' [MA 2]

(6c) 佳佳睡著了，圓圓上鄰家看電視去了。
Jiājia     shuì-zháo  le,      Yuányuan   shàng    lín-jiā
Jiajia     sleep-ACH  CRS      Yuanyuan   move.to  neighbour-home
kàn        diànshì=qu    le.
watch      TV=DIR_ITIVE  CRS
'Jiajia is asleep, Yuanyuan has gone to a neighbour's place to watch TV.' [MA 9]

Table 2 shows the distribution of some of the patterns involving the ventive and itive motion morphemes *lái* (*lai*) and *qù* (*qu*) in this novel.

**Table 2:** Deictic motion morphemes *lái* (*lai*) and *qù* (*qu*) in a 1980 novel.

|  | *lái/ lai* | *qù/ qu* | total | Motion-cum-purpose |
|---|---|---|---|---|
| Deictic verb *lái/qù* without goal NP/ purpose VP[5] | 22 | 10 | 32 | |
| The verb *láidào* 'come to' |  |  | 1 | |
| **Motion-cum-purpose patterns without locative goal NP** |  |  |  |  |
| Motion-cum purpose pattern A: *lái/qù* + purpose VP | 15 | 24 | 39 | (76,5%) |
| Motion-cum purpose pattern B: purpose VP + *lai/qu* | 1 | 10 | 11 | (21,5%) |

---

**5** This figure includes deictic motion verbs used alone, with a time expression, an aspect marker, in a relative clause, a presentational sentence, a focus construction *shì … de* etc. Only forms encoding directed motion are counted. More grammaticalized uses of *lái* and *qù* to introduce a purpose clause without any translational motion involved, where the markers might be translated as 'in order to', have been excluded here, after checking dubious sentences with a native speaker. The semantic development at play here is beyond the scope of the present paper, although it is important to grasp the link between deictic motion and purpose. Deictic directionals that occur after manner or cause of motion such as *ná-lai* 'bring', or after path verbs and path directionals such as *chū-lai* 'come out' or *ná-hui-lai* 'bring back', are not included in Tables 2 and 3.

**Table 2** (continued)

|  | lái/lai | qù/qu | total | Motion-cum-purpose |
|---|---|---|---|---|
| Motion-cum purpose pattern C: *lái/qù* + purpose VP + *lai/qu* | – | 1 | 1 | (2%) |
| Subtotal |  |  | 51 | 51 |
| **Deictic motion patterns including a locative goal NP** |  |  |  |  |
| *lái/qù* + locative goal NP | 1 | 12 | 13 |  |
| *láidào* + locative goal NP |  |  | 7 |  |
| *dào* + locative goal NP + *lai/qu* | 2 | 2 | 4 |  |
| *shàng* + locative goal NP + *lai/qu* | – | 1 | 1 |  |
| **Deictic motion patterns including a locative goal NP and a purpose VP** |  |  |  |  |
| *lái/qù* + locative goal NP + purpose VP | – | 2 | 2 |  |
| *dào* + locative goal NP + *lái/qù* + purpose VP | 1 | 2 | 3 |  |
| *shàng* + locative goal NP + *lái/qù* + purpose VP | – | 1 | 1 |  |
| *dào* + locative goal NP + purpose VP + *lai/qu* | – | 1 | 1 |  |
| *shàng* + locative goal NP + purpose VP + *lai/qu* | – | 1 | 1 |  |
| Subtotal |  |  | 8 |  |
| **Total number of patterns of deictic motion with purpose** |  |  | 59 | 59 |

These data illustrate the complex interaction between the motion-cum-purpose patterns and the motion expressions involving various kinds of path verbs and a goal NP in the spatial domain. It also shows the wide array of patterns that are attested in Standard Chinese. Such variation is at its utmost in the standard language which, as a *koinè*, mixes northern, central and southern patterns.

The fact that Pattern B is sometimes considered "colloquial" actually speaks to the formation of Modern Written Chinese, an agglomerate of northern, central and sometimes even southern patterns (see Feng 2009 for an elaborate analysis of what he calls "Modern Written Chinese"). Table 3 shows the distribution of these patterns in a Standard Mandarin TV series "Ten Years of Marriage", produced at the beginning of the 21st century. Table 4 confirms the tendency discussed in Lu 1985 (see Table 1 above): the frequency of Pattern B is indeed higher in spoken data.

**Table 3:** Deictic motion morphemes *lái* (*lai*) and *qù* (*qu*) in a 2003 TV series[6] (10 episodes, about 7.5 hours).

| | VEN *lai* | IT *qu* | total *lai/qu* | Motion-cum-purpose |
|---|---|---|---|---|
| Deictic V *lái/qù* without goal NP/ purpose VP | 80 | 80 | 160 | |
| **Motion-cum-purpose patterns without locative goal NP** | | | | |
| Motion-cum purpose pattern A: *lái/qù* + purpose VP | 18 | 39 | 57 | |
| Pattern A (variant): Path verb + *lái/qù* + purpose VP | 16 | 19 | 35 | |
| Subtotal Pattern A | | | 92 | (41,3%) |
| Motion-cum purpose pattern B: purpose VP + *lai/qu* | 18 | 92 | 110 | (49,3%) |
| Motion-cum purpose pattern C: *lái/qù* + purpose VP + *lai/qu* | 2 | 13 | 15 | |
| Pattern C (variant): Path verb + *lái/qù* + Purpose VP + *lai/qu* | 2 | 4 | 6 | |
| Subtotal Pattern C | | | 21 | (9,4%) |
| Subtotal | | | 223 | 223 |
| **Deictic motion patterns including only a locative goal NP** | | | | |
| *lái/qù* + locative goal NP | 2 | 33 | 35 | |
| *dào* + locative goal NP + *lai/qu* | 4 | 3 | 7 | |
| *shàng* + locative goal NP + *lai/qu* | 1 | 3 | 4 | |
| *láidào* + locative goal NP | | | 1 | |
| *lái/qù* + locative goal NP + *lai/qu* | 3 | 0 | 3 | |
| **Deictic motion patterns including a locative goal NP and a purpose VP** | | | | |
| *lái/qù* + locative goal NP + purpose VP | 3 | 19 | 22 | |
| *lái/qù* + locative goal NP + purpose VP + *lai/qu* | 2 | 2 | 4 | |
| *dào* + locative goal NP + *lái/qù* + purpose VP | 6 | 7 | 13 | |
| *shàng* + locative goal NP + *lái/qù* + purpose VP | 1 | 1 | 2 | |

---

[6] Table 3 shows data taken from a 2003 TV series intitled *Jiéhūn shí nián* 'Ten Years of Marriage' (director: Gāo Xīxī, 20 episodes of about 48 minutes in duration, abbreviated as [JH]). Other examples in this chapter are taken from the following TV series: *Pínzuǐ Zhāng Dàmín de xìngfú shēnghuó* 'Loquacious Zhang Damin's Happy Life' (2000, director: Shěn Hǎofàng, 20 episodes of about 45 minutes each, abbreviated as [PZ]), and *Lǎo-Mǐ jiā de hūnshì* 'Mi Family's Marriages' (2013, director: Zhào Chényáng, 32 episodes, abbreviated as [LM]). The number after the abridged title in the reference of an example refers to the episode.

**Table 3** (continued)

|  | VEN<br>*lai* | IT<br>*qu* | total<br>*lai/qu* | Motion-<br>cum-purpose |
|---|---|---|---|---|
| *dào* + locative goal NP + purpose VP + *lai/qu* |  | 1 | 3 | 4 |
| *shàng* + locative goal NP + purpose VP + *lai/qu* |  | – | 8 | 8 |
| *dào* + locative NP + *lái/qù* purpose VP + *lai/qu* |  |  | 1 | 1 |
| *shàng* + locative NP + *lái/qù* purpose VP + *lai/qu* |  | 1 | – | 1 |
| Subtotal |  |  | 55 | 55 |
| **Other motion-cum-purpose patterns** |  |  |  |  |
| *dào* + locative goal NP + purpose VP |  |  | 3 |  |
| *shàng* + locative goal NP + purpose VP |  |  | 2 |  |
| Subtotal |  |  | 5 | 5 |
| **Total number of patterns of deictic motion with purpose** |  |  |  | 283 |

**Table 4:** Distribution of Patterns A, B and C in two Standard Mandarin corpora for simple patterns (without goal NP).

| corpus \ pattern | Type of corpus | A | B | C | Total |
|---|---|---|---|---|---|
| By Middle Age | Novel | 76,5% | 21,5% | 2% | 51 |
| Married Ten Years (1–10) | TV drama | 41,3% | 49,3% | 9,4% | 223 |
|  |  |  |  |  | 274 |

These data confirm Lù's observations (Lù 1985, showed in Table 1) on the distribution of itive Patterns A and B in various types of corpora reflecting Beijing Mandarin. In order to allow an easier comparison with our data, we reorganized Lù's data in Table 5.

**Table 5:** Distribution of Patterns A and B in northern Mandarin spoken and written corpora (based on Lù 1985).

| corpus \ pattern | Type of corpus | A | B | Total |
|---|---|---|---|---|
| Chén Jiàngōng's work | short stories | 37 (62,7%) | 22 (37,3%) | 59 |
| Lǎo Shě's plays | drama | 128 (49,2%) | 132 (50,8%) | 260 |
| Crosstalks/ interviews | oral | 10 (7,7%) | 120 (92,3%) | 130 |
| Total |  |  |  | 449 |

## 2.2 Pattern A: [motion verb + purpose VP]

Pattern A [Deictic motion verb + purpose VP] is widely described in reference grammars and usually analyzed as a canonical subtype of Serial Verb Constructions (hereafter SVC). It is introduced in the early stages of teaching in Chinese classes (for instance Cheung 1994: 42 introduces it as a case of "verbal expressions in series, of the purpose type[7]).

Pattern A is the "historical" pattern, attested throughout the history of Chinese (Liáng 2007b, Zhāng 2010, Liú 2012, Yáng 2012[8]). It is consistent both with the VO order which prevails in most varieties of Sinitic, and with the iconicity which is considered by some linguists as being an important principle explaining many word order phenomena in Modern Chinese (see Tai 2002 and the discussion below in section 2.4). In Pattern A [deictic motion verbs *lái/qù* + purpose VP], the deictic motion verbs fully retain their verbal features: the motion-cum-purpose pattern is a mere extension of the allative pattern 'go to goal NP',[9] where the itive or ventive verb is directly followed by a purpose VP instead of a goal locative argument NP.

One of the characteristics of Pattern A is that any verb expressing directed motion may be followed by a purpose VP. Deictic verbs may be followed either by a goal NP, a purpose VP, or both, as shown in (7). In order for non-deictic path verbs to take a purpose VP, they must be followed either by a locative goal NP or by a deictic directional, as shown in (8) and (9).

(7a) 去法國(留學)  
 *qù Fǎguó (liúxué)*  
 go France (study)  
 'go to France (to study)'

(7b) 來(法國)工作  
 *lái (Fǎguó) gōngzuò*  
 come (France) work  
 'come (to France) to work'

---

**7** As convincingly showed by Paul (2008), there is no consensus in the field of Chinese linguistics on the definition of SVCs and their inventory. For practical reasons, we still sometimes refer in this chapter to Pattern A of motion-cum-purpose pattern as a SVC.

**8** This refers to patterns, not to the semantics of each deictic motion verb throughout history. For instance the itive motion verb *qù* has undergone a radical semantic change: see Cui 2005 for a discussion.

**9** See for instance Haspelmath (1989), who traces the origin of 'to' infinitives to purposive action nominals with, as a first step, the extension from the local allative meaning to the meaning of purpose, as in (a) Mary went to Sabina's apartment > (b) Mary went to take photos of Sabina > Mary bought a camera to take photos of Sabina. In the case of Chinese, however, it is unclear whether we are dealing with a similar evolution. Cui (2005: 112) suggests for instance that analogy with purpose VPs may have played some role in the evolution of the argument structure of deictic motion verbs, which did not take locative NPs as their arguments in Archaic Chinese.

(8a) 回法國(看病)  
    huí    Făguó  (kànbìng)  
    return  France  (see.a.doctor)  
    'return to France (to see a doctor)'

(8b) 進校園(停車)  
    jìn    xiàoyuán  (tíng chē)  
    enter  campus  (park car)  
    'enter the campus (to park the car)'

(9b) 回來看病  
    huí-lai    kànbìng  
    return- $DIR_{ven}$  see.doctor  
    'come back to see a doctor'

(9b) 進去停車  
    jìn-qu    tíng  chē  
    enter- $DIR_{itive}$  park  car  
    'go in to park the car'

An important difference between goal NPs and purpose VPs, though, lies in the fact that, in the spatial domain, bimorphemic path verbs such as *huí-lai* 'come back' must split: the deictic directional is in northern Mandarin displaced to after the goal-NP, a split that does not apply to purpose VPs.

(10) *回來法國  
    \**huí-lai*    *Făguó*  
    \*return-$DIR_{VEN}$  France  
    Intended meaning: 'come back to France'

(11) *回看病來  
    \**huí*    *kànbìng*    *lai*  
    \*return  see.a.doctor  $DIR_{VEN}$  
    Intended meaning: 'come back to see a doctor'

Pattern A, i.e. a deictic motion verb followed by a purpose VP, is observed in other VO languages such as French, with a finite motion verb, and a nonfinite purpose VP (allative preposition à 'to' is compulsory before a goal NP, but does not appear before purpose VPs).

(12) Je  descends    acheter  le    journal.  
    1SG  descend.1s.PRS  buy.INF  DEF  newspaper  
    'I go down to buy the newspaper.'

Pattern A is the only pattern available for motion-cum-purpose in Vietnamese, a strongly analytic VO language often described as "serializing", according to Li's comparative study on Chinese and Vietnamese SVCs (Lǐ 2016: 163–164: Vietnamese morphology does not tell us whether we deal with a finite or non-finite form). This correlation was noticed by Yáng (2012, 2013), who investigated the non-Sinitic VO and OV languages spoken in and around China (his study includes

Manchu, Dongxiang, Mongolian, Uighur, Lhasa Tibetan, Qiang, Pumi, Yi, Hmong-Mien – or Miao-Yao languages, Kam-Tai languages and Mon-Khmer languages) and found a high correlation between a VO vs. OV order and the respective order of the purpose VP and the morpheme (verb or affix) expressing deictic motion in motion-cum-purpose sentences. Yáng (2012, 2013) also insists on the correlation between the encoding of deictic motion to a goal (go + locative goal NP), and the encoding of deictic motion in construction with a purpose VP (go + purpose VP).

What we know about Pattern A in Sinitic languages fits with the observations on the characteristics of motion-cum-purpose patterns made by Schmidtke-Bode (2009: 94) in his cross-linguistic survey of purposive clauses:

> What all of the motion-cum-purpose constructions have in common is a relatively high degree of integration into the main clause, as compared to their non-motion purposive counterparts. They are usually more economical by virtue of containing less linguistic material, and are often described by authors as complements rather than adjuncts. As such, they are more closely integrated into the main clause because they fill a syntactic argument position.[10]

## 2.3 Patterns B and C: Northern Mandarin's "particles of purpose"

Pattern B [purpose VP + *lai/qu*], as opposed to Pattern A, is specific to northern Mandarin and typically occurs in dialogues. A map published in the *Linguistic Atlas of Chinese Dialects* (Cáo 2008, vol. 3, map 78) shows a rather complex and intricate distribution of Patterns A, B and C, but confirms Pattern A as the only attested pattern in Min and Yue-speaking areas.[11] Dialect background is indeed a key factor accounting for the distribution of these patterns.

---

**10** Studies on the French pattern encoding motion-cum-purpose illustrated in (12) also support this observation: Charolles & Lamiroy (2002) list a set of formal features that indicate a high degree of syntactic integration of the non-finite predicate into the VP. This issue would require a separate investigation. We are at least dealing here with a striking similarity in terms of word order between purpose VPs on one hand, and locative goal NPs functioning as object arguments of deictic motion verbs on the other hand.

**11** According to Carine Yiu, who has constructed a large database on sentences expressing motion events in Hong Kong Cantonese, only Pattern A is attested in colloquial Cantonese (p.c.). Adeline Tan, an Inalco PhD candidate, confirmed that only Pattern A is attested in Chaozhou, a southern Min variety of Sinitic spoken in Guangdong (p.c.). Note, however, that Pattern A is also predominant in some Mandarin areas, in Southern Mandarin for instance, and even in some varieties of Central Plains Mandarin spoken in southern Hebei or in Henan. Therefore, the dis-

On the other hand, the fact that Pattern B is typical of the informal, spoken language (see Table 1 above) may explain why it remains largely understudied in spite of being widely attested in Standard Mandarin literary texts and in popular media (it is, for instance, rarely taught in Chinese language classes). Nevertheless, the status of ventive *lai* and itive *qu* in Pattern B has been discussed in some major reference grammars, and contradictory analyses have been put forward. Below is a selection of major works on this topic.

Chao (1968: 479) dedicated a section of his seminal work *A Grammar of Spoken Chinese* to **particles of purpose**, i.e. "final particles expressing purpose", that should be distinguished from directional complements, but later studies did not follow his analysis.

Zhū (1982: 165–167) acknowledges that in Pattern B the deictic motion verbs have undergone grammaticalization, while still considering *qu* 'go' to be a verb in a serial verb construction (in Chinese *liánwèi jiégòu* or *liándòng jiégòu*) in both A and B patterns. Lù (1985, 1989), Fàn (1998, Chapter 5) and Gān and Gān (2009) take the same stance. Such an analysis entails that we are dealing with SVCs where the motion predicate and the purpose predicate may appear indifferently as the first or as the second predicate without any significant change of meaning. This is far from satisfying, for at least two reasons. First, in Pattern B, the form encoding deictic motion undergoes phonetic weakening, a prosodic characteristic of grammaticalization in northern varieties of Mandarin.[12] This indicates a loss of phonetic integrity of the original verbal morphemes.

Second, as noted in Chao (1968: 480), there exists a "redundant" or "blended" Pattern C (see (1c) and (2c) above), which also supports the hypothesis of a different grammatical function for each of the deixis-related forms which appear in these specific paradigms. In the following example (13), the first sentence is a question using Pattern B, the answer uses Pattern C, the "blended" pattern [come + purpose VP+ come], where the first *lái* is a full verb. The second toneless *lai* therefore clearly requires a treatment other than "second predicate of a SVC". Example (14) illustrates Pattern C for *qù* and *qu*.

---

tribution of Pattern A and Pattern B cannot be reduced to an opposition between Mandarin vs. non-Mandarin dialects.
**12** Mainstream Chinese dialectology usually distinguishes the Jin dialects spoken in most of the Shanxi province and in northern Shaanxi from the Mandarin dialects. Jin dialects, however, share many grammatical features with northern Mandarin dialects. Besides, a recent description of Mandarin dialects (Qian 2010) does include a chapter on Jin. In the present study, Jin dialects are included in "northern Mandarin".

(13) 你幹嘛來了？
    *Nǐ   gàn  má=lai      le?*
    2SG  do   what=come   CRS
    來取貨來了。
    *Lái  qǔ    huò=lai     le.*
    come take goods=come  CRS
    'What are you coming for?' 'I came to take goods [to sell them outside].' [JH 6]

(14) 怎麼樣啊？        啊？
    *Zěnmeyàng  a?    Á?*
    how.be      SFP   INTJ
    這不是去看工作去了嗎？怎麼樣，覺著？
    *Zhè  bú   shì  qù  kàn   gōngzuò=qu  le    ma?*
    now  NEG  be   go  look  work=go     CRS   Q
    *zěnmeyàng,      juézhe?*
    how.be           feel
    '– How did it go? – What? – Didn't you go to look for a job? How did it go?' [LM 2] (Lǎo-Mǐ asks his daughter when she comes home)

One of the grounds for an analysis of this pattern as a blended pattern is that – just as we noted before for sentences (8a) and (8b) – the motion verbs allowed before the purpose VP in Pattern A are not limited to deictic verbs: they may consist in a bimorphemic path verb, like *chū-lai* 'come out' in the following sentence, taken from a late-nineteenth-century chivalric fiction written by a novelist from a Manchu family. In example (15) the moving entity, the Young Master, is traveling away from home to settle family matters.

(15) 我的爺，你可是出來作甚麼來了？
    *Wǒ   de   yé,   nǐ   kě  shì  chū-lai      zuò  shénme=lai  le?*
    1SG  GEN  lord  2SG  Q   be   exit-DIR$_{VEN}$  do   what=come   CRS
    'My master, what is it you came to do? (Literally: 'what did you come out to do?')
    (Wen Kang: *The Tales of Heroic Sons and Daughters*, chapter 3)

Sentence (15) is one of the examples quoted by Fáng (1992: 520) in a section of his grammar dedicated to *lai* and *qu* as aspectual particles (*dòngtài zhùcí*). Fáng (1992: 466, 520) points out that this sentence is grammatically correct without the sentence-final *lai* (this is true for other sentences illustrating our Patterns B and C, including examples with itive *qu*). He notes that in sentences such as (15), the second occurrence of *lai* 'come' is unstressed, and directed motion has been expressed by the verb *chū-lai* 'come out'. He then argues that sentence-final *lai* conveys a feeling of dynamism (*dòngtàigǎn*) and emphasizes an action in progress (*dòngzuò zhèngzài jìnxíng*). The evidence provided to support this analysis of *lai* and *qu* in Patterns B and C as aspectual particles, though, is scarce and unsatisfying. Fáng's discussion – which incidentally also involves other uses of *lai* and *qu* that should rather be analyzed as directionals – shows how problematic these purpose particles are. This probably comes from the fact that we are dealing with grammaticalized function words that do not correspond to any acknowledged grammatical category in the language.

To conclude this review of the various analyses put forward in previous studies, let us turn to some descriptions which group together purpose particles and deictic directionals and use the label "directional" for both. The next section also illustrates the semantic difference between particles of purpose and deictic directionals when they appear in the same environment.

## 2.4 Particles of purpose and deictic directionals in northern Mandarin

Standard Mandarin deictic directionals consist of two unstressed, grammaticalized morphemes (ventive *lai* and itive *qu*). These deictic directionals often combine with a path verb like in *chū-lai* 'come out' in (15) above. They may also combine with a path directional and form a bimorphemic directional such as *chu-lai* 'out, towards the speaker', as illustrated in (16) with the verb *bān* 'move, carry'.

(16)  裏屋那上下鋪呢，搬出來，擱在這角上。
 Lǐ-wū           nà         shàng-xià-pù         ne,
 inside-room  DEMdist  up-down-berth       TOP
 bān-chu-lai,                 gē    zai   zhè      jiǎo=shang.
 move-DIRout-DIRven,  put  at    DEMprox  corner=on
 'That two-level bed in the inner room, let's move it out [towards us], and put it in this corner here.' [PZ 2]

Deictic directionals may also in Standard Mandarin combine directly with a verb that expresses the manner or the cause of motion. For instance, the verb *ná* 'take in one's hands', when followed by *-lai* or *-qu*, conveys the meaning of 'bring' or 'take towards another location'. It is noteworthy that Mandarin directionals (*qūxiàng bǔyǔ*) are considered as a subtype of resultative complements (*jiéguǒ bǔyǔ*), which usually encode the change of location of the patient (Liú 1998: 2) in the case of a transitive verb. This is the case in examples (17) and (18).

(17) 去，拿來我看看。
　　　Qù,　ná-lai　　　wǒ　 kàn-kan.
　　　go　 take-DIR_VEN　1SG　look-RDP
　　　'Go, bring it to me so I can have a look.' [JH 3]

(18) 這錢你拿去吧。
　　　Zhè　　　qián　　nǐ　　ná-qu　　　　ba.
　　　DEM_PROX　money　2SG　take-DIR_ITIVE　SUG
　　　'Take this money (away, don't refuse).' [JH 18]

Deictic directionals show the same phonetic weakening as Pattern B's particles of purpose. Most of the time, the semantics of the purpose predicate in the motion-cum-purpose Pattern B are sufficient to rule out a directional reading for *lai* or *qu* (as in examples (1), (2), or (14) above). However, with verbs such as *ná* 'take in one's hands', when the patient of the verb is covert, the linear chain of morphemes may be identical and create an ambiguity. Sentences such as (19), where the purpose VP is 'take (the notebook with the) homework' will be interpreted as a motion-cum-purpose sentence, where the itive motion is extrinsic to the process.[13]

(19) 去去去，拿作業去！
　　　Qù　qù　qù,　ná　　zuòyè=qu !
　　　go　go　go　take　homework=go
　　　'Go! Go and take your homework.' (and bring it back here) [JH 3]

It's worth contrasting (19) with (20).

(20) 你看，快拿去！
　　　Nǐ　　kàn,　kuài　　　ná=qu !
　　　2SG　look　quickly　take=go
　　　'Look! Go take it quickly!' (Situation: the father tells her daughter to go and take her notebook and bring it back. This sentence is uttered after (19), so the patient NP may remain covert.) [JH 3]

---

[13] Although it is grammatical in northern Mandarin for patient NPs to be inserted between the verb and the deictic directional in an imperative sentence, this word order would be unlikely for an NP denoting a specific entity known to both the speaker and the addressee (such as 'your homework' here). In this latter case, the patient NP would typically be located before the verb (like in (18)), with or without preposition *bǎ*.

The sequencing of *ná* 'take' and *qu* here recalls (18). However, in (18) the meaning is 'take away': *qu* is a typical directional, which encodes the deictic orientation of the motion of the patient. In (20), on the other hand, the meaning is 'go and take/go to take': *qu* encodes the deictic motion of the agent in a motion-cum-purpose construction, and this motion is extrinsic to the process 'take in one's hands'. Lù (1989) provides a list of the verbs which may be followed both by the ventive directional *lai* and by the particle of purpose *lai*. The formal identity, in terms of similarity of linear sequence [V + *qu* / *lai*], between directional compounds and motion-cum-purpose patterns was nicely illustrated in an anecdote reported in Chao (1968: 479): Hu Shi, a leader of the national language movement (born in Anhui, in central China), mistook in a conversation a motion-cum-purpose pattern *qǔ=lai* 'come and take' for a directional compound 'bring' involving the verb *qǔ* 'take'.[14]

Let us now look at (21) and (22), taken from the same TV drama as examples (19) and (20). They illustrate Pattern A and Pattern C, respectively, with the same verb *ná* 'take in one's hands'.

(21) 要不，我去拿。
Yào-bù,   wǒ    qù    ná.
if-not    1SG   go    take
'If needed, I will go get it.' [JH 17]

(22) 要多少？我去拿去。
Yào    duōshao?    Wǒ    qù    ná=qu.
want   how.much?   1sg   go    take=go
'How much do you need? I will go get it.' [JH 6]

This short presentation of the similarity of deictic directionals with the morphemes marking deictic motion in motion-cum-purpose Pattern B will make it easier to understand why some descriptions may analyze *lai* and *qu* in Pattern B as a directional (*qūxiàngcí*, or a directional complement, *qūxiàng bǔyǔ*). This point of view is taken for instance by Tai (2002) in an answer to Paris and Peyraube (1993) who had raised Pattern B as a counterexample to the Principle of Temporal Sequence and to a possible iconic motivation for SVCs. Tai (2002) argues that *Wǒ mǎi shū qu.* 'I'm going to buy books.' (see 1b) is not a typical purposive clause: *qu*

---

**14** Note that in some non-standard Mandarin varieties (and in Jin dialects) spoken in Hebei and Shanxi, the motion-cum-purpose Pattern B is distinct from the V-Directional pattern in that the latter requires the insertion of a dummy resultative complement between the verb and the deictic directional (see for instance Hou and Wen 1993: 14–15, and Ke [Lamarre] and Liu 2001).

is pronounced in the neutral tone, and should rather be analyzed as a directional complement that "indicates direction of movement with respect to the hearer". Zhāng (2011: 372–373), after observing that in Pattern B, deictic motion verbs are half-way on a grammaticalization path, also considers they should be treated as directional complements. Pattern C: *Wǒ qù mǎi shū qu.* 'I'm going to buy books.' is given by Tai (2002) as another piece of evidence for considering clause-final *qu* as a directional. Such an analysis is however utterly inadequate from the point of view of the grammatical function of the morphemes encoding deictic motion, as shown in the sentences above.

Similar views may be seen in descriptions of non-standard northern dialects. For instance, a survey report describing itive and ventive grammaticalized forms in Jin dialects mentions that in Píngyáo, a Jin dialect spoken in Shānxī, the usual motion-cum-purpose pattern is Pattern C [go + purpose VP + go]. In this pattern, the clause-final itive form radically diverges from the phonetic shape of the full verb: [tɕʰy³⁵ + purpose VP + tiʌʔ¹³] (Hou 1981, Hóu & Wēn 1993: 14–15). The latter form is homomorphous with the deictic directional that appears, for example, after a path verb or a path directional in [xA³⁵ tiʌʔ¹³⁻⁵³] (descend-go) 'go down'.

Nevertheless, some studies also explicitly warn against an analysis of the deixis-related forms in Pattern B as deictic directionals. Lu (1985, note 3) mentions two reference grammars published in China in the 1980's which hold this view, and states his disagreement. The fact that *ná=qu* [take-go] takes a distinct meaning in (18) ('take it away from here') and in (20) ('go and fetch it') is indeed a strong argument against analyzing both *qu* as performing the same directional function.

A monography describing the variety of Mandarin spoken in Chéngdé (located in Hebei, about 250 km north-east of Beijing, and previously known as Jehol or Rèhé), published in the 1930's, also expressly distinguishes purposive *lai* and *qu* from deictic directionals. Mullie (1937: 172–174) pays attention to the distinct readings of some ambiguous utterances, for instance 'go and take' vs. 'take away'. He explains that directionals ('converbs' in his terms) indicate "the direction wherein than action is performed" and he translates them 'hither' and 'thither', respectively, whereas the particles of purpose discussed here are translated as 'come and ... ' or 'go and ... '.

## 2.5 Grammatical morphemes in search of a grammatical category

We believe that one of the reasons why Y. R. Chao's analysis of *lai* and *qu* as particles of purpose in Pattern B failed to get acceptance is the lack of an adequate grammatical category likely to be encoded by such "particles". Grammatical markers encode grammatical categories. We have some idea of what a deictic directional may be, but what is the grammatical category that could possibly be encoded by a marker that originates in a deictic motion verb and expresses the agent's move towards or away from the deictic center in order to accomplish some purpose expressed by the adjacent VP?

# 3 An associated motion approach to northern Mandarin's particles of purpose

Clearly, a grammatical category is needed to which Chao's "particles of purpose" can be assigned: we now propose to show that **associated motion** is a plausible candidate. After providing a brief overview of associated motion in section 3.1, we provide in section 3.2 more evidence of the grammaticalization of deictic motion verbs in the northern Mandarin Pattern B. In section 3.3, we discuss the issue of the possible motivation (language-internal vs. language-external) for the spread of Pattern B in northern Mandarin.

## 3.1 Associated motion and its markers

Associated motion was first described in Australian languages (see Koch 1984 on Kaytej, an Arandic language of Central Australia, and Wilkins 1991 on Mparntwe Arrernte, another Arandic language) but it has been documented since in other parts of the world such as America (Guillaume 2016, Vuillermet 2011), Africa (Bourdin 2006; Voisin 2013; Belkadi 2015) and Asia (Jacques 2013, de la Fuente and Jacques 2017). It is the grammatical category specifically handled by grammatical morphemes that associate a translational motion event with the non-spatial event to which the verb refers (Guillaume 2016: 81).[15]

Wilkins (1991) argues that the fact that "languages as typologically, geographically and genetically distinct as Hausa, Atsugewi and Mparntwe Arrernte possess morphemes relating main verb events to background motion events"

---

[15] Note that this definition was not devised to distinguish associated motion markers from deictic directionals in Chinese. In a compound verb such as *jiào-qu* 'call someone and make him/her go somewhere', it can be argued that the deictic directional adds a motion meaning to a non-motion verb *jiào* 'call'. However, the meaning of this compound verb differs from *jiào=qu* 'go and call (someone)'.

proves that associated motion is a "grammatical category which can be added to the list of notions such as tense, mood and aspect". The languages spoken in Australia and South America to which this category was first applied show complex systems with more than 10 associated motion markers, organized along several parameters (such as an opposition between markers referring to a motion anterior to, concomitant with, or subsequent to the event or state of affairs referred to by the verb). In many of these systems, deixis (including motion towards and away from a reference point, and motion back to home base) is a significant parameter: in their inventory of associated motion forms, many studies mention markers encoding deictic motion in order to do something, i.e. 'go and do' and 'come and do'. In other words, what we call here "motion-cum-purpose" is one of most common subtypes of associated motion among languages possessing this grammatical category, if not the most common in fact.

As pointed out by Guillaume (2016: 88), though, the concept of associated motion is now sometimes extended to languages where this category is not encoded by dedicated morphologized markers in a dedicated morphosyntactic slot. For instance, Belkadi (2015) discusses a ventive directional clitic =d in Taqbaylit Berber (spoken in northern Africa) which may, according to the semantics of the predicate it combines with, encode either direction or associated motion (of the motion-subsequent-to-action type). Voisin (2013) also describes North Atlantic languages spoken in Senegal in which deictic directionals may also be used to express associated motion of the motion-cum-purpose type (see Lamarre et al. Submitted for further discussion).

If we want to show that northern Mandarin *qu* and *lai* do indeed encode the grammatical category of associated motion, we must first provide convincing evidence that the deictic motion verbs *lái* 'come' and *qù* 'go' are thoroughly grammaticalized in motion-cum-purpose Pattern B.

## 3.2 Evidence for the grammaticalization of deictic motion verbs in northern Mandarin Pattern B

There are several pieces of evidence suggesting that *-lai* and *-qu* have in Pattern B undergone some degree of grammaticalization. We have selected three; they are listed below, together with references to Lehmann (2015) when relevant.

(i) *Phonological attrition and bondedness*

Previous studies all agree that the itive and ventive morphemes *qu* and *lai* are unstressed in Pattern B, i.e. they have lost their original tone contour. In Standard

Mandarin, the prosodic realization of unstressed syllables is conditioned by the tonal contour of the preceding syllable.[16] Loss of tonal contour is regularly associated with grammaticalization in northern Mandarin. Lù (1985) further adds that in the Beijing colloquial, *qù* [tɕʰy⁵¹] 'go' is actually often realized in Pattern B with an unrounded vowel [i] and is pronounced [.tɕʰi], another type of phonetic erosion. We consider that in Pattern B *qu* and *lai* are clitics, and therefore use "=" in the transcription and glosses to link the verb and the deictic motion morphemes *lai* and *qu*.

On the contrary, in the patterns analyzed as SVCs in most reference grammars, such as (23a), where the first predicate expresses the manner of motion, no phonetic weakening occurs in the motion predicate. Thus, the same sequence of morphemes lends itself to an SVC reading 'go by bus' in (23a), with a full tone on *qù*, and to a motion-cum-purpose reading (i.e. an associated motion reading: 'go to take a bus') in (23b), where *qu* is unstressed. This is another piece of evidence against an analysis of *qu* in (23b) as a full verb in an SVC (see Zhū 1982: 166, Lù 1985, Gān & Gān 2009 for similar observations).

(23a) 坐车去。  
     Zuò    chē  qù.  
     sit     bus  go  
     'Let's go by bus.'

(23b) 坐车去。  
     Zuò    chē=qu.  
     sit     bus=go  
     'Let's go to take the bus.'

In non-standard varieties of Mandarin, phonological attrition may go far beyond a simple loss of stress. We mentioned for instance an extreme case attested in the Pingyao dialect (Shanxi, see 2.4. above), where the itive verb is pronounced [tɕʰy³⁵] in contrast to [tiʌʔ¹³] for the itive directional and the itive marker in motion-cum-purpose Pattern C. Available descriptions of such dialects often emphasize that the itive or ventive verb is not interchangeable with the directional or the particle of purpose located after the purpose VP, and that the "weaker" form cannot be used alone.[17]

---

[16] There are prosodic consequences to the phonetic erosion of suffixes and clitics in non-standard northern Mandarin that are often more conspicuous than in Standard Mandarin: they often involve a tone sandhi on the preceding syllable. This is the case in many dialects belonging to the Jilu subgroup (spoken in Hebei and Shandong) and in some Guanzhong dialects spoken in Shaanxi, belonging to the Central Plains Mandarin group.

[17] In Jin dialects, morphemes which are not etymologically assigned to entering tone syllables (with an obstruent coda) may switch to this type of short syllable if unstressed, as in the case, for instance, of grammatical morphemes (this phenomenon is called *shūshēng cùhuà* in Chinese dialectology). This may account for the pronunciation [tiʌʔ¹³], if it is etymologically related to the

This fits with the parameter of "syntagmatic cohesion or bondedness" as described by Lehmann (2015: 157–167).

(ii) *Assertedness and argument structure*

In Pattern A, the motion predicate functions as a matrix verb, which is compatible with a "V-negation-V" type of question.

(24) 我看看牆上的鐘，問她："你去不去看電影？"
Wǒ   kàn-kan      qiáng=shang de   zhōng, wèn  tā:
1SG  look.at-RDP  wall=on     GEN  clock  ask  3SG
"Nǐ   qù-bu-qù    kàn     diànyǐng?
2SG  go-NEG-go   look.at movie
'I looked at the clock on the wall, and asked her: "Would you go to the movie?" (Wáng Shuò: *Guò bǎ yǐn jiù sǐ* [Death after a high] 3)

The interrogative sentences observed for Pattern B are Wh-type questions using interrogative pronouns of the type "come/go to do what", as in (13) above.

Furthermore, deictic motion in Pattern A is expressed by a full verb, which keeps its argument structure: a goal NP argument may be added before the purpose VP, as in examples (5a), (6a), and (7a) above. In Pattern B, the morpheme expressing the itive or ventive motion is located after the purpose VP, and no locative NP can be added after it. The only way to add a locative goal NP to Pattern B is to use a non-deictic path verb that takes the locative goal NP, as in example (6c) above, or in (33) and (34) below.

This loss of argument structure is also observed in some varieties of northern Mandarin for the locative goal NP in sentences without purpose VP. In such varieties, the ventive and itive verbs do not take goal NPs (see Tang and Lamarre 2007, Lamarre 2008) and the bimorphemic pattern introduced in example (4) in section 2.1. above prevails.

(iii) *Size of the paradigm*

Examples (8) and (9) show that in Pattern A, any path verb encoding directed motion, including both non-deictic path verbs such as *huí* 'return' or *jìn* 'enter', and compound path verbs combining a deictic and a non-deictic path element

---

deictic motion verb 'go' (this issue is still under debate). See Hei (2003) for a detailed discussion of Pattern C in Jin dialects.

such as *huí-lai* 'come back', may be interpreted as the motion predicate of the motion-cum-purpose pattern, if the following VP is semantically relevant. This is consistent with the cognitive motivation described in Schmidtke-Bode (2009: 97) for motion-cum-purpose, i.e. the "close experiential correlation between directed motion and purpose".

On the other hand, in most of the northern Mandarin dialects where Pattern B is attested, only the ventive and itive morphemes *lai* and *qu* may occur after the purpose VP to refer to a motion event having as its goal the accomplishment of some action.[18] This is consistent with the observation that as forms become grammaticalized, the paradigm they belong to tend to shrink in size. Here the deixis-related morphemes *lai* and *qu* that appear after the purpose VP in Pattern B and C form a "small, tightly integrated paradigm" (Lehmann 2000: 174, Table 4.3), whereas the list of the motion verbs in Pattern A is quite large.

(25a)  去洗手！
    *Qù    xǐ    shǒu!*
    go    wash    hands
    'Go and wash your hands!'

(25b)  洗手去！
    *Xǐ    shǒu=qu!*    [JH 6]
    wash    hands=go
    'Go and wash your hands!'

(26a)  進屋洗手。
    *Jìn-wū    xǐ    shǒu.*
    enter-room    wash    hand
    'Go/come in to wash your hands.'

(26b)  *洗手進屋。
    * *xǐ    shǒu    jìn-wū.*
    wash    hand    enter-room
    (Intended meaning) 'Go/come in to wash your hands.'

---

**18** Let us mention here a third item *zǒu* attested in northwestern Mandarin, which encodes an itive meaning in expressing hortative sentences with 1st person inclusive plural subjects 'let us go and ... '.

(27a) 回來看病
　　　*huí-lai　　　kànbìng*
　　　return-DIR_ITIVE  see.doctor
　　　'come back to see a doctor'

(27b) 看病回來
　　　*kànbìng　　huí-lai*
　　　see.doctor　return-DIR_VEN
　　　# 'come back from seeing a doctor'

(iv) *The widespread "blended" or "redundant" Pattern C*

Both Chao (1968: 479) and Zhū (1982: 165–166) mentioned redundant patterns involving two occurrences of *qu* or *lai* within the same clause as evidence for the grammaticalization of the second motion verb. To examples (13), (14) and (22) above may be added two further illustrations of motion-cum-purpose Pattern C. Sentences (28) and (29) were uttered in succession by the same female character speaking Standard Mandarin in a TV drama.

(28) 你來接我的？
　　 *Nǐ　 lái　 jiē　 wǒ　 de?*
　　 2SG  come meet 1SG  SFP
　　 'You came to meet me?' (said to her husband on coming out of her workplace and seeing him waiting on his bike to take her home) [JH 7]

(29) 我老公來接我來了。
　　 *Wǒ　 lǎogōng　 lái　 jiē　 wǒ=lai　 le.*
　　 1SG  husband　 come meet 1SG=come  CRS
　　 'My husband came to meet me.' (she informs her boss that her husband is waiting for her) [JH 7]

Sentence (30), quoted by Lǜ (1985), is taken from a Beijing spoken corpus based on interviews recorded in 1982.[19] A 50-year-old woman relates her father's last days, and reports his request: he wants her to go and fetch his younger brother so that he can see him one last time before he dies.

---

[19] This sentence is now also available along with its context in the Peking University corpus known as the PKU CCL corpus, developed by the Center for Chinese linguistics of Peking University (http://ccl.pku.edu.cn:8080/ccl_corpus/).

(30) 你一定去找你舅舅去，你趕快去找去。
 Nǐ   yídìng    qù  zhǎo   nǐ    jiùjiu=qu,
 2SG  certainly go  fetch  2SG   uncle=go
 nǐ   gǎnkuài   qù  zhǎo=qu...
 2SG  quickly   go  fetch=go
 'You must go and fetch your uncle, go immediately to fetch him ...'

In the first clause, the purpose VP is a transitive verb followed by its object (*nǐ jiùjiu* 'your uncle'); in the second clause, the object NP is covert and the associated motion marker *qu* then directly follows the verb.

We mentioned that in pattern C the first motion verb could also be a bimorphemic path verb as in (15), taken from a 19th century novel. Similar patterns are by no means rare in the dialogues to be found in modern written fiction and in films, e.g. *Wǒ chūqu kànkan qu.* 'I go out to have a look.' or *Zán jìnqu zhǎo tā qu!* 'Let's go in to talk to him!'.

## 3.3 The grammaticalization of deictic motion verbs into associated motion markers

The typological approach adopted here, which considers northern Mandarin purposive particles as resulting from the grammaticalization of deictic motion verbs into associated motion markers, is, in our view, complementary to the analysis developed in Yáng (2012, 2013). Yáng (2012) led a systematic investigation of the distribution of A, B and C patterns in historical documents, and found the first occurrences of Pattern B in Chinese translations of Buddhist sutras (ca. 4th-5th century, see also Liáng 2004; 2007a for early examples of sentences with a word order similar to modern Pattern B in the contemporary language, and Cao & Yu 2000 for a discussion of these texts). He also found that the northern Pattern B [purpose VP + *qu*] prevails in documents known to have been influenced by Altaic languages. For instance he found 70 occurrences of Pattern B vs. only three occurrences of Pattern A in the Yuan and Ming (13th to 14th century) versions of *Lǎo Qǐdà*, a Chinese textbook used by Koreans and known to reflect a northern variety of Chinese heavily influenced by Altaic languages. Some of the sentences following Pattern B were later modified to Pattern A when the textbook was reedited in the 18th century. Thus Yáng (2012) notes that Pattern B was not directly triggered by language contact with various OV Altaic languages in the Liao, Jin and Yuan dynasties (ca. 10th to 14th century), but he suggests that contact had likely been an important factor in its implementation in northern Chinese. These important findings led him to question the relative part of external and internal motivation played in the birth and development of Pattern B. In this chapter, we want to raise a few issues which need to be addressed in order to better assess the part played by language-internal vs. language-external motivation.

(i)  *Why did OV order only influence deictic motion verbs?*

Why should deictic verbs be the only motion verbs or path verbs to be influenced by the Altaic OV order? The same question arises about a similar hypothesis put forward by Hashimoto (1986) and Liú (2000) regarding the order of deictic motion verbs and the locative NP in Cantonese (deictic verb 'go/come' + locative goal) vs. northern Mandarin (*dào* + goal + itive/ventive directional), as mentioned in examples (3) and (4) above. We have already pointed out that bimorphemic path verbs like *huí-lai* 'come back' can express the motion in motion-cum-purpose Pattern A, but are not felicitous in Pattern B. To invoke the influence of OV order on a basically VO language is unconvincing, unless we can explain why this influence should be restricted to deictic motion. We believe that the associated motion approach put forward in this paper provides a satisfying solution to this problem.

We have showed that in motion-cum-purpose Pattern B, *lai* and *qu* have lost their verbal features. Therefore, we have to find a scenario which accounts for the emergence of associated motion as a new grammatical category at some stage in the history of Chinese. If this innovation was triggered by language contact, or at least if its spread may be attributed to it as documented by Yáng (2012), we are dealing with the kind of phenomenon called "gap filling" in Heine and Kuteva (2005: 124–131). After the new category develops in northern Chinese as Pattern B, it may either eliminate the old Pattern A, or coexist with it (depending on the areas and the varieties). Just as Heine and Kuteva (2005: 130) put it in their discussion of contact-induced grammatical change, Patterns A and B may, in some varieties of Chinese, coexist as alternative constructions, or they may combine "and co-occur in the same construction, thus resulting in double marking", i.e. in this case Pattern C. This scenario is also compatible with the intricate geographical distribution of Patterns A, B and C (Cáo 2008, vol. 3, map 78). Hēi (2003) showed that Pattern C, widespread today in Jin dialects, is also attested in the historical documents of the Yuan period (1279–1368, under Mongol rule), and still to be found in novels such as the *Hónglóu mèng* (*The Dream of the Red Mansion*, mid-eighteenth century). The following example is taken from the last chapters of this novel, known to reflect a more northern variety of Mandarin than the preceding chapters.

(31) 剛才二爺才去打聽去了。
    Gāngcái   Èr-yé        cái   qù   dǎtīng=qu   le.
    a.while.ago second-lord just  go   inquire=go  CRS
    'Xue Ke (= the young master) has just gone to make inquiries.'
    (*The Dream of the Red Mansion*, chapter 85)

Recent descriptions of languages spoken in areas close to China such as Rgyalrong (Jacques 2013) and Manchu (de la Fuente and Jacques 2017) confirm the observations made by Yáng (2013) on the presence, in some surrounding languages of highly morphologized strategies to encode motion-cum-purpose and on the validity of the category of associated motion in analyzing the development of Pattern B in Chinese.

(ii) *A language-internal motivation? The link with deictic directionals*

There is probably still more to say on a possible internal motivation for the development of Pattern B. Based on the data gathered up to now, it appears that two factors have presumably played a key role: the shrinking argument structure of deictic motion verbs, which in some modern varieties of northern Mandarin have lost their ability to bear a goal argument – leading to the development of bimorphemic (analytic) deictic motion verbs –, and the development of deictic directionals which allow the information on deictic motion to appear after goal NPs and purpose VPs in a clause. Internal variation within northern Mandarin shows that these parameters are closely related but not totally correlated with one another.

In other words, in the northern pattern, the development of deictic directionals occurring after the goal NP allows sentences such as [*dào/shàng* + goal NP + purpose VP + deictic directional], as in (5b) and (6c). Yáng (2012: 530) noted such patterns in Yuan documents, and our own survey confirms it at this stage as a likely 'linking pattern'. The following sentence is taken from the Ming version of one of the Korean textbooks mentioned above. In the Qing edition, a bleached path verb *dào* was added in the answer before the locative goal NP 'the pawnshop', where deictic orientation is expressed after the purpose VP (we gloss it as a directional, to be consistent with glossing in examples 5b and 6c above, further investigation are needed to determine whether it is a case of "bridging context").

(32) 你今日那裏去。
    Nǐ    jīnrì   nǎli    qù?
    2SG   today   where   go

我今日印子鋪裏儅錢去。
*Wǒ   jīnrì   yìnzipù=li   dàng   qián   qù.*
1SG   today   pawnshop=in   pawn   money   go
'– Where are you going today? – Today I am going to the pawnshop to pawn [something and get] some money'
(*Piáo Tōngshì Yànjiě*, p. 19a, 13th-14th century)

(33) 我今日到當舖裏當錢去。
*Wǒ   jīnrì   dào   dàngpù=li   dàng   qián=qu.*
1SG   today   move.to   pawnshop=in   pawn   money= DIR$_{ITIVE}$
'Today I'm going to the pawnshop to pawn [it for] money.'
(*Piáo Tōngshì Xīnshì Yànjiě* section 1–10, 18th century]

This perfectly matches sentences such as (34), taken from a modern TV drama.

(34) 下午我就上市場賣去。
*Xiàwǔ   wǒ   jiù   shàng   shìchǎng   mài=qu.*
afternoon   1SG   then   move.to   market   sell= DIR$_{ITIVE}$
'This afternoon I'll go to the market to sell them.'
[JH 5]

The exact path which lead to the emergence and to the development of Pattern B is deserving of an in-depth investigation which is beyond the scope of the present paper. However, the link between deictic directionals and associated motion, if proven, may shed some light on an interesting typological regularity in grammaticalization.

# 4 Concluding remarks and perspectives for further research

1) **Associated Motion**, a "cross-linguistic valid conceptual category" (Wilkins 1991) in languages spoken in Australia, in America, and in Africa, proves to be useful for northern Mandarin too. It provides an adequate category for grammaticalized markers expressing deictic motion in purposive patterns, which had been up to now left uncategorized. The subtype of associated motion at work in northern Mandarin is that of motion-cum-purpose, i.e. motion-prior-to-action.
2) Northern Mandarin shows a much less elaborate system than the canonical systems typical of Australian or South American languages. Its associated

motion markers are grammaticalized from **deictic verbs**. They form one of the attested motion-cum-purpose patterns used in Standard Mandarin, which competes with a more ancient pattern consisting of a full deictic motion verb followed by a purpose VP, and a blended pattern with a redundant marking of deictic motion. The coexistence of several patterns with a similar function is compatible with the output of contact-induced grammaticalization.

3) Associate motion markers in Standard Mandarin and other non-standard varieties of northern Mandarin we surveyed are homomorphous with deictic directionals. This provides an interesting research topic deserving of further exploration: language-internal motivation needs to be taken into consideration if one is to account for the emergence of a grammatical category that matches similar patterns in neighboring languages and for the lexical source of the markers "recruited" to encode it.

The close link between deictic directionals and associated motion markers has been noticed in descriptions of African languages such as Berber (Belkadi 2015 on another subtype where motion follows action). Indeed, the fact that languages exhibiting very different morphosyntactic properties (say, Somali and Japanese) have come to entrust similar functions to their ventive or itive markers, including that of encoding associated motion (also of the subtype where motion precedes action), was commented on by Bourdin (2006: 27–29) as follows: "grammaticalization along a particular pathway is notionally driven", "we are dealing with language-specific instantiations of a *bona fide* cross-linguistic category", i.e. **directional deixis**. If we manage to uncover more evidence showing the interaction of these two types of deixis-related markers in the course of the grammaticalization process they have been subjected to, we would then be dealing with a case of typological regularity in semantic change attested in languages that are otherwise typologically distant from one another.

4) The behavior of former deictic motion verbs in motion-cum-purpose patterns where they lose some of their verbal features to behave like auxiliaries has been extensively discussed for English *go get* constructions, e.g. "Go get me a coffee!" (see for instance Bjorkman 2016 for a review of the literature on this issue). In this construction, the motion verb cannot be inflected, whereas there is no such restriction in similar constructions involving motion verbs followed by a *to*-infinitive. It cannot take locative modifier either. Cardinaletti & Giusti (2001) have also described in a Sicilian dialect what they call "semi-lexical motion verbs" which form motion-cum-purpose patterns such as 'I go and fetch the bread'. In these patterns, the second verb takes an inflected form instead of an infinitive form, as it would usually do in typical motion-cum-purpose patterns.

The four motion verbs which are allowed in this "inflected construction" thus share many properties with auxiliaries: while they keep their lexical meaning concerning motion, they belong to a closed class, and cannot take a locative argument. In spite of the huge typological distance separating European languages and Chinese, some of the formal features which distinguish a "typical" motion-cum-purpose pattern (*to*-infinitives in English, *a*-infinitives in Sicilian) from "special" patterns where the motion verbs lose some of their verbal features remind us of the features discussed above for pattern B in northern Mandarin. This hints at a cross-linguistic motivation for a close integration of motion and purpose predicates. Needless to say, the morphosyntactic features exhibited by specific patterns in specific languages, together with the degree of event integration shown by the motion event and the purposive action in these patterns, have to be investigated one by one. We hope that the present study will contribute to this goal.

**Acknowledgements:** The present chapter expands on a paper entitled "An Associated Motion Approach to Northern Mandarin MOTION-CUM-PURPOSE Patterns", which was given at the 25th Conference of the International Association of Chinese Linguistics (IACL-25), Budapest, June 2017. It has benefited from discussions with and comments from many colleagues as well as comments from them. I am especially grateful to Philippe Bourdin for his careful reading of an earlier draft of this paper, and for his insightful comments and suggestions. The ideas developed in this chapter also benefited from discussions on associated motion during working sessions of a research project of the French CNRS-TUL, Typology and Linguistics Universals (FRE 2559) named "Dynamic Deixis" (2015–2018). Errors and misinterpretations remain my sole responsibility.

# References

Belkadi, Aïcha. 2015. Associated motion with deictic directionals: A comparative overview. *Soas Working Papers in Linguistics* 17: 49–76.
Bjorkman, Bronwyn. 2016. Go get, come see: motion verbs, morphological restrictions, and syncretism. *Natural Language & Linguistic Theory* 34 (1): 53–91.
Bourdin, Philippe. 2006. The marking of Directional Deixis in Somali. How typologically idiosyncratic is it? In *Studies in African Linguistic Typology*, F.K. Erhard Voeltz (ed.), 13–41. (Typological Studies in Language 64.) Amsterdam/Philadelphia: John Benjamins.
Cardinaletti, Anna, and Giusti, Giuliana. 2001. "Semi-lexical" motion verbs in Romance and Germanic. In *Semi-lexical categories: The function of content words and the content of functions words*, Norbert Corver et Henk van Riemsdijk (eds.), 371–414. (Studies in Generative Grammar.) Berlin/New York: Mouton De Gruyter.

Cao, Guangshun, and Yu, Hsiao-jung. 2000. The influence of translated later Han Buddhist Sutras on the development of the Chinese disposal construction. *Cahiers de Linguistique – Asie Orientale* 29 (2): 151–177.

Cáo, Zhìyún 曹志耘 (ed.) 2008. *Hànyǔ Fāngyán Dìtújí* [Linguistic Atlas of Chinese Dialects]. Běijīng: Commercial Press.

Chao, Yuen Ren. 1968. *A Grammar of Spoken Chinese*. Berkeley: University of California Press.

Charolles, Michel, and Lamiroy, Béatrice. 2002. Syntaxe phrastique et transphrastique : du but au résultat. In *Macro-syntaxe et macro-sémantique*, Actes du colloque international d'Århus, 17–19 mai 2001, Hanne Leth Andersen & Henning Nølke (eds.), 383–419. (Sciences pour la communication). Bern : Peter Lang.

Cheung, Samuel Hung-nin, in collaboration with Sze-yun Liu and Li-lin Shih 1994 *A Practical Chinese Grammar*. Hong Kong: The Chinese University Press.

Cuī, Dásòng. 催達送 2005. *Zhōnggu Hànyǔ wèiyí dòngcí yánjiū* [Studies on Middle Chinese Motion Verbs]. Héféi: Ānhuī Dàxué Chūbǎnshè.

de la Fuente, José Andrés Alonso and Jacques, Guillaume. 2017. Associated motion in Manchu in typological perspective. Workingpaper published on Academia Edu.

Fàn, Xiāo 范曉 (ed.) 1998 *Hànyǔ de jùzi lèixíng* [Chinese Sentence Patterns]. Tàiyuán: Shūhǎi Chūbǎnshè.

Fáng, Yùqīng. 房玉清 1992. *Shíyòng Hànyǔ yǔfǎ* [A Practical Grammar of Chinese]. Beijing: Běijīng Yǔyánxuéyuàn Chūbǎnshè. (A revised edition was published in 1992 from the Peking University Press)

Féng, Shènglì. 2009. On Modern Written Chinese, *Journal of Chinese Linguistics* 37 (1): 145–162.

Gān, Lù, and Gān, Lín. 甘露、甘霖 2009. Qiānxī yóu "lái"、 "qù" gòuchéng de liándòngjù, *Zhōngzhōu Dàxué Xuébào* [Journal of Zhongzhou University] 4: 79–81.

Guillaume, Antoine. 2016. Associated motion in South America: typological and areal perspectives. *Linguistic Typology* 20 (1): 81–177.

Hashimoto, Mantaro. 1986. The Altaicization of Northern Chinese. In *Contributions to Sino-Tibetan Studies*, John McCoy & Timothy Light (eds.) 76–97. Leiden: Brill.

Haspelmath, Martin. 1989. From purposive to infinitive – A universal path of grammaticalization. *Folia Linguistica Historica* X (1–2): 287–310 (Societas Linguistica Europaea).

Hēi, Wéiqiáng. 黑维强 2003. Jìndài Hànyǔ "qù +VP+qu" jù jiégòu lèixíng jíqí fāzhǎn [The structural type of "qù +VP+qu" and its development in pre-modern Chinese], *Lánzhōu Dàxué Xuébào* [Lanzhou University Journal] 6: 10–16.

Heine, Bernd, and Kuteva, Tania. 2005. *Language Contact and Grammatical Change*. Cambridge: Cambridge University Press.

Hóu, Jīngyī. 侯精一 1981. Píngyáo fāngyán de dòngbǔshì [Verb-Result compounds in the Pingyao dialect]. *Yǔwén Yánjiū* [Language Studies] 2: 119–127.

Hóu, Jīngyī and Wēn, Duānzhèng. 侯精一、溫端政 1993. *Shānxī fāngyán diàochá yánjiū bàogào* [A survey and research report on Shanxi dialects]. Tàiyuán: Shānxī Gāoxiào Liánhé Chūbǎnshè.

Jacques, Guillaume. 2013. Harmonization and disharmonization of affix ordering and basic word order. *Linguistic Typology* 17: 187–215.

Koch, Harold. 1984. The category of 'Associated Motion' in Kaytej. *Language in Central Australia* 1: 23–34.

Kē, Lǐsī, and Liú, Shūxué. 柯理思、劉淑學 2001. Héběi Jìzhōu fāngyán "nábuliǎozǒu" yí lèi de géshì [Potential patterns such as "nábuliǎozǒu" in the Jizhou dialect of Hebei]. *Zhōngguó Yǔwén* [Chinese Language] 5: 428–438.

Lamarre, Christine. 2008. The Linguistic Categorization of Deictic Direction in Chinese: With Reference to Japanese. In *Space in Languages of China: Cross-linguistic, synchronic and diachronic perspectives*, Dan Xu (ed.), 69–97. Cham/Heidelberg: Springer.

Lamarre, Christine, Vittrant, Alice, Kopecka, Anetta, Voisin, Sylvie, Bon, Noellie, Fagard, Benjamin, Grinevald, Colette, Moyse-Faurie, Colette, Risler, Annie, Song, Jinke, Tan, Adeline, Voirin, Clément. (Submitted) Deictic directionals revisited in the light of advances in typology. In Laure Sarda and Benjamin Fagard (eds.). *Neglected Aspects of Motion Events Description*.

Lehmann, Christian. 2015. *Thoughts on grammaticalization*. 3rd edition. Berlin: Language Science Press. (First edition 1995)

Lǐ, Hóngróng. 李紅容 2016. *Xiàndài Hànyǔ liánwèishì zhuāntí yánjiū – jiānlùn liánwèishì zài Yuènányǔ zhōng de duìyìng biǎodá yǔ jiàoxué* [A Study of Serial Verb Constructions in Contemporary Chinese. With an attention toits corresponding patterns in Vietnamese and to its teaching]. Ph. D diss., Shanghai Normal University.

Liáng, Yínfēng. 梁銀峰 2004. Hànyǔ shìtài zhùcí '*lái*' de chǎnshēng shídài jíqí láiyuán [The origins and the time of emergence of the sentence-final tense particle *lai*], *Zhōngguó Yǔwén* [Chinese Language] 4: 333–342.

Liáng, Yínfēng. 梁銀峰 2007a. Hànyǔ shìtài zhùcí '*qù*' de xíngchéng guòchéng [The emergence of the sentence-final tense particle '*qù*']. In *Hànyǔ qūxiàng dòngcí de yǔfǎhuà* [The Grammaticalization of Chinese Directional Verbs], 140–151, Shanghai: Xuélín Chūbǎnshè

Liáng, Yínfēng. 梁銀峰 2007b. Mùdì biāojì '*lái*' '*qù*' de xíngchéng guòchéng [The development of purpose markers *lai* and *qu*], *Hànyǔ qūxiàng dòngcí de yǔfǎhuà* [The Grammaticalization of Chinese Directional Verbs], 197–208, Shanghai: Xuélín Chūbǎnshè

Liú, Chénghuì. 劉承慧 2012. Shànggǔ dào zhōnggǔ "lái" zài gòushìzhōng de yǎnbiàn [The Changes of *lai* in the Frame of Constructions from Pre-Qin to Medieval Chinese], Language & Linguistics 13(2): 247–287.

Liú, Dānqīng. 劉丹青 2000. Yuèyǔ jùfǎ de lèixíngxué tèdiǎn [The typological characteristics of Cantonese syntax]. *Asia Pacific Journal of Language in Education* 3 (2): 1–30.

Liú, Yuèhuá. 劉月華 (ed.) 1998. *Qūxiàng bǔyǔ tōngshì* [Directional Complements: A Compendium]. Běijīng: Běijīng Yǔyán Wénhuà Dàxué.

Lù, Jiǎnmíng. 陸儉明 1985. Guānyú "qù VP" hé "VP qu" jùshì [On the patterns '*qù* VP' and 'VP *qu*']. *Yǔyán Jiàoxué yǔ Yánjiū* [Language Teaching and Linguistic Studies ] 4: 18–33.

Lù, Jiǎnmíng. 陸儉明 1989. "V *lái le*" shìxī [A tentative analysis of V + *lai* + *le*]. *Zhōngguó Yǔwén* [Chinese Language] 3: 161–69.

Lǚ, Shūxiāng. 呂叔湘 1980. *Xiàndài Hànyǔ Bābǎi Cí* [800 Words of Contemporary Chinese]. Běijīng: Commercial Press.

Mullie, Joseph. 1937. *The Structural Principles of the Chinese Language. An Introduction to the Spoken Language (Northern Pekingese Dialect), Volumes II and III*. Pei-p'ing: Pei-t'ang Lazarist Press.

Paris, Marie-Claude, and Peyraube, Alain. 1993. L'iconicité : un nouveau dogme de la syntaxe chinoise? *Faits de langue* 1: 69–78.

Paul, Waltraud. 2008. The *serial verb construction* in Chinese: A tenacious myth and a Gordian knot. *The Linguistic Review* 25 (3/4): 367–411.

Qián, Zēngyí. 錢曾怡 2010. *Hànyǔ Guānhuà Fāngyán Yánjiū* [Studies on Mandarin Dialects]. Jǐnán: Qílǔ Shūshè.

Schmidtke-Bode, Karsten. 2009. *A typology of purpose clauses*. Amsterdam/Philadelphia: John Benjamins.

Tai, James H-Y. 2002. Temporal sequence in Chinese: A rejoinder. In *Form and Function: Linguistic Studies in Honor of Shuanfan Huang*, Lily I-wen Su, Chin-fa Lien and Kawai Chui (eds.), 331–351. Taipei: Crane Publishing Co.

Tang, Zhengda, and Lamarre, Christine. 2007. A contrastive study of the linguistic encoding of motion events in Standard Chinese and in the Guanzhong dialect of Mandarin (Shaanxi). *Bulletin of Chinese Linguistics* 2 (1): 135–168.

Voisin, Sylvie. 2013. Expressions de trajectoire dans quelques langues atlantiques. In *Faits de Langues. Sémantique des relations spatiales*, Catherine Chauvin (ed.), 42: 131–152. Berne : Peter Lang.

Vuillermet, Marine. 2012. Une typologie en cheminement : contribution de l'ese ejja à l'étude du mouvement associé. *Lidil* 46 (Typologie et description linguistiques): 79–99.

Wilkins, David. 1991. The semantic, pragmatics, and diachronic development of associated motion in Mparntwe Arrernte. *Buffalo Papers in Linguistics* 91(1): 207–257 (SUNY – University of Buffalo).

Yáng, Yǒnglóng. 楊永龍 2012. *Mùdì gòushì* "VP qu" *yǔ SOV yǔxù de guānlián* [The purpose construction "VP qu" in Chinese and SOV order]. *Zhōngguó Yǔwén* [Chinese Language] 6: 525–536.

Yáng, Yǒnglóng. 2013. *Hànyǔ zhōubiàn yǔyán yǔ* "VP qu" *yǒuguān de yǔxù guānlián* [The word order correlations related to "VP + qu (GO)" of the languages in the vicinity of Mandarin Chinese]. *Lìshǐ Yǔyánxué Yánjiū* [Studies in Historical Linguistics] 6: 342–358.

Zhāng, Liánróng. 張聯榮 2010. *Duì shànggǔ zhì zhōnggǔ shíqī* "*lái*+VP" *jiégòu de chūbù kǎochá* [A preliminary investigation on structure "*Lái* + VP" from ancient to medieval times]. *Hànyǔshǐ Xuébào* [Journal of the History of Chinese] 10: 57–68.

Zhāng, Měilán. 張美蘭 2009. *Míng-Qīng Yùwài Guānhuà Wénxiàn Yǔyán Yánjiū* [A linguistic Study of Mandarin Documents of the Ming-Qing Period]. Chángchūn: Dōngběi Shīfàn Dàxué Chūbǎnshè.

Zhū, Déxī. 朱德熙 1982. *Yǔfǎ Jiǎnggyì* [A Course in Grammar]. Běijīng: Commercial Press.

Janet Zhiqun Xing and Axel Schuessler
# Semantic extension in Old Chinese: Direction, transitivity, and voice

## 1 Introduction

Old Chinese (OC) is the literary language of ancient China from the Shang dynasty oracle bone inscriptions (ca. 1250–1050 BC), the early Zhou dynasty bronze inscriptions and their contemporaneous classics *Shījīng* 詩經 (Book of Songs), *Shūjīng* 書經 (Book of History), and *Yìjīng* 易經 (Book of Changes), to the mid and late Zhou period historical and philosophical texts up to the unification of China starting with the Qín dynasty (221BC). While the logographic writing has changed little in the past 3000 years, the pronunciation of words, of course, has. The expression 不好 still means 'it is not good' today just as it meant 3000 years ago, but though we know that in Modern Standard Chinese it is pronounced *bù hǎo*, we cannot be absolutely sure of the pronunciation 3000 years ago; we can surmise that it probably was phonemically something like \*bə hûʔ, where the symbol ˆ in Schuessler (2007) indicates some still unknown feature that arose from Middle Chinese (MC) around 600 AD in a certain syllable type, the so-called "Division I/IV".

Since OC was not recorded in an alphabetic script, its sounds need to be reconstructed. The point of departure is the MC rhyming dictionary *Qièyùn* 切韻 (601 AD); the composition of the graphs that have been created since the beginning of writing, provides phonological clues (the 'phonetic series' or *xiéshēng* 諧聲). OC reconstruction is, unfortunately, in large measure a matter of interpretation of the graphs and other meagre data. The most plausible OC system is Baxter's (1992), predominantly based on suggestions by earlier scholars (cf. Schuessler 2009). Proliferating post-Baxter (1992) attempts are not so much based on what is actually knowable based on the data we have, but, rather, rely on stacks of hypotheses. However, today most agree (with Baxter, Schuessler, and others) that OC had an *s*-suffix, a final -ʔ, and a morphological feature of initial consonant voicing (by MC at least) which some believe to be the result of an OC nasal prefix \*N- and/or \*m-. These morphemes are the subject of this study.

This chapter will be organized as follows: Section 2 introduces and classifies data collected from Schuessler's ABC Etymological Dictionary of Old Chinese (2007). Section 3 analyzes morphological structures and morphological processes prevalent in OC. Section 4 discusses how those morphological processes relate to issues of grammaticalization and lexicalization raised in the introductory chapter of this volume, and Section 5 summaries the findings of this study.

## 2 Word types

### 2.1 Data

Based on syntactic, semantic, and discourse-pragmatic functions as well as reconstructed morphological derivations of lexical items in OC texts (from 1250 BC to 220 BC) and MC (about 600 AD), forty-eight lexical items have been collected and classified into four prototype meanings: nominal, stative, intransitive, and transitive (cf. Schuessler 2007), as summarized in Table 1. Additionally, two criteria were used when collecting the data: 1) logographic forms from OC to MC have to be the same or similar;[1] 2) morpho-phonemic cognates must share the same root form.

**Table 1:** Lexical items used for this study.

| Types | Lexical Items | # of Tokens |
| --- | --- | --- |
| Nominal | *děng* 等 'step', *guān* 棺 'coffin', *guàn* 冠 'crown', *nǚ* 女 'woman', *yī* 衣 'clothes', *yǔ* 雨 'rain', *zhōng* 中 'center', *zhǒng* 種 'seed' | 8 |
| Stative | *hǎo* 好 'be good', *hòu* 後 'be behind', *jìn* 近 'be near', *shàng* 上 'be up', *xià* 下 'be down', *xiān* 先 'be ahead', *yòu* 右 'be to the right', *yuǎn* 遠 'be far way', *zuǒ* 左 'be to the left' | 9 |
| Intransitive | *chū* 出 'to come out', *chù* 處 'to sit down', *jiàng* 降 'to descend', *jué* 覺 'to wake up', *lái* 來 'to come', *sǐ* 死 'to die', *zhǎng* 長 'to grow', *gān* 甘 'to be sweet' | 8 |
| Transitive | *bài* 敗 'to defeat', *bié* 別 'to separate', *dān* 擔 'to carry on the shoulder', *huài* 壞 'to destroy', *hán* 含 'to hold in the mouth', *jiān* 監 'to inspect', *jiàn* 見 'to see', *mǎi* 買 'to buy', *mài* 賣 'to sell', *qù* 去 'to remove', *shí* 食 'to eat', *shì* 視 'to look at', *shòu* 受 'to receive', *wēi* 威 'to scare', *wèi* 畏 'to fear', *wén* 聞 'to hear about', *xué* 學 'to learn', *yǐn* 飲 'to drink', *yǔ* 語 'to talk about', *yǒu* 有 'to have', *zhāng* 張 'to draw (a bow), *zhī* 織 'to weave', *zhí* 執 'to grasp' | 23 |
| Total | | 48 |

---

[1] Similar logographic forms refer to lexical items that share the same phonetic root of a character and whose semantic functions are historically related. For instance, *wén* 聞 'to hear' > *wèn* 問 'to ask'.

## 2.2 Verb classes

Like the English words 'dog' and 'run', the overwhelmingly monosyllabic words of OC are not marked for word class. Word class, together with meaning, is an inherent lexical characteristic. A fundamental distinction can be made between grammatical particles (yě 也, mā 嗎, hū 乎, yǐ 以/矣/已, etc.), nouns, and verbs. Particles are easily identified from their meaning and function in a sentence. Noun classification is largely notional ('dog', 'law', 'virtue' are obviously nouns; some words function both as nouns and verbs, e.g. rén 仁 verb 'be kind'; noun 'human-heartedness'). While it is possible to employ a noun syntagmatically as a verb assigning it the causative/putative meaning of 'treat someone like X,' this happens only on rare occasions. Only verbs (including nouns used as verbs) can be negated with a preceding bù 不 'not' and its verbal function can thus be identified. Here we will concerned ourselves mostly with verbs.

Verbs fall into three major categories: transitive, intransitive, and stative. They can be identified by their different syntactic behaviors.

### 2.2.1 Transitive verbs

Transitive (tr.) verbs normally require an object, as jiàn 見 'to see', or shí 食 'to eat' in (1) – (2).

(1) 孟子見梁惠王 [Mengzi I, 1]
    *Méngzǐ jiàn Liáng-Huì-wáng*
    Name see country-name-king
    'Mengzi visited king Hui of (the state of) Liang.'

(2) 日有食之 [Zuǒzhuàn, Huángōng 17th year]
    *rì    yǒu   shí zhī*
    Sun there-be eat 3SG
    'As for the sun (topic), there was (something) that ate it
    (i.e. there was a solar eclipse).'

When a transitive verb appears in a sentence without an object, there are three possible explanations: (a) the verb has a passive use, as shí 食 'to eat' >'to be eaten' in (3); (b) the verb is used intransitively, e.g. jiàn 見 'to see' as in (4); and (c) a known (and aforementioned) object may be implied. These and all other syntagmatic uses apply to any transitive verb with entirely predictable syntactic functions and meanings. Thus, a hypothetical phrase 羊食 *yáng shí* 'lit. sheep eat' could mean, depending on context: (a) passive 'the sheep was eaten', or (b) intransitive 'the sheep was eating/munching'; or (c) 'the sheep ate it' (something implied).

(3) 日食 [Zuǒzhuàn, Zhāogōng 31st year]
   rì   shí
   sun eat
   'The sun was eaten.' (i.e., there was a solar eclipse.)

(4) 視之不見，聽之不聞 [Liezi 1]
   shì   zhī bù jiàn, tīng zhī bù wén
   look-at 3SG NEG see listen 3SG NEG hear
   'What (he) looks at he does not see; what (he) listens to (he) does not hear.'

### 2.2.2 Intransitive verbs

Intransitive verbs are normally not followed by objects as illustrated by *sǐ* in (5). While an intransitive (intr.) verb can be followed by a noun, it is not the object; rather, it is almost always a verbal complement, as with *sǐ* in (6) or *chū* in 出門 *chū mén* 'come out the door' (not tr./causative: 'take out the door').

(5) 無草不死 [Shījīng 201, 3]
   wú   cǎo   bù   sǐ
   NEG grass NEG die
   '(There is) no grass that is not dying'.

(6) 余命汝死我家 [Western Zhōu Bronze Inscription]
   yú   mìng   rǔ   sǐ   wǒ   jiā
   1SG charge 2SG die 1SG home
   'I charge you to die in our family.' (i.e., 'to serve for life in our family' – this can never mean 'kill our family'.)

There are rare exceptions where a following noun is the object, thus giving the intr. verb a causative (in this case putative 'consider … ') meaning as shown in (7).

(7) 胡為而死其親乎？ [Liji, Tangong I, III, 6]
   hú   wèi   ér   sǐ   qí   qīn   hū
   how act and die POSS parent PART
   'How could (those ancients) have acted and considered their parents as if dead?'

## 2.2.3 Stative verbs

Stative verbs correspond to adjectives in Western languages, but they are, nonetheless, verbs (cf. Dong in this volume). Thus *hǎo* 好 means 'to be good, fine, beautiful' (not just 'good') and is negatable with *bù* 不 (*bù hǎo* 不好 'be not good, it is not good' is a complete sentence); this applies to all 'stative verbs': *měi* 美 'be beautiful', *gāo* 高 'be high', or *yuǎn* 遠 'be far', as in (8).

(8) 遠, 莫致之 [Shījīng 59, 1]
    *yuǎn,   mò   zhì   zhī*
    far-away NEG reach you
    '(You are) far away, and (I) cannot come to you.'

Beside their application as verbs, these words can also function as adjectives modifying a noun: *měi huá* 美華 'beautiful flower', *gāo shān* 高山 'high mountain'. When modifying verbs, such words function as adverbs: *hǎo kàn* 好看 'good to look at'.

Stative verbs can take objects, which turns them into causatives ('make/let X do … ') or putatives ('consider X to be … ', 'think X to be … '). Thus, such verbs can be distinguished from transitive verbs by their causative/putative meaning as *yuǎn* in (9)

(9) 不遠千里而來 [Mengzi 1A, 1]
    *bù   yuǎn   qiān   lǐ   ér   lái*
    NEG be-far thousand mile PART come
    'You have not considered a thousand miles too far to come.'

What has been described so far is purely syntagmatic or grammatical behavior with changes in meaning. This applies to all verbs in their respective classes, and is entirely predictable.

# 3 OC morphology

To change a word's grammatical features or valency such as transitivity, voice or direction and with it, its semantic and syntagmatic behavior, requires a morphological marking, i.e. a suffix or prefix or some kind of phonetic change in the root. None of these morphological processes are inflections in the Indo-European sense, where morphological changes correspond with semantic and syntagmatic changes. In OC, the morphological changes result in new, independent words with their own word class and corresponding syntactic/semantic behavior, even though their written forms may stay the same as they were before the change occurred.

Can a noun be changed into a verb, an intransitive or stative verb into a transitive one or a transitive verb into a causative one? As explained in Section 2, neither can be done syntactically, because the result can only be causative/putative. However, These and other changes can be accomplished with the OC suffix *-s (> MC qùshēng, one source of Modern Standard Chinese tone 4), the suffix *-ʔ (> MC shǎngshēng > Modern Standard Chinese 3rd tone), and by voicing of the initial consonant.

The grammatical/morphological functions of *-s, *-ʔ and initial voicing have been much debated for two reasons: (1) since derivations often happen to be nouns or verbs, there is a tendency to project clearly marked Indo-European-like word classes onto OC; but these derivations in OC do not behave like morphological markings in IE languages and, (2) as the functions of these morphemes tend to be elusive, we must recognize that a morpheme "B" may stand in opposition to another well-defined morpheme "A", and as such "B" may represent the diffuse catch-all category "non-A", as we shall see.

Note that these morphological derivations are not grammatical but lexical, creating new word meanings. The information about the readings of graphs or written forms in the early literature is derived from the Han period and from post-Han commentatories, such as Lù Démíng's *Jīngdiǎn shìwén* 經典釋文(JDSW, 582–589 AD). For graphs that have multiple readings, JDSW suggests the correct one for a given sentence in a classical text, whether, for example, 好 is to be read hǎo or hào, or 見 is to be read jiàn or xiàn. Two issues have been raised with the JDSW, though. Some scholars (see Downer 1959) believe that the tonal distinctions claimed by JDSW do not, in fact, go back to pre-Han times but, rather, arose later. Others, however, (e.g. Schuessler 2007; Downer 1959; Chou 1962) rely on this work (with some well-advised reservations), for reasons given by Downer (1959: 264) and Baxter (1992: 316). For example, wēi 威 'scare' and wèi 畏 'fear' must have been two distinct words and therefore already morpho-phonologically differentiated in Shang and early Zhou texts, even though wēi is often written 畏, and even though JDSW is not always definitive and is, in fact, sometimes contradictory about the correct reading. Distinctions like 'scare' vs. 'fear' or 'watch' vs. 'show' cannot have been made up by bookish post-Han scholars.

The second problem with JDSW is that, according to Lù Démíng (and later dictionaries), some graphs have more than one possible reading in a given context. Downer (1959) strictly eliminated such graphs from consideration, and so, scholars who have since relied on the nearly exhaustive material of Downer and Chou, have done the same.

## 3.1 Exoactive (increasing valency), OC *s*-suffix I (> MC *qùshēng*)

In the earliest literature, the morpheme *-s* (in some OC transcriptions *-h*) had two functions: (1) increasing valency and thus creating transitive or causative derivations, and marking extroversion, and (2) forming passives. This OC *-s* is now widely accepted. It is the only source of the MC *qùshēng* 去聲 (departing tone, one of the sources of Mandarin tone 4). The morphological role of *qùshēng* has long been noted. A systematic sorting of the different functions of this tonal derivation has been attempted by, among others, Wang (1958: 212–218), and more fully by Downer (1959) and Chou (1962: 1–96).

Downer (1959) identified 14 different functions of *qùshēng*, leaving the impression that it is used to derive any word from any other; he concedes that this may have been the case from the beginning (p. 262). After Downer and Chou, scholars have attempted to reduce the categories of *qùshēng*'s functions. Mei (2000 [1980], 2012) identified the derivation of nouns from verbs in the earliest layer of the language, and subsequently also introvert vs. extrovert (as in *mǎi* 買 'to buy' vs. *mài* 賣 'to sell'). Though his work is primarily concerned with phonology, Baxter (1992: 314ff) recognizes deverbal nouns and denominal verbs created with this suffix. Baxter & Sagart (2014: 58f) come to the same conclusion as Mei without mentioning him, but state that *-s* "is a very common suffix with many functions, only a few of which are well understood."

Schuessler's (2007) method for identifying functions for *-s* is to restrict the corpus to minimal contrasting pairs in the earliest (Western Zhou) texts (*Shījīng* 詩經, *Shūjīng* 書經, *Yìjīng* 易經). A clear and simple picture emerges from the data suggesting, therefore, that the derivation by *-s* must have been a reality then. He (Schuessler 2007: 40–46) suggests that in early (Western) Zhou literature, *-s* had two functions: to form new passive words, which could belong to almost any word class, and to derive new word meanings with increases in valency. Confusingly, this *qùshēng* (a) does not mark word classes in the Indo-European sense, but creates passive as well as transitive/causative functions, and therefore (b) by the late Zhou, the Han period and later, it seems to derive any kind of word from any other kind of word; it seems to mark derivation in general. However, when investigating the texts of the early Zhou period, functions can be clearly identified. The mix-up and blurring occurs later. Thus, it is not surprising to find the same morpheme developing transitive and passive functions, as we will explain below.

### 3.1.1 Noun > verb

This *s*-suffix increases functional valency and, as such, it derives verbs from nouns as shown in (10). A derivation may even be ditransitive (direct object with an added indirect object) as shown in (11)

(10) a. yī 衣 *ʔəi 'clothes' (all OC stared forms are OCM)
　　 b. + *-s > *ʔəi-s tr. 'to put on (clothes), wear'
　　　　 衣衣　yì yī　/ *ʔəi-s ʔəi　[Yi Zhoushu 37, 9]
　　　　 '(They) wore clothes.'

(11)　載衣之裼 [Shījīng 189, 9]
　　　 zài　yì　　zhī　　tì
　　　 then dress them wrappers
　　　 'Then (they) dressed them [the babies] in wrappers.'

### 3.1.2 Stative verb > transitive verb

The stative verb (sv.) hǎo 'be fond of' overlaps semantically with 'consider good'. Therefore, it is not wrong to say hǎo yuè 好樂 'to consider music good'. However, instead, hào is used to express a newly developed transitive meaning as shown in (12). Unlike hǎo, hào cannot mean 'cause something to be good' and is restricted exclusively to the specialized meaning 'to consider music good'. Thus, the syntactic and semantic functions of the derivation only partially overlap with the simplex morphological form.

(12)　a.　hǎo 好 *hûʔ　sv. 'to be good'
　　　 b.　+ *-s > hào 好 *hû-s　tr. 'to be fond of':
　　　　　 好樂 [Mengzi 1B, 1]
　　　　　 hào yuè
　　　　　 'be fond of music'

Another example is yuǎn 遠 *wanʔ 'be far' as illustrated in (8). It can be used putatively to express the meaning 'to consider to be far'. However, with the derivation yuàn 遠 *wan-s 'to keep at a distance, put at a distance' it is simply transitive and not causative as shown in (13a). Just like any transitive verb, yuàn can syntagmatically be used to express a passive meaning as shown in (13b) (cf. example shí 食 in (3)).

(13)　a.　遠父母兄弟 [Shījīng 39, 2]
　　　　　 yuàn　　　fùmǔ　　xiōngdì
　　　　　 keep-distance parents brothers
　　　　　 '(When a girl marries) she goes far away from parents and brothers.'
　　　　　 (She does not 'consider' parents and brothers to be distant, nor does she 'cause' them to be distant.)

b. 我思不遠 [Shījīng 54, 2]
   wǒ sī bù yuǎn
   1SG thoughts NEG far
   'My thoughts cannot be kept away.'

### 3.1.3 Intransitive verb > transitive, causative (actually 'permissive')

We have seen above that intransitive verbs can be followed by nouns which are verbal complements. But to make intransitive verbs transitive, the *s*-suffix must be attached, as shown in (14).

(14) a. *lái* 來 *\*rəʔ* or *\*rək* intr. 'to come' (in the Shījīng, the word rhymes at times with *\*-əʔ*, in other places with *\*-ək*)
     b. +-*s* > *lài* 賚 *\*rək-s* tr. ('to bring' such things as rewards:)
        'to reward'
        賚我思成 [Shījīng 302, 2]
        *lài wǒ sī chéng*
        reward 1SG these success
        '(The ancestors) reward us with these successes.'
        (ditransitive use)

### 3.1.4 Transitive verb > causative

The usual transitive use of a transitive verb cannot be causative, hence the valency-increasing *\*-s* is needed to express the meaning 'cause x …' or 'let someone do x …'. These derivations seem to be permissive causatives ('let x do y'), e.g. *mǎi* 買 *\*mrêʔ* 'to buy something' tr. > *mài* 賣 *\*mrê-s* ('to let someone buy something') 'to sell something to someone' ditransitive. Or *shí* 食 *\*m-lək* tr. 'to eat' (cf. example (2) 日有食之 'the sun had something that ate it'). 食 *\*m-lək + -s > sì* 食, 飤 *\*s-lək-s* tr. = causative ('let someone eat' >) 'to give food to, feed' as shown in (15). In this *\*m-lək ~ \*s-lək-s* set, the prefixes are remnants of the Sino-Tibetan protolanguage (cf. Tibeto-Burman *\*mlak ~ \*slak*); these prefixes were either no longer understood in OC, or were not understood as permissive, hence the addition of the productive valency-increasing suffix *\*-s*:

(15) 曷飲食之 [Shījīng 123, 1]
     *hé yìn (\*ʔəm-s) sì (\*s-lək-s) zhī*
     what drink eat PART
     'What shall (I) give them to drink and eat?'

It should be noted that some OC words have preserved the Sino-Tibetan causative *s*-prefix. This is a genuine causative marker. In most words with nasal initials, the *s*-prefix devoiced the sonorant (already in OC) and was subsequently lost (voicelessness is usually indicated by *\*h-* in reconstructions), e.g. *xuè/miè* 威 *\*hmet* 'cause destruction', derived from *miè* 滅 *\*met* 'destroy, extinguish'. Because both verbs are transitive and are often glossed 'extinguish, destroy', the causative meaning of *xuè* can be missed (or even denied, as by Sagart & Baxter 2012: 32f), yet it is clear in *Shījīng* Ode 192, 8, as shown in (16) (cf. Mei 2012: 10)

(16) 燎之方揚　*liáo zhī fāng yáng*　'When the fire is just flaming high,'
　　 寧或滅之　*níng huò **miè** zhī*　'How can anyone *extinguish* it? (*\*met*)'
　　 赫赫宗周　*hè hè Zōng Zhōu*　'The majestic Zōng Zhōu,'
　　 褒姒威之　*Bāo Sì **miè** (xuè) zhī*　'(Lady) Bāo Sì has *caused its ruin* (*\*hmet*).'

The essence of causativity is indirectness; someone extinguishing a fire by wielding a bucket of water is direct action; in (16), however, Bāo Sì did not destroy the Zhōu by direct action (e.g. by herself wielding a battle-ax), but was the cause of others doing so, therefore *\*hmet* is causative. This is true of *wén* > *wèn* in (17) and *hán* > *hàn* in (18).

(17)　*wén* 聞 *\*mən*　　tr. 'to hear, hear about'
　　　*wèn* 問 *\*məns*　tr. 'to ask someone about something'
　　　　　　　　　　　　(lit. perhaps 'let me hear about it')

(18)　*hán* 含函 *\*gə̂m*　　tr. 'have in the mouth'
　　　*hàn* 含　 *\*gə̂ms*　tr. 'to put into the mouth, resent' (is 'resent' perhaps passive because something has *been put* into the mouth?)

### 3.1.5 Introvert~extrovert pairs

A striking pattern can be seen in transitive verb pairs in which one of the verbs is introvert and transitive (whenever possible ending in *shǎngshēng* 上聲 < *\*-ʔ*) and the other, extrovert and ditransitive (i.e. increase in valency). This is the only *qùshēng* derivation that Mei (2000: 339) recognizes as old (but younger than deverbal nouns), and he classifies such pairs "endodirectional" (內向動詞 *nèixiàng dòngcí*) vs. "exodirectional" (外向動詞 *wàixiàng dòngcí*); therefore the labels 'endo-/exo-' in our terminology below. Note that both members of the pair are transitive, as illustrated in (19).

(19) a. shòu 受 *duʔ   tr. 'to receive, accept':
受年 [Oracle Bones, Menzies 1812 III]
shòu  nián
receive year
'(We will) receive a harvest.'

b. + *-s > shòu 授 *dus   tr. ('to let/have/make receive' >)
'to give someone something'
(because of later phonetic changes, the two contrasting words are homophones of shòu in Modern Standard Chinese.)
授 宗人彝 [Shūjīng 42, 27]
shòu zōng    rén   jiǎ
hand assistant master vessel
'(He) handed the vessel to the assistant master of rites.'
(lit. 'temple person') (Karlgren's 1950 translation)

Additional pairs include (20)–(22)

(20) a. mǎi 買    *mrêʔ    tr. 'to buy'
     b. mài 賣    *mrê-s   tr. ('to let buy':) 'to sell'

(21) a. shì 視    *giʔ     tr. 'to look at'
     b. shì 示視  *gi-s    tr. ('to let someone look at sth'.:) 'to show'

(22) a. yǐn 飲    *ʔəmʔ    tr. 'to drink'
     b. yìn 飲    *ʔəm-s   tr. 'give someone sth. to drink'

Inspired by Mei (2000[1980]), we use the terms 'endoactive' vs. 'exoactive' in such pairs, but use them for all derivations with the morphemes *-ʔ and *-s respectively. As we will see in Sections 3.2–3.4, there are also endo-/exo- sets that are non-active, hence "passive". These pairs could also be seen as converse antonyms, but most derivations in *-ʔ and *-s do not belong to pairs, they are not the converse of anything (see examples (27) and (28), as well as those in section 3.1).

## 3.2 Exopassive: OC s-suffix II

Another function of *-s is to form **passive** derivatives from a simplex that can be a verb or even a noun as exemplified in (23):

(23) wén 聞 *mən    tr. 'to hear about, hear', + *-s > wèn 聞 *məns
pass. 'to be heard, be heard about, be famous' (homophonous with the valency-increasing causative 問 *məns tr. 'to ask'):

    a. 聲聞于外 [Shījīng 229, 5]
       shēng wèn     yú    wài
       sound be-heard PREP outside
       '(The instruments') sound is heard from the outside.'
       (cf. *JDSW* wèn).

    b. 故聲聞過情, 君子恥之 [Mengzi 4B, 18, 3]
       gù       shēng wén     guò   qíng,   jūn-zǐ
       therefore fame reputation exceed nature superior-man
       chǐ zhī
       is-ashamed-of 3SG
       'Therefore when his fame and reputation exceed his nature (i.e. merits), the superior man is ashamed of it.'

Often, the passive derivation is a noun as shown in (23b). This has led investigators to believe that one of the functions of *qùshēng* is to derive nouns from verbs (e.g. Downer 1959; Mei 2000[1980], 2012; repeated by Baxter & Sagart 2014). Yet, all the nouns in early texts are consistently passive (testable by the English paraphrase 'the thing that *has been x-ed*', not 'the thing that *is doing the x-ing*'). Since Indo-European type word classes are, in general, unmarked in OC, the noun classification is incidental to the passive as illustrated in (24)–(25).

(24)   a.    zhī    織 *tək   'to weave' tr.
           織席以為食 [Mengzi IIIA, 4, 1]
           zhī    xí    yǐ      wéi shí
           weave mat in-order to   eat
           '(They) wove mats (in order to eat:) for a living.'

    b.  +*-s > zhì    織 *tək+s > *tək-s 'woven' adj./pass.
        織文鳥章 [Shijing 177, 4]
        zhì      wén     niǎo zhāng
        woven pattern bird emblem
        '(On our flags) were woven patterns and bird emblems.'

(25)   a.    wēi 威   *ʔui   'to scare, overawe' tr.
           格則承之庸之, 否則威之 [Shūjīng 2, 14]
           gé    zé    chéng zhī yōng      zhī,   fǒu    zé      wēi      zhī
           come then receive them employ them, not    then     frighten them

'If they (the bad people) come, one receives them and employs them; if (they do) not (come), then one has overawed them.'

b. 畏天之威 [Shījīng 272]
   wèi tiān zhī wēi
   fear heaven POSS majesty
   'fear Heaven's majesty.'

c. +*-s > wèi 畏 *ʔui-s 'be scared, be awed' transitive = 'to fear, respect' tr./pass.
   宗邑無主，則民不威 [Zuǒzhuàn, Zhuang 28]
   zōng yì wú zhǔ, zé mín bù wēi
   ancestor city NEG ruler then people NEG overawe
   'When the ancestral city has no ruler, then the people are not overawed.'

Assuming for the sake of argument that 威 in (25) is not the result of scribal confusion, but that the active wēi 'to scare' is syntactically used without an object and is therefore passive ('are not scared/overawed'), a perfectly regular grammatical usage. One could just as well have used wèi 畏 ' ... then the people are not scared/overawed' or 'do not fear', where wèi is the active intransitive use of the verb 'fear'. Thus wēi and wèi have practically the same meaning in some contexts: one is an active verb used passively (wēi 'scare' > pass. 'be scared'), the other a passive verb 'be scared, fear' used as an active intransitive. This shows how words with and without qùshēng can be confused or merge in their meanings and usages, and, at the same time, explains how the distinctions of qùshēng derivations became unraveled so that by Han times, this tone is able derive anything from anything else. This may already have started during the Western Zhou as shown in (26).

(26) a. 天明畏 [Shūjīng 27, 9]
       tiān míng wèi
       heaven bright scare/majestic
       'Heaven is bright and (scary?:) majestic.'

   b. 天明威 [Shūjīng 34,2]
      tiān míng wēi
      heaven bright majesty
      'Heaven's bright majesty'

Comparing (26a) with (26b), we can see that, in the bronze inscriptions, both wēi and wèi were usually written 畏, even though 'scare' and 'fear' certainly must have been different words.

Passive is perhaps ultimately just another facet of valency modification; it is simply a reversal of the transitive/causative. Furthermore, in other languages, a morpheme may have opposing functions, such as the *-eru* forms in Japanese whose exoactives were derived from exopassives and vice versa (Shibatani 1990: 44f).

## 3.3 Endoactive, OC suffix *-ʔ (> MC *shǎngshēng*)

As seen earlier, the OC suffix *-ʔ marks introversion in transitive verbs. This *-ʔ must be a morpheme or a suffix, although it is not widely recognized (cf. Sagart 1999: 133f; Baxter 1992: 324). It also forms word derivations that do not belong to such obvious endo/exo (transitive/ditransitive) pairs, and which can be intransitive verbs (as 'to grow' in (27b)) or nouns (as 'stairs' in (28b)). These derivations which decrease valency are active in the sense that they are not passive, and introvert in the sense that they are not extrovert (cf. 'to buy' (20)). They can also be nouns whose active nature can be tested by the English paraphrase 'the thing that *is doing the x-ing*' which contrasts with the exo-passive *s*-suffix: 'the thing *that has been x-ed*' (again, 'noun' classification is incidental).

In short, this is a catch-all suffix for derivations that are not exopassive, hence "endoactive", even though these qualities may not be self-evident, as in the English translations 'to grow' intr., 'stairs' n., 'jaw' n., 'to buy' tr., etc.

(27) a. *zhāng* 張 *\*traŋ* 'to stretch, make long, draw (a bow)', tr.
既張我弓 [Shijing 180, 4]
*jì     zhāng  wǒ      gōng*
1st-PL draw   1st-PL  bow
'We drew our bows.'

b. +*-ʔ > *zhǎng* 長 *\*traŋʔ* 'to grow' intr.
生而長, 而大 [Lüshi chunqiu 3, 5]
*shēng ér zhǎng,   zhǎng ér dà*
bore and grow,    grow and big
'(Living things) are born and grow. (They) grow and become big…'

(28) a. *dēng* 登 *\*tôŋ* 'to ascend, rise, raise' intr.
登于岸 [Shījīng 241, 5]
*dēng    yú      àn*
ascend  COMP    bank
'(He) ascended a high bank.'

b. +*-ʔ > děng 等 *təŋʔ  ('the thing that is ascending, is going up':)
'step of stairs, degree, rank' n.
降一等 [Lunyu 10, 4, 5]
*jiàng   yī   děng*
descend one step
'(He) descended one step (of a flight of stairs).'

Many underived stative and intransitive verbs end in this *-ʔ (i.e. have the MC *shǎngshēng*), e.g. *sǐ* 死 *siʔ* 'to die', *zuò* 坐 *dzâiʔ* 'to sit', *chǔ* 處 *k-hlaʔ* 'to sit down, dwell', *yuǎn* 遠 *wanʔ* 'be far', *hǎo* 好 *hûʔ* 'be good', and so on. Such verbs are inherently introvert, therefore it is possible that the redundant *-ʔ is not chance or coincidence. The *-ʔ in most words is, in all probability, a Chinese innovation; for example, the Tibeto-Burman cognate to *sǐ* 死 *siʔ* 'to die' is *si* without a glottal catch (unlike *rǔ* 汝 *naʔ* 'you' = Tibeto-Burman *naʔ*; hence the OC *-ʔ in *rǔ* is apparently of Sino-Tibetan derivation.

As we have seen above, some of these words have derivatives with *-s, so that we find again *-ʔ/ *-s pairs that are, however, not overtly introvert/extrovert: 遠 *yuǎn /yuàn* and 好 *hǎo /hào* as illustrated in (12) and (13).

## 3.4 Endopassive; voicing of initial consonant (or *N-prefix?)

The voicing of a MC initial consonant is conventionally said to create intransitives from transitive verbs (e.g. Karlgren 1950; Chou 1962: 22). However, voicing does not predictably create an intransitive from a transitive verb, but rather a new word as shown in (29).

(29) a. *jiàn* 見   *kêns*   'to see, to visit someone' tr.:
孟子見梁惠王 [Meng 1A, 1]
*Mèng-zǐ jiàn Liáng Huì wáng*
Mengzi saw Liang Hui king
'Mengzi paid a visit to King Hui of Liang.'

b. + voicing: *xiàn* 現/見   *gêns*   (Sagart *N-kens)
'to appear, show up' intr.
朝暮見 [Mengzi 2B, 6]
*zhāo   mù   xiàn*
morning evening appear
'(The official) appeared mornings and evenings.'

By comparison, a passive use of a transitive word is unmarked as illustrated in (30a) (also see 2.1). The intransitive of *jiàn* 見 'to see' does not take an object in a sentence, as shown in (30b).²

(30) a. 他日見於王 [Meng 2B, 4]
   *tā    rì    jiàn    yú    wáng*
   other day see   by    king
   'Another day, he was (seen:) received by the king.'

   b. 視之不見，聽之不聞 [Liezi 1, p. 3b]
   *shì    zhī    bù    jiàn,    tīng    zhī    bù    wén*
   view   it    NEG   see,   listen   it    NEG   hear
   'What (he) looks at he does not see; what (he) listens to (he) does not hear.'

Additional examples of voicing:

(31) a. *gān* 甘 *\*kâm* 'be sweet' intr./sv.
   甘與子同夢 [Shījīng 96, 3]
   *gān    yú    zǐ    tóng    mèng*
   sweet   with   you   same   dream
   'It is sweet to lie dreaming with you.'

   b. *gān* 甘 *\*kâm*, putative use
   飢者甘食，渴者甘飲 [Mengzi 7A, 27]
   *jī    zhě    gān    shí,    kě    zhě    gān    yǐn*
   hungry person sweet food thirsty person sweet drink
   'Someone who is starving thinks (all) food (sweet:) well-tasting; someone who is thirsty considers (all) drink (sweet:) well-tasting.'

   c. + voicing > *hān* 酣 *\*gâm* 'get drunk' intr.?
   在今後嗣王酣身 [Shujing 30, 11]
   *zài jīn    hòu-sì-wáng hān    shēn*
   at current-time successor   get-drunk body
   'Their successors in our time made themselves drunk.'

---

**2** Mei (2012: 10f) turns the argument around. He considers the voiced initial form to be the original simplex, and the voiceless one a transitive/causative derivation with an *s*-prefix which causes the devoicing. Thus he derives *zhǎng* 張 *\*traŋʔ* 'to grow tall' (his *\*s-drj-*) from *cháng* 長 *\*draŋ* 'be long', and *jiàn* 見 *\*kêns* 'to see' (his *\*s-g-*) from *xiàn* 現 *\*gêns* 'to appear'. Yet the straightforward active meanings of *bài* 'defeat', *zhǎng* 'grow' (and, better, *zhāng* 'stretch') and *jiàn* 'see' speak against Mei's argument.

When a simplex like *bài* 敗 \*prâts 'to defeat, destroy' tr. already ends in an \*-s, it cannot be changed to a passive word with an additional *s*-suffix. In such words, the voicing of the initial consonant performs that function. Downer (1959: 263) has a list of these passives, including the following examples in (32):

(32) a. *bài* 敗 \*prâts 'to defeat, destroy' tr.
何亡國敗家之有 [Mengzi 4A, 8, 1]
*hé wáng guó bài jiāo zhī yǒu*
how destruct country ruin family PART exist
'How can there exist such destruction of states and ruin of families?'

b. + voicing > *bài* 敗 \*brâts 'be defeated, be ruinous' intr./passive
東敗於齊 [Mengzi 1A, 5, 1]
*dōng bài yú Qí*
east defeat by Qi
'In the east (we) have been defeated by Qí.'

This initial voicing is a catch-all morpheme for derivations that are the opposite of exo-active, i.e. non-extrovert and non-active, hence, for the nonce, this label "endopassive". This derivation collects disparate derivations under its umbrella such as *cháng* 長 \*draŋ 'be long' sv. (this is not extrovert, and not an active verb) in (27), *xiàn* 現/見 \*gêns 'to appear' intr. (and middle voice) in (29), *hān* 酣 \*gâm 'get drunk' intr. in (31), and *bài* 敗 \*brâts 'be defeated' intr. (and pass.) in (32). The introvert+medio-passive character of these derivations is often not self-evident, e.g. *xué* 學 \*grûk 'to learn' tr. which is clearly introvert; however, is the learner, the one being taught, the logical patient?

## 3.5 Summary

Middle Chinese tones and initial voicing reflect an OC system of word derivation that marks direction and voice with concomitant semantic valency changes. A word derivation can lead to an interpretation of extrovert or "introvert" (also in the sense of not-extrovert), or active or "passive" (also in the sense of not-active). These morphemes cut through conventional grammatical/lexical categories which often obscure the original nature of the OC morpheme as summarized in (33–36).

(33) OC *-s I. Extroversion in conjunction with valency (transitivity) increase; since it contrasts with introvert morphemes, Schuessler (2007) coined the term **"exoactive"**. This derivation can manifest itself in these conventional categories:

    transitive verb      hào 好 *hû-s      'to be fond of'
    ditransitive/causative      mài 賣 *mrê-s      ('to let buy':) 'to sell'

(34) OC *-s II. Passive: since this contrasts with an introvert passive, Schuessler (2007) calls it **"exopassive"**. This derivation can manifest itself in these conventional categories:

    passive      wèn 聞      *mən-s 'to be heard'
    tr. verb      wèi 畏      *ʔui-s 'to fear, respect'
    noun      chù 處      *k-hla-s 'a place'

(35) OC *-ʔ. Non-extrovert, non-passive marker with concomitant valency decrease: **"endoactive"**. This derivation can manifest itself in these conventional categories:

    intr. verb      zhǎng 長      *traŋʔ      'to grow'
    tr. verb      mǎi 買      *mrêʔ      'to buy'
    noun      děng 等      *təŋʔ      'step of stairs'

(36) OC initial voicing (Sagart's *N-prefix). Non-extrovert, non-active marker with concomitant valency decrease: **"endopassive"**. This derivation can manifest itself in these conventional categories:

    stative verb sv.      cháng 長      *draŋ      'be long'
    passive      bài 敗      *brâts      'be defeated'
    intr. verb      xiàn 現見      *gêns      'to appear'
    tr. verb      xué 學      *grûk      'to learn'

Further research may uncover whether direction or valency is the origin of these features.

# 4 Discussion

From the analysis in Sections 2–3, we have seen that the functional shifts, between transitive and instransitive/stative, between introvert and extrovert, and between active and passive, were all triggered by syntactic, namely, word order, and pragmatic factors, such as compatibility between the verb and its thematic roles (e.g. agent, patient). Morphophonemic factors, such as syllable finals *-s, *-ʔ, and initial voicing in OC, might have contributed to some cases of semantic extension, but it was definitely not required for any of these changes to occur. This leads us to question some of the seemingly settled issues in the literature of semantic change in grammaticalization and lexicalization: (1) Are semantic changes in grammaticalization and lexicalization in typologically different languages motivated by the same factors? and (2) do typologically different languages employ different mechanisms of semantic extension in grammaticalization and lexicalization?

When discussing motivation for semantic change in grammaticalization and lexicalization, researchers (Traugott 1988: 413; Heine et al. 1991: 29; Traugott & Dasher 2002; Fischer 2007) often mention two factors: ambiguity and problem-solving. They all agree that both factors are pragmatic in nature; however, the ambiguity they describe in their studies seems different from that in Chinese. Heine and his associates have a substantial discussion on the concept, but, in general, they describe ambiguity as a stage of semantic overlapping "where the former meaning still exists while a new meaning is introduced" (1991: 248–250). In Chinese, this is not a complete picture of ambiguity. Let us look at some examples.

(37) **guān** 棺 *kwân 'coffin' > guān 棺 *kwâns 'to coffin (?), put into a coffin'
棺而出之 [Zuozhuan, Xi 28]
guān　　　ér　　chū　　　　　　zhī
put-in-coffin and set-come-outside PRON.
'(They) (coffined:) put (the corpses) into coffins and set them outside of town.'

(38) **hǎo** 好 *hûʔ 'to be good'> hào 好 *hû-s 'be fond of'
貧而好樂, 富而好禮. [Liji 27, 3]
pín　ér　hào yuè,　　　　fù　ér　hào　　　　lǐ
poor and be-fond-of music, rich and be-fond-of etiquette
'If (one) is poor, (s/he) is fond of music. If (one) is rich, (s/he) is fond of etiquette.'

In (37), we see that *guān* originally conveys a nominal meaning of 'coffin'; but when it is conjunctively used with another verb *chū* 'to set come out', the writer makes it clear that *guān*, like *chū*, conveys a verbal meaning 'to put-in-a-coffin'. Evidently, this is a process of problem-solving, namely, to solve the problem of potential ambiguity between the original nominal meaning and the newly developed verbal meaning. Similarly, *hǎo* '(to be) good' in (38) is made unambiguous not only by morphophonemic change from the *shǎng* tone to the *qù* tone, but also by discourse-pragmatics, namely, to compare and contrast two enjoyments: 'be fond of music' vs. 'be fond of etiquette'. Thus, neither *guān* in (37) nor *hǎo* in (38) can possibly be interpreted as retaining their original meaning, 'coffin' and 'to be good' respectively. We see that OC writers did not seem to leave room for semantic ambiguity among lexemes.

Compared to cases of semantic change in grammaticalization and lexicalization reported in English, we see similar motivation but a somewhat different process than that in Chinese.

(39) ***be going to*** 'intention' > *be going to* 'prediction' > *gonna* 'future'
  a. *He is **going to** buy some food.*
     他要去买食物 。
     *tā yào       qù mǎi shíwù*
     he is-going-to  go buy food

  b. *It **is going** to happen.*
     （天）要下雨了。
     *(tiān) yào    xià    yǔ    le*
     (sky) is-going-to descent rain ASP

  c. *We are **gonna** do it.*
     我们要做这件事 。
     *wǒmen   yào         zuò zhè jiàn  shì*
     1PL      be-going-to do DET CL    matter

(40) ***get*** 'to have' > *get* (+ Vpast participle) 'auxiliary'
  a. *We have **got** many fresh fruits.*
  b. *I shall **get** them either naturalized or endenizened by the Queen.*
  c. *He so far lost his temper as to **get himself called** down by the judge.*
  d. *(...) and then they go together to the church, where they give good advice to young nymphs and swains to **get married** as fast as you can.* (Goldsmith 1766)

In (39a), 'be going to' is ambiguous as to whether it conveys the early/old sense of intention or the new sense of prediction. In (39b), the prediction sense is clearer. In (39c), the ambiguity is completely gone when 'gonna' is used. If we look at Chinese *yào* 要, which is equivalent to the English 'go', we can see that it has a lexical semantic ambiguity, but not a morphological one as in 'be going to'. The same is true of *qù* 去 'to go', which has no morphological marking for semantic ambiguity.

Hundt (2001, 2012) suggests that *get*'s passive function was likely derived from its causative passive function, as shown in (40b). Givón and Yang (1994), on the other hand, claim that it was the reflexive construction as in (40c) that played a crucial role in the grammaticalization of *get*'s passive function. Regardless, it is clear that the passive function of *get* was triggered by the syntactic ambiguity between the causative/reflexive construction and the passive construction "V$_{auxillary}$ + V$_{past\ participle}$", which led to semantic reinterpretation. This ambiguity disappears along with the disappearance of the causative/reflective function – receiver of the causative action and reflective pronoun, leaving *get* to be interpreted solely as having a passive function, as shown in (40d). Comparing this to Chinese passive-like constructions, we find that the key is not so much construction ambiguity, rather the linear word order of the major thematic roles of a construction that determines the interpretation of construction meaning being active or passive, as shown in (31) and (32).

To sum up, we have seen that semantic changes in grammaticalization in both Chinese and English use similar cognitive and pragmatic factors to solve problems of ambiguity. What differs between the processes of semantic change in the two genetically and typologically different languages is the mechanism used in the process (cf. Xing 2015): Chinese relies on semantic reanalysis which is contingent on discourse and pragmatic factors, as shown in Section 3.1–3.4, whereas English relies on semantic overlapping and morphological erosion or reduction, as shown in (39–40).

## 4.1 Semantic change vs. grammaticalization

This study discusses roughly three types of semantic extensions: from introvert to extrovert, from nominal to verbal, and from active to passive. Since semantic change is an integral part of grammaticalization, though not all cases of semantic change are a process of grammaticalization, this section will focus on whether the three types of semantic change are processes of grammaticalization. First, let us examine the change from introvert to extrovert. In section 3.1.5, cases of semantic extension are given to illustrate the shift of meaning from introvert to extrovert. Notice that in all those cases, such as (19), the inherent old introvert verbal interpretation 'to receive' in (19a) does not make sense in (19b). Language users had, and still have, to rely on their cognitive and pragmatic skills to reanalyze the given lexical item, e.g., *shòu* 受/授, and its relationship to adjacent elements and to derive a new compatible meaning that fits in the context, a process of semantic reanalysis (cf. Xing 2013). The new meaning 'to make receive' is extrovert in that someone/something else is 'to receive,' not the agent or constituent of the agent who 'makes receive'. As a result, this newly developed semantic function plays a different thematic role in the sentence from its old introvert meaning. Another way to illustrate this change is from a syntactic perspective, namely, intransitive > transitive, non-causative > causative, and active > passive, as illustrated in (14–25). This leads us to conclude that the process from introvert to extrovert is an example of grammaticalization. That is to say, the extrovert meaning is more grammatical than the introvert meaning due to the fact that the former is grammatically more complex in both form and meaning than the latter (cf. Heine et al. 1991).

Unlike the first type discussed above, the second type of semantic change – from nominal meaning to verbal meaning – involves a categorical change or a change of the part of speech. From the examples illustrated in (10–11), we have seen that the lexical item, *yī* 衣 originated as a noun expressing the meaning 'clothes', extended its original meaning to transitive verbal meaning 'to wear'. This type of extension is considered a case of metonymization (Meto) by Hopper & Traugott (2003: 87), who use such terms as 'associative' and 'contiguous' to characterize the relationship between the old meaning and the extended new meaning. Furthermore, according to Heine et al. (1991: 41), when both the cognitive and the pragmatic settings are responsible for the development of new meaning, it is a process of grammaticalization. An example they use to illustrate this type of grammaticalization is the change from a static concept to a dynamic concept, as *wui* 'eye' > 'to/toward' in Papago, an indigenous American language. Here, we see the similarity between the case illustrated by Heine et al. and the one discussed in this study.

The third type of semantic change, from active to passive, seems to provide the most convincing evidence for its being motivated by syntagmatic factors, undergoing a process of semantic reanalysis, and becoming more grammaticalized. Both this study, as illustrated in examples (32–38), and a number of other studies (e.g. Xing 2013, 2015) show that the active > passive extension in Chinese fundamentally differs from any of the semantic extensions discussed in the literature of grammaticalization based on Indo-European languages. In Chinese, syntagmatics, namely, syntactic position and discourse and pragmatic factors, trigger semantic reanalysis leading to the extension from active to passive meaning (Xing 2015: 616); whereas in Indo-European languages, the primary mechanisms for semantic change are cognitive and pragmatic in nature (i.e. metaphoricalization and metonymization).

## 4.2 Semantic change vs. morphological change

We have shown in Section 2 that, when some, although not all, of the OC lexical items underwent semantic change, their newly developed semantic functions, such as extrovert transitive, causative or passive meanings, seem to be marked by a syllable final *-s, which later became a *qù* tone in MC. This kind of correlation between form and function is easy to comprehend especially for readers who have experience with languages such as Latin, Greek, and Sanskrit. The problem is that this syllable final

*-s*, unlike any of the morphemes in Indo-European languages as mentioned above, was rather elusive due to the fact that it can be used for various semantic and grammatical functions (e.g. transitive, causative, passive). Additionally, it is not consistently used for any particular function. So we argue that although the syllable final *-s* may be used as a morpheme to signal an increase in semantic valency, it is not required for any particular type of semantic change to occur, nor does it play a similar role in the traditional sense in Indo-European languages. To some extent, it has the sense of polysemy in Chinese, so we may call it a polymorpheme. It seems to us that "polymorphemism" is the key OC characteristic that has led to the typologically different paths or mechanisms of semantic change taken by Chinese grammaticalizations than those taken by Indo-European languages.

# 5 Conclusion

In this study, we have attempted to explore the path of semantic extension in OC and compare Chinese cases with their counterparts in English or other related languages when applicable. Through analysis of 48 lexemes that have undergone semantic extension, we have demonstrated that all three types of semantic shift – from introvert to extrovert, from nominal to verbal, and from active to passive – were triggered by syntagmatic factors, associated with syntactic position, cognitive, discourse, and pragmatic factors. We have argued that these types of syntagmatically triggered semantic changes are processes of grammaticalization. The absence and/or ambiguity of morphological markings on word/syllable structures appears to have contributed to the different paths that typologically different languages, such as Chinese and English, have taken.

Another issue that this study has touched upon but has not discussed in detail is the issue of directionality of grammaticalization. It is generally believed that grammaticalization proceeds in one direction – unidirectionality (cf. Lehmann 1982; Heine & Reh 1984; Heine et al. 1991). Though there have been reports of exceptional cases, a majority of cross-linguistic studies support Traugott & Koenig's (1991: 189) characterization on the unidirectionality of the process of grammaticalization "whereby lexical items in the course of time acquire a new status as grammatical, morpho-syntactic forms, and in the process come to code relations that either were not coded before or were coded differently." Examining the three types of Chinese cases of semantic change and grammaticalization discussed in Sections 2–3: introvert > extrovert, nominal > verbal, active > passive, we see that all three cases comply with the unidirectional process of grammaticalization described above by Traugott and Koenig. It should be noted, however, that Traugott and Koenig's and many others' characteristic of unidirectionality focuses on the morpho-syntactic or grammatical properties of lexical items that have undergone grammaticalization and not so much on semantic reinterpretation. Heine et al. (1991) may be the first study that substantiates the conceptual directions of lexical items under grammaticalization. According to them, semantic extension generally proceeds from concrete concepts to more abstract concepts. They also lay out a cline for metaphorical abstraction as "person > object > activity > space > time > quality" (p. 48). These characterizations of semantic change help us understand the general direction of semantic abstraction cross-linguistically. And the extensions discussed in Section 3.1.1, from nominal to verbal, appear to be good examples to support part of the proposed cline by Heine and his associates, namely "object > activity". However, their proposed metaphorical abstraction cline does not seem to account for the semantic extensions discussed in Sections 3.1.2–3.1.5. Taking the conceptual extension from stative to transitive as illustrated in (12–13) *hǎo* 好 and *yuǎn* 遠, which extended its meaning from 'good' and 'far' to 'be fond of' and 'to distance' for example, can we say the stative meaning is more abstract therefore more grammatical than the transitive meaning? Similarly, can we say that the passive meaning 'food is eaten' is more abstract than the active meaning 'to eat food' and, therefore, that the former is more grammatical than the latter? Probably not. It seems to us that it might be easier to address these questions in languages with morphological markings for grammatical functions, such as passive in Indo-European languages. In Chinese, however, neither active nor passive is morphologically marked; they only differ in terms of the importance of agent or patient in discourse: in an active construction, agent is more important, whereas in a passive construction, the patient is more important (cf. Myhil & Xing 1994). Hence, using the criteria developed on the basis of morpho-syntactic forms and metaphorical/metonymical paradigms for semantic reinterpretation is difficult to quantify which concepts in those Chinese examples are more abstract or more grammatical. With this, we conclude that more research is needed for a better comprehension of conceptual extension in grammaticalization.

# References

Baxter, William H. 1992. *A Handbook of Old Chinese Phonology*, Berlin: Mouton de Gruyter, ISBN 978-3-11-012324-1.

Baxter, William and Laurent Sagart. 2014. *Old Chinese. A New Reconstruction*. Oxford University Press.

Chou, Fa-kao [Zhōu Fǎgāo]. 周法高 1962. *Zhōngguó gǔdài yǔfǎ: goucí biān* 中國古代語法: 構詞編 [*A historical grammar of Old Chinese: Morphology*]. Taipei, Nankang: Academia Sinica.

Downer, G. B. 1959. Derivation by tone-change in classical Chinese. *BSOAS* 22: 258–290.
Fischer, Olga. 2007. *Morphosyntactic Change: Functional and Formal Perspective*. New York: Oxford University Press.
Givón, Talmy and Lynne Yang. 1994. The Rise of the English GET-passive. In Barbara Fox and Paul J. Hopper (eds.), *Voice: Form and Function*, 119-49. Philadelphia/Amsterdam: John Benjamins.
Goldsmith, Oliver. 1982 [1766]. *The Vicar of Wakefield*. Harmondsworth: Penguin.
Heine, Bernd and Mechthild Reh. 1984. *Grammaticalization and Reanalysis in African Languages*. Hamburg: Helmut Buske.
Heine, Bernd, Ulrike Claudi, and Friederike Hünnemeyer. 1991. *Grammaticalization: A Conceptual Framework*. Chicago/London: The University of Chicago Press.
Hopper, Paul J. and Elizabeth C. Traugott. 2003. *Grammaticalization*. Cambridge: Cambridge University Press.
Hundt, Marianne. 2001. What corpora tell us about the grammaticalization of voice in *get*-constructions. *Studies in Language*, Vol. 25, 1: 49–87.
Hundt, Marianne. 2002. English mediopassive constructions: a cognitive, corpus-based study of their origin, spread, and current status. Post-doctor thesis, University of Freiburg.
Karlgren, Bernhard. 1950. *The Book of Documents*. Stockholm: Bulletin of the Museum of Far Eastern Antiquities.
Lehmann, Christian. 1982. *Thoughts on Grammaticalization: A Programmatic Sketch*. Cologne: Universität zu Köln, Institut für Sprachwissenschaft.
Lù, Démíng. 陸德明 1985. *Jīngdiǎn shìwén* 經典釋文 [556–627] [Explication of the Text of the Classics]. Shanghai: Guji Chubanshe.
Mei Tsu-Lin. 梅祖麟 2000. Sìshēng biéyì zhōngde shíjiān céngcì 四聲別義中的時間層次 [Chronological Strata in Derivation by Tone-Change]. *Zhōngguó yǔwén* 6, 1980: 427–443. Reprinted in *Méi Zǔlín Yǔyánxué lùnwénjí* 梅祖麟語言學論文集. Běijīng: Shāngwù yìnshūguǎn, 2000: 306–339.
Mei, Tsu-Lin. 梅祖麟 2012. The causative *s- and nominalizing *-s in Old Chinese and related matters in Proto-Sino-Tibetan. *Language and Linguistics* 13.1: 1–28.
Myhill, John and Zhiqun Xing. 1994. A comparative study of voice in Chinese, English, and Biblical Hebrew. *Language Sciences*, Vol. 16, No. 2:253–283.
Sagart, Laurent. 1999. *The roots of Old Chinese*. Amsterdam / Philadelphia: Benjamins.
Sagart, Laurent and William Baxter. 2012. Reconstructing the *s- prefix in Old Chinese. *Language and Linguistics* 13.1: 29–59.
Schuessler, Axel. 2007. *ABC Etymological Dictionary of Old Chinese*. Honolulu: Hawai'i University Press.
Schuessler, Axel. 2009. *Minimal Old Chinese and Later Han Chinese. A Companion to Grammata Serica Recensa*. Honolulu: Hawai'i University Press.
Shibatani, Masayoshi. 1990. *The Languages of Japan*. Cambridge University Press.
Traugott, Elizabeth C. 1988. Pragmatic strengthening and grammaticalization. *Berkeley Linguistics Society* 14: 406–416.
Traugott, Elizabeth C. and Richard Dasher. 2002. *Regularity in Semantic Change*. Cambridge: Cambridge University Press.
Traugott, Elizabeth C. and Ekkehard Koenig. 1991. The semantic-pragmatics of grammaticalization revisited. In Traugott, Elizabeth C. and Bernd Heine (eds.), *Approaches to Grammaticalization*, pp. 189–218. Amsterdam/Philadelphia: John Benjamins.
Wang, Li. 王力 1958. *Hànyǔ Shǐgǎo* 漢語史稿 [*Chinese Historical Grammar*]. Beijing: Zhonghua Shuju.

Xing, Janet Z. 2013. Semantic reanalysis in grammaticalization in Chinese. In Zhuo Jing-Schmidt (ed.), *Increased Empiricism: New Advances in Chinese Linguistics*, pp. 223–246. Philadelphia/Amsterdam: John Benjamins.

Xing, Janet Z. 2015. A comparative study of semantic change in Chinese and Germanic languages. *Studies in Language*, Volume 39: 3, pp. 593–633.

Barbara Meisterernst
# A new approach to the development of deontic markers: In Pre-Modern Chinese

Studies done on the early modal system of the Chinese language are usually confined to the so-called 'can-wish' verbs (Peyraube 1999, Liu Li 2000). The reason for this is that modal verbs in Late Archaic Chinese (LAC) (5th–3rd c. BCE) almost exclusively consist of different realizations of the 'first modal' (Leiss 2008: 16) 'can,' along with a small number of verbs that express volition. Modals expressing potentiality appear as the first modals in many languages. Root readings, including true deontic readings, depend on particular syntactic environments; epistemic readings of modal auxiliary verbs are almost exclusively attested in the complement of epistemic or evaluative verbs in Late Archaic Chinese. The category of epistemic modality is predominantly expressed by speaker-oriented modal adverbs having the entire proposition in their scope. The situation changes in Early Middle Chinese (EMC) (starting around the 1st c. BCE according to the periodization employed in this approach), when the modal system develops and new modal verbs derived from lexical verbs make their appearance. This development coincides with the emergence of the source structures of the aspectual markers of Modern Chinese. In Aldridge & Meisterernst (2018) it has been proposed that the change in the aspectual system can be connected to the loss of the morphological aspectual marking of the verb. In Meisterernst (2017a), it has been hypothesized that the loss of a former aspectual morphology also had an impact on the diversification of the system of modal markers in Early Middle Chinese, inspired by a similar proposal on the development of the Germanic modal system in Leiss (2008). Despite the typological differences between Chinese and the Germanic languages, the study of the aspect-modality system on the basis of insights from the Germanic system provides strong arguments for universal constraints on the relation of aspect and modality and for universal tendencies in the development of the modal system.

# 1 Modal expressions in Late Archaic Chinese

## 1.1 Modal expression of possibility

Modal verbs of POSSIBILITY and ABILITY constitute the basis of the modal system of Chinese (Peyraube 1999, Liu 2000, Li 2001, Meisterernst 2008a, b). The modal

https://doi.org/10.1515/9783110641288-008

*kě* 可 expresses participant-external or root possibility as its basic meaning, usually involving a non-volitional subject, as in (1). The modal *néng* 能 expresses participant-internal possibility, i.e. ability with a causer or agent (volitional) subject as in (2); with a non-volitional subject, it can also express circumstantial participant-external possibility. Volitional and non-volitional subjects show different syntactic constraints. Consequently, the syntax of the subject of the modal predicate can serve to distinguish *dé* 得 and *kě* 可 from *néng* 能 on the one hand, but also the different modal values of *néng* 能 on the other. The modal *dé* most typically has an opportunity reading (Xie 2012) as in (3) and an implicative reading in past tense contexts.

(1) 宋師不整，可敗也。 *Zuozhuan, Zhuang* 10.2.1 (LAC)
 Sòng shī bù zhěng, kě bài yě
 Song army NEG in. good. order, KE defeat SFP
 'The Song army is not in good order, it can be defeated.'

(2) 父能生之，不能養之。 *Xún* 75/19/110 (LAC)
 Fù néng shēng zhī, bù néng yǎng zhī
 Father NENG reproduce OBJ, NEG NENG feed OBJ
 'The father is able to bring it to life, but he is not able to feed it.'

(3) 夫子之身，亦子所知也，唯無咎與偃是從，父兄莫得進矣。
 *Zuozhuan, Xiang* 27 (LAC)
 Fūzǐ zhī shēn, yì zǐ suǒ zhī yě, wéi Wújiù
 Master GEN person, also address SUO know SFP, COP Wujiu
 yǔ Yǎn shì cóng, fù xiōng mò dé jìn yǐ
 CONJ Yan FOC follow, father older.brother none DE enter SFP
 'The personality of the master (your father) is something you also know, he only follows Wujiu and Yan, and none of our elder relatives can get entrance.'

The etymologies of the three verbs also differ: *kě* 可 'be possible', and *néng* 能 'be able' are derived from state verbs like in (4) and (5); *dé* 得 'get, obtain, manage to, able to, (must)' on the other hand is derived from an achievement verb as in (6). This is one of the features that distinguishes the modal *dé* from the other modal verbs and leads to the hypothesis that at least parts of its function are not, in the strictest sense, modal in Late Archaic Chinese. Of the three verbs, only *néng* expresses participant-internal modality on a regular basis; in this regard it resembles volitional modals (Portner 2009). All three modals are regularly attested as lexical verbs in Late Archaic Chinese. As circumstantial modal verbs they belong to the category of Modal$_2$, this term refers to dynamic modals and is explained in the subsequent discussion. Dynamic modals are hosted in the lexical layer (e.g. Cormack and Smith 2002, Butler 2003, Tsai 2015).

a) **kě 可 as a lexical verb**
(4) 有無父之國則可也。 *Zuozhuan, Huan* 16.5.3 (LAC)
Yǒu wú     fù    zhī guó zé    kě      yě
Have not.have father GEN state then possible SFP
'If there is a country without fathers, then it is possible.'

b) **néng 能 as a lexical verb**
(5) 能信不為人下，吾未能也。 *Zuozhuan, Zhao* 1.1.13 (LAC)
Néng xìn    bù   wéi rén xià,    wú wèi   néng yě
Able believe NEG be  man below, I   NEG able SFP
'Those who are able to believe are not below others; I am not able to.'

c) **dé 得 as a lexical verb**
(6) 申侯由是得罪。 *Zuozhuan, Xi* 5.5.2 (LAC)
Shēn hóu yú   shì dé zuì
Shen hou from this get guilt
'Shenhou had incurred guilt due to this.'

## 1.2 Expressions of deontic modality

Expressions of deontic modality in the strictest sense, i.e. performative speaker/addressee oriented modals, expressing obligation, permission or prohibition, are relatively infrequent in Late Archaic Chinese; they only increase in number in Early Middle Chinese. Deontic modals have been proposed to belong to a different category than circumstantial or dynamic modals, the category of Modal$_1$, necessity modals which scope over negation. These have been analyzed as being hosted in a position in syntax different from dynamic modals (see e.g. Cormack and Smith 2002, Butler 2003, Tsai 2015).

In Late Archaic Chinese, the negative deontic value of prohibition is predominantly expressed by synthetic modal negative markers such as *wú* 無 / 毋 and *wù* 勿 'don't' as in (7a); in Early Middle Chinese these were successively replaced by analytic modal negation using a modal or a neutral NEG + modal verb, such as *wù dé* 勿得 with a modal negative marker + modal verb in (7b).

(7) a. 己所不欲，勿施於人。　*Lúnyǔ* 12 (LAC)
   *Jǐ   suǒ  bù   yù,   wù     shī    yú   rén*
   Self REL NEG wish, NEG$_{mod}$ bestow PREP man
   'What you do not wish for yourself, do not bestow on others.'

b. 勿得違戾是非，爭分曲直。　*Hou Hanshu, Nüjie* (EMC)
   *Wù    dé        wéi    lì   shì  fēi,   zhēng fēn  qū      zhí*
   NEG$_{mod}$ DE$_{mod}$ oppose rage right wrong, fight divide crooked straight
   'She may not oppose and rage against [the distinction of] right and wrong nor fight against [the distinction of] crooked and straight.'

The only way to express deontic modality in a direct way is with the deontic modal verb *bì* 必 as in (8a). In Late Archaic Chinese *bì* 必 predominantly expresses 'certainty, necessity', usually corresponding to the English 'must' and the like if verbal, and to modal adverbs such as 'certainly, necessarily' if adverbial. Two functionally different instantiations of *bì* 必 have been proposed in Meisterernst (2013): a) a deontic modal auxiliary verb *bì* 必 'must/need', and b) an epistemic modal adverb 'certainly' (Meisterernst 2013). Since it predominantly refers to future contexts, the analysis of epistemic *bì* 必 as a modal adverb and not as a modal verb is semantically more conclusive. According to e.g. Coates (1983) and Bybee et al. (1994), future reference is usually not available for modal auxiliary verbs such as the English 'must' in their epistemic reading, whereas it is the default reference with deontic modals. Syntactically, the modal adverb operates on the level of Complementizer Phrase above aspect and negation, the position typical for epistemic markers, whereas the modal auxiliary verb *bì* 必 appears below and within the semantic scope of negation as in (8b) for the deontic and (8c) for the epistemic reading of *bì*. The low position is the default position of root (circumstantial) modal auxiliary verbs in Late Archaic and Early Middle Chinese, and it is the syntactic position possibility modals occupy in unmarked contexts. The employment of *bì* as a deontic modal is subject to particular semantic constraints and it is not particularly frequent in this function in Late Archaic Chinese.[1]

---

[1] For a more detailed discussion of *bì* 必 see Meisterernst (2017a and 2017b).

(8) a. 麇曰：必立伯也，是良材。 *Zuǒzhuàn, Ai* 17 (LAC)
 *Jūn yuē bì lì    Bó yě,  shì liáng cái*
 Jun say: BI enthrone Bo SFP, this good talent
 'Jun said: "You must enthrone Bo; he is a talented man."'
 NECESSARY / NEED 'that you enthrone Bo'

b. 我不必樂，祖父已來，以此為業，若捨此事，無以自濟。
 T04n0202_p0410c *Xianyujing* (EMC)
 *Wǒ bù bì lè,   zǔfù    yǐ   lái,  yǐ cǐ  wéi  yè,*
 I  NEG BI happy, grandfather already come, YI this make work,
 *ruò shě    cǐ shì  wú    yǐ zì jì*
 if abandon this duty, not.have YI self support
 'I need not be happy [about it], but since our grandfathers this has been made our work; if we abandon this duty, we cannot support ourselves.'
 NOT | NECESSARY / NEED ⇒ 'it is possible not to be happy about it'

c. 若於身上剜千燈者，必不全濟，T04n0202_p0349c, *Xianyujing* (EMC)
 *Ruò yú shēn shàng wān    qiān    dēng zhě, bì    bù*
 If PREP body above scoop.up thousand lantern NOM, BI<sub>epistemic</sub> NEG
 *quán    jì*
 completely complete
 'If one scoops a thousand lanterns out of the body, it can certainly not be achieved completely.'

Another means of expressing deontic modality is to use a doubly negated construction with the possibility modal *kě* 可: NEG *kě(yǐ)* 可(以) NEG *v*P. This construction always codes strong deontic modality, i.e. a strong obligation 'have to, must'. In contrast to the affirmative construction with *kě (yǐ)* 可(以) it never expresses root possibility (Meisterernst 2008b). The obligation is conveyed in an indirect way precisely expressing 'it is not possible that not $p$ $\neg \Diamond \neg p$' = $\Box p$ 'it is necessary that $p$'. (9) represents the two different syntactic variants of *kě* 可. The variant in a. without *yǐ* 以 requires a passivized complement, the second variant with *yǐ* does not. In (9b) the first modal predicate is contrasted to the second modal with *bì* 必 which, in combination with negation, expresses deontic exemption, i.e. anankastic modality.[2]

---

[2] The relation of modal reading and negation will be discussed in more detail below. For a more comprehensive discussion on *bì* and negation see Meisterernst (2017b). For the term 'anankastic modality' see Sparvoli (2015).

(9) a. 君子曰：「位其不可不慎也乎！ *Zuǒzhuàn, Cheng 2*[3] (Late Archaic Chinese)
*Jūnzǐ      yuē: wèi   qí    bù   kě   bù   shèn  yě   hū*
Gentleman say: rank MOD NEG KE NEG careful SFP SFP
'The gentleman says: "Rank has to be treated with [special] care!"'

b. 四鄰諸侯之相與，不可以不相接也，然而不必相親也，
*Xún* 12/10/6 (Late Archaic Chinese)
*Sì    lín     zhūhóu   zhī xiāng yǔ,      bù   kě   yǐ  bù*
Four neighbour feudal.lord GEN mutual be.close, NEG can YI NEG
*xiāng jiē    yě, rán'ér bù   bì xiāng qīn   yě*
mutual connect SPF, but NEG BI mutual close SFP
'Regarding the relationship between [the ruler and] the feudal lords from the four neighboring directions, they must be mutually connected, but they do not have to be close to each other.'

In Early Middle Chinese, the verb *dāng* 當 'match, correspond' increasingly occurs as a deontic modal auxiliary verb 'ought, should' (Meisterernst 2011).[4]

(10) 群臣議，皆曰「長當棄市」。  *Shǐjì*: 10; 426 (EMC)
*Qún chén     yì,    jiē yuē Cháng dāng qì       shì*
All minister discuss, all say Chang DANG abandon expose.marketplace
'The ministers discussed it, and they all said: "Chang should be executed and exposed in the marketplace."'

Table 1 presents the distribution of the most relevant expressions of deontic modality. Of these, only the grammaticalization processes of KE (YI), DANG and YING as markers of deontic modality are at issue in the ensuing discussion.

---

[3] There are only seven instances like this in *Zuozhuan* and all of them have the same complement verb. In the corpus of *Zuozhuan, Lunyu, Mengzi, Xunzi* and *Zhuangzi* there are altogether 27 instances of *bùkěbù* 不可不, but there are 19 instances alone in the *Shiji*.

[4] A comprehensive discussion of *dāng* 當 in LAC and EMC has been provided in Wu Xueru 巫雪如 (2014). Wu Xueru claims that the deontic, epistemic, and the future readings of DANG are attested earlier than has generally been proposed in the literature. However, she does not distinguish strictly between modal verbs and modal auxiliaries.

**Table 1:** Modals in LAC and EMC.

|  | Modal₁: deontic necessity | Circumstantial modals: Modal₂ | Modal₂: necessity |
|---|---|---|---|
| LAC | NEG+KE/KEYI+(NEG) (may/must (not)); NEG+DE(+NEG (may/must (not)); | (NEG+)KE/KEYI (cannot); (NEG+)DE (cannot); (NEG+) NENG (not able) | BI (necessary) |
| EMC | NEG+KE/KEYI/NEG+DE(+NEG); (NEG+)DANG (NEG+)YING(+NEG) | (NEG+)KE/KEYI; (NEG+)DE; (NEG+)NENG | BI; XU (need) |

## 2 The interplay of aspect and modality

The analysis of the diachronic development of deontic modal marking proposed in this paper is, to a certain extent, based on observations made on the relation between aspect and modality and the development of the Germanic modal system, particularly in Abraham and Leiss's (2008: xiii). They propose that:

– Perfective aspect is compatible ("converges strongly") with root modality
– Imperfective aspect is compatible ("converges strongly") with epistemic modality.[5]
– Negated clauses as a rule select imperfective aspect only, without necessarily yielding epistemic modality.

Epistemic readings are difficult to obtain among German modal verbs with telic [+terminative] verbs, although this does not account for negation (Heindl 2009). Deontic and epistemic interpretations are possible with atelic [-terminative] verbs (Abraham 2009: 265). The features [+/-terminative] refer to Aktionsart or lexical aspect, i.e. the *telicity* or *boundedness* of a predicate, which refers to the natural initial and final points of a situation. Events (accomplishments and achievements) are [+terminative], bi-phasic (Abraham 2009), and compatible with the perfective aspect; states and activities are [-terminative], i.e. mono-phasic (Abraham 2009), and compatible with the imperfective aspect (e.g. Smith 1997).[6]

---

**5** Other authors (Maché 2009: 25) are less strict in their assumption with regard to the selectional restrictions of epistemic modals; under certain conditions they can also select the perfective aspect. According to him the main difference lies in the fact that epistemic modificators always operate on the propositional level, whereas non-epistemic modals modify events. His study concentrates mainly on German modals, but he includes some English modals as well.
**6** See also Vendler's (1967) seminal categorisation of lexical aspects, which distinguishes states, activities, accomplishments and achievements.

Telicity features can be checked by their respective compatibility with duration or time span adverbials. Atelic predicates are compatible with duration phrases, *for x time*, whereas telic predicates are compatible with time span adverbials *in x time*. In (11a) and (11c) the predicate is atelic and unbounded. In (11b) the quantified object shifts the verb 'run' from atelic to telic.

(11) a. Mary drove the car for an hour (-TERMINATIVE)
     b. Mary ran a mile in an hour (+TERMINATIVE)
     c. Mary ran for an hour (-TERMINATIVE)

(12) and (13) represent the event structure following Abraham (2008: 7), and the comparative structures of telicity features and modality by Abraham as summarized in Leiss (2008: 17). For the reading of modal verbs, Abraham (2008: 7 proposes a structure similar to that of telic (perfective) and atelic (imperfective) verbs. According to him, deontic events are bi-phasic, corresponding to [+TELIC/ TERMINATIVE] events, and epistemic events are monophasic corresponding to [-TELIC/TERMINATIVE] events.[7]

(12) Event structure following Abraham (2008: 7)
   a. event:     |>>>>>>>>>| ................|
                 $t_1$   $E_1$   $t_m$   $E_2$   $t_n$

   b. activity[8] (|>>>>>>>> |) or;   c. state |~~~~~~~~~~|
                  $t_1$   E   $t_n$              $t_m$   E   $t_n$

(13) Bi-phasic deontic and monophasic epistemic events
   a. |>>>>>>>>>>>>|....................|      b. |........................|
      perfective event  present state           imperfective event
   a'. |>>>>>>>>>>>>|~~~~~~~~~~~~~|      b'. |~~~~~~~~~~~~~|
       deontic event  projected future         epistemic event

In the diagrams above, $t_1$ refers to the initial point of the incremental phase $E_1$, $t_m$ refers to the initial point of the second, the resultative phase $E_2$, and $t_n$ refers to a final point of the situation. The point $t_m$ belongs to both phases.

The diachronic development of the articulate system of modal verbs has been connected to the loss of an earlier aspectual system in the Germanic languages

---

**7** See also Meisterernst (2017a).
**8** The structure of (12b-c) is a version of the structure proposed in Abraham (2008: 7) modified to fit the purpose of this study.

(Leiss 2008: 16): "Languages which have lost an elaborate aspect system tend to develop articles ... as well as a class of modals with deontic and epistemic meanings ..." Germanic modal verbs start to grammaticalize from preterite-presents, and, even more importantly for the present discussion, they tend to embed a perfective infinitive (see Leiss 2008: 18).[9] The feature of perfectivity always includes the future-projecting features typical in deontic modals (Leiss 2008: 19).

This relation is most obvious in the Germanic languages which display a particularly complex modal system. But Abraham claims that even if modal readings are not directly and overtly caused by the aspectual structures of the embedded (infinitival) complement, they are still coded by aspect (Abraham 2009: 251). Two examples from Old English (OE) and from Old High German (OHG) with deontic modals selecting perfective infinitives demonstrate this relation (from Leiss 2008: 26). The infinitive is marked as perfective (resultative) by the prefix *ge-*.

(14)  a.  OE  *thaet ic saenaessas ge-seon     mihte*
               that  I  sea-bluffs  see [PFV-see] might
               'So that I could see the cliffs.' (*Beowulf* 571)

      b.  OHG  *uuer  mag  thaz gi-horen*
               who  can  that hear [PFV-hear]
               'Who can understand that?' (*Tatian* (Masser-edition). 263, 30)

In Middle High German (MHG) the percentage of *ge*-verbs is highest when embedded by *mugen* 'may' and *kunnen* 'can' (both express possibility). It is also relatively high with *suln* 'should', but it decreases with the deontic verbs *müezen* 'must' and *dürfen* 'may' and the verb *wellen* 'want'. From Old High to Middle High German there is a tendency for *ge*-verbs to appear in contexts independent of their aspectual reading (Heindl 2009: 124). According to Heindl (idem 125) most of the *ge*-verbs attested in MHG with the verb *mugen* 'may' –but also with *kunnen* 'can' – appear when combined with negation. *Mugen* is most frequently seen with negation in contrast with the also-very-frequent verb *suln* 'should'. This picture resembles, to a certain extent, the situation in Late Archaic and Eearly Middle Chinese where the predominant modals are verbs of possibility along with the modal *dāng* 'should'. The verbs of possibility always require negation in order to obtain a deontic reading.

The following hypothesis will be proposed in this paper: Parts of the reconstructed aspectual morphology of Archaic Chinese may be comparable to the

---

**9** For a more extensive discussion and a comparison with Slavic languages see (Heindl 2009).

Germanic prefix *ge (ga)-*. The loss of the Chinese morphology may have had a similar effect on the Chinese modal system as the loss of the category of aspect had on the modals in Germanic languages, i.e. an increase in the number and functions of modal verbs and their functions.[10] The proposal is based on the following cross-linguistic insights:

a) In the Germanic languages, the complex modal system develops after the loss of aspectual distinctions. The close relation between aspectual readings of matrix and embedded verbs is evidenced by languages such as Russian or Greek (Roussou 2009).
b) The aspectual morphology reconstructed for Chinese was no longer productive in Late Archaic Chinese and it most likely started to lose its transparency at that time. This loss led to a number of changes in the syntax of Chinese.
c) Modal verbs are, to a considerable extent, confined to different realizations of the 'first modal' (Leiss 2008: 16) 'can' in the early reported stages of German and Chinese.
d) The first modal KE, which only in combination with negation and in rhetorical questions allows a deontic reading, requires passivized verbs as its complement when unmarked. These refer to a resultant state, thus showing a reading similar to the *ge*-verbs in OHG and MHG.
e) True deontic modal verbs only emerge in the Early Middle Chinese period, and systematic and context free epistemic readings of modal verbs develop even later; this is the typical grammaticalization path for modal verbs reflected, for instance, by the Germanic languages. Epistemic readings are also infrequent in MHG (Heindl 2009: 153).

This study does not focus on the semantic development of modal markers from deontic to epistemic readings, frequently at issue in studies on grammaticalization paths of modal verbs including those on Chinese modal verbs (e.g. Peyraube 1999, Li 2001). The present approach attempts to figure out the earliest stages of the development of the Chinese modal system based on Abraham and Leiss's (2008) hypothesis on the early development of the Germanic modal system. Abraham and Leiss (2008) propose a strong and possibly universal relation between the verbal aspect and either the root/deontic or the epistemic reading of a modal verb. When the Germanic languages lose the former category of aspect (especially the perfective *ge*-verbs), they start to develop an elaborate class of deontic

---

[10] See also Sybesma's (1994): the aspectual marker *–le* in Modern Mandarin and its diachronic development can functionally be compared to the Germanic prefix *ge (ga)-*, which e.g. expressed completion in Middle Dutch (Sybesma 1994: 41).

and epistemic modal verbs. Modal distinctions had previously been expressed by the interplay of aspectual and temporal markings alone. The diachronic development in the Germanic languages in contrast to other Indo-European languages obviously points to a close and possibly universal relationship between the categories aspect (lexical and/or grammatical aspect) and modality.

Meisterernst (2017) proposes that some of the functions of the reconstructed aspectual morphology of Archaic Chinese may have been comparable to the Germanic prefix *ge (ga)-*, and that the loss of derivational morphology may have had a similar effect on the Chinese modal system than the loss of the category of aspect had on modals in Germanic languages.

## 3 The historical phonology and morphology of Chinese

Studies on the historical phonology of Chinese demonstrate that Chinese must have had a kind of morphology by affixation comparable to that of related languages such as Tibetan or Burmese (Sagart 1999, Gassmann and Behr 2005, Jin 2006, and Schuessler 2007). But this morphology was, to a great extent, obfuscated by the Chinese writing system. Additionally, the Chinese morphology disappeared much earlier than in e.g. Tibetan and Burmese; it had been entirely lost at the time of the earliest Tibetan written documents (6th c. CE). According to Schuessler (2007: 41), even one of the youngest derivational morphemes, i.e. the suffix *-s*, proposed in the literature (e.g. Jin 2006) as a marker of the perfective aspect, had "become a general purpose device to derive any kind of word from another" in Archaic Chinese. In many studies the verbal morphology reconstructed for Archaic Chinese is connected to distinctions within the grammatical aspect, i.e. the perfective and the imperfective aspect, a distinction between transitive and intransitive verbs and/or causative and unaccusative verbs (see e.g. Jin 2006, Mei 1988, 2015). In Meisterernst (2016) it has been argued that the aspectual distinctions expressed by the reconstructed verbal morphology concern lexical rather than grammatical aspect. Lexical aspect, Aktionsart, is generally derived by derivational morphology (Kiefer 2010: 145), the kind of morphology proposed as typical for the Tibeto-Burman languages. The aktionsart morphology adds semantic features to the verb such as ingressivity, terminativity, iterativity, etc. (Kiefer 2010: 145). This fits well the meanings proposed for a number of derivational affixes reconstructed e.g. in Sagart (1999). Two different derivational processes have been proposed for the distinction of verbal aspects (e.g. Unger 1983, Huang 1992, Jin 2006):

a) The suffix *-s indicating perfective aspect (Haudricourt 1954, Downer 1959, Unger 1983, Sagart 1999, Jin 2006, etc.); or
b) A voiceless (imperfective) – voiced (perfective) alternation of the root initial possibly caused by a former sonorant nasal prefix or by the causative prefix *s- (Karlgren 1933; Mei 1988, Baxter and Sagart 1998, etc.).

The first of these processes, the 'derivation by tone change' sì shēng bié yì 四聲別意 is attested with words of any of the tonal categories A (píng 平), B (shǎng 上), and D (rù 入), which are transformed into Category C (qù 去).

(15) verbs with a *qùshēng* variant resulting from a reconstructed suffix *s-
    a. *chí* 治 *drɨ/dri (\*r-de)* 'govern' <> *zhì* 治 *drɨʰ (\*r-de-s)* (Jin 2006: 511) 'well-governed'
    b. *guō* 過 *kwa (\*kor)* 'pass by' <> *guò kwaʰ (\*kor-s)* 'exceed, transgress(ion)'[11]

(16) Tone Change without change of meaning[12]
    a. A *píng* 平 >>> C *qù* 去
        *guàn* 貫 kwan <> (kwanʰ) 'pass through' 'perforate' (Jin2006: 332)
    b. B *shàng* 上 >>> C *qù* 去
        *guàn* 盥 kwanʼ[13] <> kwanʰ 'wash the hands or face' (Jin 2006: 79 voicing alternation)

---

[11] Schuessler (2007: 40) argues that "Word classes like 'noun' are unmarked in CH, hence tone C does not make a noun out of a verb, as is often maintained.". Derived *qùshēng* nouns were, in fact, originally verb forms, e.g. 'resultant state' (Jin 2006), or passive forms (Schuessler (exopassives by tone the suffix *-s = Tone C)).

[12] Unger, Hao-ku, 28.3.1983, 157. It has to be conceded that the system of morphological derivation in Archaic Chinese is still very unclear and regular patterns are difficult to determine (for a discussion see e.g. Harbsmeier 2016). Nevertheless, there is some evidence that part of the morphology reconstructed for Archaic Chinese was closely related to aspectual structures. Additionally, the fact that a new aspectual system develops in Early Middle Chinese is best explained, if we assume that a former system of aspectual marking was lost at that time which forced a new system to develop; this would be a natural development in human languages. This development is coincidental with a number of changes in the syntax of Chinese at the same time, which may also be connected to the loss of morphological marking.

[13] Only Early Middle Chinese according to Pulleyblank (1991).

c. D *rù* 入 >>> C *qù* 去
   *bì* 閉 pɛt¹⁴ <> pɛjʰ 'bar a door, shut' (not in Jin 2006)

Category C is supposed to have developed from a former derivational suffix *-s* which changed into *-h* and further into the *qùshēng*. This process most likely took place at the end of the Late Archaic and in the Early Middle Chinese periods (beginning with the 1st c. BCE); the differences in pronunciation resulting from it are e.g. reflected in the *fǎnqiè* 反切 glosses to the Classics from the Han period on. Double readings and minimal pairs with readings in one of the mentioned categories and in Category C are relatively frequent. Jin (2006) proposes basically two different functions of the suffix *-s* (e.g. 2006: 317, 321, 325f): a transitivization function and a deverbalization function (Jin 2006: 325).¹⁵ For the latter, he claims that the change from verb to noun can often be subsumed under a change from the imperfective to the perfective aspect (Jin 2006). The latter form, referring to a resultant state, has subsequently been employed as an adjective or a noun, to the effect that the perfective aspect often involves a deverbalization process, resulting in deverbal adjectives and nominals (Jin 2006: 323f); sometimes this process is reflected by different graphic variants. The same process is also attested in Classical Tibetan (Jin 2006: 325, 329). The suffix (OC *-s, *-h) is probably related to the Tibeto-Burman suffix *-s* (Huang 1992, Jin 2006, Schuessler 2007: 42, etc.); this was the most productive derivational affix in Classical Tibetan and obviously had aspectual functions.¹⁶ Together with the past it also appears in the imperative, i.e. in a clearly modal and future-projecting function.

(17) | | Present | Past | Future | Imperative |
|---|---|---|---|---|
| 'finish' | Sgrub | Bsgrubs | Bsgrub | Sgrubs |

When the aspectual system of Tibetan disappeared, it was gradually replaced by a new system consisting of a copula and the development of two new markers of perfective and imperfective aspect (Saxena 1997). According to Saxena (1997: 288), in the first documents in Written Tibetan, i.e. in *Dunhuang* manuscripts from the 6th century, the Tibetan morphological aspectual system is still largely attested, although first traces of its decay can already be perceived in these

---

**14** Only Early Middle Chinese according to Pulleyblank (1991).
**15** These derivations are also discussed in Xing and Schuessler (this volume) as instantiations of transitivity, direction, and voice.
**16** This *-s* never occurs following coronal finals *d n l r s*. (In some older texts, a *-d* allomorph exists after coronal finals.)

texts. In Classical Tibetan the consistent morphological marking of tense/aspect was already lost and the same structure is used for imperfective and perfective (Saxena 1997: 291) aspects. Saxena (1997: 304) concludes that the loss of the tense/aspect system coincides with the development of a new periphrastic construction expressing distinctions formerly marked by the tense/aspect morphology. Although the new Tibetan structures are somewhat different from the new aspectual structures developing in Chinese, the emergence of a new aspectual system at the beginning Early Middle Chinese period can similarly be connected to the loss of former aspectual morphology in Archaic Chinese. This has been proposed in Meisterernst (2016) and in Aldridge and Meisterernst (2018).

Example (18) from LAC shows the alternation between a Category A and a Category C reading. The *qùshēng* reading in (18b), which developed from a former *-s/*h suffix, evidently refers to an achievement and the state resulting from a preceding telic event while the reading in (18a) is transitive and causative.

(18) a. 政以治民，刑以正邪。 *Zuǒzhuàn, Yin* 11 (LAC)
    *Zhèng    yǐ   chí (\*r-de (\*drì))mín, xíng       yǐ zhèng xié*
    Government YI regulate people,     punishment YI correct bad
    'The government is necessary in order to correct the people; the punishments are necessary to correct the bad.'

   b. ... 使為左師以聽政，於是宋治。 *Zuǒzhuàn, Xi* 9 (LAC)
    ...*Shǐ  wéi    zuǒshī yǐ    tīngzhèng, yúshì*
    Cause become *zuoshi* and manage.government, thereupon
    *Sòng zhì (\*r-de-s (drì$^h$))*
    Song ordered
    '... he made him Zuoshi and let him manage the government, and thereupon Song was well ordered.'

Another form of derivation is the 'derivation by a voicing alternation' *qīng zhuó bié yì* 清濁別意, an alternation of a voiced and a voiceless initial with functions similar to the derivation by tone change. The voicing alternation is reflected by tonal differences and/or by differences in the initial consonant in Modern Mandarin (see also Xing and Schuessler, this volume).

(19) Verbs with an alternation between a [-voice] and a [+voice] initial

| Transitive variant | | | | Intransitive, unaccusative (ergative) variant | | | |
|---|---|---|---|---|---|---|---|
| bài | paɨjʰ | 敗 | destroy | bài | baɨjʰ | 敗 | destroyed (unaccusative) |
| zhé | tɕiat | 折 | break | shé | dʑiat | 折 | broken[17] |
| jiàn | kɛnʰ | 見 | see | xiàn | ɣɛnʰ | 見 | be visible[18] |

Baxter (1992: 218, following Pulleyblank 1973) attributes the voicing effect to a pre-initial element *-ɦ provisionally reconstructed for words with a cognate with a voiceless initial. Mei (2015) on the other hand proposes that a causative prefix *s- is responsible for a devoicing effect on an originally voiced initial. A causative prefix *s- has been reconstructed for Archaic Chinese and it is also well attested in Classical Tibetan (and other Tibeto-Burman languages) together with a voicing alternation. However, only very few cases of a causative prefix can be reconstructed with certainty in Archaic Chinese (Jin 2006). The situation is different with regard to a causative suffix (Jin 2006, Wang 2013).

Several arguments can be put forward in favor of the analysis of the voiced variant as the derived one and not the basic one. The first argument comes from Jin (2006: 52f) who shows that in Tibetan, no devoicing takes place following the s- prefix. According to him (Jin 2006: 109), the causative-unaccusative alternation is based on an earlier aspectual distinction. The second argument is that the unaccusative variant is always voiced. It would be difficult to account for that if it were the base form. Xing and Schuessler (this volume) argue with the straightforward active meaning of the voiceless variant against Mei's proposal. As an argument from Indo-European languages, one could add that the unaccusative form in pairs like 'break' 'broken' is always the derived form. In many Germanic

---

[17] The Middle Chinese reconstructions follow Pulleyblank (1991). The two variants of both verbs *bài* 敗 and *zhé* 折 are discussed in Jin (2006: 82f) under the label of volitional verbs (*zìzhǔ dòngcí* 自主動詞) and in the context of causation, and transitivity. Jin assumes that the change from voiceless to voiced causes a loss of volition and of transitivity (2006: 84). This argues for a localisation of these affixes in the domain of an articulated vP on a par with Travis's (2010) proposal.
[18] The two readings of 見 are discussed in Jin (2006: 67f) under e.g. the label of agentivity (*shìshì xìng* 施事性); a voiced initial appears with a theme subject (*shòu shì* 受事), and a voiceless initial with an agentive subject (*shī shì* 施事). This analysis corresponds well to the change in the semantics of the other verbs presented in this group; however, the subject of the transitive variant of the verb *jiàn* 見 is probably better labelled as an experiencer than as an agent of the verb. According to (Jin 2006: 71), the distinctive syntactic characteristic connected with a voiced initial is the lack of a subject which functions as the actor (*dòngzuò de zuòzhě* 動作的作者) of the action expressed by the verb.

languages, the 'ga/ge' prefix has basically the same function as the supposed *N-prefix (causing voicing) or the *-s suffix in Archaic Chinese.

This alternation of voiced-voiceless initials had already been connected to different verbal functions 'intransitive/passive – transitive' in the *Jīngdiǎn shìwén* (6th c. CE); the proposed functions are similar to the aspectual alternations assumed for the more frequent suffix *-s, the source of the 'derivation by tone change'. Example (20) represents the voicing alternative with the verb *bài* 敗 'defeated, defeat', one of the verbs discussed e.g. in Mei (2015). This example seems to display the same alternation between an unaccusative and a causative variant of the verb as seen in example (18). The voiced variant is unaccusative, characterised by a theme subject; unaccusative verbs are typical telic (achievement) verbs compatible with the perfective aspect. The voiceless variant is transitive and causative.

(20) a. 蔡人怒, 故不和而敗。 *Zuǒzhuàn, Yǐn* 10 (LAC)
 *Cài rén nù, gù bù hé ér bài (\*blad-s, ɦprats)*
 Cai man angry, there NEG harmonize CONJ defeated
 'The people of Cai were angry, and therefore they were not in harmony and were defeated.'

 b. 惠公之季年, 敗宋師于黃。 *Zuǒzhuàn, Yǐn* 1 (LAC)
 *Huì gōng zhī jì nián, bài (\*plad-s, prats) Sòng shī yú Huáng*
 Hui duke GEN last year, defeat Song army at Huang
 'In the last year of Duke Hui, he defeated the Song army at Huang.'
 (see also Jin Lixin 2006: 83f)

The semantic differences between the two morphological alternations, i.e. between the reconstructed suffix *-s and a reconstructed sonorant prefix have yet to be assessed. Possibly, verbs of the first category (*-s) display distinctions between atelic and telic, i.e. resultative, and those of the second category (voicing alternation) display a distinction between causative and anticausative.[19] One argument for this could be that verbs of the second group do not seem to allow the introduction of an agent; if they are followed by a PP this usually introduces a

---

[19] Xing and Schuessler (this volume) propose that the voicing alternation is employed if the transitive variant already has an *-s suffix. However, this does not account for the possible difference in the passive constructions between verbs with the voicing alternation and those with a *-s suffix.

locative and not an agent in Archaic Chinese.[20] This would be typical for anticausative verbs. (Li Yin ms.) By contrast, at least the verb *zhì* 治 of the first category does allow the introduction of an agent as in example (21a).

(21) a. 勞心者治人，勞力者治於人； *Mengzi* 3.1.4 (LAC)
*Láo xīn zhě chí rén; láo lì zhě zhì*
Exert mind-heart REL govern man; exert strength REL
*yú rén*
governed by man
'Those who exert their minds, govern others; those who exert their strength are governed by others.'

b. 十九年春，楚子禦之，大敗於津。 *Zuozhuan, Zhuang* 19 (LAC)
*shí jiǔ nián chū, Chǔ zǐ yù zhī, dà bài yú jīn*
ten nine year spring, Chuzi fend OBJ, great defeated at ford
'In the spring of the nineteenth year, the Prince of Chu fought against them and was greatly defeated at the ford.'

These examples show the relevance of studies on historical phonology for the analysis of Chinese diachronic grammar and specifically for the analysis of the aspectual system of Chinese. If Abraham and Leiss (2008) are correct in their hypothesis on universal relations between modal readings and the aspectual feature of the complement verb, a loss of a morphological marking can be expected to induce changes in the syntax of the language.

Early Middle Chinese was subjected to a number of substantial changes. Although Chinese never was a synthetic language comparable to the Indo-European languages, a drift from a more synthetic to a more analytic language can be observed particularly in the verbal system during this period. This includes changes in light verb constructions, the emergence of resultative constructions, disyllabification processes etc. (see e.g. Huang 2014, Feng 2014, Mei Guang 2015, Hu 2016, and others), a change from synthetic to analytic modal negation, from synthetic to analytic causative constructions, the development of the source structures of the aspectual systems in the Modern Sinitic languages and more. Some of these features and their changes in historical syntax have been discussed e.g. in Lin (2001) and briefly in Feng (2014) and others. The hypothesis proposed in this paper is that these changes can be

---

**20** This situation changes later and verbs such as *bài* 敗 are permitted in the *wéi* 為 ... *suǒ* 所 passive construction. The functional distinction between the two affixes still requires more research.

attributed to the entire loss of the former derivational morphological system of Chinese. In the aspectual system, distinctions are increasingly expressed by lexical means, i.e. by aspectual adverbs and possibly by sentence final particles, before a new structure for the marking of aspect develops in the EMC period. In the modal system, the entire loss of any morphological marking of aspectual distinctions may have triggered the development of a more complex system of modal marking and the emergence of the first true deontic verbs in Chinese.

# 4 Deontic markers in Late Archaic and Early Middle Chinese

## 4.1 The first deontic modal verbs in Late Archaic Chinese and Early Middle Chinese

In Late Archaic Chinese, deontic modality is almost exclusively expressed by verbs of possibility. A deontic reading of these modals requires negation or the particular syntactic context of rhetorical questions. But negation does not necessarily yield a deontic reading. The most frequent of modal verbs expressing obligation in Late Archaic Chinese is the possibility modal *kě* 可 appearing in combination with double negation BU KE (YI) BU: 'cannot not ≫ have to, must'. In this combination, the deontic reading is mandatory, whereas with simple negation preceding KE: BU KE(YI), both deontic or circumstantial possibility readings are available. The interchange between a deontic and possibility reading can be accounted for by the fact that the negation of possibility is semantically equivalent to necessity: it is not possible that not $p \neg \Diamond \neg p' = \Box p$ 'it is necessary that $p$'. The semantic differences between possibility and necessity become particularly obvious under the scope of negation (Cormack and Smith 2002). According to the scopal features of negation, two different categories of modal verbs can be distinguished in English: Modal$_1$ which scopes over negation (necessity), and Modal$_2$ which is in the scope of negation (possibility, circumstantial readings) (Cormack and Smith 2002, also Butler 2003). Of the modal verbs of Late Archaic Chinese, only *kě* 可 will be discussed here, because it most typically obtains deontic functions. One of the reasons for this may be its particular syntactic structure, requiring a passivized resultative complement in unmarked employment. *Dé* 得 can also have deontic readings, but because it differs structurally and semantically from *kě* 可, it will not be included in the discussion. The possibility modal *néng* 能 basically expresses participant-internal ability; root (deontic) readings do not occur unless they are induced by an additional deontic marker, e.g. a deontic negative marker. The modal auxiliary verb *bì* 必 will also be excluded from the discussion because the scopal features of negation demonstrate that it remains in the lexical layer in Late Archaic and Early Middle Chinese (Meisterernst 2017b). The same accounts for the modal *xū* 須 which appears as a modal verb in Early Middle Chinese and which is syntactically and semantically similar to *bì*. Following the analysis of the modal verb *kě*, the newly emerging modal verbs *dāng* 當 and *yīng* 應 will be discussed briefly.

### 4.1.1 The modal verb *kě* 可

The basic modal reading of the verb *kě(yǐ)* 可(以) 'can, possible' is to express circumstantial root possibility (Meisterernst 2008a). This is a participant-external prospect that is due to factors and circumstances that fall outside the participant's control. In this function, it belongs to the class of 'first modals' (Leiss 2008: 16). Syntactically, it is located in the lexical layer according to Tsai's (2015) cartographic approach to modals in Chinese.

In contrast to the other modal auxiliary verbs discussed in this paper, for the complement of *kě* 可 different analyses are mandatory in LAC depending on the presence or absence of the functional head *yǐ* 以. These are:
a) *kě* 可+vP;[21] the complement verb is passivized referring to a resultant state; the internal argument of the event appears in subject position, the complement verb focuses on the change of state point; the causer (agent) of the event is not included;
b) *kěyǐ* 可以+ vP: the complement verb remains transitive or intransitive, the external argument of the complement verb appears in the subject position and can be the agent (causer) of a transitive verb, or the agent, or the experiencer (e.g. with adjectives or state verbs) of an intransitive verb. Only state verbs which can include an event variable are available for this construction.

In Early Middle Chinese, the stringent distinction between the complements of *kě* 可 and of *kě yǐ* 可以 weakens considerably (see Meisterernst 2008a) and the

---

[21] The complement of KE is not a simple VP, but has a more complex structure, which may contain a causative head and an Inner Aspect Phrase in which telicity is generated.

complement of *kě* 可 is not necessarily passivized any longer; this is exemplified in (22c).²² (22a) represents the first structure, and (22b) represents the second structure.

(22) a. 紂 可 伐 矣 。 *Shǐjì*: 3; 108 (EMC)
　　　 Zhòu kě fá　 yǐ
　　　 Zhou can attack FIN
　　　 'Zhou can/must be attacked.'

　　 b. 晉 其 可 以 逆 天 乎 ? *Shǐjì*: 39; 1653 (EMC)
　　　 Jìn qí　 kě yǐ nì　　　 tiān　 hú
　　　 Jin MOD can YI go-against Heaven FIN
　　　 '... could Jin possibly go against Heaven = it may not go against Heaven?'

　　 c. 臣 愚 以 為 可 賜 爵 關 內 侯 *Hànshū* 36: 1947 (EMC)
　　　 chén yú　 yǐ wéi kě cì　　 jué guān nèi hóu,
　　　 I　　 stupid assume can bestow rank pass inner marquis,
　　　 'I am stupid, but I assume that you can / should bestow upon him a position and make him marquis of Guannei, ...'

The possibility modal *kě* 可 is the only modal verb in Late Archaic and Early Middle Chinese which requires a theme subject and a passivized (resultative = perfective) complement on a regular basis. In this particular requirement it can be compared to the Old High German and Old English deontic verbs which have a perfective infinitive complement marked by the prefix *ge-*. Perfective infinitives with *ge-* most frequently appear with the verbs *mugen* 'may' and *kunnen* 'can', which both express possibility and are thus semantically similar to the verb *kě*. The external argument of the complement verb of *kě* can only be licensed in the presence of *yǐ*.²³ In both constructions KE+VP²⁴ and KEYI+VP, the complements selected refer to events or to states resulting from a previous event: with KEYI the complement verb retains its original lexical aspect, and with KE it always refers to an achievement, a resultant state. The complement verbs can belong to those verbs which show a morphological distinction between causative and unaccusative/resultative readings, but they do not have to. All verbs, for which either the suffix *-s* or the voicing alternation are reconstructed can appear as

---

22 For a discussion on the different analyses of this construction and the role of *yǐ* 以 see Meisterernst (2008a).
23 I will not discuss the exact functional status of *yǐ* in this paper. This is still subject to debate (e.g. Meisterernst 2008a, Djamouri 2009, Aldridge 2012). But according to Aldridge (2012) it can be analysed as an applicative head, which has the function to add an argument to the structure.
24 Capitals refer to a construction or a functional category.

the complement of KE. Thus there is no constraint with regard to a distinction between verbs that are permitted in the *yú* 於 passive in Late Archaic Chinese and those that apparently are not. Although Li Yin (ms.) shows that verbs of all situation types can appear in the *yú* passive, i.e. in passive constructions in which the agent is introduced by the preposition *yú*, the verbs with a voicing alternation, such as *bài* 敗, do not seem to be permitted in this construction (see (20) and (21)). Possibly, verbs with the voicing alternation are marked morphologically as true anti-causative verbs which are characterized by the constraint of not permitting an agent.

As already mentioned deontic readings of possibility modals first appear in combination with negation or in rhetorical questions (see Liu 2000, Li 2001, Meisterernst 2008b).[25] Following Tsai's (2015) analysis of modals in Modern Mandarin, circumstantial and deontic readings should differ syntactically. Tsai (following Rizzi 1997) proposes that the different modal readings are generated in different syntactic layers: epistemic modality is realized in the CP layer; deontic modality is realized in the TP layer, and dynamic/circumstantial modality is realized in the *v*P layer. Other approaches to the syntax of modals propose similar distinctions into two different kinds of modals (see e.g. Butler 2003). Cormack and Smith (2002) propose a functional head Pol(arity) (POS/NEG) in TP, which divides modals into two groups according to the semantic scope of negation:
1) Modal₁ in the pre-Pol (POS/NEG) position = deontic modality (necessity);
2) Modal₂ in the post-Pol position = dynamic / circumstantial) modality (possibility).

The pre-Pol position corresponds to the inflectional (TP) layer in which deontic modality is generated, and the post-Pol position corresponds to the lexical layer in which dynamic modality (possibility and root possibility) is realized (according to Tsai's cartographic approach). Since negation plays a vital role in the distinction of the different modal readings of KE, an analysis of the semantic scope of negation following Cormack and Smith (2002) will be employed to provide arguments for the different syntactic realizations of the originally dynamic modal in Late Archaic and Early Middle Chinese. The proposal of a polarity head accounts particularly well for the strong deontic reading of KE in combination with double negation.[26]

---

[25] The close connection between modal readings and negation was pointed out by Lü Shuxiang (1942).
[26] The precise syntactic analysis is not at issue here; it will be discussed in a separate study.

- Simple negation with *kě* 可: NEG *kě* 不可

In simple negation, with a negative marker preceding *kě*, the modal verb is polysemous: two different readings, the circumstantial and the deontic reading are possible. In the circumstantial possibility reading, the modal verb is in the scope of the negative marker. It can be paraphrased by: 'not possible that V': NOT [POSSIBLE V = root / circumstantial possibility. In the second reading the modal functions as a necessity operator, the negation marker is within the semantic scope of the necessity marker. This can be paraphrased by: 'necessary that not V': NECESSARY [NOT V = deontic necessity reading. The circumstantial reading is represented by (23), and the deontic necessity reading is represented by (24).

(23) a. 鼻大可小，小不可大也。 *Han Fei zi* 23 (LAC)
Bí dà kě xiǎo, xiǎo bù kě dà yě
Nose big can small, small NEG KE big SFP
'If the nose is big it can be made smaller, if it is small it cannot be made bigger.'
Paraphrase: 'it is not possible that it is made bigger': NOT [POSSIBLE

b. 此城最勝。諸方所推。不可破壞。 *Taishō* 1; no.1, p.12c (EMC)
Cǐ chéng zuì shèng, zhū fāng suǒ tuī,
This city most superior, PL direction REL press,
bù kě pòhuài
NEG can destroy
'This city is most superior: from whatever direction it is pushed against, it cannot be destroyed.'
Paraphrase: it is not possible that it can be destroyed; NOT [POSSIBLE

(24) a. 君子曰：「善不可失，惡不可長，... *Zuozhuan, Yin* 6 (LAC)
Jūnzǐ yuē: shàn bù kě shī, è bù kě cháng
Gentleman say: good NEG can neglect, evil NEG can prolong
'The gentleman says: "The good may not be neglected; the evil may not be prolonged."'
Paraphase: it is necessary that the good not be neglected ... NECESSARY [NOT

b. 我今寧當捨此身命，不可毀破三世諸佛所制禁戒。 *Taishō* 4; no.202, p.381b (EMC)
Wǒ jīn níng dāng shě cǐ shēn mìng, bù kě
I now MOD$_{epistemic}$ DANG abandon this body life, NEG can

huǐpò    sān shì    zhū fó    suǒ zhì    jīnjiè
destroy three period PL Buddha REL determine precept
'I now should rather abandon this body and life; I must not destroy the precepts which the Buddhas of the three periods determined.'
Paraphrase: it is necessary not to destroy ... NECESSARY [NOT

–Double negation with *kě(yǐ)*: NEG *kě(yǐ)* NEG 不可(以)不
The doubly negated construction NEG *kě(yǐ)* 可(以) NEG vP always codes strong deontic modality, i.e. a strong obligation 'must'; it never expresses root possibility (Meisterernst 2008b). The literal meaning of the construction is 'it is not possible that not *p* ¬◊¬ *p*', resulting in the reading of □*p* as 'it is necessary that *p*'. The deontic reading is derived from the strong positive polarity triggered by double negation. The complements in this construction do not differ syntactically from the complements of KE in its circumstantial reading. In (25), the verbs are both transitive and passivized, referring to a resultant state that must be obtained in the future; the patient of the passivized matrix verb appears in the subject position.

(25) a. 不敬二君，不可不討也。  *Zuǒzhuàn, Dìng* 6 (LAC)
Bù jìng    èr jūn,   bù kě bù tǎo    yě
NEG respectful two prince, NEG can NEG punish SFP
'... he is disrespecting the two princes, and [thus] he has to (< cannot not) be punished.'
Paraphrase: it is necessary that he be punished: NECESSARY [POS

b. 范、中行數有德於齊，不可不救。  *Shǐjì*: 32; 1505 (EMC)
Fàn, Zhōngháng shuò yǒu dé    yú    Qí, bù kě bù jiù
Fan Zhonghang often have favour PREP Qi, NEG can NEG rescue
'The Fan and Zhonghang families have often done favors to Qi; they have to (< cannot not) be rescued.'
Paraphrase: it is necessary that they be Ved: NECESSARY [POS

In (26), originally intransitive verbs appear as complement of *kě*. Since *kě* requires the internal argument of the complement verb as its subject, originally intransitive verbs are causativized in order to license an internal argument which can move up to the subject position. The complement verb again refers to a resultant state projected into the future.

(26) a. 君子曰：「位其不可不慎也乎！  *Zuǒzhuàn Chéng* 2 (LAC)
jūnzǐ    yuē: wèi    qí    bù kě bù shèn    yě hū
gentleman say position$_{theme}$ MOD NEG can NEG careful SFP SFP

'The gentleman says: "The rank has to be (< cannot not be) treated carefully!"'
Paraphrase: it is necessary that it be Ved: NECESSARY [POS

b. 親而不可不廣者，仁也； *Zhuāngzǐ* 11.5.10 (LAC)
*Qīn   ér   bù   kě   bù   guǎng   zhě,        rén         yě*
intimate CON NEG can NEG broaden REL$_{subj\_theme}$, benevolence SFP
'What is intimate but has to (< cannot not) be broadened – this is benevolence.'
Paraphrase: it is necessary that it be Ved: NECESSARY [POS

In (27), the passivization effect of KE is neutralized and the external argument of the complement verb is licensed in the subject position by the insertion of *yǐ* 以 following *kě*. In (27a) and (27b), the subject is agentive. The verbs in the complements of the modal all include an event argument. The verb in (27c) is an originally intransitive verb which remains intransitive due to the presence of *yǐ*, which is required to license an external argument as the subject of *kě*.

(27) a. 君子不可以不刳心焉。 *Zhuāngzǐ* 12.2.1 (LAC)
*Jūnzǐ   bù   kě   yǐ   bù   kū       xīn   yán*
Gentleman NEG can YI NEG cut.open heart PP
'A gentleman must (< cannot not) cut open his heart for it.'
Paraphrase: it is necessary that V: NECESSARY [POS

b. 大將軍尊重益貴，君不可以不拜. *Shǐjì*:120; 3108 (EMC)
*dà   jiàngjūn   zūn       zhòng   yì   guì,     jūn*
great general   venerable important more honour, prince
*bù   kě   yǐ   bù   bài*
NEG can YI NEG bow
'The great general is very important and is receiving more and more honours; you have to (< cannot not) bow to show him your reverence.'
Paraphrase: it is necessary that V: NECESSARY [POS

c. 齊將伐晉，不可以不懼。」 *Zuǒzhuàn Xiāng* 22 (LAC)
*Qí jiāng fá      Jìn, bù   kě   yǐ   bù   jù*
Qi FUT attack Jin, NEG can YI NEG fear
'Qi will attack Jin; we have to (cannot not) be(come) afraid.'
Paraphrase: it is necessary that V: NECESSARY [POS

Due to its characteristics of always referring to a telic (accomplishment or achievement) event, the VP in the complement of KE(YI) is bi-phasic, the condition for non-epistemic modal readings. The complement of KE can refer either to the process event $E_1$ (including $t_m$) or to the resultant state event $E_2$ (including $t_m$) with verbs which have the structure proposed for event (terminative) verbs in Abraham and Leiss (2008: XIII). In LAC, the complement of KE always refers to $E_2$; in order to refer to $E_1$, the insertion of YI is required. Temporally, the predicate has the characteristic S ≠ E (speech time is not identical with, i.e. it precedes, event time), which structure is proposed for deontic modality in Japanese by Narrog (2008) and is the general structure for deontic modality which typically refers to an obligation performed in the future.,[27]

(28)  event: | >>>[>>>>>> | .........] ........|
           $t_1$   [$E_1$     $t_m$    $E_2$]    $t_n$
              不可不       不可不
              deontic event   projected future

## 4.2 New deontic modal verbs in Early Middle Chinese

The two verbs *dāng* 當 and *yīng* 應, which grammaticalized into modal verbs in Early Middle Chinese, will be discussed in this section.

### 4.2.1 The diachronic development of *dāng* and *yīng* from Late Archaic to Early Middle Chinese

The modal function of *dāng* 當 grammaticalized from a verb with the basic meaning 'match, correspond'.[28] As a modal auxiliary verb it expresses root/deontic necessity: □p 'it is necessary that p', roughly corresponding to modal 'should' in English. *Dāng* 當 is regularly attested as a modal verb from the Han period (206 BCE – 220 CE) on.[29] It occurs predominantly in indirect suggestions uttered by the speaker with regard to the – frequently unspecified –

---

[27] According to Reichenbach's distinction into speech time (S), reference time (R), and event time (E).
[28] In Late Archaic Chinese, it can also function as a temporal and local preposition; and in Middle Chinese it can function as a future marker.
[29] For a comprehensive discussion on modal DANG see Meisterernst (2011).

agent based on laws, rules, and norms (deontic modality), but it also expresses circumstantial modality. The verb *yīng/yìng* 應 occurs almost exclusively as a full verb in Late Archaic Chinese, mostly in the meaning 'answer, react, etc.',[30] or 'deserve to', correspond to'. It only very occasionally appears as an auxiliary verb. In Early Middle Chinese, particularly in the early Buddhist literature, its employment as a modal verb increases and, simultaneously, the number of its occurrences as a full verb decreases. According to its syntactic environment, different kinds of deontic modal values, from strict deontic modality, i.e. contexts of direct command and advice, to bouletic and teleological modal values are attested; the latter rather belong to the category of circumstantial modality.[31]

(29) and (30) represent the development of *dāng* and *yīng* from lexical verbs to modal auxiliary verbs. In (29a) DANG appears as a lexical verb; in (29b) it has an unaccusative verb as its complement; in (29c) it has an unergative; and in (29d) it has a transitive verb as its complement.

(29) a. 孤子當室，冠衣不純采 (*Lǐjì* 禮記, *Qūlǐ shàng* 曲禮上)
gū zǐ dāng shì, guān yī bù zhǔn cǎi
orphan son correspond house, cap dress NEG border colourful
'And if the orphaned son has taken care of the house, his cap and clothes are not decorated with colours.'

b. 我真王嗣，當立，吾欲求之 (*Shǐjì* 史記 31,1463)
wǒ zhēn wáng sì, dāng lì, wú yù qiú zhī
I true king successor, DANG enthrone, I want require OBJ
'I am the true successor to the king who should be enthroned, and I want to insist on it.'

c. 朱公長男以為赦，弟固當出也 (*Shǐjì* 41,1754)
Zhū gōng zhǎng nán yǐwéi shè dì gù
Zhū father older son think release younger.brother certainly
dāng chū yě
DANG go.out SFP

---

30 See also Li (2004: 234f).
31 Anderl (2004: 417) assumes that *yīng* 應 also serves to express epistemic modality in the *Zǔtáng jí* and that this function was possibly "introduced by Indian Buddhist logic which was introduced to China through the translation of Sanskrit scriptures." On the other hand, the development of an epistemic reading from originally deontic readings is well attested e.g. in the Germanic languages.

'The oldest son of father Zhu thought that since there was an amnesty, his younger brother should certainly get out.'

d. 天子儀當獨奉酌祠始皇廟 (*Shǐjì* 6,266)
   tiān zǐ yí dāng dú fèngzhuó cí
   heaven son ceremony DANG alone offer.wine sacrifice
   Shǐ Huáng miào
   Shǐ Huáng temple
   'According to the rites of the Son of Heaven, you alone should offer wine as a sacrifice at the temple of Shi Huang.'

In (30a) *yīng* appears as a transitive lexical verb in a Late Archaic Chinese text, while in (30b) it appears followed by a complement which could be analyzed as either nominal or verbal. Constructions like this pave the way for the grammaticalization of a verb to an auxiliary verb. In (30c) *yīng* appears with an unaccusative verb as its complement and in (30d) with a transitive verb.

(30) a. 叔向弗應。 (*Zuozhuan, Xiang* 21, Late Archaic Chinese)
   shú xiàng fú yīng
   Shu Xiang NEG$_{tr}$ respond
   'Shu Xiang did not respond to it.'

b. 匹夫熒侮諸侯者，罪應誅，請右司馬速刑焉。 (*Kongzi jiayu* 1.1, Early Middle Chinese)
   Pǐfū yíng wǔ zhūhóu zhě, zuì yīng zhū,
   Common.man mock feudal lord NOM, crime YING punish,
   qǐng yòu sīmǎ sù xíng yán
   ask right marshal quick punish him
   'If a common man mocks the feudal lords he deserves punishment/should be punished; I ask the marshal to the right to punish him quickly.'

c. 此白象寶，唯轉輪王，乃得之耳，今有小過，不應喪失。
   *Xianyujing* (*Taishō* 4; no.202 p. 372c Early Middle Chinese)
   Cǐ bái xiàng bǎo, wéi zhuǎnlúnwáng nǎi dé
   This white elephant precious, only turn-wheel-king then get
   zhī ěr jīn yǒu xiǎo guò bù yīng sāngshī
   OBJ SFP, now have small fault, NEG YING forfeit
   'This white elephant is precious, only a wheel-turning king can obtain it; even though it has a small fault, it should not be forfeited.'

d. 王告之言：『象若不調，不應令吾乘之；
   (*Xianyujing*, *Taishō* 4; no.202, p. 372c Early Middle Chinese)
   *Wáng gào zhī yán xiàng   ruò bù  tiáo, bù  yīng líng*
   King tell OBJ say elephant if   NEG tame, NEG YING make
   *wú chéng zhī*
   me ride   OBJ
   'The king told him: "If the elephant is not tamed, you should not make me ride it."'

The modal meaning of both verbs derives from a lexical meaning implying an appropriate reaction to something. The complement verbs of DANG and YING are mostly telic agentive verbs; they can be either transitive or they can – similar to the construction with KE – appear passivized in resultative constructions. But in contrast to KE, for which a passivized complement is required in Late Archaic Chinese unless it is followed by YI, DANG and YING do not require a passivized complement. This may be connected to the fact that at the time when the latter emerged any possible morphological distinctions between causative and resultant state and/or anticausative readings had certainly become entirely opaque. Similar to the construction with KE, the modal predicates with DANG and YING show a semantic sensitivity of the subject to the complement verb rather than to the modal; this is typical for raising constructions (Lin 2011): the subjects of the complement verb and the modal verb are not identical. Apart from *néng*,[32] which is probably a control verb, modals seem rather to be raising verbs in Late Archaic and Early Middle Chinese.[33] That *kě*, *dāng*, and *yīng* are raising verbs can be evidenced by the passivization test (Ademola-Ademoye 2011): all three verbs require or allow passive constructions in their complements.

### 4.2.2 A brief discussion of *dāng* and *yīng* as deontic markers

Unlike with the strong deontic construction NEG *kě(yǐ)* 可(以) NEG *v*P and the modal auxiliary verb *bì* 必, with *dāng* and *yīng* the speaker does not necessarily expect compliance on the side of the frequently only-implied agent. As with 'should' in English, the modal force of obligation is weaker than with 'must'. The strength of obligation is induced by the strength of the ordering source for the

---

[32] The status of *dé* 得 as an auxiliary verb is unclear and begs further research.
[33] This distinction between raising and control constructions of modal verbs is difficult to maintain in Chinese (see e.g. Lin and Tang 1995), and it has been abandoned by a number of scholars.

modal. When the necessity is induced by laws and regulations, these ordering sources imply a stronger obligation than when the necessity follows predetermination by destiny (Meisterernst 2011). True epistemic values are not attested with any of these verbs in LAC and very few in EMC, unless they appear in the complement of an epistemic, for instance, an attitude verb; they do not depend on the modal.[34] In contrast to the possibility modal KE which only obtains a true deontic reading in the syntactic context of negation and rhetorical questions, YING and DANG can express deontic readings independently of any syntactic trigger. Additionally, their complements are not confined to passivized, i.e. to telic resultative complements, unless otherwise marked. Accordingly, their syntactic structure clearly distinguishes them from the deontic marker KE. Thus, they are the first verbs (apart from *bì* 必) which do not require a particular syntactic trigger to function as deontic markers. These syntactic triggers can be negation or rhetorical questions. Additionally, the verb in their complement can be either unaccusative/passive or transitive without any additional marking.[35]

– The deontic modal *dāng*

Early deontic readings of DANG are represented by (31) in sentences from the Western and the Eastern Han period respectively.[36] The complement verb in (31a) is passivized, the patient/theme appears in the subject position. In (31b), and (31c), the complement verb is transitive, so the non-overt external argument is licensed in the subject position. Similar to the construction with KE, the identification of a particular agent is irrelevant. This is the most typical employment of *dāng* 當 in its earliest instances as a modal verb. In (31c) the modal verb *dāng* is negated. In contrast to the modals of possibility, for which the readings 'NOT [POSSIBLE and NECESSARY [NOT' are not necessarily equivalent (although they are logically equivalent), this is not the case with *dāng*. The reading 'NOT [APPROPRIATE' always corresponds to the reading 'NECESSARY [NOT'. The ambiguity between the different possibility readings and the necessity of a particular trigger in order to express obligation together with the entire loss of former morphological distinctions of resultant states and passivization may well have served as a trigger for the development of a more complex modal system in early Middle Chinese and the emergence of true markers of deontic modality.

---

34 A comprehensive discussion of the development of *dāng* has been provided in Wu Xueru (2014), see note 4. Xiong and Meisterernst (2019) demonstrate that there are some early instance of epistemic readings of *dāng* already in EMC.
35 For the requirements of a deontic reading of *bì* 必, see Meisterernst (2017a). A deontic reading is not possible with a theme or patient subject of the complement verb.
36 For more examples and a more comprehensive discussion on DANG see Meisterernst (2017a and 2017b).

(31) a. 群臣議，皆曰「長當棄市」。 (*Shǐjì*: 10; 426, Early Middle Chinese)
Qún chén yì, jiē yuē Cháng dāng qì shì
All minister discuss, all say Chang DANG abandon expose.marketplace
'The ministers discussed it, and they all said: "Chang should be executed and exposed in the marketplace."'

b. 我方先君後臣，因謂王即弗用鞅，當殺之.
(*Shǐjì*: 68; 2227, Early Middle Chinese)
Wǒ fāng xiān jūn hòu chén, yīn wèi wáng jí
I ASP forward ruler put.behind vassal, therefore say king if
fú yòng Yǎng, dāng shā zhī
NEG employ Yang, DANG kill OBJ
'I am just putting the ruler first and the vassal last, and therefore I told the king that if he did not employ you, Yang, he should kill you.'

c. 說所不當道，觀所不當視，此謂不能專心正色矣。
(*Hou Hanshu, Nüjie*, Early Middle Chinese)
Shuō suǒ bù dàng dǎo, guān suǒ bù dāng shì,
Say REL NEG DANG tell, observe REL NEG DANG see,
cǐ wèi bù néng zhuān xīn zhèng sè yǐ
this call NEG able concentrate mind correct appearance SFP
'To mention what one should not tell, to observe what one should not see, this means that one is not able to concentrate the mind and to keep the appearance correct.'
Paraphrase: it is not appropriate that V: NOT [APPROPRIATE = it is necessary that not NECESSARY [NOT

(32) shows DANG as a fully developed deontic auxiliary verb. In (32a) and (32b) a direct obligation is issued towards a 2nd person addressee subject; additionally, (32b), and (32c) demonstrate that DANG precedes an adverbial *wh*-word, which argues for its high syntactic position in TP.

(32) a. 諸族姓子，悉當信佛誠諦至教，勿得猶豫.
(*Taishō* 9, no.263, p.113a, Early Middle Chinese)
Zhū zúxìng zǐ, xī dāng xìn fó chéngdì,
All good.family son, completely DANG believe Buddha truth
zhìjiào wú dé yóuyù
excellent.teaching, NEG$_{mod}$ get doubt
'All you sons of good families should believe in the Buddha's truthful and most excellent teachings, and should not have any doubts.'

b. 設有是問者。汝當云何答。 (*Taishō* 1, no.1, p.112b, Early Middle Chinese)
   Shè yǒu shì wèn    zhě, rǔ dāng yúnhé dá
   If  have this question REL, you DANG how   answer
   'If there are any with these questions, in which way should you answer?'

c. 我當云何令諸眾生心歡喜耶？ (*Pusa benyuan jian zhong*, Early Middle Chinese)
   Wǒ dāng yúnhé lìng zhū zhòng    shēng xīn  huānxǐ yé
   I   DANG how   make PL multitude living heart happy  SFP$_{quest}$
   'In which way should I make all the living beings happy in their hearts?'

The aspectual characteristics of the complement verb of DANG resemble those of KE(YI).

a) The complement verb appears in an unaccusative (passive) construction referring to a resultant state similar to the construction with *kě* 可. The theme/patient of the complement verb moves to subject position.
b) The complement appears in an agentive/causative construction without any additional marking; in its earliest instances the external argument of the agentive verb is not realized overtly. This changes particularly in the early Buddhist literature (from the 2nd c. CE on).

(33)  event:       |>>>>  [>>>>>> >|..........].......|
                   t₁     [E₁    t$_m$    E₂]    t$_n$
                          當              當
                   deontic event    projected future

- The deontic modal *yīng*

Deontic readings of YING are represented in (34). In (34a) and (34d), the complement verbs are passivized. In (34b) and (34c) the complements are transitive; in (34b) the external argument, the addressee of the obligation, appears in the subject position. In (34c) and (34d), YING occurs in combination with negation; in (34c), with simple and in (34d), with double negation. Identical to DANG, the original reading of BU YING 'not correspond (appropriately)' ⇒ NOT [APPROPRIATE' always corresponds to the reading 'NECESSARY [NOT'. The negation marker is within the semantic scope of the necessity marker and YING functions as a deontic auxiliary. In contrast to DANG, though, and similar to KE, YING also occurs in double negation: NEG+Mod$_{deontic}$+NEG ⇔ 'not appropriate that not p = it is necessary that p: ¬◊¬ p' = □p'; in these cases, an interpretation NOT NECESSARY NOT does not seem to be appropriate. Although negation is not necessary to trigger the deontic reading of YING, in cases such as (34d), the circumstantial reading derived in the lexical layer is still present. This construction may provide some evidence for a similar path of grammaticalization for all modal verbs discussed in this section. And it also provides some evidence for the existence of a polarity head dividing Modal₁ and Modal₂ with regard to the modal verbs *dāng* and *yīng*.

(34) a. 汝今為我等作平等主。應護者護。應責者責。應遣者遣。當共集米。以相供給。 (*Taisho* 1, no.1, p.38b25, Early Middle Chinese)
Rǔ  jīn   wèi wǒ děng zuò   píngděng zhǔ,   yīng hù    zhě
You now for I   PL   make equality   master, YING protect REL
hù,    yīng zé   zhě zé,    yīng qiǎn   zhě qiǎn,
protect, YING correct REL correct, YING banish REL banish,
dāng gōng   jí    mǐ, yǐ       xiāng   gōngjǐ
DANG together collect rice, in.order.to mutually provide
'You will now be the master of equality for us; those who have to be protected, protect; those who have to be corrected, correct; those who have to be banished, banish; we will collect rice in order to provide you in turn.'

b. 汝等天、人、阿修羅眾，皆應到此，為聽法故。 (*Taisho* 9, n.262, p.19b, Early Middle Chinese)
Rǔ děng tiān, rén,  āxiūluó zhòng,   jiē yīng dào  cǐ,
You PL   deva, man, Asura    multitude, all YING arrive this,
wèi tīng  fǎ     gù
for listen dharma reason
'All you devas, people, Asuras, you should all come here in order to listen to the dharma.'

c. 又人子禮，不應竭用父母庫藏令其盡也。 (*Xianyujing* T04n0202_p0411b, Early Middle Chinese)
Yòu rén zǐ  lǐ,       bù yīng jié    yòng fù    mǔ
Again man son propriety, NEG YING exhaust use   father mother
kùzàng         líng qí  jǐn    yě
treasure.house make GEN exhaust SFP
'Furthermore, according to the proper behaviour for a son, he should not completely use up his parents' treasure house and cause it to be used up completely'
NECESSARY / SHOULD [ NOT

d. 今得用施，不應不與。(*Xianyujing* T04n0202_p0392b, Eary Middle Chinese)
   Jīn  dé  yòng  shī,      bù  yīng  bù  yǔ
   Now can use    distribute, NEG YING NEG give
   'Now they can be used and distributed and they should be given.'
   Paraphrase: it is not appropriate/possible that they not be given:
   SHOULD [ POS

The aspectual characteristics of the complement verb of YING resemble those of DANG and of KE(YI).
a) The complement verb appears in an unaccusative (passive) construction referring to a resultant state similar to the construction with *kě* 可. The theme/patient of the complement verb moves to subject position.
b) The complement appears in an agentive/causative construction without any additional marking; from the earliest instances on the external argument of the agentive verb can either be overtly realized or covert.

(35) event:   | >>>> [>>>>>> >| .........] .......|
              $t_1$    $[E_1$    $t_m$   $E_2]$   $t_n$
                       應            應
              deontic event  projected future

# 5 Conclusion

Syntactically, in LAC and EMC all modal auxiliary verbs, including possibility modals and true deontic modals, seem to occupy the same position in the lexical layer below TP and aspect. But an analysis of the semantic scope of negation based on a proposal by Cormack and Smith (2002) confirms that deontic readings are actually generated in a higher position than circumstantial readings. Cormack and Smith (2002) propose a functional head Pol(arity) (POS/NEG) in TP which divides modals into two groups according to the semantic scope of negation: 1) Modal$_1$ expressing deontic modality (necessity) appears in the pre-Pol (pos/neg) position; 2) Modal$_2$, expressing possibility (dynamic/circumstantial) modality appears in the post-Pol position. The pre-Pol position corresponds to the inflectional syntactic layer in which deontic modality is generated and the post-Pol position corresponds to the lexical layer, typical for dynamic modals (possibility and root possibility circumstantial modals) according to Tsai's cartographic approach (e.g. Tsai 2015).

Of the different categories of modal verbs within the range of deontic readings only the three most prominent ones in Late Archaic and Early Middle Chinese have been discussed in this paper:
1) The modal verb of possibility *kě(yǐ)* 可(以), expressing root possibility (Modal$_2$) as its basic reading, characterized by the particular syntactic constraints of its complement, i.e. the requirement of a resultant (passivized and perfective) complement in the default case without YI.
2) The deontic modals *dāng* 當, and *yīng* 應 (ex. 2), expressing deontic modality (Modal$_1$); the complement verb is not subject to particular syntactic constraints.

The similarities and differences between the two categories are as follows:
a) All three modal verbs derive from lexical verbs and they start as modal verbs in the lexical layer (Modal$_2$), before they grammaticalize or partly grammaticalize into Modal$_1$.
b) A – possibly morphologically marked – resultant state complement is required as the default complement of KE (without YI), the 'first modal'. A resultant state, perfective reading can refer to a completed 'ideal' situation in the future typical for deontic readings without any additional marking. This may have sufficed to express the different shades of root readings with this one verb: circumstantial modal meanings are expressed in the lexical layer and deontic modal readings are expressed when the modal is raised to a polarity head in the TP layer.
c) All three modal verbs allow passivization and a resultant state complement; i.e. all three modals are raising verbs. YING and DANG allow, but do not require passivization of their complements, different from KE, which does. In contrast to KE, YING and DANG permit a transitive/causative complement without any additional licensing in their original structure. At the time of their emergence as fully grammaticalized modals any morphological differences between resultant state and causative verb forms had certainly disappeared.
d) Independent of any marking, the temporal structure of the complements is identical in all three modals; it always includes the feature of telicity.
e) Only KE(YI) requires a particular syntactic context, i.e. negation (including double negation) or rhetorical questions, in order to license a deontic reading; both YING and DANG do not require any additional syntactic licensing. The semantics of the construction NEG+YING+NEG argue for a similar basis of grammaticatization of all verbs.

Although it is very difficult to prove the connection between the loss of an aspectual morphology and the rise of new modals expressing deontic modality, there is a high probability for a temporal coincidence of this loss and the emergence of new linguistic systems to replace the lost morphology. Both a new aspectual system and a more elaborate modal system emerge at the same time, and in particular the aspectual constraints on the complement of KE, which may have been morphologically marked in Archaic Chinese, provide an indirect argument in favor of the connection between a lost aspectual morphology and the rise of an elaborate modal system. This claim is also supported cross-linguistically by the development in the Germanic languages caused by a loss of their aspectual morphology. The modal systems of languages with an explicit aspectual morphology are frequently poorer than those of languages which lost this kind of morphology. In the Russian language, which has an explicit aspectual system, the system of modal verbs is less complex than in the Germanic languages. De Haan (2006) mentions that the "main ways of expressing strong modality in Russian, for instance, are with adjectives (*dolžen*) and adverbs (*nado* or *nužno*)." In addition, Heindl (2009) discusses the verb *moč* 'can' which displays different readings according to the combination with perfective of imperfective aspect.[37]

(36) a. Ivan možet rešit'   etu zadaču (ability)
       Ivan can   solvePerf this task
       'Ivan can solve this task.' (Heindl (2009: 137,)

   b. Ty ne  možeš  postroit'   zdes' garaž (deontic possibility)
      You NEG can   build.IMPF here  garage
      'You may build a here.' (Heindl 2009: 139,)

Roussou (2009: 2815) points out different readings of the modal *bori* 'can' in Greek, which are obtained according to the aspectual features of its complement; they also arise according to "the variety of inflectional combinations in the matrix and embedded clauses." For the deontic modals in Late Archaic Chinese, I propose that all modals grammaticalize into deontic markers by upward movement to a functional category within the TP in the sense of Roberts and Roussou (2003), in which deontic modality is hosted. The deontic category of prohibition was marked by synthetic modal negative markers from the earliest documents of Chinese on. The precise syntactic derivation of these modal markers is still pending, but it can be suggested that they appear as part of a functional modal head in the TP layer in which modal markers have to be located in order to express deontic modality. The deontic values of obligation (non-negative

---

[37] In her article, Heindl (2009) particularly discusses differences in aspectual readings in combination with negation.

deontic modality) may have been expressed by a combination of morphological and lexical/functional features. The frequency of unaccusative and passive complements (subject to frequent morphological marking) of modal verbs suggests the possibility that morphologically marked verb forms were employed to express deontic modality, possibly in combination with deontic adverbs or in future contexts, before the entire loss of transparency of verbal morphology induced the development of a new and more analytical system of modal marking. But this issue still has to be confirmed by future research on the morpho-syntax of Archaic Chinese and its diachronic development.

# References

Abraham, Werner. 2008. On the logic of generalization about cross-linguistic aspect modality links. In *Modality-aspect interfaces: implications and typological solutions*, Werner Abraham and Elisabeth Leiss (eds), 3–13. Amsterdam; Philadelphia: John Benjamins.

Abraham, Werner and Leiss, Elisabeth. 2008. *Modality-aspect interfaces: implications and typological solutions*. Amsterdam; Philadelphia: John Benjamins.

Abraham, Werner. 2009. Die Urmasse von Modalität und ihre Ausgliederung. Modalität anhand von Modalverben, Modalpartikel und Modus. Was ist das Gemeinsame, was das Trennende, und was steckt dahinter? In *Modalität. Epistemik und Evidentialität bei Modalverb, Adverb, Modalpartikel und Modus*, Werner Abraham and Elisabeth Leiss (eds), 251–302. Tübingen, Germany: Stauffenburg Verlag.

Ademola-Ademoye, Feyisayo Fehintola. 2011. *A cross-linguistic analysis of finite raising constructions*. PhD Thesis, University of Kwa-Zulu Natal.

Aldridge, Edith. 2012. PPs and applicatives in Late Archaic Chinese. *Studies in Chinese Linguistics*, 33 (3): 139–164.

Aldridge, Edith and Barbara Meisterernst. 2018. Resultative and termination: A unified analysis of Middle Chinese VP-YI. In *Topics in Theoretical Asian Linguistics*, Kunio Nishiyama, Hideki Kishimoto, and Edith Aldridge (eds.). John Benjamins.

Anderl, Christoph. 2004. *Studies in the Language of Zu-Tang Ji*. PhD dissertation, Oslo: Unipub.

Baxter, William H. 2014. Baxter-Sagart. Old Chinese reconstructions. http://ocbaxtersagart. lsait.lsa.umich.edu/BaxterSagartOCbyMandarinMC2014-09-20.pdf.

Baxter, William H. 1992. A Handbook of Old Chinese Phonology. Berlin; New York: Mouton De Gruyter.

Baxter, William H. and Laurent Sagart. 1998. Word formation in old Chinese. In *New approaches to Chinese word formation*, Jerome Packard (ed.), 35–75. Berlin: De Gruyter.

Butler, Jonny. 2003. A Minimalist Treatment of Modality. *Lingua* 113: 967–996.

Bybee, Joan, Revere Perkins, and William Pagliuca. 1994. *The evolution of grammar: Tense, aspect and modality in the languages of the world*. Chicago, IL: University of Chicago Press.

Coates, Jennifer. 1983. *The semantics of the modal auxiliaries*. London and Canberra: Croom Helm.

Cormack, Annabel and Smith, Neill. 2002. Modals and negation in English. In *Modality and its Interaction with the Verbal System*, Barbiers, Sjef, Beukema Frits, can der Wurff, Wim (eds.) (Linguistik Aktuell 47 / Linguistics Today 47), 133–163. Amsterdam: John Benjamins

Downer, Gordon B. 1959. Derivation by tone-change in classical Chinese. *Bulletin of the School of African and Oriental Studies* 22(2): 258–290.

Feng, Shengli. 2014. Light verb syntax between English and classical Chinese. In *Chinese syntax in a cross-linguistic perspective*, Audrey Li, Andrew Simpson, and Dylan W-T Tsai (eds.), 229–250. Oxford: Oxford University Press.

Gassmann, Robert H. and Wolfgang Behr. 2005. *Grammatik des Antikchinesischen*. Bern, Berlin, Frankfurt am Main, Wien: Peter Lang.

De Haan, Ferdinand. 2006. Typological approaches to modality. In *The expression of modality*, William Frawley (ed.), 27–70, Berlin: Mouton de Gruyter.

Harbsmeier, Christoph. 2016. Irrefutable conjectures. A Review of William H. Baxter and Laurent Sagart, Old Chinese. A New Reconstruction. *Monumenta Serica* 64 (2): 445–504, DOI: 10.1080/02549948.2016.1259882.

Haudricourt, André G. 1954. Reconstruire le chinois archaïque. *Word* 10(2–3): 351–364.

Heindl, Olga. 2009. Negation, Modalität und Aspekt im Mittelhochdeutschen im Vergleich zum Slawischen. In: Modalität. *Epistemik und Evidentialität bei Modalverb*, Adverb, *Modalpartikel und Modus*, Werner Abraham and Elisabeth Leiss (eds.), 251–302. Tübingen, Germany: Stauffenburg Verlag.

Hu, Chirui. 2016. From implicity to explicity. In *New aspects of classical Chinese grammar, Asian and African Studies of the Humboldt University Berlin* 45, Barbara Meisterernst (ed.) 75–104. Wiesbaden, Germany: Harrassowitz Verlag.

Huang, James C-T. 2014. On Syntactic analycity and parametric theory. In *Chinese Syntax in a cross-linguistic perspective*, Audrey Li, Andrew Simpson, and Dylan W-T Tsai (eds.), 1–49. Oxford: Oxford University Press.

Huang, Kunyao. 黃坤堯 1992. *Jīngdiǎn shìwén dòngcí yìdú xīn tàn* 經典釋文動詞異讀新探 [A new investigation into verbs and pronunciation in jingdian shiwen]. Taipei: Student Book.

Jin, Lixin. 金理新 2006. *Shànggǔ Hànyǔ xíngtài yánjiū* 上古汉语形态研究 [A study of Old Chinese]. Hefei, China: HuangshanPublishing House.

Karlgren, Bernhard. 1933. Word families in Chinese. *Bulletin of the Museum of Far Eastern Antiquities* 5: 9–120.

Kiefer, Ferenc. 2010. Areal-typological aspects of word-formation: The case of aktionsart-formation in German, Hungarian, Slavic, Baltic, Romani and Yiddish. In *Variation and change in morphology: Selected papers from the 13th International Morphology Meeting*, Vienna, February 2008, Franz Rainer, Wolfgang U Dressler, Dieter Kastovsky, and Hans C Luschützky (ed.), 129–148. Amsterdam: John Benjamins.

Leiss, Elisabeth. 2008. The silent and aspect-driven patterns of deonticity and epistemicity: A chapter in diachronic typology. In *Modality-aspect interfaces: implications and typological solutions*, Werner Abraham and Elisabeth Leiss (eds.), 15–41, Amsterdam, Philadelphia: John Benjamins Pub. Co.

Li, Ming. 李明 2001. *Hanyu zhudongci de lishi fazhan* 漢語助動詞的歷史發展 [The historical development of auxiliary verbs in Chinese], PhD: Beijing Daxue.

Li, Renzhi. 2004. *Modality in English and Chinese. A typological perspective*, Boca Rota (Florida): Dissertation.com.

Li, Yin. 2018. The syntax of the verbs in the YU passive. Paper presented at a Workshop on Aspect and Modality, Berlin, August 1, 2016. unpublished manuscript.

Lin, Jo-wang and Chih-Chen J. Tang. 1995. Modals as verbs in Chinese: A GB perspective. *The Bulletin of the Institute of History and Philology* 66: 53–105.

Lin, Tzong-Hong. 2001. *Light Verb Syntax and the Theory of Phrase Structure*. PhD Thesis, UC Irvine.

Lin, T.-H. Jonah. 2011. Finiteness of Clauses and Raising of Arguments in Mandarin Chinese. *Syntax* 14 (1), 48–73.

Liu, Li. 刘利 2000. *Xian Qin Hanyy zhudongci yanjiu* 先秦漢語助動詞研究 [A study of auxiliary verbs in Pre-Qin Chinese]. Beijing: Beijing Shifan daxue chubanshe.

Lü, Shuxiang. 吕叔湘 1942. *Zhongguo wenfa yaolüe* 中国文法要略 [Concise Chinese grammar]. Beijing: The Commercial Press.

Lü, Shuxiang. 吕叔湘 2002. *Zhongguo wenfa yaolüe* 中国文法要略 [Concise Chinese grammar]. Liaoning, China: Liaoning Education Publishing House.

Mache, Jacob. 2009. Das Wesen epistemischer Modalität. In *Modalität. Epistemik und Evidentialität bei Modalverb*, Adverb, *Modalpartikel und Modus*, Werner Abraham and Elisabeth Leiss, 25–56 (eds.). Tübingen, Germany: Stauffenburg Verlag.

Mei, Guang. 梅廣 2015. *Shang Hanyu yufa gangyao* 上古漢語語法綱要 [Outlind of the grammar of Old Chinese]. Taipei: San Min Book.

Mei, Tsu-lin. 梅祖麟 1980. Sisheng bieyi zhong de shijian cengci 四声别义中的时间层次 [Temporal strata in derivation by the four tones]. *Zhongguo yuwen* 中国语文 [Studies of the Chinese Language] 6: 427–443.

Mei, Tsu-lin. 梅祖麟 1988. 内部拟构汉语三例 Neibu nigou Hanyu san li [Three examples of internal reconstruction in Chinese]. *Zhongguo yuwen* 中国语文 [Studies of the Chinese Language] 204 (3): 169–181.

Mei, Tsu-lin. 2015. Proto-Sino-Tibetan Morphology and its modern Chinese correlates. In *Oxford handbook of Chinese Linguistics*, William S-Y. Wang and Chaofen Sun (ed.), 58–67. Oxford: Oxford University Press.

Meisterernst, Barbara. 2008a. Modal verbs in Han period Chinese Part I: The syntax and semantics of *kě* 可 and *kěyǐ* 可以. *Cahiers de Linguistique Asie Orientale* 37(1): 85–120.

Meisterernst, Barbara. 2008b. Negative Markers in combination with the modal auxiliary verbs *kě* 可 and *kěyǐ* 可以. *Cahiers de Linguistique Asie Orientale* 37, (2): 197–222.

Meisterernst, Barbara. 2011. From obligation to future? A diachronic sketch of the syntax and the semantics of the auxiliary verb *dāng* 當. *Cahiers de Linguistique Asie Orientale* 40 (2): 137–188.

Meisterernst, Barbara. 2013. A syntactic analysis of modal *bì* 必: Auxiliary verb or adverb? In *Breaking down the barriers: Interdisciplinary studies in Chinese* Linguistics *and beyond*, Guangshun Cao, Hilary Chappell, Redouane Djamouri, and Thekla Wiebusch (eds.), 425–449. Taipei: Academia Sinica.

Meisterernst, Barbara. 2016. The syntax of aspecto-temporal adverbs from Late Archaic to Early Medieval Chinese. *Journal of East Asian Linguistics* 25 (2): 143–181. DOI: 10.1007/s10831-015-9140-3.

Meisterernst, Barbara. 2017a. Modality and Aspect and the Role of the Subject in Late Archaic and Han period Chinese: obligation and necessity. *Lingua Sinica* 3 (10).

Meisterernst, Barbara. 2017b. Possibility and necessity and the scope of negation in Early Middle Chinese. Paper presented at the *Linguistic Society of the University of Washington*. October, 2017.

Narrog, Heiko. 2008. The aspect-modality link in the Japanese verbal complex and beyond. In *Modality-aspect interfaces: Implications and typological solutions*, Werner Abraham and Elisabeth Leiss (eds.), 279–307. Amsterdam/Philadelphia: John Benjamins.
Peyraube Alain. 1999. The modal auxiliaries of possibility in Classical Chinese. In *Selected Papers from the Fifth International Conference on Chinese Linguistics*, Tsao Fengfu, Wang Samuel und Lien Chinfa (eds.). Taipei: The Crane Publishing Co. Ltd.
Portner, Paul. 2009. *Modality*. Oxford: Oxford University Press.
Pulleyblank, Edwin G. 1973. Some further evidence regarding old Chinese-s and its time of disappearance. *Bulletin of the School of Oriental and African Studies* 36 (2): 368–373.
Portner, Paul. 1991. *Lexicon of Reconstruction Pronunciation*. Vancouver: University of British Columbia Press.
Rizzi, Luigi. 1997. On the fine structure of the left periphery. In *Elements of Grammar*, Haegeman, Liliane (ed.), 281–338. Dordrecht: Kluwer.
Roberts, Ian and Anna Roussou. 2003. *Syntactic Change: A Minimalist approach to grammaticalization*. Cambridge: Cambridge University Press.
Roussou Anna. 2009. In The Mood for Control. *Lingua* 199: 1811–1836.
Sagart, Laurent. 1999. *The Roots of Old Chinese*. Amsterdam, Philadelphia: John Benjamins.
Saxena, Anju. 1997. Aspect and evidential morphology in Standard Lhasa Tibetan : a diachronic study. *Cahiers de linguistique – Asie orientale*, 26 (2): 281–306.
Schuessler, Axel. 2007. *ABC etymological dictionary of old Chinese*. Honolulu, HI: University of Hawaii Press.
Smith, Carlotta. 1997. *The parameter of aspect*. Dordrecht, The Netherlands: Kluwer Academic Publishers.
Sparvoli, Carlotta. 2015. Sense, sensibility and factual necessity: The deontic and the anankastic within the Chinese modal system. Paper presented at Humboldt University, Institute of Asian and African Studies, Seminar of East Asian Studies, Berlin.
Sybesma, Rint. 1994. The diachronics of verb-*le* in Chinese: Where does the perfective semantics come from? In *IIAS yearbook*, Paul van der Velde (ed.), 35–44. Leiden, Germany: International Institute for Asian Studies.
Travis, Lisa Demean. 2010. *Inner Aspect. The Articulation of VP. Studies in Natural Language and Linguistic Theory*. Dordrecht et al.: Springer.
Tsai, Wei-Tian Dylan. 2015. On the topography of Chinese modals. In *Beyond Functional Sequence*, Ur Shlonsky (ed.), 275–294. New York: Oxford University Press.
Tsai, Wei-Tian Dylan, *et al*. Modal Licensing and Subject Specificity in Mandarin and Taiwan Southern Min: A Cartographic Analysis (ms.)
Unger, Ulrich. 1983. Hao ku 好古: Sinological Circular. *Early China* 9 (10): 169–174.
Vendler, Zeno. 1967. *Linguistics and philosophy*, 1st edition. Ithaca, NY: Cornell University Press.
Wang, Yueting. 王月婷 2013. Guanyu gu Hanyu "shidong" wenti de jinyibu tantao 关于古汉语"使动"问题的进一步探讨 [Further discussion[ on causative verbs in Old Chinese]. *Yuyan kexue* 3 (2): 157–163.
Wu, Xueru. 巫雪如 2014. Shanggu zhi zhonggu "dang" zhi qingtai yuyi yu weilai shi fazhan de chongtan 上古至中古"當"之情態語義與未來時發展重探 [Comprehensive discussion on the modal and future meanings of 'dang' from Late Archaic to Middle Chinese]. *Taida Zhongwen xue bao* 4 (16): 87–142

Xie, Zhiguo. 2012. The modal uses of *de* and temporal shifting in Mandarin Chinese. *Journal of East Asian Linguistics* 21: 387–420.

Xiong, Jiajuan, Meisterernst, Barbara. 2019. The syntax and the semantics of the deontic modals *yīng* 應 and *dāng* 當 in Early Buddhist texts. In *New perspectives on Aspect and Modality in Chinese Historical Linguistics, Frontiers in Chinese Linguistics,* Barbara Meistererenst (ed.), 191–220. Springer & Peking University Press.

Zhu, Guanming. 朱冠明 2008. *Moheseng dilü qingtai dongci dongci yanjiu* 摩訶僧祇律情態動詞研究 [Investigation of the modal verbs in the Mahāsāṃghika precepts]. Beijing: Zhongguo xiju chubanshe.

Shannon Dubenion-Smith
# A typology of non-clausal postpositioning in German dialects

## 1 Introduction

In this contribution, I present results from a corpus study of non-clausal postpositioning in modern German dialects. This phenomenon, exemplified in (1) below, is the occurrence of a constituent not in its expected position in the inner field but in the postfield of the clause to which it is syntactically linked (see section 2.2 for further detail).

(1) <u>wie</u>   ich  die  Mutterstute  <u>geholt</u>  <u>habe</u>  **in  Grafenwöhr**
when  I    the  mare         fetched  have  in  Grafenwöhr
'when I fetched the mare in Grafenwöhr'                  ZWZ36[1]

In the example, the prepositional phrase (PP) *in Grafenwöhr* 'in Grafenwöhr' appears after the right boundary of the inner field, which is framed by *wie* 'when' and *geholt habe* 'have fetched', instead of in its canonical position adjacent to *ich die Mutterstute* 'I the mare'.

Most investigations of postpositioning in modern German examine the spoken and written standard (for example, Filpus 1994; Hoberg 1981; Lambert 1976; Niehaus 2016; Vinckel 2006; Zahn 1991; Żebrowska 2007). Two authors, Patocka (1997) and Westphal Fitch (2011), treat the phenomenon in dialect; however, both studies are limited to one linguistic area (Bavarian and West Central German, respectively), and the latter does not include a detailed typology. Although the current paper does not provide a comparison of postpositioning in multiple dialect areas, it offers a cross-dialectal perspective by drawing on spoken dialect texts of the Zwirner Corpus (Institut für Deutsche Sprache) from the North Low German, West Central German, and Bavarian linguistic areas. In particular, the empirical focus is *base dialects*, the most geographically restricted varieties with the greatest linguistic divergence from the standard language (Lenz 2010: 296; Schmidt 2010: 217).

---

[1] The designation that accompanies each example in the article indicates the recording in the Zwirner Corpus from which the example was drawn. See section 2.1 for further discussion of this corpus.

https://doi.org/10.1515/9783110641288-009

The primary goal of this contribution is to provide an exhaustive typology of postpositionings according to their form and function and to compare the results to those for Bavarian dialects spoken in Austria (Patocka 1997) and earlier stages of German (Sapp 2014; Niehaus 2016). In addition, the paper takes an initial look at PP postpositioning and reasons for the preponderance of this form in the dataset.

Besides providing a thorough analysis of non-clausal postpositioning, I also aim to situate the phenomenon in a cross-linguistic typological context. To this end, I draw on two works by Hawkins (1986, 2018) that deal with German and English from a comparative perspective. I contend that although these languages differ in major ways with respect to grammatical and lexical patterns, postpositioning in German – especially PP postpositioning – is an operation through which the languages come to display more similar characteristics, both in terms of surface structure and a reduction in processing load by means of particular word order configurations. In addition, the discussion of PP postpositioning offers a point of comparison to the BA-construction in Chinese that is treated in this volume (see Peyraube and Wiebusch, to appear).

The remainder of the chapter is outlined as follows. In section 2, I provide an overview of the methodology for the present study including information on data selection, criteria for analysis, and procedure.[2] Section 3 presents the analysis of postpositioned constituents, followed in section 4 by a closer examination of PP postpositioning in particular and a discussion of the phenomenon from a typological perspective. Section 5 summarizes the contribution and provides directions for further research.

## 2 Methodology

### 2.1 Data selection

Thirty randomly selected dialect recordings from the Zwirner Corpus, which was compiled between 1955 and 1972 and is accessible online through the Datenbank für Gesprochenes Deutsch (DGD), served as the empirical basis for the present study.[3] These professionally recorded spoken narrative texts were elicited from

---

[2] Because of space limitations, it was necessary to condense the methodology and exclude some details here. For a more extensive discussion, see Dubenion-Smith (2019).

[3] For further information on the corpus, see Haas and Wagener (1992), Vol. 1, Lenz (2007), Wagener and Bausch (1997: 112–114), and Zwirner and Bethge (1958). The corpus can be accessed at: https://dgd.ids-mannheim.de/dgd/pragdb.dgd_extern.welcome.

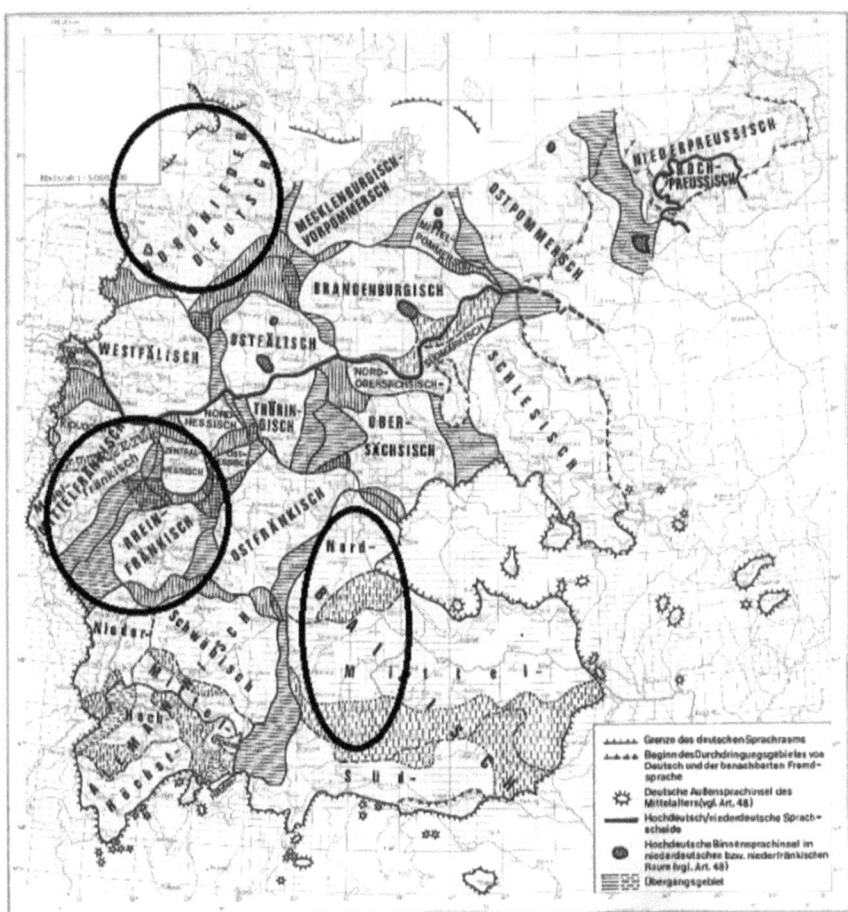

**Figure 1:** German dialect space, first decades of the 20th century. (Wiesinger 1983: 831)

autochthonous dialect speakers in an interview setting through a prompt or series of prompts and are approximately 10 minutes in length. All of the recordings have been transcribed and aligned with standardized transcriptions.

To gain a cross-dialectal perspective, I chose 10 recordings from each of the three non-contiguous linguistic areas indicated in Figure 1, namely North Low German (NLG), West Central German (WCG), and Bavarian (BAV), which represent the Low German, Central German, and Upper German regions, respectively.[4]

---

[4] These linguistic areas correspond to the regions circled in Figure 1 as follows: North Low German = *Nordniederdeutsch*; West Central German = *Mittelfränkisch*, *Rheinfränkisch*, and *Hessisch*;

Furthermore, I limited the inclusion of texts to those produced by speakers 50 years old and above and classified in the database catalogue (Haas and Wagener 1992) exclusively as *Vollmundart* 'base dialect' according to the designations set forth by the Deutsches Spracharchiv (see Pfeffer and Lohnes 1984, 1: 53). Although the recordings from the NLG (six males/four females) and WCG (five males/five females) areas are (nearly) evenly distributed with respect to sex, an even balance was not possible for the BAV area (eight males/two females) because of constraints on data selection.[5]

## 2.2 Criteria for analysis and procedure

For the present study, I adopted as the theoretical framework the *Topological Field Model* presented in Figure 2 (see Wöllstein 2010).

**prefield**   left bracket   **inner field**   right bracket   **postfield**

**Figure 2:** Topological Field Model.

The German clause can be divided into three fields (*prefield, inner field, postfield*), which are separated by the *left* and *right brackets*. In subordinate clauses, the left and right brackets are filled by conjunctions and (non)-finite verbs, respectively, and the prefield may be left unfilled or is occupied by relative pronouns and interrogative words/phrases. In main clauses, the left bracket houses finite verbs and the right bracket non-finite verbs and separable elements such as prefixes, though the latter position may remain empty. The prefield is typically filled by subjects, adverbial phrases, and embedded clauses. Finally, in canonical clauses of both types, all remaining constituents occur in the inner field, and the right bracket marks the clausal boundary. However, it is possible for material to appear not in its usual inner field position but after the right bracket in the postfield.[6] It is such postpositioned constituents – postpositionings – that are the focus of the present paper.

---

Bavarian = *Bairisch*. Note also that the Bavarian dialects treated in the study are limited to those spoken in Germany.

**5** The texts for the present contribution were selected alongside 30 regiolect texts for a separate study. Since the pool of available regiolect recordings precluded an even distribution between male and female speakers, it was necessary to adjust the selection of dialect recordings accordingly to maintain as nearly an identical ratio of male to female speakers in dialect and regiolect as possible.
**6** Note that, unlike other authors such as Patocka (1997), I do not subdivide the postfield further, for example, into a postfield and field for right dislocations; see also Zifonun et al. (1997), who

Examples (2) and (3), which involve the subordinate clause presented in the introduction and a further main clause, illustrate the division of clausal material within the Topological Field Model:

(2) subordinate clause

| pref. | LB | inner field | | RB | postf. | |
|---|---|---|---|---|---|---|
| Ø | wie | ich | die Mutterstute | geholt | habe | in Grafenwöhr |
| Ø | when | I | the mare | fetched | have | in Grafenwöhr |

'when I fetched the mare in Grafenwöhr' ZWZ36

(3) main clause

| pref. | LB | inner field | | RB | postf. | |
|---|---|---|---|---|---|---|
| die | hatten | ein | Schwein | geschachtet | bei | uns |
| they | had | a | pig | slaughtered | at | our.place |

'they had slaughtered a pig at our farm' ZW9B3

Typically, the boundary between the inner field and postfield is indicated by the presence of a constituent in the right bracket, which, together with the element in the left bracket (or prefield in the case of relative and interrogative clauses), forms what is known as a *bracket construction* (hereafter: BC).[7] Since postpositionings can be unambiguously identified as such only when this boundary is clearly defined, I therefore excluded from my analyses all main clauses in which the boundary is not overtly marked.[8]

---

propose the subdivisions *Nachfeld* 'postfield' and *rechtes Außenfeld* 'right outer field'. Because of the decisions I have made regarding the inclusion of constituents that occur after the right bracket (see the main text of the current section below), such a subdivision is not crucial in the present study.

**7** The bracket construction is a characteristic syntactic feature that German shares, for example, with Dutch but which distinguishes German from other closely related languages. In English, for example, the auxiliary and main verbs in compound tenses typically occur directly adjacent to each other, followed by objects and other constituents such as adjuncts. By contrast, these verbs are separated in German, thereby encapsulating clausal material within the inner field. Compare: *They had slaughtered a pig at our farm* vs. *Die hatten bei uns ein Schwein geschlachtet*.
**8** Besides main clause BCs in which an element in the right bracket marks the boundary between the inner field and postfield, I also included in this study BCs in which the closing element occurs at the right periphery of the inner field, namely light verb constructions, for example, *wir wussten alle mit ihm Bescheid* 'we all knew along with him' (ZW0I8) and adverbial bracket constructions, for example, *da erlebt man nichts mehr davon* 'one doesn't experience any of that any more' (ZWC38). For further discussion, see Dubenion-Smith (2019).

For the purpose of identifying postpositioned constituents and calculating rates of postpositioning, I defined the clause as the unit of measurement; more specifically, each instance of a BC. After verifying the accuracy of a transcription against the audio recording, I parsed the text to isolate the clauses and examined the BCs to determine whether or not a constituent occurs in the postfield. In this study, I considered as postpositionings only those constituents that are syntactically linked to the inner field,[9] are prosodically integrated into the preceding structure,[10] and do not have a correlate or antecedent earlier in the clause. Accordingly, I excluded afterthoughts, which form their own intonational phrase, typically after a pause (indicated below by a period), as well as appositives and cases of right dislocation:[11]

Afterthought
(4) ich   bin  wieder  zurückgekommen  .  **von   dem   Krieg**
    I     am   again   come.back          from  the   war
    'I came back from the war'                                    ZW2IO

Apposition
(5) da    habe  ich  dann  **siebzehnhundert  Mark**   zusammengebracht
    there have  I    then  seven-hundred      Marks   brought.together
    **erspartes   Geld**
    saved        money
    'I scraped together 700 Marks, savings'                       ZWE7O

Right dislocation
(6) **die**  müssen  auch  locker  gehackt  werden  **die   Kartoffeln**
    they     must    also  loose   hacked   be      the    potatoes
    'they have to be loosened up too, the potatoes'               ZW1H8

In a final step, I entered the data into databases for further analysis.

---

**9** I understand 'syntactic linkage' to mean a constituent's potential occurrence in the inner field where it fulfills a syntactic function such as adjunct or complement. Note also that the usual English term for the phenomenon 'postpositioning' is 'extraposition'. For theoretical reasons and terminological consistency in future studies that will deal with clausal constituents in the postfield, I prefer the term 'postpositioning' here. See Dubenion-Smith (2019) for further discussion.
**10** See, for example, Auer (1991), Duden (2005: 1222–1224), and Schwitalla (2012: 114–117) for discussion of the prosodic integration of postfield constituents.
**11** See Dubenion-Smith (2019) for further discussion of these types.

## 3 Typology of non-clausal postpositionings

The total dataset of 30 dialect texts consists of 5,934 clauses, 3,716 (62.62%) of which display a BC. In 326 cases, a non-clausal constituent occurs in the post-field.

Referring to the classification systems in Engel (2009a, 2009b), Patocka (1997), who bases his categorization primarily on earlier editions of Engel's works, and Zifonun et al. (1997), I identified the form and function of the 326 instances of postpositioning and organized these into groups. In the examples below, I present each function (for example, temporal adjunct) in all forms attested in the dataset (for example, PP, adverb, noun phrase [NP]). The forms appear in the order of descending frequency. See Table A.1 of the appendix for a detailed breakdown of the subtypes.

**Adjuncts**

causal – PP
(7) da    ist  es  ja    immer  mehr  brenzlig  geworden
    there is  it  PART  always more  dicey     become
    **mit  dem  Krieg**
    with  the  war
    'then it became more and more dicey because of the war'         ZWH55

causal – da compound
(8) nun  haben  wir  das alles      etwas      leichter
    now  have   we   that everything somewhat  easier
    gekriegt  **dadurch**
    gotten    through.it
    'we have thereby gotten everything somewhat more easily now'    ZW9J1

Comitative – PP
(9) die  ganze  Nacht  hatten  wir  geweint  **mit**  **den**  **Kindern**
    the  whole  night  had     we   cried    with     the      children
    'we cried the whole night with the children'                    ZWH55

Comitative – da compound
(10) da     wurde  getrunken  **dabei**
     there  was    drunk      with.it
     'there was drinking going on at the same time'                 ZWX06

Final – PP
(11) die      wo    wir  brauchen  **für**  **den**  **Kuhstall**
     which  PART  we   need      for      the      cow.shed
     'which we need for the cowshed'                                ZWC38

Instrumental – PP
(12) erst   wurde  da    Gras   gemäht  **mit**  **den**  **Sensen**
     first  was    then  grass  reaped  with     the      scythes
     'first grass was reaped with the scythes'                      ZW0M8

Locative – PP
(13) dann   wurden  die  Kartoffeln  auseinandergelesen
     then   were    the  potatoes    from.each.other.sorted
     **im**      **Keller**
     in.the    cellar
     'then the potatoes were sorted in the cellar'                  ZW1H8

Locative – adverb
(14) haben  wir  einen  ganzen  guten  Erfolg   gehabt  **dort**
     have   we   a      quite          good   success  had     there
     'we were rather successful there'                              ZW9I0

Locative – da compound
(15) da     hat's    ja    auch   Tote        gegeben  **drin**
     there  has-it   PART  also   dead.ones   given    in.it
     'there were dead ones in there too'                            ZW1P3

Modal – adverb
(16) (sie)  wird   ausgedrückt  **fest**
     it     gets   pushed.out   firmly
     'it gets pushed out firmly'                                    ZW8O8

Modal – als + NP
(17) da    kam    ich  mir   vor    **als**  **so**   **eine**  **Prinzessin**
     then  came   I    REFL  PART   as       like     a         princess
     'I felt then like a princess'                                  ZW9J1

Modal – PP
(18) gingen  wir  abends    Klock  fünf  los     **zu**  **Fuß**
     went    we   evenings  clock  five  forth   on      foot
     'in the evenings we took off at 5 o'clock on foot'             ZW9J1

Restrictive – *als* + NP

(19) da       wollte    ich   da       auch    ja      noch    gerne    hin   **als**  **Junge**
    then     wanted    I     there    also    PART    still   gladly   to    as       boy
    'as a boy I still really wanted to go there'                                       ZWX71

Temporal – PP

(20) der       sechste     ist   ertrunken    **mit**   **siebzehn**   **Jahren**
    the       sixth.one   is    drowned      with      seventeen      years
    'the sixth one drowned at the age of seventeen'                              ZWK82

Temporal – adverb

(21) die     haben    achtzehn   Pfennig   gekostet    **damals**
    they    have     eighteen   cents     costed      back.then
    'they cost 18 cents back then'                                ZWC84

Temporal – NP

(22) wenn    man    Mist      geladen   hatte    **drei**   **Tage**
    when    one    manure    loaded    had      three      days
    'when one had loaded manure for three days'                   ZW1H8

## Complements

Accusative – NP

(23) nun    wollte    er    ihm    auch    sagen    **die**   **Wahrheit**
    now    wanted    he    him    also    tell     the      truth
    'now he also wanted to tell him the truth'                     ZWT38

Prepositional[12] – PP

(24) da      wurden    die    Bauern    aufgerufen
    then    were      the    farmers   called
    **zu**   **einer**   **Demonstration**
    to       a           demonstration
    'then the farmers were called to a demonstration'              ZW2IO

---

**12** This category also includes complements of adjectives, for example, *dass die Leute sollen zufrieden sein **mit uns*** 'that the people should be satisfied with us' (ZWH55).

Prepositional – da compound

(25) da muss man immer so lange warten **darauf**
there must one always so long wait for.it
'one always has to wait so long for it'  ZWC38

Directive – PP

(26) von da aus bin ich nachher weitergereist
from there from am I afterwards further.traveled
**nach Bielefeld**
to Bielefeld
'from there I traveled on to Bielefeld'  ZWOI8

Expansive – PP

(27) da bin ich noch mitgefahren **bis nach Saarburg**
then am I still gone.with until to Saarburg
'then I kept riding along until Saarburg'  ZWH55

**Comparatives**[13] – *als* + NP

(28) wenn ihr das besser könnt **als ich**
if you that better can than I
'if you can do that better than me'  ZW2I0

**Attributive phrases** – PP

(29) ich bin Vorstand dreizehn Jahre gewesen
I am chairman thirteen years been
**von dem Verein**
of the club
'I was club chairman for thirteen years'  ZWF65

**Modal words/particles**

(30) es ist ein voller Erfolg geworden **eigentlich**
it is a full success become actually
'it actually turned out to be a complete success'  ZW910

---

**13** Note that Patocka (1997) excludes both comparatives and attributes from his counts of postpositioning since these are types of discontinuous constituents (see pp. 49–52). I include them in the present study because, like other types, they are syntactically linked to the inner field.

## Multiple postpositionings

(31) damit es nicht so warm war **für die Schafe den Tag über**
 so.that it not so warm was for the sheep the day over
 'so it wasn't so warm for the sheep during the day' ZW0G2

Table 1 shows the frequencies of the forms of postpositioning, which I calculated in two ways. First, I summed all instances of each form across the 30 texts, for example, all adverbs, and divided this sum by the total number of postpositionings ($n$ = 326). The presentation of such pooled counts here facilitates the comparison of these to results from other studies, which are reported in this manner. However, pooling data has disadvantages: 1) If the occurrence of certain forms is particularly high or low in one text, this can skew the overall counts; and 2) If the number of BCs from each text is different, which is the case here, then distributional patterns in individual texts can be under- or overrepresented in the dataset as a whole (see Baroni and Evert 2008).[14] I therefore also present equally weighted frequencies, which I calculated by first determining for every text the percentage of the total number of postpositionings that each form comprises, then averaging the percentages for each form across all 30 texts. Note that the values for the pooled and equally weighted frequencies are very similar, which indicates that in the case of the current dataset, the effect of varying text lengths is minimal and that the forms are similarly distributed across the texts.

**Table 1:** Distribution of non-clausal postpositioning by form.

| Form | Pooled Frequencies | Equally Weighted Frequencies |
|---|---|---|
| PPs, da-compounds | 211 (64.72%) | 66.74% |
| Adverbs | 45 (13.80%) | 13.08% |
| Multiple constituents | 39 (11.96%) | 11.18% |
| NPs, *als* + NP | 14 (4.29%) | 4.02% |
| Comparatives | 9 (2.76%) | 2.45% |
| Modal words/particles | 8 (2.45%) | 2.53% |
| Total dialect | 326 (100%) | 100% |

---

[14] Although it would have been possible to select a predetermined number of BCs from each text, I decided against this for two reasons. First, without parsing a recording transcription completely, it is impossible to know how many BCs it comprises. Thus, there is no way to easily pre-select texts for analysis. Second, the number of BCs to be included from each text could not exceed the number in the text with the fewest BCs, severely limiting the total amount of data in the dataset.

Before discussing the distributions, a few words about the categories and frequency counts are in order. First, the group 'multiple constituents' comprises all cases of postpositioning that involve more than one constituent, regardless of whether they are of the same type (for example, two PPs or one adverb and one PP).[15] Second, the comparative phrases occur only in the postfield, never in the inner field to which they are syntactically linked.[16] Third, the category 'modal words/particles' consists of constituents that are referred to by various terms in the German-language literature, for example, *Modalpartikeln* (Zifonun et al. 1997, 1: 58) and *Modalwörter* (Helbig and Helbig 1990) for modal words and *Abtönungspartikeln* (Zifonun et al. 1997, 1: 58–59) and *Modalpartikeln* (Krivonosov 1977) for modal particles.[17] Fourth, the category 'NPs' includes both NP complements and NPs that function as adverbial phrases, for example, *wenn man Mist geladen hatte* **drei Tage** 'when one had loaded manure for three days' (ZW1H8). Fifth, all postpositioned complement NPs are prosodically stressed. Finally, postpositioned adjectives are unattested in the dataset.

Because of the organization of results, the typologies in three relevant works on postpositioning in contemporary spoken German, namely Filpus (1994), Lambert (1976), and Zahn (1991), cannot be easily compared to those here. However, the presentation in Patocka (1997) allows for a comparison. Table 1 above showed that the vast majority of non-clausal postpositionings take the form of PPs and da-compounds. If da-compounds are removed from the calculation, the pooled percentage for the dialect data on the whole, 61.96% (202/326), is identical to that for Bavarian spoken in Austria, roughly 62% in Patocka (1997: 332).[18] The proportion of PPs in the present Bavarian data alone is somewhat lower (52.27%), but this form nonetheless comprises the majority of all postpositionings.

---

**15** This group does not include cases in which multiple constituents are coordinated, for example, *da ist es ja immer mehr brenzlig geworden* **mit dem Krieg und mit allem** 'then it became more and more dicey with the war and all' (ZWH55). In such cases, I considered only the first constituent in the postfield.

**16** While Helbig and Buscha (2013: 476–477) characterize comparative phrases as a type of "grammatical exbraciation," whereby the normal position of such phrases is the postfield, Patocka (1997: 51) emphasizes the fact that such phrases can, indeed, occur in the inner field, and Durrell (2017: 525) describes such placement as "not unusual." I have therefore not excluded comparative phrases *a priori*.

**17** Only the modal particle *auch* is attested in the dataset, for example, *ein bisschen möchte man mittun* **auch** 'one would, indeed, like to participate' (ZWK82). Although the distribution of modal words and particles differs in that the former can be fronted to the prefield while the latter cannot, I collapse the two categories here because of the low token count.

**18** Note that Patocka (1997) does not include da-compounds in his counts.

The findings in Sapp's (2014) study on postpositioning in Middle High German (MHG) and Early New High German (ENHG) and Niehaus's (2016) investigation of German from the 18th to 21st century allow for a comparison to earlier stages of the language, though the medial difference (written vs. spoken) warrants caution. Using Sapp's (2014: 135) raw data, I determined that PPs make up 64.13% of non-clausal postpositionings, a pooled proportion very close to those in the current study and Patocka's (1997). However, the next largest category in Sapp's data is NPs (17.57%), and adverbs constitute only a small share (1.32%). In addition, Sapp finds two instances of a postpositioned adjective, which together comprise a mere 0.29% of all postpositionings. This distribution stands in contrast to that in the present dialect data, in which adverbs constitute the second-largest category, NPs are represented by a very small percentage of tokens, and postpositioned adjectives are unattested.

In Niehaus's (2016: 143) data, taken from newspapers published between 1701 and 2013, PPs comprise between roughly 30% and 55% of non-clausal postpositionings and comparative constructions between 30% and 57%, depending on the time period. The former group therefore makes up a smaller proportion than in Patocka's (1997), Sapp's (2014) or the present dataset, yet is nonetheless well represented, while the prevalence of the latter contrasts starkly with the low percentage in the current study.[19] Finally, in further contrast to this investigation, but similar to Sapp (2014), Niehaus (2016: 138) finds no instances of postpositioned adverbs.

The comparison of the distribution of postpositionings in the present work to those in Patocka (1997), Sapp (2014), and Niehaus (2016) indicates first of all that the grammaticality and high frequency of PP postpositioning has remained stable over time. Likewise, postpositioned adjectives, which are unattested as postpositionings in the current dataset, also occur only rarely in earlier stages of the language. NPs and adverbs, by contrast, display a diachronic change in frequency, in opposite directions: NPs, which comprise the second largest category of postpositionings in Sapp's MHG and ENHG data, are still attested but are marked, occurring rarely and, in the case of NP complements, only when the constituent carries sentential stress. On the other hand, the proportion of postpositioned adverbs appears to have risen over time, though the observed change may be attributable to differences in modality (written vs. spoken) and not to an actual loosening of restrictions on adverbial postpositioning.

---

**19** Since Patocka (1997) and Sapp (2014) do not include comparative constructions in their analyses, no comparison to these studies can be made.

Let us now turn to the frequencies of the functions of postpositioning in the current dataset, which I calculated in the same manner as the frequencies of the forms. These are presented in Table 2.

**Table 2:** Distribution of non-clausal postpositioning by function.

| Function | Pooled Frequencies | Equally Weighted Frequencies |
|---|---|---|
| Adjuncts | 199 (61.04%) | 61.22% |
| Complements | 87 (26.69%) | 26.59% |
| Attributive phrases | 13 (3.99%) | 4.57% |
| Multiple functions | 10 (3.07%) | 2.63% |
| Comparatives | 9 (2.76%) | 2.45% |
| Modal words/particles | 8 (2.45%) | 2.53% |
| Total dialect | 326 (100%) | 100% |

The group 'multiple functions' comprises only those cases of postpositioning that consist of multiple constituents, each with a different function. I assigned cases of multiple adjuncts and complements to their respective categories.[20]

The most frequent functions in the corpus, adjuncts and complements, are also most frequent in Patocka's (1997) study. The pooled proportion of complements in Patocka's Bavarian data (32.8%) is higher than that in the data for the present study (26.07%, 85/326 overall; 18.94%, 25/132 Bavarian only), but the rate of adjuncts is almost identical (51.5% Bavarian-Patocka vs. 52.76%, 172/326 overall; 53.79%, 71/132 Bavarian only).[21]

# 4 Toward an account of PP postpositioning

A finding shared by the studies compared in the previous section to the present investigation is that, diachronically, PPs make up a large (or the largest) share of non-clausal postpositionings. Patocka (1997: 332–333) maintains that the preponderance of PPs is not necessarily attributable to an affinity of this phrase type for postpositioning, but may follow from the fact that many of the functional types

---

[20] Note that multiple attributes, comparatives, and modal words/particles do not co-occur in the dataset.
[21] For the purposes of comparison with Patocka (1997), I excluded the cases of multiple constituents from the counts of adjuncts and complements in these calculations.

occur primarily or exclusively in the form of PPs. This is the case in the present study, with 8 out of 15 functional (sub)types (not including cases of multiple postpositioning) occurring only as PPs, or as PPs and da-compounds (see appendix).

Nonetheless, PPs in my dataset not only make up the bulk of the non-clausal postpositionings, but they are also postpositioned at a relatively high rate, particularly in comparison to adverbs, the second most frequent form. To determine the rate of postpositioning of PPs and adverbs in isolation, for each text I divided the number of postpositioned PPs by the total number of BCs with a PP in the inner field or postfield, excluding all cases in which a PP and adverb appear together. I then averaged the rates across all 30 texts and repeated the procedure for the adverbs. The equally weighted mean rate of PP postpositioning in the entire dataset is 33.75% ($SD$ = 12.36%), over seven times higher than the rate of adverb postpositioning, 4.58% ($SD$ = 3.81%).

The question that arises, then, is what might account for this finding. Numerous explanations for the occurrence of postpositioning have been proposed in the literature (see Patocka 1997: 339–342 and Zahn 1991: 212–214 for an overview); in the following, I discuss three factors relevant to PPs in particular that potentially contribute to the high rate at which these are postpositioned: length, contact placement, and the attraction principle. This discussion is exploratory in nature and will not lead to firm conclusions; rather, the main goals are to determine, based on broad comparison, whether a factor might contribute to the high rate of PP postpositioning and to lay the groundwork for further investigations. Although the results are not definitive, this examination goes a step beyond previous treatments of these factors, which remain within the theoretical realm and/or do not scrutinize the data.

Patocka (1997: 332–333) considers the possibility that PPs make up the majority of postpositionings in modern Bavarian dialect because of their length but later dismisses the notion that this factor correlates with a constituent's propensity toward postpositioning (pp. 351–352). By contrast, Sapp (2014: 135–136) finds for his historical data that constituent length has a statistically significant effect on postpositioning: a length of three words or greater favors the occurrence of postpositioning, and the longer the constituent, the more likely it is to occur in the postfield. In the current data, the equally weighted mean length of PPs, based on all 30 texts, is 3.02 words ($SD$ = .69) – three times that of adverbs or right bracket elements, for example, which typically consist of a single word. Therefore, when a PP is postpositioned, a longer, heavier phrase (PP) appears after (a) shorter, lighter constituent(s) in the inner field or in the closing bracket of the BC itself.

As Niehaus (2016: 127) and Fleischer and Schallert (2011: 163) point out, Behaghel (1932: 6) captured the tendency for longer constituents to follow short ones in his *Gesetz der wachsenden Glieder* 'Law of Increasing Constituents' and invoked the principle to account for, among other phenomena, the postpositioning of PPs. More recently, Hawkins (2004), who argues that word order preferences in performance are closely linked to language processing, has explained this tendency and the processing advantage that it can afford in terms of the principle *Minimize Domains*. With respect to English, Hawkins (2004: 104–106) demonstrates how the principle can account for phenomena that are similar to German PP postpositioning vis-à-vis the placement of longer constituents after shorter ones, such as Heavy NP Shift and the preferred ordering of multiple PPs exemplified in (32a/b) and (33a/b), respectively:[22]

Heavy NP Shift
(32)  a.  Mary gave [to Bill] [the book she had been searching for since last Christmas].
      b.  Mary gave [the book she had been searching for since Christmas] [to Bill].                                       Hawkins (2004: 104)

Multiple PPs
(33)  a.  The man waited [for his son] [in the cold but not unpleasant wind].
      b.  The man waited [in the cold but not unpleasant wind] [for his son].
                                                                Hawkins (2004: 104)

In light of the evidence and theoretical insights of scholars past and present, it is likely that length contributes to the high rate of PP postpositioning in the current dataset. A thorough investigation of this factor's effect is beyond the scope of the current paper but will be the subject of future research.

A further explanation for postpositioning that has been discussed in the literature (for example, Filpus 1994: 173–175; Niehaus 2016: 124, 164–167) is contact placement, that is, the adjacent occurrence of constituents that are semantically and/or syntactically linked, which follows from Behaghel's (1932: 4) First Law (*Geistig eng Zusammengehöriges wird auch eng zusammengestellt* 'elements that conceptually belong together are placed close together'). With respect to PPs in particular, contact placement manifests itself in the appearance of the prepositional head next to its governing verb in the case of complements or, more generally, the adjacency of verbal and prepositional heads in the case of PP adjuncts to VP. This is effectuated through the postpositioning of the PP as illustrated in (34) and (35).

---

[22] See Somers Wicka and Dubenion-Smith (2009) for Phrasal Combination Domain calculations (Hawkins 2004) that demonstrate the processing advantage of analogous V-PP structures over PP-V structures in Old Saxon.

PP complement

(34) da      wurden  die  Bauern   *aufgerufen* |  zu  einer  Demonstration
     then    were    the  farmers  called       |  to  a      demonstration
     'then the farmers were called to a demonstration'                 ZW2IO

PP adjunct

(35) erst    wurde   da   Gras   *gemäht*  |  *mit*  den  Sensen
     first   was     then grass  reaped    |  with   the  scythes
     'first the grass was reaped with the scythes'                     ZW0M8

On the surface, this configuration is similar to the Chinese BA-construction, which requires that a PP complement be positioned directly after the lexical verb, which forms a quasi bracket construction with *bǎ* (see Peyraube and Wiebusch, this volume, for detailed discussion and examples).

Besides the adjacent occurrence of heads that are semantically and/or syntactically linked, Filpus (1994: 173, 239–246) argues that contact placement has additional discourse-related advantages. First, such placement enhances the clarity of sentential structure as the meaning-bearing verb appears earlier in the clause. Second, it serves as a way to effect *blockbildendes Sprechen* 'block-forming speech' (see Uhlig 1972), that is, the successive building up of linguistic chunks, which can aid in processing by organizing the clause into smaller units. Filpus views the right bracket as crucial in this process (p. 244); in examples (34) and (35) above, the verbs *aufgerufen* 'called' and *gemäht* 'reaped' signal the end of the first block, which is followed by a second block that consists of the PP only. If the PPs appeared in their canonical positions, the clauses would consist of only one longer block. Finally, note that the short-before-long processing advantage discussed above in the context of constituent length applies here as well.

If contact placement is, indeed, a factor that contributes to the preponderance of PPs in the dataset, then we would expect the rate of PP postpositioning to be higher after BCs with a verb in the right bracket than after BCs closed by a non-verbal form such as a separable prefix. To explore this hypothesis, I calculated the equally weighted mean rate of postpositioning in main clauses after BCs closed by a non-finite verb and by any other non-verbal element, in a random sample of 10 texts.[23] Similar to the calculations above, I first determined, for each

---

[23] Since subordinate clauses always display a (non)-finite verb in the right bracket, I excluded these from the analysis. I also eliminated from the counts all postpositioned da-compounds and attributive PPs as well as BCs with only a da-compound or attributive PP in the inner field. The former do not display a PP head, while the latter are complements of NPs and would not be expected to behave like PPs that are complements of or adjuncts to VP.

text, the rate of postpositioning by dividing the number of postpositioned PPs by the total number of BCs with a PP in the inner field or postfield, then I averaged the rates across the 10 texts. The equally weighted mean rate after verbs is 42.07% ($SD$ = 15.36%), nearly three times higher than after other elements, 14.68% ($SD$ = 12.02%). Given the observed difference in the expected direction, this factor merits further investigation with a larger dataset (complete set of 30 texts) and proper significance testing to determine whether the difference is statistically significant and to what extent the factor contributes to variation in postpositioning overall. In subsequent analyses, it will be important to distinguish complement and adjunct PPs and to control for the possible effect of length.

Closely related to contact placement is the attraction principle (see, for example, Filpus 1994: 157–159; Kromann 1974: 67; Patocka 1997: 352–353; Vinckel 2014: 79–81; Zahn 1991: 217), according to which a clause attracts a constituent from the inner field into the postfield. A typical case involves a postpositioned PP followed by a relative clause whose antecedent is the NP that immediately precedes it, as exemplified in (36).

(36)  die    hatten  besondere  Vorliebe  gehabt  |  für  das  Leinenzeug,
      they   had     special    preference had     |  for  the  linen
      was    hier    die        Bauern    so   in  den  Koffern..  hatten
      what   here    the        farmers   so   in  the  trunks     had
      'they had a special preference for the linen that the farmers had in their trunks'                                                          ZWT38

The postpositioning of the PP allows for the antecedent to occur adjacent to the relative pronoun, which, Filpus (1994: 157–158) and Patocka (1997: 353) maintain, increases the transparency of the utterance. In addition, this configuration gives rise to multiple linguistic blocks, the advantage of which was discussed above.

Niehaus (2016: 142) concludes on the basis of the infrequent occurrence of attraction in his dataset (only 15 cases among 223 postpositioned constituents) that this principle is not a primary explanation for non-clausal postpositioning. However, the constituents in question are not limited to PPs but also include NPs and comparative constructions. Since, as Patocka (1997: 353) points out, the attraction principle operates only on those types of constituents that already have a tendency toward postpositioning, it is necessary to consider each type separately to accurately determine what effect the principle may have. Here I examine only PPs and compare the baseline rate of postpositioning to the rate in cases of potential attraction. If the principle is operational, we would expect the latter rate to be higher than the former.

In the current dataset, there are five cases of attraction involving a PP and four further potential cases in which attraction does not occur, as illustrated in (37). These are distributed among eight different texts.

(37) da      hatte  ich  immer   zu   meinen  anderen  zwei  Schwestern
     then    had    I    always  to   my      other    two   sisters
     gesagt | die   auch keinen  Mann       mehr    hatten
     said   | who   also no      husband    more    had
     'then I said to my sisters whose husbands had also died'         ZWH55

The baseline equally weighted mean rate of PP postpositioning, calculated by dividing, for each text, the number of postpositioned PPs by the total number of BCs with a PP in the inner field or postfield, including cases in which a PP appears with another constituent but excluding the 9 cases of (potential) attraction, is 25.66% (*SD* = 10.27%). The rate of postpositioning among cases involving a PP in which the attraction principle can theoretically operate, 5/9 (55.56%), is therefore far higher than the baseline rate, which indicates that the attraction principle may, indeed, be operational with respect to PP postpositioning. However, this calculation is based on the very few tokens that occur in the dataset. In future studies, it will be necessary to examine a far higher number of cases and subject the data to rigorous statistical testing to determine whether this pattern still holds and is statistically significant.

In the context of the preliminary findings just presented, I now close this section with a brief discussion of postpositioning from a typological perspective, drawing on work by Hawkins that deals with German and English comparatively. Hawkins (1986) examines major contrasts between German and English in grammatical and lexical patterns. These include, among others, the maintenance of productive case marking on NPs in German but not in English and the conservation of clause-final verb placement (underlying SOV word order) in German but a shift to SVO order in English, which he argues is a result of case syncretism.

In more recent work, Hawkins (2018) proposes a new way of unifying these and other major contrasts between German and English. He distinguishes between syntactic, semantic, and lexical properties that are word-internal, that is, carried by words in their grammatical and lexical representations, and those that are word-external, that is, assigned through access to neighboring words. While German and English, like all languages, display both types, English has come to rely much more heavily than German on word-external properties. The major contrasts between German and English, Hawkins argues, can best be viewed as a systematic expansion of these word-external properties in English.

Hawkins (2018) observes that such word-external properties seem to be associated with a higher processing load, which is offset by word orders that result in processing domains that are as short as possible. German has retained clause-final verb placement and relies far more heavily on word-internal properties that entail less processing effort; yet the phenomenon of postpositioning, which disrupts this canonical verb placement through leakage of clausal material into the postfield, gives rise to surface structures that are more English-like and that appear, based on the preliminary results concerning PP postpositioning presented above, to also be motivated to some degree by a reduction in processing domains, in addition to other discourse-related factors. Thus, while German and English have diverged and now contrast markedly from a typological perspective, I contend that postpositioning in German is an operation through which the languages come to display more similar characteristics.

# 5 Summary and outlook

The primary goal of this contribution was to classify the 326 cases of postpositioning in 30 dialect texts from the Zwirner Corpus according to their form and function. This classification revealed that the form 'PPs/da-compounds' and function 'adjunct' comprise the majority of postpositionings and that the relative proportions, for the entire dataset as well as the Bavarian data alone, are consistent with Patocka's (1997) results for Bavarian dialects spoken in Austria. A further comparison to studies of postpositioning in earlier stages of German showed that PPs have comprised a large or the largest proportion of postpositionings over time and that the percentage of NPs has sharply decreased.

In light of the diachronic preponderance of PP postpositioning and the fact that PPs are postpositioned at a relatively high rate, I then examined this form more closely. Specifically, I considered three factors that have been proposed in the literature: length, contact placement, and the attraction principle. In my discussion, I pointed out similarities and differences between German PP postpositioning and phenomena in both a closely related language (English) and an unrelated language (Chinese). With respect to English, the similarity lies in the tendency for a longer, heavier element to occur after a shorter, lighter one as in the case of Heavy NP Shift, which is associated with a reduction in processing load. As for Chinese, the BA-construction is similar in the adjacent occurrence of a complement PP head and lexical verb, yet different in that such placement is syntactically binding, which is not the case for PP postpositioning in German. I then discussed the phenomenon of PP postpositioning from the perspective of typological contrasts between German and English, maintaining that although these languages differ in major ways with respect to grammatical and lexical patterns, through postpositioning in German the languages come to exhibit more similar characteristics, both in terms of surface structures and a reduction in processing load.

Although the initial results indicate that length, contact placement, and the attraction principle may play a role in German PP postpositioning, the findings are preliminary, and it will be necessary to expand the data pool and/or subject the data to rigorous statistical testing before firm conclusions may be drawn. One such type of statistical modelling is mixed-effects logistic regression, which allows the researcher to simultaneously evaluate the effects of multiple factors on the occurrence of a particular variable, in this case postpositioning, while taking into account the fact that multiple data points are provided by a single speaker. In future work, I intend to test the factors discussed here, as well as others such as dialect area and information structure, using this type of model. I also plan in this work to compare patterns of postpositioning in dialect to those in another form of non-standard spoken German, namely regiolect, and, in Dubenion-Smith (2019), I will expand my investigation to clausal postpositioning. Through these studies, I aim to provide a detailed variationist account of postpositioning in modern non-standard German and thereby complement the existing studies on this topic, the vast majority of which have focused solely on modern standard German or earlier stages of the language.

# Appendix

Table A.1: Breakdown of postpositioning functions and forms.

| Functions | Subfunctions/forms | | Token counts |
|---|---|---|---|
| Adjuncts (*n=199*) | causal | | 4 (2.01%) |
| | | da-compound | 2 |
| | | PP | 2 |
| | comitative | | 16 (8.04%) |
| | | da-compound | 3 |
| | | PP | 13 |
| | final | | 12 (6.03%) |
| | | PP | 12 |
| | instrumental | | 9 (4.52%) |
| | | PP | 9 |

(continued)

Table A.1 (continued)

| Functions | Subfunctions/forms | | Token counts |
|---|---|---|---|
| | locative | | 54 (27.14%) |
| | | adverb | 14 |
| | | da-compound | 1 |
| | | PP | 39 |
| | modal | | 13 (6.53%) |
| | | adverb | 7 |
| | | *als* + NP | 3 |
| | | PP | 3 |
| | restrictive | | 3 (1.51%) |
| | | *als* + NP | 3 |
| | temporal | | 61 (30.65%) |
| | | adverb | 24 |
| | | NP | 6 |
| | | PP | 31 |
| | multiple functions | | 27 (13.57%) |
| **Complements (*n=87*)** | accusative | | 2 (2.30%) |
| | | NP | 2 |
| | prepositional | | 30 (34.48%) |
| | | da-compound | 3 |
| | | PP | 27 |
| | directive | | 45 (51.72%) |
| | | PP | 45 |
| | expansive | | 8 (9.20%) |
| | | PP | 8 |
| | multiple functions | | 2 (2.30%) |
| **Comparatives (*n=9*)** | *als* + NP | | 9 (100%) |
| **Attributive phrases (*n=13*)** | PP | | 13 (100%) |
| **Modal words/particles (*n=8*)** | | | 8 (100%) |
| **Multiple postpositionings (*n=10*)** | | | 10 (100%) |

# References

Auer, Peter. 1991. Vom Ende deutscher Sätze. *Zeitschrift für Germanistische Linguistik* 19: 139–157.

Baroni, Marco, and Stefan Evert. 2008. Statistical methods for corpus exploitation. *Corpus linguistics*. In *An international handbook*, Anke Lüdeling and Merja Kytö (eds.), 777–803. Berlin: De Gruyter Mouton.

Behaghel, Otto. 1932. *Deutsche Syntax: Eine geschichtliche Darstellung*. Vol. 4. Heidelberg: Carl Winter.

Dubenion-Smith, Shannon. 2019. Clausal postpositioning in German regional language. Manuscript in preparation.
Duden 2005. *Grammatik der deutschen Gegenwartsprache. Der Duden in zwölf Bänden*. Vol. 4. 7th edition. Mannheim: Bibliographisches Institut.
Durrell, Martin. 2017. *Hammer's German grammar and usage*. 6th edition. Abingdon, Oxon; New York, NY: Routledge.
Engel, Ulrich. 2009a. *Syntax der deutschen Gegenwartssprache*, 4th edition. Berlin: Erich Schmidt Verlag.
Engel, Ulrich. 2009b. *Deutsche Grammatik*, 2nd edition. Munich: Iudicum Verlag.
Filpus, Raija. 1994. *Die Ausklammerung in der gesprochenen deutschen Sprache der Gegenwart*. Tempere: University of Tempere. (= *Acta Universitatis Tamperensis* A, 423.)
Fleischer, Jürg, and Oliver Schallert. 2011. *Historische Syntax des Deutschen. Eine Einführung*. Tübingen: Narr Verlag.
Haas, Walter, and Peter Wagener. 1992. *Gesamtkatalog der Tonaufnahmen des Deutschen Spracharchivs*. Tübingen: Max Niemeyer Verlag.
Hawkins, John. 1986. *A comparative typology of English and German: Unifying the contrasts*. London: Croom Helm.
Hawkins, John. 2004. *Efficiency and complexity in grammars*. Oxford: Oxford University Press.
Hawkins, John. 2018. Word-external properties in a typology of Modern English: A comparison with German. *English Language and Linguistics*, 1–27.
Helbig, Gerhard, and Joachim Buscha. 2013. *Deutsche Grammatik: Ein Handbuch für den Ausländerunterricht*. Munich: Klett-Langenscheidt.
Helbig, Gerhard, and Agnes Helbig. 1990. *Lexikon deutscher Modalwörter*. Leipzig: Verlag Enzyklopädie.
Hoberg, Ursula. 1981. *Die Wortstellung der geschriebenen deutschen Gegenwartssprache: Untersuchungen zur Elemenenfolge im einfachen Verbalsatz*. Munich: Max Hueber Verlag.
Krivonosov, Aleksej. 1977. Deutsche Modalpartikeln im System der unflektierten Wortklassen. In *Aspekte der Modalpartikeln: Studien zur deutschen Abtönung*, Harald Weydt (ed.), 176–216
Kromann, Hans-Peder. 1974. Satz, Satzklammer und Ausklammerung. In *Kopenhagener Beiträge zur germanistischen Linguistik*, 4. Aufsätze, 7–82.
Lambert, Pamela. 1976. *Ausklammerung in modern standard German*. Hamburg: Helmut Buske Verlag.
Lenz, Alexandra. 2007. Zur variationslinguistischen Analyse regionalsprachlicher Korpora. In *Sprachkorpora. Datenmengen und Erkenntnisfortschritt. IDS-Jahrbuch 2006*, Werner Kallmeyer and Gisela Zifonun (eds.), 169–202. Berlin and New York: Walter de Gruyter.
Lenz, Alexandra. 2010. Emergence of varieties through restructuring and reevaluation. In *Language and space. An international handbook of linguistic variation. Volume 1: Theories and methods*, Peter Auer and Jürgen Erich Schmidt (eds.), 295–315. Berlin: De Gruyter Mouton.
Niehaus, Konstantin. 2016. *Wortstellungsvarianten im Schriftdeutschen. Über Kontinuitäten und Diskontinuitäten in neuhochdeutscher Syntax*. Heidelberg: Winter Verlag.
Patocka, Franz. 1997. *Satzgliedstellung in den bairischen Dialekten Österreichs*. Frankfurt am Main and New York: Peter Lang Verlag.
Peyraube, Alain, and Thekla Wiebusch. to appear New insights on the historical evolution of differential object marking (DOM) in Chinese. In *Typological perspectives of grammaticalization & Lexicalization. East meets west*, Janet Z. Xing (ed.). Berlin and New York: Mouton de Gruyter.

Pfeffer, J. Alan, and Walter F. W. Lohnes. 1984. *Grunddeutsch: Texte zur gesprochenen deutschen Gegenwartssprache*. Überregionale *Umgangssprache aus der Bundesrepublik Deutschland, der Deutschen Demokratischen Republik,* Österreich *und der Schweiz*. Tübingen: Max Niemeyer Verlag.
Sapp, Christopher. 2014. Extraposition in Middle and New High German. *The Journal of Comparative Germanic Linguistics* 17: 129–156.
Schmidt, Jürgen Erich. 2010. Language and space: The linguistic dynamics approach. In *Language and space. An international handbook of linguistic variation. Volume 1: Theories and methods*, Peter Auer and Jürgen Erich Schmidt (eds.), 201–225. Berlin: De Gruyter Mouton.
Schwitalla, Johannes. 2012. *Gesprochenes Deutsch. Eine Einführung*. Berlin: Erich Schmidt Verlag.
Somers Wicka, Katerina, and Shannon Dubenion-Smith. 2009. *Disambiguating Clausal Structure in the Old Saxon* Hêliand. XIXth International Conference on Historical Linguistics, Radboud Universiteit Nijmegen, The Netherlands. Conference handout.
Uhlig, Eckart. 1972. *Studien zu Grammatik und Syntax der gesprochenen politischen Sprache des Deutschen Bundestages. Ein Beitrag zur deutschen Sprache der Gegenwart*. Marburg: N. G. Elwert Verlag.
Vinckel, Hélène. 2006. *Die diskursstrategische Bedeutung des Nachfelds im Deutschen: Eine Untersuchung anhand politischer Reden der Gegenwartssprache*. Wiesbaden: Deutscher Universitäts-Verlag.
Wagener, Peter, and Karl-Heinz Bausch (eds.) 1997. *Tonaufnahmen des gesprochenen Deutsch: Dokumentation der Bestände von sprachwissenschaftlichen Forschungsprojekten und Archiven*. Berlin and New York: Walter de Gruyter.
Westphal Fitch, Gesche. 2011. Changes in frequency as a measure of language change: Extraposition in Pennsylvania German. In *Studies on German-language islands*, Michael Putnam (ed.), 371–384. Amsterdam: John Benjamins.
Wiesinger, Peter. 1983. Die Einteilung der deutschen Dialekte. In *Dialektologie: Ein Handbuch zur deutschen und allgemeinen Dialektforschung, 2. Halbband*, Werner Besch, Klaus Brinker, Armin Burkhardt, Hugo Steger, Gerold Ungeheuer, and Herbert Ernst Wiegand (eds.), 807–900. Berlin and New York: Walter de Gruyter.
Wöllstein, Angelika. 2010. *Topologisches Satzmodell*. Heidelberg: Winter Verlag.
Zahn, Günther. 1991. *Beobachtungen zur Ausklammerung und Nachfeldbesetzung in gesprochenem Deutsch*. Erlangen: Palm & Enke.
Żebrowska, Eva. 2007. Korpusgestützte Syntaxforschung am Beispiel der Ausklammerung im Deutschen. *Sprachwissenschaft* 32: 101–121.
Zifonun, Gisela, Ludger Hoffmann, and Bruno Strecker. 1997. *Grammatik der deutschen Sprache*. Berlin and New York: Walter de Gruyter.
Zwirner, Eberhard, and Wolfgang Bethge. 1958. *Erläuterungen zu den Texten*. Göttingen: Vandenhoeck & Ruprecht.

## Part II: **Lexicalization**

Edward Vajda
# Ket polysynthesis, grammaticalization, and lexicalization

## 1 Introduction

A consideration of the widest possible variety of morphological types can only enrich an understanding of grammaticalization cross-linguistically. This article examines the polysynthetic Ket language of Siberia to assess how processes of grammaticalization and lexicalization have interacted with the language's templatic verb structure. Unrelated to any of its geographic neighbors for thousands of kilometers in any direction and possessing morphological traits absent from most other Eurasian languages, Ket is unusually well suited for expanding the typological horizon of the literature on grammaticalization. This chapter explains how idiosyncrasies of Ket finite verb structure influenced which morpheme classes developed new functions over time. It also demonstrates that the typical cline of semantic change that affected Ket polysynthetic verb structures appears to have been A > B > C, with no evidence that old and new meaning coexisted together in the language for any length of time. This differs from western Eurasian languages, where the cline is generally known to be A > AB > B (Heine, Claudi, Hünnemeyer 1991; Hopper & Traugott 2003), and also from East Asia's isolating languages, where it is A > AB > ABC (Xing 2015). This suggests that although the motivating factors behind grammaticalization are strong enough to affect all languages, the patterns of polysemy that typically develop in a particular language appear to depend on the language's typological profile of formal morphological complexity.

The article is structured in the following way. Section 2 provides an overview of Ket verb morphology and describes how this unusual structure evolved over time. Section 3 considers the language's diverse patterns of verb structure to identify which subtypes tended to undergo lexicalization or grammaticalization. Section 4 surveys grammaticalization patterns that affected the Ket verb base. Section 5 analyzes the etymologies of Ket predicates expressing emotional and mental states that arose by metaphorical extension from literal descriptions of activity or motion. Section 6 summarizes how lexicalization and grammaticalization pathways in Ket compare to languages with very different morphologies; it also offers a possible explanation for the similarities and differences and identifies useful directions for further research.[1]

## 2 The evolution of Ket finite verb structure

Ket is a highly endangered language spoken by a few dozen elderly people in several villages near the Yenisei River in central Siberia. It is the last surviving member of the once widespread Yeniseian family of Siberia. Unrelated to all other languages of Eurasia, Ket differs greatly from the Indo-European and East Asian languages that have informed most studies of grammaticalization. With its rigidly templatic structure, discontinuous stem, complicated verb-internal subject and object marking system, and noun incorporation (Vajda 2017a), the Ket finite verb offers a stark contrast to the fusional or agglutinating word forms of Europe and Inner Asia, as well as to East Asia's isolating morphologies. Much is now understood about the origin and development of this complex structure (Vajda and Nefedov 2015) and the areal pressures that have shaped its subsequent evolution (Vajda 2009). This section provides a basic overview of Ket morphology needed to assess the patterns of grammaticalization or lexicalization that have affected finite verbs.

Ket and its extinct daughter languages stand out in North Asia for having a strongly prefixing verb that contrasts markedly with the exclusively suffixing morphologies of all the surrounding languages (Vajda 2009, 2014). The original Proto-Yeniseian template had the following structure:

**Table 1:** The Proto-Yeniseian finite verb template.

| incorporate – OBJ – determiner(s) – 3SBJ – TAM – 1/2SBJ – verb root – TAM – ANIM.PL.SBJ |
| --- |

The TAM (tense-aspect-mood) slots on both sides of the verb root were inherited from earlier Dene-Yeniseian and show cognacy with elements of Athabaskan TAM morphology (Vajda 2017b). The incorporate slot, located near the verb's leftmost periphery, contained a noun, adjective or directional root that modifies a stem-final verb root, creating a discontinuous stem. Table 2 shows that Ket has retained most of this structure, with only two major changes: a new subject agreement slot

---

[1] I am grateful to Thekla Wiebusch for many valuable suggestions toward making this description of polysynthetic morphology easier to follow. Any remaining difficulties are due to my own deficiencies as a presenter, coupled with the wondrous complexity of the Ket finite verb.

was added verb-initially, and certain tense-aspect-mood affixes merged with the ancient verb root to create what is called the "verb base".

**Table 2:** Modern Ket finite verb template with lexical slots in bold type.

| SBJ – **incorporate** – AGR – **determiner(s)** – AGR/TAM – **verb base** – ANIM.PL.SBJ |
|---|

The portions of the template marked AGR (referring to either subject or object agreement, depending on the lexical stem) and TAM are not fully elaborated in Table 2, since the grammaticalization processes discussed in this article primarily concern the interplay between the incorporate and base. These are the verb's main lexical slots and are marked in Table 2 with boldface type, along with the determiner slot, which also belongs to the lexical stem. In many verbs the base retains the heavy lexical meaning inherited from its root component, while in others it has taken on the functions of the eroded TAM affixes that created the base through merger with the verb root. This distinction will be shown in Section 3 to be important for assessing grammaticalization and lexicalization patterns in Ket verbs.

Finally, it is important to stress that throughout this discussion of Ket finite verb morphology, the terms 'base' and 'stem' are used with intentional contrast. The **base** refers to the lexical morpheme shape nearest to the verb's rightmost edge. This slot originally contained a heavy lexical verb root, which sometimes later merged with adjacent aspectual affixes. The **stem**, on the other hand, refers to the entire array of lexical morphemes in the verb word, of which there might be as many as three discontinuous morphemes (incorporate + determiner + base), in contrast to the grammatical affixes that are interdigitated between these lexical elements.

The distinction between base and stem can be illustrated by examining examples of Ket noun incorporation. Modern Ket can express the same activity using two different verb forms, resulting in different sentence structures. One option uses a simple verb (defined as a verb with no incorporate), with a direct object expressed by an independent noun to create a simple SOV sentence with verb-internal object agreement as shown in (1). The other incorporates the object noun and deletes the object agreement marker, resulting in a discontinuous compound stem as in (2).[2]

---

[2] Unless otherwise stated, example sentences derive from my fieldwork conducted during 2005–2012 with two Southern Ket dialect native speakers Valentina Romanenkova and Marina Irikova from Kellog Village in Turukhansk District of Krasnoyarsk Krai in central Siberia. Individual lexical items can also be found in the *Comprehensive Dictionary of Ket* (Kotorova and Nefedov 2015). Tone in monosyllables is marked as follows: macron and half-long mark for high-even tone (*qōˑj* 'thick'), apostrophe for rising laryngealized tone (*qo'j* 'wish'), geminate mark for rising-falling

(1) Simple verb (without incorporated root)
    ke't    qu's    d=b-il-bed
    man     tent    3MASC.SBJ=3INAN.OBJ-PST-make
    'A man made / was making a **tent**.'

(2) Compound verb with incorporated object noun
    ke't    t=**qus**-li-bed
    man     3MASC.SBJ=**tent**-PST-make
    'A man was engaged in **tent**-making.'

The verb forms in examples (1) and (2) both contain the same verb base *bed*. Example (1) is a simple verb, in which the base and stem are virtually the same, whereas the verb stem in example (2) is compound and contains both the incorporate *qu's* 'tent' and the base *bed* 'make'.

Determiners (the middle of the three lexical slots shown in Table 2) are a set of prefixes consisting of a single consonant that can be added to either simple or compound verbs. Though many determiners are now semantically opaque (in which case they will be glossed TH for "thematic prefix"), those that retain an identifiable meaning generally modify the stem in ways similar to Latin or Russian prefixes. Determiners with identifiable meanings express shape or trajectory of the verbal event's patient- or theme-role participant; others mark distributivity (multiple participants) or pluractionality (multiple acts); still others are associated with the incorporated noun in stems expressing a transition to a new state. Example (3) shows a simple Ket verb form *-do* 'cut' ("simple" refers here and elsewhere to the absence of an incorporate):

(3) Simple stem without a determiner consonant
    ke't        kulep       d-a-b-do
    person      beard       3MASC.SBJ-PRES-3INAN.OBJ-cut
    'A man shaves (his) beard.'

Example (4) shows the same simple stem modified by two different determiner consonants:

---

tone on a long vowel (*qo:j* 'neighboring'), and grave accent for falling tone (*qòj* 'bear'). Most polysyllables have an accent-like pitch on the initial syllable, which is left unmarked. All examples reflect Southern Ket phonetics, except phonemic coda /d/ in verb bases such as *-bed* and *-ted* appears as /d/, though obstruents actually devoice in word-final pronunciation.

(4) Simple stems modified with a determiner consonant
   a. ke't    la'm    t=**t**-a-b-do
      person  board   3MASC.SBJ=**across.area**-PRES-3INAN.OBJ-cut
      'A man (person) is rough-hewing (planing) a board.'

   b. de'ŋ    qo't    t=**k**-a-b-do-n
      people  path    3MASC.SBJ=**away**-PRES-3INAN.OBJ-cut-ANIM.PL.SBJ
      'People are clearing a path.'

Historically, up to three determiners could concatenate in a single stem to combine meanings such as shape or animacy, trajectory, and pluractionality. Such combinations are now completely unproductive, and most modern stems contain a single determiner or none at all.

Examples (1)-(4) also illustrate how the modern Ket template shown in Table 2 has largely retained the Proto-Yeniseian structure shown in Table 1. One important change was the addition of a new subject person agreement slot verb-initially. The forms in (1) – (4) as well as many of those given below contain a verb-initial subject person agreement marker innovated during the evolution of modern Ket from Proto-Yeniseian during the past two to three thousand years. These markers normally surface as a prefix before vowels and as a clitic before consonants (Vajda and Nefedov 2015: 38–40). As mentioned earlier, the second innovation in template structure to arise as Ket evolved from Proto-Yeniseian involved the merger of TAM suffixes with the verb root to create the modern verb base.

The prefixing verb template inherited by Ket was strongly affected over time by the suffixal agglutinating morphology of neighboring Ewenki (Tungusic), Khanty and Selkup (Uralic), as well as Khakas and other South Siberian Turkic languages (Vajda 2009, 2017b). Only about 5% of the modern Ket verbal lexicon is comprised of simple stems consisting of a base preceded only by grammatical prefixes or determiner consonants. Simple stems, especially those lacking a determiner, belong to basic vocabulary. Relatively few verbs of this shape have survived because areal influence strongly disfavored forms without a word-initial lexical root. The same pressure also caused verb-initial subject prefixes to encliticize to any available preceding word, thus further ensuring that the verb's first syllable contains a lexical root. Example (5) shows a verb with its subject prefix encliticized to the preceding word, leaving the incorporate in phonological word-initial position:

(5) Compound stem with incorporated modifier + word final lexical verb root
   v=hu'n          a=ra             **aya**-bo-k-l-**aq**
   my=daughter     I=3FEM.SG.SBJ    **river.to.forest**-1SG.OBJ-with-PST-**walk**
   'My daughter yesterday took me inland [= walked with me from river to forest].'

The base form *-aq* in (5) originates from the erosion of intransitive prefix **ja*- plus verb root *-qod* 'walk'. The base in this stem still conveys the original lexical meaning of locomotion, which means that no grammaticalization has occurred. Similarly, no grammaticalization affected other types of compound Ket verb stems where the incorporated root modifies the verb base. In such stems, the base continues to serve as the lexical stem's semantic head. Verb bases in compound stems that retain their original lexical meanings comprise subtypes that differ according to the possible category of elements to be incorporated. Ten of the most productive of these patterns will be identified below, along with example forms.

Verb bases differ according to the possible categories of roots to be incorporated. Certain non-grammaticalized bases permit object incorporation, of which *-bed* 'make' (6a) and *-a* 'eat inanimate object' are the most prolific (6b):

(6) Examples of lexical bases that allow object incorporation
    a. *d-inus-il-bed* (coda /d/ in this and other bases actually devoiced to [t] word-finally)
       1SBJ-house-PST-make
       'I built a house.'[3]

    b. *qiːn*      *d-əːŋ-s-a-n*
       moose.PL  3SBJ-leaves-PRES-eat-ANIM.PL.SBJ
       'Moose eat leaves.'

Another example of transitivity reduction via direct object incorporation was shown in examples (1)-(2) and more can be found in Vajda (2017a: 38–62).

Only two bases allow instrument incorporation: *kit* 'smear', 'rub' in (7a); and *ted* 'hit endwise with a long object' in (7b):

(7) Examples of instrument incorporation
    a. *da=təy-i-t-ol-kit*
       3FEM.SG.SBJ=salt-3FEM.SG.OBJ-across.area-PST-rub
       'She salted her (fem-class fish).' / 'She rubbed salt on her.'

    b. *k-el-aŋ-a-ted*
       2SBJ-fish.spear-3ANIM.PL.OBJ-PRES-hit.endwise
       'You (SG) spear them (ANIM-class fish).'

---

[3] This example could also mean 'He built a house', since the pronunciation of the 1SBJ agreement prefix /di/ and 3MASC.SG.SBJ agreement prefix /du/ fall together for phononological reasons as [d] or [t] in most modern verb forms. A concise description of the extremely complex system of Ket verb-internal agreement markers can be found in Kotorova and Nefedov (2015: 38–62).

Compound stems consisting of NOUN + *k* 'on' + *tij* 'grow' express the usually pejorative meaning of 'become covered or infested with NOUN'.

(8) *əyin-ba-y-a-tij*
lice-1SG.SBJ-on-PRES-grow
'I become lice-infested.'

Four highly productive models incorporate predicate nominals into a stem consisting of determiner + base. These include: ADJ + *d* + *qan* 'become quality' in (9a); ADJ + *t* + *sin* 'make into quality' in (9b); NOUN + *k* + *bed* 'make into NOUN' in (9c); and NOUN + *t* + *aq* 'become NOUN' in (9d).

(9) Productive compound stems types with non-grammaticalized lexical bases
    a. *ugde-a-b-qan*
       long-PRES-3INAN.SBJ-become
       'It becomes long.'

    b. *d-ugde-t-a-p-sin*
       1SBJ-long-cause.transition-PRES-3INAN.OBJ-be
       'I lengthen it.' or 'I cause it to be long.'

    c. *qima*    *ares=ta*    *sul-u-k-si-bed*
       grandma   nail=3FEM.SG.SBJ   cradle.hook-3INAN.OBJ-from-PRES-make
       'Grandma makes a nail into a cradle hook.'

    d. *temn-dəŋ-t-on-oq*
       geese-1PL.SBJ-transition-PST-become
       'We turned into geese.'

Finally, *habeo*-verbs are also structured as compound stems consisting of possessed noun + base *bed* 'have':

(10) *bən-ku-l-bed*
duck-2SG.SBJ-PST-have
'You (SG) had a duck.'

At least 25% of verb stems in the *Comprehensive Dictionary of Ket* (Kotorova and Nefedov 2015) belong to one of the compound verb types with lexical base illustrated in (2) or in (5) to (10). Despite their retention of stem-final bases with heavy lexical meaning, these patterns have survived centuries of areal pressure toward suffixing because they also contain a lexical form word-initially – an incorporated noun, adjective or adverb that modifies the verb base. In such verbs, both stem-initial root and stem-final base tend to retain the literal meanings that they inherited from Proto-Yeniseian. The form in (8), *əyin-ba-γ-a-tij* 'I become lice infested', still means 'lice grow on me', and thus there was no semantic shift in the verb's lexical components. A possible exception involves the base *-bed* 'have' shown in (10). This base may derive from a merger of the stative resultative suffix *\*-ej* with the verb root *\*bed^j* 'make' (the same root that yields the base *bed* 'make' shown in 2 and 6). If this etymology is correct, then *habeo*-stems arose via the pathway: 'To me is made a tent' → 'I have a tent'. Otherwise, discontinuous, compound stems show no grammaticalization and simply involve the incorporation of secondary heavy lexical material of the sort found widely in other polysynthetic languages; see Vajda (2017a) for more discussion on the origins and productivity of each pattern.

## 3 Morphological subtypes of Ket verb stems

Examining the origin and meaning of Ket verb bases leads directly to our discussion of grammaticalization, as several bases (DO, PUT, GO) have become highly productive markers of iterativity or stativity in modern Ket in stems where they are combined with an action nominal. These bases retain their original lexical meanings of DO, GO, PUT in simple stems (which lack an incorporate) and in regular compound stems (in which the incorporate modifies the base, such as those shown in examples 6–10 above). Table 3 lists these three types of Ket finite verb stems, categorized according to the formal and functional interplay between incorporate and base. This scheme builds upon work of Soviet Ketologist E. A. Krejnovich (1968), who first subdivided Ket verbs according to location of the stem's semantic head relative to other morphemes in the word.

**Table 3:** Morphological subtypes of Ket verb stems.

---
1. Simple stems (= stems lacking an incorporate)
2. Compound stems (= stems with an incorporate that modifies the base)
3. Action-nominal stems (= stems with an incorporated action nominal)
---

Each subtype can be further subdivided according to whether the stem contains a determiner consonant, yielding six subtypes altogether. Finally, there are stems in which both incorporate and root defy semantic interpretation; these most likely originated as compound stems belonging to the second category in Table 3.

Over 60% of the individual stems listed as head words in Kotorova and Nefedov (2015) belong to one of about two dozen highly productive patterns of action-nominal stems (Type 3) in which the base functions as a sort of suffix marking transitivity or aspect. In such verbs, the main lexical meaning is expressed word-initially by the incorporated action nominal – a lexical form containing a verb root.

As an independent word outside the finite verb, the Yeniseian action nominal functions similar to either an infinitive or a participle, depending on context. Historically, it derived from the semantically corresponding finite verb in the following way: Finite stems lacking both incorporate and determiner (that is, stems with the verb base as the only lexical slot) formed their action nominal by removing all grammatical affixes and adding an action nominal prefix *si- plus suffix *-əŋ as a sort of circumfix around the bare verb root. Example (11) contains allomorphic reflexes of Proto-Yeniseian *wag^w 'drag/pull/stretch' in a finite verb form (11a) as well as in the action nominal form derived from it (11b).

(11) Simple finite verb (a) with corresponding action nominal (b)
 a. *d=b-il-**bak***
    1SBJ=3INAN.OBJ-PST-**drag**
    'I dragged it.'

 b. *si-**bagd**-eŋ* (also occurs as ***bagd**-eŋ* without the action nominal prefix *si-*)
    ANOM-**drag**-ANOM
    'dragging' or 'dragged'

Though the action nominal prefix *si- is well attested in Ket's extinct sister language Kott, it survives in Ket only in a handful of forms – a rare example being the one shown above in (11b). The action nominal suffix -eŋ survives in Ket more frequently. However, it has ceased to be productive and is often reanalyzed as a marker of pluractionality based on its coincidental homonymy with the collective noun plural suffix -eŋ; therefore, it tends to appear most often in verb forms referring to multiple participants or which express multiple actions (Vajda 2016). The fact that modern Ket action nominals no longer have easily recognizable derivational morphology has facilitated their incorporation into finite verb stems as word-initial verb roots.

Action nominals incorporated into the verb stem represent a sort of "pseudo-incorporation". True noun or adjective incorporates, like those shown earlier in examples (2) and (6) to (10), serve as secondary heavy lexical material that helps modify the verb base. By contrast, an incorporated action nominal *becomes* the stem's semantic head by replacing the base in this function. The base in action-nominal stems has entirely lost its original lexical meaning, becoming grammaticalized as a marker of aspect or transitivity (or both). In contrast to the forms shown in (1) to (10) above, where the merger of ancient TAM affixes with the ancient verb root did not entail the loss of the base's original lexical meaning, Ket verb stems with action nominal incorporation express their primary lexical meaning word-initially, so that all of the morphemes following on the right, including the base itself, serve as grammatical suffixes of one sort or another.

# 4 Grammaticalized bases in Ket action-nominal stems

Action-nominal stems can be characterized by the new, grammatical function acquired by their base and by the original lexical meaning of the verb root contained in the base.

## 4.1 Grammaticalization of verb base *bed* 'DO/MAKE' → iterative suffix *bed*

The examples in (12) below show forms representing several productive finite verb stems with action-nominal incorporation. The asterisked examples represent an attempt to reconstruct the etymological form and meaning prior to grammaticalization, while the non-asterisked examples show the form and meaning attested in modern Ket.

Grammaticalization of the base *bed* 'DO' is evident in transitive (12a)-(12b) as well as intransitive (12c)-(12d) stems:

(12) a. *\*d-akaqodəŋ-a-bed-n* (example reconstructed, not actually attested)
 \*1SBJ-river.to.forest.walking-PRES-**do**-ANIM.PL.SBJ
 \*'We engage in river-to-forest walking.'

 b. *d-aɣar-a-bed-n*
 1SBJ-river.to.forest.walk-PRES-**ITER**-ANIM.PL.SBJ
 'We walk from river to forest multiple times.'

 c. *\*d-akaqod-o-k-a-bed-n* (example reconstructed, not actually attested)
 \*1SBJ-river.to.forest.walking-3MASC.SG.OBJ-**with**-PRES-**do**-ANIM.PL.SBJ
 \*'We engage in river-to-forest walking with him.'

 d. *d-aɣar-o-ɣ-a-bed-n*
 1SBJ-river.to.forest.walk-3MASC.SG.OBJ-**TH**-PRES-**ITER**-ANIM.PL.SBJ
 'We take him from river to forest many times.'

The examples in (12) contain the action nominal *akaqodəŋ 'walking from river to forest'. This form correlates with the compound finite verb shown earlier in (5), created by compounding the directional *aka 'river to forest' with the verb root *qod 'walk', followed by the action nominal suffix *-əŋ. The modern incorporate is pronounced with local dialectal variation as ayad ~ aʁad ~ ayad ~ aʁad – with the Southern Ket variant ayar given here. Elision of the action-nominal suffix in (12b) and (12d) facilitates the incorporate's new function as semantic head of the verb stem overall. The determiner prefix in (12c), as in most of the other finite verb stem types with incorporated action nominals discussed below, has lost its lexical meaning, remaining as an obligatory though semantically opaque part of the stem. Many thousands of Ket verbs are formed using iterative -bed (or its transitive stem variant k + bed); in these forms the original base meaning of 'DO' or 'MAKE' has been entirely lost. There are no instances where such forms can be used in their etymologically literal meaning as well as in their newer, grammaticalized meaning. This follows the familiar Indo-European grammatical pathway A > AB > B and differs from the common Chinese type A > A/B > A/B/C discussed elsewhere in the present volume. This topic will be revisited in Section 6.

## 4.2 Grammaticalization of verb base *den* 'GO' → suffix *t* 'BE/UNDERGO internal state'

Another, less productive action nominal stem derivation involves using a grammaticalized base that originally meant 'GO' to express a mental or emotional state. Example (13a)-(13b) combines the high frequency simple stem *k-den* meaning 'go/leave/walk away' with the action nominal incorporate *dəʁasiŋ* '(being) happy' (< *dəq 'laugh' + *qas 'want' + action nominal suffix *-əŋ):

(13) Grammaticalization of GO → BE in compound verb stems
    a. *dəqasiŋ-u-k-a-den (example reconstructed, not actually attested)
       *laugh.wanting-3FEM.SG.SBJ-away-PRES-go
       *'Laugh-wanting she goes.'
    b. dəʁasiŋ-u-y-a-t
       happy-3FEM.SG.SBJ-TH-PRES-be
       'She is happy.'

The English translation in (13a) is contrived to provide an impression of what the underlying morpheme structure would literally mean, though there is no evidence the form was ever used to express such a meaning. The modern Ket form in (13b) expresses only the existence of the given state and cannot express actual movement through space. Minus the action nominal incorporate, the base GO (combined with determiner ɣ < k 'away') is still used as part of a simple stem to convey motion and is one of the highest frequency verbs in the language.

(14) Non-grammaticalized GO in simple verb stems
    a. *u-ɣ-á-tn* (also pronounced *u-ɣ-ó-t*)
       3FEM.SG.SBJ-away-PRES-go
       'She goes/walks/leaves.'

    b. *bo-ɣ-ón-den* (also pronounced *bo-ɣ-ón*)
       1SG.SBJ-away-PST-go
       'I went.'

## 4.3 Grammaticalization of bases *\*daq* ~ *\*da* 'PUT' → transitivity and aspect suffix

The next several example sets involve grammaticalization of PUT as a marker of transitivity and aspect. The root meaning 'put, lay' in the language ancestral to Ket had a form something like *\*daq* 'put one object' or *\*da* 'put several objects'. In contrast to their grammaticalized usage as markers of aspect and transitivity in action-nominal stems, verb bases with these shapes retain their literal meaning in simple and compound stems, where no grammaticalizion has occurred:

(15) Ket verbs with non-grammaticalized bases meaning PUT/LAY
    a. *d-es-a-b-**daq***
       1SBJ-surface-PRES-3INAN.OBJ-**put.once**
       'I put/lay it down once.'

    b. *d=d-a-b-**da***
       1SBJ=ITER-PRES-3INAN.OBJ-**put.several**
       'I put/lay them down (one after another).'

In addition to its literal usage, the ancient root meaning PUT yields a wide array of reflexes in modern Ket when grammaticalized together with adjacent aspect affixes. The resulting phonetic reduction has yielded allomorphs including: *-t* ~ *a*

/ *da* ~ *ra* / *-tn* / *-dij* ~ *rij*. The choice of variant depends on how the root interacted morphonologically with the surrounding affixes, as well as the regular Southern Ket phonological rule of intervocalic rhotacism of /d/ to [r], and perhaps on other reasons not yet determined.

Four stem patterns involving these phonologically reduced and semantically bleached forms of PUT were examined in Vajda (in press). The discussion here will concentrate on morphological aspects of their origin in connection with the grammaticalization pathway taken. In each pattern, PUT interacts not only with the immediately adjacent aspectual affixes, but also with the determiner *q-*, originally meaning 'motion or location inside'. The resulting grammaticalization has given rise to inceptives that express the beginning of an activity or the progression of an ongoing change of state. Examples (17) to (22) contain the action nominal *toʁojiŋ* 'drying', which itself is derived from the archaic noun root *\*to* ~ *\*tu* 'water'[4] + verb root *\*qoj* 'dry' + action nominal suffix *\*-əŋ*. The spontaneous event of drying out can still be expressed by the compound stem shown in (16), in which the base *qoj* 'dry' (spirantized intervocalically to *ʁoj*) retains its original function as the stem's semantic head, while *tu* acts as a regular nominal incorporate:

(16)  Compound verb stem associated with the action nominal *toʁojiŋ* 'drying'
 **tu**-t-a-b-in-ə-**ʁoj**
 **water**-transition-PRES-3INAN.SBJ-PST-3SG.SBJ[5]-**dry**
 'It dried out/became desiccated.'

### 4.3.1 Causatives and anticausative action-nominal stems with grammaticalized PUT

This subsection examines four types of stems where verb bases containing an original root meaning PUT have become markers of aspect and transitivity. In example sets (17)-(22), the elements undergoing grammaticalization appear in boldface print. The variant listed under (17a) provides a historical etymology, while (17b) illustrates actual modern usage and meaning.

---

4 The bound root *to* ~ *tu* 'water' is archaic, and Modern Ket mostly uses *ūˑl* to mean 'water'.
5 The multi-site 3rd person prefix *ə-* in this form was originally a stative/resultative or generic intransitive marker rather than an agreement marker. Please see footnote 7.

(17) Transitive single-action inceptive formed from *toʁojiŋ* 'drying' + grammaticalized PUT
    a. *\**da=toʁojiŋ-q-i-b-**daq*** (example reconstructed, not actually attested)
       \*3FEM.SG.SBJ=drying-**inside**-PRES-3INAN.OBJ-**put.once**
       \*'She puts it once into drying.'

    b. *da=toʁojiŋ-**q**-i-v[i]⁶-**t***
       3FEM.SG.SBJ=dry-**INCEPT**-PRES-3INAN.OBJ-**TRANS.MOM**
       'She starts drying it off once.'

The gloss MOM in (17b) stands for 'momentaneous', denoting single action. It contrasts with ITER in (18b) below, which stands for 'iterative'. The Ket iterative can express any action that keeps happening, whether persistent ongoing process or temporally separate series of events. Notice also that the determiner *q* 'inside' in these PUT stems has grammaticalized into a marker of inceptivity (beginning of action).

Example set (18), formed from pluractional PUT, shows the iterative partner of the single action stem in (17):

(18) Iterative transitive inceptive formed from *toʁojiŋ* 'drying' + grammaticalized PUT
    a. *\**da=toqojiŋ-**q**-a-b-**da*** (example reconstructed, not actually attested)
       \*3FEM.SG.SBJ=drying-**inside**-PRES-3INAN.OBJ-**put.many.times**
       \*'She puts it multiple times into drying.'

    b. *da=toʁojiŋ-**q**-a-b-**da***
       3FEM.SG.SBJ=dry-**INCEPT**-PRES-3INAN.OBJ-**TRANS.ITER**
       'She starts drying it off (repeatedly).' or 'She keeps drying it off.'

Inceptives derived from grammaticalized 'put inside' also occur as anti-causative intransitives, with the different base allomorph due to merger with either the change-of-state (perfectivizing) suffix -*ŋ* or stative-resultative/intransitivizing suffix -*ej*. The single-action anti-causative in (19b) is formed from *toʁojiŋ* 'drying' + grammaticalized PUT:

---

**6** The vowel [i] here is epenthetic and not part of the base -*t* (probably originally < *\*-d*). For reasons still unexplained, the transitive single-action causative base form -*t* is replaced by the suppletive form -*a* whenever directly preceded by the past-tense prefix *n*-: *t=toʁojiŋ-q-it-n-**a*** 'I started drying her off once' (1SBJ=dry-INCEPT-3FEM.SG.OBJ-PST-TRANS.MOM). This does not happen if another morpheme intervenes between past-tense *n*- and the base: *da=toʁojiŋ-q-in-di-**t*** 'She started drying me off once' (3FEM.SG.SBJ=dry-INCEPT-PST-1SG.OBJ-TRANS.MOM).

(19) Single-action anti-causative
   a. *da=toqojiŋ-**q**-s-jə-**daq**-ŋ (example reconstructed, not actually attested)
      *3FEM.SG.SBJ=drying-**inside**-PRES-3SG.SBJ[7]-**put.once**-PFV
      *'She puts herself into drying once.'

   b. da=toʁojiŋ-**q**-is-ə-**tn**
      3FEM.SG.SBJ=dry-**INCEPT**-PRES-3SG.SBJ-**INTRANS.MOM**
      'She starts drying herself off once.' or 'She starts getting dried off once.'

The iterative anti-causative formed from *toʁojiŋ* 'drying' + grammaticalized PUT in (20b) derives from the multiple action form of PUT.

(20) Iterative anti-causative
   a. *da=toqojiŋ-**q**-a-jə-**da**-ej (example reconstructed, not actually attested)
      *3FEM.SG.SBJ=drying-**inside**-PRES-3SG.SBJ-**put.many.times**-INTRANS
      *'She puts herself into drying many times.'

   b. da=toʁojiŋ-**q**-a-jə-**rij**
      3FEM.SG.SBJ=dry-**INCEPT**-PRES-3SG.SBJ-**INTRANS.ITER**
      'She keeps drying off.' or 'She starts drying (herself) off many times.'

Table 4 summarizes the complex morphophonology of action-nominal stems that have undergone grammaticalization of *q* 'inside' + PUT. The transitive-causative forms chosen (top tier) are based on the 3rd person inanimate-class object (prefix *b*-), while the intransitive/anti-causative forms (bottom tier) are based on a 3rd person animate-class singular object (prefix *jə-* ~ *ə-*).

---

[7] Originally part of the stative-resultative circumfix around the verb root, the prefix *jə-* ~ *ə-* was reanalyzed as an agreement marker for 3rd person subjects (which formerly showed zero expression in this position). It consequently disappears in forms containing 1st and 2nd person subject agreement markers: *t=toʁojiŋ-q-i-di-t* 'I start drying (myself) off' (1SBJ=dry-INCEPT-PRES-1SG.SBJ-INTRANS.MOM). See also footnote 6.

**Table 4:** Summary of transitive and anti-causative inceptives (X= action nominal; Y = object).

|  | single action → PUT + inside | momentaneous inceptive | multiple action → PUT + inside | iterative inceptive |
|---|---|---|---|---|
| Transitive stem | *-q-i-b-**daq** 'put Y into X-ing once' | q-i-v[i]-**T** ~ **A**[a] INCEPT ... TRANS.MOM 'start X-ing Y once' | -q-a-b-**da** put Y many times into X-ing | q-a-b-**DA** INCEPT TRANS.ITER 'start X-ing' |
| Intransitive stem | *-q-s-jə-**da(q)**-ŋ 'put self into X-ing once' | q-is-ə-**TN** INCEPT INTRANS.MOM 'start X-ing once' / 'start getting X-ed once' | q-a-jə-**da**-ej put (self) into X-ing many times | q-a-jə-**DIJ** (INCEPT)INTRANS.ITER 'keep X-ing' / start Xing (self) many times |

[a]See footnote 7 for a discussion of the base form alternation *t ~ a*.

### 4.3.2 Resultative action-nominal stems with grammaticalized PUT

Grammaticalization of PUT also generated "stative resultatives" – defined as verbs that express the existence of a state resulting from a prior action without narrating the action itself. Such forms occur widely in Dene-Yeniseian languages and were originally derived by adding a "stative-resultative" or "perfective-stative" circumfix around the verb root (Vajda 2017b). Stative resultatives in Ket are only formed from single action transitives like those shown in (17):

(21) Grammaticalized PUT in transitive single-action inceptive with *toʁojiŋ* 'drying'
   a. *\*da=toʁojiŋ-q-s-jə-**daq**-ej* (example reconstructed, not actually attested)
      \*3FEM.SG.SBJ=drying-**inside**-PRES-INTRANS-**put.once**-RES
      \*'She is in a state of having been put into drying'

   b. *da=toʁojiŋ-q-is-**qud*** (with base *qud* the result of unexplained metathesis)
      3FEM.SG.SBJ=dry-**TH**-PRES-**RES**
      'She is dried off.'

The form in (21b) is interesting for two reasons. First, because the grammaticalization of PUT into a marker of transitivity and aspect involved meaning present in the affixes that merged with the verb root to form the modern base, the question arises as to whether the original root PUT has grammaticalized or whether the affixes that merged with it have simply taken over as the core meaning of the base. Because these stems also involve grammaticalization of the determiner *q* 'inside' to express inceptivity – a semantic shift intrinsically connected with the original lexical meaning of the root PUT – it seems more likely that grammaticalization of the root PUT has in fact occurred, and the merger or partial merger of the aspectual affixes into bases containing PUT is secondary.

The second noteworthy aspect of PUT grammaticalizations comes to light in the examples shown in (22) below. Here, the original root *\*daq* 'put once' seems to have interacted with the stative-resultative circumfix to yield the metathesized base form *qud*, though the trigger for this change is unclear. In forms with plural subjects, the metathesis was blocked by the presence of the animate plural subject suffix *-in*, resulting in a base form of *dam* (pronounced [tam] after /s/), as shown in (22b) below:

(22) Grammaticalized PUT in a resultative stem with *toʁojiŋ* 'drying' and plural subject
  a. *\*du=toʁojiŋ-q-s-jə-**daq**-ej-in* (example reconstructed, not actually attested)
    \*3SBJ=drying-**inside**-PRES-INTRANS-**put.once**-INTRANS-ANIM.PL.SBJ
    \*'They (ANIM-class) are in a state of having been put into drying.'

  b. *t=toʁojiŋ-q-is-**tam**-in*
    3SBJ=dry-TH-PRES-**RES**-ANIM.PL.SBJ
    'They (ANIM-class) are dried off.'

  c. *toʁojiŋ-q-i-v-**əramin*** (< *toʁojiŋ-q-i-b-qud*, via replacement of *-qud* by *-ədamin*)
    dry-TH-PRES-3INAN.SBJ-**RES.PL.SBJ**
    'They (INAN-class) are dried off.'

Example (22c) shows that *-dam* spread analogically to forms with inanimate-class plural subjects, creating a fused inanimate-class stative-resultative base *-əramin* in Southern Ket. Verbs of this type are unique in having the animate-class suffix *-in* co-occurring with an inanimate-class plural subject. Here the initial /ə/ is a survival of the stative-resultative prefix *\*jə-*, a morpheme which in the animate-class plural form (22b) has elided or mixed with the preceding tense marker *s-* to yield the pronunciation [is].

Table 5 summarized the historical development of stative-resultatives with grammaticalized PUT:

**Table 5:** Ket resultative forms based on *q* 'inside' + single-action transitive PUT (X = action named by incorporated action nominal)

|  | Animate-class subject | | Inanimate-class subject | |
| --- | --- | --- | --- | --- |
| Singular subject stem | *-q-s-jə-daq-ej → 'be in the state of having been put into X.' | -q-is-ə-QUD 'be in a state of having undergone X' | *-q-i-b-ə-daq-ej → 'be in the state of having been put into X.' | -q-i-b-QUD 'be in a state of having undergone X' |
| Plural subject stem | *-q-s-jə-daq-ej-in → 'being in the state of having been put into X' | -q-is-→RAMIN 'be in a state of having undergone X' | *-q-i-b-ə-daq-ej ≠ 'being in the state of having been put into X' | -q-is-əRAMIN 'be in a state of having undergone X' |

Note that the inanimate-class plural form *-q-is-əramin* in the box on bottom right as spread analogically from animate class stems, replacing original *-q-i-b-QUD*.

## 4.4 Two action-nominal stem types with non-grammaticalized bases

The action-nominal stems with grammaticalized bases examined earlier in (13) and in (17) to (22) represent some of the most productive stem types in modern Ket, accounting for many thousands of individual verbs. The two action-nominal stem patterns shown below in (23) are likewise highly productive, but do not show grammaticalization of their bases. Both express inceptivity.

(23) Two inceptive action-nominal stems with non-grammaticalized bases
    a. *aɣar-a-ɣ-a-ʁan* (-ʁan < -qan)
       walking.from.river.to.forest-3MASC.SG.SBJ-TH-PRES-**begin**
       'He begins/starts walking from river to forest.'

    b. *aq-b-in-saŋ*
       rotting-3INAN.SBJ-PST-**begin**
       'It (suddenly/unexpectedly) began/started to rot.'

These two patterns overlap in meaning, but *qan* can combine with any action nominal, while *saŋ* is limited to uncontrolled and spontaneous changes such as rotting, falling, catching cold, and the like. Action nominals expressing involuntary changes such as *a'q* 'rotting' or *dəqŋ* 'falling' may also incorporate with *qan*, but the notion of spontaneity is lost. The base *qan* seems originally to have meant 'begin', as it also appears in inceptives with incorporated adjectives such as the example given earlier in (9a). The base *saŋ* is harder to etymologize. The same form seems to occur in the non-conjugating copular predicate *usaŋ* 'exists/ is', though the meaning of the initial syllable /u/ is opaque. It also seems to occur in the translative (TRANSL) postposition *esaŋ* 'in order to be', 'in order to do', 'in order to get', which is suffixed to nouns or action nominals to express goal of action in complex predicates expressing motion or desire; here again, the meaning of the initial syllable /e/ is unclear, so it is not possible to etymologize the spontaneous inceptive verb base *saŋ* with full confidence. Most likely, *saŋ* originally meant 'be', 'exist'; in combination with action nominals the base *saŋ* acquired a secondary meaning of inceptivity: 'rotting (suddenly) exists'. In any event, there is no evidence that either *qan* or *saŋ* grammaticalized from an earlier heavy verb root. The high frequency with which action nominals combine with these two non-grammaticalized bases – especially *qan*, since virtually any action nominal form can be compounded with it to create an intransitive inceptive stem – may have influenced the genesis of action nominal incorporation in stems with grammaticalized bases.

This concludes our discussion of grammaticalization of Ket verb bases, which is closely connected with the morphological type of stem in which the base appears. The small number of simple stems that have survived in Ket show no grammaticalization of the base. Nor do the far larger number of compound stems, with the possible exception of *habeo*-verbs in (10). The third type, action-nominal stems, contains fewer individual patterns, but each one is highly productive. All stems that incorporate action nominals display grammaticalized bases, except for the intransitive inceptives in *qan* and *saŋ* shown in (23). The base meanings *qan* 'begin' and *saŋ* 'spontaneously begin' (? < 'be', 'exist') functionally resemble light verbs that often arise from grammaticalization cross-linguistically, which may correlate with the fact that these stems seem to form a transition between Types 2 and 3.

# 5 Lexicalization of Ket verbs built with simple or compound stems

The previous section discussed action-nominal stems (Type 3 in Table 3) with grammaticalized bases, only two of which retain their original lexical meaning. However, in simple or compound stems (Types 1 or 2 in Table 3), the bases DO, GO, and PUT normally did maintain their function as heavy verb roots. The grammaticalization pathway affecting verb bases in action-nominal stems appears to be A > B > C rather than A > A/B, where both literal and figurative meanings functionally coexist. This section takes a look at lexicalized expressions of cognitive or mental states that arose metaphorically from stems expressing concrete action or motion. The verbs examined here are simple or compound stems rather than the action-nominal stems. Specifically examined are complex predicates expressing ability and intention, as well as verbs of forgetting or remembering, and the expression of ridicule, envy, or joy. Some of these stems do exhibit polysemy, with both literal and idiomatic meanings coexisting in modern usage, while others do not.

## 5.1 Verbs of ability or cognition

Expressions of ability or intention arise secondarily from more concrete meanings in many languages, and Ket is no exception. The examples in (24) show that the same predicate containing the incorporate *it-*, derived from the root **wet* 'sense', 'feel', 'understand', is used in Ket to express knowing a fact as well as the ability to perform an action:

(24) Predicates meaning 'know', 'be able' (Kotorova and Nefedov 2015: 535–536)
    a.  *bū   it-a-lam,                           at  ajtej  ke't*
        he    understand-3MASC.SG.SBJ-state.exists  I   bad   person
        'He knows I'm a bad person.'

    b.  *kəsn-əves        at   asanəj      it-pe-ram*
        Russian-PROSEC  I   conversing   understand-1SG.SBJ-state.exists
        'I can speak Russian.'

The expression of ability in (24b) likely derived from the earlier meaning of knowing a fact (24a). While this is best regarded as a form of grammaticalization, the origin of several other Ket verbs denoting internal states provide clear examples of lexicalization, and can no longer convey a literal meaning in discourse. In (25) the metaphor expressing "forget" is based on the incorporated body part noun *en-* 'mind', 'brain' plus base *suk*, which derives from a root meaning 'hook-shaped', 'bent 180%', or 'turn back in the opposite direction':

(25) *en-bo-n-suk*
     mind-1SG.SBJ-PST-turn.back
     'I forgot.' (literally, 'My mind turned back')

Example (26) expresses the recall from memory of something previously learned. It was built by adding *en-* 'mind', 'brain' to the base **wək* 'find', which reduces to *-o* in Ket but better retains its original shape as *gək* in the Yugh cognate stem meaning 'remember'

(26) *d-en-a-t-ol-o* (compare: Yugh *d-en-t-a-gək* 'he remembers it')
1MASC.SG.SBJ-mind-3MASC.SG.OBJ-TH-PST-find
'He remembered/recalled him.' (literally, 'I found him in the brain.')

The base **wək* 'find' fully retains its shape in Ket simple stem forms like *di-b-bək* 'I find it' (1SBJ-3INAN.OBJ-find). Its reduction to *-o* in the compound stem shown in (26) follows the general trend toward suffixing in stems with incorporated roots, which here has also led to phonological reduction of the word-final base. The root *suk* in (25) also occurs in Ket verbs of motion meaning 'return to starting point' (as evident from the action nominal *suyat* 'returning' < **suk* 'back' + **qod* 'walk') and verbs meaning 'push back' or 'push away' (*da-ba-t-suk* 'she pushes me away' (3FEM.SG.SBJ-1SG.OBJ-TH-turn.back). However, Ket forms meaning 'forget' or 'remember' are never used literally as verbs of motion or action and can only convey abstract mental events.

There are a number of ways to express intention in Ket, many of which involve the root *qoj ~ qas* meaning 'wish' or 'desire'. A clear case of lexicalization is shown in (27), where the etymological meaning 'raise oneself up', originally a reflexive form of the verb 'raise up/raise to adulthood' in (27a), has come to be used to mean 'intend' in (27b). This verb requires an action nominal complement marked with the translative postposition *-esaŋ*, meaning 'in order to', 'for the purpose of'.

(27) Lexicalization of 'conceive an intention' from 'raise oneself'
 a. *da=in-ku-tos*
 3FEM.SG.SBJ=PST-2SG.OBJ-raise
 'She raised you.' or 'She brought you up.'

 b. *ejiŋ-esaŋ    k-in-ku-tos*
 going-TRANSL   2SBJ-PST-2SG.SBJ-raise
 'You (SG) decided to leave.' (etymologically, 'You elevated yourself in order to go.')

Forms with multi-site subject marking such as that shown in (27b) cannot be used literally to mean 'raise oneself'. The meaning 'stand up' or 'raise oneself to a standing position' is instead expressed by the etymologically related but morphologically distinct stem shown in (28a) below. The notion of raising or rearing children can also be expressed using the unrelated stem in (28b), which contains the action nominal *tijiŋ* 'growing'.

(28) Examples of verbs with non-grammaticalized bases conveying 'rising' or 'raising'
   a. *d=h-ol-di-tes*
      1SBJ=upright-PST-1SG.SBJ-rise
      'I stood up.' / 'I got up (after sleeping).'
   b. *da=tijiŋ-q-in-di-t*
      3FEM.SG.SBJ-growing-TH-PST-1SG.OBJ-TRANS.MOM
      'She raised me (from childhood).' (etymologically, 'She put me into growing once.')

These examples of non-polysemous Ket verb stems could be multiplied, but the general trend is that Ket verbs expressing mental states or conditions normally do not retain the ability to express their literal, etymological meaning.

## 5.2 Lexicalization of expressions related to emotion

Ket has a number of idiomatic expressions for 'joking' or 'ridicule' based on a metaphor meaning 'rub with dirt'.

(29) Ket metaphors for ridicule containing the noun *ba'ŋ* 'dirt'
   a. *ba'ŋ=da          t-a-ja-yit*
      dirt=3FEM.SG.SBJ   across.area-PRES-3SG.SBJ-rub
      'She jokes around.' (literally, 'She rubs dirt on herself.')
   b. *ba'ŋ=da          b-oq-ba-t-a-b-git*   (Krejnovich 1968: 167)
      dirt=3FEM.SG.SBJ   1SG.POSS-exposed.part-1SG.OBJ-across.area-PRES-TH-rub
      'She makes fun of me.' (literally, 'She rubs exposed parts of me with dirt.')

Sentence (29a) can be used either literally or figuratively (Kotorova and Nefedov 2015: 642). Sentence (29b) was recorded only by E. A. Krejnovich in the 1960s and could not be re-elicited from my consultants during 2005–2012, so it is unclear whether it could have permitted a literal interpretation in actual usage. The verb form in (29b) is structurally unusual in that it contains a regular object marker as well as an incorporated possessed body-part term also correlated with the grammatical object. Another unsolved problem with these stems is that the original meaning of the determiners *t* (in 29a) and *t-b* (in 29b) is unclear, so that they must be glossed TH for 'thematic prefix'; the underlying meaning is probably something like '(action) across or along a surface'. Even without a full etymology, however, it is clear that the stem in (29a), at least, provides an example of an idiomatic expression that has not lost its original literal meaning and remains functionally polysemous.

Stems denoting 'envy' based on a metaphor meaning 'poke' or 'jab' also retain their literal usage. These are compound stems built with the incorporated instrument root *\*əqin-* '(sharp) branches' plus base *\*-do* 'cut', 'gouge' or *\*-ted* 'hit endwise'

(30) Ket metaphors for 'envy' (adapted from Kotorova and Nefedov 2015: 698)
 a. *d-ə:n-t-a-d-do*
  3MASC.SBJ-sharp.branches-ITER-PRES-1SG.OBJ-gouge
  'He envies me.' or 'He jabs me repeatedly with sharp branches.'

 b. *d-ə:n-ba-t-a-p-tet*
  3MASC.SG.SBJ-sharp.branches-1SG.OBJ-ITER-PRES-surface-hit.endwise
  'He envies me.' or 'He pokes me repeatedly with sharp branches.'

A number of Ket verb stems denoting emotions cannot as yet be fully etymologized, because at least one of the morphemes occupying the stem's three lexical slots (incorporate, determiner, or base) is semantically opaque. Still other stems expressing internal states or changes show no difference between the etymological meaning of their component morphemes and literal usage. An example would be compound stems meaning 'think' that combine the incorporated noun *an-* 'thought' with verb base *-bed* 'make'. Finally, there are cases where it is difficult to distinguish literal from figurative meaning in light of the Ket worldview. A number of verbs expressing anger, being evil or having a mean temperament are based on a surfeit of bile. Conversely, some verbs meaning 'cheer up', or 'improve one's mood' (31b) are based on the absence of bile.

(31) Ket evaluations of mood or temperament involving metaphors based on *qə:l* 'bile'
 a. *da=qəln-a-bed* (*qəln* < *\*qə:l* 'bile' + action nominal suffix *\*-ŋ*)
  3FEM.SG.SBJ=being.angry-PRES-ITER
  'She is angry/moody/irritable.'

 b. *da=i:lon-q-in-di-t* (*i:lon* < *\*qə:l* 'bile' + *\*pan* 'without')
  3FEM.SG.SBJ=bile.without-into-PST-1SG.OBJ-put.once
  'She cheered me up.' (literally, 'She put me into a bile-less state.')

It is difficult to separate literal from figurative meaning in such cases, since in the worldview of Kets (and many other people), having too much bile and feeling emotionally out of sorts are one and the same thing.

A final example that illustrates the difficulty of evaluating lexicalized meaning comes from fieldwork conducted in late spring of 2006, when one of our consultants, upon seeing the first insect of the season buzzing past us, suddenly exclaimed:

(32)  qajmuq=da      il-us        (Valentina Romanenkova, p.c.)
      fly=3FEM.SG.SBJ PST-melt
      'A fly melted out.' or 'A fly warmed up.'

Kets believe that insects 'melt out' or 'warm up' with the onset of spring after the long winter freeze, and it is impossible to judge objectively whether the meaning of the verb form in (32) is literal or figurative or both. Evaluating such usages in terms of polysemy or lexicalization history is simply not feasible.

This section has barely scratched the surface (pun intended) of figurative uses of Ket finite verb forms. More work should be done on documenting Ket idiomatic expressions and their etymological development. However, it is already evident that polysemous as well as non-polysemous types of lexicalization exist in Ket, though the latter predominate. This contrasts with the situation described in Section 4, where grammaticalized verb bases never allow a literal interpretation in Ket.

# 6 Summary, conclusions, and suggestions for further research

This study has analyzed the Ket finite verb to show how its structural idiosyncrasies have interacted in non-trivial ways with patterns of grammaticalization and lexicalization in the language. Most bases belonging to a particular morphological stem subtype (action-nominal stems) have undergone grammaticalization, together with semantic bleaching and phonological reductions. In addition, the lexicalization of entire stems has yielded many common expressions of emotional or mental states. The fact that the verb bases in stems containing action nominal incorporates have undergone grammaticalization is connected with the language's contact history and gradual shift from prefixing to suffixing. The grammaticalization of Ket verb bases in action-nominal stems invariably follows the pathway A > B > C, with no polysemy in evidence, though the etymologically identical bases continue to retain their literal meaning in simpler stems. Unfortunately, because the corpus of Ket language data extends back only for several decades, rather than for hundreds of years, it is not possible to ascertain whether action-nominal stems ever passed through a period of polysemy, during which both literal and grammaticalized meaning coexisted side-by-side in the speech of any particular generation. By contrast, several of the verb stems involved in idiomatic expressions of emotional or mental states examined in Section 5 do allow both literal and figurative interpretations in Ket speech as recorded over the past decade.

As a polysynthetic language, Ket differs from fusional or analytic languages of western Eurasia, on the one hand, as well as from the isolating morphologies of East Asia. The general cline of semantic change in Ket grammaticalization, in contrast to other Eurasian languages, appears to be linked to the language's formal morphological complexity. A tentative conclusion would be that increasing amounts of word-internal morphological complexity disfavors the rise of stable polysemy in grammaticalized constructions, whereas isolating morphology tends to favor it. If this is true, then differences in stable patterns of polysemy arising from grammaticalization are connected in non-trivial ways to a language's morphological type. Fusional or analytic languages typically follow the cline A > AB > B, while isolating languages instead following the cline A > AB > ABC. By contrast, semantic change in the polysynthetic Ket verb, with its much greater degree of formal complexity, appears instead to follow the general cline of A > B > C. Future studies of semantic change in other polysynthetic languages, with internal structures similar to as well as different from what has been documented for Ket, are needed to broaden the perspective on how formal morphological complexity interacts with grammaticalization and patterns of polysemy across languages.

# References

Heine, Bernd, Ulrike Claudi, and Friederike Hünnemeyer. 1991. *Grammaticalization: a conceptual framework*. Chicago: University of Chicago Press.
Hopper, Paul, and Elizabeth Traugott. 2003. *Grammaticalization*. Cambridge: Cambridge University Press.
Kotorova, Elizaveta, and Andrey Nefedov. 2015. *Comprehensive dictionary of Ket*. Munich: Lincom Europa.
Krejnovich, E. A. 1968. *Glagol ketskogo jazyka* [The Ket verb]. Leningrad: Nauka.
Vajda, Edward. 2009. Loanwords in Ket. *Loanwords in the world's languages: a comparative handbook*. Martin Haspelmath and Uri Tadmor (eds.), 471–494. Berlin/New York: Mouton de Gruyter.
Vajda, Edward. 2014. Yeniseian. *Handbook of derivational morphology*, Pavel Stekauer and Rochelle Lieber (eds.), 509–519. Oxford: Oxford University Press.

Vajda, Edward. 2016. Metathesis and reanalysis in Ket. *Proceedings of the 36th Annual Meeting of the Berkeley Linguistics Society*, Nicholas Rolle, Jeremy Steffman, and John Sylak-Glassman (eds.), 457–471. Berkeley, CA: Berkeley Linguistics Society.

Vajda, Edward. 2017a. Ket polysynthesis. *Handbook of polysynthesis*, Michael Fortescue, Marianne Mithun, and Nicholas Evans (eds.), 363–391. Oxford: Oxford University Press.

Vajda, Edward. 2017b. Patterns of innovation and retention in templatic polysynthesis. *Handbook of polysynthesis*, Michael Fortescue, Marianne Mithun, and Nicholas Evans (eds.), 906–929. Oxford: Oxford University Press.

Vajda, Edward, and Andrey Nefedov. 2015. Grammatical sketch of Ket. *Comprehensive dictionary of Ket*, Elizaveta Kotorova and Andrey Nefedov (eds.), 25–66. Munich: Lincom Europa.

Xing, Janet. 2015. A comparative study of semantic change in grammaticalization and lexicalization in Chinese and Germanic languages. *Studies in language* 39.3: 593–633.

Ken-ichi Takashima
# A lexical category in Shāng Chinese:
# V<sub>controllable</sub> vs. V<sub>uncontrollable</sub>

## Preamble

This paper examines the earliest historical phase of the Chinese language in certain of its specific aspects. The source we rely on is an extensive corpus of the so-called "oracle-bone inscriptions" (abbreviated hereinafter as "OBI"). The content of OBI is in general more ritualistic and divinatory than mundane/profane or historical. Based on archeological, astronomical, and paleographical studies, OBI can be dated to ca. 13th–11th c. BC. Their discovery, purported to have been made in 1899, in fact, transformed the thereto legendary dynasty into the first historical one: the Shāng 商 (or Yīn 殷) Dynasty (ca. 13th–11th c. BC). It had existed near the modern city of Ānyáng 安陽, Henan Province, toward the end of the Shāng-Yīn period until it was overthrown by the Zhōu 周 royal forces from the west, modern Xī'ān 西安, Shǎnxī Province.

The intention of this paper is to make clear some significant aspects of the language by means of exegetical analyses of the lexical, grammatical and semantic components of the language. The language is written in the archaic script which was succeeded by, or transformed into, the Zhōu bronze inscriptions (ca. 10th–3rd c. BC), the Zhànguó 戰國 silk and bamboo-slip writings (5th–3rd c. BC), the Qín 秦 (3rd c. BC) small-seal script, the Hàn 漢 (3rd c. BC-3rd c. AD) clerical script, and then the standard script commonly believed to have developed during the Wèi-Jìn 魏晉 period (3rd c.–5th c. AD). All the OB graphs in this paper have been transcribed using the standard script, known widely as *kǎishū* 楷書 – literally meaning "normalized/regular script".

The justification for the principal thesis of this paper – the existence of humanly controllable vs. humanly uncontrollable verbs in Shāng Chinese – reside in our perception of the people who had such an ingrained Weltanschauung that sharply dichotomized actions, affairs, and events in life into those that were considered as manageable or unmanageable. There hardly was any other option they could conceive of. It was a Weltanschauung that tended to be deterministic, and

---

**Note:** I wish to thank the participants of the Symposium (see Preface of the present volume by the editor, Janet Z. Xing) for their penetrating comments and questions. I am also much indebted to Nathan Hill and Christopher Button for their invaluable comments and suggestions to an earlier version of this paper.

that, we think, is reflected in the language of the OBI. Thus this paper addresses the rules in the use of the negatives and the so-called modal particle *qí* 其 (which we believe is both modal and aspectual). We shall attempt to show how the negatives, the word *qí*, and various verbs – controllable vs. uncontrollable ones, and successful ("success verbs") vs. trial ("attempt verbs") – are combined to produce meaningful units. The negatives discussed in the paper are the non-modal *bù* 不, *fú* 弗, and *fēi* 非; the modal *wú* 毋 and *wù* 勿, for all of which we provide commentaries on their exact natures and how they can be understood and translated into English. We will also account for the words *wú/wáng* 無/亡 'not have/there is no NP/(occasion to) V'. Grammatically, these are not negatives; they are the negative counterparts of the possessive/existential verb *yǒu* 有 'have/there is NP/(occasion to) V'. But when *wú/wáng* (some morphological distinctions are recoverable) are followed by a V, they might give a fallacious impression of them as negatives. The grammar and semantics of negatives and negative words are on the whole distinguishable.

Other related topics such as the complete absence of \**wù qí* 勿其 as opposed to the use of *wú qí* 毋其 'should not be V$_{ing}$' (§3.2), the English modal auxiliary *should* (obligative, inferential, and putative) used to translate certain expressions (§3.2), the modality of "certainty vs. uncertainty", *qí*'s syntactic function and the generation of various modal meanings, will also be discussed in the paper (§3.3).

# 1 Introduction

In his review of Takashima (2015), Smith (2016: 458) advanced the following criticism:

> Even given the difficulties and uncertainties involved in reading Shang inscriptions, it is also surprising to find a primer adopting unorthodox theory and terminology that might confuse the novice.

The "unorthodox theory and terminology" includes, among others, V$_{CONTROL}$ or V$_{UNCONTROL}$. I used this term around twenty times in that book in order to succinctly capture a distinction that nonetheless does have broader implications when analyzed in detail beyond the scope of the work. I did not imagine that it would cause any problem because the meaning of a given verb that bears a distinctive attribute of controllable as opposed to uncontrollable is specifically mentioned, and that seemed self-evident. For example, " … the word *xì* 系 'bind, tie' apparently is an action controllable verb … " (p. 8); "If we *make a sacrificial offering* of pigs to such and such ancestor", "If His Majesty *orders* X to do Y" (p. 40); "The verb *qǔ* 取... means 'to take' which seems to work in many inscriptions where ordinary nouns such as *niú* 牛 'cow', *yáng* 羊 'sheep', *shǐ* 豕 'pig', (*bái*) *mǎ* (白)馬 '(white) horse', etc. occur after this verb ... . We can also take this as a controllable verb, so that we would expect its negative counterpart to be *wù qǔ* 勿取 'should not take'. This, in fact, occurs ... " (p. 68). On the other hand, "the sun eclipsed" (p. 40) or "there is an eclipse in the sun" (*ibid.*) was, and still is, uncontrollable to any creature. Similarly, "... *shòu* 受 'receive' [as in *shòu nián* 受年 'harvest a good crop of millet'] is an action-uncontrollable verb from the viewpoint of the living" (p. 47). All these examples seemed transparent. The term "controllable" does not have anything to do with "control theory", "controller", "control sentence", "control agreement principle" (Crystal 2008: 112–3), "control/equi verb", nor with "subject-control" or "object-control" verb that are used in recent literature on GB (Trask 1995: 62–3). It is just a down-to-earth, ordinary use of the word "controllable". The term is applicable in theory to any verb that can be so classified by virtue of its lexical meaning; "un-" is just prefixed to this adjective to express negation or privation.

The first responsibility of a reviewer of any book is to read it with some care, but the actual examples cited were totally ignored, and no effort seems to have been made even to try to understand them. Also, none of a dozen errors in the book including *zhǐshì* 指示 for 指事 (p. 31) was caught or, if caught, they were not pointed out (see Appendix: Errata of Takashima 2015). The reviewer proceeded to offer: "The latter [= $V_{CONTROL}$] refers to something like 'volition'."

There is some degree of overlap in "volition" and "controllability". The term "volition" is used in the general sense of exercising, or capable of exercising, will. "Volitional verb" is used to refer to one with such an attribute. In Chinese the term is *yìyuàn huò fēiyìyuàn dòngcí* 意願或非意願動詞 according to Shěn Jiāxuān (2000: 431, 384). But my meaning is *kě kòngzhì huò bù kě kòngzhì dòngcí* 可控制或不可控制動詞 which corresponds to a "controllable or uncontrollable verb" (abbreviated hereinafter as $V_{CONTROL}$ or $V_{UNCONTROL}$). There is an appreciable difference between them. The reviewer's comment just quoted seems far less helpful to the reader than the several examples cited above.

Also, consider, for example, the verb *yuē* 曰 'say, declare' which occurs in example (6) below in which it is used as a $V_{CONTROL}$ whose subject is the king (*wáng* 王). However, it can be specified as having the non-volitional feature when, for example, it is potential as in "Two *Zǐ* can continue" (二子克延 – HJ 3269) or "S can speak" (presumably: S *kè yuē* 克曰) in which both *yán* 延 'to continue' and 曰 are $V_{CONTROL}$. Although the $V_{CONTROL}$ and its subject as a constituent frequently have the volitional or [+WILL] feature, it is not necessarily so because "S can continue" and "S can speak" are [–WILL]. But the $V_{CONTROL}$ category can still be maintained. In fact, it doesn't have to be potential to grasp the difference between V_{CONTROL}/V_{UNCONTROL} and V_{VOLITIONAL}/V_{NON-VOLITIONAL} as when we relate the act of speaking or continuing descriptively from the vantage point of a third party: "Two Zǐ continue…" and "S says…" can be non-volitional, but their actions are no doubt controllable from the viewpoint of the speaker.

However, the reviewer might have a point: the term "controllable" or "uncontrollable" is not used widely, though one does encounter it as in Yuán Yùlín (1993: 25–8) and Jacques (2017: 5). More importantly, the lexical category of V_{CONTROL} or V_{UNCONTROL} is, as noted here and there in the book, closely related, or has synergistic relationships, with the following six uses or behavioral reflexes:

(1) the use of the negatives such as *bù* 不, *fú* 弗, *fēi* 非,[1] *wú* 毋, and *wù* 勿;
(2) the use of the so-called modal particle *qí* 其;
(3) the way in which a given verb behaves in complex sentences (involving subordinate or embedded clauses);
(4) the way in which the verb and subject/topic as a unit with either the [+WILL] or [−WILL] feature behave;
(5) the way in which modality interacts with the verb specifiable as $V_{+/-controllable}$;[2]
(6) other linguistic processes.

This paper examines (1) and (2) with occasional comments on the rest.

## 2 Preliminaries to analysis

What the Shāng language users said, recorded, and why they expressed it in the way they did is well worth asking. The aim of this study is to provide answers to some aspects of these what and why questions.

---

**1** 非 is not always a negative particle. Sometimes it functions as a negative copula and sometimes as a negative in its own right. For example, 非隹烄 '(This crack) (is not⇒) does not signify that (we should conduct) a burnt sacrifice' which is the negative counterpart of 允隹烄 '(This crack) really (is⇒) signifies that (we conduct) a burnt sacrifice', found in *HJ* 34479. There are a few other examples (e.g., *Huādōng* 241), but they all occur in the inscriptions belonging to certain specific diviner groups (n. 6) and, quite importantly, occur before the copula 隹. Also, the arrow sign "⇒" in A⇒B is used to signify "A is taken as B," "A can be expressed as B," "A is interpreted as B," "A gives rise to B," or "A is abbreviated as B."
**2** This is a shortened notation of "V_{CONTROL} or V_{UNCONTROL}". This can be marked with the minus sign preceding "controllable" to mean "uncontrollable", and with the plus sign to mean "V_{CONTROL}". The "[+WILL] or [−WILL]" can also be written as "[+/−WILL]" in which the slash is to be read as "or". The more usual and seemingly standard "and/or" reading of the slash is also used in other contexts.

The Old Chinese (OC) reconstructions by Schuessler (2009) of the frequently used negatives in oracle-bone inscriptions (OBI) are as follows:

bù 不: *pə      wú 毋: *mə
fú 弗: *pət     wù 勿: *mət
fēi 非: *pəi

We have excluded the word wáng/*maŋ 亡 because this is not a negative but a verb (V) meaning "not have/there is no ... ." When 亡 is followed by a noun like lù 鹿 'deer', for instance, it means "X does not have/there are no deer." Sometimes we find it used before a V just like the other negatives, and so some classify it as a member of that category. But we treat it as the negative possessive/existential V which embeds the succeeding V. This forms a VP in the literal sense of "not have any (occasion to)/there is no (occasion to) V," in which "occasion" is a linkage dummy that is grammatically motivated, functioning something like a quasi-nominalizer. The positive counterpart of 亡 is yǒu/*wəʔ 有 'have/there is' which behaves exactly the same way as 亡 does; viz., 有+N or 有+V (⇒VP) "have/there is an (occasion to) V.[3]

There is some uncertainty in the reading of the graph 亡. If we follow the phonological tradition, it is wáng/*maŋ. When we compare its OC reconstruction with 無/无 *ma, the coda *-ŋ looks as if it was a suffix of some sort under certain conditions.[4]

---

**3** This is a literal meaning which depending on context will give such an implied meaning as "emphasis" (Takashima 1988a). Also, for the arrow sign "⇒" in A⇒B, see n. 1.
**4** Schuessler (2007: 18, 32–3, 76–7) takes the coda *-ŋ as an unproductive suffix which he calls "terminative" conveying a sense of "action with an endpoint, a goal". He gives six examples, and his first and the second ones are said to have such a meaning: "wáng 亡 OCM *maŋ 'to disappear'<wú 無 *ma 'there is no'; yáng 揚 *laŋ 'to rise, raise'<>WT: laŋ-ba 'to rise, arise' ldaŋ-ba 'get up' < WT bla 'above'." There may perhaps be a different way of interpreting the coda *-ŋ. That is, different from "terminative" or "telic", the *-ŋ in words like wàng/*maŋ 忘 'forget (some O)', wǎng/*maŋʔ 网, 罔, 網 'catch (some O) by net', and wàng/*maŋ^A 望 'hope for (some O)' might have had functioned as an *indefinite pronoun* suffixed to the stem *ma- 'not have/there is no...'. When a direct object is used after these verbs, it may be construed as co-referential to, and a further specification of, the *-ŋ (perhaps related to *ŋ- in yí/*ŋə 疑 'doubt'?). One could further scrutinize this hypothesis by comparing the "distributive/partitive" suffix *-k (Pulleyblank 1973: 122; 1995: 134–6) as in mò/*mrâk 莫 'there is nothing' (cp. it with the same *-k in its positive huò/*wâk 或 'there is some ... ', gè/*kâk 各 'each one', shú/*duk 孰 'which one'). We also need to take into consideration other words such as wǎng/*waŋ 往 'go (somewhere)' (cp. yú/*wa 于 'to, in, from O_indirect'), xíng/*grâŋ xìng/*grâŋh 行 'go to (somewhere)'. Also, when the graph 亡 is followed by a N or V, its pronunciation may have been different, presumably *ma if an N follows, and *maŋ if a V follows in which the V is embedded.

As for *fēi*/*\*pəi* 非, it is generally considered as a phonetic fusion of *bù*/*\*pə* 不 and *wéi*/*\*wi* 隹 (= 惟, 維, or 唯). If this is the case, the *hékŏu* 合口 '(closed mouth⇒)rounding' feature of the latter would have been assimilated to the same feature of the former's initial, and the vocalic quality (vocoid) of *-ə-* in *\*pəi* 非 should somehow be interpreted as more "tense/fortis" than "lax/lenis". But because schwa is articulated nearer the center of the mouth, it would seem odd for it to have such phonetic features. Wouldn't they have phonetically blocked such assimilation? Perhaps then *-ə-* might have been phonetically like [ʌ], i.e., a stressed [ə] as in English "cut" [kʌt] which is in contrast, e.g., with "about" [əbáut]. However, there may have been something other than these phonetic problems involved in the use of 非 in OBI as discussed below.

Until about twenty-five years ago, scholars were content with the interpretation that it was not until about Period III-IV (of the five-period scheme of the relative dating of OBI) that 非 made its debut in places where *bù wéi* 不隹 was expected. This gave a nice historical account for the fusion hypothesis (Jacques 2000: 215). However, we now know that the use of 非 was restricted to the inscriptions belonging to a few different diviner groups datable to as early as Period I. They consist of both the royal inscriptions (*wáng bǔcí* 王卜辭)[5] and the non-royal inscriptions (*fēiwáng bǔcí* 非王卜辭). The latter includes the "Master Zǐ 子 Group" inscriptions (689 inscribed pieces) unearthed in 1991 at Huāyuánzhuāng Locus East 花園莊東地.[6] It is possible, then, to suspect that there was a dialect mixture of some sort within the then capital city of Shāng (cf. Takashima and Yue 2000).[7] If that cannot be supported by compelling evidence, we can at least show that it was a matter of pronunciation, *\*pəwi*, *\*pəi* (or something else). It may also be a problem of representing the "mainstream" use of 不 with a similar sounding 非 in different scribal or diviner traditions, rather than a phonetic fusion *per se*.[8]

---

[5] They include a few varieties such as the Bīn 賓 Groups, Chū$_{èr}$ 出$_{二}$ Group, and Shī (or Duī) 㠯 Group.

[6] "Master Zǐ 子 Group" (Yīnxū Huādōng H3 bǔcí zhǔrén "Zǐ" 殷墟花東H3卜辭主人『子』) is distinguished from the Zǐ 子 Group inscriptions (Zǐzǔ bǔcí 子組卜辭). They belong to different "divination bureaus", though both belong to the non-royal inscriptions.

[7] The capital city is now called "Yīnxū 殷墟 'Ruins of Yīn'", located in the north-western suburb of the modern city of Ānyáng 安陽, Hénán 河南 Province.

[8] In the *Huādōng* inscriptions, there is no occurrence of *bù wéi* 不隹, but *fēi* 非 is used ten times. Four of them contrast with 不隹 – i.e., *Huādōng* 161, 234 (cp. also 122), 372, and 401. But it is significant that 非 is also used just like 不: 隹之疾子腹 'It is that (N) which is causing Lord's stomach illness' whose negative counterpart is 非隹 'It is not that (N) [which is causing Zǐ's stomach illness]' (*Huādōng* 241). This suggests that the use of 非 has more to do with its pronunciation, involving also the perennial problem of word-graph relationship.

# 3 Morphology of the negatives: *bù* 不, *fú* 弗, *fēi* 非, *wú* 毋, and *wù* 勿

The above negatives, including the assumed negative copula (非), all share the bilabial feature, one set being the stop (*\*p-*) and another its nasal counterpart (*\*m-*). As for the vowel, all have the schwa (*\*ə*) to which "NoCoda", the coda *\*-t*, or *\*-i* is added to form a syllable. If the syllabic structure of the negatives is analyzed this way, it encourages one to assume that there was some sort of morphology involved rather than that it was random or accidental. Our analysis of these negatives to follow would also support such an assumption.

## 3.1 The negatives *bù* 不 and *fú* 弗: Their interaction with modal and aspectual *qí* 其

Let us begin by considering the following pair of antithetical divination charges[9]:

(1) 甲辰卜俑貞: 今日其雨。    *HJ* 12051o
Crack making on the *jiǎchén* day [41], Rǎn tested [the following proposition against the spirit of the bone]: Today it might rain. Or: Today it might happen to rain/might be going to rain. N.B. Hereinafter we will abbreviate the bracketed portion after "tested", an interpretation of Serruys (1974: 22–3).

(2) 甲辰卜俑貞: 今日不其雨。    *Ibid.*
Crack making on the *jiǎchén* day [41], Rǎn tested: Today it might not rain. Or: Today it might not happen to rain/might not be going to rain.

This charge pair represents the positive and negative augury statements that are evidently neutral in terms of modality. The diviner charged the spirit of the turtle to respond about whether the weather would turn out to be rainy or not. Since *qí* 其 is used in both the positive and negative charges, we cannot discern any difference in attitudinal posture taken by the diviner toward what he charged orally (as understood by some specialists including myself). But notice that the negative

---

[9] The divination charges are referred to as *mìngcí* 命辭 'charging statement; charge', a modern term. They were put to the spirit believed to have resided in such bony materials as turtle plastrons or bovine scapulas. The antithetical charges are referred to as *duìzhēn* 對貞 'paired testing charges'. Most of them were uttered by the diviners affiliated with either the royal or non-royal divination bureaus.

used in (2) is *bù/\*pə* 不, a *\*p*-type variety. As mentioned earlier, *yǔ* 雨 'to rain' is an uncontrollable phenomenon. There is no instance in the OBI corpus in which 雨 is ever negated with *fú/\*pət* 弗, another *\*p*-type negative, nor with *wú/\*mə* 毋, a *\*m*-type negative.[10] There must have been reasons for all these, and we attempt to provide them in this paper.

Now consider the following charge pairs:

(3) 癸巳卜貞: 今日其雨。  *HJ* 7768
Crack making on the *guǐsì* day [30], Nan tested: Today it might (I fear) rain. (N.B. rain not desired.) Or: Today it might (I fear) happen to rain/might (I fear) be going to rain.

(4) 癸巳卜貞: 今日不雨。允不。  *Ibid.*
Crack making on the *guǐsì* day [30], Nan tested: Today it will not rain. Or: Today it will not happen to rain/is not be going to rain. [Verification, i.e., what actually happened:] Indeed it did not.[11]

Since *yǔ* 雨 is a V$_{\text{UNCONTROL}}$, 不 is expected in (4). But unlike (2) 其 is not used, except in the positive charge (3). So it is important to distinguish between the diviner's attitude toward (3) and (4). We think that the use of 其 in (3) makes a positive charge that carries a modality of doubt. It is a kind of aporia imbued with a sense of undesirability that can be deduced from the *yàncí* 驗辭 'verification' (n. 11): "*yǔn bù* 允不" (indeed it did not [rain]). Here "indeed" is taken as a confirmation of the diviner's wish that it would not rain. But notice that this is clearly based on the diviner's "presupposition", a term laden with various implications, but we use it in the rough-and-ready sense of a "self-evident assumption about some unspoken utterance". The diviner's preference for no rain is reflected in the use of 其 in (3). When 其 is used in both the positive and negative charges as in (1) and (2), any modal effect that could potentially be produced gets "cancelled out" or neutralized. Put differently, there is really no intrinsic modal meaning in 其 itself, and the word may be characterized as responding to the self-evident assumption of the diviner when we can identify what it might have been. This is an important fact about the so-called modal *qí* other scholars have not pointed out. We shall have more to say on this later.

---

[10] There are, however, several cases in which 雨 is negated with another *\*m*-type negative, *wù/mət* 勿. We will explain why that is possible in 3.2.

[11] This type of inscription is called *yàncí* 驗辭 'verifications' referring to the post-divination records of what actually transpired after the divination.

Modality has to do first and foremost with the presence of will. We have already noted that there is a measure of overlap in "volition" and "controllability". The term "volitional V" is used in the general sense of exercising will. But since the two are distinguishable,[12] we make use of both "$V_{CONTROL}$ or $V_{UNCONTROL}$" and "[+WILL] or [−WILL]". The advantage in the use of all these terms is obtained when we associate the latter feature with *qí* 其 as well as with other words such as the auxiliary potential verb *kè* 克 'can' as already observed. Consider such uncontrollable Vs as 雨 'to rain', *xué* 雪 'to snow', *fēng* 風 'to be windy', *qíng* 晴 'to be clear', and the like. They have no subject (or just an "ambient" one) to permit any [+WILL] feature as no human is involved. But when they are "modified" by 其 as in (3), it superimposes the sense of uncertainty felt by the diviner who, along with his in-group members, would be affected unfavorably by the outcome of the VP (其+V). In our freer translation of (3), we have given "Today it might, I fear, rain." That 其 indicates the undesirable alternative is buttressed by (4) where 不雨 'not rain' is echoed by 允不 'indeed it did not (rain)' in the verification as already mentioned.[13] This is a manifestation of the diviner's presupposition.

---

**12** We have already demonstrated this in the Introduction (3rd paragraph from the end). In this regard, there is a new study by a French trained philosopher-linguist (Kokubun 2017) who suggests the existence of what he calls "*chūdōtai* 中動態 'mediovoice'." This is different from the active, passive, or middle voice as in Greek or Sanskrit, and is not based on the volitional feature, but is based on whether or not the subject is *voluntarily* involved in an action. Suppose that a person was involved in a hold-up at gunpoint. The threat to his life might compel him to hand over his possessions. He might *do so* (active voice) or might be *forced to* do so (passive voice). It is quite clear that acting on or for himself (middle voice) does not apply. If the subject was *involuntarily* involved as in such a hold-up, he certainly had no positive [+WILL] of his own for whatever action he took. The subject found himself in the very *center* of a certain action, where the feature assignment of [+/−WILL] becomes a moot point since the very question of "willingness" itself is beside the point. Kokubun's *chūdōtai* 'mediovoice' thus seems to be a new voice system, and it should be distinguished from a locutionary way of handling "willingness" as in "Without volition I handed over … to the assailant." Such a "mediovoice" seems to share some common ground with our "$V_{+/-CONTROLLABLE}$". Although we cannot get deeply into here, it is instructive to distinguish "volition" from "controllability" as does Yuán Yùlín (1993: 27–31).

**13** We cannot entirely eliminate the possibility of construing 今日不雨 as "Today it *shall* not rain," where the modal "shall" is explained by Quirk *et al* (1985: 230) as: "*Shall* is in very restricted use with the 2nd and 3rd person subjects as a way of expressing the *speaker's* volition …; shall is archaic and authoritarian in tone… ." If such a translation was possible, it would signify that there are strong incantatory qualities in the diviner's mind. However, its sole basis lies in emphasizing the total message of the charges in both the positive (2) and the negative (3), as well as the verification, *all* taken together, rather than what the negative charge proper seems to say. We have chosen to take 不雨 as a simple predictive charge even though rain was not the desired alternative.

Now compare the use of *yǔ* 雨 in (3) with a verb like *zuò* 作 'to make' as in the following example:

(5) 貞: 余其作邑。                                     HJ 13503
Tested: I *will* found a settlement (here).[14]

In (5) it is easy to recognize the existence of an element of will, [+WILL], in the subject collocated with the verb *zuò* 作 'to make'. Also, 作 is a V$_{CONTROL}$ because the subject "I", here referring to the king Wǔ Dīng 武丁 (r. ca. 1230–1171 B.C.), could control his own action.[15] Another example:

(6) 貞: 呼逐从萬獲。王占曰: 其呼逐獲。                HJ 6477
Tested: If (we) issue a call to pursue (game) by way of Wàn, (they will be able to) capture (it). His Majesty, having prognosticated, declared: (We) *will* issue a call, (for they will be able to) capture (it).

There is no question that *hū* 呼 'to issue a call, call upon', used twice in (6) – first in the charge and second in the prognostication[16] – is a V$_{CONTROL}$. The second use of 呼 forms a VP with 其. Since its subject, though unexpressed, must be the 1st person, the 其呼逐 string can be specified as having the [+WILL] feature. One would think that 呼 in the charge also has the [+WILL] feature. However, since 其 is not used, there must be some difference between 呼逐 and 其呼逐. We have earlier suggested that, if the verb is uncontrollable, 其 conveys uncertainty as in (1), (2), and (3). Exactly the opposite of that should be applicable to the V$_{CONTROL}$ with the [+WILL] feature as in (5) and (6). That is, 其 conveys a sense of "determination, resoluteness". This is opposite to aporia, i.e., certainty.[17] Since the prognostication was made by the king, it seems fitting to interpret 其呼逐 as his authoritative and "official" decision.

---

[14] We also follow Quirk *et al* (1985: 230) who point out: "Especially in BrE, prescriptive tradition forbids *will* as a future auxiliary with *I* or *we*,... ." This seems now archaic particularly in American English, but "I or we *will*+V" expresses resoluteness as opposed to "I or we *shall*+V" which is plain future.

[15] The planned settlement building (*zuò yì* 作邑 'found a settlement') in Shāng and early Zhōu China was the prerogative of the king, and it was part of his expected duty to carry it out when need arose (Keightley 2012: 204; Takashima 2019: 120).

[16] This is referred to as *zhāncí* 占辭 or *zhòucí* 繇辭 that represent what was predicted by the Shāng kings and other presiding dignitaries such as the heads of powerful lineage groups of the non-royal inscriptions.

[17] In 3.3 we will explain how 其 can behave in such seemingly contradictory way as "uncertainty" and "certainty".

Let us now consider the following charge pair:

(7) 丙辰卜貞：我受黍年。 *HJ* 99950

Crack making on the *bǐngchén* day [53], Nan tested: We will (be able to) (receive:) harvest a (good) crop of millet.

(8) 丙辰卜貞：我弗其受黍年。 *Ibid.*

Crack making on the *bǐngchén* day [53], Nan tested: We might not (be able to) (receive:) harvest a (good) crop of millet.

Harvesting a good crop of millet was undoubtedly of great importance to an agrarian society like the Shāng. The subject of (7) and (8) is *wǒ* 我 'we', here taken as a collective reference to the king, dynastic elites and their associates, the recipient of a hoped-for (bountiful) harvest. *Shòu* 受 'receive' (= harvest a good crop of millet) is comparable to such other verbs as *huò* 獲 'capture (game)', *zhèng* 正 'to rectify, put ... in order' as in chastising (正⇒征) a foreign state, *zāi* 𢦏 'to smite' as in smiting a hostile state, *gǔ* 古 (⇒ 盬) 'to manage' as in managing the king's affair (盬王事 *q.v.* Takashima 2010: II.45–6, 69), etc. For these verbs we supply an implicit meaning like "can, be able to", and refer to them as "success verbs". This correlates with the *\*p*-type negatives. As mentioned in the Introduction, 受 is a V$_{UNCONTROL}$ from the vantage point of the living. The recipient was, as it were, at the mercy of a benefactor. Notice that it is negated with *fú*/*\*pət* 弗. We are thus led to conclude that, in addition to 不 in (2) and (4), another *\*p*-type negative 弗 also negates the verbs whose meanings suggest uncontrollability. So far, then, the two *\*p*-type negatives, irrespective of the coda, negate the V$_{UNCONTROL}$. We will examine one more example before considering what exactly the difference is between the two negatives:

(9) 王占曰: 吉,㞢有呼。己其伐。其弗伐，不吉。 *HJ* 6461r

His Majesty, having prognosticated, declared: Auspicious, it should be that (we) issue a call (to someone understood to follow Yuán Jiàn 爰箭[18] in attacking). On a *jǐ* day, (we) *will* launch an attack. If we do not do so, it will be inauspicious.

In (9) the VP *qí fá* 其伐 is modified by the time adverb *jǐ* 己 '*jǐ* day' (any one of the 6th, 16th, 26th, 36th, 46th, and 56th days in the sexagenary cycle). We have con-

---

[18] This name appears in a larger context on this plastron, and we assume that this person served as a military leader.

strued 己其伐 as: "On a *jǐ* day, we will launch an attack (against the enemy)."[19] This is supported by what immediately follows: "If we do not attack, it will be inauspicious." Clearly the message of the king's prognostication is: "Go ahead and take action." Note that the "success verb" reading of 其伐 and of 其弗伐 is untenable in (9) because neither "if/attack (with success)" nor "if/not/attack (with success)" accords with the main clause 不吉 'it will not be auspicious'. That is, "*If we attack with a successful outcome" and "*If we do not attack with a successful outcome" conflict with "it will be inauspicious."

If the above analysis is correct, the "success verb" reading of a given verb is by no means automatic. It depends on context (as in the above example) and on the syntactic behavior of 其. Typical word order involving the negative *fú* 弗 and 其 is 弗其伐, and more generally 弗其+V as in (8) and (39). But in (9) 其 precedes 弗, thus putting what follows under its scope. This suggests that it functions genitivally rather than adverbially as it does in the structure 弗其+V. One of the reflexes of the genitivized expressions, through its topicalization, is a conditional sentence, and the conjunctive "if" may be suitable for the main clause "it will be inauspicious."

In contrast to the "success verb", there is a subcategory of the verb referred to as "attempt verb". Setting up lexical categories such as controllable vs. uncontrollable verbs and subcategories such as "attempt" vs. "success" verbs is motivated not by whim, but by the fact that they have broader grammatical and semantic implications. For example, as analyzed in the penultimate paragraph, 伐 in 其伐 and 其弗伐 should be taken as an "attempt verb" rather than a "success verb". The same thing can be said of the verb *zāi* 甾 'to smite', an "attempt" verb in (38) but a "success" verb in (39) as we shall see it more clearly later.

Let us now compare (7) and (8) with the following examples:

(10) 貞: 我受黍年。 *HJ* 3760
Tested: We will (be able to)(receive:) harvest a (good) crop of millet.

(11) 不其受黍年。 *Ibid.*
(We) might not (be able to) (be receiving:) be harvesting a (good) crop of millet.

OBI specialists give up accounting for any difference that might have existed between 弗 and 不 when faced with examples like 弗其受黍年 in (8) and 不其受黍年

---

[19] The enemy here was most likely the Yí 夷 "barbarians" that occur on the same plastron. Also, a *jǐ* day here is probably the *jǐhài* 己亥 [36] day.

in (11). They just look at the substitution of these two negatives on the surface, and conclude that they are interchangeable (e.g., Zhāng Guìguāng 2004: 235). But they are *different* words, *different* negatives. The difference between the two is that 弗 has the coda *-t, while 不 does not. There must have been something going on here.

First, there seems no choice but to construe 其 as modulating 受 in both 弗其受黍年 and 不其受黍年. Since everything is identical except for the negatives, the modal scope of 其 can only be taken as extending to the same VP (受黍年). The uncontrollability and "success verb" interpretations of 受 must also be maintained. This would yield: "(We) might not (be able to) … a (good) crop of millet" for both 弗其受黍年 and 不其受黍年, leaving what the analyst needs to supply in the empty slot shown by the three dots. On the basis of the contrast in the rime portion of 弗 *pət and 不 *pə, as well as of 勿 *mət and 毋 *mə (to be discussed in 3.2), we have tested the idea of a "morphological formative *-t" possibly reflecting a difference in *aspect*. That is, it changes "stative" or "eventive" into "non-stative" or "non-eventive".[20] In other words, the "undynamic" nature gets changed to the "dynamic" nature by the addition of *-t in the negatives. This is not a grammatical opposition of transitive vs. intransitive verbs, but is related to aspect. Taking studies by Graham (1952, 1959, 1983), Serruys (1982), and especially Pulleyblank (1991) into consideration,[21] we have re-examined the OBI examples reckoned as displaying good contrasts as in (8) and (11), and have reached the conclusion that the *p-type negatives 不 and 弗 are best characterized as non-modal with aspectual differences between them. Let us see how this works in actual examples:

(12) 貞: 黃尹祟。 *HJ* 34790
　　　Tested: Huáng Yǐn happens to be hostile.[22]

---

[20] We will discuss the terminological issue of "stative" and "eventive" in the paragraph after example (13).
[21] Pulleyblank (1991: 34–6) provides a good summary not only of Graham's studies but also of a few others including Dobson (1959), Dīng Shēngshù (1935), Huáng Jǐngxīn (1958), and Takashima (1988).
[22] Kroll (2015: 436) glosses *suì* 祟 as "an affliction visited by spirits or demons; evil emanation, noxious influence; plague, bane, scourge" which is very close to Morohashi *et al* (1982: 2.1394). All these seem more or less applicable to OBI where it is used as both noun and verb, more frequently the latter. Takashima (2015: 113, 114) has suggested for its nominal use the word "jinx" in the VO compound *yǒu suì* 有祟 (⇒ 祟) 'there will be an [ancestor-caused] jinx'. One might translate 祟 as "to cast a spell on" (a dynamic action), but because the word is used by the diviner to present, we think, the VP (祟/不祟) in the stative/eventive aspect, we have decided against such a translation for (12) and (13).

(13)  貞：黃尹不祟。                                                                          *HJ* 34800
    Tested: Huáng Yĭn does not happen to be hostile. Or: Huáng Yĭn will not be/is not going to be hostile.

We think that (12) conveys the message: "Huáng Yĭn, one of the ancestral spirits of the Shāng kings, happens to be hostile (to the living king)" or "Huáng Yĭn will not be hostile (to the living king)." Although "stative" is normally distinguished from "eventive" (Trask 1995: 259), the distinction depends on how they are defined. The Shāng language, as we understand it, seems to render it somewhat fuzzy. An event can be presented not in the continuous state – past, present, or future – , but in the *temporary*, often momentary, state of an event. (12) does not mean "*Huáng Yĭn perpetually was/is/will be in the state of being hostile to the king." None of these is true in OBI.[23] To include "stativity" and "eventivity" in the aspectual system is motivated not merely by our stipulative definition but by the regular and predictable uses of the negative, here 不 in (13) and all the other occurrences of it so far in (2), (4), and (11). Particularly noteworthy is (4) where 不 occurs twice, its second use modified by the adverb *yŭn* 允 'indeed' as in 允不 'Indeed, it did not (rain)'. This is not a state, but an event or phenomenon that did not happen or did not occur. "It was/is/will be raining" is stative (progressive); "it rained/rains/will rain" is eventive. Further elaboration on the regular and predictable use of 不 in contrast to 弗 and vice versa is presented below.

As opposed to (12) and (13), we find the following inscriptions:

(14)  貞：黃尹祟王。                                                                          *HJ* 34580
    Tested: Huáng Yĭn will hex His Majesty.

(15)  貞：黃尹弗祟王。                                                                       *Ibid.*
    Tested: Huáng Yĭn will not hex His Majesty.

Notice that in both (14) and (15), the negative used for the verb *suì* 祟 changed from 不 to 弗. The observation made by Serruys (1982: 342) that 不 and *wú* 毋 are "used with verbs in stative, intransitive, passive functions" would lead one to infer that 祟 functions as intransitive in (13), but transitive in (15). Although that analysis works here, it fails to account for the fact that the transitive verb 受 is negated with 不 in (11), but with 弗 in (8). This example and others (e.g., [21]

---

[23] In *HJ* 3481, for instance, Huáng Yĭn appears as a benefactor in the inscription that reads: 癸未卜盾貞：黃尹保我史 'Crack making on the *guĭwèi* day [20], Dùn tested: Huáng Yĭn will protect our envoy'.

below) indicate that the criterion involved for the choice of 不 is *not* based on transitivity. We suggest that 雨, 受, 獲, and 祟 are all uncontrollable verbs which, in accordance with the grammar of OBI, first circumscribed the *\*p*-type negatives and then narrowed down the choice to 不, if the verb it negates is taken as stative/eventive, and undynamic. If the verb it negates is non-stative/non-eventive, dynamic, then 弗 is used. In terms of the aspectual theory we have been developing, the 弗其 string in (8) and (39) must have carried no sense of imminence as 弗 is not stative/eventive but dynamic. The reason there is no example of the stative/eventive verb 雨 'rain' ever negated with 弗 – mentioned in the paragraph after example [2]) – is because when it is specified as stative/eventive, it has no dynamic quality, thus forbidding the morphological formative *\*-t* to intervene.[24] By contrast, the verb 祟 does have such a dynamic quality, so that when it is so specified on the underlying level (in the mind of the diviner), it comes equipped with an object, here *wáng* 王 'king'. In this context, "to cast a spell on" as a translation for 祟 may be acceptable. The same thing can be said about the verb *hài* 害 'to harm'[25] as in the following examples:

(16)  貞: 父乙不害。                                                                    *HJ* 6115
  Tested: Fù Yǐ does not happen to be noxious (to the living king). Or: Fù Yǐ will not happen to be/is not going to be harmful (to the living king).

(17)  貞: 父乙害。                                                                        *Ibid.*
  Tested: Fù Yǐ happens to be noxious (to the living king). Or: Fù Yǐ will be/is going to be harmful (to the living king).

---

**24** As noted in n. 10, 雨 is negated with *wù/mət* 勿, but the word is not *yǔ*, but *yù* 雨 'let it rain' – this and other related issues will be dealt with in 3.2.

**25** Although the graph 𢦏 is widely accepted as standing for the word *hài* 害 'to harm' (Qiú Xīguī 1983), none of the glosses given in Morohashi *et al* (1982: 1.962), Wáng Lì (100: 222), and Kroll (2015: 150) has anything to do with affliction caused by ancestral spirits. The graph stands for some word related to *suì* 祟 'to be hostile; hex, jinx' caused by ancestral spirits (cf. also n. 22). The 𢦏 ⇒ 害 interpretation seems to have a problem in that later usages of 害 have no ancestral connection. It is not impossible that the general sense of a "harm" emanating from the malevolent ancestral spirits became generalized or a specialized meaning of "ancestor-caused harm" evolved to a general meaning of "harm". However, the 𢦏 ⇒ 害 interpretation would call for accounting for the lexicographical discontinuity. There must have been a reason for an inscription like the following to make sense: "王占曰: 亡𢦏有祟 (*HJ* 2960)." Here the graph in question is used contrastively with 祟: "His Majesty, having prognosticated, declared: There will be no 𢦏/no occasion to 𢦏, but there will be an [ancestor-caused] jinx."

(18)  乙未卜盾貞: 父乙害王。　　　　　　　　　　　　　　　　　　　　*HJ* 2231

Crack making on the *yǐwèi* day [32], Dùn tested: Fù Yǐ will cause an affliction to His Majesty.

(19)  貞: 父乙弗害王。　　　　　　　　　　　　　　　　　　　　　　　*HJ* 10601o

Tested: Fù Yǐ will not cause an affliction to His Majesty.

If the verb negated with 不 is stative/eventive and undynamic as we believe it is in (2), (4), (11), (13), and (16), the same verb negated with 弗 in (8), (9), (15), and (19) must be analyzed as non-stative/non-eventive and dynamic.

We should now like to pay attention to the problem of English translation of the negatives 不 and 弗 beyond the usual interlinear gloss "NEG" which actually misses the grammatical distinctions between the two. The latter, dynamic-aspect negative 弗, is easier to translate than the former, stative/eventive, undynamic-aspect 不, because "NEG", meaning "not" with or without some English auxiliaries – modal, non-modal, potential, etc. – will often do. But the degree to which "easiness" can be gauged seems to have much to do with the lexical nature of the verb 弗 negates, rather than with any grammatical construction in which it is used. By contrast, it is more the grammatical, aspectual, nature of 不 as stative/eventive and undynamic that contributes to the difficulty in translating 不. Recall that we have translated (1) as "Today it might rain" and (2) as "Today it might not rain." These reflect more of "eventivity" than of "stativity". But if an event could be presented not in the continuous state, but in the *temporary*, often momentary, state,[26] example (1) may be put: "Today it might happen to rain" as one possibility. Similarly, (2) as: "Today it might not happen to rain." Although these translations might capture the stative/eventive aspect of the verb "to rain", the point we wish to make is that in OBI the distinction between "stativity" and "eventivity" does not seem sharp, and that the use of 不 is triggered by such an aspectual feature as we have suggested.

If we now switch our attention to the "prospective" aspect, a temporal form likely to manifest itself in the divinatory language, what sort of meaning can we expect in 不 and 弗? First, we make a narrow definition of the prospective aspect: it is an expression of some event or action imparting a sense of "imminence" such as *be going to* or *be about to* in English. This can be contrasted with "imperfective", though no sense of imminence is assignable to it. As for the relationship

---

[26] Our argument was provided after example (12). Also, "to rain", "to snow", "to be windy", "to be sunny", and the like are neither actions nor activities; they are events imbued with stative qualities as in "rainy", "snowy", "windy", "sunny".

between prospective and stative/eventive, it would be better to examine that in the context of actual examples. We have modified our first translations of (1) and (2) in the previous paragraph. The modifications are based on an emphasis placed on the *temporary* state of "rain" as an event or happening – here perhaps better as a natural phenomenon – with which the time adverb "today" must surely be congruous. The same thing can be said of (3) and (4). The eventive-aspect interpretation of (4) 今日不雨 is, as mentioned: "Today it will not happen to rain." The prospective-aspect interpretation of (4) would be: "Today it is not going to rain" or "*Today it is not about to rain." The former translation seems acceptable, but the latter one strikes us as odd. This, we think, is due to the time span of "today" being too long as it refers to "on or in the course of this present day" (*OED*). We know that in OBI the expression *jīn rì* 今日 is used contrastively with *jīn xī* 今夕 'tonight'. There was in Shāng Chinese a macro division of time within the twenty-four hours of a day. When the sun was visible, it was referred to as 日 'day, sun; sunny', and when invisible, it was referred to as 夕 'evening, night'. "Today" covers too long a span of time to allow the diviner to express a sense of imminence. If we change *jīn rì* or *jīn xī* 今夕 to some word that indicates a shorter span of time such as, e.g., "now" or "at this moment", the prospective interpretation of both "Now/At this moment it is not going to rain" and "Now/At this moment it is not about to rain" seems acceptable, though somehwat crudely.

Also, note that *be going to* can be a prediction without any sense of imminence. If correct, the aspectual sense of imminence expressed by *not be going to* might not always be a proper translation of 不. Yet, in view of the likelihood that the Shāng diviners and kings were actually present in situations like "harvesting", "weather prediction", "ancestral scourge", etc., the prospective 不 interpretation expressed by *be going to* cannot be ruled out. In this paper we have adopted both "*not be V$_{ing}$*" and "*not happen to be V$_{ing}$*" translations intended to express stative, eventive, and prospective meanings. Now consider the following charge pair:

(20) 蜀受年。 HJ 9774
Shǔ will (successfully) harvest a (good) crop.

(21) 蜀不其受年。 Ibid.
Shǔ might not (be able to) be harvesting a (good) crop.

As we have seen, the modality of 其 varies depending on the controllability of the verb which it modulates. The sounds *pə gə (不其) and *pat gə (弗其), with different acoustic effects, may also have contributed to the aspectual interpretation of *pə 不. That is, it sounds in harmony with the prospective-aspect *gə 其. We cannot detect any sense of imminence in *pət 弗, and this, we think, is due to the coda *-t as a morphological formative which, because of its active and dynamic nature, *blocks* the stative/eventive, prospective aspect. Further examination of as many examples as possible of the *pə gə and *pət gə that are collocated with temporal adverbs would also help our understanding of the nature of the prospective aspect, but we cannot get into it in this paper.

Finally, we need to account for the fact only 不 and 弗 are used in the verifications. Several examples below (underlined) will suffice:

(22) [癸]未卜爭貞: 翌甲申昜日。之夕月有食。甲冢不雨。　　　　　　HJ 11483o
Crack making on the *guǐwèi* day [20], Zhēng tested: On the next *jiǎshēn* day [21] it will (happen to⇒) turn out to be sunny. [Verification:] That evening the moon had an eclipse. On the *jiǎ* day it was overcast, (but) it <u>did not (happen to)</u> rain.

(23) 庚寅卜: 叀子祝。不用。　　　　　　　　　　　　　　　　　Huādōng 29.3
Divined on the *gēngyín* day [27]: it should be Lord who makes the invocation ritual. (This charge) <u>was not</u> used.

(24) 甲申卜㱿貞: 婦好娩嘉。王占曰: 其隹丁娩嘉,其隹庚娩弘吉。三旬又一日甲寅娩不嘉。隹女。　　　　　　　　　　　　　　　　　　　　　HJ 14002o
Crack making on the *jiǎshēn* day [21], Nan tested: Lady Zǐ's giving birth will turn out to be felicitous. His Majesty, having prognosticated, declared: If it be on a *dīng* day that she gives birth, it will turn out to be felicitous, (but) if it be on a *gēng* day that she gives birth, that will be very auspicious. [Verification:] In thirty-one days, on the *jiǎyín* day [51] she gave birth, (but) it <u>did not turn out</u> to be felicitous. It was a girl.

(25) 乙卯卜㱿貞: 來乙亥酢下乙十伐又五,劉十。二旬又一日乙亥不酢雨。
五月。　　　　　　　　　　　　　　　　　　　　　　　　　　HJ 903o
Crack making on the *yǐmǎo* day [52], Nan tested: On the coming *yǐhài* day [12] (we) will make a *yǒu*-cutting sacrifice[27] directed to Xià Yǐ of fifteen decapitated human victims and split open ten specially reared sheep. [Verification:] In twenty one days, on the *yǐhài* day (we) <u>did not</u> make the *yǒu*-cutting sacrifice (because) it rained. Fifth month.

---

**27** For this interpretation of 酢, though with some problems, see Takashima (2010: II, 173–6).

(26) 乙丑卜王[貞]: 其逐麀獲。不往。　　　　　　　　HJ 10950o
Crack making on the *yǐchǒu* day [2], His Majesty (tested): If (we) chase *zhǎi*-deer, (we will be able to) catch (them). [Verification:] (We) did not go.

(27) 旬又一日癸亥車弗戋。之夕盟甲子允戋。　　　HJ 6834o
[Verification:] In eleven days, on the *guǐhài* day Jū [an ally] did not smite (the enemy). When that evening cut into the *jiǎzǐ* day, Jū did indeed smite them.

(28) 貞: 王其逐兕獲。弗踄兕, 獲豕二。　　　　　　　HJ 190o
Tested: If His Majesty chases water buffalos, he will (be able to) catch (them). [Verification:] (He) did not track (踄⇒阮)[28] the water buffalos, (but he) caught boars numbering two.

Four of the above examples can be accounted for by the results we have already obtained. That is, the non-modal *p-type 不 and 弗 negate a $V_{UNCONTROL}$ in (22) and (24) as one type and (27) and (28) as another. But there is an aspectual difference between the two types: the former is stative/eventive and undynamic, and that can explain (22) and (24). On the other hand, the latter type is non-stative/non-eventive and dynamic, and that can explain (27) and (28).

However, (23), (25), and (26) require different explanations. While a fuller discussion of the modal *m-type negatives – *wú*/*mə 毋 and *wù*/*mət 勿 – has to be set aside until 3.2, one can anticipate that the former negates a $V_{CONTROL}$ expressing the stative/eventive and undynamic, and the latter non-stative/non-eventive and dynamic, aspect. *Yòng* 用 'to use' in (23), *you* 肜 'to cut' in (25), and *wáng* 往 'to go' in (26) are all $V_{CONTROL}$. When these verbs are used in the verification, the deontic modality associated with 毋 and 勿 gets "neutralized" as there is no need for any modality. Pragmatically, they are in the plain "past" tense. This, we think, is due to the fundamental nature of the verification in that it is a description of the state already manifested or the action already taken. 不 signifies that the verb it negates is undynamic, while 弗 signifies that the verb it negates is dynamic.

---

**28** See Takashima (2010: II, 324–5) for the problems involved.

## 3.2 The negatives *wú* 毋 and *wù* 勿: Their interaction with modal and aspectual *qí* 其

The analyses presented in 3.1 can be extended *mutatis mutandis* to the \*m-type negatives, \*mə 毋 and \*mət 勿. That is: (1) they negate V_{CONTROL}; (2) they express a deontic modality; and (3) they express the aspectual difference between the stative/eventive, undynamic, prospective 毋 and the non-stative/eventive, dynamic, non-prospective 勿. We have used (5) and (6) as initial examples to demonstrate how the controllability feature of a verb can be recognized (*zuò* 作 'make, found' and *hū* 呼 'issue a call'), and how the kind of modality is specified. In the NEG+其+V construction as in (2), (8), (11), (21), (37), (38), and (39), however, a certain modal value must be assumed to be encoded in 其 due to the position in which 其 occurs; that is, since NEG goes with V, 其 can only be an adjunct. But unlike the \*p-type negatives (不 and 弗) this construction is limited to 毋+其+V; no \*勿+其+V is found. We will later account for such an uneven distribution. When 其 is used with 作 and 呼 which are V_{CONTROL}, it conveys a sense of resoluteness, rather than aporia. When negated it is done only by the \*m-type negatives. In this section we aim at further verifying and consolidating these results.

(29)  庚申卜王貞: 余伐邳。                                    *HJ* 68340
Crack making on the *gēngshēn* day [57], His Majesty tested: I shall launch an attack against the Pī state.

(30)  庚[申]卜王貞: 余勿伐邳。                                    *Ibid.*
Crack making on the *gēngshēn* day [57], His Majesty tested: I should not launch an attack against the Pī state.

We have observed that the verb *fá* 伐 is negated with 弗 in example (9): 己其伐。其弗伐，不吉 'On the *jǐ* day, (we) will launch an attack. If (we) do not launch an attack, it will not be auspicious'. But in (30) it is negated with *wù*/\*mət 勿. Obviously we cannot extend the same interpretation given for (9) to the above examples. As for the first use of 伐 in 己其伐, we analyzed it as an "attempt verb". Similarly, in (30) the deontic prohibitive negative 勿 'don't, should not' would make the "success verb" interpretation of 伐 unsuitable because "\*I should not launch an attack against the Pī state with a victory" is illogical. So 伐 in both (29) and (30) must be taken as an "attempt verb". The second use of the verb 伐 in (9) was analyzed likewise for the same reason; that is, "\*If we do not launch an attack with (success⇒) a victory, it will not be auspicious" is nonsensical. Reflecting all these, the following scenario may be reconstructed for (29): the king, himself acting as diviner, charged the spirit of the turtle with the exigent proposition if it gains its spiritual approval. Its negative counterpart, (30) 余勿伐邛, echoes the modality, information value (except, of course, negation), and syntactic structure of (29). To attack or not, that was the question in (29) and (30) taken together.

The following is but a pair of additional examples to apprehend the nature of controllability and the specification of a *m-type negative:

(31) 丁巳卜爭貞：呼取[29]何芻。　　　　　　　　　　　　　　　　HJ 1130
Crack making on the *dīngsì* day [54], Zhēng tested: (We) should issue a call to gather Hé's foragers (or fodder).

(32) 勿呼取何芻。　　　　　　　　　　　　　　　　　　　　　　　Ibid.
(We) should not issue a call to gather Hé's foragers (or fodder).

(31) and (32) form a *duìzhēn*, and its negative member, (32), has 勿 negating 取 (⇒聚) 'to gather' (n. 29). As such it is a $V_{CONTROL}$, but it is difficult to assign any degree of "success" quality to it. When it comes to other $V_{CONTROL}$, such as *bù* 步 'to walk, march', *yuē* 曰 'to say', and *hū* 呼 'to call', a successful or unsuccessful outcome seems irrelevant. So, the verb 聚 must belong to the "attempt" verb category.

We need to address an important issue that has to do with those cases that seem aberrant to the rule we have presented. As pointed out in n. 10, the uncontrollable V 雨 'to rain' is sometimes negated with *wù/mət* 勿. Also, *sǐ* 死 'to die', for instance, belongs to the $V_{UNCONTROL}$ category, and yet it is negated with 勿. However,

---

29 Rumination on the meaning of the verb 取 suggests that it means "to gather, collect" in OBI. Initially following the *Shuōwén* (3b/64b, 捕取也), Morohashi *et al* (1982: 1.499), Wáng Lì (2000: 99–100), I translated 取 as "take" in Takashima (2015: 68) but entered a caveat against putting any credence in such a translation because of some difficulty in understanding other inscriptions. I interpreted "take" in the sense of "take possession of something forcibly." But, 取 羊/豕/馬 may well have meant "gather sheep, pigs, horses" without necessarily having any sense of "coercion". In fact, the graph may have stood for the word *jù/*dzo?/h* 聚 'to gather', a kind of routine activity the Shāng engaged in. This word is no doubt a cognate to *qǔ* (or *qù* according to *Jīngdiǎn shìwén* 經典釋文)/*tsho?, tshô?* 取. The OC reconstructions show a contrast of the voiced and voiceless affricates, so that the graph 取 could easily have written the word 聚. If applied to the examples with the pattern: (勿)+取+$N_{proper\ such\ as\ Hé}$ 河 River Power and Yuè 岳 Mountain Power+$V_{usually\ yǔ}$ 雨 'rain', the 取⇒聚 interpretation would yield: "(We) should (or, with the negative 勿 'should not') gather/convene Hé 河 River Power (or Yuè 岳 'Mountain Power') to VP. But, by slightly rewording "gather/convene" in this context, we would get: "summon, beckon". This seems to have a slight edge over "conduct a *qǔ*-sacrifice", an instance of unsatisfactory compromise. If the 聚 interpretation does not encounter any serious obstacle, we can avoid such a compromise and adopt a consistent interpretation: "gathering, summoning" is a controllable activity the Shāng routinely engaged in as they did in "gathering (herding) their livestock".

they occur only in the prognostications, *zhàncí* 占辭 or *zhòucí* 繇辭 (n. 16) uttered by the kings or the heads of powerful lineage groups. Let us then examine a few such cases that will reveal the nature of the prognostications:

(33)　王占曰: 勿雨, 隹其風。　　　　　　　　　　　　　　　　　*HJ* 974r
　　　His Majesty, having prognosticated, declared: Don't let it rain, for [this crack] signifies that it will be windy [instead]. Or: Don't let it rain; only let it be windy.

(34)　己巳卜貞: 奚不死。王占曰: 吉, 勿死。　　　　　　　　　　　*HJ* 7340
　　　Crack making on the *jǐsì* day [6], Nan tested: Xī will not happen to die (or: will not be dying). His Majesty, having prognosticated, declared: It is auspicious, don't let him die [addressing the numen].

(35)　... 不死。子乩曰: 勿死。　　　　　　　　　　　　　　　　　*HJ* 20051
　　　... will not happen to die. Lord, having prognosticated, declared: Don't let ... die.

In (33) and (34), both belonging to the royal, Typical Bīn group divinations (王卜辭, 典賓卜辭, Period I-II), the prognosticator/seer is the king who used *wù* 勿 to negate the V (雨) in (33). But since it is here used in the sense of "let/cause it rain", the reading should be in the *qùshēng* 去聲 *yù* 雨 (supported by such a reading tradition as well). A great majority of cases of 雨 are used statively/eventively and undynamically and thus negated by *bù* 不. But (33) is different. In (34) the diviner Nan used in his charge *bù* 不 for the uncontrollable V (*sǐ* 死 'die'), which is predictable. But in the prognostication made by the king, it has changed to the deontic, prohibitive negative as if this verb were controllable. The same applies to (35) except that here the seer is the lineage head referred to as "Lord" in this non-royal, Zǐ group divination (非王, 子組卜辭 from mid-Period I). Unfortunately, there is only one reading available for this word (*sǐ*). Yet we can deduce that the nature of the divinatory language differs from the charge, *mìngcí* 命辭. The prognostication was intended not to test or verify its merit, but to influence the future. It is akin to sympathetic magic exercised by those in power such as the kings and the heads of powerful lineage groups. Differently put, the *\*p*-type negative 不 gets putatively transformed into its opposite. We can call such a process as a "controllable transformation". And that is motivated by dissimilarity in the linguistic and divinatory nature between the charges and prognostications.

We still need to account for what we can predict to be a complete absence, in fact a case of ungrammatical nexus, of *\*勿其 \*mət gə* as contrasted with the presence of grammatical 毋其 *mə gə, though in lesser quantity than 弗其 *pət gə and 不其 *pə gə.³⁰ Takashima (2010: II.52) has argued:

> When *hui* [㞢] is matched by the injunctive negative *wu* 勿 in the matching *duìzhen* sentence, the contrast is of grammatical opposition: positive vs. negative; but just as importantly, the modality of definite obligation is the same. This explains why *其㞢, *勿其, and *勿㞢 do not occur as immediate constituents. That is, these are ungrammatical because of a semantic conflict in modality. (See n. 31 for an explanation of "semantic conflict in modality".)

It has become a little clearer, we think, that although the absence of *勿㞢 may still be explained by the "modal conflict" hypothesis,³¹ that of *其㞢 and *勿其 seem to involve a kind of modal conflict that surpasses pleonasm; that is, no such concatenation as "should not" and "should not" is allowed. The absence or ungrammaticality of *其㞢 and *勿其 may be explained not only by the kind of modal conflict we are now considering but also as a problem in aspectual "concord". Within the framework of the aspectual schemes of the negatives we have been developing in this paper, aspectual features of the word 其 itself seem involved. Let us explain. Since we have interpreted the initial *m- as modal as opposed to the initial *p- as non-modal, we must perforce maintain the same interpretation for the two *m-type negatives. That is, both 毋 and 勿 are deontic, prohibitive negatives in the sense of "should not, don't" used to negate controllable, or what was thought of as controllable, verbs. But they differ in aspect; the former without any coda (as in 不) is stative/eventive, undynamic and prospective and the latter with the coda *-t (as in 弗) is dynamic. As a morphological formative *-t changes the stative/eventive, undynamic, and prospective aspect into its counterpart: non-stative/non-eventive, dynamic, and non-prospective aspect. We have, in this paper, concentrated on the modal features of the negatives and those of 其. However, it can equally be argued, as Takashima (1994) has done, that 其 is also aspectual, specifically, prospective aspect. Accordingly, we can explain not only

---

**30** For a quick check on all these, the reader is referred to Takashima (1985: 92–115), *Lèizuǎn* (2.1080–1), *Sōrui* (403), *CGDX*, and: http://ttssearch.lib.ncku.edu.tw/ttscgi/ttsweb1.exe?@@21993. According to Takashima (1985: 95, 410), Chang Ping-ch'üan (1957–72: Plastron 66[9] and 499[3]) transcribes the original inscriptions containing 勿其, but these are not trustworthy as pointed out in Takashima (2010: 228–9, 532). Professor Chang and I examined the original bones in person.

**31** There are many paired testing charges of 勿隹 'it should not be' and its typical, positive counterpart 㞢/叀 'it should be'. The string 勿隹, consisting as it does of the modal, deontic negative 勿 plus the non-modal copula 隹 'to be', makes sense as there is no modal conflict between the two. But the use of *勿㞢/叀 is precluded because of a modal conflict between "should not" and "should not (be)". This goes beyond pleonasm into ungrammaticality.

the string 不其+V 'is/will not be going to V' but also 毋其+V 'should not be going to V'. They are in perfect aspectual concord.

But why is it that *wù* 勿 alone cannot be followed by 其+V$_{CONTROL}$? The answer must have something to do with both modality and aspect. The reason why 弗其 is allowed, while *勿其 is not, must be ascribed to a modal conflict if 其 precedes, as it should, a V$_{CONTROL}$. The negative 勿 meaning "should not, don't" is used to negate a controllable, or what is thought of as a controllable, V. The modal 其 expresses a sense of resoluteness if it is used with a V$_{CONTROL}$. We have been translating such a use of 其 as "*will* (1st person), *should, shall* (2nd and 3rd person)" generally expressing a sense of determination, resoluteness. These seem to create the same kind of conflict as one that goes beyond pleonasm into unacceptability from the Shāng point of view. While further work may be desirable in order to buttress our view of 其 as an aspectual marker (on which we add a couple of favorable comments in 3.3), we have already observed that "Now/At this moment it is not about to rain" in English seems acceptable, but not "*Today it is not about to rain" (second paragraph before example [20] in 3.1). This is related to the aspect-tense (time-word) incongruity as noted earlier. Perhaps a similar thing may be said about 其 as a prospective-aspect marker and the negative *wù*. They may also be seen as a case of aspect-tense incongruity. In this connection, we raise a few more issues that have become a little clearer than before:

Let us first consider the change of the negative *wú* 毋 in *wú qí zhì* 毋其致 in (37) to the negatives *fú* 弗 before the "same" verb *zāi* 烖 in (38).

(36)  貞：百牛致。                                                      *HJ* 9214
Tested: As for the one hundred heads of cattle, (we) shall deliver (them).

(37)  貞：百牛毋其致。                                                   *Ibid.*
Tested: As for the one hundred heads of cattle, (we) *should not be delivering* (them).

(38)  王占曰：丁巳我毋其烖，于來甲子烖。旬又一日癸亥車弗烖。之夕盟甲子允烖。                                                              *HJ* 6834o
His Majesty, having prognosticated, declared: "On the *dīngsì* day [54] we *should not be smiting* [the You tribe], but on the coming *jiǎzǐ* day [1] we shall do so. [Verification:] In eleven days, on the *guǐhài* day Jū [an ally] did not smite (the enemy). When that evening cut into the *jiǎzǐ* day, Jū did indeed smite them.

The positive charge (36) and the negative charge (37) constitute a *duìzhēn* pair. If we follow the accepted view that the positive charge was uttered before the negative one, we cannot tell if the verb *zhì* 致 'to send' in (36) is aspectually or modally marked. Thus, even though we have here such a *duìzhēn* pair, when no mark can be identified, we have generally followed a minimalist's interpretation. Applied to (36), since the subject is 1st person, "shall" is warranted by the word *zhēn* 貞 'to test (the content of a charge against the bone spirit)'. This suggests that the charge is of predictive and augural nature. Following Quirk *et al* (1985: 230; cf. n. 15), "I or we *shall*+V" is taken as *plain* future. On the other hand, (37) comes equipped with the modal, stative/eventive, undynamic and prospective 毋. This is further followed by 其 modulating 致 which is undoubtedly a $V_{CONTROL}$. As for (38), both the prognostication and the verification are built around the verb *zāi* 烖 'to smite' which, when negated with 弗, should be a "success verb" as in the following example:

(39) 癸丑卜爭貞：自今至于丁巳我弗其烖囿。　　　　　　　　　　*Ibid.*
Crack making on the *guǐchǒu* day [50], Zhēng tested: Starting from the present down to the *dīngsì* day [54] (i.e., between now and the *dīngsì* day), we (?) might not (be able to) smite the You tribe.

This plastron shows that in terms of "page design" or layout (38) is inscribed seamlessly after (39),[32] signifying that these the inscriptions are closely related to each other. 弗 in (39) as a charge is in contrast to 毋 in the prognostication portion of (38). This requires an explanation of the negative swaps.

We have already noted that the charge is a testing statement addressed to the spirit of the bone for its response; the prognostication is intended not to test or verify its merit, but influence the future in many (but not all) cases; and the verification is a description of the state already manifested or the action already taken, and 不 is used to negate the intrinsically undynamic state or event. By contrast, 弗 is used to negate the inherently dynamic action. Applying these and the modal feature we have identified for \**m-*, the negative 毋 in (38) 丁巳我毋其烖, 于來甲子烖, a prognostication, may have been used to sway the spirits to sanctify that *on the coming jiǎzǐ* day the subject – "we" or "Yǐ?"[33] – would smite (the You tribe), even though the

---

[32] Keightley (1978: 46, n. 90; 87, n. 118) calls this as a "display inscription".
[33] It is common to take this as the first-person plural pronoun *wǒ* 我 'we' referring to the king, dynastic elites and their associates. However, since there is good evidence that the same graph refers to the name of a tribal/lineage group (*HJ* 248r, 6950o, 21586, etc.), it may have stood for Yǐ 義 which consists of the phonetic *wǒ*/\*ŋaih 我 and the signific 羊 referring to tribal/lineage groups. The signific 羊 is also used in Qiāng 羌, Jié 羯, Mǐ 羋, and Xī 羲 all of which refer to tribal/lineage groups. A perusal of the subjects of the VP (毋+V as IC) shows that they are usually in the 3rd person (Takashima 1985: 505). To determine which was the real subject might have been

subject *should not be* doing so on the *dīngsì* day (see infra). The *focus* here is clearly on the date, *jiǎzǐ* day, that the king hoped the smiting maneuver would succeed. So the first use of 戋 in (38) has to be a $V_{CONTROL}$ in contrast to the $V_{UNCONTROL}$ in (39). This explains the interchange of the negatives. Thus the features assignable to the first and the second use of 戋 in (38) are different along with the feature assignment of the attempt vs. success V.

The verification confirms the accuracy of the king's prognostication. We have translated the first half of the prognostication (我毋其戋) as "We (or Yì) *should not be smiting* [the You tribe]" by faithfully following our interpretation of the negative 毋 and the deontic 其 expressing certainty, determination or resoluteness. But the translation is awkward and, worse, the meaning is not all that clear. We need to clarify what might have been the intended meaning.

English has two different meanings for the auxiliary verb *should*: the obligative *should* as in "we should go" and the presumptive or inferential *should* as in "he should know the fact." Quirk *et al* (1972: 740, 784) introduces a "putative *should*", expressing an idea or plan which may not be fulfilled as in this example they provide: "The *idea* is that education for the over-sixteens *should be* improved." This is contrasted with a sentence with *will* instead of *should*: "The fact is that education for the over-sixteens *will be* improved" which "asserts the improvement as a fact, and assumes that the plan will be carried out." But they also point out: "Contrary to what might be thought, *should* in such clauses does not necessarily carry any sense of obligation,... ." If we apply these seemingly irrefutable points to 我毋其戋, we can eliminate that it expresses the obligative sense of "*ought not to be smiting*". We think that it is more cogent to interpret "We (or Yì) *should not be smiting* [the You tribe]" as a *putative* idea. This interpretation is not the same as the "presumptive or inferential *should*", and such a putative prognostication seems to agree with the focus of (38) 丁巳我毋其戋, 于來甲子戋, i.e., the "auspicious" *jiǎzǐ* day rather than the *dīngsì* day.

## 3.3 Modal *Qí* 其 revisited

We examine here only two topics regarding the modal *qí* 其 that arose in the course of discussion, but about which we deferred analysis until now. They are: (1) the nature and range of its modal meanings and (2) its syntactic function and the relationship it bears to its modal meanings.

---

intended, it would be necessary to establish the friend or foe relationship between the royal "we" and the tribal Yì, a task beyond the scope of this work.

As for (1), when 其 is used with a V$_{CONTROL}$, we have interpreted it as expressing "certainty, determination or resoluteness". But when 其 is used with a V$_{UNCONTROL}$, we have interpreted it as expressing "uncertainty, doubt". How can such seemingly contradictory interpretations be possible?

To answer this question, some theoretical framework is needed. We have adopted a fairly straightforward, epistemic/notional model of modality as described by Jespersen (1924 [1965]: 319–21) and further developed by Lyons (1968: 307–9). If we interpret their schemes in our way, modality is a kind of semantic modulation superimposed on the verb, the negatives, and other word classes. That is done by a modal "weight" thought of as moving on such scales as: (A) "necessity" and "obligation"; (B) "certainty" and "possibility"; and (C) "wish" and "intention". Each of these scales is like a balance, so that graduations are on a continuum. Since the verb does not inflect in Chinese, various modal qualities classifiable into (A), (B), and/or (C) are executed by lexical items like 其, *huì* 叀/叀 'should be (modal copula)', the *m*-type negatives, and other words. That is, the "modal weight" moves, as it were, on one or more of these three scales. The speaker/writer would assign it to a particular position on these scales depending on the attitudinal posture he has taken toward what he spoke or wrote down. In this respect, we can say that "deciphering" modal qualities in OBI is a process of *estimating* what might have been that position on these scales, a process that demands keen perceptiveness as the speaker or writer himself is unlikely to have been able to fix precise spots. Such, however, is the nature of modality, and any account of epistemic modalities can only be approximate. Keeping this in mind, we now try to see how some actual examples may be optimally interpreted. Those given below have been chosen afresh:

(40)  王其步伐夷。 *HJ* 6461
His Majesty *should* (or *shall*) march to launch an attack against the Yí.

(41)  王勿步伐夷。 *Ibid.*
His Majesty *should not* (or *shall not*) march to attack the Yí.

Since *bù* 步 'to walk, march' forms a constituent with the subject *wáng* 王 with the [+WILL] feature, it is undoubtedly a V$_{CONTROL}$. We would interpret 其 here as indicating a sense closer to obligation than to necessity; that is, the "modal weight" moves toward the "obligation" rather than toward the "necessity" side on the (A) scale. Note that in (41) 其 is matched in position with 勿, a deontic, dynamic, non-prospective *m*-type negative whose modal weight also moves on (A), but closer to its "obligation" side. It seems equally possible, however, to interpret that the modal weight moves closer to the "intention" side of the (C) scale, rather than to its "wish" side. If the subject is the 1st person wǒ 我 'we' as in *HJ* 6949, 21796, etc., this interpretation would gain further support because (41) would be comparable to (5) 余其作邑 'I *will* found a settlement' already discussed.

Let us now look at the following examples:

(42) 己亥卜貞: 何不喪眾。 *HJ* 61
Crack making on the *jǐhài* day [36], tested: Hé *will not be losing* the royal retinue.

(43) 其喪眾。 Ibid.
[Hé] *might be losing* the royal retinue.

There is little doubt that *sàng* 喪 'to lose, incur loss' is a $V_{UNCONTROL}$. Note that in (43) *qí* 其 is matched in position with *bù* 不 – a *\*p*-type stative/eventive, undynamic, prospective negative – in (42). In contrast to (40), 其 in (43) indicates a sense of uncertainty, here imbued with a sense of undesirability as we know that Hé is a lineage group affiliated with the Shāng royal house. The possible loss of the royal retinue, Shāng labor force, would have been undesirable. The modal weight seems to move on the (B) scale and is placeable closer to the "possibility" rather than to the "certainty" side. Note also that 其 is no doubt "prospective" in terms of aspect.

Finally, the following examples will reveal how the "wish" side of (C) – "wish" and "intention" – may have worked:

(44) 貞: 翌癸丑其雨。 *HJ* 16131o
Tested: On the following *guǐchǒu* day [50], it *might be going to* rain.

(45) 王占曰: 癸其雨。三日癸丑 允雨。 *HJ* 16131r
[His Majesty], having prognosticated, declared: On the *guǐ* day, it *shall be going to* rain. [Verification:] In three days, on the *guǐ* day it indeed rained.

As seen earlier, *yǔ* 雨 'to rain' is a $V_{UNCONTROL}$, and the 其 in (44) and (45), which are closely related to each other in terms of both page design/layout and content, can be safely interpreted as conveying a sense of desirability in (45). This is vouched for in the verification. The 其 in (44) carries a modality of doubt in accordance with the rule we have deduced from its use with the $V_{UNCONTROL}$. In the prognostication portion of (45), 其 does not suggest any sense of undesirability. In fact, it suggests the opposite. This, in turn, suggests that there is no specific modal value *encoded* in the 其. If so, the modal weight of the 其 in (45) must be construed as moving toward the "wish" side of (C). Aspectually considered, 其 is also prospective, and this is the reason for adding "*be going to*" to "*it shall rain*" even though the addition makes it unidiomatic in English.

As for the topic (2) – 其's syntactic function and its relationship with its various modal meanings – , we will be brief as the subject is treated in detail in Takashima (2018).

The starting point of determining the syntactic function of 其 is that it is, as accepted in standard Classical Chinese, a pronoun in its genitive case. Such a usage has its roots in OBI as in the following examples:

| | | | |
|---|---|---|---|
| *qí hú* | 其虎 | 'its tigers (tigers in that place)' | *HJ* 13505 |
| *qí huáng niú* | 其黃牛 | 'its/his/their yellow bovine' | *HJ* 36350 |
| *qí láo* | 其牢 | 'its/his/their penned bovine' | *HJ* 35828 |
| *qí xī* | 其夕 | 'that evening' | *HJ* 16131r, *Túnnán* 1059 |
| *qí yè* | 其夜 | 'that night' | *HJ* 12948r, *Túnnán* 1059 |
| *qí dōng/běi* | 其東/北 | 'its east/north' | *HJ* 28790 |
| *qí jí* | 其疾 | 'such/aforementioned illness' | *HJ* 21045 |
| *qí yà* | 其亞 | 'his/their *yà*-officers' | *HJ* 5691 |
| *qí pèi* | 其配 | 'my spouse' (in this context) | *Yīngcáng* 1864 |

We then applied the same pronominal genitive (⇒PRO GEN) 其 to those cases in which a verb follows. To give a couple of examples:

(46) 己卯卜貞：雨。王占[曰]：其雨隹壬。壬午允雨。　　　　　　*HJ* 9020
　　Crack making on the *jǐmǎo* day [16], Nan tested: It will rain. His Majesty, having prognosticated, (declared): If it rains, it will be on a *rén* day. [Verification:] On the *rénwǔ* day [19] it indeed rained.

(47) 癸酉卜亙貞：臣得。王占曰：其得隹甲乙。　　　　　　　　*HJ* 6410
　　On the *guǐyǒu* day [10] Xuān tested: The servitors will be caught. His Majesty, having prognosticated, declared: If they get caught, it will be on a *jiǎ* day or *yǐ* day.

Literally, 其雨 means "its raining" and 其得 "their being caught". These are then followed by the copula *wéi* 隹 'to be' to constitute a grammatically complete sentence. One can also construe the PRO GEN 其+V as a topic meaning "as for ... " which can be interpreted pragmatically as a conditional clause (a common phenomenon in the use of topics) meaning "if/when ... ", the interpretation we have adopted for (46) and (47).

In contrast to (46) and (47), we also find expressions without any VP after nominalized phrases. For example:

(48) 貞：我其喪衆人。 　　　　　　　　　　　　　　　　　　　　　　　HJ 500

　　　Tested: We might be losing the royal retinue and men?/! (<"Our losing the royal retinue and men").

(49) 貞：般往來，其有禍。 　　　　　　　　　　　　　　　　　　　　　HJ 42590

　　　Tested: As to Bān's to and fro, there might be misfortunes?/! (< ..., his having misfortunes).

The logical extension of the analysis adopted for (46) and (47) should lead one to construe that (48) and (49) do not have a main verb.

　　　There are languages with comparable constructions. For example, we have such commonly encountered sentences in modern Japanese as "*ame ga higashi no hō kara futte kuru no!* 雨が東の方から降って來るの! (Rain comes falling from the east!)" [with a falling intonation] or "*ame ga higashi no hō kara futte kuru no?* 雨が東の方から降って來るの? (Rain comes falling from the east?) [with a rising intonation]." The verb *kuru* 來る is nominalized by the postposition *no* の which makes these sentences verb-less. Similarly, *kore taberu no* これ食べるの!/? 'You eat this!/?' which can be a command, question, statement (explanatory), expressing sundry modal meanings. Many other examples could be cited. In terms of grammar, it is as though "VP in the disguise of NP" would result, generating a variety of modal values such as disbelief, surprise, question, wonder, command, and so on. Consider also an English expression: "His marrying that woman!/? ..." is incredible, wonderful, questionable, etc. Similarly, "His killing his beloved wife!/?" which conveys surprise, disbelief, outrage, question, etc. Sometimes there is not even any verb at all as in "What a man!" Thus, the absence of a main verb results in generating a variety of modal meanings. One might object to this by emphasizing that the nominalized verb is like the main verb and that it would be simpler to leave it at that. But simplicity cannot compromise with analyticity, and sometimes one can gain an insight into modally charged meanings as may have been intended.

　　　As already mentioned, we can exclude all the constructions of the NEG+其+V type: 不其+V, 弗其+V and 毋其+V. Since the V and the negatives are correlated and have synergetic relationships as shown in 3.1 and 3.2, the insertion of 其 between these negatives and V can only be taken as an adjunct. The 其 in the NEG+其+V construction must have become *lexicalized* to function like an adverb, an issue we cannot delve into further in this paper. So apart from these, we have double-checked all the 其+V examples with or without any object after V, as well as all the 其+V examples that are used as subordinate clauses meaning "if/when ... " or as an embedded clause like 勿雨, 隹其風 'don't let it rain, for [this crack] signifies that it will be windy'. In short, we believe that all of them can be accounted for.

# 4 Conclusions

This paper has made an effort to grasp what the speakers of Shāng Chinese thought they were saying and why they expressed it the way they did. If states, events, and actions were classified into those susceptible or unsusceptible to human control, it is reasonable to think that such a binary classification was based on the Shāng worldview. But above all a clear distinction was made between the $V_{CONTROL}$ and $V_{UNCONTROL}$.

The classification of a V into controllable or uncontrollable is interlinked with the use of bù 不, fú 弗, wú 毋, wù 勿, and modal qí 其. The use of 不其, 弗其, and 毋其 and the absence of *勿其 are all accountable through the modal and aspectual features associated with these words that are conditioned by the nature of the ensuing V (except of course *勿其). A sense of "imminent prospect" can be assigned to 不 and 毋, but not to 弗 and 勿. The latter two are active and dynamic negatives, while 不 and 毋 are stative, eventive, and undynamic for which such a meaning as "not be $V_{ing}$" or "not happen to be $V_{ing}$" has been suggested. It has also been suggested that 其 is a prospective aspect marker which goes well with the negatives 不 and 毋. We have called this "aspectual concord". However, no aspectual concord is observable in the 弗其 concatenation as in (8) and (39), and thus it is devoid of any sense of imminence.

As for the modality of 其, the word seems to have already been lexicalized in OBI as it functions like an adverb in the NEG+其+V construction, and we have elicited a sense of aporia from contextual analyses (in [2], [8], [11], [21], [39]). This obtains when 其 is used with a $V_{UNCONTROL}$, and the negative is necessarily of the *p-type (不 or 弗). Its "modal weight" moves on the "certainty" and "possibility" scale. When 其 is used with a $V_{CONTROL}$, it dictates the use of only the *m-type (毋 or 勿), often expressing a sense of determination, where its modal weight moves on the "necessity" and "obligation" scale. When 其 is used in the prognostications, it expresses a sense of hope in which the modal weight moves on the "wish and intention" scale. In all other constructions, 其 functions as PRO GEN prenominally and preverbally. In the former case, it refers to any of the 1st, 2nd, or 3rd person with genitive meanings (including "such/aforementioned" in certain contexts). Used preverbally, 其 generates a variety of modal meanings induced by ("possessivizing"⇒) nominalizing the verb.

# Appendix: Minimum Errata of Takashima (2015)

**A thoroughly revised edition of this book was published in January, 2019.**

p. 31, fn. 16, l. 7: Change "指示字" to "指事字".

p. 45, l. 6: Change "the following page" to "(below)".

p. 49, l. -4: Change 不 to 弗.

p. 68, example sentence (14): Delete 其; on l. 15 change "行" to "永".

p. 82, example (9): Change 貞 to 卜 with its translation "cracked".

p. 135, l. -8: Replace " ... do not consider 茲卟 be an abbreviation of" with "do not consider this as equivalent to 茲卜卟 ... "

p. 139, example (2): Change "*guǐchǒu* day [50]" to "*guǐhài* day [60]".

p. 144, l. 4: Change "*\*kwar*" to "*\*kwarh*".

p. 155, example sentence (1) and l. -3: Change 餌 to 自.

p. 163, l. 1, l. 3; p. 164, l. 7, 8, 10, 20, 22: Change the character 加 to 卯.

p. 164, l. 11: Change "*\*skhjagw* (?)" to "*\*hrjagw*".

# References

Baxter, William H. and Laurent Sagart. 2014. Baxter-Sagart Old Chinese Reconstruction, v.1.1 (September 20, 2014): http://ocbaxtersagart.lsait.lsa.umich.edu/BaxterSagartOCbyMandarinMC2014-09-20.pdf

CGDX Abbreviation of Guólì chénggōng dàxué *Jiǎgǔwén quánwén jiǎnsuǒ yǔ quánwén yǐngxiàng xìtóng* 國立成功大學甲骨文全文檢索與全文影像系統. Tainan: Guólì chénggōng dàxué, 1995.

Chang, Ping-ch'üan. 張秉權 1957-72. *Xiǎotún dì èrběn: Yīnxū wénzì: Bǐngbiān* 小屯第二本—殷墟文字—丙編. Vol. I, No. 1 上輯 (一), 1957; Vol. I, No. 2 上輯 (二), 1959; Vol. II, No. 1 中輯 (一), 1962; Vol. II, No. 2 中輯 (二), 1965; Vol. III, No. 1 下輯 (一), 1967; Vol. III, No. 2 下輯 (二), 1972. Taipei: Institute of History and Philology, Academia Sinica.

Crystal, David. 2008. *A Dictionary of Linguistics and Phonetics*. 6th edition. Oxford: Blackwell Publishing.

Dīng, Shēngshù. 丁聲樹 1935. *Shì fǒudìngcí fú bù* 釋否定詞弗不. *Qìngzhù Cài Yuánpéi xiānsheng liùshíwǔ suì lùnwénjí* 慶祝蔡元培先生六十五歲論文集, Vol. 2, pp. 967-96.

Dobson, W.A.C.H. 1959. *Late Archaic Chinese*. Toronto: University of Toronto Press.

Graham, Angus. 1952. A Probable Fusion Word: 勿 *wuh* = 毋 *wu*/之 *jy*. *Bulletin of the School of Oriental and African Studies*, 14, pp. 139-48.

Graham, Angus. 1959. Observations on a New Classical Chinese Grammar. *Bulletin of the School of Oriental and African Studies*, 22, pp. 556-71.

Graham, Angus. 1983. *Yún* 云 and *Yuē* 曰 as Verbs and Particles. *Acta Orientalia Havniensia*, 44, pp. 33-71.

*Huādōng* 花東. 2003. Abbreviation of *Yīnxū Huāyuánzhuāng dōngdì jiǎgǔ* 殷墟花園莊東地甲骨 (*Oracle-Bone Inscriptions from Yinxu Huayuanzhuang Locus East*). 6 Vols. Comp. by the

Institute of Archaeology, Chinese Academy of Social Sciences. Kunming: Yúnnán rénmín chūbǎnshè 雲南人民出版社.

*HJ* (= *Héjí* 合集). 1978–82. Abbreviation of *Jiǎgǔwén héjí* 甲骨文合集. 13 vols. Guō Mòruò 郭沫若 ed. Hú Hòuxuān 胡厚宣, editor-in-chief. Beijing: Zhōnghuá shūjú 中華書局.

Huǎng, Jǐngxīn. 黃景欣 1958. Qín Hàn yǐqián gǔ Hànyǔ zhōng de fǒudìngcí 'fú' 'bù' yánjiū 秦漢以前古漢語中的否定詞 '弗' '不' 研究. *Yǔyán yánjiū* 語言研究, 3, pp. 1–23.

Itō, Michiharu and Takashima, Ken-ichi. 伊藤道治、高嶋謙一 1996. *Studies in Early Chinese Civilization: Religion, Society, Language and Palaeography*. 2 vols. Hirakata 枚方: Kansai Gaidai University Press 關西外大出版社. Part I: Religion and Society (pp. 1.1–178,) is by Itō, and Part II: Language and Palaeography (pp. 1.179–505) is by Takashima.

Jacques, Guillaume. 2000. The Character 維・惟・唯 ywij and the Reconstruction of the 脂 *Zhi* and 微 *Wei* Rhymes. *Cahiers de Linguistique–Asie Orientale*, 29.2, pp. 205–22.

Jacques, Guillaume. 2017. A Note on Volitional and Non-volitional Prefixes in Gyalrong Languages. Paper uploaded on 5. 26.2017 to: https://www.academia.edu/33206495/A_note_on_volitional_and_non-volitional_prefixes_in_Gyalrong_languages

Jespersen, Otto. 1924. *The Philosophy of Grammar*. Reprinted in New York: The Norton Library, 1965.

Keightley, David N. 1978. *Sources of Shang History: The Oracle-Bone Inscriptions of Bronze Age China*. xvii+281pp. Berkeley: University of California Press.

Keightley, David N. 2000. *The Ancestral Landscape: Time, Space, and Community in Late Shang China (ca. 1200–1045 B.C.)*. China Research Monograph 53. v+209pp. Center for Chinese Studies. Berkeley: Institute of East Asian Studies, University of California.

Keightley, David N. 2012. *Working for His Majesty: Research Notes on Labor Mobilization in Late Shang China (ca. 1200–1045 B.C.), as Seen in the Oracle-Bone Inscriptions, with Particular Attention to Handicraft Industries, Warfare, Hunting, Construction, and the Shang's Legacies*. China Research Monograph 67. xxiv+507pp. Berkeley: Institute of East Asian Studies, University of California.

Kokubun, Kōichirō. 國分功一郎 2017. *Chūdōtai no sekai: Ishi to sekinin no kōkogaku* 中動態の世界: 意志と責任の考古學. Tokyo: Igaku shoin 醫學書院.

Kroll, Paul W. 2015. *A Student's Dictionary of Classical and Medieval Chinese*. Leiden: Brill.

*Lèizuǎn* 類纂. 1989. Abbreviation of *Yīnxū jiǎgǔ kècí lèizuǎn* 殷墟甲骨刻辭類纂. 3 vols. By Yáo Xiàosuì 姚孝遂・Xiāo Dīng 蕭丁. Beijing: Zhōnghuá shūjú 中華書局.

Lyons, John. 1968. *Introduction to Theoretical Linguistics*. Cambridge: Cambridge University Press.

Morohashi Tetsuji 諸橋轍次, Kamata Tadashi 鎌田正, and Yoneyama Taratarō 米山寅太郎 1982. *Kō Kanwa jiten* 廣漢和辭典. 4 vols. Tokyo: Taishūkan shoten 大修館書店.

*OED* Abbreviation of *Oxford English Dictionary*. 2$^{nd}$ ed. (CD ROM version) 2002. Oxford: Oxford University Press.

Pulleyblank, Edwin G. 1991. Some Notes on Morphology and Syntax in Classical Chinese. *Chinese Texts and Philosophical Contexts: Essays Dedicated to Angus C. Graham*, pp. 21–45. Ed. by Henry Rosemont. La Salle: Open Court.

Qiú, Xīguī. 裘錫圭 1983. Shì hài 釋害. *Gǔwénzìxué lùnjí* 古文字學論集, Chūbiān 初編. Hong Kong: Xiānggǎng Zhōngwén dàxué zhōngguó wénhuà yánjiūsuǒ 香港中文大學中國文化研究所, pp. 217–227.

Quirk, Randolf, Sidney Greenbaum, Geoffrey Leech, and Jan Svartvik. 1972. *A Grammar of Contemporary English*. London and New York: Longman.

Quirk, Randolf, Sidney Greenbaum, Geoffrey Leech, and Jan Svartvik. 1985. *A Comprehensive Grammar of the English Language*. London and New York: Longman.

Schuessler, Axel. 2007. *ABC Etymological Dictionary of Old Chinese*. Honolulu: University of Hawaii Press.

Schuessler, Axel. 2009. *Minimal Old Chinese and Later Han Chinese: A Companion to Grammata Serica Recensa*. Honolulu: University of Hawaii Press.

Schwartz, Adam C. 2013. Huayuanzhuang East I: A Study and Annotated Translation of the Oracle Bone Inscriptions. Ph.D. dissertation. Chicago: University of Chicago.

Serruys, Paul L-M. 1974. Studies in the Language of the Shang Oracle Inscriptions. *T'oung Pao*, Vol. 60, 1–3, pp. 12–120.

Serruys, Paul L-M. 1982. Towards a Grammar of the Language of the Shang Bone Inscriptions. *Zhōngyāng yánjiūyuàn guójì Hànxué huìyì lùnwénjí* 中央研究院國際漢學會議論文集, Yǔyán wénzì zǔ 語言文字組 (Taipei: Academia Sinica), pp. 313–64.

Shěn, Jiāxuān. 沈家煊 (Tr. 譯) 2000. *Xiàndài yǔyánxué cídiǎn* 現代語言學詞典. Beijing: The Commercial Press. Chinese translation of David Crystal, *A Dictionary of Linguistics and Phonetics*. Oxford: Blackwell Publishing, 1997.

*Shuōwén* 說文. 1963. Abbreviation of *Shuōwén jiězì* 說文解字. Xǔ Shèn 許慎. Redaction of Xú Xuàn 徐鉉. Reprint of the 1873 edition by Chén Chāngzhì 陳昌治 (based on 1809 edition by Sūn Xīngyǎn 孫星衍). Also called "*Dà Xúběn* 大徐本." Reprinted in Beijing: Zhōnghuá shūjú 中華書局.

Smith, Adam. 2016. [Review of] Ken-ichi Takashima: *A Little Primer of Chinese Oracle-Bone Inscriptions with Some Exercises. Bulletin of the School of Oriental and African Studies*, Vol. 79, 2, pp. 457–8.

*Sōrui* 綜類. 1971. Abbreviation of *Inkyo bokuji sōrui* 殷墟卜辭綜類, by Shima Kunio 島邦男. Tokyo: Kyūko shoin 汲古書院.

Takashima, Ken-ichi. 高嶋謙一 1985. *Yīnxū wénzì bǐngbiān tōngjiǎn* 殷墟文字丙編通檢 (*A Concordance to Fascicle Three of Inscriptions from the Yin Ruins*). Taipei: Institute of History and Philology, Academia Sinica.

Takashima, Ken-ichi. 高嶋謙一 1988. Morphology of the Negatives in Oracle-Bone Inscriptions. *Computational Analysis of Asian and African Languages* (Tokyo: National Inter-University Research Institute of Asian and African Languages and Cultures), 30, pp. 113–133. For a revised and enlarged version, see Itō and Takashima (1996: 364–82).

Takashima, Ken-ichi. 高嶋謙一 1988a. An Emphatic Verb Phrase in the Oracle-Bone Inscriptions. *Bulletin of the Institute of History and Philology*, Vol. 59, Pt. 3 (In Memory of Dr. Fang Kuei Li), pp. 653–694.

Takashima, Ken-ichi. 高嶋謙一 1994. The Modal and Aspectual Particle *Qi* in Shang Chinese. *Papers of the First International Congress on Pre-Qin Chinese Grammar*, pp. 479–565. Ed. by Robert H. Gassmann and He Leshi 何樂士. Changsha: Yuèlù shūshè 岳麓書社.

Takashima, Ken-ichi. 高嶋謙一 1996. See Itō and Takashima (1996: Part II).

Takashima, Ken-ichi and Anne O. Yue. 高嶋謙一、余靄芹 2000. *Studies in Early Chinese Civilization: Religion, Society, Language and Palaeography*. 2 vols. Hirakata 枚方: Kansai Gaidai University Press 關西外大出版社. Part I: Religion and Society (pp. 1.1–178,) is by Itō, and Part II: Language and Palaeography (pp. 1.179–505) is by Takashima.

Takashima, Ken-ichi. 高嶋謙一 2010. *Studies of Fascicle Three of Inscriptions from the Yin Ruins*, Vol. I: General Notes, Text and Translations (殷墟文字丙編研究, 上冊: 解說・隸定・英譯) (translations up to plastron #259 by Paul L-M. Serruys 司禮儀); Vol. II: New

Palaeographical and Philological Commentaries (殷墟文字丙編研究, 下冊: 註釋•古文字語言學新探). Taipei: Institute of History and Philology, Academia Sinica.

Takashima, Ken-ichi. 高嶋謙一 2010a. A Reconstruction of Shang Joint Rituals. *Festschrift Dedicated to the 73rd Birthday of Professor Jerry Norman* (羅杰瑞先生七秩晉三壽慶論文集), pp. 453–472. Ed. by W. South Coblin (柯蔚南) and Anne O. Yue (余靄芹). Hong Kong: Institute of Chinese Civilization, Chinese University of Hong Kong.

Takashima, Ken-ichi. 高嶋謙一 2015. *A Little Primer of Chinese Oracle-Bone Inscriptions with Some Exercises*. Wiesbaden: Harrassowitz Verlag.

Takashima, Ken-ichi. 高嶋謙一 2016. The Original Function and Meaning of *Qí* 其 as Reflected in the Language of Oracle-Bone Inscriptions. *Festschrift in Honor of the 80th Birthday of Professor Ting Pang-hsin* (《丁邦新先生八秩壽慶論文集》). Submitted to Hong Kong University of Science and Technology.

Takashima, Ken-ichi. 高嶋謙一 2018. The Original Function and Meaning of *Qí* 其 as Reflected in the Language of Oracle-Bone Inscriptions. In the *Frontiers in the Study of Sinitic and Sino-Tibetan Languages: Festschrift in Honor of Professor Ting Pang-Hsin on His 80th Birthday* 《漢語與漢藏語前沿研究——丁邦新先生八秩壽慶論文集》. Ed. by Chen Zhongmin 陳忠敏, Cheung Hung-Nin Samuel 張洪年, Ho Dah-an 何大安, Sun Jingtao 孫景濤, and Yiu Yuk-man Carine 姚玉敏. Beijing: Social Sciences Academic Press (社會科學文獻出版社), pp. 59–87.

Takashima, Ken-ichi. 高嶋謙一 2019. *A Little Primer of Chinese Oracle-Bone Inscriptions with Some Exercises*. 2nd edition (revised and enlarged). Wiesbaden: Harrassowitz Verlag.

Takashima, Ken-ichi and Anne O. Yue. 高嶋謙一、余靄芹 2000. Evidence of Possible Dialect Mixture in Oracle-Bone Inscriptions. *Memory of Professor Li Fang-Kuei: Essays of Linguistic Change and the Chinese Dialects*, pp. 1–52. Ed. by Ting Pang-Hsin 丁邦新 and Anne O. Yue 余靄芹. Taipei: Institute of Linguistics [Preparatory Office], Academia Sinica.

Trask, R.L. 1995. *A Dictionary of Grammatical Terms in Linguistics*. London and New York: Routledge.

*Túnnán* 屯南. 1980. Abbreviation of *Xiǎotún nándì jiǎgǔ* 小屯南地甲骨. 5 vols. Beijing: Zhōnghuá shūjú 中華書局.

Wáng, Lì. 王力 (Editor-in-chief) 2000. *Wáng Lì gǔhànyǔ zìdiǎn* 王力古漢語字典. Beijing: Zhōnghuá shūjú 中華書局.

*Yīngcáng*. 1985. Abbreviation of *Yīngguó suǒcáng jiǎgǔjí* 英國所藏甲骨集. Beijing: Zhōnghuá shūjú 中華書局.

Yuán, Yùlín. 袁毓林 1993. *Xiàndài Hànyǔ qíshǐjù yánjiū* 現代漢語祈使句研究. Beijing: Běijīng dàxué chūbǎnshè 北京大學出版社.

Zhāng, Guìguāng. 張桂光 2004. *Gǔwénzì lùnjí* 古文字論集. Beijing: Zhōnghuá shūjú 中華書局.

Chaofen Sun
# Non-specific degree: Chinese gradable adjectives

## 1 Introduction

This paper is an in-depth study of Chinese[1] adjectives in light of distribution of degree words (Bolinger 1972) in the predicate position. A Chinese gradable adjective lexicalizes a non-specific degree. The strongest evidence comes from the fact that an adjective like *gāo* 'tall' does not have a form for the comparative or superlative degree like its English counterparts *tall, taller, tallest:* the same adjective *gāo* without any specific morphological marker can occur in direct, or indirect comparative constructions. A construction with its standard marked by a prepositional *bǐ* 'than' is treated as a direct comparative in this paper, and those without such a preposition are treated as indirect comparative. This paper demonstrates through the distributions of the degree modifiers and answers to yes/no questions that the claim (現代漢語虛詞例釋 *xiàndài hànyǔ xūcí lìshī* 1986,[2] Liu 2010, inter alia) that a bare Chinese adjective indicates a covert positive degree and the adverb *hěn* is an overt positive degree marker is neither well motivated by facts nor does it provide a full account. Evidence will be given to demonstrate that degree adverbs like *hěn* 'very', *fēicháng* 'very, very', *chāo* 'super', etc. are neither meaningless grammatical forms nor positive degree markers per se, but they are degree words from an ordered set co-occurring with a gradable adjective to form an adjectival construction with a specific degree meaning. Bare adjectives cannot simply be comparative as has been claimed by some (Sybesma 1999, Liu 2010, inter alia). This claim does not explain the constraints on bare adjectives in general. It says nothing either with respect to the obligatory presence of *hěn* 'very' in *wǒ \*(hěn) hǎo* 'I am well' when answering a greeting like *How are you?* in Chinese. The greeting *nǐ hǎo* 'hello' is actually a wish in which the adjective signifies an infinite meaning. A Chinese wish must be made, for cultural/pragmatic

---

[1] The term "Chinese" in this paper refers to the present-day Standard Modern Chinese *pǔtōnghuà* in China. The English word *Mandarin*, originally coined for *guānhuà* meaning "language of the officials," is considered anachronistic and thus not used in this paper for the reason that the term *guānhuà* is no longer commonly used in Chinese speaking communities including in mainland China, Taiwan, Hong Kong, Singapore, etc.
[2] *Xiàndài Hànyǔ Xūcí Lìshī* (Examples interpreting function words in Modern Chinese). 1982. Class of 1955 and 1957 of the Department of Chinese, Peking University (eds), Beijing: Commercial Press.

https://doi.org/10.1515/9783110641288-012

reasons, without any limit in terms of degree and, thus, demands an adjective of a non-specific degree, cf., *zhù (\*zuì) hǎo* 'All the best!' or *zhù shēngrì (\*hěn) kuàilè* 'Happy birthday!' etc. Note that the counterparts of the ungrammatical Chinese greetings are all good in English, *All the best* in the superlative or *a very happy birthday* with a degree word. This study, therefore, finds that open-scale adjectives are unlimited in terms of degree. Closed-scale meanings implying maximal/minimal degrees must appear in the form of de-adjectival verbs or in negation. Therefore, unlike in English, there is no positive absolute adjective in Chinese. This paper claims that the non-specific degree lexicalized in gradable adjectives typologically distinguishes Chinese from English as two different adjectival systems.

There have been many studies on Chinese adjectives[3] in light of the string (Li & Thompson 1981, Paul 2005, Sun 2017, inter alia), i.e., a noun phrase with the string: adjective (*de*) noun. Whereas this is certainly a most common phenomenon, the ADJ NOUN sequence is nevertheless complicated by compounding and debates on the function of the nominal modification marker *de* 的 in Chinese. For example, in (1) the adjective *bái* 'white' can optionally co-occur with *de* with the same meaning, i.e., 'white paper'. However, without *de* it is ambiguous in (1a). Paul (2005)[4] suggests that the Chinese modification marker *de* instantiates a functional category on the noun phrase tree, and that adjectives with *de* are interpreted as signaling an accessory property while those without are interpreted as having a defining property. In light of the data given in (1), such a claim actually fails to provide a full account. Given such a claim, the adjective *bái* with the same meaning 'white' should then be, at the same time, an accessory property for *paper* in the case with *de* and a defining property in the case without *de*. Furthermore, the claim is really paradoxical if the meaning of 'unused' in the *de*-less version is treated as a defining property for *paper*, as *paper*, used or not, is *paper*. As far as the meaning of *paper* is concerned, 'unused' hardly defines the thing signaled by the noun.

---

[3] Guo (2002) notes from his corpus study that Chinese adjectives are distinguishable from verbs as a lexical category. What he called "quality" adjectives, treated interchangeably as simple/gradable adjectives in this paper, make up 5.4%, or 2355 items out of a total of 43,330 words in his corpus. Moreover, 99.47% of the 2355 items are used as predicates of sentences with 98% modifiable by *hěn* 'very' and 94% negatable by *bù* 'not' as *bù gāo* 'not tall' in (25b). Thus, the propensity to co-occur with *hěn* 'very' and negator *bù* are taken to be two distinct features of Chinese adjectives.

[4] This paragraph on the constructional effect of the ADJ (*de*) Noun sequence was added at the suggestion of an anonymous reviewer of the paper.

(1) a. 白紙  b. 白的紙
       bái-zhǐ       bái de zhǐ
       white paper   white paper
       'unused/white paper'  'white paper'

As a matter of fact, an adjective in the ADJ (*de*) N sequence inevitably entails a certain relationship with its following noun, (Sproat and Shih 1988, Liu, F 2016, Sun 2017, inter alia). However, a thorough investigation of the constructional effect of the strings concerned would have taken us far afield from the main objective of this paper, i.e., to uncover the general nature of the Chinese adjectives. In order to avoid the complications posed by the challenges of these NP strings noted in above, the focal attention of this paper is on the adjectives themselves, particularly those in the predicate position.

Section 2 discusses how Chinese adjectives can be divided into two subgroups: gradable adjectives that can be modified by a degree word and ungradable adjectives that cannot. Section 3 is a demonstration of the inadequacy of treating Chinese gradable adjectives as having a covert positive degree. The section is also a display of evidence showing that Chinese gradable adjectives lexicalize a non-specific degree. Degree words in Chinese function to construct an adjectival phrase with a specific degree value. Section 4 deals with the lexically infinite nature of open-scale adjectives. Section 5 presents arguments to demonstrate that with the typologically distinct non-specific degree there is no truly closed-scale adjectives. Section 6 demonstrates that the non-specific degree is still part of the conventional meaning of a set of adjectives that are of closed-scale only in negation, but not part of the meaning of the de-adjectival verbs that do contain closed-scale meanings. Section 7 concludes the paper with a schematic description of the adjectives that contain closed-scale meaning only in negation.

## 2 Ungradable and gradable adjectives

Zhu (1984)[5] noted two classes of Chinese adjectives: those that signal *xìngzhí* 'quality' (2) and those that express *zhuàngtài* 'manner' (3). The two classes are distinguishable by their distributional properties with respect to degree words such as *hěn* 'very'. Whereas the former can co-occur with degree words as shown

---

[5] This refers to the publication date of a book that was essentially a lecture series by Professor *Zhū Déxī* originally delivered in 1961–62.

in (2b), the latter, as shown in (3b), cannot. In this paper, the "quality" adjectives, or "simple adjectives" as they are also commonly referred to in the field (Liu 2010, Lin & Peck 2016), are treated as gradable adjectives, and the so-called "manner" adjectives are treated as ungradable. Following Kennedy (2007a), I assume that gradable adjectives are those that can map their arguments onto some abstract measurement in terms of degrees from a set of totally ordered degree words including *hěn*. These two classes are coded as such in the lexicon as two unpredictable subcategories of adjectives.

(2) a. 大、好、乾净、偉大
 *dà, hǎo, gānjìng, wěidà*
 'big, good, clean, great'

 b. 很大、很好、很乾净、很偉大
 *hěn dà, hěn hǎo, hěn gānjìng, hěn wěidà*
 'very big, very good, very clean, very great'

(3) a. 雪白、綠油油、灰不溜秋、乾乾净净
 *xuě-bái,   lùyóu-yóu,   huī-bù-liū-qiū,   gān-gān-jìng-jìng*
 snow-white, green-oil-oil, grey-no-slippery-autumn, dry-dry-clean-clean
 'extremely white, fresh and green, grey and dull, extremely clean'

 b. *很雪白、 *很綠油油、 *很灰不溜秋、 *很乾乾净净
 **hěn xuě-bái,   *hěn lù-yóu-yóu,   *hěn huī-bù-liū-qiū,*
 very snow-white, very green-oil-oil, very grey-no-slippery-autumn,
 '*very snow-white, very fresh and green, very dark,
 **hěn gān-gān-jìng-jìng*
 very dry-dry-clean-clean
 very clean'

Ungradable adjectives can be further divided into at least two sub-classes: unproductive and partially motivated, both of which are characteristics of lexicalization (Brinton and Traugott 2005). For example, in (3a) the idiomatic expression *huī-bù-liū-qiū* grey-no-slippery-autumn 'very dark' does not result from the totality of the meanings of its component morphemes. As a matter of fact, the relationship between the form and meaning is rather opaque; even though the color *huī* 'grey' can be construed as relevant, the rest of the sequence *-bù-liū-qiū* grey-no-slippery-autumn 'very dark' is unanalyzable. It is therefore an arbitrary expression like any lexical item. *Lù-yóu-yóu* green-oil-oil 'fresh and green' is similarly unproductive. Even though the meaning of *lù* 'green' clearly has a great deal to do with the meaning of the sequence, it is still totally unanalyzable in relating the meaning of 'oil' to the meaning of 'fresh'. Such a combination is an unproductive formation, as *yóu-yóu* can hardly be attached to another color term to produce a meaning of 'fresh'.

However, the other two examples in (3) are partially motivated. In *xuě-bái* snow-white *snow* is used to semantically strengthen the 'whiteness' of something, as the naturally formed *snow* falling from the sky in winter is always white. But such a semantic strengthening is still only partially motivated as *snow* is not the only thing on earth that is naturally white. *Gān-gān-jìng-jìng* is a reduplicated form of the gradable adjective *gān-jìng* 'clean' in (2). It is partially motivated as it is quite common to reduplicate an adjective to strengthen its conventional meaning. However, there are actually two fixed patterns of adjectives with four syllables consisting of the duplicated gradable *gānjìng* in (2a) in an AABB pattern *gān-gān-jìng-jìng* in (3a) and the duplicated ungradable *xuě-bái* in (2a) used in an ABAB pattern *xuě-bái-xuě-bái* 雪白雪白.

Furthermore, the examples in (4) show that *měilì* and *gān-jìng* can be modified by a degree word *hěn* 'very' and are thus gradable adjectives. But while the former can be reduplicated in neither AABB, nor ABAB, pattern, the latter can only reduplicate in the AABB pattern. Thus, the reduplication pattern is somewhat arbitrary and not totally predictable. Therefore, the reduplicated forms are treated as ungradable adjectives in this paper.

(4) a. 很美麗  
    *hěn měilì*  
    very pretty  
    'very pretty'

b. 很乾净  
    *hěn gānjìng*  
    very clean  
    'very clean'

(5) a. *美美麗麗  
    **měiměilìlì*  
    pretty-pretty-elegant-elegant  
    *intended:* 'very pretty'

    *美麗美麗  
    **měilìměilì*  
    pretty-elegant-pretty-elegant

b. 乾乾净净  
    *gān-gān-jìng-jìng*  
    'very clean'

    *乾净乾净  
    **gān-jìng-gān-jìng*

All Chinese ungradable adjectives cannot directly occur in the predicate position, as shown in (6b). Whereas the gradable adjective *gānjìng* in (6a) in the predicate position can occur alone, the ungradable reduplicated form cannot without going through a nominalization process (Li & Thompson 1981, Zhan & Sun 2013) with a *shì ... de* construction in (6c).

(6) a. 這件衣服乾淨
    *zhe-jiàn yīfú gān-jìng*
    DEM-CL clothes dry-clean
    'This clothing is clean.'

   b. *衣服乾乾淨淨
    **yīfú gān-gān-jìng-jìng*
    clothes dry-dry-clean-clean

   c. 衣服（是）幹幹淨淨的
    *yīfú(shì) gān-gān-jìng-jìng de*
    clothes be dry-dry-clean-clean NOM
    'This clothing is very clean.'

Moreover, the reduplicated form cannot occur in an explicit comparative construction such as those shown in (7b and 7d). Therefore, reduplicated forms like *gān-gān-jìng-jìng* should be properly classified as ungradable adjectives despite their semantically strengthened meaning.

(7) a. 這件衣服比那件乾淨
    **zhe-jiàn yīfú bǐ nà-jiàn gān-jìng*
    DEM-CL clothes COMPAR DEM-CL clean
    'This clothing is cleaner than that.'

   b. *這件衣服比那件幹幹淨淨
    **zhe-jiàn yīfú bǐ nà-jiàn gān-gān-jìng-jìng*
    DEM-CL clothes COMPAR DEM-CL dry-dry-clean-clean

   c. 今天比昨天開心
    *jīntiān bǐ zuótiān kāi-xīn*
    today COMPAR yesterday open-heart
    '(I am) happier today than (I was) yesterday.'

   d. *今天比昨天開開心心
    **jīntiān bǐ zuótiān kāi-kāi-xīn-xīn*
    today COMPAR yesterday open-open-heart-heart

Not all ungradable adjectives belong to the type of semantic strengthening noted above. There are ungradable adjectives like those in (8) that cannot be modified by degree words or occur in the predicate position independent of the *shi ... de* construction.

(8) a. 副，人工、共同、軍用、國營、私立、單項
   *fù réngōng gòngtóng jūnyòng guóyíng sīlì dānxiáng*
   vice artificial common military state-run private single case

   b. *很副，*很人工，*很共同，*很軍用，*很國營，
   *很私立, *很單項
   *hěn fù, *hěn réngōng, *hěn gòngtóng, *hěn jūnyòng, *hěn guóyíng,
   very vice, very artificial, very common, very military, very state-run,
   *hěn sīlì, *hěn dānxiáng
   very private, very single case

In sum, Chinese adjectives in the lexicon are lexicalized into two types in (9): gradable and ungradable. They are distinguishable as the former can co-occur with a degree word while the latter cannot. Furthermore, adjectives as idiomatic expressions can be reduplicated to strengthen a certain property, albeit in an unpredictable manner. The remainder of this paper demonstrates how and why Chinese gradable adjectives should be properly recognized as lexicalizing a non-specific degree.

(9) a. ADJ$_{\text{gradable, non-specific degree}}$
   b. ADJ$_{\text{ungradable}}$

## 3 Chinese gradable adjectives lexicalize a non-specific degree

It has been claimed (*xiàndài hànyǔ xūcí lìshī* 1982, Sybesma 1999, Liu 2010, Lin & Peck 2016, inter alia) that Chinese gradable adjectives are in various ways associated with a covert positive degree in implicit comparison (more below in this section). According to these scholars, in contrast to English in which a gradable adjective like *tall* can be analyzed as having a positive degree, a Chinese gradable adjective like *gāo* 'tall' as in (10a) only denotes a covert positive degree (Liu 2010) and is unacceptable without an overt positive degree (Liu 2010) marker *hěn* 'very' as in (10b).

(10) a. ??他高⁶
 ??*tā gāo*
 3SG tall
 'He is tall.'

 b. 他很高
 *tā hěn gāo*
 3SG very tall
 'He is very tall.'

Sybesma (1999: 27–28) says that

> [O]ne of the differences between Mandarin adjectives and their European counterparts is that, while for the latter the positive degree is the unmarked option, for the former the comparative is. Consequently, in European languages the comparative is morphologically marked whereas in Mandarin the positive degree is. The most neutral 'positive degree marker' is *hěn*. ... [W]e find that *hěn* has two different functions. One is that of an intensifier like the English *very*. The other function might be paraphrased as a marker of the positive degree. As an intensifier *hěn* is stressed, as a positive degree marker it is not.

However, a closer examination of the Chinese data shows that the views on Chinese adjectives noted by the scholars cited above may not actually be correct. First of all, it is a mystery why a positive adjective has to be understood as only covertly so without the degree marker *hěn* in (10b). In a comparative construction neither the English *very* (alone without *much*) nor the Chinese *hěn* in (11b) is allowed. In both cases, the English *tall* and the Chinese *gāo* are positive. So the fact is that the bare adjective *gāo* in Chinese may be just as positive as its Engish counterpart *tall*. It is then entirely possible that the necessary presence of the degree word *hěn* in (10b) before *gāo* has to do with a reason unrelated to the positive degree of an adjective.

(11) a. 他比我高
 *tā bǐ wǒ gāo*
 3SG COMPAR 1SG tall
 'He is taller than me.'

---

6 This paper follows the established practice of using double question marks ?? to show an even more unacceptable utterance than a somewhat unacceptable utterance marked by a single question mark? Those that are marked with a star * are totally unacceptable.

b. *他比我很高
*tā bǐ wǒ hěn gāo
3SG COMPAR 1SG very tall
'*He is very taller than me.'

Second, the sentences in (12a and b) show that a positive adjective *gāo* 'tall' is negatable by *bù*. Obviously, the two sentences with, and without, *hěn*, are meaningfully different. That is, *tài* in (12b) carries, in addition to positivity, a degree value that is absent in *bù gāo* (12a). Furthermore, the sentence in (12c) shows that *hěn* as a degree word does not provide a positive degree, as the *bù gāo* it modifies remains negative.

(12) a. 他薪水不高
*tā xīnshuǐ bù gāo*
3SG salary NEG tall
'His salary is not high.'

b. 他薪水不太高
*tā xīnshuǐ bù tài[7] gāo*
3SG salary NEG too tall
'His salary is not very high.'

c. 他薪水很不高
*tā xīnshuǐ hěn bù gāo*
3SG salary very NEG tall
'*His salary is very not high.' 'His salary is very low.'

In order to make his argument work, Liu (2010) contends that *bù gāo* 'not tall' is actually the positive *ǎi* 'short/low' and, therefore, *hěn* is still an overt positive degree marker for *ǎi*. The problem with this claim is that *bù gāo* does not entail *ǎi* 'short/low'. For example, *gāo* in both sentences (13) retains some sort of 'tall' implication after the negation of *gāo* as the second clauses suggest.

(13) a. 他虽然不高，但是也不矮
*tā suīrán bù gāo, dànshì yě bù ǎi*
3SG though NEG tall, but also NEG short
'Although he is not tall, he is not short either.'

---

7 After the negator *bù*, *hěn* is collocationally unacceptable. *Tài* as an adverb implying a comparative degree is preferred.

b. 他雖然不高，可是在班裏還算是高的
   *tā suīrán bù gāo, kěshì zài bānli hái suàn shì gāo de*
   3SG though NEG tall, but in class still count be tall NOM[8]
   'Although he is not tall, in his class he still counts as tall.'

In fact, the data in (14) reveal that Chinese adjectives are all positive and the covert/overt contrast is not a well-motivated proposition as the primary meaning of *hěn* 'very' is to simply signal a specific degree value. The data in (14) clearly demonstrate that the bare adjective *hǎo* 'good' is just as positive as the bare verb *qù* 'go' in answering a yes/no question. Note that neither *hǎo* 'good', nor *qù* 'go', is correct if the answers are literally translated into English according to the original adjectival, or verbal, meanings. This parallelism between a verb and an adjective in answering a yes/no question positively raises serious doubts about the treatment of Chinese gradable adjectives as only having a covert positive degree meaning.

(14) a. 這樣好不好？　　　好！
       *zheyàng hǎo bù hǎo?*　　*hǎo,*
       DEM good not good　　　good
       'Is this all right?'　　　'Yes!' '*good'

   b. 你去不去？　　　去
      *nǐ qù bù qù?*　　*qù*
      2SG go not go　　　go
      'Will you go?'　　　'Yes' '*go'

Still another issue is Sybesma's claim that a bare Chinese adjective should be taken as simply signaling a comparison while *hěn* 'very' should be taken as a positive degree marker. Following his logic, one may assume that when *hěn* is present, it is simply a matter of positivity. The data in (15) show that with, or without, the presence of the degree word *hěn*, the adjective *dà* is positive. The difference is not, in fact, about positivity. Though there is not a degree word in (15a), and though there is a specific degree value associated with *hěn* in (15b), the positivity of the adjective *dà* is a constant in both.

---

[8] NOM in the gloss stands for the grammatical marker of a nominalizer.

(15) a. 這個房間大
      *zhe-ge fángjiān dà*
      DEM-CL room big
      'This room is big.'

   b. 這個房間很大
      *zhe-ge fángjiān hěn dà*
      DEM-CL room very big
      'This room is very big.'

Example (15b) is actually an implicit comparison (Lin & Peck 2016). The gradable adjective *dà* denotes the property of *big* in comparison with a certain standard in context. In other words, the one marked by the degree marker also marks a comparison situation. Kennedy (2007a: 3) observes that "[w]ithin linguistic semantics, a fruitful line of research has developed that analyzes the positive form as a relation between the degree to which an object possesses some gradable concept measured by the predicate and a context dependent STANDARD OF COMPARISON based on this concept." He (2007b: 157) distinguishes implicit comparison from explicit comparison, repeated here in (16–17):

(16) Implicit Comparison
     Establish an ordering between objects x and y with respect to gradable property g using the positive form by manipulating the context in such a way that the positive form is true of x and false of y.

(17) Explicit Comparison
     Establish an ordering between objects x and y with respect to gradable property g using a morphosyntactic form whose conventional meaning has the consequence that the degree to which x is g exceeds the degree to which y is g.

Paradis (2001) and Lin & Peck (2016) argue that comparison is implicit in scalar adjectives. In this light, both sentences in (15) are cases of implicit comparison, as they establish an ordering between the size of *fángjiān* 'this room' and the size of a context dependent (including possible speaker-subjective attitude) standard with respect to the gradable property *big*. The difference is that the presence of a degree marker *hěn* in (15b) results in a degree that is absent in (15a). The adjective *dà* in both sentences is undoubtedly positive.

The question to answer then is what kind of positive degree *dà* 'big' denotes in (15). The contrast in (18) suggests that a bare gradable adjective in the predicate position has a positive degree without any specific value. The one in (18b) with an equally positive but the degree marker *hěn* is totally infelicitous in this context as the question is specifically about something that is indefinitely big in the world, but not about something that has a specific degree, i.e., *very big*.

(18) 世界上什麼大？
*shìjiè-shang shénme dà*
world-up what big
'What is big in the world?'

    a. 天大
      *tiān dà*
      sky big
      'The sky is big.'

    b. ??天很大
      *tiān hěn dà*
      sky very big
      'The sky is very big.'

But then, how do we know *hěn* 'very' signals a specific degree? In (19), a scale is proposed to characterize an ordered set of degree words that range from a negative degree signified by *bù* to a maximal degree. The scale includes degree words like *bǐjiào* 'compare/relative' near the minimal end to *zuì* 'superlative' near the maximal.

(19) An ordered set of degree words for gradable adjectives

超 太/ 最/ 極 挺 / 很 比較/ 還/ 有點 不
*chāo tài/ zuì / jí tǐng/ hěn bǐjiào/ hái/ yǒudiǎn bù*
'super, most, extremely, very, very, very, compare, still, somewhat, not'
←-----------------------------------------------------------------------→

Accordingly, in (20a) *hǎo*, as an open-scale gradable adjective without any qualification, indicates a non-specific, positive degree of 'good.' It is negated by *bù* in (20b) to display a negative degree. But for the rest of the data in (20), *hǎo* is qualified by a degree word from *bǐjiào* 'compare' in (20c) to *chāo* 'super' in (20g). The examples in (20c & 20f) show that the comparative and superlative degree meanings are part of this ordered set of degrees.

(20) a. 這裏咖啡好
    *zheli kāfēi hǎo*
    DEM coffee good
    'The coffee here is good.'

b. 這裏咖啡不好
    *zheli kāfēi bù hǎo*
    DEM coffee NEG good
    'The coffee here is not good.'

c. 這裏咖啡比較好
    *zheli kāfēi bǐjiào hǎo*
    DEM coffee relative good
    'The coffee here is all right.'

d. 這裏咖啡很好
    *zheli kāfēi hěn hǎo*
    DEM coffee very good
    'The coffee here is very good.'

e. 這裏咖啡非常好
    *zheli kāfēi fēicháng hǎo*
    DEM coffee not-common good
    'The coffee here is very, very good.'

f. 這裏咖啡最好
    *zheli kāfēi zuì hǎo*
    DEM coffee most good
    'The coffee here is best.'

g. 這裏咖啡超好
    *zheli kāfēi chāo hǎo*
    DEM coffee super good
    'The coffee here is super good.'

Note that the order of the degree words on the scale of (19) is not changeable, and thus the strengths of the degree meanings are fixed and increase when moving up the scale. That is, *fēicháng hǎo* 'very, very good' is a stronger degree with respect to the property of *good* than *hěn hǎo* 'very good', and, similarly, *zuì hǎo* 'most good' is stronger than *fēicháng hǎo,* as well as *hěn hǎo,* and so on and so forth. For this reason, the degree words in (19) can be conveniently used to establish an ordering between objects x and y with respect to a certain gradable property. In (20) the degree words establish orderings of different nature between *the coffee here* and an implicit standard of *coffee* in context with respect to the gradable property *good*. The key is that a specific degree (a certain ordering between x and y) value that is at least as great as the standard of this implicit comparison is not part of the lexical meaning of *hǎo* 'good' but is rather context-dependent, or measured "on the fly" (Kennedy 2007a), so to speak.

However, when the standard of comparison is marked by a preposition *bǐ* in (21), the adjective *dà* has no marking of any kind comparable to the *-er* suffix in English. In this paper it is treated as direct comparison.[9] Furthermore, (21b) demonstrates that the gradable adjective *dà* 'big' cannot be marked by any of the degree words on the scale in (19). That is, the ordering between objects x and y with respect to a gradable property is signaled in a direct manner but context-dependent only in (20) where an appropriate degree word is selected without a standard of comparison in the sentence.

(21) a. 這個房間比那個房間大
    *zhe-ge fángjiān bǐ    nèi-ge fángjiān dà*
    DEM-CL room COMPAR   DEM-CL room big
    'This room is bigger than that room.'

  b. 這個房間比那個房間*很/*非常大
    *zhe-ge   fángjiān bǐ    nèi-ge fángjiān *hěn/*fēicháng   dà*
    DEM-CL   room COMPAR   DEM-CL room very/very, very     big
    '*This room is very/very, very bigger than that room.'

Two observations can be made about the Chinese comparison constructions here. First, the degree words with specific meanings on the ordered set given in (19) can only establish an ordering between two entities in indirect comparison in which the standard of comparison is absent in the sentence and largely dependent on context. Second, the gradable adjectives do not lexically denote a specific degree in either direct, or indirect, comparison. It follows, therefore, that Chinese gradable adjectives lexically signal a non-specific degree. The Modern Chinese idiom in (22) attests to the above two observations. Using the negation *méiyǒu* with a superlative degree word *zuì*, a world in which everyone is only striving to be good is established. Interestingly, the gradable *hǎo* 'good' with a non-specific degree meaning, cannot be modified by a degree word such as *hěn* 'very' from the ordered set in (19). Rather, the degree word *gèng* 'even', that has no place on

---

[9] I want to thank an anonymous reviewer who pointed out that Chinese comparative is generally recognized as a language with implicit comparison (Kennedy 2007b) typology, as the adjectives carry no morphological marker.

the ordered scale in (19), must be used to signal a situation without any specific degree.

(22) 没有最好，只有更/*很好
*méiyǒu zuì hǎo   zhǐ yǒu gèng/*hěn hǎo*
No most good,  only has more good
'There is no best; [there is] only better.'

As a matter of fact, *gèng* (22–23) unlike any degree word with a specific degree meaning, can occur in direct comparison as well, as the gradable adjective there also carries a non-specific positive degree meaning. In an English explicit comparison construction, the adjective cannot be modified by a specific degree word either, *\*He is very taller than me*.

(23) 他比我更/*很高
*tā  bǐ   wǒ  gèng/*hěn gāo*
3SG than 1SG even/very tall
'He is even taller than me.'

In short, Chinese gradable adjectives without any modifier are positive without the fictitious contrast between covert and overt positive degrees. But, more importantly, they are non-specific in terms of degree, as no morphological suffix like the English *–er* or *–est* attaches to an adjective. Such a typological distinction is captured in (24) as English gradable adjectives lexicalize degree meanings morphologically like the regular *good*, comparative *better*, and superlative *best* (*more/-er* and *most/-est* for other adjectives).

(24) | Gradable adjectives | English | Chinese |
| --- | --- | --- |
| specific degree | + | – |

Chinese gradable adjectives lexicalize a non-specific positive degree. Therefore, any adjectival phrase with a bare gradable adjective in the predicate position is still of a non-specific degree (25a). At the same time, an adjectival phrase denoting a specific degree is grammatically constructed out of a combination of a gradable adjective and a degree word, noted as [DegW] in (25b), from the ordered set of degree words in (19). (25b) is a description of the grammatical process used in forming an adjectival phrase with a specific degree word. (25c) is a schema for an adjectival phrase in which a gradable adjective is modified by the non-specic if degree word *gèng* 更 'even' noted as [Non-DegW].

(25) a. [ADJ_gradable]            ↔  Adjectival Phrase_non-specific degree
     b. [DegW, ADJ_gradable]      ↔  Adjectival Phrase_specific degree
     c. [Non-DegW, ADJ_gradable]  ↔  Adjectival Phrase_specific degree

# 4 Non-finite nature of open-scale adjectives

The gradable adjectives *gāo* 'tall' and *hǎo* 'good' noted above are commonly graded by degree words like *hěn* 'very', *fēicháng* 'very, very', etc. in the predicate position according to a certain contextually determined standard. The order of the degree words on the scale is determined by the degree elements they denote. Kennedy & McNally (2005: 352) observe that

> ...the structure of the (ordered) set of degrees – the scale itself – is also linguistically significant. In theory, several different structural features could be important, including whether a scale is finite or infinite, whether it is dense or discrete, whether it contains minimal or maximal elements or not, and so forth. Determining the full range of structural variation in scales that natural languages are sensitive to would require an empirical investigation that goes beyond the scope of a single article, however, so our strategy here is to focus on just one of these parameters: whether a scale is OPEN (lacks a minimal element, a maximal element, or both) or CLOSED (has minimal and maximal elements).

There are two main scalar patterns for gradable adjectives cross-linguistically: open scale and closed scale. In (26a & b) the adjectives *hǎo* 'good', *huài* 'bad', *gāo* 'tall', and *ǎi* 'short' are all of open scale and can together form idiomatic expressions containing a pair of negated antonyms, while *gān* 'dry', *shī* 'wet', *kōng* 'empty', and *mǎn* 'full' in (26c & 26d) carry a non-specific degree positively but a specific degree with a closed-scale reading in negation. Therefore, they cannot form such a construction of negated antonyms. The antonyms of the former group with an open-scale pattern do not completely negate each other, whereas the antonyms of the latter group do completely. In the next section, it will be demonstrated that the closed-scale meanings also come through when the latter group are used as a de-adjectival verb. Interestingly, the former and latter groups all carry a non-specific degree in a positive statement. The latter group is treated as covert closed-scale adjectives (more see section 5).

(26) a. 不好不壞
       *bù hǎo bù huài*
       NEG good NEG bad
       '(It) is just so-so.'

b. 不高不矮
   *bù gāo bù ǎi*
   NEG tall NEG short
   '(He) is of the right height.'

c. ??不乾不濕
   ??*bù gān bù shī*
   NEG dry NEG wet
   '*(It) is neither dry nor wet.'

d. *不空不滿
   **bù kōng bù mǎn*
   NEG empty NEG full
   '*(It) is neither empty nor full.'

This section demonstrates that the open-scale adjectives are actually non-specific without any degree meaning. Many specific uses of Chinese adjectives can then follow from this hypothesis as it naturally motivates the pragmatic triggers for constraints on some special expressions in various discourse contexts. Kennedy (2007a) notes that implicit comparison is vague and context-dependent. It is widely known that gradable adjectives used alone in the predicate position frequently result in unacceptability without the degree marker *hěn*. To a large extent such a restriction has motivated the problematic claim that *hěn* is a positive degree marker for Chinese adjectives (Sybesma 1999, Liu 2010, inter alia). Note that open-scale adjectives that lack a minimal or maximal degree can easily be taken to be unlimited, or infinite, in terms of degree. Treated as a case of indirect comparison in this paper, the bare *gāo* in (27a) is odd because it is rather difficult to take a person's height as having an infinite degree. The basketball player *Yao Ming*, perhaps 7.6 feet tall, may be truly a very tall person. Yet, a man, no matter how tall he can be, still cannot – not even metaphorically – be taken as having the potential to become infinitely tall. In comparison to buildings, mountains, and other things that can be described as *tall*, 7.6 feet is really not that tall at all. Therefore, the degree word *hěn* simply removes the infinite denotation from a gradable adjective by changing it into a construction with a degree value from an ordered set with specific degree values consistent with a speaker's opinion. The sentence in (27b), still a case of indirect comparison, is good because it is located in a context, or in a possible world, in which there are only two people. It is a context particularly conducive to a crisp judgement as the difference in height between *Yao Ming* and *I*, the standard of comparison, can be easily determined. (27a) without a degree word is unacceptable as no context conducive to a crisp judgement is available.

(27) a. 姚明*(很)高
　　　 *yáomíng \*(hěn) gāo*
　　　 Name (very) tall
　　　 'Yao Ming is (very) tall.'

　　 b. 姚明高，我不高
　　　 *yáomíng gāo wǒ bù gāo*
　　　 Name　 tall, 1SG NEG tall
　　　 'Yao Ming is tall; I am not.'

Second, the treatment of *hěn* as an overt positive degree marker provides no ready answer to why, in answering *How are you?* in Chinese, *hěn* must be present in (28b) but absent with the same gradable adjective *hǎo* in a good wish as in (28a) that is functionally equivalent to the English *hello*. It follows that, as *nǐ hǎo* and *wǒ hěn hǎo* are both positive, the necessary absence, or presence, of *hěn* in (28) suggests that something other than a matter of overt positive degree is at work.

(28) a. 你（\*很）好！
　　　 *nǐ (\*hěn) hǎo!*
　　　 2SG very good
　　　 'Hello!'

　　 b. 你最近怎麼樣？　　　 我\*（很）好！
　　　 *nǐ zuìjìn zěnme yàng?*　 *wǒ \*(hěn) hǎo!*
　　　 2SG recent how things　 1SG (very) good
　　　 'How are you?'　　　　　 'I am (very) well!'

In Chinese, perhaps due to a cultural or pragmatic reason, an open-scale adjective sometimes must not be limited to any specific degree meaning. Therefore, *hǎo* 'good' in (28a) can never be modified by a degree word. It seems that such a cultural constraint is played to the fullest in making a good wish. That is, a good wish must not co-occur with any degree word, i.e., not any limiting specific degree. Note that in English, a good wish is commonly made either in the superlative degree, or with the degree word *very*, cf., *all the best! I wish you a very Happy Birthday!* But nothing with a specific degree is possible in a Chinese wish \**zhù zuì hǎo* 'wish you the best' or \**zhù hěn hǎo* 'wish you to be very well' as in (29a & b). Although the literal English translation of an idiomatic Chinese birthday wish to a senior citizen given in (29d), *I wish you a life of 10,000 years without end,* may seem a mouthful, or even laughable, to a Westerner, the literal gloss fully corroborates the non-specific-degree hypothesis for Chinese gradable adjectives, as the limit of *10,000 years* is cancelled by *without end*.

(29) a. 你（*很）好！
 *nǐ (\*hěn) hǎo*
 2SG very good
 'Hello!'

 b. 祝（*很、*最）好！
 *zhù (\*hěn, \*zuì) hǎo*
 wish very most good
 '(I) wish (you) well!'

 c. 祝你生日（*很）快樂！
 *zhù nǐ shēngrì (\*hěn) kuàilè*
 wish 2SG birthday very happy
 '(I) wish you a happy Birthday!'

 d. 祝您萬壽無疆！
 *zhù    nín          wàn    shòu    wú jiāng*
 wish 2SG 10,000 year no     boundary
 '(I) wish you a very, very long life!'

## 5 Chinese closed-scale adjectives

The non-existence of the negated antonymous construction noted in (26) for the covert closed-scale adjectives suggests that they may be distinguishable from open-scale adjectives by the maximal, or minimal, degrees. However, in this section I will show that non-specific degree remains the dominant factor over proportional meanings in the morphosyntax of Chinese gradable adjectives in the predicate position, corroborating the hypothesis that all Chinese gradable adjectives are lexically of a non-specific degree. The closed-scale meanings for this set of adjectives can be realized only if they are negated (26) or used as a de-adjectival verb.

First of all, just like open-scale adjectives, adjectives similar to the English ones with a closed-scale structure can be used in explicit comparison, as the maximal degree adjective *kōng* 'empty' with a standard marked by *bǐ* in (30) confirms.

(30) 這個房間比那個房間空
 *zhe-ge   fángjiān bǐ       na-ge fángjiān kōng*
 DEM-CL room COMPAR DEM-CL room empty
 'This room is emptier than that room.'

Pertaining to the notions of maximal/minimal degrees, however, these Chinese adjectives do not truly have a closed-scale structure like their synonymous adjectives in English where there is finer co-occurrence constraints associated with proportions. They, nevertheless, remain subject to distributional constraints just as open-scale adjectives are, and are primarily sensitive to the non-specific degree rather than the maximal/minimal degrees.

Bolinger (1972) and Kennedy & McNally (2005) note, among many, three different English degree modifiers–*well*, *much*, and *very*–with largely complementary distributions. *Very* has a standard-raising effect depending on how the initial standard is determined in a context. *Much*, as a degree modifier, is very close to *very* but is restricted to minimum-standard absolute adjectives or totally closed scales. Finally, *well*, as a degree modifier, is felicitously used with adjectives that have totally closed scales.[10]

(31) a. Martin Beck was well/??much/??very acquainted with the facts of the case.
b. Their vacation was ??well/much/??very needed.[11]
c. Al was ??well/??much/very surprised by the results of the election.

The meaning of the English *much* refers to an amount that one argument has over another as in the English *much taller*. But no comparable Chinese degree word denoting an amount is found to target the distinctive degree value in the English *much*, as *gèng* 'even', the closest Chinese degree word, is used to modify any gradable adjective without a specific degree reading with a meaning closer to *even* than *much*. The English adjectives *acquainted* (31a) and *needed* (31b) denote some maximal or minimal degrees respectively. Furthermore, there are no temporally bounded deverbal adjectives in Chinese. The degrees with respect to the maximal/minimal degrees in *shúxī* 'acquaint', *xūyào* 'need' and *chījīng* 'surprised' in (31) are, remarkably, signaled by the same *hěn* 'very' from the ordered scale, thus revealing a Chinese system in which adjectives need not be discriminatively collocated to different degree words in the same ways their counterparts in English must. *Hěn*'s uses, as a degree word, then need not depend on the maximal/minimal degrees of the adjectives but can provide a specific degree value to an adjectival phrase that has a gradable adjective with s non-specific

---

**10** The examples in (31) are taken from Kennedy & McNally's paper and abridged by me for the purposes of quick reference; any inappropriateness or error in these examples is completely my responsibility.
**11** Elizabeth Traugott (p.c.) pointed out to me that given a highly uncommon context, *needed* can be modified by *very*.

degree. *Hěn* is perhaps the most grammaticalized of the degree words in marking a default ordering between two entities.

(32) a. 這個案子小馬很熟悉
      *zhe-ge ànzi xiǎomǎ hěn shúxī*
      DEM-CL case Name very acquaint
      'Mr. Ma was well acquainted with this case.'

   b. 假期他們很需要
      *jiàqī tāmen hěn xūyào*
      vacation 3PL very need
      'They need the vacation very much.'

   c. 選舉的結果讓我很喫驚
      *xuánjǔ de jiéguǒ ràng wǒ hěn chījīng*
      election DE result let 1ST very surprise
      'The results of the election very much surprised me.'

Furthermore, according to Kennedy & McNally (2005) and Kennedy (2007a), there are four kinds of English scalar patterns: open scale, lower closed scale, upper closed scale, and closed scale as exemplified in (33) (taken from Kennedy & McNally 2005: 355). The contrasts show that *tall/short* with an open-scale pattern in (33a) without a minimal, or a maximal, element does not collocate with the adverb *completely*. (33b & c) may have a minimal but no maximal element or vice versa, and the antonyms thus have opposite acceptability when collocating with the adverb *fully*. Adjectives in (33d) have both maximal and minimal elements, and the antonyms are totally compatible with the proportional degree modifier '100%'.

(33) a. Open scale: *Her brother is completely ??tall/??short.*
   b. Lower closed scale: *The pipe is fully ??bent/straight.*
   c. Upper closed scale: *We are fully certain/??uncertain about the results.*
   d. Closed scale: *The room is 100% full/empty.*

But the grammatical statuses of the similar Chinese sentences in (34), mirroring the meanings of the English patterns in (31), are once again quite different. The proportional adverb 百分之百 '100%' can co-occur with neither the Chinese open-scale adjectives *gāo/ǎi* 'tall/short', nor the covert closed-scale *wān/zhí* 'bent/straight' or *kōng/mǎn* 'empty/full'. The unacceptability probably follows from the lexicalized non-specific degree meaning of all the gradable adjectives. The contrasts between the English antonyms in (33b & c) are completely absent in Chinese (34b & 34c) as there is no difference in acceptability. Obviously, this set of data reveal once again that, with respect to scalar patterns, Chinese and English synonymous adjectives behave differently with respect to the degree words. Chinese gradable adjectives generally do not restrict the degree words in light of maximal/minimal elements like the English adjectives do.

(34) a. *他弟弟百分之百高/矮
    tā    dìdi     bǎifēnzhībǎi   gāo/ǎi
    3SG   brother  100%           tall/short
    '??Her brother is 100% tall/short.'

  b. 管子完全??彎/??直
    guǎnzi   wánquán   ??wān/??zhí
    pipe     fully     bent/straight
    'The pipe is fully ??bent/straight.'

  c. 我们對結果完全肯定/不肯定[12]
    wǒ-men   duì   jiéguǒ   wánquón   kěndìng/bù kěndìng
    1PL      to    result   fully     certain/uncertain
    'We are fully certain/??uncertain about the results.'

  d. 房間百分之百??滿/??空
    fángjiān   bǎifēnzhībǎi   ??mǎn/??kōng
    room       100%           full/empty
    'The room is 100% full/empty.'

As can be seen, just like the open-scale adjectives, a specific degree marker is necessary for these covert closed-scale adjectives as non-specific degree is part of their lexical meanings.

# 6 De-adjectival verbs

Although the gradable adjectives in Chinese cannot co-occur with proportional degree adverbs, it is noteworthy that unacceptable sentences such as those in (34) all become acceptable if they are used with the sentence-final perfect marker *le* (a verb phrase clitic) as seen in (35). The hidden closed-scale patterns for *wān/zhí* 'bent/straight', and *mǎn/kōng* 'full/empty', have surfaced and can all be mod-

---

[12] *kěndìng* 'certain' may not be an adjective but a verb, or auxiliary, in Chinese. This may significantly contribute to its acceptability in (34c).

ified by proportional adverbs, either *bǎifēnzhībǎi* '100%' or *wánquán* 'fully' as in (35) and (36). This suggests that similar adverbials with maximum/minimum standards in English can co-occur with Chinese de-adjectival verbs marked by the sentence-final *le* signaling "currently relevant state, CRS" (Li & Thompson 1981, Smith 1997, Lin & Peck 2016, inter alia). Please note that in (35a) *wān* 'bent' is a lower closed-scale pattern in English, and 100% *bent* in Chinese actually connotes that the item is 100% certainly bent, even if it is just a little bit so. It does not imply any specific proportion of bentness, or straightness. Nevertheless, the meanings of (35b) ambiguously refer to the proportional values with respect to the property signified by the adjectives or the proportion of certainly on the part of the speaker.

(35) a. 管子完全/百分之百彎/直*（了）
    guǎnzi wánquán/ bǎifēnzhībǎi wān/zhí *(le)¹³
    pipe fully 100% bent/straight CRS
    'The pipe is now fully/100% bent/straightened.'

  b. 房間完全/百分之百滿/空*（了）
    fángjiān wánquán/ bǎifēnzhībǎi mǎn/kōng *(le)
    room fully 100% full/empty CRS
    'The room is now completely/100% full/empty.'

It is proposed here, then, that, when co-occurring with a *le* indicating a change of state, *wān* 'bent' and *zhí* 'straight' in (35a) are no longer typical adjectives but verbs indicating a result of change of state as signaled by *le*. That is, the resulting state after the event of bending a pipe is a bent pipe. Thus, the non-specific degree for a gradable adjective is totally absent in this verbal use. In other words, an adjective without a specific degree implication fails to provide a standard basis for a crisp judgement on proportion. Nevertheless, once a gradable adjective is used as a de-adjectival verb, it then denotes a resulting state that constitutes an absolute standard of proportion. As a de-adjectival verb, the non-specific degree meaning accompanying a gradable adjective is totally absent. This open-scale adjectives *gāo/ǎi* 'tall/short' in (36) are good because as the change-of-state predicates are condusive to a crisp judgement with a clear standard. The two otherwise open-scale adjectives *gāo/ǎi* 'tall/short' are both used as de-adjectival verbs and similarly cannot occur with a proportional adverb *bǎifēnzhībǎi* '100%' without the sentence-final *le*.

---

**13** Following Li & Thompson (1981), the perfective aspect marker -*le* is glossed as PFV and currently relevant perfect aspect marker *le* as CRS.

(36) 她弟弟百分之百高/矮*（了）
    tā   dìdi    bǎifēnzhībǎi  gāo/ǎi*   (le)
    3SG  brother  100%          tall/short  CRS
    'Her brother is now 100% taller/shorter.'

This hypothesized absence of an interfering non-specific degree in (36) is further supported by the data in (37) where a proportional degree word modifies a gradable adjective after a specific degree is qualified by *hěn* 'very'.

(37) a. 他弟弟百分之百很高/矮
       tā   dìdi    bǎifēnzhībǎi  hěn   gāo/ǎi
       3SG  brother  100%          very  tall/short
       'Her brother is 100% very tall/short. (in Chinese)'

    b. 這根管子百分之百很彎/直
       zhe-gen  guǎnzi  bǎifēnzhībǎi  hěn   wān/zhí
       DEM-CL   pipe    100%          very  bent/straight
       'The pipe is 100% very bent/straight. (in Chinese)'

    c. 房間間百分之百很滿/空
       fángjiān  bǎifēnzhībǎi  hěn   mǎn/kōng
       room      100%          very  full/empty
       'The room is 100% very full/empty. (in Chinese)'

Kennedy (2007a) observes that the English *empty* is a maximum standard adjective but, in a certain context, allows something less than a maximum standard in the sentence. For example, *The theater is empty tonight* describes a situation in which there are actually a few people in it, thus without reaching the maximum standard of *empty*. He describes this kind of use as context-dependent imprecise use of absolute adjectives.[14] However, the distributions of the adjectives in (34–37) demonstrate that there may not be any positive absolute adjective in Chinese, and the closed-scale meanings come from negation in (26) and temporally bound de-adejctival verbs, and adjectives. All gradable adjectives are used systematically just like the open-scale adjective, presumably because of the lexicalized indefinite degree meaning. Note that all of them must be either modified by a degree word like *hěn* 'very' or de-adjectivized into a verb to highlight proportions. This is far from accidental. As a matter of fact, there are no absolute adjec-

---

[14] They are variously known as "loose talk" (Unger 1975) or "pragmatic halos" (Lasersohn 1999) as well.

tives like the English *excellent, marvelous, wonderful, absolute,* etc. that cannot be modified by degree words in Chinese. Chinese gradable adjectives across the board (35–37) are context-dependent with respect to the uses of an appropriate degree word from the scale in (19). Such a typological feature is related to the non-specific degree of Chinese gradable adjectives, an observation that, having not been previously noted elsewhere, is discussed for the first time in this paper. Although the English adjectives in (38) are not discussed in Kennedy & McNally (2005), or Kennedy (2007a, b), they are probably closed-scale gradable adjectives in English but not so in Chinese. Although they can be used in direct comparison (38a), in Chinese *yōuxiù* 'excellent', unlike its English counterpart, can be modified by *hěn* 'very'.

(38) a. 你比他優秀
      *nǐ   bǐ       tā    yōuxiù*
      2SG  COMPAR  3SG  excellent
      'You are more excellent than he is.'

b. 你*(很)優秀
      *nǐ   \*(hěn)  yōuxiù*
      2SG  very     excellent
      '*You are very excellent.'

The examples in (39) are provided to show that even the adjective meaning *absolute* is not an absolute one but has a non-specific degree in Chinese, as it must co-occur with a degree word just like any open-scale adjective. This restriction is far from exceptional in cases motivated by pragmatics.

(39) a. ??你這樣說絕對
      *??nǐ  zheyàng  shuō  juéduì*
      2SG  DEM-CL  say   absolute
      '*Your saying it this way is absolute.'

b. 你這樣說比较絕對
      *nǐ  zheyàng  shuō  bǐjiào  juéduì*
      2SG  DEM-CL  say  compare  absolute
      '??Your saying it this way is relatively absolute.'

c. 你這樣說很絕對
      *nǐ  zheyàng  shuō  hěn  juéduì*
      2SG  DEM-CL  say  very  absolute
      '??Your saying it this way is very absolute.'

d. 你這樣説非常絕對
   nǐ    zheyàng  shuō  fēicháng  juéduì
   2SG  DEM-CL   say    not-often  absolute
   '??Your saying it this way is very, very absolute.'

e. 你這樣説最絕對
   nǐ    zheyàng  shuō  zuì   juéduì
   2SG  DEM-CL   say    most  absolute
   '??Your saying it this way is most absolute.'

f. 你這樣説超絕對
   nǐ    zheyàng  shuō  chāo   juéduì
   2SG  DEM-CL   say    super  absolute
   '??Your saying it this way is super absolute.'

Kennedy (2007a: 36) proposed an Interpretive Economy constraint, given in (40), to account for the imprecise uses, allowing for context dependent truth conditions only as a last resort. That is, the conventional meaning of *empty* normally denotes a certain maximum standard, and only in some specific contexts, can it be pragmatically motivated to deviate from the maximum standard, i.e., in the sentence *The theater is empty tonight* where the adjective *empty* is allowed in a particular context, in spite of the existence of a few people in the theater.

(40) Interpretive Economy
Maximize the contribution of the conventional meanings of the elements of a sentence to the computation of its truth conditions.

But the data in (35–39) demonstrate that what dominates the co-occurrences between Chinese gradable adjectives and degree words is not the general scalar property but the non-specific degree meaning systematically lexicalized into all Chinese gradable adjectives. Therefore, the maximum/minimum standard required by the conventional meanings of *empty* to the computation of the truth conditions must include some non-specific degree meaning for the covert Chinese closed-scale adjectives. The non-specific degree for open-scale adjectives gives rise to an infinite degree meaning because of the unlimited scalar meaning. But the covert closed-scale adjectives with the maximal/minimal degree meanings only contain the non-specific degree meaning without the infiniteness of open-scale adjectives, thus disallowing their occurrence without either a degree word or a sentence-final *le*. The data in (41a) once again show that the bare adjective *empty* in *The theater is empty today* behaves just like any gradable adjective in

Chinese, systematically requiring a specific degree marker and does not allow the imprecise reading that is permissible in English.

(41) a. ??今天劇場空
   *??jīntiān jùchǎng kōng*
   today theater empty
   'The theater is empty today.'

   b. 今天劇場比較空
   *jīntiān jùchǎng bǐjiào kōng*
   today theater compare empty
   'The theater is relatively empty today.'

   c. 今天劇場很空
   *jīntiān jùchǎng hěn kōng*
   today theater very empty
   'The theater is very empty today.'

   d. 今天劇場非常空
   *jīntiān jùchǎng fēicháng kōng*
   today theater very-very empty
   'The theater is very, very empty today.'

   e. 今天劇場最空
   *jīntiān jùchǎng zuì kōng*
   today theater most empty
   'The theater is emptiest today.'

*Kōng*, an adjective somewhat similar to the English *empty*, is nevertheless allowed to have the closed-scale meaning as a de-adjectival verb with the sentence-final perfect marker *le* in (42a). It is important to note that the non-specific degree is only part of the conventional meaning of a gradable adjective. But used as a de-adjectival verb, *kōng* does not contain a non-specific degree constraint. The *yībàn* 'half' in (42b) is presumably a syntactic object of the de-adjectival transitive verb *kōng* signaling a specific measureable value, testifying to *kōng*'s verbal status here.

(42) a. 今天劇場空了
   *jīntiān jùchǎng kōng le*
   today theater empty CRS
   'The theater is emptied.'

b. 今天劇場空了一半
   *jīntiān jùchǎng kōng le yībàn*
   today theater empty PFV one-half
   'The theater is half empty.'

c. 今天劇場空得很
   *jīntiān jùchǎng kōng de hěn*
   today theater empty DE very
   'The theater is extremely empty.'

(42c) is still another verbal construction, namely, Verb$_{intransitive}$-得很, Verb-*de hěn*, in which there must be an intransitive verb. The de-adjectival verb *kōng* 'empty' can occur without an object in this construction to indicate a situation in which *kōng* is still aptly used to describe a theater with only a few people in it, similar to the imprecise use of the English closed-scaled *empty*. In other words, the non-specific degree lexicalized in a Chinese gradable adjective does not exist in a de-adjectival verb. Note that the Verb$_{intransitive}$-*de hěn* construction is rather productive as is suggested by the data in (43). In these verbal cases, the non-specific degree is no longer relevant to the uses of de-adjectival verbs in signaling a highly subjective, or context-dependent, belief/attitude with respect to the maximum/minimum standard of a certain property.

(43) a. 棍子彎得很
       *gùnzi wān de hěn*
       rod bend DE very
       'The rod was completely bent.'

   b. 我好得很
      *wǒ hǎo de hěn*
      1SG good DE very
      'I am extremely well.'

   c. 姚明高得很
      *yáo míng gāo de hěn*
      NAME tall DE very
      'Yao Ming is extremely tall.'

   d. 他絕對得很
      *Tā juéduì de hěn*
      3SG absolute DE very
      '(His attitude) is irrationally absolute.'

The schemas in (44) describe a. an intransitive verbal construction denoting a change-of-state with a de-adjectival verb like those in (42a) and (42b), a transitive verbal construction with a syntactic object of measurement as in (42b).

(44) a. [(NP) [DE-ADJ $le_{CRS}$] ↔ [(Theme) [BECOME < ADJ >]]]$_S$
     b. [(NP) [DE-ADJ NP] ↔ [(Theme) [ DE-ADJ [MEASURE]]]]$_S$

The schema in (45) describes an even more grammaticalized construction, i.e., the V$_{intransitive}$-*de hěn* construction, in spite of the imprecise uses, regularly denotates a maximum, or minimum, standard in relation to a property signaled by a de-adjectival verb (43).

(45) [(NP) [DE-ADJ-*de hěn*] ↔ [(Theme) [BECOME-[ADJ]$_{maximum/minimum\ standard}$]$_S$

# 7 Conclusion

In summary, this paper proposes that Chinese gradable adjectives that lexicalize a non-specific degree are typologically quite different from English adjectives. Such a hypothesis, in comparison with the others in the available literature, appears to provide a stronger and better account of Chinese adjectives. It is assumed that many of the obligatory uses with, or without, a degree word in various contexts follow from the non-specific degree that is part of the conventional meanings of gradable adjectives. Whereas open-scale adjectives with a lexical non-specific degree meaning are commonly used in good wishes and special contexts requiring no limit of degree must not co-occur with a degree word, open-scale adjectives as such must otherwise co-occur with a degree word from an ordered set to designate a specific degree with respect to a property. They can be used with proportional degree words only as de-adjectival verb or marked by a degree word with a specific degree meaning. Although non-specific degree is primarily a lexical feature of Chinese gradable adjectives, all of the gradable adjectives can be used in a special V-得很, V–*de hěn*, construction, linking to an absolute maximum/minimum standard denoted by this construction.

According to Kennedy & McNally (2005) and Kennedy (2007a), closed-scale adjectives should include maximum/minimum elements corresponding to absolute standards. Interestingly in the Chinese adjectival system, unlike that in English, all positive gradable adjectives are relative without absolute maximum/minimum elements as they are regularly used with degree words. Furthermore, Chinese does not have deverbal adjectives like *done, acquainted,* etc. collocating with different degree words like *well, much, very*. Thus, corresponding Chinese adjectives are modified by the same set of degree words for open-scale adjectives. Proportional degrees are signaled by de-adjectival verbs, not by bare adjectives. Furthermore, the set of adjectives like *mǎn* 'full', *kōng* 'empty', *gān* 'dry', *shī* 'wet', etc. that, in positive form, are relative like open-scale adjectives, can signal closed-scale meanings only when used as de-adjectival verbs or negated. Whereas further work is needed to uncover the exact reasons for this phenomenon, (46) is a schematic description of the scalar properties of these covert closed-scale adjectives. The dots in the parantheses denotates the hidden nature of the boundedness of a covert closed-scale adjective accounting for the fact that they are used just like any open-scale adjective with a lexicalized non-specific degree without implying any absolute maximum/minimum standard. The use of a degree word in each instance is totally determined by a context-dependent standard in indirect comparison.

(46)  (.)___*chāo*___*zuì*___*fēicháng*___*hěn*___*bǐjià*___(.)
       super   most   very-very   very   comparatively

However, the hidden boundedness of these set of adjectives manifest themselves when they are negated or used as de-adjectival verbs.

**Acknowledgements:** I want to thank editor of the volume, an anonymous reviewer, Professor Elizabeth Traugott, and Professor Jee Young Peck whose valuable comments have helped me see many logical problems and inconsistencies in my earlier drafts. I am also grateful to all of my colleagues and friends who have given me valuable comments and suggestions after hearing my presentations of earlier versions of this paper at Stanford, Tsinghua University, Beijing Language University, Nankai University, Western Washington University, San Francisco State University, and at the 2018 IACL conference at the University of Wisconsin in Madison. Still I am solely responsible for all the remaining problems and issues in this paper.

# References

Bolinger, Dwight. 1972. *Degree Words*. The Hague and Paris: Mouton.
Brinton, Laurel J. and Elizabeth Closs Traugott. 2005. *Lexicalization and Language Change*. Cambridge: Cambridge University Press.
Guo, Rui. 郭銳 2002. *Xiandai Hanyu Cilei Yanjiu* (A study of lexical categories in Modern Chinese). Beijing: Commercial Press.
Kennedy, Christopher. 2007a. Vagueness and grammar: the semantics of relative and absolute gradable adjectives. *Linguistics and Philosophy* 30.1: 1–45.
Kennedy, Christopher. 2007b. Modes of comparison. *Proceedings of the Annual Meeting of the Chicago Linguistic Society* 43.1: 141–65.

Kennedy, Christopher and Louise McNally. 2005. Scale structure and the semantic typology of gradable predicates. *Language* 81.2: 345–81.
Larserohn, Peter. 1999. Pragmatic halos. *Language* 75.3: 522–51.
Li, Charles N. and Sandra A. Thompson. 1981. *Mandarin Chinese: A Functional Reference Grammar*. Berkeley: University of California Press.
Lin, Jingxia and Jeeyoung Peck. 2016. Classification of Mandarin Chinese simple adjectives: A scale-based analysis of their quantitative denotations. *Language and Linguistics* 17.6: 827–55.
Liu, Chen-Sheng Luther. 2010. The positive morpheme in Chinese and the adjectival structure. *Lingua* 120.4: 1010–56.
Liu, Feng-his. 2016. Syntactic sources of adjectives in Mandarin Chinese. *Studies in Chinese Linguistics* 33-1: 39–54.
Liu Yuehua, Wenyu Pan, and Wei Gu. 劉月華、潘文娛、劉韡 2004. *Shiyong Xiandai Hanyu Yufa* (A practical grammar of Modern Chinese). Beijing: Commercial Press.
Paradis, Carita. 2001. Adjectives and boundedness. *Cognitive Linguistics* 12.1: 47–65.
Paul, Waltraud. 2005. Adjectival modification in Mandarin Chinese and related issues. *Linguistics* 43–4: 757–93.
Peck, Jeeyoung, Jingxia Lin, and Chaofen Sun. 2013. Aspectual classification of Mandarin Chinese verbs: a perspective of scale structure. *Language and Linguistics* 14.4: 663–700.
Rappaport Hovav, Malka and Beth Levin. 2010. Reflections on manner/result complementarity. In Edit Doron, Malka Rappaport Hovav and Ivy Sichel (eds), *Syntax, Lexical Semantics, and Event Structure*. Oxford and New York: Oxford University Press.
Smith, Carlotta. 1997. *The Parameter of Aspect*. Dordrecht, The Netherlands: Kluwer Academic Publishers.
Sproat, Richard and Shih, Chilin. 1988. Prenominal adjectival ordering in English and Mandarin. In James Blevins and Juli Carter (eds.), *Proceedings of NELs* 18–2: 465–89. Amherst, MA: GLSA.
Sun, Chaofen. 2017. The grammar of Chinese nouns. In Istvan Kecskes and Chaofen Sun (eds), *Key Issues in Chinese as a Second Language Research*, 145–61. New York & London: Routledge.
Sun, Chaofen and Ming Chew Teo. 2017. Temporally closed situations for the Chinese perfective LE 了. In Rachel Giora and Michael Haugh (Eds.), *Doing Intercultural Pragmatics: Cognitive, Linguistic, and Sociopragmatic Perspectives on Language Use*, 233–55. Berlin and Boston: De Gruyter Mouton.
Sybesma, Rint. 1999. *The Mandarin VP*. Dordrecht, Netherlands: Springer.
Traugott, Elizabeth Closs and Graeme Trousdale. 2013. *Constructionalization and Constructional Changes*. Oxford: Oxford University Press.
Unger, Peter. 1975. *Ignorance*. Oxford: Clarendon Press.
Wang, William S-Y. 1965. Two aspect markers. *Language* 41.3 457–70.
Zhan, Fangqiong and Chaofen Sun. 2013. A copula analysis of shì in the Chinese cleft construction. *Language and Linguistics* 14.4: 755–89.
Zhu, Dexi. 朱德熙 1984. *Yufa Jiangyi* (Lecture notes on Chinese grammar). Beijing: Commercial Press.

Yancheng He and Fuxiang Wu
# Compounding word-formation in Ahou Gelao

## 1 Introduction and preliminaries

The Gelao language is one member of the Kra branch of the Tai-Kadai family. As one of its dialects, Ahou Gelao is the native language of the Gelao people inhabiting Hongfeng Village of Pudi Township, Dafang County, on the eastern edge of the Yunnan-Guizhou Plateau in the western part of Guizhou Province, China. Being a member of the Tai-Kadai family, Ahou Gelao is an analytic and tonal language. It shows SVO word order typology and head-initial pattern in nominal phrases. Within the nominal phrase, all modifiers except numerals follow the modified head, with demonstratives coming last. This is just the opposite of Chinese. For more detailed descriptions of the language see He (2008, 2012). Even though Ahou Gelao is genetically unrelated to Chinese, it displays similarities with Chinese in quite a few ways due to areal diffusion, with compounding being one of the similar properties. Specifically, compounding serves as the key morphological process in Ahou Gelao; the same is true in Mandarin Chinese (Ceccagno and Basciano 2007: 207–208, Dong 2011: 8, Tham 2015: 306).

From a typological point of view, this paper provides a brief survey of the compounding processes in Ahou Gelao, touching upon (1) the criteria for distinguishing compounds from phrases, (2) syntactic and semantic relations of constituents in compounds, and (3) compounding in different word classes. In addition, a brief introduction is provided into the lexicalization and/or grammaticalization in the compounding process, as well as the motivation for and mechanism of lexicalization. In short, we will relate the compounding process with the processes of lexicalization and/or grammaticalization throughout the paper where applicable.

Before probing the details of compounding in Ahou Gelao, a brief overview of some related theoretical and terminological issues is necessary. We will begin with compounding and then mention two relevant issues: lexicalization and grammaticalization. After that, we will briefly mention the lexical category classification in Ahou Gelao.

Regarding the definition of compound, there seems to be no consensus among scholars. Just as Lieber and Stekauer (2009: 6) claim, in spite of extensive research into compounds and compounding processes, there are hardly any universally accepted criteria for determining what a compound is. The reasons why it is difficult to come up with a satisfying and universally applicable definition for compound, as Lieber and Stekauer (2009: 4) identify, are twofold. Firstly, the elements that make up compounds in some languages are not free-standing words, but rather stems or roots. Secondly, it is not always easy to make a clean distinction between compounds on the one hand and derived words or phrases on the other.

The criteria for distinguishing between a syntactic construction and a compound are not well established. Possible criteria proposed so far include phonological (stress, vowel harmony, the sandhi process, tonal pattern s, vowel deletion or reduction, etc.), morphological (the behavior of the compound with respect to inflection, presence of linking elements or special formatives, the loss of syntactic dependency markers, special constituent order), syntactic (syntactic impenetrability, inseparability, and inalterability), semantic (non-compositionality, degree of lexicalization or listedness in the lexicon), and orthographic (written as a single orthographic word).[1] None of these are foolproof or cross-linguistically applicable but language-specific.

The study of compounds involves many aspects and issues, including, but not limited to, headedness, exocentricity, productivity, the lexical category of the constituents (and the whole compound as well). The grammatical and semantic relationships of the constituents, and thus the classification of the whole compound, along with the relationship between compounding and other morphosyntactic phenomena such as incorporation, serial verbs, phrasal verbs, and the like complicate their study as well.

As a type of word formation, the process of compounding, as revealed by some recent studies such as Lehmann (2002), Packard (2004), Brinton and Traugott (2005), Lightfoot (2011), Wischer (2011), among others, can be closely interrelated with the processes of lexicalization and/or grammaticalization. While it is plausible that compounding may correlate with lexicalization, as they both are usually closely associated with the lexicon, it may be not so easy to see the relation of compounding, if there is one, to grammaticalization. For this reason, a look at the relation of lexicalization to grammaticalization will, perhaps, help understand the correlations between compounding and grammaticalization.

Compared with grammaticalization, scholarly attention that has been paid to lexicalization is relatively recent and relatively sparse. And, as Lightfoot (2011: 438) puts it, it was largely through the recognition of much language change phenomena associated with grammaticalization that scholars began, by the early years of the 21st century, to take more notice of the seemingly opposite or parallel type of change we call lexicalization. In a sense, the study of lexicalization is a by-product of that of grammaticalization.

---

[1] For detailed discussion see introductory works such as Aikhenvald (2007), Lieber and Stekauer (2009), among others.

Lightfoot (2011) is a relatively recent and thorough overview of representative works to date on lexicalization with regard to grammaticalization, and various commonalities and differences between the two are examined. The article profiles how notions such as these of grammaticalization and lexicalization in the literature have varied, and how relatively recently more of a consensus exists. " ... they began to differentiate types of lexicalization, often from degrammaticalization. Degrammaticalization came to mean more that which is somehow an opposite process to grammaiticalization, and thus began to free lexicalization from that oppositional sense."(Lightfoot 2011: 442) Now more and more scholars recognize that there are broader and narrower notions of lexicalization, the broader one entailing anything entering the lexical inventory, and the narrower one including only those gradual and unmotivated types of lexicalization.

Outlining the main readings of lexicalization mainly from a diachronic or synchronic sense, Hohenhaus (2005) holds that lexicalization in the diachronic sense includes formal changes (formal lexicalization) and demotivation or loss or addition of semantic features (semantic lexicalization).

The notions and nature of (narrow) lexicalization with respect to grammaticalization are best summarized by Brinton and Traugott (2005), as indicated by the definitions they provide for these two types of changes:

> Lexicalization is the change whereby in certain linguistic contexts speakers use a syntactic construction or word formation as a new contentful form with formal and semantic properties that are not completely derivable or predictable from the constituents of the construction or the word formation pattern. Over time there may be further loss of internal constituency and the item may become more lexical. (Brinton and Traugott 2005: 96)

> Grammaticalization is the change whereby in certain linguistic contexts speakers use parts of a construction with a grammatical function. Over time the resulting grammatical item may become more grammatical by acquiring more grammatical functions and expanding its host-classes. (Brinton and Traugott 2005: 99)

Similarities and differences between these two types of changes are indicated in the definitions. Clearly, (narrow) lexicalization is not the reverse change of grammaticalization, contrary to the traditional view that grammaticalization and lexicalization are quite distinct, even opposite processes. Instead, lexicalization along with grammaticalization can be working together. "Again, it is not excluded that lexicalization and grammaticalization occur jointly in a given case." Lehmann (2002: 16) claims, using English *wanna* and *gonna* as cases in point, stating that in the former the combination of a lexical and a grammatical morpheme lexicalizes to a modal, in the latter, the combination of semi-grammaticalized *going* with a grammatical morpheme is lexicalized and further grammaticalized .

Similar phenomena are quite common in Chinese (Wu 2005; Dong 2011), where a syntactic combination of two adjacent words (lexical or grammatical, even clitic) tends to lexicalize into a new lexeme, with the grammatical word or clitic further grammaticalizing into an intra-word component of the new lexeme. Parallel changes, as observed by Wu (2005), are also attested in some languages of the Tai-Kadai family and Hmong-Mien family in China which are similar to Chinese in morpho-syntactic typology.

With the 'degenerate' resultative $V_2$ endings such as $-dào$ 到 'attain' in gestalt $V_1$-$V_2$ words as an illustrating example of grammaticalization in modern Mandarin, Packard (2004: 262) discusses the relationship between lexicalization and grammaticalization and draws a similar conclusion that the lexicalization of morphemes often involves their grammaticalization.

An important point to keep in mind about the relationship between lexicalization and grammaticalization is that, just as Packard (2004: 264) points out, "although they are highly correlated and do often co-occur, they are nonetheless demonstrably independent phenomena."

Now we turn to the topic of the correlations between the processes of compounding and grammaticalization. As Wischer (2011: 356) points out, if grammaticalization is a process by which linguistic elements change into constituents of grammar, or by which grammatical items become more grammatical in time, and on the other hand, if word formation processes, such as compounding, derivation, conversion, clipping, or blending, 'allow for the production of new lexical items', we would have to propose that grammaticalization and word formation must be distinct processes, possibly even contradictory or mirror images.

After elucidating the relationship between grammaticalization and such processes of word formation as derivations and phrasal compounds, Wischer (2011: 364) claims that word formation, though usually closely associated with the lexical domain of a language, is in various ways interrelated with processes of grammaticalization, the reason for which seems to lie in the fuzzy relationship between lexicon and grammar. Specifically, as Wischer (2011: 362) argues, the formation of such 'phrasal compounds' as *instead of, somebody, look up, write down*, etc., whereby a lexical word has lost its original lexical meaning and has become an integral part of a new grammatical word, is rightly treated as grammaticalization. On the other hand, due to their univerbation and idiomaticization, they are similarly subject to a lexicalization process. "Finally, the formation of phrasal compounds can be accompanied by a grammaticalization process, which may affect the whole construction or only part of it."(Wischer 2011: 364)

Like many other analytic languages, Chinese in particular, word classes in Ahou Gelao are largely determined by their syntactic properties. Accordingly, twelve word classes can be identified: nouns, verbs, adjectives, adverbs, pronouns, demonstratives, classifiers, prepositions, numerals, particles, interjections and conjunctions. Despite the fact that adjectives and verbs (intransitive verbs particularly) share many commonalities, including the ability to take aspect markers and to be followed by a modifier of degree or other modifiers, it remains helpful to distinguish adjectives from verbs in Ahou Gelao, as adjectives manifest other syntactic properties that can distinguish them as a separate word class. One of these properties is that they can uniquely be reduplicated in an A-B-B pattern, e.g. $liaŋ^{31}$ (black)-$ʔlən^{33}ʔlən^{33}$ ($ʔlən^{33}$ 'dark') 'pitch black', $wa^{31}$ (yellow) -$jy^{13}jy^{13}$ ($jy^{13}$ 'peach') 'golden yellow', $ləu^{31}$ (blue)-$ɣuŋ^{33}ɣuŋ^{33}$ ($ɣuŋ^{33}$ 'sound') 'deep blue', among others. For more discussion on lexical category classification in Ahou Gelao see He (2012).

# 2 The criteria for distinguishing compounds from phrases

Compounding in Ahou Gelao can be roughly defined as a formation process based on the combination of two or more independent morphemes that results in the formation of a unitary word. Here "independent" does not necessarily mean that the components need to be free, as it is often the case that each part of a compound may be either free or bound as a result of diachronic changes such as lexicalization and grammaticalization. To adopt Aikhenvald's (2007: 24) expression, "compounding involves word-formation based on the combination of at least two potentially free forms".

In Ahou Gelao, compounds display some behaviors and properties that help distinguish them from phrases. These characteristics are mainly of four types: (1) phonological; (2) morphological; (3) morpho-syntactic and (4) semantic. They are illustrated in turn below.

## 2.1 Phonological criteria

Ahou Gelao compounds often form one phonological word and are characterized by single stress. Concordant with the head-modifier pattern of Ahou Gelao phrases, compounds in this language are usually stressed on the head of two elements, e.g. ´$haŋ^{33}.tiɔ^{13}$ 'dawn/daybreak' versus ´$haŋ^{33}$ ´$tiɔ^{13}$ 'the day is falling/dawning'. This can also be proven by the fact that contrastive stress can only fall on the stress center (the head) of a compound. In other words, it is the whole compound rather than the individual elements contrasted that is stressed. If the contrasted components of the compounds are stressed, it will result in a phrase reading. For example, the compounds $tɔ^{55}nɛ^{31}.ʔna^{55}$ (earth-wet) 'mud/wet earth' and $tɔ^{55}nɛ^{31}.xəu^{13}$ (earth-dry) 'dry earth' are both based on the noun $tɔ^{55}nɛ^{31}$ 'earth', and both place the stress on this first element. If the two are contrasted, the contrastive stress falls on the stress centers (the head) of the two compounds (in both cases on $tɔ^{55}nɛ^{31}$ 'earth'), rather than on the parts of the compounds that are different, namely $ʔna^{55}$ and $xəu^{13}$. However, if the same structures are taken as phrases, contrastive stress is free to fall on the parts that differ. So, like a single word, compounds present only a single possible position for contrastive stress.

In the case of a predicate-complement (V-C) compound, the complement receives the main stress (see Section 3.3). This may seem contradictory to the head-stressed pattern mentioned above, but it turns out that the semantic head falls on the complement rather than on the preceding verb. In other words, the complement carries the main meaning to be expressed. Thus it is, in fact, still consonant and concordant with the head-stressed pattern. For instance, in the compound $tiɔ^{13}lin^{31}$ (fall-late) 'lag behind; be late', the main meaning 'being late' is carried by the second (complement) constituent $lin^{31}$, with the first (predicate) element $tiɔ^{13}$ functioning as something like a copular or linking verb.

Another kind of phonological mark on compounds in Ahou Gelao is the widespread tone sandhi 353 on the head of the structure used to indicate that it is a unitary word rather than a phrase. For instance, the plain sequence $haŋ^{33}\ lin^{31}$ (day-back/late) is usually interpreted as 'the next day' whereas the changed tone sequence $haŋ^{353\sim33}lin^{31}$ has developed the more specialized meaning of 'tomorrow'. Parallel examples are $gaŋ^{31}\ naŋ^{33}$ (like-this) 'like this' vs. $gaŋ^{353\sim31}naŋ^{33}$ 'how/however', $xən^{33}\ naŋ^{33}$ (NCL.HU-this)[2] 'this one (person)' vs. $xən^{353\sim33}naŋ^{33}$ 'who/whoever', among others. In a sense, the variant tone 353 can be regarded as a mark indicating the ongoing process of lexicalization, which turns the whole structure into a unitary compound.

Noting that tone sandhi of this type generally involves the depletion of a whole syllable, which in most cases is $nei^{55}$ 'to, for, of', a widely-used verb-derived grammatical morpheme (serving as a syntactic dependency marker being its major function; see more details below). As a matter of fact, diachronically, it is safe to say that where there is a tone sandhi of this type, there is the depletion of a whole syllable, though the original structure and the particular syllable therein may be not so easily reconstructed or traced back, due to the lack of a transitional stage that can link them to the current tone sandhi form. So, perhaps

---

[2] Abbreviations are listed on the front pages of this volume.

it would be more appropriate to say that it is the depletion of a whole syllable that gives rise to the tone sandhi, as this conforms to the process of lexicalization or grammaticalization that leads to phonological reduction on the one hand and semantic specification on the other. In other words, this rising-and-falling tone 353 is a relic or trace of the particle $n\varepsilon i^{55}$ in the predominant 'head + $n\varepsilon i^{55}$ + complement' syntactic pattern during its lexicalization into a compound. Specifically, the grammatical morpheme $n\varepsilon i^{55}$ is fusing with the head (usually a nominal or verbal element) that comes before it when the whole syntactic construction is lexicalized into a compound. This may be considered a process of morphologization, a process whereby an originally autonomous word becomes a bound morpheme.[3] As Hopper and Traugott (1993: 131) point out, "the beginnings of morphologization must be sought in repeated use of syntactic constructions". It is the frequent syntactic collocation of a particular word class with a particular type of clitic that most typically leads to morphologization (Hopper and Traugott 1993: 132).

## 2.2 Morphological criteria

Compounds in Ahou Gelao can be recognized on some morphological grounds. One of these morphological properties is that, in most cases, compounds belong to the same word class as their first (head) members, for instance, $k^ह un^{55} dia^{33}$ (generation-young) 'younger generation' ([N + Adj]N), $\chi a^{13} \eta^{55}$ (head-river) 'riverhead' ([N + N]N), $ha\eta^{33} z u^{13}$ (day-grow) 'birthday' ([N + V]$_N$), as can be seen from the following discussions on the structure of compounds. This may be attributable to and concordant with the head-modifier structure of phrases in this language, as mentioned earlier.

A second morphological property characteristic of Ahou Gelao compounds is the absence of the aforementioned syntactic dependency marker $n\varepsilon i^{55}$, e.g. $l\varepsilon i^{55} wa^{33}.\chi a^{13} \gamma ui^{31}$ (girl-heaven) 'fairy' < $l\varepsilon i^{55} wa^{33}\ n\varepsilon i^{55}\ \chi a^{13} \gamma ui^{31}$ 'lady from heaven'. Sometimes, the deletion of this marker is incomplete but has left a trace on the head which causes it to undergo a tone sandhi into 353, as mentioned earlier, e.g. $ma^{33} hye^{353\ \sim 13}.xuai^{33} liai^{13}$ (vehicle/machine-spin.hemp) 'spinning wheel' < $ma^{33} hye^{13}\ n\varepsilon i^{55}\ xuai^{33}\ liai^{13}$ 'machine for spinning hemp'. This can be seen as a transient stage in the development of a syntactic structure into a unitary compound word, an ongoing process of lexicalization of a non-word unit into a word, with form and meaning evolving harmoniously and form undergoing morphological reduction and meaning specialization.

---

[3] We would like to thank Prof. Janet Z. Xing for reminding us of this term.

Some compounds in Ahou Gelao can be identified by the presence of some linker morphemes. These compounds are restricted to some cardinal numerals, namely, 11 to 19 (or some compound terms based on these numerals), and 110,000 to 190,000. Specifically, the compounds for 11 to 19 are formed in a way that the units precede the tens on the one hand and a classifier (generally $ma^{33}$ is used in simple counting but other classifiers will be used instead when used with specific nouns) must insert itself between one and the other, thus giving rise to $sɿ^{55}ma^{33}ɕe^{13}$ (one-$ma^{33}$-ten) '11', $səu^{33}ma^{33}ɕe^{13}$ (two-$ma^{33}$-ten) '12', $tɿ^{33}ma^{33}ɕe^{13}$ (three-$ma^{33}$-ten) '13', etc. In other words, the classifier $ma^{33}$ here serves no function other than that of a linker, infixed to numerals from 11 to 19. In addition, the form for 'ten' used in this pattern is exclusively realized as $ɕe^{13}$, different from its other form, $hye^{13}$. The figures 20 to 90 are expressed as $səu^{33}hye^{13}$ (two-ten) '20', $tɿ^{33}hye^{13}$ (three-ten) '30', $pau^{33}hye^{13}$ (four-ten) '40', etc., while the numerals in between as $səu^{33}hye^{13}sɿ^{55}$ (two-ten-one) '21', $səu^{33}hye^{13}tɿ^{33}$ (two-ten-three) '23', etc.

Parallel to the pattern of 'one-$ma^{33}$-ten' for teens, the forms for 110,000 to 190,000 are constructed in a similar way, with $ɣuaŋ^{13}$ '10,000' serving as the intervening linker, thus resulting in $sɿ^{55}ɣuaŋ^{13}ɕe^{13}$ (one-$ɣuaŋ^{13}$-ten) '110,000', $səu^{33}ɣuaŋ^{13}ɕe^{13}$ (two-$ɣuaŋ^{13}$-ten) '120,000', $tɿ^{33}ɣuaŋ^{13}ɕe^{13}$ (three-$ɣuaŋ^{13}$-ten) '130,000', etc.[4]

## 2.3 Morpho-syntactic criteria

With the exception of the linker morphemes mentioned above, other morphemes usually cannot be inserted in between the components of a compound, nor is a pause possible between two immediate constituents of a compound (since a compound in Ahou Gelao can ultimately be analyzed as consisting of two immediate constituents), without giving rise to a phrase interpretation. For example, the compound $ɣuaŋ^{31}.ʔue^{33}guaŋ^{33}laŋ^{33}$ (wind-whirl.round.and.round) 'whirlwind/cyclone,' allows the insertion of no other morphemes between the two immediate constituents of $ɣuaŋ^{31}$ 'wind' and $ʔue^{33}guaŋ^{33}laŋ^{33}$ 'whirl round and round'. The insertion of any morpheme – the syntactic dependency marker $nɛi^{55}$ mentioned above, for instance – will turn the whole structure into the phrase 'wind of the whirling-round-and-round type'. Nor is a single pause or hesitation allowed therein either of which will render it as 'wind is whirling round and round'.

Similarly, components of compounds cannot be modified separately. So, the compound $mm^{31}.bm^{33}χən^{33}$ (rain-pass.road) 'shower (of rain)' can only take a modifier as a whole, e.g. $[mm^{31}bm^{33}χən^{33}]ɬiuŋ^{33}$ 'big shower (of rain)', and

---

[4] See He (2008, 2012) for more information on the numeral system in Ahou Gelao.

not *[mɯn³¹ɬiuŋ³³]bɯn³³χən³³ 'heavy rain is passing through the road', or *mɯn-³¹bɯn³³[χən³³ɬiuŋ³³] 'the rain is passing through the big road'.

Furthermore, components of compounds cannot undergo co-referential deletion. Therefore, one has to say mɯn³¹ʔai³³ sɔ³³ mɯn³¹ɬiuŋ³³ (drizzle or heavy.rain) 'drizzle or heavy rain' instead of *mɯn³¹ʔai³³ sɔ³³ ɬiuŋ³³ 'the rain is small or big'. However, some compounds having numerals as their components seem to allow the numeral parts to undergo co-referential deletion in coordination with simple juxtaposition, e.g. ma³³-ʕɛ³¹.-sau¹³-lai³¹ 'August, September' (literally 'the eighth, ninth month'). But it turns out that this co-referential deletion pattern is not productive, as it carries quite a few conditions: (i) it is restricted to the simple juxtaposition of only two members, (ii) the numerals involved are limited to 1 to 10, and (iii) the numbers have to be adjacent in sequence though to which two adjacent numbers the deletion can be applied seems to be idiomatic and unpredictable, as seen in, say, mau³¹-miaŋ³¹ 'five, six' which is more acceptable than miaŋ³¹-tɛ³³ 'six, seven'.

## 2.4 Semantic criteria

Although not all compounds are idiomatic in meaning, idiomaticity, or non-compositionality of the meaning of the entire unit can still be used as a semantic criterion for compounds. Generally, the meaning of a compound in Ahou Gelao is not the simple accumulation of the meanings of its components and thus not always predictable. For example, qʰa⁵⁵tsʰuai³³ (excrement-cat), literally 'cat's excrement', means 'mould/mildew', which is hard to predict from the combined meanings of its components. Similar examples are mɯn³¹ʔau¹³ (rain-white) 'hail', sau³³χɛ³³ (share/divide-family) 'live apart', guai³¹qʰɛ¹³ (year-foot) 'previous years', among others. While, in general, this is the rule, there are some compounds whose meaning can be intuited from the sum of the meanings of its components: kʰuŋ⁵⁵dia³³ (generation-young) 'younger generation', lɛ³¹nia¹³ (do-accompany) 'keep company' and yuaŋ³¹ʔue³³guaŋ³³laŋ³³ (wind-whirl-round.and.round) 'whirlwind/cyclone' can serve as illustrating examples. As a matter of fact, "...the degree of relatedness between the meaning of a compound and the meaning of its parts forms a continuum"(Li and Thompson 1981: 48). This may be related to such factors as degree of lexicalization, frequency of use and contextual appropriateness, as is the case in Mandarin Chinese as pointed out by Dong (2011: 39–47) and some other Chinese scholars.

In fact, just as Benczes (2006: 184) points out, frequency of use and degree of lexicalization can influence the ways that novel compounds and existing compounds are processed: "Hence novel words will be processed in terms of their constituents, while already existing words will vary to the degree to which they are processed by their constituents and as a whole, depending on their frequency or degree of lexicalization."

So far, criteria from four aspects have been provided for distinguishing compounds from phrases. However, none of these criteria are universally valid, and it is more reliable to use the integration of all these criteria to distinguish between compounds and phrases.

## 3 Syntactic and semantic relations of constituents in compounds

Like many other Tai-Kadai and Sino-Tibetan languages in the area, Mandarin Chinese in particular (Dong 2011, Packard 2004), compounding is the major device on which the lexical stock of Ahou Gelao is built and by which it is augmented. Being a major and productive morphological process, compounding can be divided into several types based on different parameters or dimensions such as freedom of parts, whether its meaning is synthesizable or lexical, whether it is endocentric or exocentric in construction, whether it is syntactic or non-syntactic, and functional classes of constituents. And the principles by which compounds can be classified are, by and large, mutually independent and thus form several dimensions of cross-classification. For the sake of practicality and convenience, we shall choose and illustrate the most important dimensions in detail while noting other dimensions only when they appear to be particularly relevant.

As can be seen below, compounds in Ahou Gelao are superficially quite similar to phrases, since the structures of these words largely arise from the lexicalizations of syntactic structures.[5] Sometimes the same sequence of constituents may correspond either to a phrase or a compound. For example, $za^{13}$ 'ask' plus $ma^{33}$ 'wife' can be either a verb phrase 'ask one's wife' or a compound word 'propose marriage', depending on the syntactic environment in which they appear. As suggested by Anderson (1985: 46), compound classification can refer either to formal structure or to the semantic relations between a compound's components. So in this section, we will focus on the syntactic relations between components in compounds in detail while referring to their semantic relations only briefly, as this treatment appears to be more effective in displaying the syntactic correspondence between compounds and phrases.

---

**5** This is also true of Mandarin Chinese, as pointed out by Sinologists, e.g. Chao (1968), Packard (2004) and Dong (2011).

One should keep in mind, however, that, though most of the time the structures and rules of compounding are comparable to those of phrasal construction, compounding may sometimes display some morphological processes that are applicable only to compounds, due to their semantic unpredictability and idiosyncrasy as a result of lexicalization. This can probably further be ascribable to the 'description-name' distinction proposed by Bauer (1983: 142), to the effect that while descriptions have to be coherent or compositional, names merely have to be associated with an appropriate denotatum. According to Bauer, while there may be a parallel between word-formation and phrase formation in the way that syntactic collocation determines meaning, the two processes exhibit important differences, the crucial one being that sentences and phrases describe while lexemes name.

The syntactic relations between compound constituents in Ahou Gelao include the following five types: head-modifier, predicate-object, predicate-complement, subject-predicate, and coordinate, on which the classification of five corresponding types of compounds is based.[6] These five types of compounds will be stated and illustrated in turn below, along with a brief indication of the semantic relations between their components. The functional class of each type of compound as well as its components is also indicated.

## 3.1 Head-modifier compounds

The bulk of Ahou Gelao compounds are of this type. The first element serves as the center/head of the compound with the second, the modifier of the head, serving as a further explanation or restriction of it. In other words, head-modifier compounds are left-headed. The head of such compounds is generally a noun (1a-l) or nominal element (classifier) (1m-s) while the modifier can be a noun (1a-d), a verb (1e-h), an adjective (1i-l), a determiner (1m-n), etc. When the modifier is a transitive verb, the head is its semantic patient (1e, f). When it is an intransitive verb or adjective, the semantic role of the head can be anything other than patient (1g-l). In any case, the word class of such compounds as a whole is usually determined by the head and thus functions as a noun or nominal element. For example:

(1) a. $\chi\varepsilon^{33}\gamma u i^{31}$ (family-sky) 'heaven' [N-N]$_N$
    b. $ts^h \eta^{55} q^h \varepsilon^{13}$ (step-foot) 'footstep; footprint' [N-N]$_N$
    c. $q^h \partial n^{33} h y e^{33}$ (medicine-fire) 'gunpowder' [N-N]$_N$
    d. $\chi a^{13} \eta^{55}$ (head-river) 'riverhead' [N-N]$_N$

---

6 Compounds in Mandarin Chinese display similar syntactic structures (see Chao 1968, Dong 2011).

|  |  |  |  |  |
|---|---|---|---|---|
| e. | mɔ³³tiaŋ¹³ | (rice-cook) | 'congee/gruel' | [N-V]_N |
| f. | li¹³ta¹³ | (child-embrace) | 'adopted child' | [N-V]_N |
| g. | haŋ³³zu¹³ | (day-grow) | 'birthday' | [N-V]_N |
| h. | ŋ⁵⁵jye¹³ | (water-spew/overflow) | 'spring; fountain' | [N-V]_N |
| i. | kʰuŋ⁵⁵dia³³ | (generation-young) | 'younger generation' | [N-Adj]_N |
| j. | yəu³³wa³¹ | (people-new) | 'bride/bridegroom' | [N-Adj]_N |
| k. | χei⁵⁵le¹³ | (iron-raw) | 'pig iron' | [N-Adj]_N |
| l. | hu⁵⁵liaŋ³¹ | (cloud-dark) | 'cloudbank' | [N-Adj]_N |
| m. | haŋ³³naŋ³³ | (day-this) | 'today' | [CL-Det]_N |
| n. | ga³¹xe³³ | (corner-what) | 'where' | [CL-Det]_Pron |
| o. | lai³¹liuŋ³³ | (CL.FLT-land) | 'land' | [CL-N]_N |
| p. | lai³¹xaŋ⁵⁵ | (CL.FLT-ice) | 'ice' | [CL-N]_N |
| q. | lau³³wa³¹ | (LCL-village) | 'hamlet; village' | [CL-N]_N |
| r. | lau³³liuŋ¹³ | (LCL-county) | 'county; county town' | [CL-N]_N |
| s. | lau³³ke³³ | (LCL-street) | 'bazaar; fair; market' | [CL-N]_N |

Compounds of this type can be built and extended in a recursive fashion, but still with the head always appearing before the modifier and the whole compound functioning as a noun. It is worth noting that the modifiers in this case are not limited to the head-modifier type but include compounds of the predicate-object and predicate-complement types (2f-j). Of course, the degree of recursion allowed is restricted by certain rules or conditions, which merit in-depth research.

| (2) | a. | χɛ³³ɣui³¹ʔiu⁵⁵ | (family-sky-aged) | 'Heaven; God' | [[N-N]_NAdj]_N |
|---|---|---|---|---|---|
|  | b. | liuŋ³¹ŋəu³³wa³¹ | (vegetable-flower-yellow) | 'lily flower (as vegetable)' (lit. 'vegetable with yellow flower') | [N[N-Adj]_N]_N |
|  | c. | qʰən³³qʰɛ³³ʔau¹³ | (herb-chicken-white) | 'Chinese ground orchid' | [N[N-Adj]_N]_N |
|  | d. | kʰaŋ³³tɕʰe¹³ŋ³³ | (grass-tail-dog) | 'green bristlegrass' | [N[N-N]_N]_N |
|  | e. | ye³¹tɕʰe³³ɕiu³³ | (hole-corner-eye) | 'canthus' | [[N-N]_NN]_N |
|  | f. | ŋəu³³ɕin⁵⁵lei³¹ | (flower-lead-ox) | 'morning glory' | [N[V-N]_V]_N |
|  | g. | ŋ⁵⁵tiɔ¹³ɬiu¹³ | (water-fall-cliff) | 'waterfall' | [N[V-N]_V]_N |
|  | h. | mm³¹bm³³χən³³ | (rain-cross-road) | 'shower (of rain)' | [N[V-N]_V]_N |
|  | i. | ŋ⁵⁵.ʔue³³.guaŋ³³laŋ³³ | (water-swirl-round.and.round) | 'whirlpool' | [N[V-Adv]_V]_N |
|  | j. | ɣuaŋ³¹.ʔue³³.guaŋ³³laŋ³³ | (wind-swirl-round.and.round) | 'whirlwind' | [N[V-Adv]_V]_N |

As can be seen from these examples, an interesting property of this head-modifier type of compounds is that they are quite parallel in syntactic structure to phrasal constructions which are characterized by the left-headed rule, namely, heads preceding their modifiers.

## 3.2 Predicate-object compounds

Compounds of this type are also quite productive in Ahou Gelao. Most of them have the internal structure [V-N]ᵥ, with the verb as the head of the compound and the noun as the object of it. Most of these compounds function as intransitive verbs and only a few can be used as transitive verbs. The semantic interpretation of these compounds is often idiomatic and idiosyncratic rather than transparent and straightforward. For example:

(3) a. $tɕɔ^{33}səu^{33}$ (read-book) 'study; attend school' [V-N]ᵥ
 b. $liɔ^{13}q^hε^{13}$ (get up-foot) 'set off; start (a journey)' [V-N]ᵥ
 c. $q^ha^{33}ɕiu^{33}$ (see-eye) 'see' [V-N]ᵥ
 d. $za^{13}dɹ^{31}$ (listen-words) 'obedient; biddable' [V-N]ᵥ
 e. $sau^{33}χε^{33}$ (share/divide-family) 'live apart' [V-N]ᵥ
 f. $ɲi^{33}χau^{13}$ (feel-sleepiness) 'feel sleepy' [V-N]ᵥ
 g. $ŋe^{13}χau^{13}$ (sleep-sleepiness) 'sleep' [V-N]ᵥ
 h. $dyai^{31}ɬiau^{55}$ (think-heart) 'intend; want' [V-N]ᵥ
 i. $ɳe^{13}vu^{31}$ (adhere-hand) 'lose (to)' [V-N]ᵥ
 j. $ʕa^{31}vu^{31}$ (release-hand) 'let go of; pardon' [V-N]ᵥ
 k. $tsʰaŋ^{33}diuŋ^{31}$ (set trap-forest) 'trap animal' [V-N]ᵥ
 l. $ty^{13}diuŋ^{31}$ (chase-forest) 'go hunting' [V-N]ᵥ
 m. $lε^{31}zuŋ^{33}$ (do-song) 'sing' [V-N]ᵥ
 n. $liai^{33}ɬiau^{55}$ (turn-heart) 'regret' [V-N]ᵥ
 o. $tiɔ^{55}ye^{33}$ (appear/evolve-sickness) 'get sick; fall ill' [V-N]ᵥ
 p. $zaŋ^{13}γuaŋ^{31}$ (pull-tendon) 'get cramp' [V-N]ᵥ
 q. $q^həu^{33}təu^{33}$ (hang-paper) 'commemorate the dead by hanging paper at the tombs' [V-N]ᵥ
 r. $ɓ^{13}.sɔ^{33}ʔɔ^{55}$ (change-body) 'menstruate' [V-N]ᵥ
 s. $mε^{13}lin^{31}$ (find-back) 'tail after; track' [V-N]ᵥ

It appears that all these examples have undergone reanalysis in their meanings via metaphorical or metonymic extension, which have led them to become lexicalized to a certain degree. Both metaphor and metonymy are a variety of figurative use of language. What distinguishes a metaphorical use or metonymic use of an expression is the relationship between the figurative meaning and the literal meaning. Metaphor involves a relation of resemblance or analogy, i.e. "seeing something as something else". Unlike metaphor, metonymy involves a relation of association, i.e. "using one entity to refer to another that is related to it". For instance, $liai^{33}tiau^{55}$ (turn-heart) 'regret', whereby, with "decision" viewed as "heart", the meaning of "regret" is seen as "turning one's heart", is a case of metaphorical extension. On the contrary, $q^hau^{33}tau^{33}$ (hang-paper) 'commemorate the dead by hanging paper at the tombs', using the action of "hanging paper" to refer to the event/custom of "commemorating the dead by hanging paper at the tombs", illustrates a metonymic extension.

As a matter of fact, metaphor and metonymy can be viewed as the main mechanisms of the lexicalization of compounds. Based on a thorough and systematic analysis of exocentric compounds, which have been marginally treated, compared to endocentric compounds, Benczes (2006: 184) claims that metaphor and metonymy can be employed in systematic ways to create exocentric compounds of noun-noun combinations. The main difference between endocentric compounds and exocentric compounds, Benczes (2006: 184) argues, "is not transparency of meaning, but creativity: the latter represents a type of nominal construction that has been coined by a more imaginative, associative and creative word formation process, based on conceptual metaphor and metonymy."

Most of the above-listed examples are more lexicalized than some other examples (3f, g) which still display relatively more syntactic interpretation. Some (3a, d) may even have a syntactic phrase reading in the proper context. For instance, when $za^{13}dr^{31}$ and $tɕɔ^{33}sau^{33}$ appear in the utterance (4) where they express concrete actions, they should be analyzed as syntactic phrases, whose meaning can be taken literally as 'listen to (the teacher's) words' and 'read books' respectively.

(4) $ʔa^{33}m̩^{31}$   $kɔ^{13}$   $t^han^{353\sim31}nan^{33}$   $za^{13}$   $dr^{31}$   $tɕɔ^{33}$   $sau^{33}$   $hau^0$.
    2SG.TOP  be.at  here                    listen  words  read   book  CNS
    'You just stay here listening to (the teacher's) words and reading books.'

The compounds in examples (3h-j) and (3s) are the only compounds that display the highest degree of lexicalization, as they have developed into transitive verbs and can take nominal elements as their objects. In other words, if the compounded words are transitive verbs, they possess a higher degree of lexicalization than those that are intransitive.

The striking property of these compounds is that their nouns (objects) are indefinite in reference. They lack individuality and referentiality and appear as bare nouns. This is a crucial point because it can spell out the distinction between compounds and syntactic phrases of identical structure [V-N]$_V$. In other words, the Ns of syntactic phrases of [V-N] structures are usually definite in reference. Following are two illustrating examples:

(5) a. $q^hua\mathrm{\tilde{\imath}}^{33}$  $s\mathrm{\partial}u^{33}$  $gua\mathrm{\tilde{\imath}}^{31}$  $b\varepsilon^{33}$  $ma^{33}$-  $\eta\mathrm{\partial}u^{31}$  $ts^h\varepsilon^{55}$
ago two year DEF CL.AUG snake invite
$ma^{33}$-  $\eta^{33}$  $\mathrm{z}iu^{33}$  $ts^ha\eta^{33}$  $\mathrm{?}\varepsilon^{33}$  $\mathbf{za^{13}ma^{33}}$,
CL.AUG wasp go for 3 propose.marriage
$me^{33}$  $\mathrm{z}iu^{33}$  $za^{13}$  $l\varepsilon i^{55}$  $wa^{33}$  $ha^{13}$  $la^{33}$  $\mathrm{z}u^{13}$.
INTN go ask CL.DIM woman CL.KNW SRN Zhang
'In ancient times, a snake asked a wasp to be his matchmaker, as he wanted to make proposals to the girls of the Zhang family.'

b. $ts^h\imath^{55}$  $ha^{33}$  $kun^{13}$  $\eta uan^{31}$  $tian^{55}$  $t\varepsilon^h i^{33}$,  $p\mathrm{\sigma}^{55}$
take CL.VLU jarl silver bury CONT husband
$\mathrm{?}\varepsilon^{33}$  $\mathbf{za^{13}}$  $\mathbf{ma^{33}}$  $\mathrm{?}\varepsilon^{33}$,  "$han^{13}\varepsilon a^{13}$  $m^{31}$
3 ask wife 3 portion 2SG
$me^{33}$  $d\mathrm{z}ai^{31}xe^{33}$  $li^{33}$?"
INTN time-INDF use
'After burying the pot (full of silver), the husband asked his wife, "When will you use your share?"'

The sequence $za^{13}$ (ask)-$ma^{33}$ (wife) in (5a) forms a compound as there is no definite reference to the noun $ma^{33}$ here. By contrast, the same sequence in (5b) can only be construed as a syntactic phrase, with the definite nominal phrase $ma^{33}$ $\mathrm{?}\varepsilon^{33}$ (his wife) appearing as the object of the verb $za^{13}$. In fact, the second $za^{13}$ and its object $l\varepsilon i^{55} wa^{33} ha^{13} la^{33}$-$\mathrm{z}u^{13}$ in (5a) can also serve as a good illustration, where the predicate-object structure forms a phrasal construction instead as the object is obviously definite in reference. In fact, phonologically, there is a logical pause between the verb and its object in a phrasal construction while such a pause is impossible in a compound reading.

As for the verbal elements of these compounds, they are quite low in activity and transitivity. They are largely verbs of cognition or sensation with abstract meanings. Even though there are verbs of concrete actions like "hang" in (3q), these "concrete" meanings do not apply to the meaning of the gestalt compounds in a straightforward manner. Rather, they have been generalized and abstracted via metaphorical or metonymic extension before their lexicalization from a phrase to a compound. To put it in another way, the more concrete action the verbal element expresses and the higher the individuality the object element displays, the lower the degree of lexicalization of the overall compound. " ... the lexicalisation potential of such a compound is quite low because it is based on a very temporary relationship."(Benczes 2006: 31)

Similar semantic constraints on the lexicalization of the predicate-object type of phrases into compounds in Mandarin Chinese are revealed (Dong 2011: 158–187).

## 3.3 Predicate-complement compounds

The predicate-complement compounds are [V-V]$_V$ in structure, with the second element (verb) serving as the complement to the first. The second verb is usually (but not necessarily) an intransitive verb (including adjectives). Semantically, the second element (verb) lends various dimensions to the action described by the first verb such as completion, state, direction, degree, and manner, among others. The word class of such compounds is evidently verb or adjective. For example:

(6) a. tiɔ⁵⁵ʔe³³ (appear/evolve-good) 'good-looking; beautiful' [V-Adj]$_{Adj}$
　　b. tiɔ¹³lin³¹ (fall-late) 'lag behind; be late' [V-Adj]$_{Adj}$
　　c. ŋe¹³ne¹³ (sleep-get) 'fall asleep' [V-V]$_V$
　　d. ʔluŋ⁵⁵ne¹³ (meet-get) 'encounter; come across' [V-V]$_V$
　　e. ʔlau⁵⁵tɔ³³ (remember-arrive) 'remember' [V-V]$_V$
　　f. ʔe³³kʰi³³ (good-eat) 'be delicious' [Adj-V]$_{Adj}$
　　g. ʔe³³saŋ¹³ (good-look) 'good-looking' [Adj-V]$_{Adj}$
　　h. ʔe³³bm³³ (good-pass) 'happy' [Adj-V]$_{Adj}$
　　i. ʔla⁵⁵lɛ³¹ (know-do) 'know how; be capable' [V-V]$_{Adj}$
　　j. lɛ³¹nia¹³ (do-accompany) 'keep company' [V-V]$_V$
　　k. hi¹³lɛ³¹ (call-do) 'be called; having a name'[7] [V-V]$_V$
　　l. qʰɔ⁵⁵lin³¹ (hit-roll) 'roll about' [V-V]$_V$
　　m. qʰɔ⁵⁵tai¹³ (hit-broken) 'break into pieces' [V-Adj]$_V$
　　n. lɛ³¹ʐa³¹ (do-wrong) 'make a mistake' [V-Adj]$_V$
　　o. juai¹³ʔe³³ (say-good) 'promise; plight' [V-Adj]$_V$
　　p. zaŋ¹³ʔlɛ¹³ (stretch-lazy) 'stretch (the body)' [V-Adj]$_V$
　　q. tau¹³tɕʰi¹³ (tease-get angry) 'tease; provoke' [V-Adj]$_V$

Compounds of this predicate-complement type are relatively less productive. Comparatively they are less lexicalized than some other types of compounds, as

---

**7** This compound functions as a copula, taking a nominal object, e.g.:

(i) 　lei⁵⁵-nɛ³¹　　　ʔe³³　　hi¹³lɛ³¹　　tuŋ⁵⁵jyn³³.
　　　CL.DIM-name　3　　be.called　Dongyun
　　　'His name is [called] Dongyun'.

can be seen from the relatively transparent and straightforward compositionality of their semantics. Phrases of this predicate-complement type can be divided into different subclasses according to whether the predicate element is a transitive or intransitive verb or an adjective. Those with a transitive predicate element seem to have a higher probability of being lexicalized into compound words.

## 3.4 Subject-predicate compounds

In compounds of this type, the N syntactically functions as the subject of the V, which in turn functions as the predicate. Compounds of this class share some but not all the characteristics of the head-modifier type of compound, as they share with the latter the internal structure of [N-V] or [N-Adj]. But they are verbs or adjectives and they usually function as a predicate, differing from the head-modifier type whose grammatical categories are nominal in nature. Structurally, they are [N-V]$_{V/Adj}$ or [N-Adj]$_{V/Adj}$ whereas head-modifier type are [N-V]$_N$ or [N-Adj]$_N$. Again, the structure of this type of compound is generalized from that of corresponding phrasal constructions, as subjects in Ahou Gelao typically precede their predicates. The meanings of compounds of this kind, however, are often idiosyncratic, displaying a higher degree of lexicalization. Again, as can be seen from the examples below, they may have been abstracted through metaphorical extension (7a-l, n, o) or metonymic extension (7m, p, q), or they may have undergone other types of semantic changes.[8] To illustrate, consider here just two examples of ɬiau$^{55}$dai$^{13}$ (heart/liver-full) 'satisfied' and ɣui$^{31}$laŋ$^{31}$ (sky-sound) 'thunder'. In the first case, the sensation domain "satisfaction" is understood via the physical domain "heart-content", so the meaning of the compound ɬiau$^{55}$dai$^{13}$ involves a metaphorical change. In the latter case, because the whole "sky-sounding" is used to refer to the specific part "thundering", the compound ɣui$^{31}$laŋ$^{31}$ thus reveals a metonymic change.

Like the predicate-complement type, the class of subject-predicate compounds is relatively closed, as it consists mainly of verbs or adjectives describing mental activities or propensity. Interestingly, these compounds are largely

---

[8] A thorough and detailed analysis of the metaphorical and metonymic change of compound meaning is no easy job and far beyond the scope of this paper. Readers are invited to refer to Benczes (2006) for full details on how metaphor and metonymy can influence a compound's meaning.

connected with and formed using references to internal organs, particularly the 'heart' or the 'liver'.[9] For example:

(7) a. ɬiau⁵⁵ʔe³³ (heart/liver-good) 'kind-hearted' [N-Adj]$_{Adj}$
 b. ɬiau⁵⁵dia³³ (heart/liver-small) 'timid' [N-Adj]$_{Adj}$
 c. ɬiau⁵⁵χaŋ³³ (heart/liver-bitter) 'painstaking; hard' [N-Adj]$_{Adj}$
 d. ɬiau⁵⁵dʑɔ³¹ (heart/liver-straight) 'straightforward' [N-Adj]$_{Adj}$
 e. ɬiau⁵⁵waŋ³¹ (heart/liver-disorder) 'sick' [N-Adj]$_{Adj}$
 f. ɬiau⁵⁵ʔai³³ (heart/liver-tiny) 'careful; cautious' [N-Adj]$_{Adj}$
 g. ɬiau⁵⁵ɬiuŋ³³ (heart/liver-big) 'courageous' [N-Adj]$_{Adj}$
 h. ɬiau⁵⁵tai¹³ (heart/liver-full) 'satisfied' [N-Adj]$_{Adj}$
 i. ɬiau⁵⁵yua³¹ (heart/liver-high) 'pleased; glad' [N-Adj]$_{Adj}$
 j. ɬiau⁵⁵ʔau¹³ (heart/liver-white) 'depressed' [N-Adj]$_{Adj}$
 k. ɬiau⁵⁵dʑn¹³ (heart/liver-vicious) 'evil; malicious' [N-Adj]$_{Adj}$
 l. ɬiau⁵⁵jye¹³ (heart/liver-boil/overflow) 'enraged' [N-V]$_{Adj}$
 m. qʰɛ¹³hui⁵⁵ (foot-fast/early) 'active; keen' [N-Adj]$_{Adj}$
 n. χəu¹³liu³³ (price-rough/hard) 'expensive' [N-Adj]$_{Adj}$
 o. χəu¹³dɔ³³ (price-even) 'cheap; inexpensive' [N-Adj]$_{Adj}$
 p. haŋ³³tiɔ¹³ (day-fall) 'dawn' [N-V]$_V$
 q. γui³¹laŋ³¹ (sky-sound) 'thunder' [N-V]$_V$

One striking property of this subject-predicate combination is that the predicate is limited to intransitive verbs or adjectives, as illustrated by these examples. And it turns out that those phrases with an adjective predicate are easier to lexicalize than those with an intransitive predicate.

Semantically, the constraints on the lexicalization of this subject-predicate type of phrase include (1) the subject having to be [-animate], [-volitional] and [-referential]; (2) the predicate having to be [-controllable] and [-accomplished]. As can be seen in the examples, the subjects turn out to be nouns denoting body parts ("heart", "liver", "foot"), objects ("price") or natural phenomena ("day", "sky"), which share the semantic feature of [-animate]. Closely related to this [-animate] feature are the features [-volitional] and [-controllable], which implies that the subjects are, semantically, a theme that has neither volition nor control over the action or state denoted by the predicate. According to general understanding, a theme is a participant that is located or is undergoing a change of location (motion). It may also be the locus of an action or property that does not undergo a change. In the latter case, the semantic feature [-accomplished] is implied. Take

---

[9] Note that 'heart' and 'liver' are homophones in Ahou Gelao, all called ɬiau⁵⁵. One may as well say that they regard the heart and liver as one and the same organ.

the compound $\gamma ui^{31}la\eta^{31}$ (sky-sound) 'thunder' for example, the theme "sky" is the locus of the action "making sounds", with the whole compound denoting an ongoing action or state, involving no change of state. With regard to the feature of [-referential]: it means that the subject in the compound has to be non-referential in meaning, referring to no specific entity in the world. The subject ɬ$iau^{55}$ 'heart/liver' in the compound ɬ$iau^{55}dia^{33}$ (heart/liver-small) 'timid', for instance, makes no reference to any specific heart/liver in the real world. Accordingly, the whole compound does not refer to any fact or event of a specific heart/liver being small but rather the property of being timid. On the contrary, if the subject ɬ$iau^{55}$ has referential meaning and refers to some specific heart/liver in the real world, then the entire word sequence ɬ$iau^{55}dia^{33}$ will not be a compound but a phrase referring to a fact or event of a specific heart/liver being small. To sum up, the [-referential] status of the subject in a subject-predicate compound is a key point in distinguishing it from a phrase with identical word sequence.

Similar syntactic and semantic constraints on the lexicalization of subject-predicate phrases in Mandarin Chinese have been revealed (Dong 2011: 192–197).

Note that the word class of the compound of $ha\eta^{33}ti\mathfrak{o}^{13}$ 'dawn' (7p) and $\gamma ui^{31}la\eta^{31}$ 'thunder' (7q) can also be a noun.

## 3.5 Coordinate compounds

As opposed to compounds of the head-modifier type, coordinate compounds consist of two equal members of the same lexical class, neither of which can be identified as the head. Such compounds usually belong to the same word class as their members, though, in rare instances, the compound may function as a different word class than its members. Semantically, components of these compounds are closely related, being either (a) synonyms, (b) antonyms or (c) parallels. Thus, the integrated meaning of these compounds cannot be regarded as the simple sum of the meanings of their components. In this sense, coordinate compounds differ from coordinate phrases which are interpreted as a logical conjunction of 'A and B' or disjunction of 'A or B'. In addition, the order of the two elements in a compound is fixed and cannot be reversed. For this reason, the principle used to interpret coordinate phrases is not applicable to coordinate compounds. Coordinate compounds in Ahou Gelao are not productive. Following are some examples:

(8) a. $q^h\varepsilon^{13}vu^{31}$ (foot-hand) 'craftsmanship' [N-N]$_N$
 b. ɬ$iu\eta^{33}$ɬ$iau^{55}$ (stomach-heart) 'mood; state of mind' [N-N]$_N$
 c. ɕ$iu^{33}liu^{13}$ (eye-face) 'appearance; feature; profile' [N-N]$_N$

| | | | |
|---|---|---|---|
| d. | wa¹³me³¹ | (father-mother) | 'parents' | [N-N]ₙ |
| e. | pɔ⁵⁵ma³³ | (husband-wife) | 'husband and wife; couple' | [N-N]ₙ |
| f. | niuŋ³¹ʔin⁵⁵ | (elder sister-younger sister) | 'sisterhood' | [N-N]ₙ |
| g. | te³³zɔ¹³ | (elder brother-younger brother) | 'brotherhood, brothers' | [N-N]ₙ |
| h. | qʰən¹³nia¹³ | (guest-companion) | 'relatives, kin' | [N-N]ₙ |
| g. | guai³¹lai³¹ | (year-month) | 'age; years; time' | [N-N]ₙ |
| h. | baŋ³³liuŋ³³ | (paddy field-dry field) | 'cropland' | [N-N]ₙ |
| i. | ʔɛ¹³dia³³ | (many/much-few/little) | 'amount; how much' | [Adj-Adj] Pron |
| j. | xəu¹³ʔui¹³ | (dry-tender) | 'discuss; talk over' | [Adj-Adj]ᵥ |
| k. | ha³³ʔluŋ⁵⁵ | (open-meet) | 'attend/hold a meeting' | [V-V]ᵥ |
| l. | ʃau¹³tiaŋ⁵⁵ | (pull out-plant) | 'transplant; replant' | [V-V]ᵥ |
| m. | liuŋ³³yən³¹ | (steal-look) | 'pry' | [V-V]ᵥ |

Many of these compounds have undergone metaphorical generalization or metonymic changes in their compounded meanings. Some (8i-j) have even undergone conversion, with adjectives turning into nouns in (8i) and verbs in (8j). This reveals that these compounds have a higher degree of lexicalization.

As can be seen from these examples, components of these compounds in Ahou Gelao are largely nouns, and these nominal elements are generally abstract nouns and non-referential. In the case of concrete nouns, they have to be abstracted or generalized through metaphorical or metonymic extension before they can be lexicalized. If the components are adjectives, they have to undergo conversion for lexicalization. When the components are verbs, they are all transitive. In terms of the semantic relations between the components, those combinations in which the two components are synonyms or parallels lexicalize more easily than those with two antonymic components, as the latter combination needs to undergo class shift in order to achieve lexicalization. For example, the compound noun $qʰɛ¹³vu³¹$ (foot-hand) 'craftsmanship', lexicalizes from the combination of two parallel nominal components 'foot' and 'hand', whereas the compound pronoun $ʔɛ¹³dia³³$ (many-few) 'how much; how many', lexicalizes from the combination of two antonymic adjectival components 'many' and 'few'. In the latter case, a class shift of the two components from adjective to pronoun is required for the lexicalization. There is no class shift in the former case, as both the components and the whole compound are nouns.

Dong's (2011: 101–141) and other scholars' studies unveil similar syntactic and semantic constraints on the lexicalization of coordinate phrases in Mandarin Chinese.

# 4 Compounding in different word classes

In this section, we will classify and analyze compounds by both their word class and that of their components. In Ahou Gelao, compounds can be classified into the following word class types: (1) nominal compounds; (2) verbal compounds; (3) compound adjectives; (4) compound adverbs; (5) compound numerals; and (6) compound pronouns. Their properties will be elaborated briefly in order.

## 4.1 Nominal compounds

The classification of nominal compounds can operate within two traditional sets of parameters: (i) whether a compound denotes a subclass of items described by one of its elements or not (*endocentric* vs. *exocentric*), and whether it is a coordinate structure (which falls under the exocentric umbrella); and (ii) whether it contains a verbal root or not (*root compounds* vs *synthetic compounds*) (Aikhenvald 2007: 31).

### 4.1.1 Endocentric, exocentric and coordinate compounds

An endocentric compound refers to a subclass of items whose meaning is connected to one of its constituents. This constituent can be treated as the head of the compound. For instance, $haŋ^{33}zu^{13}$ (day-grow) 'birthday' is a sort of day, $ŋəu^{33}yua^{33}$ (flower-sun) 'sunflower' is a sort of flower, $yəu^{33}wa^{31}$ (people-new) 'bride/bridegroom' is a sort of woman/man, etc.

The semantic relationship between the components of endocentric compounds is largely genitive, part-whole or generic-specific, e.g. $yəu^{33}.lau^{33}wa^{31}$ (people-LCL-village) 'villagers' (literally 'people of/from village'), $lai^{31}ɕi^{33}$ (CL.FLT-tree) 'leaf' (literally 'leaf of tree'), $ne^{13}ŋəu^{33}$ 'petal' (literally 'petal of flower'), $lai^{31}liuŋ^{33}$ (CL.FLT-dry.land) 'land'. What is worth mentioning here is that the generic-specific type of meaning relation abounds in Ahou Gelao, as indicated by the last example of $lai^{31}liuŋ^{33}$ 'land', where the classifier $lai^{31}$ serves as the head (something generic) while the following noun $liuŋ^{33}$ as the modifier (something specific), to the effect that 'land is categorized as something flat'. About half of the nominal compounds are of this type.

Another situation is one in which one component may modify the other, e.g. $daŋ^{31}wa^{31}$ (sugar-yellow) 'brown sugar', $k^həu^{33}zi^{33}$ (buckwheat-wild) 'wild buckwheat', $ŋəu^{33}ŋ^{55}$ (flower-water) 'water lily'.

An exocentric compound is one in which the final meaning is different from either of its components. For example, $\eta^{55}\chi\varepsilon i^{55}$ (water-iron), literally 'iron water', means 'steel', differing from either 'water' or 'iron'. Similarly, neither $sa^{33}hye^{33}$ (spark-fire) 'shooting star', and $s\partial u^{33}\mathfrak{s}\varepsilon^{31}ts^{h}ai^{33}$ (literally 'being poor for eight generations', used as the name of a boy in a story) can be reduced or traced back to either one of their components.

Coordinate nominal compounds in Ahou Gelao generally consist of two juxtaposed nouns which denote a unitary concept, as illustrated in the above-listed examples such as $q^{h}\varepsilon^{13}vu^{31}$ (foot-hand) 'craftsmanship', $\text{\textit{łiuŋ}}^{33}\text{\textit{łiau}}^{55}$ (stomach-heart) 'mood; state of mind', $\varepsilon iu^{33}liu^{13}$ (eye-face) 'appearance; profile', $wa^{13}me^{31}$ (father-mother) 'parents', $p\mathfrak{o}^{55}ma^{33}$ (husband-wife) 'husband and wife; couple', etc. Kinship terms happen to be the category in which coordinate compounds of this type abound. Occasionally coordinate compounds may consist of two juxtaposed adjectives, for example, $\text{\textit{ʔ}}\varepsilon^{13}dia^{33}$ (many/much-few/little) 'amount' (8i) and $x\partial u^{13}\text{\textit{ʔ}}ui^{13}$ (dry-tender) 'discuss; talk over' (8j) shows. As illustrated by the examples, coordinate compounds can be considered a kind of exocentric compound since their meanings refer to a unitary concept that equals that of neither component. As a matter of fact, compounds with highly non-compositional meaning are quite difficult to analyze, as they get lexicalized in such a way that the semantic relations between their parts becomes obscured.

### 4.1.2 Root compounds and synthetic compounds

Root compounds are those that do not have a verb base or root, while synthetic compounds consist of a verbal root with its argument (Aikhenvald 2007: 31).

The typical argument in synthetic compounds is an intransitive subject, as indicated by such examples as $\eta^{55}jye^{13}$ (water-spew) 'fountain', $k^{h}u\eta^{55}dia^{33}$ (generation-young) 'younger generation', $y\partial u^{33}wa^{31}$ (person-new) 'bride/bridegroom', $\chi\varepsilon i^{55}l\varepsilon^{13}$ (iron-raw) 'pig iron', $hu^{55}lia\eta^{31}$ (cloud-dark) 'cloudbank', $\text{\textit{łiau}}^{55}\text{\textit{ʔ}}e^{33}$ (heart-good) 'kind-hearted', among others. The compounding with a direct object, however, is rather restricted, with sparse examples such as $li^{13}ta^{13}$ (child-embrace) 'adopted child; foster child' and $m\mathfrak{o}^{33}tia\eta^{13}$ (rice-cook) 'congee/gruel'. This is probably because the OV order in these compounds is the reverse of the normal VO order in a clause; thus the O argument appears in the canonical position of an S (subject of an intransitive verb) or an A (subject of a transitive verb). The result – three arguments appearing in the same slot – is too heavy an information burden for mental processing.

Similarly, a transitive subject can hardly become compounded without the co-occurrence of the direct object, e.g. $pu^{55}mu^{33}pe^{13}$ (CL.ML.GRN-pick-pocket) 'pickpocket', $pu^{55}sɿ^{33}ʔmɛ^{33}$ (CL.ML.GRN-castrate-pig) 'pig castrator/gelder', $pu^{55}dzn^{33}yəu^{33}$ (CL.ML.GRN-rob-people) 'bandit'. A few compounds seem to become compounded only in the company of the transitive subject, such as $pu^{55}nia^{13}$ (CL.ML.GRN-accompany) 'friend/companion', $yəu^{33}ŋ̊e^{13}$ (person-acquaint.with) 'acquaintance', $pu^{55}χɛ^{353\sim13}jin^{31}$ (CL.ML.GRN-craftsman-kill) 'butcher', but a closer look reveals that the direct objects are omitted or implied in context, probably because there is a range of items rather than a single one available to be chosen as the candidate for the argument.

It so happens that the oblique constituent of instrument gets compounded rather productively. The instrumental argument is mostly coded with the widespread classifiers $ʔa^{33}$ 'thing for doing something' and $lɛi^{55}$ 'tiny thing for doing something' (glossed as CL.INS and CL.DIM respectively), with the structure patterning as CL + Verb. In fact, most of the names for utensils, artifacts and other tools are compounded in this pattern, e.g. $ʔa^{33}tsən^{55}$ (CL.INS-cut) 'scissors', $ʔa^{33}sən^{33}$ (CL.INS-comb) 'comb', $ʔa^{33}tʰiaŋ^{33}$ (CL.INS-cover) 'cover/lid', $lɛi^{55}bɔ^{13}hye^{33}$ (CL.DIM-peck-fire) 'percussion cap holder (of a gun)', and $lɛi^{55}tɕʰe^{55}χaŋ^{33}$ (CL.DIM-poke-tobacco) 'tobacco pipe poker', among others.

Other oblique constituents that can be compounded include a locative (2g-h) or a temporal (1g). A few more illustrating examples: $pu^{55}ty^{13}diuŋ^{31}$ (CL.ML.GRN-chase-forest) 'hunter' (literally 'the man who chases game in the forest'), $haŋ^{33}kʰi^{33}$ (day-eat) 'auspicious day' (literally 'the day on which people eat a banquet'), and $ti^{33}haŋ^{33}jin^{31}qʰɛ^{33}$ (three-day-kill-chicken) 'the custom of offering a chicken to the Child-bringing Goddess three days after an infant's birth'.

### 4.1.3 Other parameters of nominal compounding

Syntactically, nominal compounds in Ahou Gelao are mainly of the head-modifier type, as can be seen above. Coordinate compounds are relatively less widespread.

As for the freedom of the components, nominal compounds – especially endocentric, exocentric and coordinate compounds – often consist of free forms. On the other hand, nominal compounds can also be of a type wherein one of its members may come from a closed class and be a bound morpheme. Classifiers appear to be the prime source as the bound morphemes in nominal compounds of this type, as stated and illustrated above. Deictic pronouns or demonstratives can also be the bound parts of this type of nominal compound: $haŋ^{33}naŋ^{33}$ (day-this) 'today', $ʔa^{33}ŋuai^{33}naŋ^{33}$ (CL.GNR-moment-this) 'now'.

Compared with verbal compounding and compounding in other word classes, nominal compounding is quite productive in both type frequency and token frequency. But even within nominal compounds, the degree of productivity varies from one type to another, as illustrated above.

Nominal elements (nouns or classifiers) involved in compounding are usually non-referential. Nominal compounds can be formed from phrases, such as the above-mentioned examples $səu^{33}ɕɛ^{31}tsʰai^{33}$ (literally 'poor-for-eight-generations', the name of a boy in a story) and $tɿ^{33}haŋ^{33}jin^{31}qʰɛ^{33}$ 'the custom of offering a chicken to the Child-bringing Goddess three days after an infant's birth' (literally 'three-day-kill-chicken').

## 4.2 Verbal compounds

Verbal compounds are sequences of verb roots which result in the creation of a single verb with shared arguments (Aikhenvald 2007: 32). Ahou Gelao combines verb compounding and serial verb construction with the main difference between the two being that verbal compounds form one grammatical and one phonological word while serial verb constructions consist of several independent grammatical and phonological words. In other words, verb compounding is root serialization while serial verb construction is verb serialization. As a matter of fact, verb compounding and verb serialization are two stages on a continuum, with the latter getting lexicalized into verbal compounds (He 2011).

Verbal compounds in Ahou Gelao are mainly of two types, namely, the predicate-complement (V-C) ones seen in Section 3.3 and the parallel/coordinate ones seen in Section 3.5. The type of subject-predicate structure outlined in Section 3.4 is sparsely attested (see examples 7p-q). Since V-C compounds are very productive and substantially outnumber coordinate compounds in Ahou Gelao, we will limit our focus to V-C compounds.

### 4.2.1 Formal features of V-C compounds

Generally, the complement receives the main stress, as: $sau^{55}ʔe^{33}$ (handle-good) 'manage to do with; handle', $ʔluŋ^{55}n̯e^{13}$ (meet-touch) 'encounter; come across', $ʔləu^{55}tɔ^{33}$ (remember-arrive) 'remember'. On one occasion where the complement is a dissyllabic morpheme and the second syllable has a neutral tone, the stress falls on the first, as: $li^{33}.kui^{33}ʑi^{13}$ (use-finish) 'use up'.

The verb and the complement tend to form a close unit, such that the whole combination takes no inserted element. And the components cannot be negated separately.

## 4.2.2 Common types of complements

While complements tend to separate into certain types, the preceding verb, as we will see, can be almost any verb. As a rule, verbs having a very general meaning appear to have a greater variety of complements than verbs that have a specific meaning. Thus, $lɛ^{31}$ 'do, make', $q^hɔ^{55}$ 'hit, strike', and $sau^{55}$ 'do/deal with; tackle' take as complements adjectives such as $ʔe^{33}$ 'good' and $za^{31}$ 'wrong', and resultative complements such as $kui^{33}zi^{13}$ 'complete' and $łai^{13}$ 'broken (to bits)'. Verbs of motion and physical action naturally take directional complements. Adjectives mostly take complements of degree. What follows is the description of the common types of complements in Ahou Gelao.

The most frequent type of complement is the resultative complement. In this type of verbal compound, the complement signals the result of the preceding verb. It often describes the state of the object affected by the verb. Since the grammatical meaning of a complement is 'result', the complement tends to be an adjective rather than an action verb. Here are some illustrating examples: $lɛ^{31}za^{31}$ (do-wrong) 'make a mistake', $q^hɔ^{55}łai^{13}$ (hit-broken) 'break into bits', $q^hɔ^{55}gun^{31}$ (hit-dead) 'beat to death; kill', $k^he^{13}ʔe^{33}$ (alter-good) 'improve'.

One characteristic of resultative compounds is that they cannot be modified by post-posed adverbs of degree such as $tsa^{31}sɿ^{31}$ 'substantially' and $haŋ^{33}$ 'awfully', since they do not match adverbs of degree semantically. On some occasions when a V-Adj combination happens to be modified by an adverb of degree, the combination would be interpreted as a syntactic construction rather than a compound. To clarify: if a V-Adj structure can be modified by an adverb of degree, it is the complement (the adjective) alone that will be modified rather than the whole unit. For instance, the above-mentioned resultative compound $k^he^{13}ʔe^{33}$ (alter-good) 'improve', if followed by $haŋ^{33}$ 'awfully', the whole structure will be rendered as $k^he^{13}$ [$ʔe^{33}$ $haŋ^{33}$], meaning 'changing is much better; changing is preferably good'.

The number of common resultative complements could amount to more than 30. Most of them can combine with the three verbs with very general meaning mentioned above, namely, $lɛ^{31}$ 'do, make', $q^hɔ^{55}$ 'strike', and $sau^{55}$ 'do/deal with; tackle'. Here are some representative common resultative complements: $ʔe^{33}$ 'good/correct', $ty^{13}$ 'bad', $za^{31}$ 'wrong', $q^huai^{33}$ 'early', $lin^{31}$ 'late', $le^{31}$ 'far', $liu^{33}$ 'near', $łai^{13}$ 'broken', $gun^{31}$ 'dead', $dɔ^{33}$ 'level/even', $bɛ^{13}$ 'toppled', $dzy^{33}$ 'gone through', $hɛ^{13}$ 'clean'.

There are a few complements which express the phase of an action described in the preceding verb rather than some result in the action. These complements are termed 'phase complements' by Chao (1968: 446). We here adopt his term. What follows is the most important phase complements.[10]

a. -$kui^{33}zi^{13}$ 'finish/thorough' denotes the thoroughness/completion or the fullest extent of the action: $hue^{33}$-$kui^{33}zi^{13}$ (sell-complete) 'sold out', $k^{h}i^{33}$-$kui^{33}zi^{13}$ (eat-complete) 'eat up', $li^{33}$-$kui^{33}zi^{13}$ (use-complete) 'use up'.

b. -$paŋ^{13}$ 'obtain/get' denotes accomplishment or successful completion of the action of the verb: $tɕɔ^{33}$-$paŋ^{13}$ (learn-get) 'manage to learn', $ȵaŋ^{13}$-$paŋ^{13}$ (catch-get) 'manage to catch'.

c. -$ȵe^{13}$ as an ordinary resultative complement means 'hit the mark; touched the essential point', where it usually requires the perfective aspect -$kɔ^{0}$, as: $χəu^{33}$-$ȵe^{13}$-$kɔ^{0}$ (count-got.at) 'have made just the right guess/count; have guessed/counted correctly'. As a phase complement, it means 'touched; got at; successful after an attempt': $ʔluŋ^{55}$-$ȵe^{13}$ (meet-got.at) 'encounter; come across; meet with'.

d. -$ʔe^{33}$ means 'good' when used independently. As a phase complement, it conveys the meaning of 'completing the task signaled by the preceding verb', quite similar to but not identical with the meaning of -$kui^{33}zi^{13}$ 'finish/thorough'. Examples: $q^{h}ɔ^{55}$-$ʔe^{33}$ (hit-good) 'complete the task of hitting', $lɛ^{31}$-$ʔe^{33}$ (do-good) 'complete the task of doing'.

e. -$tɔ^{33}$ means 'arrive/reach' when used independently as verb (a Chinese loan). As a phase complement, it carries the meaning of 'succeed in finishing the task signaled by the preceding verb', quite similar to the meaning of -$ȵe^{13}$ 'successful after an attempt' in (c). It is quite limited in scope of combination and occurs with only a few verbs of perception, e.g. $ʔləu^{55}$-$tɔ^{33}$ (remember-arrive) 'succeed in remembering, think of'.

f. -$tɕ^{h}i^{33}$ is a loan from Chinese qǐ 'rise', but it cannot be used independently as a verb in Ahou Gelao. As a phase complement, it means 'to get something done in a short period or in a slight manner', e.g. $q^{h}a^{33}$-$tɕ^{h}i^{33}$ $pa^{33}$.$mau^{13}$ (put-up CL.CNV-hat) 'put on one's hat', $pu^{55}$-$tɕ^{h}i^{33}$ $pa^{33}$.$dʑəu^{31}$ (put-up CL.CNV-clothes) 'put on one's clothes', $t^{h}iaŋ^{33}$-$tɕ^{h}i^{33}$ $pa^{33}$.$ŋau^{33}$ (close-up CL.CNV-door) 'just shut the door', $q^{h}ɔ^{55}$-$tɕ^{h}i^{33}$ $laŋ^{31}$.$luŋ^{31}$ (beat-up CL.RND-drum) 'just beat the drum'.

g. -$tau^{33}$ is a loan from Chinese dǎo 'topple', and again it cannot be used independently as a verb in Ahou Gelao. As a phase complement, it combines with only a few verbs to express the state of doing an action or the state as

---

**10** Note that most of these phase complements, especially those that can still be used independently, also occur as ordinary resultative complements. See Chao (1968: 446–450) for detailed descriptions of similar phenomena in Mandarin Chinese.

a result from an action, e.g. $k^h i^{33}$-$tau^{33}$ (eat-up) 'the state of eating', $ze^{31}$-$tau^{33}$ (adhere-up) 'the state of being connected'.

h. -$t^h yai^{33}$ means 'settle, decide on' when used independently as verb. As a phase complement, it means 'to bring (a matter) to an end' or 'get something settled', e.g. $ts^h ən^{33}$-$t^h yai^{33}$ (buy-settle) 'settle the purchase, get the purchase finally settled'.

Directional complements are also quite common. The structure of a directional verbal compound can be schematized as $V_1$-$V_2$, where $V_1$ implies a displacement, and $V_2$ (which may itself be a compound) signals the direction in which the subject moves as the result of the displacement. There are two types of directional complements:

(i) Those using the verbs $luŋ^{31}$ 'come – hither' and $ʑiu^{33}$ 'go – thither/away'.[11] Apart from being main verbs themselves, $luŋ^{31}$ 'come' and $ʑiu^{33}$ 'go' as complements denote motion toward or away from the speaker respectively, e.g. $ts^h ɿ^{55}$-$luŋ^{31}$ (take-come) 'bring', $ts^h ɿ^{55}$-$ʑiu^{33}$ (take-go) 'take away', $tiu^{55}$-$luŋ^{31}$ (send-come) 'send over here', $tiu^{55}$-$ʑiu^{33}$ (send-go) 'send away'.

(ii) Those that for double complements are formed with one of the type (i) directional verbs preceded by one of the six motion verbs, i.e. $ʔi^{33}$ 'ascend – up', $ɕɔ^{55}$ 'descend – down', $t^h iuŋ^{13}$ 'enter – in', $diau^{13}$ 'exit – out', $bɯ^{33}$ 'cross – over', and $(tau^{13})dzən^{31}$ 'return – back'. In other words, these six motion verbs cannot be used singly as directional complements but have to be followed by a type (i) directional verb. Thus, if we take any one of these six motion verbs, say, $ʔi^{33}$ 'ascend', and combine it with either member of type (i), we get two new double directional complements: $ʔi^{33}$-$luŋ^{31}$ (ascend-come) 'up toward the speaker'; $ʔi^{33}$-$ʑiu^{33}$ (ascend-go) 'up away from the speaker'. Since there are six members of the motion verb category and two members in the type (i) category, we have a total of twelve double complements. Here are some examples: $hy^{13}.dzən^{31}$-$luŋ^{31}$ (fly-return-come) 'fly back toward the speaker'; $χa^{55}.diau^{13}$-$ʑiu^{33}$ (pour-exit-go) 'pour out away from the speaker'; $suai^{33}.ʔi^{33}$-$ʑiu^{33}$ (run-ascend-go) 'run up away from the speaker'; $ɕin^{55}.bɯ^{33}$-$luŋ^{31}$ (lead-cross-come) 'lead over to the speaker'.

It should be noted, however, that in most cases, these six motion verbs tend to take a locative object and thus the whole unit ceases to be a compound and turns, instead, into a phrase or serial verb construction, e.g. $ts^h əu^{33}$ $ɕɔ^{55}$ $ŋ^{55}$ $ʑiu^{33}$ (push-descend-water-go) 'push down into

---

[11] We indicate in the gloss first the independent meaning (before the dash) and then the directional meaning (after the dash).

the water away from the speaker', $t^hai^{31}$ $ɕɔ^{55}$ $pa^{55}$ $luŋ^{31}$ (carry-descend-beneath-come) 'carry down (to the ground) toward the speaker', $suai^{33}$ $ʔi^{33}$ $ʑe^{31}$ $ʑiu^{33}$ (run-ascend-hill-go) 'run up the hill away from the speaker'.

## 4.3 Compounding in other word classes

Compound adjectives are also common in Ahou Gelao, as adjectives constitute an open class in this language. Adjectives form compounds that are structurally similar to the verbal compounds mentioned above, namely, the predicate-complement (V-C) type discussed in Section 3.3, the subject-predicate type in Section 3.4, and the parallel/coordinate type in Section 3.5. In terms of productivity, like verbal compounds, the predicate-complement (V-C) type of compound adjective appears to be mostly productive. The subject-predicate type is also productive in some sense, although it is restricted to certain classes of nouns (see Section 3.4). As can be seen in Section 3.5, the parallel/coordinate type of compound adjective is quite rare, as two adjectives may get compounded into a pronoun (e.g. $ʔɛ^{13}dia^{33}$ (many/much-few/little) 'how much; how many') or a verb (e.g. $xəu^{13}ʔui^{13}$ (dry-tender) 'discuss; talk over'). Here we will just make some comments on the V-C type of compound adjective.

As seen in the examples in Section 3.3, the V-C type of compound adjective can be classified into two subtypes according to the relative position of the adjective in relation to the verb in the compound, namely, (1) V-A type, e.g. $tiɔ^{55}ʔe^{33}$ (appear-good) 'good-looking; handsome; beautiful'; and (2) A-V type, e.g. $ʔe^{33}saŋ^{13}$ (good-look) 'good-looking; beautiful'. The latter can be called a purposive complement, as the meaning conveyed in the structure can be described as "good/hard/knowing for something". And the adjectives that can appear in this position form a rather closed class of just three or four members. In both cases, the whole compound can be modified by adverbs of degree such as $t^hai^{13}$ 'too', $tsa^{31}sɿ^{31}$ 'substantially', and $haŋ^{33}$ 'awfully', since it functions as an adjective.

Compound adverbs in Ahou Gelao are rather restricted, with most of them being manner adverbs. Structurally they are of the predicate-complement type by and large: $gaŋ^{354\sim31}naŋ^{33}$ (like-this) 'anyhow', $gaŋ^{31}naŋ^{33}$ (like-this) 'in this way, like this', $gau^{354\sim31}vu^{33}$ (like-that) 'like that', $gau^{31}vu^{33}$ (like-that) 'in that way', $ts^hən^{55}lin^{31}$ (follow-back) 'afterwards, subsequently', $ga^{13}tɕ^hi^{33}$ (seize-up) 'hastily/hurriedly', $tɹ^{31}tɔ^{33}$ (reach-up) 'subsequently', $χɔ^{33}tau^{33}$ (be.with-up) 'together', $ʑe^{31}tau^{33}$ (adhere-up) 'closely, continuously', etc. Note that the formation of these compound adverbs, whereby a lexical word has lost its original lexical meaning and has become an integral part of a new grammatical word, obviously involves grammaticalization. On the other hand, due to their univerbation and idiomaticization, they are rightly treated as lexicalizations from syntactic constructions. In fact, some of these compound adverbs, $ze^{31}tau^{33}$, for instance, may undergo grammaticalization into prepositions, thus exhibiting a case of polygrammaticalization, as illustrated soon below.

Compound adverbs of the subject-predicate type or other types can scarcely be found, e.g. $q^h\varepsilon^{13}hui^{55}$ (foot-quick) 'quickly, immediately', $sɿ^{55}\chi ən^{33}$ (one-road) 'together'.

Compound numerals are very widespread and productive. In fact, numerals in Ahou Gelao are compounded to such an extent that it makes the class of numerals virtually open. For more information on numeral systems in this language, see He (2008, 2012) as well as Section 2.2 above.

Compounding of prepositions is also occasionally attested. It is worth noting that, like the compound adverbs mentioned above, compound prepositions are also of the predicate-complement type: $m\varepsilon^{13}lin^{31}$ (find-back) 'after, along', $ts^hən^{55}$-$lin^{31}$ (follow-back) 'after, along', $\chi ɔ^{33}tau^{33}$ (be.with-up) 'together with', $ze^{31}tau^{33}$ (adhere-up) 'after (somebody)', $ŋan^{13}tau^{33}$ (aim-up) 'toward; against', etc. As a matter of fact, quite a few of them are cognates. These data seem to display a development or grammaticalization path from verbal compounds to compound adverbs or compound prepositions. We present here one example to illustrate the different uses of the compound $ze^{31}tau^{33}$ as a verb (9), an adverb (10), and a preposition (11), respectively:

(9)  səu³³   tʰaŋ³¹   tʰiɔ⁵⁵ɕau¹³       ɕɛ³¹   **$ze^{31}$-$tau^{33}$**   tiº.
     two    NCL.ST   geomantic.site    TOP    adjoin-PHS                EXPL
     'And the two geomantic sites adjoin (one another), as you may know.'

(10) sɿ⁵⁵    guai³¹   hui³³   səu³³   li¹³,    səu³³   li¹³    tɔº
     one     year     bear    two     child    two     child   all
     ʔiu³³   lɛi⁵⁵-   hɔ⁵⁵,   **$ze^{31}tau^{33}$**   hui³³   miaŋ³¹-guai³¹-ɕe¹³.
     COP     CL.YNG   man     nonstop               bear    six-year-ten
     '(His wife) bore two children per year, both boys, and continued to give birth (in this way) for sixteen years without stop.'

(11) wa¹³qʰɛi¹³   ʔɛ³³   tɔº     **$ze^{31}tau^{33}$**   ty¹³,    tyai¹³-tɕʰi³³    ma³³
     uncle (MEB)  3      thus    closely               chase    ignite-PHS       NCL.CLD
     liau³¹   **$ze^{31}tau^{33}$**   ʔɛ³³   ty¹³.
     torch    after                 3      chase
     'His uncle just chased (him) closely, ignited a torch and chased after him.'

Compound pronouns in Ahou Gelao also exist. In this language, most of the personal pronouns have three forms: basic, reflexive and topic ones. Generally the reflexive and topic forms of these personal pronouns are the combination of the basic forms with the two noun classifiers $ha^{33}$ (CL.VLU) (used to describe valued or appreciated persons, animals or objects) and $ʔa^{33}$ (CL.GNR) (a generic classifier, used for general objects or things)[12] respectively. To put it in another way, the reflexive and topic forms derive diachronically from combining the corresponding basic forms with these two classifiers: for example, the topic form of first person singular $ʔa^{33}zi^{55}$ (1SG.TOP) < $ʔa^{33}$ (CL.GNR) + $zi^{55}$ (1SG), the topic form of first person plural $ʔa^{33}te^{33}$ (1PL.TOP) < $ʔa^{33}$ (CL.GNR) + $te^{33}$ (1PL), the reflexive form of first person plural $ha^{33}te^{33}$ (1PL.REFL) < $ha^{33}$ (CL.VLU) + $te^{33}$ (1PL).[13]

Apart from personal pronouns, definite pro-forms and indefinite-interrogative pro-forms themselves are also compounds in structure. To be specific, these pro-forms come from the combination of two syntactic constituents. In fact, these types of compound pro-forms are quite frequent in Ahou Gelao. As He (2012: 87) puts it, they are compounds formed through the combination of demonstratives/determiners with words from other classes. In other words, these pro-forms generally consist of two different syntactic elements, with one ($naŋ^{33}$, $vu^{33}$, $bɛ^{33}/jye^{33}$, $xe^{33}$, $ʔa^{33}xe^{33}/a^{31}xe^{33}$) being a determinative/determiner and indicating the function of the pro-forms (demonstrative or indefinite) and the other ($xən^{33}$, $sən^{33}$, $pʰa^{13}$, $sɿ^{55}$, $ga^{31}$, $tʰaŋ^{31}$, $sa^{13}/dzai^{31}$, $ga^{31}$) denoting their category or scope (person, thing, place, time, manner, quantity, etc.). Some of them can still be analyzed as being in a transitional stage on the path from phrases to lexicalized compounds. Note that most of these compounds manifest the tone sandhi 353 as discussed in Section 2.1. These pro-forms are shown in Table 1.

Table 1: The common demonstrative pro-forms in Ahou Gelao.

| Gloss | Definite | | | Indefinite-Interrogative |
|---|---|---|---|---|
| | Proximate | Distal | Recognitional | |
| Human | $xən^{353~33}naŋ^{33}$ 'this (person)' | $xən^{354~33}vu^{33}$ 'that (person)' | | $xən^{353~33}a^{31}xe^{33}$ 'what (person)'; $ʔia^{33}lo^{33}$ 'who' |
| Animal | $sən^{353~33}naŋ^{33}$ 'this (animal)' | $sən^{353~33}vu^{33}$ 'that (animal)' | | $sən^{353~33}a^{31}xe^{33}$ 'what (animal)' |
| Animate | $pʰa^{353~13}naŋ^{33}$ 'this (being)' | $pʰa^{353~13}vu^{33}$ 'that (being)' | | $pʰa^{353~13}a^{31}xe^{33}$ 'what (being)' |

---

**12** For a more detailed discussion on classifiers in Ahou Gelao, see He (2012).
**13** For a more detailed discussion on this issue, see He (2012, 2014).

**Table 1** (continued)

| Gloss | Definite | | | Indefinite-Interrogative |
|---|---|---|---|---|
| | Proximate | Distal | Recognitional | |
| Inanimate | sɿ$^{55}$naŋ$^{33}$ 'this (thing)' | sɿ$^{55}$vu$^{33}$ 'that (thing)' | sɿ$^{55}$bɛ$^{33}$ 'that (thing)' | sɿ$^{55}$xe$^{33}$; sɿ$^{55}$a$^{31}$xe$^{33}$ 'what (thing); whichever' |
| Place | tʰaŋ$^{353\sim31}$naŋ$^{33}$ 'this (place); here' | tʰau$^{353\sim31}$vu$^{33}$ 'that (place); there' | | tʰaŋ$^{353\sim31}$a$^{31}$xe$^{33}$; tʰaŋ$^{353\sim31}$ga$^{31}$xe$^{33}$; ga$^{31}$xe$^{33}$ 'what (place); where; wherever' |
| Time | ʔa$^{33}$ŋuai$^{33}$naŋ$^{33}$ 'this (time); now' | | sa$^{13}$bɛ$^{33}$ 'that (time)' | sa$^{353\sim13}$a$^{31}$xe$^{33}$ 'what (time); when; whenever' |
| Manner | gaŋ$^{353\sim31}$naŋ$^{33}$ 'like this' | gau$^{353\sim31}$vu$^{33}$ 'like that' | gau$^{353\sim31}$bɛ$^{33}$ 'like that' | gaŋ$^{353\sim31}$naŋ$^{33}$ 'however' |
| Quantity | qʰən$^{55}$naŋ$^{33}$ 'this many (much)' | | | ʔɛ$^{13}$dia$^{33}$ 'how many; how much' |
| Reason | | | | lɛ$^{31}$sɿ$^{55}$xe$^{33}$; lɛ$^{353\sim31}$xe$^{33}$ 'do what; why' |

No other word classes are found to have a compounding tendency in Ahou Gelao.

# 5 Summaries and findings

Herein, we have offered a brief discussion of compounding in Ahou Gelao specifically discussing (1) the behaviors and properties that help distinguish them from phrases, (2) the syntactic and semantic relations of their constituents, and (3) compounding in different word classes. We have also related the compounding process to the process of lexicalization and/or grammaticalization, touching upon the degree and possibility of and the constraints on the lexicalization of phrases or syntactic constructions into compounds. The main findings can be summarized as follows:

(1) Behaviors and properties that help distinguish compounds from phrases include:
   (i) Ahou Gelao compounds often form one phonological word and are characterized by single stress which falls on the head of the compound. The widespread tone sandhi 353 on the head of the structure is another kind of phonological mark on compounds;

(ii) Morphologically, a compound (a) belongs to the same word class as its first (head) member, attributable to and concordant with the head-modifier structure of phrases, (b) loses the syntactic dependency marker *nei*[55] between two elements, which makes the compound become more lexicalized, or (c) utilizes some special linker morphemes;

(iii) Morpho-syntactically, other morphemes usually cannot be inserted between the components of a compound, nor is a pause possible between the two elements. Similarly, components of compounds cannot be modified separately, nor can they undergo co-referential deletion;

(iv) Semantically, the meaning of a compound is generally not the simple sum of the meanings of its components. This correlates with the degree of lexicalization of the compound. Metaphor and metonymy are the main forces that shape the semantic interpretations.

(2) The syntactic and semantic relations of the constituents of compounds.

(i) The structures and rules of compounding are generally comparable to those of phrasal constructions, but compounding may sometimes display some morphological processes that, as a result of lexicalization, are applicable only to compounds.

(ii) The syntactic relations between constituents of compounds are of five types: head-modifier, predicate-object, predicate-complement, subject-predicate, and coordinate, which match five corresponding phrasal types. They display differences with respect to the degree and possibility of and the constraints on the lexicalization of the combination.

(iii) The head-modifier type of compound appears to be the most widespread and productive one. The word class of such compounds as a whole is usually determined by the head and thus functions as a noun or nominal element.

(iv) The predicate-object compounds are also quite productive. Most of these compounds function as intransitive verbs. There exist constraints on the lexicalization of the combination on the part of both the predicate and the object.

(v) Predicate-complement compounds are a third productive type. They are [V-V]$_V$ in structure. Semantically, the complement provides various dimensions such as completion, state, degree, and manner, among others. Those with a transitive predicate have a higher probability of lexicalization into compound words.

(3) Compounding in different word classes.

(i) Nominal compounding is quite productive, compared with verbal compounding and compounding in other word classes. But even within nominal compounds, the degree of productivity varies from one type to another. Nominal compounds often consist of free forms, but there are also types wherein one of the members may come from a closed class and can be a bound morpheme.

(ii) Endocentric compounds are rather widespread in Ahou Gelao. Exocentric compounds are quite productive, in the sense that they are coined by a more creative process based on conceptual metaphor and metonymy. Coordinate nominal compounds generally consist of two juxtaposed nouns. Coordinate compounds are essentially exocentric compounds since their meanings refer to a unitary concept that equals that of neither component.

(iii) The typical argument in synthetic compounds is an intransitive subject, but the compounding with a direct object is very restricted. A transitive subject can rarely be compounded without the co-occurrence of the direct object. The oblique constituent of instrument gets compounded rather productively.

(iv) Verbal compounds in Ahou Gelao are mainly of the predicate-complement (V-C) type and the complements tend to separate into various types, with the most frequent being resultative complements. Directional complements are also quite common.

(v) Compound adjectives are also common in Ahou Gelao. They are structurally similar to verbal compounds.

(vi) Compound adverbs in Ahou Gelao are rather restricted, with most of them being manner adverbs. Structurally they are, by and large, of the predicate-complement type.

(vii) Compound numerals are very widespread and productive.

(viii) Compounding in prepositions is also occasionally attested. Structurally, they are also of the predicate-complement type. Verbal compounds, compound adverbs and compound prepositions appear to be diachronically related.

(ix) Compound pronouns in Ahou Gelao also exist, with definite pro-forms and indefinite-interrogative pro-forms occurring quite frequently.

# References

Aikhenvald, Alexandra Y. 2007. Typological distinctions in word-formation. In *Language Typology and Syntactic Description (Volume III: Grammatical categories and the lexicon)* (2nd edition), Timothy Shopen (ed.), 1–65. Cambridge: Cambridge University Press.

Anderson, Stephen R. 1985. Typological distinctions in word formation. In *Language Typology and Syntactic Description (Volume III: Grammatical categories and the lexicon)*, Timothy Shopen (ed.), 3–56. Cambridge: Cambridge University Press.

Bauer, Laurie. 1983. *English Word-Formation*. Cambridge: Cambridge University Press.
Benczes, Reka. 2006. *Creative Compounding in English: The Semantics of Metaphorical and Metonymical Noun-Noun Combinations*. Amsterdam & Philadelphia: John Benjamins.
Brinton, Laurel J. and Elizabeth Closs Traugott. 2005. *Lexicalization and Language Change*. Cambridge: Cambridge University Press.
Ceccagno, Antonella and Bianca Basciano. 2007. Compound headedness in Chinese: an analysis of neologisms. *Morphology* 17: 207–231.
Chao, Yuen-ren. 1968. *A Grammar of Spoken Chinese*. Berkeley and Los Angeles: University of California Press.
Dong, Xiufang. 董秀芳 2011. 词汇化：汉语双音词的衍生和发展（修订本）[Lexicalization: The Origin and Evolution of Chinese Disyllabic Words (Revised Edition)]. Beijing: Commercial Press.
He, Yancheng. 何彦誠 2008. 红丰仡佬语概况 [A brief introduction of Hongfeng Gelao language]. *Minority Languages of China* 6: 66–79.
He, Yancheng. 何彦誠 2011. 红丰仡佬语连动结构的词汇化 [On the lexicalization of serial verb constructions in Hongfeng Gelao]. *Minority Languages of China* 4: 29–33.
He, Yancheng. 何彦誠 2012. *A Grammar of Ahou Gelao*. Postdoctoral diss., Institute of Linguistics, Chinese Academy of Social Sciences.
He, Yancheng. 何彦誠 2014. 红丰仡佬语的人称代词系统 [Personal pronoun system in Hongfeng Gelao]. *Minority Languages of China* 1: 13–20.
Hohenhaus, Peter. 2005. Lexicalization and institutionalization. In *Handbook of Word-Formation*, Pavol Stekauer and Rochelle Lieber (eds.), 353–373. Dordrecht: Springer.
Hopper, Paul J. and Elizabeth C. Traugott. 1993. *Grammaticalization*. Cambridge: Cambridge University Press.
Lehmann, Christian. 2002. New reflections on grammaticalization and lexicalization. In *New Reflections on Grammaticalization*, Ilse Wischer and Gabriele Diewald (eds.), 1–18. Amsterdam & Philadelphia: John Benjamins.
Li, Charles N. and Sandra A. Thompson. 1981. *Mandarin Chinese: A Functional Reference Grammar*. Berkeley: University of California Press.
Lieber, Rochelle and Pavol Stekauer. 2009. Introduction: status and definition of compounding. In *The Oxford Handbook of Compounding*, Rochelle Lieber and Pavol Stekauer (eds.), 3–18. Oxford: Oxford University Press.
Lightfoot, Douglas. 2011. Grammaticalization and lexicalization. In *The Oxford Handbook of Grammaticalization*, Heiko Narrog and Bernd Heine (eds.), 438–449. Oxford: Oxford University Press.
Packard, Jerome L. 2004. *The Morphology of Chinese: A Linguistic and Cognitive Approach*. Cambridge: Cambridge University Press.
Tham, Shiao Wei. 2015. Resultative verb compounds in Mandarin. In *The Oxford Handbook of Chinese Linguistics*, Williams S-Y. Wang and Chaofen Sun (eds.), 306–321. Oxford: Oxford University Press.
Wischer, Ilse. 2011. Grammaticalization and word formation. In *The Oxford Handbook of Grammaticalization*, Heiko Narrog and Bernd Heine (eds.), 356–364. Oxford: Oxford University Press.
Wu, Fuxiang. 吴福祥 2005. 汉语语法化演变的几个类型学特征 [Some Typological Features of the Grammaticalization Changes in Chinese]. *Chinese Language* 6: 483–494.

# Subject Index

absolute adjective  11, 320, 338, 342, 343
accusative form  105, 106, 107, 119
action nominal  140, 264, 265, 267, 268, 269, 274, 275, 277, 278
adjective  10, 75, 76, 82, 87, 88, 92, 94, 96, 97, 169, 203, 225, 239, 242, 243, 258, 264, 265, 275, 285, 355, 361, 366, 367, 368, 370, 372, 375, 378
adjunct  9, 142, 235, 236, 237, 244, 250, 302, 312
affix  30, 38, 39, 96, 97, 142, 201, 203, 205, 207, 259, 265, 268, 269, 272
agreement (subject, object)  259
ambiguity  183, 184, 185, 187, 219
analogy  105, 117, 364
anaphoric  60, 62
animacy  29, 121, 124
animate (class)  271, 274
anthropocentrism  82
anti-causative  211, 270, 271, 272
antonym  175, 334, 339
areal diffusion  11, 351
argument structure  121, 134, 140, 152, 157
aspect/aspectual  34, 36, 37, 39, 40, 45, 46, 47, 48, 103, 191, 194, 197, 201, 202, 203, 206, 207, 210, 221, 223, 225, 265, 295, 301, 305, 306, 310, 313, 136, 360
associated motion  9, 132, 149, 150, 151, 155, 156, 157, 158, 159

*bǎ* 把  103, 109 (See also DOM)
*bǐ* 比 'than'  319
blending  354
bracket construction  235, 247
Buddhist translations  115

cataphoric  65
causative  24, 112, 168
certainty  205, 284, 292 (See also uncertainty)
charges (*míngcí* 命辭)  289, 304
*chí* 持  5, 8, 103
*chūdōtai* 中動態 'mediovoice'  291
circumstantial  192, 193, 194, 208, 209, 211, 212, 213, 216, 221, 223, 224

classifier  5, 18, 20, 22, 24, 25, 26, 27, 28, 32, 33, 34, 35, 36, 39, 41, 42, 43, 48, 49, 361, 371, 373, 380
class shift  370
clause
– conditional  311
– main  66, 142, 234, 235, 247, 294
– subordinate  234, 235, 247, 312
clerical script (*lishū* 隸書)  283
cline  1, 17, 18, 19, 20, 21, 30, 37, 72, 80, 188, 257, 281
clipping  354
clitic  1, 39, 44, 131, 150, 151, 261, 340, 354, 357
close-scale adjectives  321, 334, 337, 340, 344, 347, 348
comitative  104
comparative constructions  66, 243, 248, 319
complement  8, 10, 103, 117, 118, 119, 120, 125, 132, 142, 145, 147, 155, 168, 173, 191, 195, 196, 199, 200, 208, 209, 210, 213, 214, 215, 216, 217, 218, 219, 221, 223, 224, 225, 226, 236, 239, 242, 243, 244, 246, 247, 248, 250, 251, 277, 338, 356, 357, 361, 362, 366, 367, 374, 375, 376, 377, 378, 379, 382, 383
complex word  29
compositional  62, 361
compositionality  367
compound (compounding)
– compound adjective  371, 378
– compound adverb  371, 378, 379, 383
– compound numeral  371, 379, 383
– compound preposition  379, 383
– compound pro-form  380
– compound pronoun  370, 371
conjunct  63
connotative meaning  83, 84, 85, 97
constituent order  11
constraints  11, 31, 35, 38, 102, 103, 121, 122, 123, 192, 194, 224, 225, 234, 319, 335, 338, 366, 368, 369, 370, 381, 382
contact-induced change  156, 159
conversion  96

coordinate compound  369, 371, 372, 373
copular  275, 356
co-referential deletion  359, 382

*de* 的 (nominal modification marker)  320
*de* 得-adjectival verbs  11, 320, 321, 334, 337, 341, 345, 346, 347, 348
definiteness  18, 22, 24, 25, 34, 35, 42, 101, 123, 124
degrammaticalization  353
degree of lexicalization  352, 359, 364, 365, 367, 370, 382
degree of productivity  374, 382
degree words  319, 321, 322, 324, 330, 331, 332, 333, 334, 338, 340, 343, 344, 347
deictic directional  9, 132, 133, 134, 135, 140, 141, 145, 146, 147, 148, 149, 150, 157, 158, 159
deictic motion verb  8, 132, 134, 136, 140, 141, 142, 143, 148, 149, 150, 152, 155, 156, 157, 159
deictic orientation  147, 157
deixis  62, 64, 148, 150, 153
demonstratives of
– degree  7, 56, 57, 71
– manner  7, 56, 57, 65, 71
– quality  7, 56, 57, 71
demonstratives (use)
– anaphoric  60, 62, 63, 64
– cataphoric use  61
– exophoric  7, 58, 60, 61, 62, 66, 67, 70, 71, 72
demotivation  353
denotation  75, 79, 80, 81, 82, 83, 85, 88, 91, 97, 335
denotative meaning  7, 83, 84, 85, 91, 97
denotatum  361
deontic  9, 191, 193, 194, 195, 196, 197, 198, 199, 200, 208, 210, 211, 213, 215, 216, 218, 219, 220, 221, 224, 225
depletion  356
description  7, 19, 27, 29, 41, 56, 67, 75, 79, 80, 81, 82, 85, 86, 88, 91, 143, 145, 148, 157, 257, 258, 262, 301, 307, 321, 333, 348, 351, 375
diachrony  101, 126

dialect  3, 8, 9, 39, 40, 41, 104, 125, 132, 134, 143, 147, 148, 151, 153, 159, 231, 232, 233, 234, 242, 243, 245, 250, 251, 267, 288, 351
direct comparison  332, 335, 343, 348
directional complement  112, 119, 143, 147, 148, 375, 377
directional compound  147
direct object  101, 103, 107, 109, 110, 112, 117, 119, 121, 123, 124, 171, 259, 262, 287, 372, 373, 383
disposal forms (See also DOM)
– *broad* disposal  112, 115
– *giving* disposal  109, 110, 117, 120
– *making* disposal  109, 111, 117
– *narrow* disposal  112, 115
– *placing* disposal  109, 110
ditransitive constructions  112
DOM (differential object marking)  43, 101, 102, 121, 126
*duìzhèn* 對貞 'antithetical/paired testing charges'  289, 303, 306

eclipse  285, 300
enclitic  43
endo-active  175, 178, 182
endocentric  360, 364, 371, 373
endocentric compound  364, 371
endo-directional (內向動詞 *nèixiàng dòngcí*)  174
endo-passive  181, 182
eventive  295, 296, 298, 299, 301, 302, 304, 310
exo-active  181
exocentric  360, 371, 373
exocentric compound  364, 372, 383
exo-directional (外向動詞 *wàixiàng dòngcí*)  174
exo-passive  178
exophoric  61, 62
extrovert  9, 171, 174, 178, 181, 182, 185, 186, 187

feminine (agreement class)  31
formal structure  360
frequency  37, 55, 103, 104, 125, 133, 135, 237, 243, 267, 275, 359

*ge*-prefix  199, 200, 201, 206
*give*-marker  104
goal  2, 10, 41, 71, 110, 112, 120, 133, 134, 135, 137, 140, 141, 142, 152, 156, 157, 160, 232, 245, 250, 275
*go get* constructions  159
gradable adjectives  10, 11, 320, 321, 336, 337, 339, 342, 344, 347
grammaticalization  1, 2, 3, 4, 5, 6, 7, 8, 10, 11, 49, 72, 107, 111, 113, 115, 116, 118, 119, 120, 122, 124, 125, 126, 132, 134, 143, 148, 149, 155, 158, 159, 166, 183, 184, 185, 186, 187, 188, 200, 217, 222, 281, 351, 352, 353, 354, 355, 357, 379, 381

habeo-verb  263, 275
Han (period)  170, 171, 177
headedness  352
head-initial  11, 351
head-modifier  355, 357, 361, 363, 367, 369, 373
*hékǒu* 合口 'closed mouth'  288
*help*-marker  104
*hěn* 很 'very'  319, 321, 323, 325, 328, 330, 332, 334, 338, 342, 343
historical phonology  201, 207

iconicity  31, 140
idiomaticity  359
idiosyncratic (idiosyncrasy)  29, 361, 363, 367
inanimate  26, 29, 42, 101, 122, 123, 262, 271, 273, 274
inceptivity  270, 273, 274, 275
indefinite pronoun  287
indirect comparison  332, 335, 348
inferential  36, 308
inflection  41, 49, 169, 352
inscriptions
– non-royal (*fēiwáng bǔcí* 非王卜辭)  288
– royal (*wáng bǔcí* 王卜辭)  288
instrumental form  105, 106
intransitive  4, 44, 87, 168, 170, 173, 177, 178, 179, 185, 201, 206, 209, 213, 214, 262, 266, 270, 271, 275, 295, 296, 346, 347, 355, 361, 363, 364, 366, 367, 368, 372
introvert  9, 171, 174, 178, 179, 181, 182, 185, 187

iterativity (iterative verb)  201, 264
itive  8, 131, 132, 135, 136, 139, 140, 143, 144, 145, 146, 148, 150, 151, 152, 153, 156

*jiāng* 將  5, 8, 103
*Jīngdiǎn Shìwén* 經典釋文  170, 303
*jù/*dzoʔ/h* 聚 'to gather'  303
juxtaposition  30, 359

*kǎishū* 楷書  283

language contact  125, 155, 156
left-headed  361, 363
lexeme (lexicon)  3, 4, 6, 18, 184, 187, 261, 352, 354, 361
lexical category  286, 351, 352, 355
lexicalization  10, 11, 18, 32, 36, 49, 56, 166, 183, 184, 281, 322, 351, 352, 353, 354, 355, 356, 357, 359, 360, 364, 365, 367, 368, 369, 370, 379, 381
lexical replacement  119
lexical subjectification  81, 82, 92, 93, 97
linking element  352
logographic form  166
loss of morphology  202

manner of motion  151
mechanism  9, 11, 33, 47, 49, 75, 82, 92, 97, 105, 183, 185, 186, 187, 351, 364
mediovoice (*chūdōtai* 中動態)  291
metaphorical (extension)  55, 257, 363, 364, 365, 367, 370
metonymic (extension)  55, 363, 364, 365, 367, 370
*mìngcí* 命辭 'charge/charging statement'  289, 304
modal (modality)  3, 191, 192, 193, 196, 209, 215, 218, 219, 222, 223, 224, 225, 242, 244, 289, 291, 299, 302, 353
momentaneous verb  270
monosyllabic  103, 167
morphological criteria  358
morphological derivation  166, 170, 202
morphological process  11, 165, 169, 351, 360, 361

morphology 9, 19, 29, 30, 36, 38, 39, 40, 41, 45, 46, 48, 49, 191, 200, 201, 224, 257, 258, 259, 281, 289
morpho-phonemic cognates 166
motion-cum-purpose 8, 142, 160
motivation 11, 18, 31, 147, 149, 153, 156, 157, 159, 351

negation 2, 11, 68, 70, 120, 123, 152, 193, 194, 195, 197, 199, 200, 207, 208, 209, 211, 212, 213, 219, 221, 223, 224, 285, 320, 321, 327, 332, 334, 342
negatives
– dynamic *fú* 弗 284, 289, 294, 313
– *m-type: *wú* 毋 and *wù* 勿 290, 301, 302
– *p-type: *bù* 不, *fú* 弗, and *fēi* 非 290, 301, 302, 313
– stative/eventive *bù* 不 295, 297, 298, 304, 305, 313
nominal compound 371, 372, 373, 374
non-compositional 352, 359, 372
non-referential 369, 370, 374
nouns (nominal class) 374
numeral 11, 18, 20, 26, 27, 28, 33, 34, 35, 36, 41, 42, 351, 355, 358, 359

object 2, 3, 5, 7, 8, 63, 75, 79, 80, 81, 82, 85, 96, 126, 155, 177, 258, 259, 262, 278, 285, 312, 329, 346, 361, 365, 366, 375
objective 81, 83, 95, 321
obligative (obligation) 193, 195, 208, 213, 215, 218, 219, 220, 221, 225, 305, 308, 309, 313
oblique 373, 383
open-scale adjectives 320, 321, 337, 338, 339, 340, 341, 344, 347, 348
oracle-bone inscriptions (*jiǎgǔwén* 甲骨文) 287
orthographic criteria 352
OV order 109, 142, 156, 372

passive 9, 23, 24, 171, 172, 175, 176, 177, 178, 181, 182, 185, 186, 187, 188, 218, 219, 296
past tense 192
paths of grammaticalization 68, 71
path verb 134, 135, 136, 137, 141, 144, 145, 148, 152, 155, 156, 157

patient-subject sentences (*shòushì zhǔyǔ jù* 受事主語句) 112
perfective 18, 20, 32, 33, 34, 41, 197, 199, 201, 203, 204, 206, 210, 224
perfective (perfectivizing suffix) 270
perfective-stative (verb form) 272
periodization 102, 191
permissive 173
phase complement 376, 377
phonetic weakening 132, 143, 146, 151
phonological criteria 357
phrasal compound 354
phrasal construction 361, 363, 365, 367
phrasal verb 352
plural 20, 37, 42, 43, 45, 265, 273, 274, 380
polygrammaticalization 379
polymorpheme 187
polysemy 5, 7, 63, 97, 187, 257, 276, 280, 281
polysynthesis 10, 281
possessive (form) 55, 124, 284, 287
possibility 9, 11, 24, 193, 194, 195, 199, 208, 209, 210, 211, 212, 213, 219, 223, 224, 226, 291, 298, 310
postfield 9, 231, 234, 235, 236, 237, 242, 245, 249
postposition (postpositioning) 2, 3, 9, 252, 275, 312
potential 126, 183, 248, 249, 285, 291, 298, 335, 366
pragmatics 2, 18, 19, 32, 43, 49, 84, 183, 343
predicate-complement 356, 361, 362, 366, 367, 374, 378, 379, 382
predicate-object 362, 363
prefix 45, 46, 47, 48, 49, 165, 173, 174, 202, 205, 206, 234, 260, 261, 262, 265, 267, 273
prefix **m*- 165
prefix **N*- 165, 179, 182
prepositional phrases 9, 10
prepositions 8, 23, 103, 106, 116, 119, 120, 122, 355, 383
present tense 67
presupposition 290, 291
problem-solving 183
prognostication (*zhāncí* 占辭 or *zhòucí* 繇辭) 292, 304

propositional anaphors  63
prosecutive case (See also prolative case)
prosody  143, 151
purpose  , 8, 20, 32, 112, 119, 142, 160, V, 140
purposive complement  378
putative  167, 168, 170, 172, 304, 308

*Qièyùn* 切韻  165
quantifiers  107
*qùshēng* 去聲  171, 304

reanalysis  9, 19, 21, 46, 48, 49, 185, 363
referentiality  364
regular script (*kǎishū* 楷書)  283
resultative complement  112, 145, 147, 208, 219, 375
resultative compound  375
resultative (verb)  33
resumptive pronoun  107, 122, 124
root compound  371, 372
root serialization  374

sandhi  352, 356, 357, 380
semantics
– semantic change  5, 7, 10, 18, 72, 75, 80, 81, 83, 88, 93, 95, 97, 183, 185, 186, 187, 281, 367
– semantic constraints  121, 125, 366, 369, 370
– semantic criteria  359
– semantic extension  2, 7, 9, 183, 185, 186, 187, 188
– semantic overlapping  183, 185
– semantic reanalysis  18, 19, 21, 46, 48, 49, 185, 186
– semantic relation  11, 351, 360, 361, 370, 372, 381, 382
– semantic role  361
sentential connectives  64
serial verbs  352
Shang Dynasty  165, 170, 283
*shǎngshēng* 上聲  174
should  308, 309 (See also obligative, inferential, and putative)
silk and bamboo-slip writings (*jiǎnbó* 簡帛)  283

singular (number)  31
small-seal script (*xiǎozhuàn* 小篆)  283
space deixis  62
specialization  87, 357
specificity  101, 123
stative-resultative (verb)  270, 272, 273
stative (verb and adjective)  166, 169, 172
stativity (of verb)  296, 298
stress  151, 243, 355, 356, 381
subject  8, 17, 30, 42, 44, 46, 68, 85, 110, 112, 116, 117, 153, 192, 194, 205, 206, 209, 210, 213, 214, 218, 219, 220, 221, 224, 226, 234, 246, 249, 251, 258, 261, 271, 273, 277, 285, 291, 292, 293, 307, 309, 311, 338, 354, 367, 368, 369, 372, 374, 378, 383
subjective  83, 85, 95, 329, 346
subject-predicate  361, 367, 368, 369, 378, 379, 382
subordinator  63
suffixes
– suffix *-s  170, 171, 173, 187, 201, 202, 203, 206, 210
– suffix *-ʔ  170, 171, 175, 178
– suffix *-h  169
synchrony  101
syntactic
– change  105
– collocation  357, 361
– constituent  380
– criteria  102, 358
– dependency  352, 356, 357, 358, 382
– relation  360, 361, 382
– compound  295, 351
synonym  104, 338, 340, 369, 370
syntagmatic  1, 9, 18, 20, 43, 167, 169, 172, 186, 187

TAM (tense-aspect-mood)  47, 258, 259, 261, 265
targets of grammaticalization  71
thematic (derivational affix)  56, 57, 72, 182, 185
token frequency  79, 374
tonal language  11, 351
tonal pattern  352

tone  20, 38, 41, 42, 131, 148, 150, 151, 170, 171, 177, 183, 186, 202, 204, 206, 259, 291, 356, 357, 374, 380, 381
topic  10, 17, 18, 26, 67, 122, 143, 159, 167, 251, 267, 284, 286, 294, 308, 311, 354, 380
Topological Field Model  235
transitive (verb)  44, 87, 155, 167, 170, 172, 173, 174, 178, 179, 182, 186, 209, 213, 216, 217, 296, 345, 347, 361, 363, 364, 372, 382
transitivity  VII, 34, 44, 123, 165, 169, 182, 203, 205, 262, 265, 268, 272, 297
translative (postposition)  275, 277
type frequency  373

unaccusative  201, 205, 206, 210, 216, 217, 221, 223, 226
uncertainty (See also certainty)
unergative  216
ungradable adjectives  321
unidirectionality  1, 17, 187, 188
univerbation  354, 379

valency  169, 171, 178, 181, 182, 187
ventive  131, 132, 136, 140, 143, 145, 147, 148, 150, 151, 152, 156, 159
verbal features  140, 156, 159
verb compounding  374
verb serialization  374

verb (types)
– abstract verbs  107
– controllable verbs  10, 294
– *give* verbs  18, 22, 23, 24, 32, 33, 48, 101, 104, 110, 112, 117
– *help* verbs  104
– perception verbs  102
– *take* verbs  5, 8, 103, 104, 107, 109, 113, 118, 147, 285, 303
– uncontrollable  10, 284, 285, 290, 291, 294, 297, 303, 304, 313
– verbs of attempt  284
– verbs of success  284, 293
voicing  9, 42, 165, 170, 179, 204
voicing alternation  204, 205, 206, 210, 211
volition  191, 192, 205, 285, 291
VO order  134, 140, 372
vowel harmony  352

word formation  11, 37, 38, 352, 353, 354, 364
word order  3, 20, 25, 30, 121, 122, 125, 135, 140, 142, 146, 155, 182, 185, 232, 246, 250, 294, 351

*xiéshēng* 諧聲  165

*yàncí* 驗辭 'verification, verifying statement'  290

Zhou (Dynasty)  165, 170, 171, 177

# Language Index

Ahou Gelao  11, 351, 354, 355, 356, 357, 358, 359, 360, 361, 363, 367, 369, 370, 371, 372, 373, 374, 375, 376, 378, 379, 380, 381, 383
Altaic languages  8, 125, 132, 155
Archaic Chinese  9, 103, 109, 111, 119, 199, 140, 201, 202, 204, 205, 206, 207
Athabaskan languages  258

Beijing dialect  151
Berber  150, 159

Cantonese  25, 38, 48, 60, 104, 131, 142, 156

Dene-Yeniseian (family)  258, 272

English  2, 6, 7, 10, 29, 30, 36, 48, 55, 56, 58, 59, 60, 61, 63, 64, 65, 66, 67, 69, 70, 72, 75, 81, 96, 97, 107, 159, 160, 167, 176, 184, 185, 187, 194, 197, 199, 208, 210, 215, 218, 232, 235, 236, 246, 249, 250, 267, 284, 288, 292, 298, 306, 308, 311, 312, 319, 320, 325, 326, 328, 332, 333, 336, 337, 338, 339, 340, 341, 343, 345, 346, 347, 353
European Languages  , 1, 2, 7, 48, 56, 58, 59, 60, 62, 64, 66, 67, 68, 69, 71, 72, 160, 187, 201, 205, V
Ewenki  261

Finnish  65
French  2, 30, 59, 65, 66, 69, 141, 142, 160, 291

Gāndhārī  125
Gelao  2, 11
German  2, 3, 6, 9, 36, 48, 56, 57, 58, 59, 62, 63, 65, 66, 67, 69, 70, 107, 190, 191, 197, 198, 199, 200, 206, 210, 216, 225, 231, 232, 233, 234, 235, 242, 243, 246, 249, 250, 251, 282
Germanic languages  199, 200, 201, 225

Hmong-Mien  26, 142, 354
Hmong-Mien language  26

Japanese  2, 7, 56, 58, 59, 60, 62, 63, 64, 65, 66, 67, 68, 69, 71, 72, 159, 178, 215, 312
Jilu Mandarin  134
Jin dialects  143, 148, 152, 156

Ket  2, 4, 5, 6, 10, 47, 48, 49, 257, 258, 259, 260, 261, 262, 264, 265, 266, 267, 268, 269, 270, 272, 273, 274, 275, 276, 277, 278, 279, 280, 281, 289
Khakas  261
Kra  11, 351

Late Archaic Chinese  104, 109, 110, 191, 192, 193, 194, 196, 200, 208, 211, 215, 216, 217, 218, 225
Late Han Chinese  113
Latin  31, 56, 59, 186, 260

Mandarin  , 5, 7, 11, 20, 25, 39, 40, 56, 59, 60, 68, 69, 71, 72, 103, 122, 123, 131, 142, 146, 171, 319, 326, 351, VII, 359, 360, 366, 369
Manchurian  125
Medieval Chinese  3, 5, 8, 102, 103, 110, 112, 115, 116, 124, 125
Middle Chinese  9, 88, 91, 93, 165, 181, 191, 193, 194, 196, 199, 200, 202, 203, 204, 205, 207, 208, 215
Modern Chinese  VII, 2, 5, 103, 117, 124, 140, 191, 319
Modern English  63, 69, 70
Mongolian  125

Northern Chinese dialects  132, 156
Northern Mandarin  , 131, VII, 143

Old Chinese (OC)  VII, 9, 36, 49, 76, 79, 85, 91, 92
Old English  165, 287

Papago 186
Polish 59, 64
Prâkrit 125

Romanian 120
Russian 66, 200, 225, 260
Sanskrit 125, 186, 216, 291
Selkup 261
Semelai 39, 43, 44, 45, 49
Shāng Chinese , VIII
Sinitic languages 24, 25, 26, 38, 39, 48, 49, 103, 104, 123, 124, 131, 133, 207
Sino-Tibetan 173, 174, 179, 360
South Siberian Turkic 261
Southern Min 103, 104, 142
Spanish 2, 59, 69
Standard Mandarin 8, 102, 123, 132, 133, 137, 139, 143, 145, 147, 151, 154, 159

Tai-Kadai 11, 351, 360
Taiwanese 131
Tangwang Chinese 唐汪漢語 39
Thai 34
Tibeto-Burman 173, 179

Uighur 125
Uralic (family) 261

Vietnamese 38, 141

Weining Ahmao 26, 27, 28, 29, 39, 41, 42, 43, 49
Wu dialects 25, 104

Xunxian Chinese 浚县漢語 40, 41

Yabem 45, 46, 48, 49
Yeniseian (family) 47, 49, 258, 261, 264, 265

www.ingramcontent.com/pod-product-compliance
Lightning Source LLC
Chambersburg PA
CBHW031411230426
43668CB00007B/278